Taxing America

Wilbur D. Mills, Congress, and the State, 1945–1975

Taxing America offers a new interpretation of the American state between 1945 and 1975 by tracing the career of Wilbur D. Mills, chairman of the House Ways and Means Committee from 1958 to 1974. Blending methodological insights from history, political science, and sociology, Julian Zelizer provides one of the first comparative histories of income taxation, Social Security, and Medicare in this study of the seminal role Mills played in the national tax agenda as he negotiated between the tax policy community and Congress.

Taxing America lays out four innovative arguments about the expansion of the state during the postwar period: (1) Congress played a crucial role in the institutionalization of the state after World War II; (2) policy communities helped encourage policymaking by creating a link between Congress and other parts of the state; (3) taxation was central to postwar liberalism and its domestic agenda by offering a means of providing moderate economic and social assistance without stimulating a conservative backlash; and (4) a fragile alliance between influential fiscal conservatives and the state was instrumental in expanding support for the policies of the tax policy community.

Julian E. Zelizer is Assistant Professor of History and Public Policy at the State University of New York at Albany. He received his B.A. from Brandeis University and his Ph.D. from The Johns Hopkins University. He was a Research Fellow at the Brookings Institution. He has published articles in *The Journal of Policy History*, *Reviews in American History*, and *Documentary Editing*, and contributed a chapter to the book *Funding the Modern American State: The Rise and Fall of an Era of Easy Finance, 1941–1995*, edited by W. Elliot Brownlee (Cambridge University Press and Woodrow Wilson Center Press, 1996).

Taxing America

Wilbur D. Mills, Congress, and the State, 1945–1975

Julian E. Zelizer

PUBLISHED BY THE PRESS SYNDICATE OF THE UNIVERSITY OF CAMBRIDGE
The Pitt Building, Trumpington Street, Cambridge, United Kingdom

CAMBRIDGE UNIVERSITY PRESS
The Edinburgh Building, Cambridge CB2 2RU, UK   http://www.cup.cam.ac.uk
40 West 20th Street, New York, NY 10011-4211, USA   http://www.cup.org
10 Stamford Road, Oakleigh, Melbourne 3166, Australia

First published 1998

Printed in the United States of America

Typeset in New Baskerville 10/12 pt, in Quark Xpress™ [BTS]

A catalog record for this book is available from the British Library

Library of Congress Cataloging-in-Publication Data

Zelizer, Julian E.
Taxing America: Wilbur D. Mills, Congress, and the state,
1945–1975 / Julian E. Zelizer.
p.   cm.
Includes index.
ISBN 0-521-62166-6 hb
1. Mills, Wilbur D. (Wilbur Daigh), 1909–   .   2. Taxation – United
States – History.   3. United States.   Congress.   House.   Committee on
Ways and Means – History.   I. Title.
HJ2381.Z45   1998
336.2'00973 – dc21   98-21974
CIP

ISBN   0 521 62166 6 hardback

For my parents, Viviana and Gerald,
with love and appreciation

Contents

Key to Collections

COHP	Columbia University Oral History Project (New York, New York)
DEL	Dwight D. Eisenhower Library (Abilene, Kansas)
HTL	Harry S. Truman Library (Independence, Missouri)
JFKL	John F. Kennedy Library (Boston, Massachusetts)
JMIC	John Manley Interview Collection (in the author's possession). These documents are also in the Lyndon B. Johnson Library.
LBJL	Lyndon B. Johnson Library (Austin, Texas)
NA	National Archives: Papers of Ways and Means and Joint Committee on Internal Revenue Taxation (Washington, D.C.)
NAS	National Archives: Records of the Social Security Administration (College Park, Maryland)
NAT	National Archives: General Records of the Department of the Treasury (College Park, Maryland)
NPM	National Archives: Nixon Presidential Materials (College Park, Maryland)
RMP	Robert J. Myers Papers, Wisconsin Historical Society (Madison, Wisconsin)
SSP	Stanley S. Surrey Papers, Harvard University Law Library (Cambridge, Massachusetts)
WCP	Wilbur J. Cohen Papers, Wisconsin Historical Society (Madison, Wisconsin)
WMPC	Wilbur D. Mills Papers Collections (Conway, Arkansas)

Congress granted me access to the Committee collections, and to the transcripts of the *Executive Sessions of the House Committee on Ways and Means* from 1958 to 1972. During these top-secret sessions, the committee met behind closed doors, joined only by staff members and invited experts, to write the final legislation before putting it up for a vote in the House. Under the regulations of Congress, I could not take notes while reading the transcripts, nor could I cite the material directly. Nonetheless, I was able to read the entire collection – unedited – and I have relied on it throughout this book. Scholars who want to examine this extraordinary material should contact Ways and Means.

The John Manley interviews were conducted largely between 1964 and 1969 for his groundbreaking book, *The Politics of Finance*. I am indebted to John Manley for generously providing me with copies of these interviews. Because I cannot name the source of my quotations as a result of an agreement between Manley and his subjects, I refer to them as "one Republican" or "an HEW official." Their names are on the interviews, which were conducted with the following people.

Democrats

Ross Bass (Tennessee), James Burke (Massachusetts), Dante Fascell (Florida), Richard Fulton (Tennessee), William Green (Pennsylvania), Martha Griffiths (Michigan), Albert Syndey Herlong (Florida), William Pat Jennings (Virginia), Eugene Keogh (New York), Cecil King (California), Philip Landrum (Georgia), Lee Metcalf (Montana), Wilbur Mills (Arkansas), George Rhodes (Pennsylvania), Dan Rostenkowski (Illinois), Clark Thompson (Texas), Albert Ullman (Oregon), Charles Vanik (Ohio), John Watts (Kentucky).

Republicans

Bruce Alger (Texas), James Battin (Montana), Jackson Betts (Ohio), George Bush (Texas), Harold Collier (Illinois), Barber Conable (New York), Thomas Curtis (Missouri), Stephen Derounian (New York), Herman Schneebeli (Pennsylvania), James Utt (California).

Congressional Staff

Albert McCauley, Professional Staff; Mark Talisman, Administrative Assistant to Charles Vanik; Richard Wilbur, Assistant Minority Counsel; David West, Assistant Minority Counsel; William Quealy, Assistant Minority Counsel.

Department of the Treasury

Donald Lubick, Tax Legislative Counsel; Stanley Surrey, Assistant Secretary.

Department of Health, Education, and Welfare

Wilbur Cohen, Assistant Secretary; Charlie Hawkins, Legislative Reference Officer, Welfare Administration (SSA); Robert Myers, Chief Actuary of Social Security; Michael Stern, Special Aide to Wilbur Cohen.

Acknowledgments

Writing about a community of experts has made me extremely conscious of the many people who have shaped this book. Since the beginning, I have received sage advice, strong encouragement, and invaluable support from friends, colleagues, and research institutions. I hope that *Taxing America* lives up to their expectations and that they all feel their efforts were worthwhile.

One of my greatest acknowledgments goes to James Kloppenberg, my undergraduate mentor at Brandeis University, who has continued to inspire me. I first saw him speak at an orientation for prospective students. Working closely with him since then, I have had an opportunity to be associated with one of the nation's finest intellectual historians. As a mentor, a colleague, and a friend, Jim has played a crucial role in my intellectual development and in the creation of this book.

At graduate school, a number of scholars helped me to become a professional historian. Foremost, Louis Galambos read through several drafts of this work. From the beginning, he has encouraged me to put forth my arguments with conviction and vigor, even when they stimulated a heated response. Lou said on several occasions that my skin would become thick and that my research would profit from the risks of innovation. Several years later, my skin feels a lot thicker, and I believe that this work has benefited from his advice.

Dorothy Ross helped me to understand how the study of political discourse could provide important insights into the operations of the modern American state. Dorothy, along with her husband Stanford, helped me to develop strategies to use Mills as a window into the relationship between political culture and the American state.

While I was at Johns Hopkins, JoAnne Brown, Ronald Walters, and J.G.A. Pocock provided helpful advice along the way.

All the participants in the Woodrow Wilson International Center Workshop, which produced *Funding the Modern American State*, were instrumental at an early stage in this project. Their comments helped me to structure the basic narrative of my work and to see where my understanding of Mills fit within the existing scholarship. I am grateful to W. Elliot Brownlee for giving me the opportunity to participate in the workshop and for taking a chance on a young scholar interested in the politics of taxation.

At the Brookings Institution, Sarah Binder, Robert Katzmann, Thomas Mann, Kent Weaver, Joseph White, and Margaret Weir sharpened my understanding of the legislative process and helped me to develop my arguments about the implications of this history for current political debates. As a historian, I was honored to work with political scientists of such high esteem.

I would especially like to thank my fellow Research Fellows – Gary McKissick, Eric Patashnik, and Carolyn Wong – who supported me throughout a challenging year. Gary, Eric, and Carolyn never failed to express enthusiastic support, and our conversations enabled me to see how my work addressed different projects within the political science community.

Since leaving Brookings, I have exchanged a thousand e-mails with Eric Patashnik, now a political scientist at Yale University. His insightful reading of this book improved the analysis immeasurably, and his support and friendship have made the academy a better place to be. I look forward to future collaborations with him.

My colleagues in the Department of History and the Rockefeller College of Public Affairs at the State University of New York at Albany have provided a stimulating environment within which to complete this work. I thank the Department of History for inviting me into this institution that devotes an extraordinary amount of energy to the study of public policy. Its confidence in my ability to make the history of public policy interesting to broader audiences was very encouraging during the final stages of this book.

Brian Balogh, Edward Berkowitz, Meg Jacobs, Ira Katznelson, and Jessica Korn dedicated a significant amount of their time to reading entire drafts of the book. Their cogent analysis of my work led me to broaden my arguments and to deepen my narrative. Meg has also been a great conference partner and fellow traveler in the excitement and frustrations of political history.

Several colleagues provided useful comments on particular chapters or conference papers based on material in the book – among them, Paula Baker, Philip Ethington, Elizabeth Faue, Robert Lieberman, Robyn Muncy, and Robert Myers.

Several archivists, curators, and historians guided me through the collections that constitute the basis of this book, including Raymond Smock, Robert Frizzel, William Davis, and David de Lorenzo.

I thank the anonymous reader at Cambridge University Press whose advice on my analysis of Congress resulted in improvements to the book.

Ronald Cohen, my manuscript editor, provided sage advice on the presentation of this book. His enthusiasm and comments made the final stages a stimulating process. And I thank Frank Smith at Cambridge for his work as editor and his encouragement. Since my work was a doctoral dissertation in its earliest incarnation, Frank has remained a strong supporter of this project. He has been an ideal editor.

Several institutions have made this book possible – The Brookings Institution, the Everett Dirksen Center for Congressional Research, the Eisenhower World Affairs Institute, the Harry S. Truman Library Institute, the John F. Kennedy Library, the Johns Hopkins University, and the Lyndon B. Johnson Library. I thank them all.

Woodrow Wilson Center Press allowed me to incorporate material into Chapters 1, 3, 4, 5, and 6 that appeared in "Learning the ways and means: Wilbur Mills and a fiscal community, 1954–1964," in *Funding the Modern American State, 1941–1945: The Rise and Fall of the Era of Easy Finance,* ed. W. Elliot Brownlee (Cambridge: Cambridge University Press and Washington, D.C.: Woodrow Wilson Center Press, 1996), 289–352. Penn State University Press granted me permission to include material in Chapter 2 that appeared in "'Where Is the Money Coming From?': The Reconstruction of Social Security Finance, 1939–1950," in *The Journal of Policy History,* 9, No. 4 (Fall 1997): 399–424. My thanks to both presses.

My parents, to whom this book is dedicated, have been great friends, models, and supporters since they brought me into this world. As teachers and writers, both have shown me why intellectual pursuits are valuable in contemporary society. They had never wavered in their support of my professional aspirations, and for that I will always be grateful.

With all my heart, I want to thank my wife, Nora K. Zelizer, for all she has done. Nora has been my best friend for the last seven years. We have shared many special moments since meeting during the first week of graduate school. Although she did not enter into our relationship with the intention of becoming a Wilbur Mills expert, Nora has provided incredible advice on each page of this book, from its first incarnation as a graduate seminar paper to the final version of this manuscript. More important has been Nora's influence on me as a person. Through her intelligence, her warmth, and her enthusiasm, Nora has opened up countless aspects of living that I had never perceived before we met. In short, she has transformed me into a much different and better person. I am thankful every day that I found such a wonderful woman, and I look forward to our continuing adventures.

Introduction

Building a State in America

"A critical turning point" were the words one official used to describe President Lyndon Johnson's showdown with Wilbur Mills over the Great Society in the summer of 1968.[1] For almost two years, the administration had unsuccessfully lobbied Congress to enact a tax increase. At first, Johnson claimed the increase was needed to finance the war in Vietnam without depleting funds from the Great Society. By the winter of 1968, administration economists also warned that the increase was absolutely essential if Congress wanted to end sky-rocketing inflation. The tax increase could provide a shield protecting Johnson's domestic accomplishments while preventing further price increases.

But Wilbur Mills, the powerful chairman of the House Ways and Means Committee – the committee in charge of income taxation and Social Security – refused to support the measure until the administration agreed to a significant reduction in domestic spending. Mills said the deflationary effects of a tax increase would be negated should the government pour money back into the economy through public spending. He also contended that Congress needed to tighten its own spending belt before asking citizens to do the same. Mills insisted that Johnson had to choose between guns or butter.

In exchange for the tax increase, President Johnson accepted more than $6 billion in spending cuts (from a federal budget of about $184 billion), significantly weakening the Great Society. Johnson had little choice in his decision since Mills had accumulated enough political capital to block the tax increase should the administration refuse his demands. As the Speaker of the House complained, the chairman had "blackmailed" the administration and the Democratic leadership.[2] Even worse, Mills walked away from the battle without any notable scars, while the president emerged as

---

[1] Joseph Califano to Lyndon Johnson, 2 May 1968, LBJL, White House Central File, Box 54, File: LE/FI 11-4, 5/1/68–5/15/68.

[2] John McCormack (D-MA) cited in Barefoot Sanders to Lyndon Johnson, 9 May 1968, LBJL, White House Central File, Box 54, File: LE/FI 11-4, 5/1/68–5/15/68.

the man who sold out the poor to finance a bloody war in the jungles of Southeast Asia.[3]

For those who remember Mills's drunken escapades in the Tidal Basin, this historic confrontation with Lyndon Johnson seems inconceivable. For those who worked with the chairman during the prime of his career, however, the confrontation was unforgettable.[4] Either way, the struggle hints at the critical role Mills played in the development of the American state during a crucial period in its history, a period that began with a significant expansion during the New Deal and ended with political reform in the 1970s.

During this transformation of the American state, the Cold War pushed the nation into a new role in international affairs, while it helped legitimize the permanent need for a strong government at home. The Cold War also led federal officials from both parties to expand the budget to an unprecedented size to pay for military operations and domestic activities related to the war. Economic growth brought rising wages and improved living conditions to many segments of the nation: home ownership grew by almost half, while average incomes rose by more than 50 percent. Amidst prosperity, organized labor and capital reached an accord that centered on collective bargaining. Citizens excluded from the comforts of this era participated in national movements that demanded an end to racial, ethnic, and gender discrimination.[5]

Economic growth generated a constant stream of revenue into the federal government. Each increase in an individual's income resulted in a corresponding increase in the individual's tax contribution; rising income also brought more revenue into Social Security. As a result, Congress found itself with an excess of revenue without raising taxes or cutting spending. Between the 1940s and 1970s, other factors produced automatic revenue, including periodic reductions in the massive defense budget. Given the size of the military expenditures (over 14 percent of GDP by 1953), small reductions produced considerable revenue. Together, this income thrust policymakers into a discussion over reducing taxes or increasing spending. This stands in sharp contrast to the early 1990s, when a combination of diminished revenues, large national deficits and debt, and entrenched bud-

---

[3] Irving Bernstein, *Guns Or Butter: Lyndon Johnson's Presidency* (New York: Oxford University Press, 1995).

[4] This battle was most recently recalled during the debates over the balanced budget in 1996. See Joseph A. Califano, Jr., "Balancing the Budget, L.B.J. Style," *The New York Times*, Sunday, 31 December 1995, section E; Sander Vanocur, "When Mills Balked," *The New York Times*, 4 January 1996.

[5] James T. Patterson, *Grand Expectations: The United States, 1945–1974* (New York: Oxford University Press, 1996).

getary commitments produced a debate that centered on the trade-off between spending reductions and increased taxation.[6] In the postwar period, however, it seemed to many officials that an ever-expanding economic pie could prevent such difficult debates. Congress could distribute a benefit to one group of citizens without imposing a direct cost on another group.

During this period, the state increased in size and scope on an unprecedented scale in American life. Broad segments of society – including the poor, the physically disabled, elderly retirees, middle-class consumers, private investors, and corporations – came to depend on social and economic assistance from the federal government, including public welfare, contributory old-age insurance, disability insurance, macroeconomic income-tax adjustments, and tax breaks.

CHALLENGES AND OBSTACLES

These policies were not achieved without considerable challenge. Throughout the twentieth century, state-builders encountered formidable obstacles. First, the nation's anti-statist culture caused politicians and citizens to resist any sizable expansion of centralized government. Born in a revolution against central government, American political culture was rooted in the concepts of popular sovereignty, local democracy, and individual autonomy.[7] Although this cultural bias was not immutable, and contradictory pro-government sentiment did emerge, anti-statism and a devotion to minimal taxation imposed limits on state-building.[8] Among most business leaders,

[6] C. Eugene Steuerle, "Financing the American state at the turn of the century," in *Funding the Modern American State, 1941–1995: The Rise and Fall of the Era of Easy Finance*, ed. W. Elliot Brownlee (Cambridge: Cambridge University Press and Washington, D.C.: Woodrow Wilson Center Press, 1996), 409–444; Paul Pierson, *Dismantling the Welfare State? Reagan, Thatcher, and the Politics of Retrenchment* (Cambridge: Cambridge University Press, 1994), 149–155.

[7] James T. Kloppenberg, "The Virtues of Liberalism: Christianity, Republicanism, and Ethics in Early American Political Discourse," *Journal of American History* 74, No. 1 (June 1987): 9–33.

[8] Gareth Davies, *From Opportunity to Entitlement: The Transformation and Decline of Great Society Liberalism* (Lawrence: University Press of Kansas, 1996), 10–53; Morton Keller, *Regulating a New Economy: Public Policy and Economic Change in America, 1900–1933* (Cambridge, MA: Harvard University Press, 1990); David T. Beito, *Taxpayers in Revolt: Tax Resistance During the Great Depression* (Chapel Hill: University of North Carolina Press, 1989); Charles Lockhart, *Gaining Ground: Tailoring Social Programs to American Values* (Berkeley: University of California Press, 1989), 23–25; Ellis Hawley, "Social Policy and the Liberal State in Twentieth Century America," in *Federal Social Policy: The Historical Dimension*, eds. Donald T. Critchlow and Ellis W. Hawley (University Park: Pennsylvania State University Press, 1988), 117–141; Terrence J. McDonald,

moreover, "a sense of suspicion toward the state has managed to survive the most impressive and decisive political triumphs."[9] Even when domestic programs were enacted, they were often locally administered, limited in coverage, stigmatized, under-financed, and vulnerable to retrenchment.

The second challenge involved the fragmented institutional structure of government. The constitutional separation of powers, the doctrine of federalism, and a paucity of civil servants created numerous opportunities for particular interest groups to undermine public policies. Without a centralized system of governance, state-builders were forced to push their proposals through various levels of government. This required exhaustive efforts by those who hoped to maintain public policies over long periods of time.

Despite these obstacles, the state achieved a significant presence in the United States during the second half of the twentieth century. Amidst the crisis of the Great Depression and World War II, the Roosevelt administration had presided over the creation and expansion of an unparalleled number of federal programs including welfare, labor protection, old-age pensions, unemployment compensation, rural development, income taxation, and price controls. In the process, these programs continued to strengthen the executive branch, a process that had begun during the progressive era.[10] In the national crisis, Roosevelt and his allies found an opportunity to expand government, while their opponents, inside and outside of Congress, were generally muted. Historian Doris Kearns Goodwin concludes that by 1945, "Big government – modern government – was here to stay. The new responsibilities of government amounted to nothing less than a new relationship between the people and those whom they chose for service, a new understanding, a revised social contract, one framed within the democratic limits of the original understanding, but drastically changed in content."[11]

The Parameters of Urban Fiscal Policy: Socioeconomic Change and Political Culture in San Francisco, 1860–1906 (Berkeley: University of California Press, 1986); Alan Brinkley, *Huey Long, Father Coughlin, & The Great Depression* (New York: Vintage Books, 1983); Barry D. Karl, *The Uneasy State: The United States from 1915 to 1945* (Chicago: The University of Chicago Press, 1983); Morton Keller, *Affairs of State: Public Life in Late Nineteenth Century America* (Cambridge, MA: Harvard University Press, 1977); James Holt, "The New Deal and the American Anti-Statist Tradition," in *The New Deal: The National Level*, eds. John Braeman, Robert H. Bremner, and David Brody (Columbus: Ohio State University Press, 1975), 27–49.

[9] David Vogel, *Kindred Strangers: The Uneasy Relationship Between Politics and Business in America* (Princeton: Princeton University Press, 1996), 30.

[10] Sidney M. Milkis, *The President and the Parties: The Transformation of the American Party System Since the New Deal* (New York: Oxford University Press, 1993).

[11] Doris Kearns Goodwin, *No Ordinary Time: Franklin & Eleanor Roosevelt: The Home Front in World War II* (New York: Touchstone Books, 1994), 625–626.

But the survival of the expansionist state after 1945 was not guaranteed. Although crises had enabled Roosevelt to develop the infrastructure of the state, its institutionalization remained uncertain, and its future depended on support within Congress, especially among committee chairmen such as Wilbur Mills who had the legislative muscle to protect and expand programs. Even in the Great Depression, many new programs had been administered at the state and local level, and several major policies were dismantled once the economy recovered. The state's capacity to raise revenue had remained limited until the war.[12] During the immediate postwar period, opponents intensified their attacks on the legacies of the New Deal and World War II.[13] At the local level, some citizen's groups attempted to stifle the implementation of programs such as neighborhood integration and public housing.[14]

In the workplace, management attempted to curtail the scope of labor regulations. At the same time, the National Association of Manufacturers mounted a public relations campaign against domestic programs, while the business press expressed strong reservations about all government intervention.[15] While NAM mounted an anti-statist and anti-labor campaign, millions of blue collar workers – a key constituency in the New Deal coalition – procured benefits and job security from the corporation. Beginning in World War II, the union movement and welfare capitalists constructed elaborate systems of private benefits within their institutions, ranging from health insurance to workers' pensions, that offered an attractive supplement, or alternative, to the welfare state. Subsidized by government benefits

[12] Alan Brinkley, *The End Of Reform: New Deal Liberalism In Recession And War* (New York: Alfred A. Knopf, Inc., 1995); Brian Balogh, *Chain Reaction: Expert Debate & Public Participation In American Nuclear Power, 1945–1975* (Cambridge: Cambridge University Press, 1991), 11–13; Anthony J. Badger, *The New Deal: The Depression Years, 1933–40* (London: Macmillan Education Ltd, 1989), 299–312; Mark H. Leff, *The Limits of Symbolic Reform* (Cambridge: Cambridge University Press, 1984); Karl, *The Uneasy State,* 80–182; Herbert Stein, *The Fiscal Revolution in America,* revised edition (Washington, D.C.: AEI Press, 1990), 39–130; Ellis W. Hawley, *The New Deal and the Problem of Monopoly* (Princeton: Princeton University Press, 1966).

[13] David Plotke, *Building a Democratic Political Order: Reshaping American Liberalism in the 1930s and 1940s* (Cambridge: Cambridge University Press,1996), 190–262.

[14] Thomas J. Sugrue, *The Origins of the Urban Crisis: Race and Inequality in Postwar Detroit* (Princeton: Princeton University Press, 1996), 209–258.

[15] Elizabeth Fones-Wolf, *Selling Free Enterprise: The Business Assault on Labor and Liberalism, 1945–1960* (Urbana: University of Illinois Press, 1994); Robert Griffith, "Forging America's postwar order: Domestic politics and political economy in the age of Truman," in *The Truman Presidency,* ed. Michael J. Lacey (Cambridge: Cambridge University Press and Washington, D.C.: Woodrow Wilson International Center for Scholars, 1989), 57–88; Nora K. Moran, "Visions of Management: The American Business Press in the Postwar Era, 1945–1985" (Ph.D diss., Johns Hopkins University, 1997).

such as tax breaks, this private welfare state weaned blue collar support away from the American state.[16] After 1938, an alliance of congressional conservative southern Democrats and Republicans possessed enough votes to become an ongoing source of opposition to social policy, particularly concerning labor and civil rights.[17] To preserve and expand the state, supporters needed to overcome resistance at multiple levels of politics.

Yet scholars know relatively little about the accomplishments in American state-building during the postwar period. Most historians and historical social scientists have focused on the failures of American state-building, explicitly or implicitly portraying the West European and Canadian states as normative, and have provided sophisticated analyses showing how the nation's fragmented government and its anti-statist culture hampered policymaking.[18] In short, most scholars have begun with the question, "Why did the American state achieve so little in the twentieth century?" In answering this question, they have provided a comprehensive history of the policies and policymakers who failed to achieve their goals in the twentieth century. We thus know much about the roads not taken in postwar American politics.[19] This book takes a different approach.

Taxing America begins with the question, "How did the American state achieve what it did between 1945 and 1975, despite the nation's anti-statist culture and despite its fragmented political institutions?"

---

[16] Michael K. Brown, "Bargaining for Social Rights: Unions and the Reemergence of Welfare Capitalism, 1945–1952," *Political Science Quarterly*, 12, No. 4 (Winter 1998): 645–674; Sanford M. Jacoby, *Modern Manors: Welfare Capitalism Since the New Deal* (Princeton: Princeton University Press, 1997); Nelson Lichtenstein, "Labor in the Truman Era: Origins of the 'Private Welfare State,'" in *The Truman Presidency*, 128–155.

[17] Clyde P. Weed, *The Nemesis of Reform: The Republican Party During the New Deal* (New York: Columbia University Press, 1994), 168–203; Ira Katznelson, Kim Geiger, and Daniel Kryder, "Limiting Liberalism: The Southern Veto in Congress, 1933–1950," *Political Science Quarterly* 108, No. 2 (1993): 283–302; David L. Porter, *Congress and the Waning of the New Deal* (Port Washington: National University Publications, 1980); James T. Patterson, *Congressional Conservatism and the New Deal: The Growth of the Conservative Coalition in Congress, 1933–1939* (Lexington: University of Kentucky Press, 1967).

[18] For an excellent critique of this tendency and a cogent review of the literature on state-building, see Theda Skocpol, *Protecting Soldiers and Mothers: The Political Origins of Social Policy in the United States* (Cambridge, MA: The Belknap Press of Harvard University Press, 1992), 1–66.

[19] Michael B. Katz, *The Undeserving Poor: From the War on Poverty to the War on Welfare* (New York: Pantheon Books, 1989); Margaret Weir, *Politics and Jobs: The Boundaries of Employment Policy in the United States* (Princeton: Princeton University Press, 1992); Jill Quadagno, *The Color of Welfare: How Racism Undermined the War on Poverty* (New York: Oxford University Press, 1994); Brinkley, *The End of Reform*.

Wilbur Mills's experiences provide four important historical answers to this question.

Congress and the state

Congress played a crucial role in the institutionalization of the state. Nowhere was this clearer than with taxation. After all, taxation was central to state-building: Politicians extracted money from citizens to pay for government. Unlike the way it handled issues such as foreign policy, Congress never ceded its constitutional jurisdiction over taxation to the executive branch, not even during World War II.[20] As a result, Congress continued to exert tremendous influence over taxation throughout the century.

Without understanding the history of Congress it is impossible to understand the evolution of national tax policy during this period.[21] Between 1945 and 1975, Congress influenced tax politics through the decentralized committee system, which created an insulated arena for representatives from both parties and from competing regions to achieve difficult compromises without public scrutiny.[22] The specialized committee system dispersed power throughout Congress while simultaneously enhancing the power of the representatives who became committee chairmen (many of whom were senior southern Democrats). Within the House of Representatives, for example, committee chairmen maintained authority over committee staffs, they created and dismantled subcommittees, they controlled the committee agenda and parliamentary procedure, they scheduled committee proceedings, and they served as the floor managers for committee bills.[23]

Although committees had been an important part of Congress since the eighteenth century, the power of committee chairmen increased dramatically during the twentieth century. Traditional sources of congressional leadership, such as the Speaker of the House and the Democratic Caucus, had weakened significantly by World War II as a result of institutional and partisan reform. Within a congres-

[20] Bartholomew H. Sparrow, *From the Outside In: World War II and the American State* (Princeton: Princeton University Press, 1996), 33–66; 97–160; 270.

[21] On the historiography of congressional studies, see Joel Silbey, "The Historiography of the American Legislative System," in *Encyclopedia of the American Legislative System: Studies of the Principal Structures, Processes, and Policies of Congress and the State Legislatures Since the Colonial Era*, ed. Joel Silbey (New York: Charles Scribner's Sons, 1994), 281–299.

[22] Richard F. Bensel, *Sectionalism and American Political Development, 1880–1980* (Madison: University of Wisconsin Press, 1984), 175–255; 317–367; 403–412.

[23] Richard Fenno, *Congressmen in Committees* (Boston: Little, Brown & Company, 1973).

sional system that valued specialized expertise and revolved around
seniority, moreover, committee chairmen secured strong positions
within the House as they mastered particular areas of policy. Committee chairmen also served for longer terms following the war;
approximately 60 percent of committee chairmen held their positions for more than five years, and almost a dozen served for over a
decade.[24] These chairmen provided the type of continuity within
national government that political executives and bureaucrats had
long contributed in Western Europe.[25] As a result of their position,
chairmen such as Mills were a formidable presence at all stages of
policymaking process.

Policy communities

The second answer from Mills's career to the question of the
American state's achievements concerns the role that policy communities played in helping to facilitate policymaking despite the fragmented structure of the state. In particular, they offered an arena
where congressional leaders would interact with other members of
the state on a regular basis. A policy community, according to one
political scientist, "hums along on its own, independent of such political events as changes of administration and pressure from legislators'
constituencies."[26] To shape policies at every stage of the tax-writing
process, Mills worked closely with a specialized tax community whose
members included political party officials, leaders and experts from
umbrella business and financial associations (such as the Chamber
of Commerce), staff members of the executive and congressional
branch, bureaucrats and administrators, university professors, independent specialists, editors and writers of the specialized policy
media, and participants in think tanks.[27]

Ultimately, policy communities needed to sell their ideas to committee chairmen. Mills often identified with and operated through
the tax community. By balancing the competing needs of its members
and translating their ideas into concrete legislative victories, he

---

[24] Steven S. Smith and Christopher J. Deering, *Committees in Congress*, 2nd edition
(Washington, D.C.: Congressional Quarterly Inc., 1990), 39–45.

[25] Joseph White and Aaron Wildavsky, *The Deficit and the Public Interest: The Search for
Responsible Budgeting in the 1980s* (Berkeley: University of California Press and New
York: Russell Sage Foundation, 1989), 544.

[26] John W. Kingdon, *Agendas, Alternatives, and Public Policies* (Glenview, Illinois: Scott,
Foresman, 1984), 124.

[27] Although in earlier work I have referred to this group as the "fiscal policy community," I have decided that "tax policy community" better defines the boundaries and
the agenda of the membership.

expanded his influence in the state. Similar to his interaction with members of Congress and their interest groups, Mills hammered out compromises with the tax community, the tax men of Washington, D.C. The community traded information, agendas, and networks to the president, as opposed to the interest groups that tended to exchange money and constituents for political support.[28] The relationship between Mills and the community was unbalanced. Although Mills benefited from negotiating with this community to expand his influence in policymaking, as chairman of Ways and Means he could maintain his power simply by sitting on the chairmanship. The policy community, on the other hand, depended on Mills to achieve any legislative success. Nonetheless, through a strong working relationship, both partners in this marriage could increase their influence and productivity.

The tax community included three factions, categorized as Social Security, Growth Manipulation, and Tax Reform.[29] As chairman of Ways and Means, Mills negotiated with, and participated in, all three factions. The Social Security faction promoted contributory social insurance as the most generous form of government assistance that could be maintained within the nation's anti-statist culture. The growth manipulation faction argued that adjustments to the income-tax code, especially stimulative rate reductions, offered an effective form of economic policy. While members of this faction argued over questions of timing and size, they all agreed that tax manipulation surpassed government regulation, aggressive monetary policy, or public spending as a means of boosting economic growth. The tax reform faction supported an ongoing, incremental reform process in which Congress would periodically cleanse the tax code by eliminating as many tax breaks as possible. By demonstrating its willingness to control the system, according to this faction, Congress could maintain political support for a progressive, growth-oriented tax code and for the tax breaks that Congress deemed essential on economic and political grounds.

Together, these factions constituted a larger community that

[28] It is interesting to note that recent scholarship suggests that interest groups also engaged in the politics of information and agenda-setting. See Gary McKissick, "Issue Manipulation: Interest Group Lobbying and the Framing of Policy Alternatives" (Ph.D. diss., University of Michigan, 1997) and Theda Skocpol, *Boomerang: Clinton's Health Security Effort and the Turn Against Government in U.S. Politics* (New York: W.W. Norton, 1996), 133–172.

[29] These are labels that I have given to the various factions of the community. The factions at the time perceived themselves within these distinct groupings. While the members would certainly classify their interests around these typologies, the actual labels are my own construction.

achieved considerable influence within the tax-writing committees during Mills's career. Although the names of the faction members – such as Robert Ball, Andrew Biemiller, Wilbur Cohen, Henry Fowler, Walter Heller, Robert Myers, Joseph Pechman, Herbert Stein, Stanley Surrey, and Laurence Woodworth – meant little to the average voter in New York or Arkansas, they were members of a community that helped design several monumental pieces of legislation, including the Revenue Acts of 1962 and 1964, Medicare in 1965, the Tax Reform Act of 1969, and the Social Security Amendments of 1972. The community was the product of a distinct historical period, an era that was characterized largely by economic growth, the Cold War, and the decentralized congressional committee system.

A "culture of tax policy" provided a considerable degree of coherence to this community. This political culture included a distinct discourse with its own vocabulary and conceptions of the political economy, certain types of social interactions between members of government, and established ways of learning the political process.[30] One scholar has defined the term "political culture" as "the underlying assumptions and rules that govern behavior in the political system . . . the political ideals and operating norms of a polity . . . the manifestation in aggregate form of the psychological

---

[30] My understanding of the term "political culture" comes from the following works: Kathryn Kish Sklar, *Florence Kelley & The Nation's Work: The Rise of Women's Political Culture, 1830–1900* (New Haven: Yale University Press, 1995); Frank Dobbin, *Forging Industrial Policy: The United States, Britain, and France in the Railway Age* (Cambridge: Cambridge University Press, 1994); Philip J. Ethington, *The Public City: The Political Construction of Urban Life in San Francisco, 1850–1900* (Cambridge: Cambridge University Press, 1994); Michael McGerr, "Political Style and Women's Power, 1830–1930," *The Journal of American History* 77, No. 3 (December 1990): 864–885; Robert Kelley, "The Interplay of American Political Culture and Public Policy: The Sacramento River as a Case Study," *Journal of Policy History* 1, No. 1 (1989): 19; Paula Baker, "The Domestication of Politics: Women and American Political Society, 1780–1920," *American Historical Review* 89, No. 3 (June 1984): 620–647; Jean Baker, *Affairs of Party: The Political Culture of Northern Democrats in the Mid-Nineteenth Century* (Ithaca: Cornell University Press, 1983); Daniel Walker Howe, *The Political Culture of the American Whigs* (Chicago: University of Chicago Press, 1979). In their book, *A History of Taxation and Expenditure in the Western World* (New York: Simon and Schuster, 1986), Carolyn Webber and Aaron Wildavsky argue that political culture offers the best way to understand the tax and spending systems of particular nations across time and space. Although their work provides one of the most comprehensive histories of fiscal policy and a powerful argument for the influence of political culture on policy, their book plays down the relevance of institutional design, special interests, and policy. Their definition of culture is vague, and broad characterizations are used to label entire portions of a population. I attempt to use a much more specific definition of culture, by focusing on the particular culture of a distinct group within the U.S. government.

and subjective dimensions of politics . . . the product of both the collective history of a political system and the life histories of the members of the system. . . ."[31]

By examining such important issues as language, rituals, and attitudes, the history of political culture reveals how the unexamined assumptions of political actors played a pivotal role in political development. Political discourse was an important aspect of the community. The postwar discourse helped Mills and other policymakers to communicate and to devise substantive policies. It also led Mills to conceive of himself as involved in a common intellectual and political project with other policymakers.[32] Policy communities worked most effectively with the individuals and organizations who embraced the main aspects of their culture and with those who had access or who held key institutional positions of power. These communities, according to one analysis, "effectively express cultural norms about appropriate political strategies, tactics, and actions."[33]

Taxation as liberal policy

The third answer from Mills's career to how the American state achieved so much involves the centrality of taxation to postwar liberalism and its domestic agenda. Taxation was much more than a purely technical, administrative endeavor at the periphery of political life.[34] Through taxation, Mills and the community were able

---

[31] Cited in Jo Freeman, "The Political Culture of the Democratic and Republican Parties," *Political Science Quarterly* 101, No. 3 (1986): 327–328.

[32] In discussing political discourse, I draw on Dorothy Ross, *The Origins of American Social Science* (Cambridge: Cambridge University Press, 1991) and J.G.A. Pocock, *Virtue, Commerce, and History: Essays on Political Thought and History, Chiefly in the Eighteenth Century* (Cambridge: Cambridge University Press, 1985), 1–34.

[33] David Knoke, Franz Urban Pappi, Jeffrey Broadbent, Yutaka Tsujinaka, *Comparing Policy Networks: Labor Politics in the U.S., Germany, and Japan* (Cambridge: Cambridge University Press, 1996), 218. For theoretical discussions about policy communities, see the following: Frank R. Baumgartner and Bryan D. Jones, *Agendas and Instability in American Politics* (Chicago: University of Chicago Press, 1993); Paul Burstein, "Policy Domains: Organization, Culture, and Policy Outcomes," *Annual Review of Sociology* 17 (1991): 327–350; Jack L. Walker, "The Diffusion of Knowledge, Policy Communities, and Agenda Setting: The Relationship of Knowledge and Power," in *New Strategic Perspectives on Social Policy*, eds. John E. Tropman, Milan J. Dluhy, and Roger M. Lind (New York: Pergamon Press, 1981), 75–97.

[34] *Taxing America* builds on an emerging school of literature that pays closer attention to the role of taxation in American state-building, which includes the following work: Brownlee, ed., *Funding the Modern American State, 1941–1995*; John J. Coleman, *Party Decline in America: Policy, Politics, and the Fiscal State* (Princeton: Princeton University Press, 1996); Sheldon D. Pollack, *The Failure of U.S. Tax Policy: Revenue and Politics* (University Park: Pennsylvania State University Press, 1996); Theda Skocpol, *Social*

to sell various economic and social programs within the nation's anti-statist culture. As the chairman of a tax-writing committee, Mills perceived the relevance of taxation to both social welfare and economic policy. Mills pressured, and often coerced, liberal policymakers to fashion an agenda that was politically and economically viable within Congress. This agenda centered around contributory, wage-related social insurance, moderate macroeconomic fiscal policy, and a growth-oriented tax code.

Between the 1940s and 1970s, Mills and the tax community transformed federal taxation from a revenue-raising device into a mechanism for earmarking government benefits and for managing economic growth. The first area where taxation was central to postwar liberalism was social welfare policy. Regarding social welfare, Mills grasped that strong income-transfer programs, such as Social Security, required sound revenue-raising mechanisms to finance them. Taxes were not just incidental to social programs, Mills understood, and they could serve as a mechanism that guaranteed strong political support. Mills and the community ensured that Old-Age and Survivors' Insurance remained the centerpiece of U.S. social welfare. The "pay-as-you-go" earmarked tax system became an essential component of the success of Social Security during this period as it legitimized the absence of a means test. It helped secure broad middle class support and it seemed to ensure that Congress had to raise enough taxes to cover the cost of annual benefits. Congress defended the exclusive symbolic link between the Social Security tax and the social insurance benefit, thereby eliminating the possibility of directly financing Social Security pensions through general revenue. For government officials, this decision strengthened the insurance component of Social Security since they felt the payroll tax distinguished the programs it financed. Once it secured this link, the community began

Policy in the United States: Future Possibilities in Historical Perspective (Princeton: Princeton University Press, 1995); Richard Richards, *Closing the Door to Destitution: The Shaping of the Social Security Acts of the United States and New Zealand* (University Park: The Pennsylvania State University Press, 1994); Christopher Howard, "The Hidden Side of the American Welfare State," *Political Science Quarterly* 108, No. 3 (1993): 403–436; Ronald King, *Money, Time, and Politics: Investment Tax Subsidies and American Democracy* (New Haven: Yale University Press, 1993); Ann Shola Orloff, *The Politics of Pensions: A Comparative Analysis of Britain, Canada, and the United States, 1880–1940* (Madison: University of Wisconsin Press, 1993); Robert Stanley, *Dimensions of Law in the Service of Order: Origins of the Federal Income Tax, 1861–1913* (New York: Oxford University Press, 1993); Sven Steinmo, *Taxation and Democracy: Swedish, British, and American Approaches to Financing the Modern State* (New Haven: Yale University Press, 1993); Skocpol, *Protecting Soldiers and Mothers*, 112–130; Cathie J. Martin, *Shifting the Burden: The Struggle over Growth and Corporate Taxation* (Chicago: University of Chicago Press, 1991).

an intensive campaign to expand social insurance to an increasingly middle-class constituency while reducing welfare.

But the success of the earmarked tax system was not automatic. It was challenged repeatedly on many grounds – by those who wanted a more expansive program, by those who wanted to undermine the program by eliminating this powerful tax, or by others who believed on economic grounds that this tax was inefficient. Throughout his career in Congress, Mills would devote a great deal of his time working with the Social Security faction of the community to protect this earmarked tax system and its "pay-as-you-go" structure. Mills would be successful until the very end of his career – between 1969 and 1972 – when politics and the popularity of the program overwhelmed the system.

The historical scholarship on Social Security has focused on benefits, particularly on the racial and gender dynamics behind who received different types and amounts of benefits. This research argues that the two-track structure of Social Security tended to benefit white male retirees, who had been industrial wage-earners, and their dependent wives (social insurance), while Social Security provided meager assistance to single women, African-Americans, and the unemployed (public assistance).[35] *Taxing America* focuses on the question of taxation with respect to Social Security, especially on the fiscal mechanisms through which policymakers distinguished social insurance from public welfare.

Without these symbolic distinctions, social insurance would not have been as attractive, as generous, or as desirable. One main reason

[35] Robert C. Lieberman, "Race and the Organization of Welfare Policy," in *Classifying By Race*, ed. Paul Peterson (Princeton: Princeton University Press, 1995), 156–187; Gwendolyn Mink, *The Wages of Motherhood: Inequality in the Welfare State, 1917–1942* (Ithaca: Cornell University Press, 1995); Alice Kessler-Harris, "Designing Women and Old Fools: The Construction of the Social Security Amendments of 1939," in *U.S. History as Women's History: New Feminist Essays*, eds. Linda Kerber, Alice Kessler-Harris, and Kathryn Kish Sklar (Chapel Hill: University of North Carolina Press, 1995), 87–106; Nancy Fraser and Linda Gordon, "'Dependency' Demystified: Inscriptions of Power in a Keyword of the Welfare State," *Social Politics* 1, No. 1 (Spring 1994):4–31; Linda Gordon, *Pitied But Not Entitled: Single Mothers and the History of Welfare* (New York: The Free Press, 1994); Quadagno, *The Color of Welfare* and Jill Quadagno, *The Transformation of Old Age Security: Class and Politics in the American Welfare State* (Chicago: University of Chicago Press, 1988); Rickie Solinger, *Wake Up Little Susie: Single Pregnancy and Race Before Roe v. Wade* (New York: Routledge, 1992); Katz, *The Undeserving Poor* and Michael Katz, *In the Shadow of the Poorhouse* (New York: Basic Books, 1982); Ann Shola Orloff, "The Political Origins of America's Belated Welfare State," in *The Politics of Social Policy in the United States*, eds. Margaret Weir, Ann Shola Orloff, and Theda Skocpol, (Princeton: Princeton University Press, 1988), 65–80; James Patterson, *America's Struggle Against Poverty, 1900–1985* (Cambridge, MA: Harvard University Press, 1981).

citizens and politicians privileged social insurance was the perception that it was an earned right. As a result, claimed the policymakers, its benefits did not create dependency on the government. This definition of the policy was not inherent to the benefit, but had to be constructed through a complex tax system with its symbols and its rhetoric. Mills's career thus provides a stronger understanding of how social insurance and public welfare were distinguished and defined within the state. By focusing on taxation, I reconstruct the discourse that was used among tax policymakers during most of the debates over social welfare, thereby providing a richer sense of the culture and logic that drove these important decisions. Mills's career suggests that issues other than race and gender – the issues on which most historical studies have focused – were also crucial to the development of Social Security and to the intentions of those who constructed the program.[36] In particular, policymakers sought to create an expansive social insurance program grounded in a distinct system of contributory finance that could withstand the anti-statist culture of the United States.

The second area where taxation became central to postwar liberal governance involved economic policy. Mills discerned that the manipulation of tax rates and the creation of tax breaks enabled the government to help manage the economy indirectly without infringing on the prerogatives of economic institutions. Unlike the nineteenth-century state that relied on the court system and tariffs for particular regional industries, or the period between 1900 and 1945 when the state added regulatory commissions and administrative agencies, the postwar state relied increasingly on macroeconomic fiscal policy to intervene in the national economy from the late-1940s to the mid-1970s.[37]

[36] For an insightful critique of the racial analysis of Social Security history, see Gareth Davies and Martha Derthick, "Race and Social Welfare Policy: The Social Security Act of 1935," *Political Science Quarterly* 112, No. 2 (Summer 1997): 217–235.

[37] For different strategies for government intervention in the economy that took hold before the 1940s, see the following: William J. Novak, *The People's Welfare: Law and Regulation in Nineteenth-Century America* (Chapel Hill: The University of North Carolina Press, 1996); Brinkley, *The End of Reform*; Judith Goldstein, *Ideas, Interests, and American Trade Policy* (Ithaca: Cornell University Press, 1993); Christopher L. Tomlins, *Law, Labor, and Ideology in the Early American Republic* (Cambridge: Cambridge University Press, 1993); Ellis W. Hawley, *The Great War and the Search for a Modern Order: A History of the American People and Their Institutions, 1917–1933*, 2nd edition (New York: St. Martin's Press, 1992), and Hawley, *The New Deal and the Problem of Monopoly*; William E. Forbath, *Law and the Shaping of the American Labor Movement* (Cambridge, MA: The Belknap Press of Harvard University Press, 1991); Steven Skowronek, *Building a New American State: The Expansion of National Administrative Capacities, 1877–1920* (Cambridge: Cambridge University Press, 1982); Keller,

By this point in history, moreover, "fiscal policy... meant tax policy."[38]

The World War II mass tax, made permanent in peacetime through the recodification of 1954, had a major impact on Mills and the community. Indeed, the revised code in 1954 validated the direction taxation had taken during World War II and the Korean War – toward high progressive rates, the use of numerous tax breaks for non-wage income, and dependence on withholding on wages at the source. Following the enactment of the mass tax, policymakers could no longer ignore the macroeconomic impact of income taxation. Through its permanent high tax rates and its massive withholding system, the federal government would continue to absorb billions of dollars each year from the national economy. Through its complex system of tax breaks, moreover, the federal government would have considerable influence on national private investment decisions. The recodification confirmed that the income tax had become much more than a revenue-raising mechanism. Although government officials of earlier historical periods were aware that taxation affected matters such as capital investment and regional industry, they did not deliberately manipulate taxation to help manage the national economy. The postwar period was different. Income-tax policy was used as a macroeconomic tool through which expert officials could stimulate national economic growth or restrain excessive expansion.

From 1955 through 1964, Mills conducted several congressional hearings that promoted this concept in political debate. Meanwhile, the practical experience of constantly rewriting the code forced congressional representatives to acknowledge the immense economic impact of each technical provision. Like Medicare, the Revenue Acts of 1962 and 1964 represented an important achievement for Mills and his colleagues. To stimulate economic productivity and private investment and to achieve full employment, the Revenue Acts enacted the largest postwar tax reductions to that date (and the largest until 1981) and, for the first time, openly endorsed temporary peacetime deficits in non-recessionary times. The legislation also gave rise within Congress to a crucial concept of tax reform. According to the experts, incremental reform would create a more favorable climate for economic growth and "horizontal equity," the notion that equal incomes should pay equal taxes, and that there should thus be

Regulating a New Economy and *Affairs of State*; Robert Wiebe, *The Search for Order, 1877–1920* (New York: Hill and Wang, 1967); Samuel P. Hays, *The Response to Industrialism, 1885–1914* (Chicago: University of Chicago Press, 1957).

[38] Steinmo, *Taxation & Democracy*, 136.

fewer distinctions between different types of income. Importantly, tax reform did not attempt to destroy the tax-break system with the hidden benefits it bestowed on powerful interest groups and political constituencies. Rather, it aimed to preserve the income-tax structure by distinguishing "legitimate" tax breaks, defined as those provisions that were currently endorsed by the leaders of the tax community and Congress, from those that could no longer be defended effectively. These efforts culminated in the concept of "tax expenditures," which posited that the government actually spent money through a hidden budget of tax breaks for individuals and organizations.

Fiscal conservatism and the state

Finally, the fourth lesson from Mills's career involves the active role of fiscal conservatives in building tax policies of the American state between the New Deal and the 1970s.[39] During this period, several influential fiscal conservatives entered into a fragile alliance with the state. By the 1960s, fiscal conservatism meant more than a strict adherence to balanced budgets. Many fiscal conservatives in government, particularly those within the Democratic Party, supported a state that used moderate tax reductions to stimulate economic growth, even if the reductions required occasional deficits; they supported a state that limited non-defense general-revenue expenditures; and they supported a state that provided contributory social insurance for the elderly. Fiscal conservatives such as Mills hesitantly accepted the growth of a particular version of centralized govern-

---

[39] Thus far, little attention has been given to the role of fiscal conservatism in the growing historical literature on conservatism since the 1930s. The only exception comes from the political scientist James D. Savage, whose *Balanced Budgets & American Politics* (Ithaca: Cornell University Press, 1988) provides an interesting account of the importance of balanced budgets before the New Deal and since the 1980s, but provides less analysis of the crucial period in between. On the history of conservatism, see the following: E.J. Dionne, Jr., *Why Americans Hate Politics* (New York: Simon & Schuster, 1991); Charles W. Dunn and J. David Woodward, *The Conservative Tradition in America* (Lanham, Maryland: Rowman & Littlefield, 1996); Godfrey Hodgson, *The World Turned Right Side Up: A History of the Conservative Ascendancy in America* (Boston: Houghton Mifflin, 1996); Paul Gottfried and Thomas Flemming, *The Conservative Movement* (Boston: Twayne Publishers, 1988); David Green, *Shaping Political Consciousness: The Language of Politics in America from McKinley to Reagan* (Ithaca: Cornell University Press, 1987); George H. Nash, *The Conservative Intellectual Movement in America Since 1945* (New York: Basic Books, 1976); and "AHR Forum: The Problem of American Conservatism," *American Historical Review* 99, No. 2 (April 1994): 409–452.

ment. The state offered them enticing political opportunities. For example, Social Security enabled congressional representatives to distribute generous "self-supporting" benefits to constituents, to increase their power within the Democratic party and among moderate Republicans, and to avoid being marginalized as reactionaries while continuing to defend fiscal restraint.

Although many fiscal conservatives accepted the need for substantial government expenditures and occasional budget deficits, they still dedicated themselves to restraining the long-term growth of government through the power of the purse. The congressional tax-writing committees were institutions that promoted fiscal conservatism within the state. Congress had delegated to members of these committees, particularly the chairmen, the responsibility of controlling tax rates, the national debt, and annual deficits. Fiscal conservatives expressed ongoing concern about the detrimental effect of deficits on consumer prices, national savings, and the international stability of the dollar. As a result, they tended to define policy debates in terms of budgetary cost, tax burdens, and potential effect on the deficit. In doing so, fiscal conservatives stood out amidst the "era of easy finance," and foreshadowed the type of debate that would dominate the 1990s.

The organization of the book

The convergence of these aspects of Mills's experience – the influence of Congress, the relevance of a specialized tax policy community and its culture, the centrality of taxation to postwar liberalism and its domestic policy, and the alliance between fiscal conservatives and the state – frames the narrative of *Taxing America*. My account of Mills and the community is divided into three sections.

Part I explores the development of the tax policy community, and the ways in which Mills began to use his relationship with members of this community to enhance his influence from inside Congress. This part also discusses the political discourse that helped to unite the tax community throughout Mills's tenure in Congress.

Part II turns to state-building and public policy. Once the community had formed and obtained positions of power, it needed to translate its agenda into public policy. The narrative thus focuses on how the tax community transformed federal taxation from being primarily a redistributive and revenue-raising device into a mechanism to stimulate economic growth and earmark government benefits. Drawing on Mills's work, this section also examines how some fiscal conservatives came to terms with the state on specific legislative battles.

Part II also explores how policies restructured politics.[40] Once enacted, policies often took on a life of their own, beyond the control or original expectations of those who had created them. Provisions such as Social Security and tax breaks created a sense of entitlement among recipients that fueled demands for liberalization. Mills and the community constantly dealt with the tensions produced by this dynamic; this became most evident in the debates over Medicare and tax reform.

Part III examines congressional reform, the disintegration of the tax community, the unraveling of its tax system, and the flight of fiscal conservatives from their alliance with the state.

To understand the history of the political, economic, and professional elites who dominate this story, my analysis draws on the methodology of social and cultural history, which has focused on social communities and social movements. Scholars of state-building have generally played down the social history of political elites. Rather, they have focused on macroeconomic forces that drove institutional development or on individual leaders isolated from any social context. *Taxing America* looks at the social and cultural history of the political elites who constructed the state's tax policies during the postwar period.

This type of analysis sheds new light on the development of political institutions. It pays close attention to the role of personal networks, contingency, and human agency in the rather abstract process of state-building. By examining the importance of a policy community and its culture, *Taxing America* shows that personal networks and individual choices were instrumental in the development of the state – an aspect of political history that the "new institutionalism" has tended to play down. I emphasize the interaction between these networks, their discourse, and the institutional structures within which they operated.[41]

---

[40] Pierson, *Dismantling the Welfare State?* 39–41.

[41] Some social scientists have started to explore the relationship between ideas and institutions. See Margaret Weir, "Ideas and the politics of bounded innovation," in *Structuring Politics: Historical Institutionalism in Comparative Analysis*, eds. Sven Steinmo, Kathleen Thelen, and Frank Longstreth (Cambridge: Cambridge University Press, 1992), 188–216; M. Stephen Weatherford with Thomas B. Mayhew, "Tax Policy and Presidential Leadership: Ideas, Interests, and the Quality of Advice," *Studies in American Political Development* 9, No. 2 (Fall 1995): 287–330; Paul J. Quirk, "In Defense of the Politics of Ideas," *The Journal of Politics* 50, No. 1 (February 1988): 31–41.

SHAPING THE POLICY AGENDA

Most scholars who have discussed Mills have taken his power for granted or have focused on the process through which he maintained this power.[42] They have not analyzed how Mills learned to exercise his power or how he expanded his influence beyond the official duties of the chairmanship. As a result, scholarly accounts of the period present Mills and his committee as "obstacles" to modern fiscal and social welfare policymaking. Like most accounts of Congress, they suggest that the chairman derived his power exclusively from his ability to block presidential initiatives and to remain outside the state policymaking process.[43]

Framed by an analysis of how Congress shaped the development of the state, *Taxing America* examines how Mills expanded his influence by working *within* the tax policy community and not just *against* it. By learning the skills of modern congressional politics, and by learning to work both with the policy communities that had emerged

---

[42] *Taxing America* takes a different approach than John Manley's classic study of Mills and the Ways and Means committee in Manley's *The Politics of Finance: The House Committee on Ways and Means* (Boston: Little, Brown, 1970). Manley's work used a Parsonian model to explain how Mills achieved such power during the 1960s. Mills did so, according to Manley, through a consensus-building approach to issues, through his actual expertise, and through the value system of the committee. Manley, however, was interested primarily in timeless processes, and his study largely picked up after 1964, once Mills had achieved his power, and ends before 1972, when his power came under intense challenge. By developing a more comprehensive historical interpretation of Mills and viewing the 1960s in the context of the 1950s, I hope to show that Mills's success was anything but inevitable or consensual: Mills had to learn how to be influential as chairman. His growing influence during this period stemmed from two important factors that Manley neglects: First, he developed a close relationship to the policymaking community outside of Congress; second, he mastered the discourse that shaped that community. My concept of Mills's mastery of the "discourse" encompasses, but is broader than, Mills's "actual expertise," which Manley stressed. Unlike Manley, I examine critically the notion of "expertise" as a construct within a larger political culture and as a part of an ongoing discourse about the nature of politics in the postwar era. Finally, I focus much of my analysis on the policies that Mills passed, rather than just the process through which he devised them. In my analysis, those policies structured Mills's subsequent politics as much as vice versa.

[43] For works that tend to present Mills in this light, see Martin, *Shifting the Burden*, 81–106; Steinmo, *Taxation & Democracy*; Howard Winant, *Stalemate: Political Economic Origins of Supply-Side Policy* (New York: Praeger, 1988); Stein, *The Fiscal Revolution in America*; Stein, "The fiscal revolution in America, part II: 1964–1994," in *Funding the Modern American State, 1941–1995*, 201–209; Robert M. Collins, "Growth Liberalism in the Sixties," in *The Sixties: From Memory to History*, ed. David Farber (Chapel Hill: University of North Carolina Press, 1994), 11–44; Lawrence C. Pierce, *The Politics of Fiscal Policy Formation* (Pacific Palisades, California: Goodyear Publishing Company, 1971); 135–178.

during this period and the powerful interests that predated them, Mills helped to shape tax policies from their conception to their enactment.[44] Mills used the "positive power" of the chairmanship in addition to its "negative power." Positive power revolved around extra-procedural tactics such as using policy information for political advantage, building alliances with talented staff and experts, and exploiting personal relationships.[45] Negative power included procedural tactics such as blocking a bill from coming to the House floor and establishing limits on debate. In exercising positive power, Mills's relationship with the tax community reveals how, in some arenas, Congress continued to influence the entire policymaking process during the period of the "Imperial Presidency."[46]

Mills operated effectively in three different political arenas: the tax policy community, Congress, and his congressional district. Within Congress, for example, Mills crafted the technical substance of bills so that they gained broad bipartisan support in the tax-writing committees, in the House, and in the Senate.[47] Mills's thirty-eight years in Congress (including his reelection after the Fanne Fox scandal), moreover, reveals his popularity among voters in the second district of Arkansas.

Taxing America focuses on Mills's relationship with the tax policy community, considering the other two arenas as they relate to the first. Before legislation reached the House floor, Mills struggled to influence the issues that would dominate the policy agenda, how particular pieces of legislation would be packaged, and which policy alternatives would be ignored. This complex process, which social scientists have labeled "agenda-setting," required skillful intellectual and rhetorical negotiation.[48] By bringing his legislative skills to the

[44] The process of "social learning" within the state has been explored in two important volumes from the Woodrow Wilson Center: Michael Lacey and Mary Furner, eds., *The State and Social Investigation in Britain and the United States* (Cambridge: Cambridge University Press and Washington, D.C.: Woodrow Wilson Center Press, 1993) and Furner and Barry Supple, eds., *The State and Economic Knowledge: The American and British Experiences* (Cambridge: Cambridge University Press and Washington, D.C.: Woodrow Wilson International Center For Scholars, 1990).

[45] The concept of positive and negative power was developed in Smith and Deering, *Committees in Congress*, 10–13.

[46] Arthur M. Schlesinger, Jr., *The Imperial Presidency* (New York: Popular Library, 1974) and *The Cycles of American History* (Boston: Houghton Mifflin Company, 1986), 277–336. See also James L. Sundquist, *The Decline and Resurgence of Congress* (Washington, D.C.: The Brookings Institution, 1981).

[47] Manley, *The Politics of Finance.*

[48] Kingdon, *Agendas, Alternatives, and Public Policies,* 3–4; 206–209; Nelson W. Polsby, *Political Innovation in America: The Politics of Policy Innovation* (New Haven: Yale University Press, 1984).

agenda-setting process, Mills brokered compromises among the various factions of the tax community. He shaped the policy agenda and packaged legislation so that numerous members of the community could perceive it as a partial victory.

While participating in the agenda-setting process, Mills acted both as a political chameleon and a political sphinx. As a chameleon, he absorbed the interests, the ideas, and the language of each faction in the tax community. By immersing himself in each faction, Mills was able to define the policy agenda so to appear as a partial validation of their efforts. As a sphinx, Mills refused to commit himself to any particular proposal until the very end of deliberations. This strategic approach entailed more than evasiveness. Rather, it enabled Mills to fulfill his duty as a legislative leader by fostering negotiation and designing compromise. As a chameleon and a sphinx, Mills brought his legislative skills to the intellectual world of policymakers. In the end, his relationship with the tax community remains one of the most distinctive aspects of his tenure on Ways and Means, and it offers considerable insight into the process through which policy communities and congressional committees developed the nation's public policy, its political agenda, and its governmental institutions.

At the same time, Mills packaged the policy agenda and legislation so that the ideas of the policy community would be politically attractive to members of Congress and their interest groups. As chairman of Ways and Means, Mills faced numerous pressures, ranging from the president to party leaders to powerful interest groups to policy experts to constituents. One of the most important aspects of Mills's career involved his negotiations with these conflicting pressures. The relationship between the tax community and the other sources of pressure created a constant tension in Mills's career. That tension offers crucial insights into the complexities of the state during the postwar period.

Besides advancing his own power within Congress, Mills developed and promoted a larger policy agenda. Foremost, he remained committed to the principles of fiscal conservatism, insisting that balanced budgets and low taxation were essential political objectives. While he was determined to limit the long-term cost of programs and minimize the negative impact of government on private markets, Mills gradually accepted the permanence of the state in many areas of life. By the time he became chairman, he supported a contributory social insurance program based on earmarked taxes and wage-related benefits, as well as macroeconomic fiscal policies that helped to stimulate growth through rate adjustments and tax breaks. In short, Mills wanted to help maintain the presence of a federal government that adhered to the nation's anti-statist, individualist, and fiscal values. Mills sought affordable federal assistance without a welfare state.

Any historical book that focuses on a particular individual raises several questions about the role of that individual in history. For example, did Mills and the policy community matter, or would tax policy have been the same during this period had they never existed? This counterfactual question is not the type of inquiry that frames this study. Certainly, Mills and the tax community were influential during their time in power. We can glean through historical documents that Mills and members of the community held positions of power, that they were involved in tax policymaking in the executive and congressional branch, and that there was a convergence between their agenda and the policies that emerged.

There are other important questions concerning the role of the individual in history. Did Mills direct the community, or did the community direct him? Did Mills lead the Congress, or did he follow the dictates of representatives and senators? Was there something distinctive about Mills's influence, or did the chairmanship of Ways and Means produce the same type of leader over time regardless of who held the chairmanship? For the historian, the answer to all of these questions is "all of the above." Mills at times helped lead the community, yet he was also profoundly influenced by the community. Mills often steered the House of Representatives and Ways and Means on matters of taxation, yet he also crafted legislation to secure the votes of members. Both looked to each other and both were interdependent in their quest to secure power. For a historian interested in the richness of political development, Mills's career reminds us that it is essential to stress the tensions between human agency and the context within which individuals operated.

Regarding the dejure power of Ways and Means, every chairman of the committee had access to political power as a result of his statutory authority. Nonetheless, different chairmen have done different things with their power; they have also chosen vastly different policies to support while asserting that power. There has been a difference between the dejure and defacto power of the chairmanship. Some, such as Chairman Ullman during the 1970s and Chairman Archer during the 1990s, have acquiesced to the demands of the party leadership or the president. Others, such as Mills or Chairman Rostenkowski, were more aggressive in shaping legislation at all stages of the policymaking process; they even were willing to challenge a president from the same party, as Mills did when he engaged Johnson in 1968 over the War on Poverty. The same dynamic can be seen when considering the different legacies of the presidents of the United States, all of whom shared a similar formal position of power, but each of whom accomplished very different legacies with that power and witnessed changes in the institution of the presidency over time.

The impact of individuals within their larger institutional and cultural context should not be underestimated by students of politics. Since this is not a biography, I have focused on those aspects of Mills's career that are relevant to the larger themes of this book and that best capture his role in American political history. To examine these crucial topics comprehensively, I do not focus on issues such as highway construction policy or Mills's battle with alcoholism. These I will leave to his biographer. With these issues in mind, let us begin our exploration into the complex world of the American state during the postwar period.

PART ONE

Learning the Ways and Means

1

An Arkansas Traveler Comes to Washington

When Representative William Oldfield (D-AK) visited his district during the 1910s, he frequently dined with local political and business leaders. In this group of elites was the banker Ardra Pickens Mills, whose son Wilbur was privileged to attend some of these meetings. During these and other encounters, Oldfield inspired Wilbur to point his career toward politics. As a member of the House Committee on Ways and Means, Wilbur Mills later recalled, Oldfield was "well liked, very influential, and to a young boy he seemed like a very important man."[1] Oldfield's prestige was rooted in the cosmopolitan world of Washington, D.C., a world far removed from Mills's rural, agricultural hometown.

For Mills to follow in Oldfield's footsteps, he needed a considerable amount of knowledge about the operation of the federal government. After being elected to Congress in 1938, Mills began to learn. He encountered an institution that was still dominated by political parties and interest groups. As a young congressional representative, Mills obtained his political education from established Democrats such as Sam Rayburn (D-TX) and congressional staffers such as Colin Stam. This chapter examines the process through which Mills entered into congressional politics, and it looks at a generation of professionals who came into government alongside him.

By the early 1950s, this Arkansas traveler would be prepared to join a generation of policy experts whose professional training, political environment, and political beliefs had stimulated them to come to Washington. Together, they would coalesce into the tax policy community. Ultimately, Mills's generation would transform William Oldfield's political world by forging new ties between Congress and technocratic expertise, by transforming taxation into a central component of economic and social policy, and by demonstrating that fiscal conservatism and state-building were not incompatible.

---

[1] "Wilbur Mills . . .'Mr. Taxes' in the Congress," *Newsweek*, 14 January 1963, 16.

FROM KENSETT TO CONGRESS

The year 1909 was an important one for government officials who were building the American state. Between May and August, Congress drafted a constitutional amendment granting the federal government the authority to impose taxes on the proceeds of any "lawful business." By 1913, the states ratified this amendment, giving Congress the power to collect a federal income tax.

The summer of 1909 was also important for Ardra Pickens Mills and Abbie Daigh, a young couple who lived in Kensett, Arkansas. Located in White County, approximately fifty miles northeast of Little Rock, Kensett was a small farming town (population 1,444) that stood near the intersection of the Missouri-Pacific Railroad Line. Here, the Mills owned a local country store that sold everything from house plants to horse collars.[2] On May 24, 1909, Abbie gave birth to Wilbur Daigh, the first of three children; soon after, the Mills had a second boy, Roger Q., and a girl named Emma. In the next few years, the A.P. Mills General Store prospered, enabling the Mills to purchase a lucrative cotton gin. During the Great Depression, Ardra entered the financial business when he rescued the Bank of Kensett by purchasing its falling stock. With Ardra as its president, the bank eventually prospered.

Ardra and Abbie encouraged the intellectual development of their precocious first son. By age eleven, they had taught him double-entry bookkeeping; in his teens, they sent him to the reputable Searcy High School, where Mills "wore over-alls and long, black stockings, and the Searcy boys laughed at him and called him a 'country boy.' "[3] But Mills graduated as valedictorian in 1926 and left behind friends such as Bill Dickey, future Hall of Fame player for the New York Yankees, as he set out to extend his education.

Mills enrolled in Hendrix College, a small coeducational Methodist institution located on a low hill in Conway, Arkansas. Founded in the 1880s, Hendrix maintained a strong liberal arts curriculum that placed great emphasis on history, English, math, and foreign languages.[4] By 1900, the U.S. Office of Education cited Hendrix for having higher academic standards than any other college or university in Arkansas; in 1929, the American Association of Universities placed Hendrix on its approved list. Despite his rigorous academic schedule, Mills participated in so many social activities that his class elected him to its "Hall of Fame." He served as president of

[2] "An Idea on the March," *Time*, 11 January 1963, 21.
[3] "Wilbur Mills: What's His Tax Strategy?" *Nation's Business*, February 1968, 50.
[4] J.J. Propps, "Memories of Hendrix College," *The Arkansas Historical Quarterly* XXVIII, No. 1 (Spring 1969): 49–72.

Tau Kappa Alpha, the national debating fraternity, and as president of the Franklin Literary Society. Mills also became the business manager and managing editor of the *Bull Dog*, a college weekly, and joined the Dramatic Club.

In 1930, Mills graduated as the salutatorian of his class. Mills's peers had recognized his strong intellectual capacities. As his roommate later recalled, "[Mills] was always interested in government and, frankly, from the very beginning, the tax structure . . . his powers of concentration were just far beyond the ordinary."[5] At graduation, the yearbook noted under Mills's picture: "His splendid grades are indicative of much 'gray matter'. Wilbur walks life's straight paths and is a boon companion for anyone who is 'down and out'. . . ."[6] His exceptional record at Hendrix was good enough to get him into Harvard Law School. In 1930, Mills left for Cambridge, planning to specialize in corporate law and to "learn how to talk to President Roosevelt."[7]

At Harvard, Mills's classmates included Leon Keyserling, Gerald Morgan, and Fred Scribner, all of whom became top-level government officials. Keyserling would lead the Council of Economic Advisors under President Truman, while Morgan and Scribner served as top-level officials under President Eisenhower. But law school was "a constant grind" for the Arkansan. Besides an intense workload, he felt "out of his element" in the social circles of the Northeast.[8] During his graduate career, Mills developed few friendships within his class, and he earned poor grades in many of his classes. Although colleagues and reporters often assumed that Mills had earned an L.L.B, he actually left Cambridge during his final semester, without finishing his degree, to work as a cashier in the family bank during the Depression.[9] During his years at Harvard, Mills had thus grappled with a major source of tension that would continue to influence him. As a colleague once said: "Mills comes from a little town of 2,500, which is a small rural town, but he nevertheless is a Harvard Law

[5] William Rudy, "Wilbur Mills: Power on the Potomac," *New York Post*, 12 July 1971.
[6] Joe Purcell, "The Wilbur Mills Story," *The Arkansas Lawyer* 6, No. 2 (March 1972): 50.
[7] Kay Goss, "Wilbur D. Mills: A Public Life and Historic Career," the Wilbur D. Mills Memorial Foundation. This pamphlet is distributed at the Wilbur D. Mills Archives in Conway, Arkansas.
[8] Lawrence O'Brien, interview with Michael Gillette, 24 July 1986, LBJL, Oral History Interview Collection, Tape XI, 49. Fred Scribner later said, "I just can't remember Wilbur at Harvard at all." See "Wilbur Mills . . . 'Mr. Taxes' in the Congress," 17.
[9] Stephen A. Merrill, *Wilbur D. Mills: Democratic Representative from Arkansas* (Washington, D.C.: Grossman Publishers, 1972), 2.

School graduate who has got an incisive mind." To understand him, the colleague said, you had to "understand those 'inconsistent' factors."[10]

When Mills left Harvard, he opted for a career that would bring those "inconsistent factors" to the surface. In 1934, after having been admitted to the Arkansas bar the previous year, Mills launched his political career. He became a probate judge in White County through an unexpected electoral victory over long-time incumbent, Foster White. Mills's campaign attacked White's "courthouse gang" for its exorbitant expenditures and corruption. He promised to clear the county of three-quarters of its debt by the end of his first year. If he failed, he would refuse his salary during his second year. Although Mills fulfilled the pledge, he still reduced his salary from $3,600 to $2,000.[11] Mills had demonstrated his commitment to fiscal conservatism to the electorate.

During his judicial tenure, Mills obtained a candid view into the volatile world of southern politics, a world that was very different from his idealized, childhood visions. Arkansas maintained a "one-party system in its most undefiled and undiluted form." This system involved corruption, and operated through personal connections, not textbook processes. Local elites who could deliver the vote dominated the state's political factions. The "confusion and paralysis" of this complex system caused "clean government" and "corruption" to occupy the minds of the electorate.[12] Mills manipulated this atmosphere to his advantage. On the one hand, he played on the fears of the electorate by painting himself as a "reformer" against the corrupt establishment. On the other hand, he still operated within the system to develop needed programs.

Despite his growing political presence, Mills was not a physically imposing person: he stood at about five feet eight inches; he maintained a stocky figure, fluctuating between 170 and 180 pounds; he combed back his thin brown hair with a smooth gel and wore thick-rimless "Benjamin Franklin" glasses; and he spoke with a bass, raspy voice. Mills's clean looks and his respectful manners reportedly attracted many young women. One of them, Clarine (Polly) Billingsley, who worked as a postmistress in Kensett, began to date

---

[10] Wilbur Cohen, interview with David McComb, 8 December 1968, LBJL, Oral History Interview Collection, Tape 1, 18. See also Lawrence O'Brien, interview with Michael Gillette, 24 July 1986, 49–50.

[11] "Judge Wilbur D. Mills of Searcy Makes Announcement For Congress," *The Melbourne Times*, 10 June 1938; C.P. Lee Jr., "White County Judge Says 'No' Successfully," *The Arkansas Gazette*, 26 April 1936.

[12] V.O. Key, Jr., *Southern Politics in State and Nation* (New York: Alfred Knopf, 1950), 183–204.

young Mills. On May 27, 1934, they were married and took a one night honeymoon in the Albert Pike Hotel, Little Rock, then returned to work the next morning. The couple moved into a modest white bungalow home that overlooked the tracks of the Doniphan, Kensett & Searcy Railway.

In 1938, Mills's career blossomed when Arkansas voters elected him to represent the largely white and rural Second Congressional District, which included the northern Ozark Mountains, the small farm country of central Arkansas, and the plantation region of the Mississippi delta.[13] The Second District was one of the poorest and least populated in the country, with most voters having extremely low incomes and minimal education; unions were virtually non existent.[14] Arkansas itself was one of the least industrialized states in the 1930s, and by the end of World War II it had some of the most stringent anti-union laws in the country. Together with Alabama, Mississippi, and South Carolina, Arkansas consistently placed at the bottom of per capita income and average annual wage per production worker for southern states and the nation.[15]

When the voters of this impoverished region chose the twenty-nine-year old Mills to represent them, he became the second youngest member of the House of Representatives. Once elected, Mills and his wife moved into a small apartment in Washington on Connecticut Avenue near the National Zoo, while keeping their house in Arkansas. Mills undertook a brutal work schedule: He spent almost twelve hours a day at the office, rarely attended Washington cocktail parties, and used his free time to scan the daily newspapers and analyze specialized economic reports. He frequently returned to his district to speak to constituents and their interest groups. Grasping the importance of a good relationship with the district, Mills continued throughout his career to spend much time delivering speeches to Arkansan organizations. He often used these speeches to send messages to Washington.

Determined to achieve power and influence within Congress, Mills followed the Democratic establishment and learned the ways and means of Capitol Hill. In the process, he concentrated on the politics of taxation, an issue that had captivated his interest since his days as county judge.

[13] For the best data on the district, see Merrill, *Wilbur D. Mills*, 5–10.

[14] *CQ Census Analysis: Congressional Districts of the United States* (Washington, D.C.: Congressional Quarterly Service, 1964), 1787; 1809; 1835; U.S. Department of Commerce, *Congressional Data Book (Districts of the 88th Congress)* (Washington, D.C.: Department of Commerce, 1963), 21–29.

[15] Calvin Hoover and B.U. Ratchford, *Economic Resources and Policies of the South* (New York: Macmillan, 1951), 49; 116–117; 411.

DEMOCRATS AND LOBBYISTS

Mills kept an open mind about how Washington worked. On meeting Vice-President John Nance Garner, Mills confessed, "I just don't know anything." Garner replied, "Shake hands with me boy. That makes you the smartest man who ever came to Washington."[16] Mills took that comment to heart. He understood that the federal government had its own norms, and to succeed he would have to understand them thoroughly. Although he remained too low on the seniority ladder to exercise much power during the 1940s, Mills steadily advanced his education in the politics of taxation.

The Democrats place Mills on Ways and Means

Mills learned a great deal about the congressional process, particularly the role of political parties and interest groups. Within Congress, political parties helped politicians secure office, achieve electoral stability, and obtain important government positions. Party officials could thus influence the types of legislation representatives would support.[17] The Democrats eased Mills's way into the government through the committee system. Each party maintained a Committee on Committees – for the Democrats it was Ways and Means – that assigned newly elected members to committees and reassigned members who wanted to transfer. Leadership positions within committees, moreover, were parceled out according to seniority. Since institutional reforms had weakened the Speakership of the House in 1911 and the Democratic Caucus in 1915, committees had decentralized the House by removing decision-making authority from any individual leader and dispersing legislative power among specialized panels of representatives.[18]

The Democrats placed Mills on the House Banking and Currency Committee in 1939. But in his second term, Mills attempted to earn

---

[16] "Key Man in Medicare Battle," *Medical World News* 6, No. 7 (February 1965): 33.

[17] Randall B. Ripley, "The Party Whip Organizations in the United States House of Representatives," *American Political Science Review* LVIII, No. 3 (September 1964): 561–576; Gary W. Cox and Mathew D. McCubbins, *Legislative Leviathan: Party Government in the House* (Berkeley: University of California Press, 1993); Martin Shefter, *Political Parties and the State: The American Historical Experience* (Princeton: Princeton University Press, 1994).

[18] Richard F. Fenno, Jr., *Congressmen in Committees* (Boston: Little, Brown, 1973); Richard F. Bensel, *Sectionalism and American Political Development, 1880–1980* (Madison: University of Wisconsin Press, 1984); Richard W. Bolling, *Power in the House: A History of the Leadership of the House of Representatives* (New York: Dutton, 1968); Nelson W. Polsby, "The Institutionalization of the U.S. House of Representatives," *American Political Science Review*, 62 (March 1968): 144–168.

a seat on the prestigious Ways and Means. He neglected to discuss his plans with the Democratic leadership, and as a result, he was soundly defeated. When House Speaker Sam Rayburn heard about this situation, he asked the young Arkansan, "Why didn't you tell me you wanted on the Ways and Means Committee? I'd have put you on my list . . . You can have the next vacancy."[19] Mills took that advice, and on October 15, 1942, the Democrats placed him on Representative Doughton's (D-NC) Ways and Means Committee. Doughton and Rayburn, an irritable and shy individual who stood at five feet six inches, sported a balding head, and rarely smiled, tended to place representatives on Ways and Means who came from safe districts and who adhered to Democratic interests – namely, free trade and the oil depletion allowance.[20] Although Mills was younger than most members of Ways and Means, Rayburn and Doughton decided that he displayed the characteristics needed to join the committee.[21]

Rayburn adopted the young Arkansan as one of his "boys."[22] He assigned a senior Democratic House member, Edward Cox (D-GA), and the Democratic Comptroller of the General Accounting Office, Lindsey Warren, to "chaperon" Mills and to instruct him on the "norms" of the House.[23] Meanwhile, Rayburn taught Mills some simple axioms: "Don't ever talk until you know what you're talking about," and "If you want to get along, go along."[24] He cautioned against the advice of intellectuals who "never won an election or met a payroll."[25] The Speaker also urged Mills to maintain a clean image in the public eye; he warned him never to take a drink in public, or else, "they see you taking one drink they will swear that you were drunk and it will get out on you that you were drinking too heavily."[26] Finally, Rayburn introduced Mills to up-and-coming Democrats, such

---

[19] Wilbur Mills, interview with Anthony Champagne, 13 March 1986, Sam Rayburn Library (Bonham, Texas), 10.

[20] Fenno, *Congressmen in Committees*, 25; John Manley, *The Politics of Finance: The House Committee on Ways and Means* (Boston: Little, Brown, 1970), 15–58.

[21] The exact reason why Rayburn decided to place Mills on the committee remains unclear. But given the strict guidelines Rayburn followed when judging others to join, Rayburn must have decided that Mills would protect the crucial Democratic positions, that he came from a safe congressional seat, and that he would continue to follow the party line in the future.

[22] Wilbur Mills, interview with Joe Frantz, 2 November 1971, LBJL, Oral History Interview Collection, 1.

[23] Wilbur Mills, interview with Anthony Champagne, 17–19.

[24] Ibid.; "I Love This House," *Time*, 2 February 1959, 13.

[25] Cited in Robert C. Wood, *Whatever Possessed the President? Academic Experts and Presidential Policy, 1960–1988* (Amherst: University of Massachusetts Press, 1993), 6.

[26] Wilbur Mills, interview with Anthony Champagne, 7.

as Lyndon Johnson, in his late-afternoon "board of education." There they spent hours plotting legislative strategies over bourbon and water.[27] While collaborating with Rayburn, Mills also learned the importance of tailoring bills so that they would be likely to receive a solid House majority. Assuring a majority required constant interaction with party leaders and the committee chairman.

Rayburn's lessons taught Mills about the norms of Congress: specialization and apprenticeship. The first norm led congressional representatives to specialize on issues that came before the committee. Members were encouraged to develop a monopoly of knowledge in one area of policy as a way to distinguish themselves. In the process of acquiring this knowledge, new members were required by the second norm to serve an apprenticeship as they learned from senior members about Congress. New representatives refrained from participating in committee deliberations or on the House floor. The second norm reinforced the first by prodding new committee members to defer to senior representatives who had some expertise.[28] Giving importance to specialization and apprenticeship – norms that are integral to most professions – reflected the professionalization of Congress that was taking place at the time.[29]

Mills remained generally loyal to the Democrats. He assisted Rayburn with difficult tax matters ranging from national policy to local constituent problems.[30] Speaking to constituents, he praised the Democrats for introducing programs to develop electricity, provide bank insurance, and assist farmers. During World War II, Mills supported the increased wartime tax burden imposed by Congress: "Taxes are a very vital part of a war-time price control program and, therefore, a major part of the responsibility of keeping prices down belongs to Congress."[31] Mills usually adhered to the party line, even

[27] Norman Miller, "Mills & the Tax Bill," *The Wall Street Journal*, 22 January 1968; Murray Seeger, "Reports & Comment," *Atlantic Monthly*, August 1971, 13.

[28] Donald R. Matthews, *U.S. Senators and Their World* (New York: Vintage Books, 1960); Steven S. Smith and Christopher J. Deering, *Committees in Congress*, 2nd edition (Washington, D.C.: Congressional Quarterly Inc., 1990), 40; Fenno, *Congressmen in Committees*, 79–80; Polsby, "The Institutionalization of the U.S. House of Representatives."

[29] For discussions of specialized knowledge and the professions, see Andrew Abbott, *The System of Professions: An Essay on the Division of Expert Labor* (Chicago: University of Chicago Press, 1988); JoAnne Brown, *The Definition of a Profession: The Authority of Metaphor in the History of Intelligence Testing, 1890–1930* (Princeton: Princeton University Press, 1992); Paul Starr, *The Social Transformation of American Medicine* (New York: Basic Books, 1982); Magali Sarfatti Larson, *The Rise of Professionalism: A Sociological Analysis* (Berkeley: University of California Press, 1977).

[30] Wilbur Mills to Sam Rayburn, 13 October 1949, WMPC, unprocessed; JMIC; "Economic Statesman: Wilbur Daigh Mills," *The New York Times*, 20 December 1957.

[31] Wilbur D. Mills, "The Relation of Taxes to Our Economy," 1943, WMPC, Box 218, File 2.

when it threatened his standing in his district. During the 1948 presidential election, for instance, Mills was the only Arkansan congressman who defended the Democrats and President Truman against
Strom Thurmond's attack on their civil rights platform. While admitting that he was "embarrassed" by the "one mistake of the present
administration – Civil Rights," Mills urged his supporters to vote for
the Democrats, whose economic policies were sound and who would,
in the end, protect states' rights. Mills also warned that Thurmond's
independent party might undermine political stability by preventing
any party from winning a solid majority: "We do not want to go
the way of France do we? Let us work within established parties –
clean house if necessary, but not throw all overboard and jump over
after it."[32]

In his voting record, Mills followed the pattern of most moderate
southern Democrats: Except on civil rights and labor issues, he generally supported the party's domestic policies, including Social Security, highway development, and federal aid for the prevention of water
pollution.[33] Mills also voted in favor of Democratic anti-communist
measures, and supported Truman's foreign policy initiatives, including Greek-Turkish aid and NATO. Mills supported the Marshall Plan
as a program "calculated to strengthen capitalism."[34] In 1948, Mills
voted for Harold Knutson's (R-MN) 20 percent tax reduction only
after the Ways and Means added two important Democratic provisions, income-splitting and an increase in special exemptions for the
aged and blind.[35] Between 1954 and 1964, Mills would earn an
average party unity score that was seven percentage points higher
than the average for all House Democrats.[36]

Learning about lobbyists

Interest-group politics, which constituted the second major aspect of
congressional politics learned by Mills, consisted of alliances between
congressional committees and interest groups.[37] Interest groups were

---

[32] Wilbur Mills, "What is Best for Arkansas Politically," 26 October 1948, WMPC, Box
218, File: Mills Speeches (In District) Radio Town Hall Meeting October 26,
1948/2; Mills, interview with Anthony Champagne, 1–2.

[33] On southern Democrats, see Ira Katznelson, Kim Geiger, and Daniel Kryder, "Limiting Liberalism: The Southern Veto in Congress, 1933–1950," *Political Science
Quarterly* 108, No. 2 (1993): 283–302.

[34] Wilbur Mills to Paul Glines, 22 March 1948, WMPC, Box 222, File: HR 29 Civil
Rights Proposal (Poll Tax) (L) 1948 (2).

[35] Harold Knutson to Wilbur Mills, 6 April 1948, WMPC, unprocessed.

[36] Everett Felix Cataldo, "The House Committee on Ways and Means" (Ph.D. diss., The
Ohio State University, 1965), 178–179.

[37] Political scientists call these relationships "iron triangles" by stressing the interdependence of interest groups, congressional committees, and agencies. But the IRS

most active whenever their particular tax matters were in question. Because of the large number of organizations interested in tax policy, lobbyists were either directly or indirectly a constant presence in the deliberations. One of the most important roles of lobbyists was to push tax breaks through the committees, since these tax breaks were extremely difficult to eliminate once they had been established. The mineral depletion allowance, for example, was a tax break that had saved the oil industry billions of dollars since 1926 by compensating companies for the high cost of exploratory drilling. Since its enactment, powerful organizations such as the American Petroleum Institute had guarded this provision. Immediately on arrival at Ways and Means, Mills encountered the power of these interest groups and their intimate relations with the committee. Rayburn and Doughton allowed only Democrats who supported the oil tax break to be placed on Ways and Means. Mills was no exception to that rule, and understood the need to protect the oil industry from any drastic change in the tax code.[38]

Rayburn taught Mills the parliamentary skills needed to balance the demands of interest groups, tax-collecting agencies, and the Democratic Party. Meanwhile Colin Stam, who headed the staff of the Joint Committee on Internal Revenue Taxation [JCIRT], helped Mills learn how to use expertise in his new job. Stam was "a 'big man' – a husky six-footer with a $17\frac{1}{2}$ shirt collar and a pleasant, scholarly face of equally generous proportions."[39] Stam had received his B.A. from Washington College in 1916 and his L.L.B from Georgetown University in 1922. Following five years as an attorney at the Bureau of Internal Revenue between 1922 and 1927, Stam joined the JCIRT as an assistant counsel after graduating from law school. He gradually worked his way up the committee staff, and became chief of staff of the JCIRT in 1938.

Like other committee members, Mills relied on Stam and the JCIRT staff for information on tax policy. In 1926, Congress had created the JCIRT composed of five House members and five senators, with the chairmen of the tax-writing committees traditionally rotating control of the JCIRT. While the committee did not have any legislative authority, its staff provided Ways and Means and the Senate

---

did not have the same type of vested interest in a particular interest group or loophole as the Department of Agriculture, for example, had in the American Farm Bureau Federation and price supports. Although "iron triangle" is a useful term to describe many federal policies, it fails to explain the highly factionalized interest-group politics of taxation.

[38] JMIC.

[39] John L. Connolly, "Colin F. Stam – The Individual," in *Essays on Taxation: Contributed in Memory of Colin F. Stam* (New York: Tax Foundation, 1974), 2.

Finance Committee with enhanced expertise to design legislation. The staff included lawyers, accountants, and economists, who earned a reputation in Congress for their bipartisan, technical analysis of the tax code.[40]

As head of the staff, Stam provided Mills with the analytical skills needed to propose policies that tax administrators could enforce and that interest groups would accept. To help him in this task, Stam served as a conduit of information between the interest groups, committee members, and Mills. During these years, Mills paid close attention to Stam's interaction with fellow committee members. As one colleague recalled, Mills was "learning very quickly" as he watched "older colleagues" and absorbed "the techniques of both how to deal with the problem and the information."[41]

Mills later explained in an interview:

> I was told by everyone in those days that my job was to learn the jurisdiction of the committee, and that took a lot of work. So, I undertook to memorize the Internal Revenue Code, and almost did, I guess. I spent an awful lot of time studying it, and Social Security legislation, reciprocal trade legislation, debt legislation, welfare programs, unemployment compensation, all these matters that were within the jurisdiction of the Ways and Means Committee. I was told that if I was to have any influence in the House, it would depend upon the members feeling that I had knowledge of the subject matter superior to their knowledge, that my judgment was sound and so on. If I developed that kind of reputation, then people would follow me in my presentation of legislation. So, I endeavored to try to do that.[42]

By the late-1940s, Wilbur Mills had learned a great deal about the role of parties, interest groups, and congressional staff in policymaking. These lessons were crucial to Mills's development because these actors would remain integral to the process throughout his career, even when new types of policy experts entered into the congressional fray.

[40] Mary Etta Boesl, "Joint Taxation Committee," in *The Encyclopedia of the United States Congress*, eds. Donald C. Bacon, Roger H. Davidson, and Morton Keller (New York: Simon & Schuster, 1995), 837–840; Michael J. Malbin, *Unelected Representatives: Congressional Staff and the Future of Representative Government* (New York: Basic Books, 1980); Manley, *The Politics of Finance*, 319.

[41] Wilbur Cohen, interview by David McComb, 8 December 1968, LBJL, Oral History Interview Collection, Tape 1, 27.

[42] Wilbur D. Mills, interview with Lewis E. Weeks, 13 August 1980, Hospital Administration Oral History Collection, Library of the American Hospital Association (Chicago, Illinois, 1983), 5.

THE HOUSE COMMITTEE ON WAYS AND MEANS

Through his appointment to Ways and Means, Mills joined one of the most prestigious institutions in Congress. Whereas the Senate Finance Committee was also powerful, its role was to amend and modify the basic proposals put forth by Ways and Means.[43] By 1942, Ways and Means had jurisdiction over Social Security, income taxation, trade, and the national debt ceiling. The Constitution (Article I, Section 7) ensured that this kind of revenue-raising legislation would always emanate from the House. Unlike other policy areas, such as defense, taxation was one area that Congress refused to delegate authority over to the executive branch during the twentieth century. The history of the committee provides some insight into its power.

The history of Ways and Means

The committee became a formal standing committee in 1802, in charge of expenditures and revenue. During the 1830s, Ways and Means secured control of the nation's tariff programs. Amidst the turmoil of the Civil War, Ways and Means reached the height of its power in the nineteenth century. Under the chairmanship of Republican Thaddeus Stevens from Pennsylvania, the committee passed the first federal income tax (although it was dismantled following the war) and helped to establish a national currency.[44] As its workload grew beyond reasonable limits, the House decided to delegate some responsibility away from the committee. In 1865, the House voted to create a separate Appropriations Committee to handle expenditures and a Committee on Banking and Currency to manage national finance.[45]

Despite this, Ways and Means maintained considerable power during the twentieth century. Between the 1860s and the 1920s, the committee focused on tariffs and excise taxes. Tariffs constituted the major source of revenue for the United States. Congressional Republicans, along with a handful of Democrats from industrial regions, promoted protectionist policies. For the Republicans, protectionism emerged as the centerpiece of the party's economic policy. Through-

---

[43] Timothy Conlan, "Senate Finance Committee," *The Encyclopedia of the United States Congress*, 837–840.

[44] Randall Strahan, "House Ways and Means Committee," in *The Encyclopedia of the United States Congress*, 2112–2114.

[45] George B. Galloway, *History of the House of Representatives*, 2nd ed. (New York: Crowell, 1976), 59.

out this period, high tariffs generated an ongoing government surplus and provided congressional representatives with a lucrative benefit that they could distribute to select industries in their district.[46] The Republicans relied on tariff revenue to build a generous program of Civil War veterans benefits that cemented voter allegiance to their party.[47]

Ways and Means empowered

Several institutional changes took place between 1910 and 1942 that strengthened the committee. First, the congressional reforms of 1910 and 1911 reduced the power of the Speaker of the House and placed Ways and Means at the center of the party system. After 1911, Ways and Means served as the Democratic Committee on Committees, making all committee appointments for the party. By gaining the power to make these appointments for the Democrats, Ways and Means took over one of the most important functions of congressional leadership: helping to define the success of a representative by providing or restricting access to everything from political prestige to district benefits.[48] The Speaker had to work with the chairman of Ways and Means to exert influence on appointments. Second, in 1919, Republicans prohibited the majority floor leader from chairing a legislative committee. As a result, the chairman of Ways and Means would be selected only through the seniority system; the House also increased committee membership from fifteen to twenty-five representatives. Third, the committee increased its access to expertise. In 1918, a committee bill established the Legislative Drafting Service to help any committee draft legislation, and in 1926 Congress created the JCIRT. Fourth, the dominance of the seniority system between 1939 and 1973 made advancement within Ways and Means fairly

---

[46] Charles W. Calhoun, "Political Economy in the Gilded Age: The Republican Party's Industrial Policy," *Journal of Policy History* 8, No. 3 (1996): 291–309; Morton Keller, *Affairs of State: Public Life in Late Nineteenth Century America* (Cambridge, MA: Belknap Press of Harvard University Press, 1977), 376–380; Sheldon D. Pollack, *The Failure of U.S. Tax Policy: Revenue and Politics* (University Park: Pennsylvania State University Press, 1996), 46.

[47] Theda Skocpol, *Protecting Soldiers and Mothers: The Political Origins of Social Policy in the United States* (Cambridge, MA: Belknap Press of Harvard University Press, 1992), 102–151; Megan J. McClintock, "Civil War Pensions and the Reconstruction of Union Families," *The Journal of American History* 83, No. 2 (September 1996): 456–480.

[48] Kenneth A. Shepsle, *The Giant Jigsaw Puzzle: Democratic Committee Assignments in the Modern House* (Chicago: University of Chicago Press, 1978).

automatic once a representative was on the committee, thereby weakening the influence of external support.[49]

Mills joined Ways and Means at a time when the decentralized committee system was becoming fully entrenched. The Legislative Reorganization Act of 1946 reduced the number of standing committees in the House, expanded the committee staff, and reduced the number of committee assignments for most members to one. To help Congress keep up with the expertise of the executive branch, the act authorized all standing committees to hire a staff of up to four professional and six clerical workers; it also strengthened the Legislative Reference Service. The number of congressional staffers doubled between 1946 and 1956. Finally, the Legislative Reorganization Act implemented some procedural changes that strengthened the role of committee chairmen.[50]

Increasing its policy jurisdiction, Ways and Means enlarged the federal tax system and regained considerable control over federal expenditures between World War I and World War II. Following World War II, Congress created a mass tax with high rates and low exemptions (top rates reached 94 percent for individuals and 40 percent for corporations), and a withholding system that covered 74 percent of the population.[51] As the tax imposed high rates on a growing percentage of the population, each tax break became more valuable to the taxpayer and more costly to the Treasury. Through the complex system of tax breaks, Ways and Means maintained its own system of hidden expenditures.[52] Since the New Deal, the committee also gained control of the Social Security system, including Unemployment Insurance, Old-Age and Survivors' Insurance, Old-Age Assistance, Aid to the Blind, and Aid to Dependent Children. Roo-

---

[49] Richard F. Bensel, *Sectionalism and American Political Development, 1880–1980* (Madison: University of Wisconsin Press, 1984), 346–351.

[50] Smith and Deering, *Committees in Congress*, 39. See also David C. King, "Legislative Reorganization Acts," in *The Encyclopedia of the United States Congress*, 1279–1280; Susan Webb Hammond, "Congressional Staffs," in *The Encyclopedia of the American Legislative System: Studies of the Principal Structures, Processes, and Policies of Congress and the State Legislatures since the Colonial Era*, ed. Joel Silbey (New York: Scribner's, 1994), 785–800.

[51] Pollack, *The Failure of U.S. Tax Policy: Revenue and Politics*, 64; John F. Witte, *The Politics and Development of the Federal Income Tax* (Madison: University of Wisconsin Press, 1985), 110–130.

[52] W. Elliot Brownlee, "Reflections on the history of taxation," in *Funding the Modern American State, 1941–1995: The Rise and Fall of the Era of Easy Finance*, ed. W. Elliot Brownlee (Cambridge: Cambridge University Press and Washington, D.C.: Woodrow Wilson Center Press, 1996), 40; Stanley S. Surrey, *Pathways to Tax Reform: The Concept of Tax Expenditures* (Cambridge, MA: Harvard University Press, 1973).

sevelt had placed the Social Security program under the tax-writing committees because the constitutional power of the government to tax could protect the program from the conservative Supreme Court. Roosevelt also hoped to win over the committee chairmen who had initially shown half-hearted support for the proposal.[53] In terms of institutional growth, Social Security was a political coup for Ways and Means. Together, control over these indirect and direct expenditures placed Ways and Means in competition with Appropriations. By the early 1970s, Ways and Means would be responsible for over 40 percent of federal spending.[54]

A "control committee"

Ways and Means, moreover, was one of the most respected committees in the House. Along with the Rules and Appropriations Committees, Ways and Means was what political scientist David Mayhew has called a "control committee." Given the interest and constituent pressures that most members of Congress faced, representatives depended on the "control committees" to maintain the institutional integrity of the House despite the particular interests of its members. Mayhew argued that Ways and Means was essentially "hired to put a damper on particularism in tax and tariff matters and to protect what members call the 'actuarial soundness' of the social security program . . . control committees are like governors on what can all too easily become a runaway engine."[55] Committee members, according to one interview-based study, perceived themselves as a "Congressional braintrust"; they talked about each other by using adjectives such as "scholarly," "studious," "extremely intelligent," and "good students."[56]

[53] C. Eugene Streuerle, *The Tax Decade: How Taxes Came to Dominate the Public Agenda* (Washington, D.C.: Urban Institute Press, 1992), 82–83.

[54] Cited in Catherine E. Rudder, "The House Committee on Ways and Means," *Encyclopedia of the American Legislative System*, 1033.

[55] David R. Mayhew, *Congress: The Electoral Connection* (New Haven: Yale University Press, 1974), 154–158. Despite his brilliant analysis, Mayhew does not explain why legislators within the control committee failed to act according to their own self-interest and why they were interested in the "internal currency" of Congress, such as respect and power among other representatives. As one critic, William Muir, explained, "Since the controlling assumption of his analysis is that legislative members have an interest in nothing but reelection, his invocation of institutional maintenance arrangements might strike one as insupportable in theoretical terms." William K. Muir, Jr., *Legislature: California's School for Politics* (Chicago: University of Chicago Press, 1982), 182–185. I contend that there are alternative motivations that shaped the actions of some committee chairmen, in addition to reelection, to explain the respect for members of Ways and Means.

[56] Cataldo, "The House Committee on Ways and Means," 52. Regarding similar sentiments among members of the House Appropriations Committee, see Aaron

Congressional representatives wanted Ways and Means to make the type of decisions that they themselves found difficult. Congress granted special rules to the committee, and accepted certain secretive operational tactics that helped Ways and Means to overcome interest-group pressure and pass substantive legislation. The closed rule, for example, prevented the House from making any amendments to Ways and Means legislation. Members could only vote yes or no on the entire bill or send the bill back to the committee for it to be reconsidered.[57] The practice remained central to committee politics from 1940 until the 1970s.[58] During the mid-1960s, one Ways and Means Democrat explained the importance of the rule as follows: "It'd be suicide if you ever tried to write a tax or social security bill on the floor. We sit in there surrounded by experts to keep us from going off on a tangent so you can imagine what would happen on the floor. We cooperate to write a good bill partly because of the closed rule. We get consensus."[59]

To help Ways and Means maintain internal discipline, both parties tended to appoint moderates to the twenty-five-member committee. "Ways and Means members are," according to the political scientist John Manley, "pragmatic in their outlook on politics, patient in their pursuit of objectives, unbending on few things, and inclined to compromise on all but the most basic issues."[60] Though the panel often denied the requests of particular representatives, members understood that Congress as an institution depended on the committee to make such decisions. Through a reputation of "fiscal responsibility," moreover, the members gained a considerable amount of political capital within a culture that valued technical expertise and incremental change.[61]

When one representative noted in the 1960s that Ways and Means was the "fountainhead of the economic structure," he may have been exaggerating.[62] By the late 1940s, however, Ways and Means had secured a central position within the state. Strengthened by the expansion of the income tax, by Social Security, and by congressional reform, Ways and Means maintained jurisdiction over some of the most important programs in government. When Mills obtained a position on this prestigious committee, he encountered the type of

Wildavsky, *The Politics of the Budgetary Process*, 3rd edition (Boston: Little, Brown, 1979), 47–56.
[57] Fenno, *Congressmen in Committees*, 18.
[58] Witte, *The Politics and Development of the Federal Income Tax*, 111.
[59] Manley, *The Politics of Finance*, 72.
[60] Ibid., 47.
[61] JMIC; Joseph Barr to Claude Desautels, 25 February 1963, SSP, Box 177, File 2.
[62] JMIC.

professional fortune that eluded many politicians throughout their entire careers.

A NEW GENERATION OF POLICYMAKERS

Mills resembled many of the other tax policymakers who reached professional maturity during the 1950s. Most of them were white middle-class males, who had been born between Theodore Roosevelt's reelection in 1904 and the conclusion of World War I in 1918. Although they were raised in families of diverse ethnic and regional backgrounds, once they attended the universities, their social experiences were similar. What held these men together was their professional education and their entrance into politics just as the national state became a significant presence in American life. The biographies of these future members of the tax policy community provide the generational context within which Mills rose to power.

The lawyers

Some were legal scholars immersed in theoretical analysis of the tax code; they had been trained to focus on the way statutory language affected tax evasion. Among them, Stanley Surrey was the most prominent in his field. Surrey, born in Manhattan on October 3, 1910, began his career in 1932 after receiving his L.L.B from Columbia University. In law school, he became known as a "relentless questioner."[63] Although Surrey joined a law firm in 1933, he (like other young lawyers during the Depression) decided to move to Washington. There, he worked as a counsel for the National Recovery Administration between 1933–35 and for the National Labor Relations Board in 1936–37.

Following a few short-term positions in academia, Surrey returned to public service as a counsel for the Treasury in 1942–44 and in 1946–47. In 1950, he left Washington to accept a position as professor of Law at Harvard University, where he maintained a busy schedule. Besides teaching, Surrey directed a program on international taxation from 1953 to 1961; he served as the chief reporter for the American Law Institute Income Tax Project between 1948 and 1961; he was a special counsel to the Ways and Means Subcommittee on Internal Revenue Administration in 1951–52; and he assisted the Department of Treasury in its studies on the tax code in 1953–54. By the mid-1950s, academic scholars and government officials regarded Surrey as a leading expert on fiscal issues. His 1957 publication, "The

[63] Donald Lubick, interview with Julian Zelizer, 16 May 1994, 2–3.

Congress and the Tax Lobbyist – How Special Tax Provisions Get Enacted," earned widespread praise for its insightful critique of the alliance between lobbyists and representatives.[64]

Although not as well-known as Surrey, Mortimer Caplin was another major figure in the world of tax law. Born six years after Surrey, Caplin received most of his education at the University of Virginia, where he obtained a law degree in 1940. After graduation, Caplin clerked for a federal judge on the United States Court of Appeals; in September 1941, he joined a prominent New York law firm. After World War II service in the Navy, he returned to his practice as a corporate lawyer, but his military experience had "some real bearing" on his thinking and led him to "engage in deep study, writing, things of that sort." While remaining at his firm, Caplin completed a doctoral program at New York University, studying with such notable figures as Randolph Paul. He then obtained a job at the University of Virginia in August 1950, where his students included Robert and Edward Kennedy.[65] Colleagues praised Caplin's publications on the tax code in the 1950s.

Other members of this generation, who were not in the intellectual circles familiar to Surrey and Caplin, spent most of their early careers as tax practitioners. For instance, Henry "Joe" Fowler practiced law within the federal government. Fowler, who was born in 1908, was a conservative Virginian in manner, speech, and temperament. He attended Roanoke College in Salem, Virginia, and received a law degree from Yale in 1932. After a short stint on the staff of the Reconstruction Finance Corporation, Fowler served as a counsel for the Tennessee Valley Authority. In 1939, he moved into Congress as chief counsel for the Committee on Education and Labor. Two years later, he jumped back into the federal bureaucracy, working as a special counsel to the Federal Power Commission. While at the FPC, Fowler made a name for himself when he helped negotiate an agreement with Canada to develop the St. Lawrence Seaway Project.

In September 1941, the administration invited Fowler to become

---

[64] Stanley S. Surrey, "The Congress and the Tax Lobbyist – How Special Tax Provisions Get Enacted," *Harvard Law Review* 70, No. 7 (May 1957): 1145–1182. See also, Surrey, "Current Issues in the Taxation of Corporate Foreign Investment," *Columbia Law Review* 56, No. 6 (June 1956): 815; Surrey, "The Income Tax Base For Individuals," 21 November 1957 (Paper Presented at the Tax Institute Symposium on Income Tax Differentials) in NA, RG 233, Box 6342, File: Income Tax Rates.

[65] Mortimer Caplin, interview with Julian Zelizer, Washington, D.C., 13 June 1994; Mortimer Caplin, interview with Shelley Davis and Kecia McDonald, 18–25 November 1991, Internal Revenue Service, Internal Revenue Service Oral History Interview, 1–5.

assistant general counsel of the Office of Production Management, which soon became the War Production Board. He stayed with the agency until early 1944, when he accepted an appointment as economic adviser to the U.S. Mission for Economic Affairs in London. Later that year, Fowler returned to the United States as special assistant to a vice-chairman of the War Production Board on International Economic Affairs. In 1946, Fowler entered private practice in a Washington firm specializing in corporate and administrative law, but he was soon back in government. In the fall of 1951, he became administrator of National Production Authority in the Department of Commerce. Soon after, he succeeded Manly Fleischmann as the presidentially appointed administrator of the Defense Production Administration, and in late 1952 he became director of Defense Mobilization at the request of Truman. In January 1953, Fowler returned temporarily to private practice.[66]

The economists

Although Washington economists were often at odds with lawyers such as Fowler, they too played an important role in this new generation of policymakers. While lawyers tended to focus on questions of tax compliance, evasion, and equity, economists expressed particular interest in the relationship between the taxation and economic growth. Arthur Burns, for example, took Washington by storm, serving in a wide array of positions. Born in 1904, Burns had completed his doctoral work in economics at Columbia University, simultaneously working on the research staff of the National Bureau of Economic Research. Once he obtained his Ph.D., he joined the Bureau full-time and helped the Commerce Department draw up the index of leading economic indicators in 1938.[67] He served as the Bureau's director of research from 1945 to 1953.[68] He was a successful scholar who enjoyed the kind of quantitative analyses that the Bureau produced.

Burns accepted Eisenhower's offer to chair the Council of Economic Advisors. Sherman Adams, who described Burns as having "a glassy stare through thick lenses, peering out from under a canopy of unruly hair parted in the middle, a large pipe with a curved stem,"

---

[66] Henry Fowler, interview with David McComb, 10 January 1969, LBJL, Oral History Interview Collection.

[67] For the best analysis of Burns, see Wyatt C. Wells, *Economist in an Uncertain World: Arthur F. Burns and the Federal Reserve, 1970–1978* (New York: Columbia University Press, 1995), 7.

[68] "Arthur Burns," DEL, Records of the Council of Economic Advisors, Box 1, Folder: [Administrative] CEA, Biographies, Council Members and Staff.

and others in the administration were impressed with Burns's knowledge.[69] As chairman, Burns retained a deep commitment to "objectivity," and championed an empirical, inductive approach to economics. He often said that he preferred to draw conclusions from observable facts, rather than from theoretical, abstract models. He took a cautious approach to politics, refusing to use the chairmanship aggressively. During a rare appearance before the Joint Economic Committee, for example, Burns insisted that his testimony remain off the record.[70] While chairing the council, he also served on the president's Advisory Board on Economic Growth and Stability and on the Cabinet Committee on Small Business. After working with the Eisenhower administrations, Burns returned to Columbia University to teach economics.

Along with Burns, Herbert Stein helped to solidify the "economic expertise" of his generation. Stein, born in Detroit, Michigan, on August 27, 1916, earned his A.B. from Williams College in 1935 and pursued graduate work at the University of Chicago. The New Deal and World War II brought Stein to Washington. In 1938 and 1939, he worked as an economist for the FDIC, moving to the National Defense Advisory Commission in 1940. After one year with the NDAC, Stein served on the War Productions Board from 1941 to 1944 at the same time as Henry Fowler, and then with the Office of War Mobilization and Reconversion in 1945. After the war, Stein stayed inside Washington, D.C. He immediately joined the Committee of Economic Development, a group of politically moderate business leaders who supported the use of fiscal policy to manage growth. In 1947, Stein helped write the CED's *Taxes and the Budget*, and in 1948, *Monetary and Fiscal Policy for Greater Economic Stability*. These publications strongly influenced fiscal policy discussions by articulating a moderate version of Keynesianism that many policymakers found attractive.[71] He also published *U.S. Government Price Policy during the World War* (1938), *Jobs and Markets* (1946), and *Policies to Combat Depression* (1956), and served as associate director of research for the CED from 1948 to 1956. He became director of research in 1956.

[69] Cited in Robert M. Collins, *The Business Response To Keynes, 1919–1964* (New York: Columbia University Press, 1981), 154.

[70] Arthur Burns to Paul Douglas, 3 February 1956, and Douglas to Burns, 27 February 1956, DEL, Arthur F. Burns Papers, Box 96, Folder: Congressional Correspondence 1956 (2). See also Burns, "An Economist in Government," *Columbia University Forum*, 1, No. 1 (Winter 1957): 4–6.

[71] Collins, *The Business Response To Keynes, 1929–1964*, 115–172; Herbert Stein, *The Fiscal Revolution in America*, revised edition (Washington, D.C.: AEI Press, 1990), 197–240.

Walter Heller, who spent much of his career in a different theoretical and ideological camp, also became an influential economist
in Washington. After completing his undergraduate work at Oberlin
College and earning his Ph.D. at the University of Wisconsin, Heller
worked as a financial economist for the Treasury Department (alongside Surrey) from 1942 to 1946. That year, he moved into academia,
as a professor of economics at the University of Minnesota, where he
remained until Kennedy's election. As a professor, Heller's reputation
rested on his support of a demand-centered Keynesianism that
emphasized the manipulation of taxes and spending to stimulate
economic growth. While in academia, Heller maintained his connection to government through several channels. In 1947–48, he was
the chief of internal finance for the U.S. Military Government in
Germany; between 1952 and 1960, he was a consultant for the U.N.,
the CED, and the U.S. Census Bureau; and between 1955–1960 he
assisted the Minnesota Department of Taxation and served as a tax
advisor to the governor.[72]

One of Heller's closest friends was another prominent economist,
Joseph A. Pechman. Pechman earned his prestigious reputation as
the director of Economic Studies at the Brookings Institution from
1962 to 1983. "He was one of the small and talented group of scholars and academics," *The Washington Post* later noted, "who, in the two
decades after World War II, introduced the political world to modern
economic theory and its implications for national growth."[73] Born in
1918 in New York City, Pechman graduated from the City College
of New York in 1937 and went on to receive a doctoral degree in
economics from the University of Wisconsin.

From the start of his career, Pechman was determined to apply
his academic knowledge to the world of politics. In 1941, the
young economist moved to Washington and worked for the Office
of Price Administration. When he returned from a tour of duty
in Europe with the army, Pechman joined the tax staff of the
Department of Treasury until 1953. Following a year of teaching
and research at the Massachusetts Institute of Technology, Pechman
worked for the staff of the Council of Economic Advisors in 1954.
From 1956 to 1960, when he joined Brookings, Pechman assisted
the Committee on Economic Development, where he collaborated
with Walter Heller, who was then a consultant to the CED.[74]

---

[72] Edward S. Flash, Jr., *Economic Advice and Presidential Leadership: The Council of Economic Advisors* (New York: Columbia University Press, 1965), 176.

[73] Editorial, "Joseph A. Pechman," *The Washington Post*, 23 August 1989.

[74] Hobart Rowen, "The Passing of a Tax Purist," *The Washington Post*, Sunday, 3 September 1989, section H; Stuart E. Eizenstat, "Joe Pechman: A Passion For Fairness,"

During these years, Pechman developed a passion for and expertise in the cause of tax reform.

The civil servants

A young group of civil servants was also increasingly prominent by the early 1950s. In Social Security, two men, Wilbur Cohen and Robert Myers, moved up the federal bureaucracy as Mills climbed the congressional ladder. Cohen grew up in Milwaukee, Wisconsin, where he was born in 1913. In 1934, he graduated from the University of Wisconsin with a degree in economics. On graduation, Cohen worked as a research assistant to Professor Edwin Witte, the executive director of the president's Cabinet Committee on Economic Security. Thereafter, he remained in Washington as a technical advisor to Arthur Altmeyer, chairman of the Social Security Board, helping to devise legislative proposals and evaluate the administration of programs.

While heading this division, he held positions on several federal advisory groups. In 1946–47, he served as director of research to the Advisory Committee on Universal Training; between 1950 and 1951 he chaired the Wage Stabilization Board's Tripartite Committee on Health, Welfare, and Pensions, which formulated economic stabilization policies for employee benefit plans. In 1953, Cohen became the director of the Social Security Administration's Division of Research and Statistics. In addition, he represented the United States at six international conferences. In 1956, Cohen left Washington temporarily to become professor of Public Welfare Administration at the University of Michigan. But, he maintained close ties to the federal government, corresponding regularly with policymakers such as Mills. Colleagues were overwhelmed with Cohen's technical knowledge on a broad range of issues; as one recalled, "he was a ball of fire who had the advantage of knowing the subject intimately and, consequently, having the opposition arguments equaling Wilbur Mills'. He had the ability to communicate with Congress. He also had the knowledge so you could feel comfortable in a meeting discussing strategy or substance."[75] Cohen worked closely with Robert

The Washington Post, 2 September 1989; "Joseph A. Pechman, 1918–1989," The Brookings Review, Fall 1989, 3; "Joseph A. Pechman Is Dead at 71," The New York Times, 21 August 1989; "Joseph A. Pechman, 71, renowned economist," The Washington Times, 21 August 1989.

[75] Lawrence O'Brien, interview with Michael Gillette, 24 July 1986, LBJL, Oral History Interview Collection, Interview XI, 37. For a full biography of Cohen, see Edward D. Berkowitz, Mr. Social Security: The Life of Wilbur J. Cohen (Lawrence: University Press of Kansas, 1995).

Ball, another member of this generation and a key Social Security policymaker.

Robert Julius Myers, another specialist in Social Security, has been described as an individual who "delighted in the technical nooks and crannies of the program . . . a stickler for detail and intellectual rigor."[76] Myers was born in Lancaster, Pennsylvania, in 1912. He obtained his undergraduate degree at Lehigh University in 1933 and his M.S. at the University of Iowa in 1934. Between 1934 and 1946, he served as an actuary for the Committee on Economic Security, the Railroad Retirement Board, and the Social Security Board. Myers prepared the vital actuarial estimates for the Social Security Act of 1935; according to one Social Security expert, the original old age insurance proposals included a number of options, labeled M-1, M-2, up to M-9. "M" stood for Myers and "M-9" meant Myers's "ninth shot at it."[77]

After ten years in Social Security, Myers obtained a position under W.R. Williams, chief actuary of the Social Security Administration (SSA) in 1946. The following year, Williams became embroiled in a public conflict with several administrators over the use of insurance rhetoric to describe the program. When Williams quit his position, Myers took over as chief actuary, a position he retained until 1970. Myers's job was to translate the policy proposals of others into actuarial terms. Myers insisted that actuaries should be the "eyes and brains" of SSA; without their guidance, the program might lose its actuarial soundness.[78] Although Myers was not a political operative, his analyses carried great weight in Congress by lending statistical credibility to political proposals.

On federal tax matters, professional staffer Laurence Neal Woodworth became the preeminent civil servant in his field. More than any other individual, Mills would come to rely on Woodworth as a confidant and advisor. Woodworth, who was born in Loudenville, Ohio, in 1918, earned his A.B. at Ohio Northern University in 1940 and his M.S. in government management at the University of Denver in 1942. At his first job, Woodworth served as a research analyst for the Civil Research Institute in Kansas City. In 1943, he moved to the Tax Foundation, one of the leading professional think tanks on tax policy at that time. In 1944, Colin Stam hired Woodworth as an economist for the Joint Committee on Internal Revenue Taxation; as one

[76] Edward Berkowitz, "Introduction," in *Social Security After Fifty: Successes and Failures*, ed. Edward Berkowitz (New York: Greenwood Press, 1987), 8.

[77] Cited in Martha Derthick, *Policymaking for Social Security* (Washington: The Brookings Institution, 1979), 55.

[78] Jerry Cates, *Insuring Inequality: Administrative Leadership in Social Security, 1935–1954* (Ann Arbor: University of Michigan Press, 1983), 92–93.

lawyer recalled, "Larry was technically so confident that Stam had to have him."[79]

Woodworth was not well known outside his own office until the mid-1950s because Stam discouraged his staff from writing or speaking at tax meetings. Privately, however, Woodworth conversed with politicians, public finance economists, tax lawyers, and interest groups on a regular basis. Woodworth, said colleagues, was "a great student of the tax law," a man with an unusually broad knowledge of the tax code; he had a keen "awareness of its details and historical lore." In addition, he gained an "intimate" knowledge of Congress, including its operations, its personalities, and its institutional "mystique."[80] When Stam's influence waned in the House during the early 1960s, Woodworth emerged from the shadows to become highly influential on matters of tax policy.

The interest-group officials

As Woodworth wrote tax policies, he encountered a new type of interest-group official. Within the AFL-CIO, for example, the bureaucratic structure of the organization and the complex process of administrative politics required a different type of individual than George Meany or Walter Reuther, who had dominated media headlines. These new influential officials included Andrew Biemiller, Stanley Ruttenberg, and Nelson Cruikshank. Biemiller, who received his B.A. from Cornell in 1926, served as an instructor of history at the University of Pennsylvania. At the age of twenty-six, he moved into politics and union organizing when he accepted an invitation in 1932 from the Socialist Party in Milwaukee to set up an educational program at the Southside Socialist Education Center. There he taught labor economics and labor history, as well as public speaking. He also was a reporter for the socialist daily, *Milwaukee Leader*. During World War II, Biemiller was the labor vice-chairman for the War Production Board, and in 1944 he was elected to Congress and served as a Democratic Representative for Wisconsin in 1945 and 1946 and again in 1949–50. On his arrival at Congress, Speaker Sam Rayburn coached him on parliamentary procedures.[81] Following this brief legislative stint, Biemiller worked for two years as a consultant on labor affairs

[79] Donald Lubick, interview with Julian Zelizer, 16 May 1994, 13.

[80] Stanley S. Surrey, "Tribute to Dr. Laurence N. Woodworth: Two Decades of Federal Tax Policy Viewed from This Perspective," *National Tax Journal* XXXII, No. 3 (September 1979): 227; Mortimer Caplin, interview with Julian Zelizer, 13 June 1994.

[81] Andrew Biemiller, interview with James R. Fuchs, 29 July 1977, HTL, Oral History Interview Collection, 12–15.

to the secretary of Labor and as a special assistant to the Secretary of the Interior, before he was hired as a legislative lobbyist for the AFL. In 1956, the AFL-CIO appointed this outspoken and commanding lobbyist to be the director of its legislative department.

While Biemiller publicly articulated AFL-CIO policy, Director of Research Stanley Ruttenberg and Nelson Cruikshank formulated it. Ruttenberg was a soft-spoken man who had been raised in a coal-mining town in western Pennsylvania, and whose brother Harold became a leading voice for the Steel Workers Organizing Committee. After military school in Virginia, Ruttenberg attended the University of Pittsburgh, graduating with a B.S. in 1937. Joining the CIO that year, Ruttenberg moved his way up the union movement by way of staff positions. He served as the assistant to CIO director of Research Ralph Hetzel. Then, after an interlude in the army during World War II and two more years in research for the CIO, he was promoted to Director of Research and Education in 1948. He went on to become the AFL-CIO's Director of Research in 1955. In addition to his work at the AFL-CIO, Ruttenberg was active in numerous organizations involved with fiscal policymaking, including the National Planning Commission and the National Bureau of Economic Research.[82] Under President Kennedy, Ruttenberg was brought into the Department of Labor. On Social Security, Ruttenberg deferred to Nelson Cruikshank, a former minister who had attended the Union Theological Seminary. In the 1930s, Cruikshank worked for the WPA and Farm Security Administration, and in World War II, for the War Manpower Commission. In 1944, Cruikshank joined the AFL, where he worked closely with Wilbur Cohen to learn the technical nuances of payroll taxes and wage-related benefits. Cruikshank became the organization's leading expert on Social Security, and in 1955 he was named the director of the AFL-CIO's Department of Social Security.[83]

The tax men

From Stanley Surrey to Nelson Cruikshank, Wilbur Mills encountered a generation of policymakers who were united by their professional education.[84] Their universities promoted a scientistic ethos that

[82] Julian E. Zelizer, "From Wildcats to Technocrats: The AFL-CIO, 1955–65," 19 October 1995 (paper presented to the 1995 North American Labor History Conference).

[83] Berkowitz, *Mr. Social Security*, 54–55.

[84] William Strauss and Neil Howe have called this the "G.I. Generation." They point out that four members of this generation became President of the United States – Lyndon Johnson (born 1908), Ronald Reagan (1911), Richard Nixon (1913), and

stressed specialization, quantitative data, and technocratic analysis.[85] They took courses, moreover, with professors who valued objectivity, not advocacy, as their cherished ideal for their students. The experts, according to this ethos, were modern heroes who promoted the "public interest" through rational, disinterested knowledge. These lessons continued in graduate school, where mentors explained to them the importance of esoteric knowledge, not just as an ideal, but as an essential tool for advancing through occupational hierarchies.[86] Almost all of these men finished their higher education between 1932 and 1942.

Their graduation from the universities coincided with the expansion of the federal government during the New Deal and World War II. Mills's generation took advantage of this situation by acquiring its first jobs in the new administrative apparatuses of the state; there, they applied their "technical" skills to "political" situations. In doing so, they helped consummate the marriage that occurred, as one historian has argued, between the professions and the federal government.[87] After these formative years, they dedicated their careers to the preservation of this important relationship.

During the 1950s, these men refined their abilities to negotiate the "technical" and "political" aspects of federal institutions. Some, including Surrey, Cohen, and Fowler, did so by returning to private practice, where they kept apprised of the latest advances in their specialty. At the same time, they stayed involved with the federal government through professional think tanks, national interest groups, and trade associations. Several of these men were also consultants to the Treasury and Congress and participated regularly in congressional hearings. Meanwhile, other members of this generation,

John Kennedy (1917). William Strauss and Neil Howe, *Generations: The History of America's Future, 1584–2069* (New York: William Morrow, 1991), 262–265.

[85] On the importance of technocratic expertise in academic thought, see Burton J. Bledstein, *The Culture of Professionalism: The Middle Class and the Development of Higher Education in America* (New York: W.W. Norton, 1978); Guy Achlon, *The Invisible Hand of Planning: Capitalism, Social Science, and the State in the 1920s* (Princeton: Princeton University Press, 1984); Dorothy Ross, *The Origins of American Social Science* (Cambridge: Cambridge University Press, 1991); Morton J. Horwitz, *The Transformation of American Law 1870–1960: The Crisis of Legal Orthodoxy* (New York: Oxford University Press, 1992); Jerold S. Auerbach, *Unequal Justice: Lawyers and Social Change in Modern America* (New York: Oxford University Press, 1976), 74–101; 158–230.

[86] Mary O. Furner, *Advocacy and Objectivity: A Crisis in the Professionalization of American Social Science, 1865–1905* (Lexington: University of Kentucky Press, 1975).

[87] Brian Balogh, "Reorganizing the Organizational Synthesis: Reconsidering Modern American Federal-Professional Relations," *Studies in American Political Development* 5, No. 1 (1991): 119–172.

including Myers and Woodworth, worked for the government on a full-time basis, building networks in Washington.

Unlike the New Dealers, who saw themselves as pathbreakers creating new forms of government, this generation tended to define their role as pragmatists and technocrats who sought to institutionalize, expand, or modify what already existed. By the time they entered public service, most were Democrats, with a handful of moderate Republicans, who perceived the New Deal as having established an appealing framework for governance. At the same time, following World War II and the start of the Cold War, they celebrated the values of liberal individualism and castigated the collectivism and direct government controls of communism. By the late 1950s, this generation would emerge as the major players within the tax community.

THE PROMISE OF EXPERTISE

By the middle of the Truman presidency, Mills had reached a position high enough on the seniority ladder to have a significant influence on committee policy. During the 1940s, he had gained a better sense of the policymaking process through his work with Democrats, interest groups, and congressional staff. Understanding these groups was crucial to Mills because they would continue to exert tremendous influence even as the process was transformed in the 1950s and 1960s. Once Mills obtained a seat on the coveted Ways and Means, he could build on his political knowledge and move up the hierarchy of this powerful committee.

Like others in his generation, Mills developed a faith in the value of specialized expertise. The federal tax code, Mills said, depended on the knowledge of economists and accountants: "Those of the interested public who because of training and experience have a knowledge of taxation and the ways in which it affects our economy . . . it is the duty of tax men, whether in public or private life, to inform the American people of the consequences of continuing to deal with the federal tax structure and the demands for particular relief which it engenders on a case by case basis."[88] Mills boasted that his committee consulted regularly with "the outstanding scholars, the leading tax experts and the leading economists in the nation . . . We wanted the benefit of their brainpower, and their scholarship. . . ."[89] Through technical knowledge, Mills argued, experts and politicians

[88] Wilbur D. Mills, "Remarks before the Society of Public Accountants," September 1958, WMPC, Box 775, File 9.

[89] Wilbur D. Mills, "Remarks before the Fourth Annual Recognition Banquet," 9 November 1964, WMPC, Box 591, File 2.

could design a restrained federal state that provided limited social welfare benefits and helped direct economic growth.

Mills's generation was also well versed in economic and legal theories that emphasized the role of the government in maintaining market stability. On leaving the university, Mills and his colleagues cut their professional teeth on the expanding institutions of the American state during the New Deal and World War II. They had experienced the crisis of the Great Depression, and concluded that the federal government must play a permanent role in the nation. "Do not be misled," Mills warned in 1948, "economic policies of Government both at home and in international relations determine to a great extent these periods of prosperity and depression."[90] Mills's generation was adept at operating within public bureaucracies and willing to use some type of government intervention to influence the economy.

As a result of its professional training and its political beliefs, Mills's generation believed that technocratic knowledge could diminish partisanship, weaken the influence of interest groups, and curtail the authority of political elites. Once these officials accepted the permanence of the state, they turned to technical knowledge as a mechanism for minimizing the arbitrary authority that developed in centralized political institutions. As the historian Theodore Porter argued: "A decision made by the numbers . . . has at least the appearance of being fair and impersonal. Scientific objectivity thus provides an answer to a moral demand for impartiality and fairness."[91] This logic ignored the social basis of technocratic knowledge and downplayed the ways in which technocratic discourse ignored other types of dialogue about politics. Nonetheless, it provided hope for policymakers who accepted a federal state but feared communism.

Beyond this general consensus, however, Mills's policy agenda remained vague. Focusing on securing his position in Congress, Mills adhered closely to Rayburn's famous axiom – "Don't ever talk until you know what you're talking about" – hesitating to articulate a clear vision of domestic policy. Two major legislative developments, the Social Security Amendments of 1950 and the Internal Revenue Recodification of 1954, pushed Mills to define his policy agenda more clearly. This legislation determined the key issues and established the larger context for policy debates during the next three decades.

[90] Mills, "What is Best for Arkansas Politically."
[91] Theodore M. Porter, *Trust in Numbers: The Pursuit of Objectivity in Science and Public Life* (Princeton: Princeton University Press, 1995), 8.

2

"Where is the Money Coming From?"[1]

Because of its earmarked tax system, the insurance portion of Social Security achieved a special status within the American state between 1950 and 1972. Although much of the logic behind the system was based on misconceptions – the notion that the program resembled private insurance or that a clear distinction existed between payroll tax revenue and general revenue – the misconceptions legitimatized social insurance in the minds of policy experts, politicians, and recipients.[2] As a result of the Social Security tax, they claimed, recipients did not receive something for nothing, nor did Congress feel as if it were building a massive welfare state. The tax system proved essential in defining old-age insurance as distinct from welfare and to legitimatizing the exclusion of a means test; the tax enabled citizens and politicians to perceive payments as an earned benefit. Through contributory old-age insurance, the state would forge a strong alliance with the elderly and their descendants, both with retirees who received cash payments and with middle-class families who did not have to finance their parents' retirement years.[3]

Wilbur Mills's first major political battle centered on Social Security. During the first ten years of his congressional career, the earmarked tax system behind Social Security had come under intense fire. When an early reaction emerged against some aspects of Social Security taxation during the 1940s, many social insurance advocates seemed willing to compromise on important aspects of the program.

---

[1] This quotation comes from Representative Noah Mason (R-IL), who was describing the key issue behind any decision on social welfare. U.S. Congress, House Committee on Ways and Means, *Social Security Legislation: Hearings*, 85th Cong., 2nd sess., 1958, 56.

[2] Cheryl Zollars and Theda Skocpol, "Cultural Mythmaking as a Policy Tool: The Social Security Board and the Construction of a Social Citizenship of Self Interest," in *Political Culture and Political Structure: Theoretical and Empirical Studies*, ed. Frederick D. Weil, vol. 2 (1994): 381–408.

[3] John Myles, *Old Age in the Welfare State: The Political Economy of Public Pensions*, revised edition (Lawrence: University Press of Kansas, 1989).

When Mills started his tenure on Ways and Means in 1942, the program's financial principles were up in the air. By 1943, Congress had undermined two of the main fiscal mechanisms that distinguished Old-Age and Survivors' Insurance (OASI) from other forms of welfare. Foremost, Congress had abolished the mandate that required a large annual surplus of Social Security tax revenue in order to build a substantial reserve. Moreover, it authorized the use of direct general-revenue finance to pay for benefits when payroll taxes became insufficient. These actions blurred the thin line that separated old-age insurance from public welfare. The battle to resolve this dilemma would shape Mills's outlook on Social Security taxation for the rest of his career. Not only did he learn how symbols and rhetoric could build political support for government programs, but he found that the particular revenue source behind expenditures was crucial to their success or failure. Mills and his colleagues redesigned the earmarked tax system into the "pay-as-you-go" structure that defined the program until 1972. The tax system constituted a seminal compromise between fiscal conservatism and the American state and secured support from the middle class for its "earned" benefits.

Mills learned about these aspects of domestic policy through his work with Wilbur Cohen, Robert Ball, and Robert Myers, who had advanced in the Social Security Administration during the 1930s and 1940s, and Nelson Cruikshank, who became the AFL-CIO's chief expert on Social Security. This new generation of advocates placed greater emphasis on the centrality of the earmarked tax system in order to protect the program from political attack. As they formed into the Social Security faction of the tax community, Cohen, Ball, Myers, and Cruikshank worked closely with Mills to preserve the earmarked tax system that distinguished old-age insurance from welfare.

EARMARKED TAXES AND THE NEW DEAL

When the Roosevelt administration introduced earmarked taxation into the New Deal, it built on an old tradition. According to political scientists Carolyn Webber and Aaron Wildavsky, the leaders of Athens had relied on earmarked taxes to simplify the collection and distribution of revenue and to control government costs. Earmarked taxes, Webber and Wildersky argue, constituted a conservative method of public finance: "With earmarking there is no question about how resources will be used, because the use is specified. Availability of funds determines amounts spent; unless there is a large surplus in an earmarked fund, balances act as a check on spending, for when revenues are depleted, expenditure for the fund's specified purpose

must stop."[4] By the twentieth century, however, national political institutions had come to rely on modern budgeting techniques.[5]

The Social Security Act of 1935

To a limited extent, however, earmarked taxes regained prominence
at the federal level during the New Deal. Through the Social Security Act of 1935, federal officials began to use earmarked taxes to distinguish an entire category of government benefits.[6] By earmarking
taxes, policymakers designated a particular revenue source to a particular type of expenditure. This practice stood in contrast to general-
revenue financing, through which particular expenditures were
financed by consolidated, non-earmarked monies. When Congress
enacted Social Security, it divided the program into two tracks, each
characterized by the type of tax that paid for its benefits.

The public assistance track included Old-Age Assistance (OAA),
Aid to the Blind, and Aid to Dependent Children (ADC). Even
though federal funding for welfare represented a significant innovation, public assistance relied on a traditional system of finance. Congress paid for benefits through general revenue raised primarily by
personal and corporate income taxes. Like other general-revenue
programs, policymakers feared that benefits might become too

---

[4] Carolyn Webber and Aaron Wildavsky, *A History of Taxation and Expenditure in the
Western World* (New York: Simon and Schuster, 1986), 120–121.

[5] James D. Savage, *Balanced Budgets & American Politics* (Ithaca: Cornell University
Press, 1988), 121–160.

[6] There were many precedents within the United States for the use of earmarked taxes
to pay for contributory programs. On the federal level, there was a series of smaller
programs for selected government workers that used a "contributory system" of
finance. These included programs for employees of the federal and District of
Columbia governments (1920); officers of the Foreign Service (1924); workers on
the Panama Canal (1931); employees of Federal Reserve Banks and the Federal
Reserve retirement system (1934); and railroad workers (1934). On the state level,
the Wisconsin unemployment program required firms to pay taxes into its reserve,
which then funded benefits to workers when they were unemployed. Finally, in the
private market, the insurance industry provided a model for the use of earmarked
contributions. But, the Social Security Act marked a dramatic departure in scale and
scope from anything that had existed in the past at the federal level. For the best
work on the origins of earmarked taxes before the 1930s in the United States and
abroad, see the following: Richard Richards, *Closing the Door to Destitution: The Shaping
of the Social Security Acts of the United States and New Zealand* (University Park: Pennsylvania State University Press, 1994), 17–46; Peter Baldwin, *The Politics of Social Soli-
darity: Class Bases of the European Welfare State 1875–1975* (Cambridge: Cambridge
University Press, 1990); G. John Ikenberry and Theda Skocpol, "The Road to Social
Security," in Skocpol's *Social Policy in the United States: Future Possibilities in Historical
Perspective* (Princeton: Princeton University Press, 1995), 136–166.

generous over time; they sometimes invoked Civil War pensions as an example of how noncontributory programs tended to become mired in corruption and partisan politics.[7] Congress did not have to raise a specific tax each time it raised a noncontributory benefit, nor did recipients contribute anything directly to the program. To combat these problems, Congress imposed strict controls on OAA and ADC, including means-testing and low benefits, and the states were to administer the program. Although welfare experts spent the next fifty years debating the expansion of benefits, few of them challenged its basic method of finance.[8]

In contrast, the social insurance track, Old-Age and Survivors' Insurance and Unemployment Compensation, stimulated a continuous debate about the program's tax source.[9] Since the inception of Old-Age Insurance in 1935, Congress had imposed a monthly tax on the gross income of employees to pay for monthly benefits; both workers and their employers shared this tax burden. By paying the Social Security tax, participants would "earn" the right to their benefits; general revenue, moreover, could not be used to pay for the program.[10] Administrators claimed that the payroll tax revenue was placed into a trust fund (created in 1939), which Congress would use

---

[7] Theda Skocpol, *Protecting Soldiers and Mothers: The Political Origins of Social Policy in the United States* (Cambridge, MA: The Belknap Press of Harvard University Press, 1992), 533.

[8] The main exception involves the debates over a negative income tax between 1964 and 1971. See Daniel P. Moynihan, *The Politics of Guaranteed Income: The Nixon Administration and the Family Assistance Plan* (New York: Random House, 1973); Jill Quadagno, *The Color of Welfare: How Racism Undermined the War on Poverty* (New York: Oxford University Press, 1994), 117–134.

[9] Although Chapter 4 turns briefly to the issue of unemployment compensation, which constituted the other "social insurance" program, *Taxing America* focuses on Old-Age Insurance.

[10] On the debates over the payroll tax during the New Deal, see Mark Leff, *The Limits of Symbolic Reform: The New Deal and Taxation, 1933–39* (Cambridge: Cambridge University Press, 1984), 45–47; 275–286; Edward D. Berkowitz, *America's Welfare State: From Roosevelt to Reagan* (Baltimore: The Johns Hopkins University Press, 1991), 13–65; Robert J. Myers, "Pay-As-You-Go Financing for Social Security is the Only Way to Go," *Journal of the American Society of CLU & CHFC* (January 1991): 52–58; Ann Shola Orloff, *The Politics of Pensions: A Comparative Analysis of Britain, Canada, and the United States, 1880–1940* (Madison: University of Wisconsin Press, 1993); Richards, *Closing the Door to Destitution*, 17–46; 111–154; Robert M. Ball, *Social Security Today and Tomorrow* (New York: Columbia University Press, 1978); Otto Eckstein, "Financing the System of Social Insurance," and Joseph A. Pechman, "Discussion of the Paper by Otto Eckstein," in *The Princeton Symposium on the American System of Social Insurance: Its Philosophy, Impact, and Future Development* (New York: McGraw-Hill, 1968), 47–73. Colin Gordon examines the corporate response to this legislation in *New Deals: Business, Labor, and Politics in America, 1920–1935* (Cambridge: Cambridge University Press, 1994), 240–279.

in future years to pay for personal retirement benefits. Wage-related benefits were said to guarantee the connection between the individual's contributions and the benefits he received.[11] Unlike public assistance, these benefits were to be administered by the federal Social Security Board. During the early years of the program, Social Security administrators directed intense public relations efforts to promoting the concept of contributory old-age insurance and earned benefits among the citizenry.[12]

The payroll tax constituted the heart and soul of Old-Age Insurance. According to the Social Security Act, the payroll "contribution" was a direct tax on the wage income of workers in covered occupations. While the tax applied to all wage income, no matter how small or large, the Act imposed a maximum limit on the amount of wages on which taxes could be collected (this was called the earnings or wage base). By contributing this payroll tax during their productive years, according to Roosevelt, retirees would feel as if they had earned their benefits. "Those taxes were never a problem of economics. They are politics all the way through," Roosevelt explained. "We put those payroll contributions there so as to give the contributors a legal, moral, and political right to collect their pensions and their unemployment benefits. With those taxes in there, no damn politician can ever scrap my social security program."[13] After a challenge in 1937, the Supreme Court validated this system by declaring the old-age insurance tax constitutional.

Under the terms of the Social Security Act, the Bureau of Internal Revenue would begin collecting payroll taxes in 1937. The Treasury was to place the taxes into the general-revenue fund, like all other tax revenue, where the funds could be used for anything from building battleships to constructing roads.[14] Nonetheless, the law required that Congress make an annual appropriation into the old-age reserve account that was sufficient to preserve a self-supporting system. In

[11] Jerry Cates, *Insuring Inequality: Administrative Leadership in Social Security, 1935–1954* (Ann Arbor: University of Michigan Press, 1983), 16–17; Martha Derthick, *Policymaking For Social Security* (Washington: The Brookings Institution, 1979), 252–287; 339–368; W. Andrew Achenbaum, *Social Security: Visions and Revisions* (Cambridge: Cambridge University Press, 1986).

[12] Zollars and Skocpol, "Cultural Mythmaking as a Policy Tool," 381–408; Brian Balogh, "Securing Support: The Emergence of the Social Security Board as a Political Actor, 1935–1939," in *Federal Social Policy: The Historical Dimension*, eds. Donald T. Critchlow and Ellis W. Hawley (University Park: Pennsylvania State University Press, 1988), 55–78.

[13] Cited in Arthur M. Schlesinger, Jr., *The Age of Roosevelt: The Coming of the New Deal* (Boston: Houghton Mifflin, 1959), 308–309.

[14] Ralph T. Compton, *Social Security Payroll Taxes* (New York: Commerce Clearing House, 1940), 31.

1935, "self-supporting" meant a reserve large enough so that if the program ceased operating, all benefits earned at that time could be paid from the reserve.[15] The program would thus never need to depend directly on general revenue. Roosevelt and Secretary of the Treasury Henry Morgenthau insisted on a "self-supporting" system despite the desire of the Committee on Economic Security, which had written the administration proposal, to include a substantial future general-revenue subsidy. It was crucial to Morgenthau and the president that Social Security be fiscally conservative for political and moral reasons. Morgenthau intended the deflationary tax system to commit future officals to a particular policy design. Along with Roosevelt, he believed that the self-financing tax system would guarantee the program's long-term solvency and help to define these payments as "earned benefits" that the elderly were entitled to receive. Moreover, Social Security taxes could lower the operating deficit since they would be invested in government securities.[16]

The founders of Old-Age Insurance claimed that scheduled taxes would exceed the cost of benefits over the long-term. Roosevelt and Morgenthau were adamant on building a reserve fund to protect the federal budget from deficits in future decades: "It is almost dishonest," Roosevelt told Secretary of Labor Francis Perkins, "to build up an accumulated deficit for the Congress of the United States to meet in 1980. We can't do that. We can't sell the United States short in 1980 any more than in 1935."[17] Contemplating that the cost of benefits would reach approximately $3.5 billion by 1980, the founders established a tax schedule that could finance 60 percent of these expenditures at a combined tax rate of 6 percent for the employer and employee. The excess of tax revenue collected during the early years of the program would create a reserve of $47 billion by 1980, which was sufficient to finance the remaining cost of benefits; Congress would invest the revenue in U.S. interest-bearing bonds. Under this byzantine system, in which the government invested its own monies in itself, workers could theoretically receive benefits that were equivalent to their tax contributions, with interest;

---

[15] Robert J. Myers, "Methodology Involved in Developing Long-Range Cost Estimates for the Old-Age, Survivors, and Disability Insurance System," May 1959, Actuarial Study No. 49, RMP, unprocessed, 48–49; Myers, "Actuarial Aspects of Financing Old-Age and Survivors Insurance," *Social Security Bulletin* 16, No. 6 (June 1953): 7; Myers to Wilbur Cohen, 11 January 1950, WCP, Box 33, Folder 3.

[16] Eric M. Patashnik, "Unfolding Promises: Trust Funds and the Politics of Precommitment," *Political Science Quarterly*, 112, No. 3 (Fall 1997): 439; Mark H. Leff, "Taxing the 'Forgotten Man' ": The Politics of Social Security Finance in the New Deal," *The Journal of American History*, 70, No. 2 (September 1983): 359–381.

[17] Cited in Schlesinger, *The Age of Roosevelt*, 309–310.

the Social Security Administration claimed that U.S. bonds were the "safest investment in the world."[18]

THE PERILS OF UNCERTAINTY, 1937–1948

Within two years of the enactment of Social Security, however, strong opposition had mounted against collecting a surplus of revenue. First, Keynesian economists warned that the surpluses and the taxes themselves would drain consumer purchasing power. Reserves, they said, were unnecessary because the government always had the power to tax and because "policyholders" could not withdraw their contributions. Second, the popular Townsendite movement promoted flat pensions that offered more generous benefits. Third, fiscally conservative legislators and business leaders feared that Congress would use the surplus for extravagant public expenditures; instead, they preferred lowering the corporate tax burden. Finally, many financial analysts cautioned that large reserves meant higher costs to those who paid the income tax that financed the interest on the federal bonds.[19]

Congress abandons large surpluses

In response to these challenges, Congress, using the Social Security Amendments of 1939, abandoned the principle of accumulating large reserves. Among the financial stipulations, the amendments legally earmarked payroll taxes by creating the Federal Old-Age and Survivors' Insurance Trust Fund; payroll tax revenue was to be placed directly into the fund and used for nothing else.[20] The amendments also established a Board of Trustees to report whenever the reserve exceeded three times the program's cost.[21] Although not

---

[18] Social Security Administration, "Facts About the Trust Fund of the Federal Old-Age and Survivors Insurance System," January 1950, NAS, Office of the Actuary, Box 37, File: 705, 1950.

[19] Sheryl R. Tynes, *Turning Points in Social Security: From "Cruel Hoax" to "Sacred Entitlement"* (Stanford: Stanford University Press, 1996), 60–120; Carolyn L. Weaver, *The Crisis in Social Security: Economic and Political Origins* (Duke, N.C: Duke Press Policy Studies, 1982), 102–124; Edward D. Berkowitz, "The First Advisory Council and the 1939 Amendments," in *Social Security After Fifty: Successes And Failures*, ed. Edward D. Berkowitz (New York: Greenwood Press, 1987), 55–78.

[20] Wilbur Cohen to Myer Jacobstein, 31 August 1948, WCP, Box 28, Folder 4.

[21] Myers, "Actuarial Aspects of Financing Old-Age and Survivors Insurance"; Myers, "Old-Age, Survivors, and Disability Insurance Provisions: Summary of Legislation, 1935–1956," *Social Security Bulletin* 20, No. 7 (July 1957); 3–8; James S. Parker, "Financial Policy in Old-Age and Survivors Insurance, 1935–1950," *Social Security Bulletin* 14, No. 6 (June 1951): 3–10; Myers to Cohen, 11 January 1950, WCP, Box 33, Folder 3.

specifically stated in the law, this implied that the system would be run on a "pay-as-you-go" basis, with a little money to be deposited in a contingency reserve fund. To reduce the program's surplus by almost one-half, the tax-writing committees increased benefits, expanded coverage to widows and children of those participants who died before reaching the retirement age, and froze the tax rate at 2 percent.[22] Congress renamed the program Old-Age and Survivors' Insurance (OASI).

Politically, Congress was eager to reduce the actuarial surplus because this meant increasing benefits without raising taxes. By boosting cash benefits and expanding coverage to those constituents who were not yet in the program, representatives could strengthen support within their districts. The extension of coverage was particularly appealing during a period when many representatives did not yet have constituents who received Social Security. Of course, there were limits to this electoral payoff. After all, constituents perceived the benefits as an earned right, not as a government benefit, and politicians had defined their own role as brokers between the contributions and benefits of citizens in this social insurance system. Nonetheless, representatives were aware that any type of monies that arrived to citizens via the federal government increased political satisfaction among the electorate. Congress thus agreed to abandon the plan for accumulating large reserves in the trust fund.

Without the original concept of a "full" reserve, policymakers could now only rely on the symbolic value of the payroll tax, or the absence of direct general-revenue funding, to distinguish OASI finance from public assistance and to justify the exclusion of a means test. Although OASI was to be financed in the same fashion as all other public expenditures, with one group of citizens paying for the benefits of another group, most government officials explained the payroll tax was a special type of tax that entitled the contributor to receive a specific type of benefit in future years. According to the Social Security Board, the tax provided the "psychological basis" for OASI: Unless every benefit recipient "makes a contribution, no matter how small, the whole system of Social Security, with relatively fixed benefits payable as a matter of right, would be jeopardized."[23] Or, as Marion Folsom, a business executive from Eastman Kodak, explained:

---

[22] U.S. Congress, House Committee on Ways and Means, *Social Security Act Amendments of 1939*, 76th Cong., 1st sess., 1939.

[23] U.S. Department of Treasury, Division of Tax Research, "The Extension of Old-Age and Survivors Insurance to the Self-Employed," 5 December 1945, HTL, Papers of Fred Vinson, Roll 19. See also Wilbur Cohen to Professor Milton Handler, 12 October 1949, WCP, Box 29, Folder 4.

The contributions which an individual makes give him the feeling that he has earned the benefits as a right. This avoids and eliminates the need for a means test and the fear of being an object of charity . . . Sharing in the cost of the benefits should give the individual a better understanding of their value and of the workings of our economic system. It also helps to offset a tendency on the part of the individual to look toward the government for support. He realizes, too, that any increase in benefits may involve an increase in contributions.[24]

While general revenues meant welfare, payroll taxes meant earned benefits. Indirectly, the program had already been compromised because the government used general revenue to finance the interest on the securities in the trust funds, and used general revenue to supplement the pensions of workers who were close to retirement when the program started. Nonetheless, policymakers distinguished these cases from direct general-revenue finance, which, in their minds, constituted the biggest threat to the integrity of social insurance.

The threat of general revenue

Nonetheless, the 1939 amendments left open the possibility of using general revenue to pay for OASI.[25] Even Henry Morgenthau, who had been the strongest advocate for a full reserve in 1935, now suggested that "general tax revenues may be substituted – without substantial inequity – for a considerable proportion of the expected interest earnings from the large reserve contemplated by the present law."[26] Without the full reserve, Congress would have to pay for the benefits of current retirees either by raising payroll tax rates on working citizens or by using general revenues.[27] The 1939 amendments neither authorized nor excluded either option. By failing to resolve this issue, Congress left Social Security in a state of grave uncertainty.[28]

---

[24] Marion Folsom, "Greater Security For Your Old Age," 21 December 1948, NAS, RG 47, Office of the Actuary, Box 26, File: Folsom.

[25] Robert J. Myers, "Estimates of the Reserves Under the Old-Age Insurance System in the United States," 18 September 1950, NAS, RG 47, Office of the Actuary, Box 37, File: 705, 1950.

[26] Technical Staff of the Office of the Secretary of the Treasury, "Questions and Answers on Social Security," 11 March 1949, HTL, Papers of John W. Snyder, Box 85, Folder: Questions and Answers on Social Security.

[27] Robert Myers to Wilbur Cohen, 11 January 1950, WCP, Box 33, Folder 3; Myers, "The Financial Principle of Self-Support in the Old-Age and Survivors Insurance System," April 1955, Actuarial Study No. 40, RMP, unprocessed.

[28] Roy Blough to Secretary Vinson, 28 February 1946, HTL, Papers of Fred Vinson, Roll 19.

The tax-writing committees aggravated this situation by maintaining a tax freeze throughout the 1940s. Congress justified its position on the basis of several factors: the small number of elderly persons receiving old-age insurance benefits, the surplus that had accumulated since 1937, and the rising wartime payrolls that resulted in larger Social Security tax collections.[29] Starting in January 1942, Roosevelt refrained from making any official Social Security proposals.[30] The tax freeze, according to Robert Myers, chief actuary of the Social Security Administration, found "unanimous" support from "Government, labor, and business representatives."[31]

Myers sensed a problem that would divide the Social Security faction of the tax community. This division pitted administrators, whose survival depended on the growth of generous and broad benefits, against the program's financial guardians (SSA actuaries and the tax-writing committees), who depended on an earmarked tax system that could control long-term costs and prevent any strain on income taxation. Social Security actuaries, according to Myers, felt intense pressure at this time from their bureaucratic leaders to avoid raising the issue of long-term cost. As Myers complained: "There is the very serious limitation that the general philosophy of planners is to utterly disregard costs, if this might prove a deterrent. The planners also are not willing to face the problems and difficulties which an analytical actuarial mind will usually bring forth. Rather, the attitude is that any word of adverse criticism denotes a reactionary attitude or, in other words, you must all be in favor of it or all against it with no midway positions."[32] Although Mills and Myers found a solution in 1950, this cleavage created serious friction within the tax community during the next two decades, and would explode into open conflict after 1972.

Worse still for fiscal conservatives, the tax-writing committees adopted the Vandenberg-Murray amendment (1944), which authorized general-revenue appropriations into the Social Security trust fund when the cost of benefits exceeded the amount of payroll tax

---

[29] Mark H. Leff, "Speculating in Social Security Futures: The Perils of Payroll Tax Financing, 1939–1950," in *Social Security: The First Half-Century*, eds., Gerald D. Nash, Noel H. Pugach, and Richard F. Tomasson (Albuquerque: University of New Mexico Press, 1988), 243–278; The American Forum of the Air, "Should We Freeze the Social Security Tax?" 5 December 1944, NAT, RG 56, Office of Tax Policy, Box 40, File: Social Security Finance.

[30] Bartholomew H. Sparrow, *From the Outside In: World War II and the American State* (Princeton: Princeton University Press, 1996), 42–43.

[31] Robert Myers to W.R. Williamson, 24 October 1946, NAS, RG 47, Office of the Actuary, Box 40, File 750.

[32] Robert Myers to G.W. Calvert, 10 July 1947, NAS, RG 47, Office of the Actuary, Box 26, File C.

revenue.[33] The subsidy was scheduled to begin in about fifteen years, when the government finished paying off the cost of the war and reconversion; the percentage of general revenue would increase gradually until it represented about one-third of total annual expenditures; Myers warned that the subsidy could even reach three-quarters of tax collections under certain conditions.[34] When the House voted to repeal the amendment in 1946, the Senate voted against repeal. The following year, Treasury officials accepted a temporary continuation of the tax freeze, and assumed an eventual federal contribution to the program.[35] In 1947, the Republican Congress voted to reduce future scheduled Social Security tax increases.[36]

Within the context of these developments, Robert Ball headed the staff of an Advisory Council on Social Security, which issued a series of reports in 1948 on the condition of the program. The Council, set up by the Senate Finance Committee, argued that the best way to reduce dependency on public welfare was to expand contributory social insurance into a universal program. The council proposed expanding Social Security to cover rural farm workers, domestic employees, and the self-employed.

Besides raising benefits and expanding coverage, the Council recommended an immediate increase in the tax rate to $1\frac{1}{2}$ percent for employers and employees. Congress, according to the Council, should increase the tax rate to $2\frac{1}{2}$ percent when the cost of benefits exceeded taxes. Thereafter, a modified "pay-as-you-go" system would

[33] U.S. Congress, House Committee on Ways and Means, *Social Security Amendments of 1949: Report Number 1300*, 81st Cong., 1st sess., 1949, 4. For brief scholarly discussions of the Murray amendment, see F.J. Crowley, "Financing the Social Security Program – Then and Now," U.S. Congress, Joint Economic Committee, Subcommittee on Fiscal Policy, *Studies in Public Welfare: Paper No. 18*, 93rd Cong., 2nd sess., 1974, 29–32; Wilbur Cohen, "Financing," 1960, WCP, Box 72, Folder 6; Derthick, *Policymaking For Social Security*, 240–241; Leff, "Speculating in Social Security Futures," 243–279, and Leff, "Historical Perspectives on Old-Age Insurance: The State of the Art on the Art of the State," in *Social Security After Fifty*, 29–55.

[34] Wilbur J. Cohen, "Cost Factors Under the Wagner-Murray and Dingell Bills," 26 July 1943, WCP, Box 40, Folder 2; Robert Myers to Robert Ball, 17 June 1949, NAS, RG 47, Office of the Actuary, Box 38, File: 710; Myers, "Estimates of the Reserves Under the Old-Age Insurance System in the United States."

[35] Acting Secretary of the Treasury to James Webb, 1 August 1947, HTL, White House Bill File, Box 29, Folder: 6 August 1947 [H.R. 3813–H.R. 4079]; Technical Staff of the Office of the Secretary of the Treasury, "Questions and Answers on Social Security," 11 March 1949, HTL, Papers of John W. Snyder, Box 85, Folder: Questions and Answers on Social Security.

[36] Edward D. Berkowitz, "Social Security and the financing of the American state," in *Funding the Modern American State, 1941–1995: The Rise and Fall of the Era of Easy Finance*, ed. W. Elliot Brownlee (Cambridge: Cambridge University Press and Washington, D.C.: Woodrow Wilson Center Press), 157.

be maintained through a general-revenue contribution whenever benefits exceeded taxes. The Council added that the general-revenue subsidy should never exceed one-third of the benefit disbursements.[37] Such a contribution could be legitimized on the grounds that the social insurance system was gradually taking over a major part of the "burden" for caring for the aged, widows, and dependent children from public assistance.[38]

Together, the Vandenberg-Murray amendment and the tax freeze had jeopardized one of the key distinctions of social insurance. Congress had not only eliminated the accumulation of reserves, but had also authorized the use of general revenue to pay for a portion of OASI benefits. Although no one suggested that old-age pensions be means-tested, Congress had threatened the tax system that rationalized the distribution of government benefits regardless of need. During the next two years, Ways and Means and the Social Security Administration teamed up to reestablish the stability of the payroll tax. Their efforts to prevent general revenue from "contaminating" social insurance began in the winter of 1949, when Ways and Means conducted hearings on a new series of proposals to broaden coverage in OASI.

FINANCING THE EXPANSION, 1949–1950

As America entered the 1950s, federal officials initiated a campaign to expand social insurance and to eliminate most noncontributory public assistance. There were many factors behind this campaign. Some were microeconomic and ideological: Collective bargaining for private pensions led corporate employers to support public pensions to minimize their own costs; a higher cost-of-living fueled a demand for higher benefits; and government officials were more willing to expand contributory social insurance for retirees who had "earned" their benefits rather than to poor citizens in need of government handouts. Other factors were macroeconomic: Rising incomes had generated enough revenue so that officials could raise benefits without a major increase in the tax rate; wartime inflation had weakened the buying power of benefits; and the World War II labor market had brought many workers from the South, who had been in jobs not

---

[37] Wilbur Cohen and A.J. Altmeyer, 23 March 1948, WCP, Box 28, Folder 2; Robert J. Myers, "Actuarial Cost Estimates for Proposals of Social Security Administration and Advisory Council," 14 January 1948, RMP, Box M83-106, unprocessed.

[38] Robert J. Myers, "Material for the Meeting of the Advisory Council on Social Security," 12–13 March 1948, NAS, RG 47, Office of the Actuary, Box 5; U.S. Department of Treasury, "Comments on Congressman Reed's Statement on the Old-Age Insurance System," 29 March 1939, NAT, RG 56, Office of Tax Policy, Box 36, File: Social Security and Relief.

covered by Social Security, to work in Northern industrial jobs that were covered. Meanwhile, there was a substantial revenue surplus because more people were paying for benefits than were receiving them.[39] These developments coincided with congressional elections, which provided an incentive for representatives from both parties to provide constituents with more cash.[40]

OAA grows faster than OASI

But the prospects for this expansion were uncertain. Since the founding of Social Security, social insurance planners feared that progressively funded public assistance benefits might emerge as the main component of the welfare system.[41] During the 1940s, moreover, welfare was expanding at a faster rate than OASI.[42] When representatives promised to increase benefits for the elderly, they meant OAA assistance, not OASI.[43] Because OASI covered a limited segment of the work force, rural agricultural laborers, domestic workers, state and local government employees, and the self-employed still relied on public assistance.[44] In 1949, the federal government spent almost three times as much on welfare as it did on insurance; the average OAA payment, for example, was 70 percent more than the average insurance benefit.[45] At the state level, there was strong

[39] In 1940, less than 1 percent of the elderly population received Social Security benefits. Weaver, *The Crisis in Social Security*, 126.

[40] This paragraph is drawn from the following works: Tynes, *Turning Points in Social Security*, 99–120; Nelson Lichtenstein, "From Corporatism to Collective Bargaining: Organized Labor and Eclipse of Social Democracy in the Postwar Era," in *The Rise and Fall of the New Deal Order 1930–1980*, eds. Steve Fraser and Gary Gerstle (Princeton: Princeton University Press, 1989), 140–145; Beth Stevens, "Blurring the Boundaries: How the Federal Government Has Influenced Welfare Benefits in the Private Sector," in *The Politics of Social Policy in the United States*, eds. Margaret Weir, Ann Shola Orloff, and Theda Skocpol (Princeton: Princeton University Press, 1988), 123–148; Quadagno, *The Color of Welfare*, 155–173; Berkowitz, *America's Welfare State*, 50–65; Berkowitz, "Social Security and the financing of the American state," 148–193; Weaver, *The Crisis in Social Security*, 125–143; Cates, *Insuring Inequality*, 50–85.

[41] Cates, *Insuring Inequality*, 105.

[42] Derthick, *Policymaking for Social Security*, 273; Berkowitz, *America's Welfare State*, 55–65; Cates, *Insuring Inequality*, 104–153; Jules H. Berman, "State Public Assistance Legislation," *Social Security Bulletin* 12, No. 12 (December 1949): 3–10.

[43] Robert Ball, Audio Recording, 1996, Social Security Administration, Office of Library (Baltimore, Maryland).

[44] Kenneth Finegold, "Agriculture and the Politics of U.S. Social Provision: Social Insurance and Food Stamps," in *The Politics of Social Policy in the United States*, 215–216.

[45] Derthick, *Policymaking for Social Security*, 271–274; Wilbur Cohen to Herbert Seibert, WCP, Box 66, Folder 5.

political support for the neo-Townsendite movement, based on
Dr. Francis Townsend's 1930s campaign, that had emerged. This
movement called for generous flat pensions to the elderly that would
be progressively financed through general revenue.[46] Given these
factors and statistics, advocates of social insurance feared that their
program would be swamped by the continued growth of elderly
welfare. As one administration staffer acknowledged, "Because of our
failure to develop a much stronger social insurance system than
we now have, it is nip and tuck as to whether . . . advocates of a
general pension system may win out in the race between insurance
and pensions."[47]

The proposal to expand OASI

To avoid this outcome, the Social Security Administration lobbied
Congress for an expansion of coverage and benefits that would once
and for all establish the primacy of OASI over Old-Age Assistance. In
response to the election of 1948 that kept Harry Truman in the pres-
idency and enabled the Democrats to retake both chambers of
Congress, the Democratic party supported a massive expansion of
Social Security. Between February and April 1949, Chairman Robert
Doughton's (D-NC) Ways and Means conducted public hearings.
Doughton teamed up with Arthur Altmeyer, the commissioner of
Social Security, to argue that an expansion of social insurance
was crucial to eliminating the need for public assistance.[48] Most
hearing participants agreed. Mills, for example, warned that "the
longer Congress delays coverage under title II, the greater grows the
momentum for increased assistance under title I."[49] By extending
OASI benefits to domestic servants, farm workers, and the self-
employed, he argued, Congress could reduce the demand for

---

[46] Derthick, *Policymaking for Social Security*, 220–221.

[47] Staff Comments, "Memorandum for Mr. Murphy: Expansion and Extension of Social
Security System," 14 February 1949, WCP, Box 28, Folder 8. This document is also
in HTL, Files of Charles S. Murphy, Box 27, Folder: Social Security [Folder 2]. See
also W.R. Williamson to Robert Myers, 26 March 1949, RMP, Box M86-W3,
unprocessed.

[48] U.S. Congress, House Committee on Ways and Means, *Social Security Act Amendments
of 1949: Hearings*, 81st Cong., 1st sess., 1949, 1081–1083; 1221. See also Arthur
Altmeyer, "Old-Age, Survivors, and Disability Insurance," *Social Security Bulletin*, 12,
No. 4 (April 1949): 3–15; Richard Neustadt to Gerhard Colm, 16 December 1949,
HTL, Papers of Richard Neustadt, Box 1, Folder: Chron. Files, 1947–1956; Mr.
Kirby to Mr. Lynch, 9 November 1948, HTL, Papers of L. Laszlo Ecker-Racz, Box 1,
Bound Book.

[49] U.S. Congress, House Committee on Ways and Means, *Social Security Act Amendments
of 1949: Hearings*, 81st Cong., 1st sess., 1949, 1390.

government handouts to the elderly.[50] Social insurance, added Myers, helped those workers who had been excluded from the burgeoning private pension system.[51]

The convergence of the proposed expansion with the tax freeze and the Vandenberg-Murray amendment forced Congress to confront the issue of general revenue. Until the tax source behind OASI was clearly defined by Congress, its proponents would have difficulty selling social insurance as an earned benefit. As Mills lamented, "The present program is not sound, and the present rate of taxation provided to maintain that program is not sound."[52] Indeed, Myers now estimated that the general-revenue subsidy might be over $6.5 billion by the year 2000.[53]

Policymakers came down on both sides of the general-revenue debate. Some administrators and economists supported the use of non-earmarked monies. Foremost, the Council of Economic Advisors argued that an eventual Treasury contribution offered an "economically sound and desirable course." Among themselves, they concluded that "in an economy whose vigor depends upon a high relative level of consumption, a social insurance scheme which depends entirely upon payroll taxes which bear on consumption is an anachronism which can defeat the most fundamental purpose of social security."[54] Likewise, Robert Ball concluded that "the Government's obligation to eventually make up the deficit of contribution of older workers and those who in the early years contribute at less than the actuarial rate should be explicitly stated in the legislation."[55] "For social insurance just as for private annuities," Ball wrote, "it is much easier for both workers and employers to pay a more or less level rate over a working lifetime." He continued to recommend a constant low tax rate combined with a general-revenue subsidy.[56] On similar grounds, the CIO

[50] Wilbur Cohen to Arthur Altmeyer, 15 April 1948, WCP, Box 28, Folder 2; Robert Myers to M.A. Linton, 22 April 1949, RMP, Box M86-W3, unprocessed.

[51] Robert Myers to John Corson, 24 August 1949, RG 47, Office of the Actuary, Box 26, File: CO.

[52] U.S. Congress, House of Representatives, *Congressional Record*, 81st Cong., 1st sess., 5 October 1949, 13905.

[53] Robert Myers to Wilbur Cohen, 25 February 1949, RMP, Box M83-106, unprocessed; Myers to Carl Curtis, 5 May 1949, RMP, Box M86-43, unprocessed; Myers, "Question Raised By Mr. Byrnes," 5 April 1949, RMP, Box M83-106, unprocessed; Myers to Wilbur Cohen, 4 June 1947, RMP, Box M83-106, unprocessed; Myers to Cohen, 24 June 1947, RMP, Box M83-106, unprocessed.

[54] Gerhard Colm and David Christian to Leon Keyserling, 25 January 1949, HTL, Papers of Leon Keyserling, Box 9, Folder: Social Security Program.

[55] Robert M. Ball, "What Contribution Rate for Old-Age and Survivors Insurance?" *Social Security Bulletin* 12, No. 7 (July 1949): 9.

[56] Cited in Derthick, *Policymaking For Social Security*, 240.

and AFL each proposed a provision allowing the balance of future costs to be paid through general revenue.[57]

But most Ways and Means members shied away from the general-revenue approach. The thought of placing non-earmarked tax money into the system seemed to undermine the basic premise of contributory social insurance. Members also wanted to avoid any future income-tax hikes that might be required should they abandon the self-supporting system. Before expanding OASI, they insisted on restoring the connection between the payroll tax and the insurance benefit. Robert Kean (D-NJ), for example, warned that if the committee wanted "to pay to the individual as a matter of right, and then if we start to take out of the general tax revenues money which he has not earned through his insurance premiums, which would go to rich and poor alike, there ought to be a needs requirement which is entirely contrary to the idea of this whole system."[58] Similarly, Noah Mason (R-IL) argued that he was fooling his constituents "if I am promising them certain benefits which they will only partially pay for and the rest comes out of the air – as most of them think, when it comes out of the general Treasury."[59]

Mills caught the eyes of Washington pundits by helping to resolve this debate. As he joined the deliberations and worked with Myers, Ball, and Cohen, the Social Security faction of the tax community started to coalesce. Indeed, Mills stepped into a vacuum that existed within the House of Representatives on Social Security. Until the late 1940s, the Social Security Board had taken charge of the program. Chairman Doughton had displayed little interest in Social Security, and only a handful of representatives, such as Jere Cooper (D-TN), had emerged as congressional experts on the subject. Even though he was still a junior member of the committee, Mills, a fiscal conservative who supported contributory social insurance, joined this small group by virtue of his knowledge and his networks with the Social Security Administration. Although Wilbur Cohen and Robert Ball remained skeptical of Mills's allegiance to the program, they came to recognize him during this legislative battle as the influential voice on Social Security within Congress.

Mills and Myers work on actuarial matters

Together, Mills, Cohen, Ball, and Myers found a compromise between the actuarial fears of fiscal conservatives and the expansionary desires

---

[57] William Green to President Truman, 14 January 1949, HTL, Official Files 121-A, Box 665, Folder: O.F. 121-A, Unemployment Insurance, Social Insurance (May 1949–Feb. 1949).

[58] U.S. Congress, House Committee on Ways and Means, *Social Security Act Amendments of 1949: Hearings*, 81st Cong., 1st sess., 1219.   [59] Ibid., 1236.

of administrators. Mills began this effort within Congress by publicly confessing his "guilt" for accepting what "now appears to be a very ill-advised thing over the years, not permitting the original tax rate provided in the 1935 and 1939 acts to go into effect, but continuing to agree with the Senate that it should be frozen at 1 percent of payroll each on employer and employee."[60] Behind the scenes, he worked closely with Myers to reestablish a close actuarial balance for the "pay-as-you-go" program. At Doughton's request, Myers worked on loan from the Social Security Administration as an actuary for Ways and Means. Mills and Myers were a formidable team. On the one hand, Mills pushed Myers toward producing politically feasible data. On the other hand, Myers provided Mills with a respected technician whose vast knowledge intimidated Mills's opponents. In 1949, these opponents even included top administration officials who privately acknowledged that "the tendencies toward weakening the contributory principle are not necessarily bad and . . . there is a certain amount of political appeal in not pressing the issue."[61]

While designing the proposed expansion in 1950, this dynamic tax duo took several steps toward strengthening the payroll system. Most importantly, Mills wanted to force Congress to pay for OASI entirely through the payroll tax with monthly contributions paying for monthly benefits. Unlike previous estimates, their new data assumed that there would not be any federal subsidy from general revenue in the short- or long-term.

While determining who should be covered by the program, they always began with the question of cost, after which they considered the issue of "rights" or "need."[62] For example, Myers criticized the rec-

---

[60] U.S. Congress, House of Representatives, *Congressional Record*, 81st Cong., 1st sess., 5 October 1949, 13905. Also cited in Leff, "Speculating in Social Security Futures," 266. See also Colin Stam to Wilbur Mills, 28 May 1949, WMPC, Box 38, File: HR 6000.

[61] Richard Neustadt to Charles Murphy, 14 July 1950, and Murphy to Wilbur Mills, 14 July 1950, HTL, Papers of Richard Neustadt, Box 1, Folder: Chron. Files, 1947–1956. See also David Christian to Leon Keyserling, 2 February 1949, HTL, Papers of Leon Keyserling, Box 9, Folder: Social Security Program; Myers to M.A. Linton, 7 April 1949; Myers to Gordon McKinney, 11 April 1949; Linton to Myers, 20 April 1949; Myers to Reinhard Hohaus, 21 April 1949; Myers to Mills, 27 April 1949; Myers to Linton, 3 May 1949; the aforementioned documents are in RMP, Box M86-43, unprocessed; and Derthick, *Policymaking for Social Security*, 55–58.

[62] For a glimpse into the actuarial discourse, see the following documents: U.S. Congress, House Committee on Ways and Means, *Actuarial Cost Estimates for the Old-Age and Survivors Insurance System as Modified by the Social Security Act Amendments of 1950*, 27 July 1950, H4488 (Committee-Print); Robert Myers to Wilbur Cohen, 25 January 1950, WCP, Box 29, Folder 6; Myers to Cohen, 25 February 1949; Myers, "Question Raised By Mr. Byrnes," 5 April 1949; Myers to Wilbur Cohen, 2 November 1949; Myers, "Actuarial Cost Estimates on H.R. 6000," 2 November 1949. All the aforementioned documents between Mills and Myers are located in RMP, Box M83-106,

ommendation made by the Advisory Council in 1948 that a level tax rate should be supplemented by a general-revenue subsidy on "equitable grounds." Myers warned because actuarial cost estimates were never "precisely determinable," the amount of federal money needed to pay for OASI could climb much higher than Robert Ball and the Council had expected.[63] The viability of long-term actuarial estimates would continue to be a controversial issue within the Social Security faction.

Mills and Myers used conservative estimates to guarantee the actuarial soundness of their proposals. For example, they relied on a graduated contribution rate that would meet all benefit payments and produce a moderate excess income for seventy-five years. By dealing with seventy-five-year periods, the two men hoped to avoid the short-term focus that had produced the tax freeze of the 1940s.[64]

Another one of their favorite devices was the "level earnings assumption," whereby they did not anticipate any increase in wage levels, even though the long-range trend of wages had been upward since 1890. Should wages continue to rise, as most economists agreed they would, the "unanticipated surplus" of taxes could provide Congress with enough revenue to liberalize benefits or expand coverage without raising taxes.[65] Under the level-wage assumption, Myers also estimated that Congress would not increase payroll tax rates or the

unprocessed. See also, Myers to Mills, 29 March 1949; Myers to Mills, 15 April 1949; Myers to Mills, 26 April 1949; Myers to Mills, 27 April 1949; Myers to Mills, 5 May 1949; Myers to Mills, 9 May 1949; Myers to M.A. Linton, 22 April 1949; Myers to Reinhard Hohaus, 26 April 1949; Myers to Gordon McKinney, 11 April 1949; Linton to Myers, 20 April 1949, RMP, Box M86-43, unprocessed; Myers to Mills, 23 April 1949, NAS, RG 47, Office of the Actuary, Box 1, File: HR 2893.

[63] Robert Myers to Ida Merriam, 15 July 1949, RG 47, Office of the Actuary, Box 38, File: 710.

[64] Robert J. Myers, "Methodology Involved in Developing Long-Range Cost Estimates for Old-Age, Survivors, and Disability Insurance System," May 1959, Actuarial Study No. 49, and Myers, "Long-Range Cost Estimates for the Old-Age and Survivors Insurance: 1954," Actuarial Study No. 39, RMP, unprocessed; U.S. Congress, House Committee on Ways and Means, *Social Security Act Amendments of 1949: Report Number 1300*, 81st Cong., 1st sess., 1949, 32; Myers to Wilbur Cohen, 25 February 1949, RMP, Box M83-106, unprocessed; Myers to Wilbur Mills, 5 May 1949, RMP, Box M86-43, unprocessed; Myers to Wilbur Cohen, 5 January 1949, WCP, Box 28, Folder 7; Myers to W.R. Williamson, 24 October 1946, NAS, Office of the Actuary, Box 40, File: 750.

[65] Robert J. Myers, "Underlying Factors in Long-Range Actuarial Cost Estimates for OASDI System," 8 June 1962, RMP, Box M83-106, unprocessed; Myers to Wilbur Cohen, 16 December 1948, WCP, Box 28, Folder 6; Myers to Cohen, 21 May 1948, WCP, Box 41, Folder 3; Myers, interview with Peter Corning, 8 March 1967, COHP, Interview #1, 7–8; Myers to Jacob Perlman, 6 May 1949 and Perlman to Cohen, 21 April 1948, NAS, RG 47, Office of the Actuary, Box 17, File: 1950–1946.

wage base; if it did, representatives would once again find themselves with an "unanticipated surplus." According to Mills and Myers, this conservative assumption contained the size of guaranteed future benefits below the level of taxes that would most likely be collected; it postponed benefit increases until economic conditions actually brought in necessary revenue under existing tax rates. Without this assumption, Myers recalled, "it would make a static program look less expensive and, therefore, you could liberalize the benefits. That's not right – you're counting the chickens before they've hatched. So I stood strong against that." Mills, according to Myers, "was very strongly in favor of this procedure" because he wanted to be able to go to Congress and say "this system is in actuarial balance after what we've done."[66] The assumption still left room for future representatives to enact politically attractive liberalizations within, what they believed would be, reasonable tax limits once economic conditions allowed it.

The Social Security Amendments of 1950

Based on the work of Mills, Myers, Ball, and Cohen, Ways and Means reported out a bill to the House in August 1949. The opening paragraphs of their report began with the difficult choice facing Congress: "There are indications that if their insurance program is not strengthened and expanded, the old-age assistance program may develop into a very costly and ill-advised system of noncontributory pensions, payable not only to the needy but to all individuals at or above retirement age who are no longer employed." The time had come, the committee proclaimed, to "reaffirm the basic principle that a contributory system of social insurance in which workers share directly in meeting the cost of the protection afforded is the most satisfactory way of preventing dependency."[67] The bill expanded coverage to over 11 million people and raised benefits for present and future retirees. The amendments promised benefits for retirees who were newly eligible to the program as the result of its expansion, but who had never contributed taxes into the system as a result of their initial exclusion. Like

---

[66] Robert J. Myers, interview with Larry DeWitt, 14 March 1996 and 8 July 1996, Social Security Administration, Office of Library, 13–14.

[67] U.S. Congress, House Committee on Ways and Means, *Social Security Act Amendments of 1949: Report Number 1300*, 81st Cong., 1st sess., 1949, 2–3. See also The Advisor by Unemployment Benefit Advisors, Inc., 16 June 1949, WCP, Box 36, Folder 3; The Advisor by Unemployment Benefit Advisors, Inc., "Status of Deliberations in Ways and Means – Second Chapter," 5 July 1949, WCP, Box 36, Folder 3; Wilbur Cohen to Edwin Witte, 28 September 1949, WCP, Box 29, Folder 3.

the 1939 amendments, this liberalization further reduced the projected surplus by several billion dollars.[68]

To finance these changes, the legislation ended the tax freeze and
eliminated the Vandenberg-Murray amendment.[69] The decision to
exclude general revenue from the program, according to Wilbur
Cohen, cut across ideological lines: "They all – the liberals and the
conservatives – went for a completely self-supporting system. Let's
not get into a Government subsidy."[70] The committee recommended
"a tax schedule which . . . will make the system self-supporting . . . as
nearly as can be foreseen under present circumstances." Recognizing
that future results might differ from the estimates made at the time,
Ways and Means stipulated that Congress should adjust the tax
schedule when needed. Through this system, Myers explained, "no
appropriated monies other than contributions from workers and
employers will, over the long-run, be needed to pay the benefits (and
also the administrative expenses)."[71] Additionally, the committee
raised the wage base to $3,600, far below the amount sought by the
administration.[72]

During the debate on the House floor, Ways and Means members
conveyed the sense of crisis that gripped Social Security policymakers. Kean, for example, warned that "we are at the crossroads.
The old-age assistance program has grown by leaps and bounds. More
than twice as many of our older citizens are receiving old-age assistance as are receiving payments under OASI."[73] This proposal would
protect OASI by restoring the integrity of the payroll tax, the political glue that held the contributory system together. The hope of Ways
and Means, Kean concluded, was that the "old-age assistance program
will gradually taper off as more and more people become qualified
under OASI."[74]

But it was Mills who captured the political imagination of the
House. In his presentation, he explained that social insurance offered
federal assistance without creating a welfare state:

[68] Acting Assistant Director, Legislative Reference to William Hopkins, 24 August 1950,
    HTL, White House Bill File, Box 75, Folder: August 28, 1950 [H.R. 6000-Folder 1].
[69] U.S. Congress, House Committee on Ways and Means, *Social Security Act Amendments
    of 1949: Report Number 1300*, 81st Cong., 1st sess., 1949.
[70] Wilbur Cohen, "Bureau Directors' meeting with Commissioner," 15 August 1949,
    WCP, Box 36, Folder 3.
[71] Myers, "The Financial Principle of Self-Support in the Old-Age and Survivors Insur-
    ance System."
[72] Oscar Ewing to President Truman, 6 July 1949, HTL, Files of Charles S. Murphy,
    Box 27, Folder: Social Security.
[73] U.S. Congress, House of Representatives, *Congressional Record*, 81st Cong., 1st sess.,
    4 October 1949, 13835.
[74] Ibid., 13837.

We have heard an awful lot in recent months about the development of the welfare state. It is significant that we hear that charge every time any legislation is presented to the Congress which has to do with the welfare of an individual. I challenge the statement that the creation of machinery providing security against need in old age constitutes a welfare state or is in the direction of a welfare state. If we should adopt some of these grandiose schemes which have been submitted to the House in the form of a bill providing for the payment of pensions to individuals who have reached the age of 65, whether they need those benefits or not, as some of our colleagues have signed a discharge petition to do so, we might be proceeding in the direction of a welfare state [here, Mills is referring to the variants of the Townsend Plan]. But when we call upon the individual during his productive years to lay aside, in the form of a contribution, out of his wages and earnings an amount of money which will enable an agency of the Government to provide him with benefits after he becomes 65 years of age, or when he becomes disabled at less than 65 years of age, how can it be said that we are doing something for that individual for nothing?[75]

Mills insisted that the taxpayer was at least "entitled to say" that he was "buying and paying for that security" against need in his old age, even if he had not actually done so.[76]

Such arguments were effective. On October 5, 1949, the House passed the bill by a vote of 333 to 14 after a "splendid demonstration of teamwork" by committee Democrats.[77] The Senate postponed action until 1950. After five months of study, the Senate Finance Committee reported out a bill in May 1950, which the Senate passed by a vote of 81 to 2 following a well-orchestrated campaign by Wilbur Cohen.[78] Soon after, the conference report passed both chambers on August 28, 1950.

The Social Security Amendments of 1950 extended coverage to approximately 10 million workers, including portions of the nonprofessional self-employed, agricultural workers, employees of nonprofit institutions, and domestic servants. The benefit amounts

[75] U.S. Congress, House of Representatives, *Congressional Record*, 81st Cong., 1st sess., 5 October 1949, 13905.

[76] Ibid. Also cited in Derthick, *Policymaking For Social Security*, 249.

[77] Charles S. Murphy to President Truman, 6 October 1949, HTL, Files of Charles S. Murphy, Box 27, Folder: Social Security.

[78] Richard Neustadt to Stephen Spingarn, 21 May 1950, HTL, Papers of Richard Neustadt, Box 1, Folder: Chron. Files, 1947–1956.

were roughly doubled, a reflection in the changes in wage levels and cost of living since the 1939 amendments; the retirement test (the amount of earnings permitted beneficiaries if they were to receive benefits) was notably liberalized.[79] This expansion helped to cement an alliance between the state and the elderly through a social provision that appeared self-supporting and distinct from welfare; it also showed members of Congress that these types of benefits could be raised significantly without any apparent cost to the taxpayer.

Despite all the rhetoric about a race to defeat welfare, the amendments increased the scope of public assistance: Until the government had expanded OASI to a sufficient level, most representatives agreed on the continued need for noncontributory welfare. In 1950, Congress created grants-in-aid, called "vendor payments," that partially financed medical providers for needy citizens.[80] Congress also created a new category of federal grants-in-aid, as opposed to a 1943 proposal for a federally administered program, for needy individuals who were permanently and totally disabled. And they increased the rate of federal participation in elderly welfare, OAA.[81]

Most importantly, the amendments transformed the "financial philosophy" of OASI by resolving the uncertainty about the role of general revenue.[82] In short, Myers explained, Congress now intended that "the system should be completely self-supporting from the tax income provided. Accordingly, the provision for potential government contribution to the system, which had been incorporated in 1943, is eliminated."[83] The Social Security Amendments of 1950 affirmed a "pay-as-you-go" approach by eliminating the Vandenberg-Murray amendment, by raising the wage base, and by establishing a graduated tax schedule that would meet the cost of the program for the next seventy-five years.[84] The small excess of tax contributions

[79] Robert J. Myers, "Old-Age, Survivors, and Disability Insurance Provisions: Summary of Legislation, 1935–1958," Social Security Bulletin 22, No. 1 (January 1959): 18; Wilbur J. Cohen, "The Social Security Act Amendments of 1950: Legislative History of the Coverage Provisions," n.d., WCP, Box 249, Folder 3.

[80] Wilbur J. Cohen, "The Need for More Adequate Financing of Medical Assistance," n.d., WCP, Box 49, Folder 2; Ruth White, "Vendor Payments for Medical Assistance," Social Security Bulletin 13, No. 6 (June 1950): 3–10.

[81] Richard Neustadt to Charles Murphy, 14 July 1950, HTL, Papers of Richard Neustadt, Box 1, Folder: Chron. Files, 1947–1956.

[82] Myers, "The Financial Principle of Self-Support in the Old-Age and Survivors Insurance System."

[83] Myers, "Estimates of the Reserves Under the Old-Age Insurance System in the United States."

[84] U.S. Congress, House Committee on Ways and Means, Actuarial Cost Estimates for the Old-Age and Survivors Insurance System as Modified by the Social Security Act Amendments of 1950, 27 July 1950, H4488 (Committee-Print), 3–12; U.S. Department of

over benefits in the early years was to be deposited in the trust fund. The money was invested in government bonds, and equaled the amount needed to pay benefits in months when unexpected increases in benefits or decreases in tax revenues, or both, resulted in expenditures greater than revenues; the contingency reserve would most likely be used in the case of a severe economic recession.[85]

Drawing on the Ways and Means report, the Conference Committee recognized that long-range cost estimates could not be precise and that adjustments in the tax schedule might be necessary in the future. The committee recommended that the system be financed by an increasing tax schedule that of necessity would rise higher than the level tax rate that Robert Ball had endorsed.[86] Finally, the committee did not suggest that earmarking taxes should be used in all areas of fiscal policy. As one official explained: "A guiding principle of fiscal policy should be that the Government expends its funds where they are needed most, regardless of the source of the funds."[87] But earmarking taxes, according to the committee, could be used when there was a clear correlation between the benefit and the tax.[88]

The amendments secured an exclusive link between the payroll tax and the insurance benefit, thereby eliminating the possibility of financing OASI through general revenue. Congress redistributed money across generations, from the paychecks of wage-earners to the pockets of retirees who received substantially more than they had paid in taxes. For fiscal conservatives such as Mills, this decision appeared to strengthen OASI because they felt the payroll tax distinguished the programs it financed by limiting cost and avoiding the dole. Policymakers often acknowledged that these distinctions were primarily symbolic. Some of the economic arrangements were a fiction. Mills, for example, admitted to the House that "the net effect upon the individual who pays a tax is the same whether it is a social-security tax or an income tax: His income is decreased by the amount of the tax and

Treasury, Tax Advisory Staff of the Secretary, "Financing Social Security," 18 January 1952, HTL, Papers of L. Laszlo Ecker-Racz, Box 6, Bound; Robert Myers to Wilbur Cohen, 10 November 1949 and Myers to Cohen, 2 November 1949, in NAS, RG 47, Office of the Actuary, Box 2, File: 1949.

[85] Robert J. Myers, "Financing Policy," 1954, DEL, Papers of Oveta Culp Hobby, Box 60, Folder: Background Book For 1954 Hearings, OASI.

[86] Robert J. Myers, "Old-Age, Survivors, and Disability Insurance: Financing Basis and Policy Under the 1958 Amendments," *Social Security Bulletin* 21, No. 10 (October 1958): 15–21.

[87] Richard Neustadt to the Director, 14 December 1949, HTL, Papers of Richard Neustadt, Box 1, Folder: Chron. Files, 1947–56.

[88] Wilbur D. Mills, "Remarks to the Pulaski County Bar Association," 30 October 1964, WMPC, Box 591, File: Mills, Speeches.

so is his purchasing power. That is simple mathematics."[89] Regardless, they continued to encourage the belief that the payroll tax was the key feature that separated OASI from other forms of welfare: In their rhetoric, policymakers did not even call the payroll tax a "tax," but referred to it as a "contribution."[90] Once they established this distinction, they began an intensive campaign to expand social insurance and to eliminate federal participation in public assistance programs. "The amendments of 1950," Robert Ball explained several decades later, "really saved the concept of contributory social insurance in this country."[91]

THE LEGACY OF THE AMENDENTS

Other factors besides symbolic distinctions created the strong congressional support for the amendments. Throughout the summer of 1950, for example, Truman had been pushing Congress to raise income taxes in order to prevent inflation and to pay for the Korean War.[92] But Congress resisted such an unpopular action, especially during an election year. In fact, some representatives called for a tax reduction through lower excise taxes and expanded tax breaks. More fiscally conscientious representatives, however, designed subtle mechanisms for raising revenue; Mills, for example, proposed a speed-up in the collection of corporate tax payments.[93] Within this context, the Social Security Amendments offered an alluring anti-inflationary weapon that provided tax increases that were rhetorically disguised as higher "contributions" for benefits.[94]

[89] U.S. Congress, House of Representatives, *Congressional Record*, 83rd Cong., 2nd sess., 18 March 1954, 3525.

[90] Technical Staff of the Office of the Secretary of the Treasury, "Questions and Answers on Social Security," 11 March 1949, HTL, Papers of John W. Snyder, Box 85, Folder: Questions and Answers on Social Security; U.S. Congress, House Committee on Ways and Means, *Social Security Act Amendments of 1949: Hearings*, 81st Cong., 1st sess., 1949, 1371.

[91] Robert Ball, Audio Recording, 1996, Social Security Administration.

[92] President Truman to Senator Walter George, 25 July 1950, HTL, Official Files, Box 700, Folder: O.F. 137 (March–April 1951).

[93] David Bell to Charles Murphy, 23 May 1950 and Mr. Lynch to Secretary John Snyder, 21 June 1950 in HTL, President's Secretary's Files, Box 160, Folder: Treasury, Secy of (folder 2); Joseph Pechman to L. Laszlo Ecker-Racz, 7 March 1950, HTL, Papers of L. Laszlo Ecker-Racz, Box 2, Bound; L. Laszlo Ecker-Racz to Assistant Secretary Graham, 31 May 1950, HTL, Papers of L. Laszlo Ecker-Racz, Box 1, Bound; "Representative Mills Would Balance Budget By Speeding Up Corporation Tax Collections," 17 May 1949, WMPC, Box 701, File 1; Press Release, 17 May 1949, WMPC, Box 707, File 1 and Box 40, File 1; JMIC.

[94] Gerhard Colm and David Christian to Leon Keyserling, 25 January 1949, HTL, Papers of Leon Keyserling, Box 9, Folder: Social Security Program.

Nonetheless, most fiscal policymakers appear to have based their decisions and their deliberations on the need to reestablish the primacy of social insurance and to retain its distinction from the welfare payments associated with stigmatized members of American society. Within months, their plan appeared to be a success. By February 1951, the number of elderly citizens on insurance surpassed those on assistance. The number on the old-age assistance rolls had decreased approximately 65,000 as of June 1951, from the high of September 1950.[95]

Dwight Eisenhower's presidential election in 1952 brought in a Republican Congress for only the second time since 1933. Nevertheless, Congress continued its expansion of Social Security with strong bipartisan support. In 1952 and 1954, Congress extended coverage to over 10 million workers, including farm operators and the professional self-employed (except doctors, lawyers and dentists), provided coverage to employees of state and local government, liberalized retirement tests, and increased real benefits by an additional 12.5 percent. In addition, the 1954 amendments raised the contribution schedule to meet the increased cost of the benefit changes and to correct an "actuarial insufficiency" that had been discovered in the relationship between benefit distribution and tax intake.[96] Like Truman, Eisenhower perceived the political advantages that could be reaped from the continued expansion of this social program for the elderly.

There were still attacks on the "self-supporting" system. Representative Carl Curtis's (R-NE) Subcommittee on Social Security, for example, issued a report that attacked the claims that Social Security was modeled after private insurance. According to the report, "contractual rights" were nonexistent, and benefit claims had occasionally been eliminated by the SSA. The subcommittee insisted that Social Security was a "conditional" right, always subject to legislative change. It submitted a legislative proposal that threatened to overturn the entire system.[97] These fierce attacks, however, caused a backlash

[95] Wilbur J. Cohen, "Should Old-Age Assistance Again Outpace Old-Age Insurance?" WCP, Box 249, Folder 3; Robert J. Myers, "Long-Range Trends in Old-Age Assistance," *Social Security Bulletin* 16, No. 2 (February 1953): 13–15; "Public Assistance: Effect of the Increase in Current Old-Age and Survivors Insurance Benefits," *Social Security Bulletin* 14, No. 9 (September 1951): 3–6.

[96] Myers, "The Financial Principle of Self-Support in the Old-Age and Survivors Insurance System." Myers, "Long-Range Cost Estimates For Old-Age and Survivors Insurance: 1954," Actuarial Study No. 39, RMP, unprocessed.

[97] Edward D. Berkowitz, *Mr. Social Security: The Life of Wilbur J. Cohen* (Lawrence: University Press of Kansas, 1995), 71–94. Within the Treasury, there were also economists who continued to support alternatives to the payroll tax to finance a portion

against Curtis's position from supporters of Social Security, including Mills, Wilbur Cohen, and even Eisenhower.[98] Although the report was correct in its critique of the program, the subcommittee failed to grasp the importance, both to the providers and to the recipients of social insurance, of the language that symbolically distinguished their benefits from welfare.

By 1954, OASI had become a centerpiece of U.S. domestic policy. Meanwhile, public assistance programs diminished in size. The average monthly number of elderly receiving OAA declined at a steady rate; the average monthly number of families on ADC dropped significantly until 1955.[99] The amendments of 1950 had allowed this to take place by reestablishing the connection between the payroll tax and social insurance, guaranteeing that the system would exclude general revenue from its system of finance.[100] Once this marriage had been consummated, policymakers could package OASI as an effective alternative to socialism or the welfare state.

The 1950 amendments continued to shape the politics of Social Security for the next three decades. The amendments set social insurance on a path of long-term incremental growth. When Mills took over Ways and Means in 1958, a consensus had already formed around OASI: Bureaucrats, think-tanks, congressional representatives, interest groups, experts, and both parties now fought to liberalize "self-supporting" social insurance and to eliminate public

of social insurance. See U.S. Department of Treasury, Tax Advisory Staff of the Secretary, "Financing Social Security," 18 January 1952, HTL, Papers of L. Laszlo Ecker-Racz, Box 6, Bound.

[98] See Wilbur J. Cohen, interview with Maclyn P. Burg, 31 March 1976, DEL, Oral History Interview Collection, 16–22; L.A. Minnich Jr., "Legislative Leadership Conference," 17–19 December 1953, DEL, Ann Whitman File, Legislative Meetings Series, Box 1, Folder: Legislative Meetings – 1953(6) [August–December]; Dwight D. Eisenhower to J. Earl Schaefer (Boeing Airplane Company), 30 September 1954, DEL, Ann Whitman File, DDE Diary Series, Box 8, Folder: September 1954 (1); Eisenhower to the Director of the Bureau of the Budget, 5 November 1953, DEL, Ann Whitman File, DDE Diary Series, Box 3, Folder: November 1953 (3); George Humphrey to Dwight Eisenhower, 5 November 1953, DEL, Ann Whitman File, Administration Series, Box 20, Folder: Humphrey, George M. 1953 (2); Arthur Burns to the Eisenhower Cabinet, 17 May 1954, DEL, Ann Whitman File, Cabinet Series, Box 3, Folder: Cabinet Meeting of April 2, 1954; Robert J. Myers, "Financing Policy," 1954, DEL, Papers of Oveta Culp Hobby, Box 60, Folder: Background Book For 1954 Hearings, OASI; "Extracts From Secretary of the Treasury Humphrey's Press Conference," 21 May 1953, DEL, White House Central Files, Official Files, Box 172, Folder: 9 May 1953.

[99] Berkowitz, America's Welfare State, 92–93.

[100] Robert J. Myers, "Financing Policy," 1954, and Myers, "The Interrelationship of the OASI Contribution Schedule and the Long-Range Cost Estimates," 22 October 1953, DEL, Papers of Oveta Culp Hobby, Box 60, Folder: Background Book For 1954 Hearings, OASI.

assistance. Building on the earmarked tax system, Congress expanded social insurance to unprecedented levels. While the earmarked tax system reenergized social insurance, it also imposed certain long-term restrictions for advocates of expansion. These limitations became apparent when Mills resisted disability insurance on the grounds that the benefits would undermine the fiscal soundness of Social Security. Although Congress enacted disability insurance in 1956, along with a separate trust fund, the battle over the program left many Social Security advocates with a better sense of how difficult it would be to expand benefits within this distinct system of finance.

For Mills and other fiscal conservatives, these types of constraints were the great legacy of the 1950 legislation. The Social Security tax system revealed the imprint of fiscal conservatism by imposing certain long-term restrictions on the program. First, the tax system limited the type of benefit that Congress could distribute. Wage-related benefits were needed to justify the earmarked tax system and to maintain the insurance myth. Second, the tax system imposed a ceiling on the amount of benefits that the government could provide. Policymakers and legislators insisted on a balanced budget principle for Social Security, meaning that the federal government should only distribute, or plan to distribute, as much in benefits each month as it raised in taxes each month, leaving aside a small amount for a contingency reserve. Conservative actuarial assumptions, in their minds, protected the fiscal soundness of the program by limiting the size of scheduled long-term benefits to a level below taxes, by avoiding liberalizations based on erroneous economic prognostications, and by forcing representatives to consider the long-term cost of each liberalization. Given its institutional design, the finance system raised the threat of a "solvency crisis" each time retirement benefits cost more than taxes.[101] Ironically, critics later attacked many features of this tax system, such as the level-wage assumption, for masking the cost of the program and for creating incentives for Congress to incrementally expand benefits without considering the long-term cost.[102]

Cohen, Ball, Myers, and Mills continued to be influenced by the Social Security Amendments of 1950 because it had helped to distinguish them as the experts on Social Security finance and because the amendments had determined that payroll taxes would be the sole source of revenue for OASI benefits. By doing so, the amendments distinguished OASI from welfare even as they transformed the program into one of the largest and most popular components of the American state.

---

[101] Paul Pierson, *Dismantling the Welfare State? Reagan, Thatcher, and the Politics of Retrenchment* (Cambridge: Cambridge University Press, 1994), 64–73.

[102] Derthick, *Policymaking for Social Security*, 51–52.

3

"Taxation of Whom and for What?"[1]

After surviving the twists and turns of Social Security in 1950, Mills still had much to learn about federal taxation. When he decided to specialize in tax policy, he had selected one of the most challenging issues in domestic politics. The American state relied on a complicated system of multiple taxation, each tax with its own logic, history, and rules. To succeed on Ways and Means, Mills needed to master the intricacies of each particular tax. Just as he spent the 1940s learning about the use of earmarked payroll taxes, Mills spent the 1950s studying the economic and political functions of the income tax.

In response to the recodification of 1954, which validated the World War II tax system in peacetime, Mills helped to organize a series of congressional studies and hearings on tax reform and on the relationship between taxation and economic growth. The studies found that the manipulation of income taxation could provide economic assistance to private investors and consumers while avoiding the direct management of business institutions, as under communism. Through the studies on taxation and economic growth, Mills also helped to promote into Congress a new type of political elite to represent the public interest. Until the 1940s, two organizations had secured the right to claim that they represented the citizen within the tax policymaking process: interest groups and political parties. Economic experts still had limited access to the congressional leadership despite their gains within the executive branch.[2] Speaker Sam Rayburn (D-TX), for example, rarely consulted with economists, and regularly turned to Mills for advice on tax issues. Although Senate Majority Leader Lyndon Johnson (D-TX) developed a wider network

---

[1] Leon H. Keyserling, *Taxation Of Whom And For What: "Tax Reform" Versus Tax Reform* (Washington D.C.: Conference on Economic Progress, 1969), HTL, Papers of Leon H. Keyserling, Box 56, Folder: Taxation Of Whom And For What.

[2] For the limited access economists encountered in debates over tariff policy at the turn of the century, see Judith Goldstein, *Ideas, Interests, and American Trade Policy* (Ithaca: Cornell University Press, 1993), 91–94.

of expert advisors on taxation, his network did not include many economists.[3]

During the postwar period, new types of policymakers gained access to the tax policymaking process with the help of Mills and his committee; professional actuaries, for example, increased their clout in Congress through the expansion of Social Security. The new policymakers also came from the sort of policy-making channels that one political scientist has called "issue networks," which were populated by staff members of the executive and congressional branches, university academics, independent specialists, publishers and editors of the specialized policy media, and participants in professional think tanks.[4] Between 1954 and 1957, the studies on taxation and economic growth helped to bring together members of the leading issue networks with officials from political parties and interest groups. As a result, they formed into the tax reform and growth manipulation factions of the tax community by identifying themselves as the "leading experts" on these issues and by endorsing new approaches to federal taxation. In the next two decades, the tax reform faction promoted a continuing process of reforming tax breaks to maintain the integrity of the growth-oriented tax code. Meanwhile, the growth manipulation faction focused on adjusting tax rates to stimulate economic productivity, private investment, and consumer demand.

By the late-1950s, the tax community had emerged. Two factors helped the experts to enter into the relatively closed world of tax politics. First, new public policies required new types of policymakers. The tax recodification of 1954 guaranteed that the World War II income-tax system would play a major role in the peacetime economy: Through high rates, taxes absorbed billions of dollars from private markets, even in times of peace; through large tax breaks that privileged certain types of income, the tax structure influenced private investment decisions. In tax policy, new types of policymakers were sought in policy debates once it became clear that the federal tax system would continue to have a significant impact on the economy even after the Korean War ended. Discussions about macroeconomics also became more prevalent simply because the tax

---

[3] Iwan W. Morgan, *Eisenhower Versus "The Spenders": The Eisenhower Administration, the Democrats and the Budget, 1953–1960* (New York: St. Martin's Press, 1990), 34; Robert C. Wood, *Whatever Possessed the President? Academic Experts and Presidential Policy, 1960–1988* (Amherst: University of Massachusetts Press, 1993), 6.

[4] Hugh Heclo, "Issue Networks and the Executive Establishment," in *The New American Political System*, ed. Anthony King (Washington, D.C.: American Enterprise Institute, 1978), 90–121.

system was actually capable of influencing so many aspects of the national economy.

The second factor behind the success of tax experts involved political entrepreneurs within the state who secured positions for new types of policymakers. The empowerment of experts in tax politics was not just a product of their professional strength or the centrality of expertise to the national culture. Rather, politicians within the state empowered experts for their own political objectives, such as advancing their influence or promoting their agenda and interests. Mills enhanced his position within the state by bringing issue networks into the deliberations on the macroeconomic impact of taxation and on tax reform. Mills even started to package himself as a "fiscal expert," and worked closely with other experts to strengthen his political position within the House. In doing so, Mills's subcommittees helped to cement a role for the "fiscal expert" to represent the public, in addition to interest-groups and party leaders, in congressional tax policymaking.

RECODIFYING THE CODE

The road to recodification began in World War II. Until the 1940s, the income tax had been peripheral to the American state. Thirty years after its adoption, no more than 6 percent of the population had ever been required to pay an income tax.[5] During World War II, however, the income tax moved to the front and center of the federal revenue system. The changes were so dramatic that Secretary of the Treasury Henry Morgenthau had orchestrated an extensive public relations campaign, through radio and newspapers, to sell the mass tax to the American public. During a Disney animated short commissioned by the Treasury, entitled *The New Spirit*, a radio announcer told Donald Duck: "[It is] your privilege, not just your duty, but your privilege to help your government by paying your tax and paying it promptly." Or as Irving Berlin sang in a jingle, "I Paid My Income Tax Today."[6]

The World War II tax system

The impact of the new tax system was dramatic. "The war," Mills said, "wrought great changes in the American economy and its institutions.

---

[5] Mark H. Leff, *The Limits of Symbolic Reform: The New Deal and Taxation, 1933–1939* (Cambridge: Cambridge University Press, 1984), 287.

[6] Carolyn C. Jones, "Mass-based income taxation: Creating a taxpaying culture, 1940–1952," in *Funding the Modern American State, 1941–1995: The Rise and Fall of the*

Among these were "basic, structural revisions in our Federal tax system."[7] Between 1939 and 1944, prosperity and the advent of withholding increased the number of Americans paying federal income taxes from 4 million to nearly 44 million; corporate and individual taxes increased from 1 percent of the GNP in 1939 to 8 percent in 1943. Maximum tax rates on personal income reached 94 percent. By 1945, the state was collecting over $19 billion in personal income taxes (compared with $1 billion in 1939) and $16 billion in corporate taxes.[8] By 1950, moreover, the federal income tax produced over 51 percent of the revenue collected at all levels of government, compared with only 16 percent in 1940.[9] Added to these statistics was the feeling that millions of workers experienced when they encountered the federal state directly, often for the first time, through regular deductions from their paychecks.

The World War II income-tax system constituted a seminal stage in the development of the American state and its revenue system. "Mass taxation had replaced class taxation," according to one historian, as the federal government "came to dominate the nation's revenue system."[10] New policies stimulated new conceptions of federal taxation. As the income tax touched large numbers of workers and businesses on a regular basis and removed billions of dollars from the economy, policymakers perceived new aspects of taxation. By the end

---

Era of Easy Finance, ed. W. Elliot Brownlee (Cambridge: Cambridge University Press and Washington, D.C.: Woodrow Wilson Center Press, 1996), 121–125.

[7] Wilbur D. Mills, "The Challenge of Federal Tax Policy in 1957: Address before the Seventeenth Annual Federal Tax Dinner of the Federal Tax Forum," 6 December 1956, WMPC, Box 781, File 1.

[8] These figures were complied from the following works: U.S. Treasury Department, Tax Advisory Staff of the Secretary, "Factors to be Considered in the 1951 Individual Income Tax Program," 1951, HTL, Papers of L. Laszlo Ecker-Racz, Box 5, Bound; Joseph Pechman, "Effect of Built-In Flexibility and Rate and Exemption Changes on the Yield of the Federal Individual Income Tax During a Recession," 30 October 1953, DEL, Arthur Burns Papers, Box 107, Folder: Fiscal and Monetary – N.B.E.R Conference on Policies to Combat Depression, 1953 (1); Randolph E. Paul, *Taxation in the United States* (Boston: Little, Brown, 1954); Herbert Stein, *The Fiscal Revolution in America*, revised edition (Washington, D.C.: AEI Press, 1990); Leff, *The Limits of Symbolic Reform*; John F. Witte, *The Politics and Development of the Federal Income Tax* (Madison: University of Wisconsin Press, 1985); John H. Makin and Norman J. Ornstein, *Debt and Taxes: How America Got into its Budget Mess and What to Do About It* (New York: Time Books, 1994); Iwan W. Morgan, *Deficit Government: Taxing and Spending in Modern America* (Chicago: Ivan R. Dee, 1995); Bartholomew H. Sparrow, *From the Outside In: World War II and the American State* (Princeton: Princeton University Press, 1996), 97–160.

[9] W. Elliot Brownlee, "Tax regimes, national crisis, and state-building," in *Funding the Modern American State*, 93.

[10] Ibid., 93.

of World War II, it was virtually impossible to ignore the impact of taxation on the economy.

Moderate Keynesian economists, who believed in the occasional use of deficit-inducing tax reductions to stimulate growth, were among the first to respond to these changes in the 1940s. Some economists within government had introduced a new series of comprehensive statistics on the Gross National Product in 1941, which improved their mathematical ability to determine what types of fiscal policies would strengthen national consumer demand.[11] In 1947, the Research and Policy Committee of the Committee on Economic Development published "Taxes and the Budget: A Program for Stability in a Free Economy." In this document, widely circulated among tax experts, the CED proposed the concept of a high-employment balanced budget, which would create deficits automatically when unemployment rose above a certain level and a small surplus when unemployment fell below an acceptable level. Herbert Stein, one of the authors of "Taxes and the Budget," explained: "The normal practice would be to balance the budget in normal conditions, that the automatic variations of the deficit or surplus that came with variations of the economy would be accepted, but that except in extreme circumstances there would be no positive steps to change expenditures or tax rates to deal with actual or forecast recessions or booms."[12]

The fiscal effect of the Cold War

Despite a series of controversial rate reductions during the reconversion period, Congress retained the basic wartime income-tax structure: The top tax rate for individual income hovered around 90 percent until 1964.[13] With no end in sight to the Cold War and its high

---

[11] Herbert Stein, *Presidential Economics: The Making of Economic Policy From Roosevelt to Clinton*, 3rd edition (Washington, D.C.: American Enterprise Institute, 1994), 67.

[12] Ibid., 79–81.

[13] Witte, *The Politics and Development of the Federal Income Tax*, 136; Sheldon D. Pollack, *The Failure of U.S. Tax Policy: Revenue and Politics* (University Park, The Pennsylvania State University Press, 1996), 67–78; Committee on Taxation, Business Advisory Council, "Interim Report," 14 February 1947, HTL, Papers of John W. Synder, Box 32, Folder: Taxes – General (Folder 5); John Clark to President Truman, 31 March 1948, HTL, Papers of John P. Clark, Box 2, Folder: Letters and Memoranda to the President, 1948–1949; "Memorandum on the Outlook for Tax Reduction," 19 May 1947, HTL, Papers of John W. Synder, Box 31, Folder: Taxes – General (Folder 4); Council of Economic Advisors to the President, 7 December 1948, HTL, Papers of John D. Clark, Box 2, Folder: Letters and Memoranda to the President, 1948–1949; Charles Murphy to Leon Keyserling, 19 December 1949, HTL, Papers of Leon H. Keyserling, Box 8, Folder: White House Contacts – Charles Murphy.

military expenditures, the government became dependent on the revenue that the income tax produced.[14] To pay for the Korean War, for example, the Revenue Act of 1951 raised marginal top rates on the individual income tax to 91 percent, while corporate rates hit an all-time high of 70 percent. In total, tax revenues mushroomed from 14.8 percent of GNP in 1950 to 19.3 percent of GNP in 1952.[15] Unlike his Republican predecessors after WWI, Eisenhower refused to dismantle the wartime income tax following the end of the Korean War.[16] Eisenhower, like Truman, remained more committed to balancing budgets than reducing taxes. As a result, the budget was balanced in fiscal years 1947, 1948, 1949, 1951, 1956, 1957, and 1960; deficits in the remaining years merely averaged about 1 percent of GNP.[17]

The Cold War produced pressure for high levels of public spending that required high rates of taxation. Defense spending skyrocketed during the 1950s.[18] In 1957, Congress approved defense expenditures that were $3 billion higher than the amount the president had requested. Eisenhower felt impotent before the defense establishment, and failed, despite a vigorous campaign, to curb the rise of military spending during the final years of his presidency.[19] On leaving office, the president warned that a "military-industrial complex" gripped the federal budget. By perpetuating the crisis atmosphere of World War II, the Cold War defense system built a political base of conservatives and liberals that safeguarded the mass tax from retrenchment.

[14] President Truman to Robert Doughton, 14 November 1950, HTL, Official Files, Box 700, Folder: O.F. 137 (March–April 1951); "Statement of Secretary Snyder before the Senate Committee on Finance," 4 December 1950, HTL, Papers of L. Laszlo Ecker-Racz, Box 3, Bound; Charles S. Murphy to President Truman, 14 May 1951, HTL, Papers of Richard E. Neustadt, Folder: Chron. Files, 1947–1956; Truman to Walter George, 25 July 1950, HTL, Official Files, Box 700, Folder: O.F. 137 (March–April 1951). "Revenue Sources for the Balance of the President's 1951 Program," n.d.; "Economic Projections as Background for 1951 Tax Policy"; "Statement of Secretary Snyder," 5 February 1951; "The Dangers in Delaying the 1951 Tax Legislation," 5 February 1951, U.S. Department of Treasury, Tax Advisory Staff of the Secretary, 6 June 1951. Aforementioned documents all in HTL, Papers of L. Laszlo Ecker-Racz, Box 5, Bound.

[15] Morgan, *Deficit Government*, 61.

[16] "Eisenhower Quotes on Tax Reduction," October 1953, DEL, White House Central File, Official File, Box 760, Folder: Tax Matters 1952/1954 (2). See also Committee for Economic Development, "Limits to Taxation," 17 April 1953, DEL, Arthur Burns Papers, Box 108, Folder: Fiscal and Monetary – Taxation and Government Expenditure, 1953.

[17] Morgan, *Deficit Government*, 56.

[18] C. Eugene Steurele, "Financing the American state at the turn of the century," in *Funding the Modern American State, 1941–1995*, 420.

[19] Morgan, *Eisenhower Versus "The Spenders,"* 74–98; 127–151.

Congress distributes tax breaks

Neither the Cold War nor the increases in domestic expenditures discouraged Congress from its continuing expansion of the intricate system of tax breaks. After all, no representative felt personally responsible for the budgetary cost that any one tax break imposed on the government; nor did any single tax break pose an unbearable cost on federal coffers. Even the popular concept of the "tax loophole" implied that Congress did not anticipate the consequences of its legislation, but that astute tax lawyers had manipulated laws to their advantage. Since 1913, the tax-writing committees had gradually developed a complex tax-break system that used tax exemptions, deductions, and exceptions to achieve economic as well as political goals.[20] Unlike Social Security taxes, income-tax rates were only applied against taxable income – income after deductions and exceptions.

To help influential interest groups and voting constituencies escape their legal obligations, congressional representatives enacted provisions that narrowed the definition of taxable income; some significant tax breaks involved the treatment of capital gains income, oil exploration costs, tax-exempt securities, and undistributed corporate profits.[21] One of the first tax breaks was the exemption of interest on state and local bonds. In 1913, Congress decided to exempt the interest from these bonds, which were a key source of revenue for local and state governments, to persuade the states to ratify the income-tax amendment.[22] Some of the narrower breaks afforded the type of particularistic protection that had been provided by nineteenth-century tariffs.

Allowing the committee to exempt individuals and corporations from specific responsibilities, these provisions functioned as a hidden system of government expenditures that remained under the tight control of the tax-writing committees.[23] "In the aggregate," Mills lamented, "they add up to a substantial amount of income on which

---

[20] Brownlee, "Tax regimes, national crisis, and state-building in America," 60–101.

[21] For the history of tax breaks up through the 1950s, see Witte, *The Politics and Development of the Federal Income Tax*; Paul, *Taxation in the United States*; Gene Smiley and Richard H. Keehn, "Federal Personal Income Tax Policy in the 1920s," *The Journal of Economic History* 55, No. 2 (June 1995): 285–303.

[22] Sven Steinmo, *Taxation & Democracy: Swedish, British, and American Approaches to Financing the Modern State* (New Haven: Yale University Press, 1993), 75.

[23] The concept of "tax expenditures" was developed by Stanley S. Surrey in *Pathways To Tax Reform* (Cambridge, MA: Harvard University Press, 1973). See also William F. Hellmuth and Oliver Oldman, *Tax Policy and Tax Reform: 1961–1969, Selected Speeches and Testimony of Stanley S. Surrey* (Chicago: Commerce Clearing House, 1973).

tax legally need not be paid."[24] When interest groups realized that rates were going to remain over 90 percent, they intensified their pressure to narrow the definition of taxable income.[25] New England business executives, for example, told Truman that accelerated depreciation rates (a provision that allowed businesses to write off the cost of obsolete plant equipment) would enable the textile industry to modernize its facilities and to boost the regional economy.[26] Or, as a Treasury economist explained the expansion of another tax break, the liberal treatment of capital gains income: "The present broad definition of capital gains permits large amounts of income from profit-seeking transactions and personal effort to escape the full application of the income tax, and encourages taxpayers to exert increasing pressure upon the courts and Congress to enlarge further the area of income eligible for capital gains treatment. The results are to erode the base of the income tax, to create gross inequities, and to impair the morale of the larger body of taxpayers."[27]

One of the most contested tax breaks centered on the life insurance industry. Before 1921, Congress taxed the companies through the "total income" approach, which treated them like all other corporations. Thereafter, under pressure from industry lobbyists, Congress adopted the "net-investment income" approach, which only considered a percentage of the firms' investment income as taxable.

[24] Wilbur D. Mills, "How Your Income Taxes Can Be Cut," *Nation's Business*, November 1959, 72–76.

[25] For confidential discussions of the most notorious tax breaks, as well as proposals to create new ones, see: United States Department of Treasury, Tax Advisory Staff of the Secretary, "Possible Methods of Revising 1948 Estate and Gift Tax Legislation," Box 1; "Tax Incentives to Investment Abroad," Box 2; "Special Depletion Allowance," Box 2; "The Estates of Henry and Edsel Ford: A Case Study in the Disposition of Accumulated Wealth," 7 March 1952, Box 6; "Tax Issues in 1953," 15 December 1952, Box 7. All the aforementioned documents are in bound books in HTL, papers of L. Laszlo Ecker-Racz. See also Mr. Oram to Colin Stam, 8 May 1950, HTL, Box 1, Bound; Matthew Woll [Vice President and Chairman of the Committee on Taxation, American Federation of Labor] to President Truman, 11 January 1951, HTL, Official File, Box 700, Folder: O.F. 137 (March–April 1951).

[26] Assistant to the President to the Secretary of the Treasury, 9 September 1949, HTL, Official Files, Box 699, Folder: O.F. 137 (1 of 2). See also "Report of Meeting of the Treasury and Joint Committee Staffs," 26 February 1945, HTL, Papers of Roy Blough, Box 8, Folder: Treasury – Joint Committee Staff Meetings; Roger Milliken to C.D. Jackson [Special Assistant to the White House], 23 December 1953, DEL, White House Central File, Official File, Box 760, Folder: Tax Matters 1952/54 (2).

[27] "Need for a Narrower Definition and Fuller Taxation of Capital Gains to Accompany High Level Taxation of Ordinary Income," 1951, HTL, Papers of L. Laszlo Ecker-Racz, Box 5, Bound; Arthur Burns to Marion Folsom, 13 October 1953, DEL, Arthur Burns Papers, Box 97, Folder: Department of Treasury, 1953.

At first, the Treasury relied on an individual, company-by-company method to determine the taxable income of each corporation, based on its net investment income minus a specified percentage of its own required insurance reserves for policyholders. During World War II, the Treasury switched to a more lenient, industry-wide approach of defining taxable investment income. Although the new law produced $27 million in its first year of operation, it eventually resulted in no tax whatsoever on the industry. From 1948 until 1958, Congress superimposed a temporary measure, which it had to renew annually, that produced higher revenues.[28]

The revision of the tax code

Tax breaks received considerable attention when Congress decided to rewrite the tax code in 1954 – the first major revision of the code since 1913 – in response to changes in the types of income and benefits that were being paid.[29] By 1953, for example, even the most astute experts were unclear how to treat income-in-kind, including Social Security benefits, unemployment insurance, private pensions, employee death and disability benefits, and health care programs. Additionally, the nation's economic structure had changed dramatically since 1913.[30] This caused all sorts of problems for Ways and

[28] U.S. Congress, House Committee on Ways and Means, Subcommittee on Internal Revenue Taxation, *Report on the Taxation of Life Insurance Companies*, 31 December 1958, H1416 (Committee – Print), 1–4; U.S. Congress, House Committee on Ways and Means, Subcommittee on Internal Revenue Taxation, *Taxation of Income of Life Insurance Companies: Hearings*, 85th Cong., 2nd sess., 1958, 2–5; Claris Adams and Eugene Thore to Wilbur Mills, 21 November 1957, WMPC, unprocessed; U.S. Department of Treasury, Tax Advisory Staff of the Secretary, 6 December 1949, HTL, Papers of L. Laszlo Ecker-Racz, Box 1, Bound; John Synder to Robert Doughton, 10 October 1949, and "The tax treatment of life insurance companies," 16 September 1949, HTL, John Synder Papers, Box 31, Folder: Taxes – General (Folder 2); U.S. Department of Treasury, Tax Advisory Staff of the Secretary, "Record of Discussion with Life Insurance Industry," 24 October 1949, HTL, Papers of L. Laszio Ecker-Racz, Box 1, Bound; "Taxation of Life Insurance Companies," DEL, Bryce Harlow Papers, Box 23, Folder: Taxation-Life Insurance Companies; Fred Scribner to Maurice Stans, 17 March 1958, NAT, RG 56, Office of Tax Policy, Box 20, File: Life Insurance Legislation; "Survey of Texas Life Insurance Companies with Large Amounts of Policy Loans," 1956, NAT, RG 56, Office of Tax Policy, Box 20, File: Tax Avoidance.

[29] "Rep. Mills Outlines Plans for Technical Revision of Code: Opposes Tax Cuts Now," *The Journal of Taxation*, February 1957, 112–115.

[30] For a list of the issues discussed during the hearings, see Staff, Joint Committee on Internal Revenue Taxation, *Part I Summary Of Recommendations Contained In The Testimony Presented Before The Committee On Ways and Means Relative To General Revenues*, January 1954, H41318 (Committee – Print). On the changing structure of the

Means. The tax code, for example, failed to distinguish clearly between the different types of business organizations that now existed: corporations with income earned abroad, multinational corporations, service industries, partnerships, holding companies, closely held corporations, and tax exempt organizations.[31] The lengthy process of recodification fostered a new level of awareness of how tax breaks had become incorporated into every facet of the economy.

In exchange for the progressive income-tax structure, interest groups insisted that more types of income needed to be protected from an excessive tax burden. From June to August 1953, Congress and the Department of Treasury conducted extensive investigations in an effort to solve these problems by rewriting the code. During these investigations, interest groups mobilized to show that their tax breaks could be justified on economic grounds. Under Chairman Daniel Reed (R-NY), Ways and Means divided the code into fifty major areas. Teams of staff members from the Treasury, the House Legislative Counsel, the Joint Committee on Internal Revenue Taxation, and the Internal Revenue Service were each assigned sections. Working closely with executive agencies, interest groups, and other committees, these groups spent over 300,000 man-hours devising policy changes. Surrey and Adrian de Wind, a private attorney, served as consultants. The groups built on the expert studies that had been completed by the Joint Committee on Internal Revenue Taxation for Postwar Taxation. Since 1945, numerous experts had been brought in by Colin Stam from outside the Treasury and Congress to participate in the studies of the Joint Committee on Postwar Taxation.[32]

economy during the postwar years, see the following works: Michael Bernstein and David Adler, eds., *Understanding American Economic Decline* (Cambridge: Cambridge University Press, 1994); Michael Bernstein, *The Great Depression: Delayed Recovery and Economic Change in America, 1929–1939* (Cambridge: Cambridge University Press, 1987); David M. Gordon, Richard Edwards, and Michael Reich, *Segmented Work, Divided Workers: The Historical Transformation of Labor in the United States* (Cambridge: Cambridge University Press, 1982); John K. Galbraith, *The Affluent Society* (Boston: Houghton Mifflin, 1958); Harold G. Vatter, *The U.S. Economy In The 1950s* (New York: Norton, 1963); Alfred D. Chandler, Jr., *Strategy and Structure: Chapters in the History of the American Industrial Enterprise* (Cambridge: Cambridge University Press, 1962).

[31] Witte, *The Politics and Development of the Federal Income Tax*, 149.

[32] Staff, Joint Committee on Internal Revenue Taxation, *Part I Summary Of Recommendations Contained In The Testimony Presented Before The Committee On Ways and Means Relative To General Revenues*, January 1954, H41318 (Committee – Print), 1; U.S. Congress, Subcommittee of the Committee on Ways and Means, *Internal Revenue Investigation: Hearings*, 3 February–13 March 1953; "Extracts From Secretary of the

While the groups met, Ways and Means held public hearings. More than 500 witnesses testified on subjects ranging from selective federal excise levies to individual tax exemptions. Meanwhile, committee members reviewed over 17,000 separate suggestions for tax revisions. There were extensive discussions on issues ranging from depreciation and amortization to research and development expenditures to the double taxation of dividends. Most of those who testified on dividends, for instance, recommended relief from double taxation by way of either a credit or a higher deduction on dividend income.[33] On August 14, the final day of the hearings, there was even discussion of reforming the oil depletion allowance. But the committee postponed any final decisions. Reed announced that a revision of the "antiquated" tax laws would be the "first order of business" for the following year.

In January 1954, the administration offered twenty-five proposals, which had been written largely by top Treasury officials and Colin Stam. The proposals included liberalized tax treatment for depreciation, research and development expenses, and retained corporate earnings.[34] The proposals gained support in part because the nation

Treasury Humphrey's Press Conference," 21 May 1953, DEL, White House Central Files, Official Files, Box 172, Folder: 9 May 1953; "Eisenhower Quotes on Tax Reduction," 1953, DEL, White House Central File, Official File, Box 760, Folder: Tax Measures 1952/1954 (2); Colin Stam to Wilbur Mills, 15 March 1954, WMPC, unprocessed; Stam to Mills, 2 April 1954, WMPC, unprocessed; "Rep. Mills Outlines Plans for Technical Revision of Code: Opposes Tax Cuts Now," 112–115. For notes on the previous studies, see: Mr. Shere to Secretary John Synder, 12 June 1947, HTL, John Synder Papers, Box 31, Folder: Taxes – General (Folder 2); Henry Morgenthau to Harry Truman, 16 April 1945, HTL, President's Secretary's File, Box 138, Folder: General File: Tax Data; "Reports of Meeting with the Joint Committee Staff," 26 February 1945–8 December 1945, HTL, Papers of Roy Blough, Box 8, Folder: Treasury – Joint Committee Staff Meetings; Witte, *The Politics and Development of the Federal Income Tax*, 146.

[33] Staff, Joint Committee on Internal Revenue Taxation, *Part I Summary Of Recommendations Contained In The Testimony Presented Before The Committee On Ways and Means Relative To General Revenues*, January 1954, H41318 (Committee – Print), 1.

[34] George M. Humphrey, "Remarks to First Fall Luncheon of The National Press Club," 16 September 1953, DEL, George M. Humphrey Papers, Roll 13, Folder 69; Humphrey, "Statement by Treasury Secretary Humphrey before Joint Committee on the Economic Report," 2 February 1954, and "Statement By Secretary Humphrey," 25 February 1954 in DEL, George M. Humphrey Papers, Roll 13, Folder: 70; Secretary Humphrey, "Lower Taxes for YOU," DEL, Files of Gerald Morgan, Box 8, Folder: Tax; U.S. Department of Treasury, Press Release, 25 February 1954, DEL, White House Central Files, Official File, Box 760, Folder: 1954 (1); L.A. Minnich Jr., "Legislative Leadership Conference," December 17–19, 1953, DEL, Ann Whitman File, Legislative Meetings Series, Box 1, Folder: Legislative Meetings – 1953 (6) [August–December]; *Economic Report of the President: Transmitted to*

was suffering from a severe recession. Although the recodification had been devised without regard to short-term economic conditions, its potential stimulative effects enticed legislators eager to improve the economy. The proposed legislation also excited legislators who would be able to distribute tax breaks to interest groups by way of the law. Between January and March, Ways and Means drafted the measure in closed door sessions. The committee reported a bill that retained top individual rates of 91 percent, and corporate rates of 52 percent.

Interest groups left their footprints all over the legislation, which contained $1.5 billion in new tax breaks. Each tax break provided an important benefit to particular interests, from the oil industry to middle-class homeowners, by relieving them legally of the tax responsibilities that existed under the progressive rate structure. For people with moderate income, the recodification included increased deductibility of medical expenses, a new tax credit for retirement income, a new deduction for child care expenses to widows and mothers whose husbands were "mentally or physically defective," a formal exemption of health and accident benefits and sick pay, deductibility of interest on installment purchases, and the liberalization of income-splitting benefits. For people with higher income, the breaks included an increase in the amount of income that could be deducted as charitable donations, a credit and an exclusion for dividend income, and a provision allowing certain partnerships the option of being taxed as corporations. For business, the bill enacted accelerated depreciation allowance, an extended period in which operating losses could offset profit, and higher depletion allowances.[35]

Democrats, now a congressional minority, opposed the legislation on several grounds. First, the tax breaks would create a substantial deficit without any promise of increased federal revenues in coming years. Second, they threatened to increase the complexity of the tax code. As Mills explained: "I fear that taxpayers are going to find so many rules, limitations, and qualifications, that it will be

---

Congress, January 1954, DEL, Ann Whitman File, Administration Series, Box 13, Folder: Economic Report, January 1954 (1), 77.

[35] Most of this paragraph is drawn directly from Witte, *The Politics and Development of the Federal Income Tax*, 146–147. See also, U.S. Congress, House of Representatives, *Congressional Record*, 83rd Cong., 2nd sess., 17 March 1954, 3420–3429; The White House Press Staff, "Statement by the President," 16 August 1954 and Secretary George Humphrey to Rowland Hughes [Director, Bureau of the Budget], 6 August 1954, DEL, White House Office, Reports to the President on Pending Legislation Prepared by the White House Records Office, Box 32, Folder: 8/16/54.

practically impossible for them to intelligently fill out a tax return."[36] Instead of creating new tax breaks, he argued, Congress should reduce the overall rates and simplify the code.[37] Finally, Reed's bill provided most of the relief to the upper-income brackets; for instance, Democrats said, the committee chose liberalized depreciation rates for business while rejecting higher exemptions for lower income groups.[38] On the House floor, Mills asked his colleagues: "How can you justify reducing one individual's tax under this bill by over $10,000 and declining to reduce the tax of another by $120 . . . Are we so blind to fairness, are we so blind to understanding . . . Have we reached that stage in American History?"[39] Reed, however, disagreed. Should the House increase exemptions, he warned, "serious consideration" would be given "to allowing the revision measure to die."[40]

Although the Democrats mounted a stinging attack on the bill for its "trickle down" economics and its implicit acceptance of deficits, the Republicans pushed the measure through Congress. Drawing on the rhetoric of sacrifice, Eisenhower continued to attack liberalized rates of exemptions for low-income workers as establishing a dangerous precedent: "When the time comes to cut income taxes still more, let's cut them. But I do not believe that the way to do it is to excuse millions of taxpayers from paying any income tax at all . . . I simply do not believe for one second that anyone privileged to live in this country wants someone else to pay his fair and just share of the cost of his Government."[41]

In promoting the final bill, Reed told his colleagues that "this bill represents a complete overhaul of all our revenue laws, the first since the enactment of the income tax . . . It is designed to achieve a peacetime expansion of the economy which we have hitherto been

---

[36] U.S. Congress, House of Representatives, *Congressional Record*, 83rd Cong., 2nd sess., 18 March 1954, 3527.

[37] Ibid., 3526.

[38] Jack Martin [Administrative Assistant to the President] to Secretary George Humphrey, 24 March 1954; President Eisenhower to Senator Douglas, 15 March 1954; Douglas to Eisenhower, 19 February 1954, all in DEL, White House Central File, Official Files, Box 760, Folder: 1954 (1). See also Richard Musgrave, "Federal Tax Reform and the Taxation of Low and Middle Incomes," 16 October 1953, DEL, White House Central File, Official File, Box 760, Folder: Tax Matters 1952/1954 (2); "Minutes of Cabinet Meeting," 5 March 1954, DEL, Ann Whitman File, Cabinet Series, Folder: Cabinet Meeting of March 5, 1954.

[39] U.S. Congress, House of Representatives, *Congressional Record*, 83rd Cong., 2nd sess., 18 March 1954, 3527.

[40] L.A. Minnich, Jr., to Mr. Dodge, 15 March 1954, DEL, Ann Whitman File, Legislative Meetings Series, Box 1, Folder: Legislative Meetings 1954 (2) [March–April].

[41] Cited in Witte, *The Politics and Development of the Federal Income Tax*, 148.

able to achieve only in time of war." Through accelerated depreciation, the legislation would "have far-reaching economic effects.
Incentives resulting from the changes are vital in order to help create
thousands of jobs each year and to maintain the present high levels
of investment in plant and equipment. The bill will make it possible for management to assume risks which they would otherwise
not take."[42]

Some tax breaks enacted through the recodification had an immediate economic impact. For example, the acceleration of depreciation fueled the growth of suburban shopping malls once the provision
took effect in 1956. The provision permitted real estate developers
to write off the costs of new business buildings rapidly and to claim
losses against unrelated income. A tax shelter industry emerged
around new suburban commercial development. Investors discovered
that they "could build a structure, claim 'losses' for several years while
enjoying tax-free income, then sell the project for more than they had
originally invested."[43]

In the end, the recodification validated the direction taxation had
taken during World War II – namely, high progressive rates, numerous tax breaks for non-wage income, and withholding at the source
on wages. Although Congress would enact some minor reductions following the Korean War, the system never returned to the low rates
and the narrow tax base of the prewar period. This legislation transformed the debates about income taxation. Before the 1950s, these
debates had focused primarily on balancing the budget, raising
revenue, and redistributing income.[44] Now that the mass income tax
had been incorporated into the infrastructure of the state, Congress

---

[42] U.S. Congress, House of Representatives, *Congressional Record*, 83rd Cong., 2nd
sess., 17 March 1954, 3420–3424. See also George Humphrey, "Remarks at Tax Institute of the University of Texas School of Law," 1 October 1954, DEL, George
Humphrey Papers, Roll 13, Folder: 70; President Eisenhower to Senator Douglas, 15
March 1954, DEL, White House Central File, Official File, Box 760, Folder: 1954 (1).

[43] Thomas W. Hancett, "U.S. Tax Policy and the Shopping-Center Boom of the 1950s
and 1960s," *American Historical Review* 101, No. 4 (October 1996): 1082–1110.

[44] W. Elliot Brownlee, "Economists and the formation of the modern tax system in the
United States: The World War I crisis," in *The State and Economic Knowledge: The
American and British Experiences,* eds. Mary O. Furner and Barry Supple (Cambridge:
Cambridge University Press and Washington, D.C.: Woodrow Wilson International
Center for Scholars, 1990), 401–435; Brownlee, "Social investigation and political
learning in the financing of World War I," in *The State and Social Investigation in
Britain and the United States,* eds. Michael J. Lacey and Mary O. Furner (Cambridge:
Cambridge University Press and Washington, D.C.: Woodrow Wilson Center Press,
1993), 323; Leff, *The Limits of Symbolic Reform,* 93–168; Alan Brinkley, *Voices of Protest:
Huey Long, Father Coughlin & The Great Depression,* (New York: Vintage Books, 1982),
61–81; Stein, *The Fiscal Revolution in America,* 6–130; Morgan, *Deficit Government,*
1–54.

turned its attention to another important issue: the economic effect of income-tax policies.

TAXATION AND THE ECONOMY

By the final years of the Truman presidency, Mills had reached a high enough position on the seniority ladder to have a significant influence on committee policy, especially since Speaker Sam Rayburn and Chairman Robert Doughton depended on Mills for advice on tax issues.[45] News reporters relied on Mills on a daily basis as their main "off-the-record" source of committee information on taxation.[46] From 1954 to 1957, Mills used his political skills to become deeply involved with the tax policy community. He chaired the subcommittees on fiscal policy for the Ways and Means Committee and the Joint Economic Committee. Responding to the Internal Revenue Code of 1954, with its high statutory rates and its unprecedented number of tax breaks, these subcommittees conducted several important studies on the economic implications of reforming tax breaks and the manipulation of tax rates and spending.

The Ways and Means Committee hearings

Mills started to build a reputation for his tax expertise through these studies. On Ways and Means, Mills directed a series of comprehensive hearings and investigations into the possibilities of tax reform. He brought in prominent professors of law and economics, including Stanley Surrey, Harvey Brazer, Thomas Atkeson, Randolph Paul, Richard Musgrave, and Joseph Pechman, who formed a network around reforming tax breaks such as the depletion allowance, business expense deductions, and foreign income. By "reform," members of this network referred to an ongoing negotiation process in which Congress would eliminate some controversial and outdated tax breaks in exchange for creating new breaks that they claimed were justified on economic and political grounds. Under the proper leadership, Ways and Means could make the difficult tradeoffs between interest groups that preserved the integrity of the system. Through these studies, Mills gained a better understanding of how tax breaks affected private investment and of how incremental reform was essential in order to maintain the integrity of a growth-oriented tax code.

[45] Morgan, *Eisenhower Versus "The Spenders,"* 34.
[46] Louis Cassels, "This Man Shapes Your Tax Bill," *Nation's Business*, March 1956, 34–35.

The Subcommittee on Internal Revenue Taxation, for example, conducted several studies aimed at correcting "technical errors" in the revenue code, errors that were costing the government and taxpayers millions of dollars. Together, the members and their staff drafted proposals to eliminate scores of "unintended" advantages in the current tax laws, including tax breaks that allowed owners of oil property to pay lower taxes by selling their property for limited periods and permitted investors to cut tax corners by buying stock in Canadian investment companies.[47] Economist Richard Musgrave lent support to these efforts by updating his 1948 study of the effective tax burden, revealing the regression at the bottom rates, proportionality in the middle levels, and progression at the top.[48] The studies also examined tax-exempt institutions and cooperatives, retirement income for people not covered by pensions, tax treatment of income derived from abroad, deferred compensation plans, and income from cancellation of indebtedness.[49] Mills's efforts were complemented by the Cabinet Committee on Small Business, directed by CEA chairman Arthur Burns. This committee designed reforms to ease the tax burden on small business and foster capital accumulation.[50]

The subcommittee's studies produced the Technical Amendment Act, proposed by Ways and Means in July 1957. The legislation corrected a slew of technical errors that had been incorporated into the revenue code. By closing as many tax breaks as possible, Mills argued, Congress could enact sound rate reductions: "If we could apply the same rules to all income, the rate of tax would not have to

[47] "Tax Changes Are Coming," *Nation's Business*, November 1956, 100; Bradley H. Patterson, Jr., "Minutes of Cabinet Meeting," 29 April 1955, DEL, Ann Whitman File, Cabinet Meeting Series, Box 5, Folder: Cabinet Meeting of April 29, 1955.

[48] "Impact of Taxes," *Business Week*, 19 November 1955, 78.

[49] "Tax Changes Are Coming"; *Congressional Quarterly Almanac*, 84th Cong., 1st sess., 1955, 424; Wilbur Mills, "Remarks before the Arkansas Association of Public Accountants Concerning the Internal Revenue Code of 1954," 1955, WMPC, Box 783, File 13; "Rep. Mills Outlines Plans for Technical Revision of Code: Opposes Tax Cuts Now," 112–115; U.S. Congress, House of Representatives, *Congressional Record*, 85th Cong., 2nd sess., 1958, 1205; Jack Anderson [Administrative Assistant to the President] to Representative H.R. Gross, 17 February 1959, DEL, White House Central File, Official File, Box 761, Folder: 1959–1960.

[50] See Jim Hagerty to President Eisenhower, 1 January 1957, DEL, Ann Whitman File, Box 9, Folder: Burns, Dr. Arthur F. 1956–57 (1); "Second Progress Report by the Cabinet Committee on Small Business," 31 March 1958, DEL, Ann Whitman File, Administration Series, Box 33, Folder: Small Business-Cabinet; Arthur Burns to President Eisenhower, 12 May 1958, DEL, Ann Whitman File, Administration Series, Box 9, Folder: Burns, Dr. Arthur F. 1958–59 (1); Raymond Saulnier to President Eisenhower, 16 December 1960, DEL, Ann Whitman File, Administration Series, Box 32, Folder: Saulnier, Raymond J. 1960.

be so high." He added: "The rates have to be so high if we are to derive the present amount of revenue because the base to which we apply those rates is not as large as it would be in the absence of the exceptions we have made in the past to the general rule."[51] Through reduction and reform, Congress could preserve the integrity of the income-tax system and the willingness of Americans to pay their obligations.

Mills and Thomas Curtis (R-MO) also directed a more specialized project through the Special Subcommittee on the Taxation of Life Insurance Companies, which met with representatives from the JEC and the Treasury, state insurance commissioners, industry representatives, and independent experts. In 1954, the staff of the subcommittee on life insurance taxation, together with influential insurance lobbyists, helped Mills and Curtis write a quantitative position paper that led to a revised temporary law in 1955.[52] The revised formula still permitted much of the industry's income, particularly underwriting profits (premium payments), to escape taxes.[53] Additionally, the law allowed companies to deduct a higher percentage of their net investment income from the tax returns. As a result, only 12–15 percent of net investment income was taxable.[54] Although this legislation left the problem of a permanent solution to future committees,

[51] "Here's Outlook For Taxes: A Nation's Business Interview with Rep. Wilbur D. Mills," *Nation's Business*, February 1957, 104.

[52] Wilbur Mills and Thomas Curtis, "The Mills-Curtis Plan For The Taxation of Life Insurance Companies," 1956, WMPC, Box 294, File: H.R. 7201-Ways and Means Committee 1956/8; Curtis, "The House Committee on Ways and Means: Congress Seen Through a Key Committee," *Wisconsin Law Review* 1966, No. 1 (Winter 1966): 138; Thomas Martin to Mills, 17 July 1954, WMPC, Box 294, File 16; U.S. Congress, House Committee on Ways and Means, Subcommittee on Internal Revenue Taxation, *Taxation of Income of Life Insurance Companies: Hearings*, 85th Cong., 2nd sess., 1958, 2–5; Subcommittee on Internal Revenue Taxation, House Committee on Ways and Means, *Report on the Taxation of Life Insurance Companies*, 31 December 1958, H1416 (Committee – Print); Paul Clark to Mills, 29 June 1956, WMPC, Box 293, File: 21 H.R. 7201-Ways and Means Comm, 1956/1; Gerard Brannon to Mills, 20 March 1959; Brannon to Mills, 3 February 1959; Department of Treasury, Press Release, 10 April 1958; Eugene Thore to Mills, 21 November 1957; Thore to Robert Anderson, 20 November 1957; Thore to Mills, 18 December 1958; Mills to Thore, 22 December 1958; Thore to Mills, 24 February 1959; Claris Adams to Mills, 31 January 1959; Adams to Mills, 3 February 1959. Aforementioned documents all in WMPC, unprocessed.

[53] U.S. Congress, House Committee on Ways and Means, "Press Release," 16 September 1958, WMPC, unprocessed.

[54] U.S. Congress, House Committee on Ways and Means, Subcommittee on Internal Revenue Taxation, *Report on the Taxation of Life Insurance Companies*, 31 December 1958, H1416 (Committee – Print), 1; U.S. Congress, House Committee on Ways and Means, Subcommittee on Internal Revenue Taxation, *Taxation of Income of Life Insurance Companies: Hearings*, 85th Cong., 2nd sess., 1958, 3.

the studies built up the analytical base for the tax-writing committees to devise future tax reforms.

These accomplishments earned Mills a reputation within Congress as being the "brain" behind the Ways and Means.[55] Although he did not yet control the chairmanship of Ways and Means, Mills used these studies of the tax code to enhance his role within Congress and build his professional reputation within Washington. He achieved his success by collaborating with committee staffers, interest-group representatives, and a handful of academic experts. To assist him in studying other "technical amendments" to the code, Mills set up specialized advisory groups consisting of selected experts and business leaders. These groups studied particular sections of the tax code, including problems with corporations, partnerships, tax-exempts, and estates under the guidance of the committee staff.[56] Finally, Mills corresponded with scholars, such as Thomas Atkeson of the College of William and Mary, about proposals to simplify tax returns.[57] In the same way that Mills carved a professional niche through Social Security in 1950, he mastered income taxation between 1954 and 1957 and demonstrated his expertise.

While conducting the subcommittee hearings, Mills developed ties to the Treasury. Foremost, he made important contacts with such officials as Robert Anderson, Russell Harrington, Marion Folsom, and Dan Throop Smith. Commissioner of Internal Revenue Russell Harrington, for example, provided Mills with quantitative analyses about the cost of tax breaks, about structural problems with the Internal Revenue Service, and the administrative feasibility of various

[55] JMIC; Bernard J. Lammers, "The Role of Congressional Tax Committees" (Ph.D. diss., Columbia University, 1967), 142.

[56] "Rep. Mills Outlines Plans for Technical Revision of Code: Opposes Tax Cuts Now," 112–115; U.S. Congress, House Committee on Ways and Means, *Technical Amendments to Internal Revenue Code: Hearings*, 84th Cong., 2nd sess., 1956; Charles MacLean, Jr., "Problems of Reincorporation and Related Proposals of the Subchapter C Advisory Group," *Tax Law Review* 13, No. 4 (May 1958): 407–437. See also the following documents from the WMPC, unprocessed: Leo Irwin to Wilbur Mills, 1 February 1954; Irwin to Mills, 12 October 1956; Mills to George Humphrey, 16 November 1956; Staff, House Ways and Means Committee, Subcommittee on Internal Revenue Taxation, *Staff Data: Suggested Problems For Advisory Group on Subchapter C*, 3 December 1956; Norris Darrell to Mills, 28 December 1956; Department of Treasury, "Technical Information Release," 2 January 1957; Colin Stam to Mills, 8 January 1957; Irwin to Jere Cooper and Mills, 8 February 1957; Fred Scribner to John Moss, 21 February 1957; Mills to James Casner, undated; Stam to Mills, 14 August 1957. See also James Riddell to Stanley Surrey, 24 October 1956, and Surrey to Sherwin Kamin, 12 December 1956 and Surrey to James Riddell, 30 October 1956, SSP, Box 20, File 4.

[57] Thomas Atkeson to Wilbur Mills, 21 November 1956, WMPC, unprocessed.

reforms.[58] Mills developed a particularly close relationship with Dan Throop Smith, assistant secretary for tax policy from 1953 until 1960; together, they devised various proposals for rate reductions and tax credits to stimulate private investment without distorting the "free operation" of the market. They also worked on reforms in areas such as the treatment of dividend income and capital gains.[59]

Besides personal contacts, Mills gained a strong understanding of how the Department of Treasury operated as a policymaking institution. Despite the creation of the Council of Economic Advisors in 1946, the Treasury remained the most important income-tax organization within the executive branch. Inside the Treasury, Mills learned that the most influential officials were the assistant secretary, the under-secretary, and the IRS commissioner, because these insiders negotiated the demands of "technical" and "political" experts in order to formulate and administer the laws. During the 1950s, Mills and his staff developed a strong connection to the office of the assistant secretary, which synthesized the academic analyses of the Office of Tax Analysis and the Tax Legislative Counsel with the political strategies of the secretary.[60]

The Joint Economic Committee studies

Meanwhile, Mills's bipartisan subcommittees on the Joint Economic Committee conducted two major studies of fiscal policy. Congress had created the Joint Economic Committee in 1946 to enhance the economic expertise of the legislative branch. Although the committee lacked the statutory power to report legislation, its staff and members offered "in-house" expert analysis to Congress on taxation and the budget. The Joint Economic Committee, chaired by former eco-

---

[58] Colin Stam to Wilbur Mills, 13 May 1957; Russell Harrington to Mills, 19 April 1957; Harrington to Mills, 12 March 1957, and Leo Irwin to Members of the Subcommittee on Internal Revenue Taxation, 2 April 1957; Harrington to Mills, 11 March 1958; Harrington to Mills, 23 May 1957; Harry Byrd, 10 April 1958; Mills to George Humphrey, 16 November 1956; Mills to Humphrey, 27 February 1957; Marion Folsom to Mills, 21 January 1954; Russell Train to Mills, 3 December 1956; Train to Mills, 5 February 1957, all in WMPC, unprocessed. See also Mills to Folsom, 13 January 1954, WMPC, Box 759, File 2; Folsom to Mills, 9 December 1953, WMPC, Box 759, File 12; Folsom to Mills, 20 March 1953, WMPC, Box 759, File 12.

[59] L.A. Minnich, Jr., "Minutes of Cabinet Meeting," 8 July 1955, DEL, Ann Whitman File, Cabinet Meeting Minutes, Box 5, Folder: July 5, 1955; Wilbur Mills to Dan Throop Smith, 2 January 1957; Smith to Mills, 18 October 1956; Smith to Mills, 5 July 1956; Smith to Mills, 5 July 1956 all in WMPC, unprocessed.

[60] Thomas J. Reese, *The Politics of Taxation* (Westport, Connecticut: Quorum Books, 1980), 13; Lawrence Pierce, *The Politics of Fiscal Policy Formation* (Pacific Palisades: Goodyear Publishing Company, 1971).

nomics professor Senator Paul Douglas (D-IL), "gave liberals a platform to criticize the administration's macroeconomic policy."[61] The
committee built a case for a more aggressive macroeconomic policy
than Eisenhower, who focused almost exclusively on balancing the
budget, could accept.[62]

The first study conducted by Mills's subcommittee, which first met
in December 1955, examined the criteria for evaluating tax policies
in relation to economic growth; the subcommittee included Douglas,
Representative Thomas Curtis (R-MO), and Senator Barry Goldwater
(R-AZ). The hearings, according to Mills, dealt only with the "economic" aspects of taxation, as opposed to the "political" or "technical" questions that had dominated previous congressional inquiries.[63]
The subcommittee arranged several panels to hear testimony on
taxation and the economy. One panel focused on tax policy and its
relation to short-run economic stabilization and long-run economic
growth. Another panel investigated the possibilities of tax reform,
analyzing, for instance, the potential effect of a rate reduction on consumption and investment. Other panels discussed the effect of recent
fluctuations in the federal tax base.[64] During each particular session,
the experts attempted to push representatives to examine the economic effect of each provision.[65]

The subcommittee concluded that a permanent rate reduction was
essential to achieving long-term growth in the 1950s and the 1960s.
Efficient policies, according to the staff, would result in remarkable

[61] Morgan, *Eisenhower Versus "The Spenders,"* 32.

[62] Ibid.

[63] "Official Verbatim Transcript of Hearings before Joint Committee on the Economic
Report: Subcommittee on Tax Policy," 24 May 1955, HTL, Papers of Grover Ensley,
Box 1, Folder: Official Verbatim Transcript of Hearings before the Joint Committee
on the Economic Report, Jan.–Dec. 1955, 17; 63.

[64] U.S. Congress, Joint Economic Committee, Report to the Congress, 25 August 1955,
WMPC, Box 700, File 11; Paul Douglas to Wilbur Mills, 13 September 1955, WMPC,
Box 701, File 1; John Morris, "Democrats Map New Tax Survey," *The New York Times*,
5 May 1955; U.S. Congress, Joint Economic Committee, Subcommittee on Tax
Policy, "Tax Policy for Economic Growth and Stability," 1955, WMPC, unprocessed;
"Impact of Taxes," *Business Week*, 19 November 1955, 78–86; "Official Verbatim Tran-
script of Hearings before Joint Committee on the Economic Report: Subcommittee
on Tax Policy," 24 May 1955, HTL, Papers of Grover Ensley, Box 1, Folder: Official
Verbatim Transcript of Hearings before the Joint Committee on the Economic
Report, Jan.–Dec. 1955.

[65] "Official Verbatim Transcript of Hearings before Joint Committee on the Economic
Report," 24 May 1955, HTL, Papers of Grover Ensley, Box 1, Folder: Official Ver-
batim Transcript of Hearings before the Joint Committee on the Economic Report,
Jan.–Dec. 1955; "Report of Hearings of the Subcommittee on Tax Policy," 15–16
December 1955, NAT, RG 56, Office of Tax Policy, Box 33, File: Federal Tax Policy
for Economic Growth and Stability.

rates of growth by 1965: national production would increase by 50 percent, the standard of living would rise at least 30 percent, and the nation would achieve a total production exceeding $535 billion.[66] Mills's colleagues also felt that temporary reductions were an effective mechanism for ending a recession. Although they concluded that in 1955 economic conditions did not warrant a rate reduction, the members agreed that if it became "apparent that expansion of economic activity is slowing, and that a higher rate of increase in total demand is required to make full use of our growing productive capacity . . . we would be in a position to reduce taxes."[67] Arthur Burns explained that a tax reduction was a much "sounder method" of dealing with mild recessions than increases in general-revenue expenditures.[68] This reflected his conservative preference for indirect economic interventions that benefited the upper- and middle-income brackets.

Despite endorsing mild stimulative tax reductions, Mills concluded that Congress should wait to see the results of increased defense spending and Federal Reserve actions.[69] "If during the coming months it becomes apparent that inflationary forces have subsided and that a stimulus to total demand is needed to maintain full use of our growing productive capacity," Mills said, "we will be in a position to enact a carefully balanced program of tax reduction and thereby provide continuing impetus for further real growth in the economy. Tax reductions should be postponed, however, until actual events

---

[66] "Official Verbatim Transcript of Hearings before Joint Committee on the Economic Report: Subcommittee on Tax Policy," 24 May 1955, HTL, Papers of Grover Ensley, Box 1, Folder: Official Verbatim Transcript of Hearings before the Joint Committee on the Economic Report, Jan.–Dec. 1955, 12–13. See also Louis Shere to Arthur Burns, 26 January 1956, DEL, Records of the Council of Economic Advisors, Box 16, Folder: Joint Committee on the Economic Report, Hearings, January 1956.

[67] Cassels, "This Man Shapes Your Tax Bill," 35. See also Collis Stocking to the Council of Economic Advisors, 17 March 1955, DEL, Records of the Council of Economic Advisors, Box 16, Folder: Joint Committee on the Economic Report [1955], Policy Suggestions; Arthur Burns to President Eisenhower, 25 June 1956, DEL, Ann Whitman Files, Administration Series, Box 9, Folder: Burns, Dr. Arthur F. 1956–57 (3); L.A. Minnich, Jr., "Minutes of Cabinet Meeting," 27 February 1957, DEL, Ann Whitman Files, DDE Diary Series, Box 21, Folder: Feb '57 Miscellaneous (1); Louis Shere to Arthur Burns, 26 January 1956, DEL, Records of the Council of Economic Advisors, Box 16, Folder: Joint Committee on the Economic Report Hearings [January 1956]; "Minutes of Cabinet Meeting," 2 April 1954, DEL, Ann Whitman File, Cabinet Series, Box 3, Folder: Cabinet Meeting of 2 April 1954.

[68] Arthur Burns, "The Current Business Recession," 22 March 1958, DEL, Ann Whitman File, Administration Series, Box 2, Folder: Robert B. Anderson (3).

[69] John J. Coleman, *Party Decline in America: Policy, Politics, and the Fiscal State* (Princeton: Princeton University Press, 1996), 145.

indicate this occasion for them."[70] A few participants were frustrated with this decision. They believed that a temporary tax cut was needed to stimulate the economy. This tension – like the one that existed between Social Security administrators and fiscal conservatives – delineated the conflict that continued within the tax community during the 1960s. Some policymakers, such as the University of Minnesota economist Walter Heller, were eager to enact temporary tax cuts on the basis of short-term prognostications. Other policymakers, such as Mills, expressed reluctance, and demanded stronger evidence before accepting such policies.

Two years later, the subcommittee examined the role of expenditure policies in economic growth and inflation. As Mills told Congress, "Government spending may have a significant impact on the conditions for achieving economic stability. Our experience during war and defense emergency periods has shown that some types of government outlays may provide a sharp spur for the technological progress upon which our economic growth is based. . . ." He added: "The Subcommittee's present study is directed at improving and refining our knowledge of the complex relationships between the scope and character of Government activity and that of the private sectors in our economy."[71] Tax and spending, the subcommittee concluded, must be considered together.[72] To help do this, the subcommittee formed several panels to look at topics that included efficiency in government expenditures, procedures for determining the value of spending programs, the problem of "automatic" expenditures, and improved methods for calculating what effect expenditures had on economic growth.[73] While the subcommittee called for greater

[70] Mills, "The Challenge of Federal Tax Policy in 1957."

[71] "Introduction By Wilbur D. Mills, Chairman of Subcommittee on Fiscal Policy," WMPC, Box 702, File 9.

[72] Philip Taylor to the Council of Economic Advisors, 29 January 1957, DEL, Records of Council of Economic Advisors, Box 16, Folder: Joint Committee on the Economic Report, Hearings 1957.

[73] U.S. Congress, Joint Economic Committee, Subcommittee on Fiscal Policy, "Hearings on Federal Expenditure Policy for Economic Growth and Stability," 8 November 1957, WMPC, Box 702, File 9; Norman Ture to Wilbur Mills, "Draft of Subcommittee's Report," 18 June 1957, WMPC, Box 703, File 1; Mills to the Members of Congress, 28 June 1957, WMPC, unprocessed; Mills, "Introduction By Wilbur D. Mills, Chairman Subcommittee on Fiscal Policy," undated, WMPC, Box 702, File 9; "No Time For Nodding," *The Christian Science Monitor*, 2 March 1957; "Toward a Fuller Economy," *The Washington Post*, 3 March 1957; Kenneth Roose to the Council of Economic Advisors, 30 January 1957, and Philip Taylor to the Council of Economic Advisors, 4 February 1957, DEL, Records of the Council of Economic Advisors, Box 16, Folder: Joint Committee on the Economic Report; "'Stabilizer' for Smooth Business Sailing," *Newsweek*, 17 June 1957, 81.

control of federal expenditures, Mills added, "I would not say that our problem is blindly cutting expenditures as such. Our problem is rather evaluating expenditure programs."[74]

These two JEC studies helped to open the doors of political influence to a new generation of individuals and organizations from the various issue networks on taxation.[75] Although parts of these networks had existed before World War II, their numbers increased significantly in the postwar era, and achieved a new level of cohesion.[76] By the mid-1950s, certain issue networks were starting to negotiate with political parties and interest groups over formulating fiscal policy. Aware of this development, Mills helped mediate between the issue networks and congressional politics.

The Mills subcommittee did this by soliciting oral testimony and scholarly papers written by the leading experts in several of the tax networks that took shape during these years.[77] Panels were set up with particular issue networks in mind. One network – the one that included Walter Heller; Herbert Stein, director of research for the Committee on Economic Development; and Paul Samuelson, an

---

[74] Wilbur D. Mills, "Fiscal and Monetary Policy as Factors in Economic Growth: Address to the National Association of Mutual Savings Banks," 2 December 1958, WMPC, Box 775, File 5.

[75] See pages 43–53.

[76] The following works discuss the proliferation of professional experts, staff, bureaucrats, and think tanks after World War II: Herbert Stein, "The Washington Economics Industry," *The American Economic Review* 76, No. 2 (May 1986): 1–10; Ellen Herman, *The Romance of American Psychology: Political Culture in the Age of Experts* (Berkeley: University of California Press, 1996), 124–152; Michael A. Bernstein, "American economics and the American economy in the American century: Doctrinal legacies and contemporary policy problems," in *Understanding American Economic Decline*, 361–393; Susan Webb Hammond, "Congressional Staffs," in *Encyclopedia of the American Legislative System: Studies of the Principal Structures, Processes, and Policies of Congress and the State Legislators Since the Colonial Era*, ed. Joel Silbey (New York: Scribner's, 1994), 785–800; Donald R. Kennon and Rebecca M. Rogers, *The Committee on Ways and Means: A Bicentennial History 1789–1989* (Washington: U.S. Government Printing Office, 1989), 215–357; James A. Smith, *The Idea Brokers: Think Tanks and the Rise of the New Policy Elite* (New York: Free Press, 1991); Reese, *The Politics of Taxation*; Brian Balogh, *Chain Reaction: Expert Debate and Public Opinion in American Commercial Nuclear Power, 1945–1975* (Cambridge: Cambridge University Press, 1991), 21–59; Jeffrey H. Birnbaum, *The Lobbyists: How Influence Peddlers Get Their Way in Washington* (New York: Random House, 1992); Henry J. Aaron, *Politics and the Professors: The Great Society Perspective* (Washington D.C.: Brookings Institution, 1978).

[77] U.S. Congress, Joint Economic Committee, Subcommittee on Fiscal Policy, "Press Release," 25 April, 9 May, and 24 June 1955, WMPC, Box 700, File 10–11; U.S. Congress, Joint Committee on the Economic Report, Subcommittee on Tax Policy, "Minutes of Meeting of the Subcommittee on Tax Policy," 5 May 1955, WMPC, Box 700, File 10; "Impact of Taxes," *Business Week*, 19 November 1955, 78–86.

economist at MIT – focused on Keynesian macroeconomic policies to promote economic growth. Another network scrutinized proposals to stimulate private investment, ranging from liberalized depreciation to lower capital gains taxes to investment credits. This network included the university professors Arthur Burns, E. Cary Brown, and Paul McCracken, the government and think-tank economists Dan Throop Smith, Gerhard Colm, and Raymond Saulnier, the interest group experts George Terborgh and Emerson Schmidt, and the accountant Maurice Peloubet. A fourth network, which included Otto Eckstein and Arnold Soloway, analyzed the relationship between expenditures and economic growth. Wilbur Cohen, Robert Ball, and Robert Myers led a fifth network on the taxation of the elderly.

As Mills tried to incorporate these networks into congressional politics, he worked extensively with a group of federally employed economic experts. Grover Ensley, executive director of the JEC, and Norman Ture, the JEC economist, helped with the studies and provided Mills with in-depth analyses of current research on taxation and spending.[78] During the studies, Ensley acted as a liaison to the economics departments of several major universities while building close ties to interest groups and research organizations such as the Tax Foundation. After meeting with these organizations, Ensley briefed JEC members on economic conditions to help them define their policy options.[79] Ture worked even more closely with the subcommittee. With a master's degree in economics and four years of experience at the Treasury, Ture had been recruited by Ensley to the JEC in 1955.[80]

Through these studies, Mills learned how his relationship with

---

[78] Norman Ture to Wilbur Mills, 7 October 1957, WMPC, Box 702, File 9; Ture to Mills, 11 September 1957, WMPC, Box 703, File 1; Ture to Mills, 13 September 1957, WMPC, Box 703, File 4; Ture to Mills, 20 December 1956, WMPC, unprocessed; Grovner Ensley to Mills, 16 May 1956, WMPC, Box 701, File 2; Ensley to Mills, 23 May 1957, WMPC, Box 701, File 8; "Official Verbatim Transcript of Hearings before Joint Committee on the Economic Report: Executive Session," 2 February 1955, HTL, Papers of Grover Ensley, Box 1, Folder: Official Verbatim Transcript of Hearings before the Joint Committee on the Economic Report, Jan.–Dec. 1955, 11–19.

[79] Grover Ensley, interview with Richard Allan Baker, 1 November 1985, JFKL, Oral History Interview Collection, 60–75; Ensley to Wilbur Mills, 14 November 1956, and Ensley, "A General Preview of the Tax Outlook For 1957: Address to the Fourth Annual Conference on the Economic Outlook, University of Michigan, Ann Arbor," 15 November 1956, WMPC, Box 701, File 1; Ensley to Senator Douglas, 22 March 1955, WMPC, Box 701, File 2; Ensley to Mills, 2 June 1955, WMPC, Box 700, File 10; Ensley to Mills, 14 October 1955, WMPC, Box 700, File 11.

[80] Paul Douglas to Wilbur Mills, 22 January 1955, and Grover Ensley to Douglas, 22 March 1955, WMPC, Box 701, File 2.

experts such as Ture could strengthen his political position in Washington. At the JEC, Ture was instrumental in setting up the studies and determining which experts were qualified to participate.[81] He also wrote background reports on the proposals submitted to the committee, providing Mills with "factbooks" and questions to use at the hearings. Mills learned how to benefit from Ture's expertise without becoming dependent on him. Ture recalled, "He [Mills] could glance at two or three questions [provided to him for the hearings] and immediately pick up on the train of thought." Once Mills had read the questions, "he would take them over himself and would never have to look down at the paper again." Ture added: "And it also did not come out as a committee member dutifully and sometimes with great difficulty reading the prose of some other staff member. It was Wilbur Mills asking the questions, and twisting them and using them to bring out what he wanted to see brought out."[82] When the hearings were completed, Ture wrote the reports synthesizing the materials from the studies with other data that he had gathered from executive departments and research institutions.[83]

The hearings helped Mills to understand the delicate process of creating the impression of an "objective" expert forum for congressional policymaking. In August 1955, Senator Douglas complained to Mills that the experts for the JEC hearings were weighted on the side of business, since industrial representatives had "much larger personnel than those who take the public view, and their interest being concentrated, they have much more determination and time to propagandize their views." Douglas asked Mills to "counterbalance" the special interests with the public view. Mills and Ture denied this

---

[81] Norman Ture to Wilbur Mills, 22 October 1955 and Mills to Ture, 28 October 1955, WMPC, Box 700, File 10; U.S. Congress, Joint Committee on the Economic Report, Subcommittee on Tax Policy, "Minutes of Meeting of the Subcommittee on Tax Policy," 5 May 1955, WMPC, Box 700, File 10; "Official Verbatim Transcript of Hearings before Joint Committee on the Economic Report: Subcommittee on Tax Policy," 24 May 1955, HTL, Papers of Grover Enlsey, Box 1, Folder: Official Verbatim Transcript of Hearings before the Joint Committee on the Economic Report, Jan.–Dec. 1955, 1–11.

[82] Norman Ture, interview with Julian Zelizer, Washington, D.C., 13 December 1993.

[83] Norman Ture to Wilbur Mills, "Draft of Subcommittee's Report," 18 June 1957, WMPC, Box 703, File 1. See also Ture to John Hoghland II, Acting Assistant Secretary for Congressional Relations, Department of State, 24 September 1957, WMPC, Box 705, File 13; Ture to Mills, 13 September 1957, WMPC, Box 703, File 4; Mills to Ture, 31 August 1956, WMPC, Box 700, File 10; Dan Throop Smith to Mills, 5 July 1956; Ture to Mills, 17 September 1956; Mills to Throop Smith, 18 September 1956; Throop Smith to Mills, 1 October 1956; Ture to Mills, 18 October 1956; E.J. Engquist, Jr., to Mills, 25 October 1956; Engquist, Jr., to Mills, 4 January 1957, all in WMPC, Box 700, File 9.

charge. Nonetheless, Mills told Douglas and Ture that in the future they should "avoid as much as possible the implication or charge" that they were weighting the panels. Mills noted: "I want all segments of our economy to be permitted to voice their opinions, as I am sure you do."[84]

Stressing his commitment to "objectivity," Mills frequently urged that policy decisions "be based on careful economic analysis, rather than on the popular catch phrases" that were "frequently and indiscriminately attached to legislative proposals."[85] He wrote Eugene Keogh (D-NY), for example, that "our type of hearings are more a seminar affair than the type of hearings that are conducted by our Committee [Ways and Means] where anyone who desires is permitted to testify."[86] When presenting his report to Congress, Mills explained that efficient policies "can be properly discharged only by level-headed searching scrutiny of facts, in which all those participating keep partisan considerations subservient to the interests of the country as a whole."[87] In this particular study, Mills boasted: "Tax experts from all over the country, representing every shade of opinion and professional background, made valuable contributions to this study. The staff of the Committee brought together a huge mass of statistics on the operation of our tax system and its effects on the nation's economic development."[88]

Reactions to the JEC hearings were mixed. Some party leaders seemed troubled. One reporter observed, "recent studies by the two subcommittees have been conducted on such a lofty nonpolitical plane that some of Mr. Mills' Democratic friends have privately accused him of catering to the economic intellectuals of the business and educational world to the detriment of his own party's interests."[89] But most policymakers were more impressed with Mills's innovative "panel of experts" approach to congressional politics. One journal

[84] Mentioned in Wilbur Mills to Paul Douglas, 8 August 1955; Douglas to Mills and Norman Ture, 1 August 1955; John Lehman to Mills, 3 August 1955, all in WMPC, Box 700, File 10; "Official Verbatim Transcript of Hearings before Joint Committee on the Economic Report: Executive Session," 6 December 1955, HTL, Papers of Grover Ensley, Box 1, Folder: Official Verbatim Transcript of Hearings before the Joint Committee on the Economic Report, Jan.–Dec. 1955. For a similar dispute, see Wright Patman to Mills, 6 December 1955 and Mills to Patman, 7 December 1955, WMPC, Box 700, File 11.

[85] "Congressional Group Urges Budget Surplus Be Used to Cut Debt Instead of Taxes, If Business Boom Holds," *The Wall Street Journal*, 30 December 1955.

[86] Wilbur Mills to Eugene Keogh, 9 September 1955, WMPC, Box 700, File 9.

[87] Wilbur Mills to the Congress, 28 June 1957, WMPC, Box 703, File 1.

[88] Wilbur D. Mills, "Let's Strengthen the Income Tax," 1955, WMPC, Box 408, File: 16.

[89] "Economic Statesman: Wilbur Daigh Mills," *The New York Times*, 20 December 1957.

commented that the JEC hearings "were so scholarly in tone and so completely lacking in partisan strife that reporters soon quit covering them."[90] Similarly, *Business Week* claimed that "in the scholarly atmosphere scrupulously maintained at these hearings, economists exchange views with the same freedom they would have in a university seminar."[91] An economist, reviewing for the *American Economic Review*, called the committee report an "impressive compendium," and noted that "economists owe a considerable debt" to these studies. The reviewer believed that "dozens of the papers could, in my judgement, have been appropriately published in this *Review* or other leading journals. There is here an almost embarrassing abundance." His only regret was that the studies, as a government document, would not reach a wider audience inside and outside the economics profession.[92]

Mills's reputation for valuing expertise started to crystallize as a result of these studies. Politicians and academics praised Mills. Heller wrote Mills: "The tax hearings a couple of years ago broke new ground in the organization and procedure of Congressional inquiries into fiscal policies . . . Thanks to your leadership, and Norman Ture's skillful planning and follow-through, a significant advance in American fiscal thinking has been scored."[93] Even Harvard's Stanley Surrey, in an article that criticized the legislative tax process, cited Mills's subcommittee as an "excellent illustration of what can be done to increase understanding of tax issues."[94] Reactions were so favorable that the JEC could not satisfy the demand from academic and government officials for the subcommittee's printed compendium of papers.[95] Such success encouraged Mills to maintain close relationships with individuals who were crucial to the new tax community. Surrey, for instance, corresponded frequently with Mills about the treatment of foreign income.[96]

---

[90] Cassels, "This Man Shapes Your Tax Bill," 66.

[91] Cited in Grover Ensley, interview with Richard Allan Baker, 1 November 1985, 73. See also "Looking At Tax Effects," *Business Week*, 21 May 1955, 20–31.

[92] Howard R. Bowen, "Federal Tax Policy for Economic Growth and Stability," *American Economic Review* XLVI, No. 3 (June 1956): 465–467.

[93] Walter Heller to Wilbur Mills, 16 December 1957, WMPC, Box 775, File 5. These boxes in the WMPC are filled with letters of praise for Mills's work from people ranging from professors of law and economics to congressional representatives.

[94] Stanley S. Surrey, "The Congress and the Tax Lobbyist – How Special Tax Provisions Get Enacted," *Harvard Law Review* 70, No. 7 (May 1957): 1172. See also Surrey to Wilbur Mills, 13 December 1955, WMPC, Box 700, File 11.

[95] U.S. Congress, Joint Economic Committee, "Minutes From Meeting of Joint Economic Committee," 13 January 1958, WMPC, Box 701, File 1, 3.

[96] Stanley Surrey to Wilbur Mills, 13 December 1955, WMPC, Box 700, File 11; Mills to Surrey, 4 May 1956; Surrey to Mills, 14 May 1956; Mills to Surrey, 21 May 1956;

FORMULATING AN AGENDA

These hearings, by introducing Mills to new policymakers and to new policy ideas, pushed him to define his legislative agenda. Mills still considered himself to be a fiscal conservative. He believed that balanced budgets and low taxation were essential long-term political objectives, although he gradually acknowledged that the government needed room to maneuver in the short run. Mills accepted the permanence of the state in America, but he was determined to design fiscal restraints that would limit the long-term cost of programs and minimize the negative effect of government on private markets. As a fiscal conservative, Mills tended to define programs in terms of budgetary cost rather than rights or needs.

An American state

Mills lambasted conservatives who still called for an end to the federal government. "We must," Mills explained, "continue to rely on public policies and actions to provide the setting in which the free expression of private incentives basic to the successful operation of our enterprise system will result in a rate of growth consistent, both in the short and long run, with stability in the price level."[97] He dismissed critics who wanted to dismantle the federal income tax. Mills warned audiences that the "restrictive impact" of the tax system had been "grossly exaggerated." After all, he said, during the ten years since the end of World War II, the United States had enjoyed "rates of economic growth which is the envy of the entire world." According to Mills, the JEC studies demonstrated that there was no "statistical fact or theory" to support the argument that the federal tax had significantly damaged personal incentives. The fact that Karl Marx had advocated progressive income taxation during the nineteenth century (a criticism leveled by some conservatives), Mills explained, did not itself "make the tax undesirable" or "a seditious instrument for undermining the free-enterprise system." If politicians adopted a "guilt-by-association test," Congress would have to eliminate Social Security, collective bargaining, unemployment compensation, workmen's compensation, public school education and other programs and institutions that were "basic to the health and vigorous functioning of our free, competitive, private enterprise economy."[98]

Surrey to Mills, 19 November 1956; Surrey to Mills, 1 February 1957; Mills to Surrey, 4 February 1957; Surrey to Mills, 7 February 1957; Mills to Surrey, 11 February 1957; Surrey to Mills, 25 March 1957, all in WMPC, unprocessed.

[97] Wilbur D. Mills, "Federal Tax Policy and the Economic Challenges of 1957: Address before the Tax Executives Institute," 18 February 1957, WMPC, Box 780, File: 12.

[98] Mills, "Let's Strengthen the Income Tax."

Mills told another audience: "The economy's performance since the end of World War II confirms the importance of sound public policy in providing the setting in which this spirit can impel our private enterprise economy to new achievements. A major instrument of this public policy has been the Employment Act of 1946 and the Executive and Congressional machinery which it established."[99] Despite his frequent attacks on excessive farm supports and their budgetary cost (regardless of the numerous agricultural interests in his district), Mills acknowledged that "government participation in agricultural programs over the past forty years has been necessary and no doubt has helped in the difficult economic adjustment in agriculture."[100]

Fiscal policy

Even as a fiscal conservative, Mills started to recognize the necessity of active fiscal policy; the experts involved in the JEC and Ways and Means studies were clearly having an effect on his rhetoric. Mills's hesitant acceptance of occasional deficits signaled an important stage in his development. He told the Chamber of Commerce, "My thought has been that over a number of years we should operate our fiscal affairs in the black but that we should not necessarily try, year in and year out, to be in the black. We must recognize the need on occasion for tax reduction as a stimulus when our economy is turning down and we are losing the momentum and progress that we have had."[101] While insisting that taxes should not "go up and down like hemlines," Mills agreed that Congress should use moderate tax adjustments on occasion, rather than higher expenditures or government regulation, to ensure economic growth and a high employment, balanced budget.[102]

---

[99] Wilbur D. Mills, "Federal Tax Policy and Economic Growth," 1 May 1956, WMPC, Box 783, File: 20.

[100] Wilbur D. Mills, "Remarks at the Annual Meeting of Arkansas Division, Associated Milk Producers, Inc.," 24 July 1971, WMPC, Box 417, File 6. See also Mills, "The Challenge for Re-Direction of Farm Policy: Address to American Farm Federation," 11 December 1957, WMPC, Box 775, File 2.

[101] "Here's Outlook For Taxes," 33.

[102] Mills expressed many of these views during a battle over a proposed temporary reduction to combat the 1958 recession. Although Mills opposed the reduction, he did so on the grounds that the economy was recovering from its slump. He did not refute the notion that tax reductions were necessary if economic conditions called for them. See the following: Wilbur Mills to William Martin, 13 January 1958, WMPC, Unprocessed; Allen Drury, "Capital Expects Economic Review To Be Optimistic," *The New York Times*, 20 January 1958; "Recession Is a Fighting Word," *Business Week*, 25 January 1958, 28; Charles Sieb, "How Congress Looks at Tax Cuts," *Nation's Business*, March 1958, 40.

Before audiences in Washington, New York, and Arkansas, Mills elaborated his position. During a speech to tax professionals in Manhattan, for example, he explained some of the logic behind his emerging view of tax policy:

There is, I venture to say, not a single economic activity which is not affected and conditioned by our Federal tax laws. Evidence of the enormous impact of the Federal tax system is constantly brought to the attention of the Congress and the Administration by demands from taxpayer groups for tax revisions, and these demands are constantly increasing in scope and complexity. The professional journals of lawyers, accountants, and economists are replete with instances of the way in which taxes affect decision-making at the personal and business level . . . In short, without losing sight of the basic purpose of Federal taxation – raising revenue to defray the expense of government – there is an ever-widening awareness of the significance of the Federal tax structure in shaping the complexion of our economic growth.[103]

Although Mills preferred to focus on the revenue-raising function of taxation, he acknowledged that "when the Federal Government activities represent over one-fifth of the national income, the manner in which those activities are financed will have significant economic consequences."[104] In a bold statement for a fiscal conservative, Mills explained:

It is generally agreed, for example, that when the private economy is not fully using available resources, reducing taxes relative to spending will have a stimulating effect. It is also agreed that when the economy is pressing hard on available resources, increasing taxes relative to spending will help to repress inflationary pressures. Once the level of Government spending has been determined, changing the level of tax receipts is an effective way to minimize economic fluctuations. We cannot afford to neglect this important tool, since these fluctuations represent significant obstacles to the attainment of our objective of steady economic growth.[105]

Mills also strongly endorsed the automatic stabilizing effect of the federal income tax and other federal programs, such as unemploy-

[103] Mills, "The Challenge of Federal Tax Policy in 1957."
[104] Mills, "Federal Tax Policy and Economic Growth."
[105] Ibid.

ment compensation: "Under our present tax system . . . when a business downturn occurs, taxes automatically fall, leaving more purchasing power in private hands. This cushions the downturn and makes it easier to reverse."[106] Speaking of the period before the 1950s, Mills recalled toward the end of his life: "Strange thing, just how little we used to know about the effect upon the economy of either increases in taxes or decreases in taxes. You can't have adjustments of any size within your tax structure without having some effect, one way or another, on your economy. Used to be they never thought of that." [107]

Through a flexible income-tax system that sustained high rates of growth, Mills claimed, the United States would show the world that "contrary to the basic premise of communism that a capitalistic system can not adjust to the needs of masses of the people," the United States could "grow more rapidly than the totalitarian, communistic systems."[108] His acceptance of automatic stabilizers, moderate tax adjustments, and temporary deficits, instead of higher public spending, reflected a bipartisan trend of policymakers and legislators during these years.[109] To avoid drastic action, Mills said that a permanent rate reduction (from a range of 91–20 percent to 70–10 percent) tied to expenditure control and revenue-raising reforms would eliminate the "drag" of high taxes on investment and demand.[110] Lower rates and fewer tax breaks would also bring a degree of "fairness" to the tax code.[111]

---

[106] Mills, "Let's Strengthen the Income Tax"; Mills, "Fiscal and Monetary Policy as Factors in Economic Growth."

[107] Wilbur D. Mills, interview with Lewis E. Weeks, 13 August 1980, Hospital Administration Oral History Collection, Library of the American Hospital Association (Chicago, Illinois, 1983), 16.

[108] "Official Verbatim Transcript of Hearings before Joint Committee on the Economic Report: Subcommittee on Tax Policy," 24 May 1955, HTL, Papers of Grover Ensley, Box 1, Folder: Official Verbatim Transcript of Hearings before the Joint Committee on the Economic Report, Jan.–Dec. 1955, 13–14.

[109] Robert M. Collins, *The Business Response to Keynes, 1929–1964* (New York: Columbia University Press, 1991), 142–209; Coleman, *Party Decline in America*; Herbert Stein to members of the Subcommittee on the Maintenance of High Employment and Advisors, 23 December 1953, DEL, Arthur Burns Papers, Box 106, Folder: Fiscal and Monetary – C.E.D [Committee For Economic Development] Depression Study, 1953 (1).

[110] "Transcript of Hearings before the Joint Committee on the Economic Report," 24 January 1955, HTL, Papers of Grovner Enlsey, Box 1, Folder: President's Economic Report – Transcript of Hearings – Pres. Econ. Report 1/24/55, 48–58; 70–78.

[111] Mills, "Federal Tax Policy and Economic Growth."

Tax reform

Mills's language of tax reform closely resembled that of Stanley Surrey and Joseph Pechman; it included specific proposals for eliminating foreign tax havens, tightening the definition of capital gains, reducing the oil-depletion allowance, and increasing the restrictions on travel and entertainment deductions. To maintain the integrity of the progressive income tax, Congress needed to cleanse the revenue code periodically by eliminating tax breaks that had become obsolete or that encouraged inefficient investments.[112] At the same time, reformers should narrow the definition of taxable income in areas where private investment was stifled by high rates.[113] Ongoing reform would maintain the integrity of the system while avoiding the need for any radical change in policy: "Instead of childishly radical proposals for scrapping the income tax or severely restricting it, we should lend our mature efforts to conserving its desirable features and in so doing transform it into a more effective instrument for promoting sound and steady economic growth."[114]

Contributory social insurance

Mills also wanted to expand contributory social insurance by increasing taxes and paying higher benefits to more recipients. Since 1950, he had come to believe firmly that the program should remain self-supporting and that monthly benefits and payroll tax revenue should be tied together. The earmarked tax system offered a conservative

[112] Mills, "The Challenge of Federal Tax Policy in 1957."

[113] These views were later summarized in Wilbur D. Mills, "Are You A Pet Or A Patsy?" *Life*, 23 November 1959, 62. For a good look at Mills's discussion of taxation, see Mills, "Preface," *Virginia Law Review* 44, No. 6 (October 1958): 835–838; "Keep The Income Tax But Make It Fair," *U.S. News & World Report*, 27 July 1956, 68–80; "Here's Outlook For Taxes," 32–109; Mills, "The Relation of Taxes to Our Economy: Speech," undated, WMPC, Box 218, File 2; Mills, "Remarks of Mr. Mills before the Arkansas Association of Public Accountants Concerning the Internal Revenue Code of 1954"; Mills, "Federal Tax Policy for Economic Growth"; Mills, "Remarks of Wilbur Mills to the Section of Taxation of the American Bar Association," 25 August 1956; Mills, "Remarks of the Honorable Wilbur D. Mills before the National Automobile Dealers' Association," 14 November 1956, WMPC, Box 781, File 2; Mills, "Let's Strengthen The Income Tax"; Mills, "Federal Tax Policy and the Economic Challenges of 1957"; Mills, "Factors in Tax Reduction and Revision: Address to the American Tax Foundation," 2 December 1957, WMPC, Box 775, File 5; Mills, "Remarks of the Honorable Wilbur D. Mills before the Society of Public Accountants," September 1958, WMPC, Box 775, File 9; "High Taxes and Good Sense," *Newsweek*, 11 June 1956, 90.

[114] Mills, "Let's Strengthen the Income Tax."

method of financing Social Security by limiting the potential growth
of the program because Congress had to raise as much money each
year as it paid out in benefits. The earmarked tax system, moreover,
defined old-age pensions as an earned benefit rather than as a form
of welfare for the needy. For Mills, the soundness of Social Security taxation would remain his "overriding consideration" about the
program, even more than its economic impact.[115] As he would tell the
House in 1960:

> There must be revenue in the fund in time and over a period
> of years to pay for those benefits that we think our people are
> entitled to receive . . . we are not discussing small matters when
> we discuss amendment of the Social Security Act; we are dis-
> cussing terrifically large matters because of their application to
> so many people, and because of the great number of important
> policies that are involved in carrying on this program. It is there-
> fore essential, and those who are most interested in social secu-
> rity have always pointed out, that it is most important, absolutely
> essential, that we keep this system as actuarially sound as possi-
> ble . . . [if the program became actuarially unsound] someone
> is going to have to pay taxes to make up these deficiencies
> between the tax contributions and benefit payments. It is no
> secret where this money will come from. It will inevitably come
> in large measure from the young people in their twenties and
> thirties who are relatively new additions to America's work force;
> it will come from the pay-roll taxes imposed on generations not
> yet born.[116]

Welfare and defense

In sharp contrast, Mills hoped to curtail public assistance expenditures that encouraged "dependency" and "government centraliza-
tion" while destroying the family. Although Mills shared a traditional
conservative aversion to deficit spending, he specifically targeted
welfare expenditures that were financed through the general revenue.
Like others in the tax community, Mills mounted rhetorical attacks on
deficits while displaying flexibility toward "uncontrollable" military
and social insurance expenditures. To be sure, Mills lamented "how
terribly expensive maintaining 'nonwar' is today . . . the dreadful
grinding cost of continual suspense and of goods and services fore-
gone to pay for a fireworks display for the stars." Nonetheless, he sup-

[115] U.S. Congress, House of Representatives, *Congressional Record*, 86th Cong., 2nd sess.,
22 June 1960, 13809.
[116] Ibid., 13812–13814.

ported Cold War defense spending as unavoidable. "Unless there is a marked change in world tensions and reduction in Soviet effort," Mills told Congress, "neither of which is now a realistic prospect, we must be prepared to maintain a pretty steadily rising defense effort in the years to come."[117] These contrasting views on contributory social insurance, defense spending, and means-tested public assistance continued to define Mills's agenda throughout his career.

Reflecting on the JEC and Ways and Means studies, Mills often compared the entire tax-writing process to the court system. Like a court, the tax-writing committees needed to make decisions on the basis of objective evidence. But most of the material presented, he warned, "does not lend itself to the making of decisions in accordance with the criteria that are as objective as those generally available in other forums." With the exception of "presentations that emanate largely from academic circles," most of the information was derived from sources having "some direct personal interest" in the legislation. As a result, Mills sought the advice of professionals whose "impartial and objective" knowledge could help his colleagues grapple with the technical and substantive aspects of taxation.[118]

BACK IN THE DISTRICT

Most of Mills's ideological positions meshed with his basic political interest – the needs of his district and Arkansas. By 1957, the rural and agricultural state of Arkansas was profiting from a variety of federal programs. Foremost, the agricultural support system that had been constructed during the New Deal was essential to the livelihood of many farmers, including those in Mills's district. Military spending and army bases had helped to lift Arkansas out of its economic depression during World War II and helped to accelerate the process of industrialization.[119] Like other southern and southwestern states during the war, Arkansas underwent one of the largest relative gains nationally in manufacturing capital expansion.[120] Military spending

---

[117] Mills, "Factors in Tax Reduction and Revision." See also Wilbur D. Mills, "Remarks to the Veterans of Foreign War," 21 June 1958, WMPC, Box 776, File 1.

[118] Wilbur D. Mills, "The Role of the Organized Bar in Federal Tax Legislation: Remarks before the American Bar Association," 10 November 1962, WMPC, Box 591, File: Mills Speeches.

[119] C. Calvin Smith, *War and Wartime Changes: The Transformation of Arkansas, 1940–1945* (Fayetteville: University of Arkansas Press, 1986).

[120] Bruce J. Schulman, *From Cotton Belt to Sunbelt: Federal Policy, Economic Development, and the Transformation of the South, 1938–1980* (New York: Oxford University Press, 1991), 104; Randall Bennet Woods, *Fulbright: A Biography* (Cambridge: Cambridge University Press, 1992), 88.

continued to sustain many parts of Arkansas throughout the Cold War; one of the state's largest industries – aluminum processing – earned millions of federal dollars for the construction of military airplanes. For much of Mills's career, the Second District was home to corporations dependent on the military, such as the Aluminum Company of America, the Reynolds Metals Corporation, and the Aerojet General Corporation. Aerojet, for example, was involved in the development of first-stage motors for the Navy's advanced submarine-launched Polaris missile and second-stage motors for the Air Force's Minuteman strategic missiles.

Similar to much of the South, the industrialization, mechanization, and urbanization of Arkansas, combined with the great migration of African-Americans, undermined many of the racial and economic structures, particularly the plantation system with its wealthy planter class and black tenancy base, that previously fueled white opposition to all types of federally administered social programs.[121] Following the redistricting of 1960, Mills's formerly rural district included electrical equipment production, printing and publishing, and banking; 65.8 percent of the district population was classified as "urban" in census records by the early 1960s.[122]

By 1961, federal payments constituted 24.1 percent of Arkansas' state and local general revenue, well above the national average of 14.1 percent.[123] Arkansans were also beneficiaries of the expansion of Social Security when OASI incorporated non-industrial employees, still the dominant type of worker in the state. All of Arkansas, moreover, benefited from the interstate highway system, which was developed during the second half of the 1950s. The interstate highway program helped to modernize the state's underdeveloped road system through an infusion of federal funds; Mills had been central to the creation of this program. Finally, Arkansas business benefited from the oil depletion allowance because the processing of petroleum was the state's third largest industry.[124] These types of federal pro-

---

[121] Numan V. Bartley, *The New South 1945–1980* (Baton Rouge: Louisiana State University Press, 1995), 105–146; 261–297; Earl Black and Merle Black, *Politics and Society in the South* (Cambridge, MA: Harvard University Press, 1987), 23–72; Jack Temple Kirby, *Rural Worlds Lost: The American South 1920–1960* (Baton Rouge: Louisiana State University Press, 1987); Jill Quadagno, "From Old-Age Assistance to Supplemental Security Income: The Political Economy of Relief in the South, 1935–1972," in *The Politics of Social Policy in the United States*, eds. Margaret Weir, Ann Shola Orloff, and Theda Skocpol (Princeton: Princeton University Press, 1988), 252–262.

[122] Stephen A. Merrill, *Wilbur D. Mills: Democratic Representative from Arkansas* (Washington, D.C.: Grossman Publishers, 1972), 7.

[123] Schulman, *From Cotton Belt to Sunbelt*, 119.

[124] Writers' Program of the Works Progress Administration in the State of Arkansas, *Arkansas: A Guide to the State*, 2nd edition (New York: Hastings House, 1948), 70.

grams in Arkansas gave Mills ample electoral reasons, in addition to his own ideological development, to accept the permanence of the modern American state.

THE POSTWAR TAX POLICYMAKERS

Building on the foundation provided by the recodification of 1954, Mills's generation of policymakers had begun to redefine the terms of the debate over tax policy. No longer wedded to the concept of income taxation as exclusively a revenue-raising device or a redistributive mechanism, federal officials began to consider how adjustments in the tax law could encourage economic productivity, private investment, consumer demand, and full employment. In the modern American political system, the income tax was a key policymaking institution. Certainly, policymakers differed as to how aggressive the government should be in its manipulation of taxation. While some officials were enthusiastic about the possibilities, others, such as Mills, accepted the idea of working within the existing system with hesitation.[125] Nonetheless, Mills and his colleagues all acknowledged that the income tax played a major role in the nation's political economy.

Just as they distinguished social insurance from public welfare, they defined the manipulation of income taxation as a unique method to manage economic growth, one that avoided the direct management of market institutions. Through the adjustment of tax rates, Congress could stimulate consumer demand and private investment without resorting to the intrusive mechanisms used in communist regimes or in wartime, such as price controls or microeconomic industrial regulation. The government could also stimulate private investment through tax breaks that exempted certain types of income from the high tax burden; these laws provided a strong incentive for particular forms of investment. To maintain the integrity of this system, Mills and his colleagues concluded, Ways and Means should support an ongoing process of incremental reform to distinguish "legitimate" breaks from those that lacked strong economic or political justification. Ways and Means had been granted the procedural mechanisms and had developed a culture that encouraged members to make these tough decisions.

The Ways and Means committee and JEC studies also helped a young generation, including Mills, gain a sense of themselves as a policymaking community. The studies on fiscal policy offered an educa-

---

[125] For a critique of those who were overly enthused with possibilities of manipulating taxation, see Thomas B. Curtis, "The Economic Effects of Federal Taxation," *Tax Review* XVII, No. 5 (May 1956): 17–20.

tional forum in which its members could engage colleagues with their ideas. With the help of these committees, policymakers from specialized issue networks gradually began to coalesce. They interacted on a regular basis with the members of the political parties and interest groups. These efforts were complemented by the community-building work of the Department of Treasury, the Department of HEW, presidential task forces, and cabinet committees.

From this process emerged a distinct policy community, which included a new generation of policymakers, as well as a new type of policymaker. Although there were varying degrees of involvement and different levels of power within the community and although serious ideological divisions existed among its three factions, they operated within a circumscribed policymaking arena and shared a common political language. Together, they would be partially responsible for the Social Security and income-taxation policies of the 1960s. Between 1958 and 1961, Mills learned how to use the resources of the community to expand on his role as chairman of Ways and Means.

4

The Legislative Mills, 1958–1961

Following the death of Chairman Jere Cooper (D-TN) in 1957, Mills became chairman of Ways and Means. When a reporter asked Speaker Sam Rayburn (D-TX) if this meant that Mills had a promising future in Washington, Rayburn snapped in response: "When you're chairman of the Ways and Means Committee, you've already arrived!"[1] Rayburn understood that Ways and Means had maintained an influential role in national politics throughout the twentieth century because of its power to write tax legislation. When Mills became chairman of this committee, he stepped into an important position. As chairman, Mills could accept or reject presidential tax proposals, he supervised an elaborate tax and expenditure system, and he had access to one of the most talented staffs in Congress. He could also depend on a committee whose membership was relatively consensual and pragmatic.[2]

Mills joined a long list of representatives who had shared the title of "powerful chairman of Ways and Means." During the twentieth century, the position had been filled by such notable individuals as Sereno Payne (R-NY), Oscar Underwood (D-AL), Claude Kitchin (D-NC), Joseph Fordney (R-MI), William Green (R-IA), Willis Hawley (R-OR), James Collier (D-MS), Robert Doughton (D-NC), Harold Knutson (R-MN), Daniel Reed (R-NY), and Jere Cooper (D-TN). Every chairman of Ways and Means had access to power because of his position. Nonetheless, these chairmen had done different things with their power. Some, such as Payne, acquiesced in the demands of the party leadership. Others, such as Kitchin, were more aggressive in shaping legislation.

The biggest distinction between the chairmen involved the chang-

---

[1] John Cauley, "Mills of Arkansas, Powerful Voice in Congress," *The Kansas City Times*, 22 August 1961; "The Man Who Steers Tax Policy," *Business Week*, 22 March 1958, 59.

[2] John F. Manley, *The Politics of Finance: The House Committee on Ways and Means* (Boston: Little, Brown, 1970), 45–63; Richard F. Fenno, Jr., *Congressmen in Committees* (Boston: Little, Brown, 1973), 2–5; 83–94.

ing role of Ways and Means within the American state. By the time Mills became chairman in 1958, the committee was different than it had been at the beginning of the century. Although the internal structure of the committee remained similar, the institutional context within which it operated had been transformed. First, Social Security and the postwar income tax placed national government programs of unprecedented size under the wings of Ways and Means. Second, institutional reforms freed the committee chairman from the tight grip of the Speaker of the House and the Democratic caucus. Through the decentralized committee system, most committee chairmen found much greater autonomy within Congress than in the early 1900s. Finally, the sheer number of policymakers and organizations involved in national politics – ranging from congressional staff to bureaucrats to think tanks to university and independent economists – mushroomed after 1932. As a result, the policymaking process became denser and more complicated. These changes presented Mills with different types of challenges and responsibilities than those of his predecessors.

Mills learned immediately on taking over Ways and Means that he needed to do more than just hold a powerful congressional position to maximize his influence in the national state. To shape successful policies, Mills needed to master the art of congressional politics, an art that changed as the state expanded. Congressional politics became more complex and difficult to control. Congressional leaders had to tailor legislation that would allow representatives to support bills in spite of an unprecedented number of demands, ranging from constituents who expected more government services to policy communities that aggressively promoted their agendas.

Mills spent the first three years of his chairmanship improving his ability to balance these demands. In doing so, he learned how to make full use of the special procedural rights granted to Ways and Means, of his relationship to the tax community, and of his technical expertise to achieve parliamentary success. By linking technical knowledge to congressional power, Mills expanded his influence inside the American state.

NO-WAYS AND BY NO-MEANS

Congressional leadership required the ability to forge consensus among competing factions. Although Mills had demonstrated his intellectual skills during the 1950s, there were uncertainties about his proficiency at uniting opposing sides behind legislation. In his early attempts to do so, Chairman Mills failed.

Failing as chairman

The first bill he proposed as chairman provided for a $1.5 billion, sixteen-week extension of unemployment compensation for workers whose benefits had expired during the 1958 recession and for workers in noncovered industries. The measure authorized federal grants from general revenue to finance this expansion. Abnormal levels of unemployment, according to Mills, justified this temporary departure from the contributory principle.[3] Ways and Means passed the bill by a vote of 16 to 7. But Mills did not package the measure properly, leaving it open to charges of being a "raid on the general funds" that threatened to destroy the contributory principle underlying unemployment compensation.[4] Until 1958, an earmarked tax was the sole source of federal funding for the program, thereby distinguishing the benefits from welfare. The Mills bill relied on general revenue. In short, argued Howard Smith (D-VA), the legislation represented "undisguised, unabridged, and unabashed socialism."[5] Persuaded by the opposition, the House soundly rejected the committee bill, and a coalition of southern Democrats and Republicans substituted a weak version of the proposal.[6]

[3] U.S. Congress, House Committee on Ways and Means, *Temporary Unemployment Compensation Act of 1958,* 23 April 1958, H1656 (Committee – Print); U.S. Congress, House Committee on Ways and Means, *Emergency Extension of Federal Unemployment Compensation Benefits: Hearings,* 85th Cong., 2nd sess., 1958; John McCormack to Wilbur Mills, 11 March 1958, WMPC, unprocessed; "H.R. 12065," 1958, and "Memorandum for Filing-Legislative Folder on H.R. 11326 (Mr. Mills) Relating to Additional Unemployment Compensation Benefits," 1958, and Gerard Brannon to Leo Irwin, 25 March 1958, all in NA, RG 233, 85th Cong., Box 638, File: HR 12065 (1 of 9); Mills to Howard Smith, 22 April 1958, NA, RG 233, 85th Cong., Box 638, File: HR 12065 (3 of 9).

[4] L.A. Minnich, Jr. to Maurice Stans, 22 April 1958; Minnich, "Notes on Legislative Leadership Meeting," 22 April 1958; Minnich, "Legislative Leadership Meeting: Supplementary Notes," 25 March 1958; and "Legislative Leadership Meeting: Supplementary Notes," 18 March 1958. Aforementioned documents are in DEL, Ann Whitman File, Legislative Meetings Series, Box 3, Folder: Legislative Minutes 1958 (2) [March–April]. See also John Morris, "President Fights Jobless Pay Bill," *The New York Times,* 23 April 1958; "President Proposes $600 Million Speedup in Spending; Asks Same Amount in Program to Extend Jobless Pay," *The Wall Street Journal,* 26 March 1958; Felix Belair, Jr., "Eisenhower Asks Fund To Prolong Pay For Jobless," *The New York Times,* 26 March 1958; "President Gives Governors Outline of Plan to Extend Jobless Pay," *The Wall Street Journal,* 20 March 1958.

[5] U.S. Congress, House of Representatives, *Congressional Record,* 85th Cong., 2nd sess., 30 April 1958, 7747–7749; Daniel Reed, Press Release, 18 April 1958, NA, RG 233, 85th Cong., Box 638, File: HR 12065 (1 of 9); U.S. Congress, House Committee on Ways and Means, *Temporary Unemployment Compensation Act of 1958,* 23 April 1958, H1656 (Committee – Print).

[6] In an off-the-record interview, Mills later claimed that he did not really lose the bill because the House rejected the part of the legislation – funding benefits for uncov-

The unemployment compensation failure in 1958 revealed the limits of power for committee chairmen within the nation's fragmented political system. Although Mills grasped the arcane logic of the unemployment compensation tax, and despite his dejure power as chairman of Ways and Means, he failed to create a coalition. The gap between technical and parliamentary expertise, skeptics warned, was something Mills needed to overcome. Following this crushing defeat, even Mills's strongest supporters questioned his skills as chairman.[7] In other legislative battles over highway construction and Treasury bond interest rates, for example, Mills again proved incapable of pushing a bill through swiftly or even of maintaining control of his committee.[8] Some Washington pundits began to label Ways and Means as the "No-Ways and By No-Means" committee. *Time* magazine described Mills's performance during his first years as chairman as "inept."[9]

Learning to lead the committee

Confronting these professional challenges, Mills quickly learned how to "read" the needs of his fellow representatives and to "sell" them

ered workers through general revenue – that he had known they would reject. Mills claimed to have added that section of the measure to distract attention away from the more moderate sections, which he and the Eisenhower administration had sought all along. Ultimately, the moderate sections passed. This statement, however, seems at best a rationalization for the devastating loss: Mills had always been aware of the severe blow to a committee chairman that resulted from such major defeats, and it seems highly unlikely that he would set himself up for a loss at such an early stage of his career. Regardless of his intentions, the defeat raised many questions among policymakers and the media about his abilities, thus tarnishing his reputation.

[7] JMIC.

[8] "Rayburn Sees No Bond Rate Ceiling Vote This Session," *The Wall Street Journal*, 27 August 1959; John Morris, "Democrats Study A New Bond Plan," *The New York Times*, 18 January 1960; Editorial, "Frozen in Politics," *The Wall Street Journal*, 26 April 1960; "House Unit Urges Approval of Compromise Bill to Revoke $4\frac{1}{4}\%$ Ceiling on Some Bonds," *The Wall Street Journal*, 2 March 1960; "House Foes of Compromise Bond Rate Bill Win Indefinite Delay; Treasury Asks Action," *The Wall Street Journal*, 17 March 1960; "Democrats Stall Mills' Compromise On Rate Ceiling," *The Wall Street Journal*, 18 February 1960; "House Unit Votes Compromise Bill On Bid to End Bond Rate Ceiling," *The Wall Street Journal*, 24 February 1960; Editorial, "No Compromise With Reason," *The Wall Street Journal*, 29 February 1960; *Congressional Quarterly Almanac*, 86th Congress., 1st Session, 1959, 273–275; U.S. Congress, House of Representatives, *Congressional Record*, 86th Cong., 1st sess., 1959, 18157–19378.

[9] "Decline & Fall," *Time*, 7 September 1959, 11; "Tax Overhaul Plan," *The Wall Street Journal*, 29 June 1959; Charles Sieb, "Steering Wheel of the House," *The New York Times*, Sunday, 18 March 1962, Section 6; Robert Novak, "Ways & Means Woe," *The Wall Street Journal*, 12 January 1962; "Wilbur Mills. . . . 'Mr. Taxes' in the Congress," *Newsweek*, 14 January 1963, 14–18.

his proposed policies. He developed a keen awareness of the multiple policy pressures that influenced them. Success depended on his ability to exchange rewards skillfully in return for support, without sacrificing the integrity of complex fiscal legislation. After the unemployment compensation fiasco, Mills would never again allow a bill out of his committee until he was certain that it would pass his committee and the House. As the chairman once said: "There's no point in bringing out a bill just for show, knowing it will be beaten on the floor . . . our job is to work over a bill until our technical staff tells us it is ready and until I have reason to believe that it is going to get enough support to pass."[10] Mills went to extraordinary lengths to ensure the support of a vast majority in the committee. He depended on the positions of committee members to indicate the support a measure would receive on the House floor: "I think if I can get a vast majority of the membership of the Ways and Means Committee to agree on something, that I've got a vast majority of the House to agree on the same thing."[11]

The political scientist John Manley found that Mills learned to nurture the votes of his committee and their interest groups, and to tailor bills to ensure majorities in the House. To secure the support of his committee, for example, Mills made extensive use of "Members' Bills," one of the purest examples of interest-group politics. Every year, time was allotted to committee members to propose minor, "technical" provisions that benefited one of the specific interest groups that supported them. These bills usually passed unanimously and, under special rules, without opposition in the House. Mills brought these bills to the House floor under the "consent calender," created for "noncontroversial bills," preventing any debate. Some examples of Members' Bills included a refund on self-employment taxes for a particular individual and the suspension of export duties on a specific metal.[12]

Through Members' Bills, Mills played the game of interest-group politics by distributing small benefits that did not impose a dramatic budgetary cost when considered individually but that were important to particular members of the committee and their supporters. Members' Bills placated committee members who at other times were asked to support loophole-closing reform. Throughout the 1960s and early 1970s, Mills used Members' Bills on a regular basis as tools through which to generate support for his leadership.

---

[10] Sieb, "Steering Wheel of the House." See also Douglas Cater, "The Ways and Means of Wilbur Mills," *The Reporter*, 29 March 1962, 26.

[11] Both quotations are cited in Fenno, *Congressmen in Committees*, 115.

[12] Manley, *The Politics of Finance*, 79–81.

To ensure passage of more comprehensive legislation, Mills also consciously avoided the partisanship of previous chairmen, particularly Robert Doughton, who had chaired the committee between 1933 and 1953.[13] Instead, Mills developed a bipartisan norm that Manley called "restrained partisanship." Mills stressed that "partisanship should not interfere with a thorough study and complete understanding of the technical complexities of the bills under consideration."[14] The chairman achieved this difficult task by working closely with committee Republicans, especially ranking Republican John Byrnes (R-WI). He refused to meet privately with Rayburn or the Democratic caucus to devise legislation.[15] The alliance between Mills and Byrnes was part of a bipartisan trend during the 1960s of Democratic chairmen and ranking Republicans working on a consensual basis; other partnerships included William Fulbright (D-AR) and George Aiken (R-VT) on the Senate Foreign Relations Committee and William M. McCulloch (R-OH) and Emanuel Celler (D-NY) on the House Judiciary Committee.[16]

Redefining the Social Security Amendments of 1958

Mills modeled this consensual approach to politics on the successful moments of his first year as chairman. Whereas the unemployment fiasco served as a reminder of how not to handle a bill, the Social Security Amendments of 1958 became a prototype of how to maintain stable coalitions and how to work with the tax community to achieve legislative success. The pressure to reform Old-Age, Survivors, and Disability Insurance began when the increased cost-of-living weakened the economic value of cash benefits.[17] According to the experts, people who retired after 1954 were receiving insufficient benefits, and some were even forced onto public assistance.[18] To correct this deficiency, Wilbur Cohen, then a professor of social work at the University of Michigan, proposed an increase in benefits to be

---

[13] JMIC; Bernard J. Lammers, "The Role of Congressional Tax Committees" (Ph.D. diss., Columbia University, 1967), 365–368.

[14] Manley, *The Politics of Finance*, 64–68.

[15] JMIC.

[16] David R. Mayhew, *Congress: The Electoral Connection* (New Haven: Yale University Press, 1974), 104.

[17] Old-Age and Survivors' Insurance (OASI) became Old-Age, Survivors, and Disability Insurance (OASDI) in 1956 when Congress enacted a program for the disabled that was financed through a separate trust fund. For clarity, I will still refer to the Old-Age and Survivors Insurance portion of the program as OASI.

[18] U.S. Congress, House Committee on Ways and Means, *Social Security Amendments of 1958: Report*, 85th Cong., 2nd sess., 1958, 4.

financed through a higher wage base and a reformed investment procedure for the trust fund. Besides pressing for an increase in cash payments, Cohen contemplated an increase in widow's and children's benefits, a liberalized retirement test, and a higher family maximum for benefits. Further improvements depended on the willingness of Congress to raise payroll taxes.[19]

Early on, however, the Department of Health, Education, and Welfare warned of a veto from Eisenhower for any tax increase intended to finance higher OASI benefits.[20] As a compromise, Secretary of HEW Marion Folsom proposed that Congress raise the wage base to finance a temporary increase in benefits based on a sliding scale: Those who retired before 1955 would receive a raise of 8 percent, those who retired before 1957 would receive a raise of 5 percent, those who retired in 1957 and 1958 would receive a raise of 3 percent.[21] Folsom's plan intrigued Mills, especially as it had been designed by the trusted Robert Myers.[22] Some officials also assumed that Mills was adhering to a "Texas" agreement between Senate Majority Leader Lyndon Johnson (D-TX), Rayburn, and Secretary of the Treasury Robert Anderson that there be no major tax changes in 1958.[23] During a meeting with Andrew Biemiller and Nelson Cruikshank from the AFL-CIO on July 3, Mills said that he wanted to move forward with the plan with one exception: The

[19] Wilbur Cohen to Wilbur Mills, 8 January 1958, WCP, Box 64, Folder 5. See also Cohen to Mills, 1 July 1957 in WCP, Box 64, Folder 5; Robert J. Myers, "Cost Estimate for Raising the Maximum Earnings Base to $6,000 and Increasing the General Benefit Level by 25%," 19 February 1957, RMP, Box M83-106, unprocessed.

[20] L.A. Minnich, Jr., "Minutes of Cabinet Meeting," 6 June 1958, DEL, Ann Whitman File, Cabinet Meeting Series, Box 11, Folder: Cabinet Meeting of June 6, 1958; Cohen, "Materials for the Study of Factors Influencing the Social Security Amendments of 1958," 10 September 1958, WCP, Box 251, Folder 1. See also Wilbur J. Cohen, "The Social Security Amendments of 1958: Another Important Step Forward," 17 October 1958, WCP, Box 251, Folder 1; U.S. Congress, House Committee on Ways and Means, *Social Security Legislation: Hearings*, 85th Cong., 2nd sess., 1958, 3–42, 554–555.

[21] Robert Myers to the Secretary, 13 June 1958, RMP, Box M83-106, unprocessed; U.S. Congress, House Committee on Ways and Means, *Social Security Legislation: Hearings*, 85th Cong., 2nd sess., 1958, 7–15; Staff Secretary, "6/10/58," DEL, White House Office, Office of the Staff Secretary, Legislative Meeting Series, Box 5, Folder: L-49 (3); L.A. Minnich, Jr. to Maurice Stans, 10 June 1958, DEL, Ann Whitman File, DDE Diary Series, Box 33, Folder: June 1958-Staff Notes (3); L.A. Minnich, Jr., "Minutes of Cabinet Meeting," 6 June 1958, DEL, Ann Whitman File, Cabinet Meeting Series, Box 11, Folder: Cabinet Meeting of June 6, 1958.

[22] Robert Myers to the Secretary, 2 June 1958, and Myers to Charles Schottland [Commissioner of Social Security], 10 June 1958 and Schottland to the Secretary, 11 June 1958 and Myers to the Secretary, 13 June 1958, RMP, Box M83-106, unprocessed.

[23] Cohen, "Materials For The Study of Factors Influencing The Social Security Amendments of 1958."

benefit increase would be across the board, rather than targeted, because the latter might be too difficult for representatives to explain to their constituents.

Mills monitored the proposal as it was designed. Although Social Security policymakers such as Cohen, Myers, and Robert Ball had developed ties with Mills before he became chairman, they now had even more of an incentive to consult with him regularly. Before committing himself to any proposal, Mills met with Cohen on July 10 in Washington. Within the privacy of Mills's office, Cohen warned that the taxless, temporary increase established a dangerous precedent for politicians to revert to the fiscally irresponsible practices of the 1940s. The professor, moreover, had been told that Chairman Harry Byrd (D-VA) of the Senate Finance Committee opposed considering any legislation, particularly a temporary increase, until the Advisory Council of Social Security Financing completed its report in 1959.[24] Stirred by these arguments and worn out from a trying year, Mills turned to Cohen and said, "You know more about this than I do. You may be right. See if you can work it out." Within hours, Cohen recommended a *permanent* 10 percent benefit increase for *all* retirees, a raise in the taxable wage base, and a tax-rate increase scheduled for 1960.[25] Of course, an across-the-board benefit increase to constituents during an election year held significant appeal to Mills.

Once the proposal reached his committee, Mills helped redefine the legislation in a manner that would command stronger support in Congress. Besides his ability as chairman to secure or block votes, Mills demonstrated his understanding of the dynamics behind Social Security and his skill at crafting legislation. During the executive sessions between July 15 and July 26, Mills attempted to overcome the division that existed between Folsom and Cohen, and even more

[24] L.A. Minnich, Jr., "Minutes of Cabinet Meeting," 28 March 1958, DEL, Ann Whitman File, Cabinet Meeting Series, Box 10, Folder: Cabinet Meeting of March 28, 1958.

[25] Cohen, "Materials For The Study of Factors Influencing The Social Security Amendments of 1958." This section of my analysis draws heavily on Edward D. Berkowitz, *Mr. Social Security: The Life of Wilbur J. Cohen* (Lawrence: University Press of Kansas, 1995), 348; Berkowitz, "Social Security and the financing of the American state," in *Funding the Modern American State, 1941–1995: The Rise and Fall of the Era of Easy Finance* (Cambridge: Cambridge University Press and Washington, D.C.: Woodrow Wilson Center Press, 1996), 178–183. Berkowitz provides an excellent analysis of the battle between Cohen and Folsom over the temporary benefits; he also develops a nuanced description of the relationship between Cohen and Mills. However, Berkowitz plays down the issue of the actuarial deficit. We both rely extensively on the document in the Wilbur Cohen Papers, "Materials For The Study of Factors Influencing . . . ," which provides a detailed behind-the-scenes look at this legislative battle.

important, their congressional allies.[26] To avoid another defeat, Mills quickly repackaged the rhetoric of the legislation into less controversial terms: He shifted the debate away from the issue of "inadequate benefits" and toward the problem of "actuarial deficits."

The chairman understood the political payoff for legislation that protected the actuarial soundness of Social Security, even if it meant raising payroll taxes. "We ought to keep on strengthening social security whenever possible," Mills told reporters. "But we also must keep the program on an actuarially sound basis."[27] After all, workers paid their "contribution" with the expectation that the program would remain sound through their own retirement. As the Princeton Opinion Research Corporation found in an extensive survey for the National Association of Manufacturers: "The results of the poll indicate widespread acceptance of the social security program, a willingness to pay its costs, a desire to see it liberalized, and a conviction that it is sound."[28] Members of Congress thus gained electoral support not only by distributing immediate benefits to recipients, but by voting to protect the actuarial soundness of the tax system that was said to guarantee the future benefits of current contributors. This differed from the income-tax system in that citizens did not perceive a direct, concrete benefit that would result for themselves from a tax hike.

Throughout the committee sessions, Mills continued to package the legislation in actuarial terms by focusing on a report by the Board of Trustees of OASI that revealed a short-term and long-term deficit in the program.[29] Mills invited Robert Myers to help him explain the condition of the trust fund to the committee behind closed doors. In the short-run, for the first time in eighteen years since benefits were first paid, current income to the OASI trust fund was slightly less than current expenditures. If no changes were made, expenses were likely to exceed income in each year until 1965. In the long-run, revised actuarial estimates of the OASI provisions of the 1956 law showed an increase in the actuarial imbalance of the program from 0.20 percent to 0.57 percent of payrolls.[30] Even Myers

[26] Robert Myers to Charles Schottland, 14 July 1958 and Wilbur Cohen to Wilbur Mills, 10 July 1958 in RMP, Box M83-106, unprocessed; Myers to Cohen, 24 February 1958, WCP, Box 65, Folder 2.

[27] Louis Cassels, "This Man Shapes Your Tax Bill," *Nation's Business*, March 1956, 66.

[28] Roy L. Swift to Robert Ball, 19 September 1958, NAS, RG 47, Bureau of Old Age and Survivors Insurance, Correspondence of Director Victor Christgau, Box 6, Folder: Incoming Correspondence July–September 1958.

[29] Wilbur J. Cohen, "The Social Security Amendments of 1958: Another Important Step Forward," 17 October 1958, WCP, Box 251, Folder 1.   [30] Ibid.

admitted that the program was further out of balance than he had anticipated.[31]

Although these figures seemed minute to the untrained eye, to Social Security experts they meant a great deal. For Mills, the numbers suggested that there were serious problems with the self-supporting system: In the short-run, the link between payroll tax revenue and social security insurance benefits seemed tenuous; in the long-run, the link was less certain than it had been at any time since 1949. While the administration insisted that there was "no cause for concern about the long-range financial condition of the program," Mills bombarded the committee with statistics that proved otherwise.[32] As he later reiterated on the House floor, without the tax increase Congress might have to "dip into the general funds of the Treasury for those amounts."[33] Most representatives accepted these ominous actuarial predictions as a matter of fact because, as Cohen later recalled, Mills was "probably the only man out of the five hundred and thirty five people in Congress" who completely understood "the actuarial basis of Social Security." Unlike other legislators, Cohen added, Mills was "completely conversant with the basis for making the actuarial estimates and all of the factors that enter into it."[34]

The chairman convinced his committee and the House that the expansion of benefits offered an effective method for protecting the soundness of the payroll tax, rather than vice versa. Mills based his argument on two propositions. First, the benefit increase served as a sweetener for raising the tax rates. Second, the tax increase would raise enough money to pay for increased benefits, to eliminate the short-term imbalance, and to reduce the long-term deficit.[35] This

[31] Robert Myers to the Secretary of HEW, 2 June 1958 and Myers to Charles Schottland, 17 January 1958, RMP, Box M83-106, unprocessed; U.S. Congress, House Committee on Ways and Means, *Social Security Legislation: Hearings*, 85th Cong., 2nd sess., 1958, 7–9; U.S. Congress, House Committee on Ways and Means, *Social Security Amendments of 1958: Report*, 85th Cong., 2nd sess., 1958, 2–27; Myers, "Old-Age, Survivors, and Disability Insurance: Financing Basis and Policy Under the 1958 Amendments," *Social Security Bulletin* 21, No. 10 (October 1958): 15–21.

[32] Cohen, "Materials for the Study of Factors Influencing the Social Security Amendments of 1958"; Cohen, "The Social Security Amendments of 1958: Another Important Step Forward." For the administration's views on this issue, see U.S. Congress, House Committee on Ways and Means, *Social Security Legislation: Hearings*, 85th Cong., 2nd sess., 1958, 9–11; Cohen, "Information from Trustees Report Indicating Actuarial Imbalance on Intermediate Cost Basis is not an Immediate Problem nor the Most Likely Possibility," 1 August 1958, WCP, Box 270, Folder 5.

[33] U.S. Congress, House of Representatives, *Congressional Record*, 85th Cong., 2nd sess., 31 July 1958, 15733.

[34] Wilbur Cohen, interview with David McComb, 8 December 1968, LBJL, Oral History Interview Collection, Tape 2, 7–8 and Tape 1, 27.

[35] U.S. Congress, House of Representatives, *Congressional Record*, 85th Cong., 2nd sess., 31 July 1958, 15734; Robert J. Myers, "Certain Actuarial Aspects of OASDI Amend-

logic solved the puzzle of how to overcome the disagreement between Folsom and Cohen. By the end of the sessions, all participants agreed on the need to eliminate the deficit and pay for new benefits through a tax increase.[36] Mills was so persuasive that John Byrnes, who usually resisted payroll-tax increases, lobbied the committee to start this increase one year earlier than the date Cohen had proposed. Likewise, the administration dropped its threat to veto the tax increase, realizing it had little support in Congress.[37]

On July 28, Ways and Means reported a bill to the House that included a permanent, across-the-board 7 percent increase in benefits, an increase in the total monthly benefits that could be paid to one family, an extension of coverage to dependents of disabled workers, a raise in the wage base from $4,200 to $4,800, a liberalization of the retirement test, and a payroll-tax increase effective in 1959.[38] Three days later, the House passed the legislation by an overwhelming vote of 375-2. By the time the Senate debated the amendments, the old-age insurance provisions had ceased to be an issue. The only remaining conflict centered on the administration's opposition to the provisions that Mills helped incorporate into the bill, provisions that increased federal public assistance payments to poor southern states such as Arkansas. In the end, Mills and Senator Robert Kerr (D-OK) forced the president to back down on

ments uder Consideration by Ways and Means Committee," 25 July 1958, RMP, Box 83–106, unprocessed; U.S. Congress, House Committee on Ways and Means, *Social Security Amendments of 1958: Report*, 85th Cong., 2nd sess., 1958, 26.

[36] Wilbur J. Cohen and Fedele F. Fauri, "The Social Security Amendments of 1958: Another Significant Step Forward," WCP, Box 251, Folder 3; Cohen, "Materials for the Study of Factors Influencing the Social Security Amendments of 1958"; U.S. Congress, House Committee on Ways and Means, *Social Security Amendments of 1958: Report*, 85th Cong., 2nd sess., 1958, 3; "Financing Old-Age, Survivors, and Disability Insurance: Report of the Advisory Council on Social Security Financing," *Social Security Bulletin* 22, No. 2 (February 1959): 3–11; Robert J. Myers, "Methodology Involved in Developing Long-Range Cost Estimates for the Old-Age and Survivors, and Disability Insurance System," Actuarial Study No. 49, May 1959, RMP, unprocessed.

[37] Cohen, "Materials for the Study of Factors Influencing the Social Security Amendments of 1958"; Nelson Rose to Maurice Stans, 25 August 1958 and Dan Throop Smith to Wilbur Mills, 10 July 1958, NAT, RG 56, Office of Tax Policy, Box 38, File: Social Security Amendments of 1958. For Byrnes's fears about the high levels of payroll tax rates, see his remarks in the U.S. Congress, House of Representatives, *Congressional Record*, 85th Cong., 2nd sess., 31 July 1958, 15746.

[38] Myers, "Certain Actuarial Aspects of OASDI Amendments Under Consideration by Ways and Means Committee"; U.S. Congress, House Committee on Ways and Means, *Social Security Amendments of 1958: Report*, 85th Cong., 2nd sess., 1958; Phillip Hughes to President Eisenhower, 23 August 1958, DEL, White House Office, Reports to the President on Pending Legislation Prepared by the White House Records Office, Box 138, Folder: 8/28/58.

this issue. On August 28, President Eisenhower signed the bill into law.[39]

During the debates, the chairman had learned that technical expertise and legislative skills were not incompatible. By working with members of the Social Security faction of the tax community, such as Cohen and Myers, Mills expanded his influence in shaping policy. Mills's success at redefining the legislation in terms of "actuarial deficits" rather than "benefit increases" garnered considerable support within his committee. For Mills, this realization constituted an important stage in his professional development. By mastering the relationship between his technical expertise and legislative skills, he increased his clout in Congress. Furthermore, by selling the expansion of OASDI benefits as a partial solution to actuarial deficits, the legislation allowed him to preserve his identity as a "hardline tax man" while adding to it a reputation as a "defender of social security."[40] Shrewd parliamentary maneuvers such as these, combined with his understanding of public policy and his commitment to negotiating compromise, helped Mills achieve considerable success during the remainder of his career.

Taking control of Ways and Means

As Mills became an effective leader, he earned the trust of numerous representatives and consolidated his position on Ways and Means. In 1961, for example, he centralized control by eliminating Ways and Means' various subcommittees. Under Mills, the final markups of tax legislation were completed in executive sessions that were open only to committee members (without their personal staff) and a handful of Treasury or Social Security Administration experts. "The sessions," according to one scholar, "were long and grueling, and although all committee members were invited to participate, in practice a subgroup did the vast majority of the work. Tax bills typically started as concepts that were discussed in arduous detail and then drafted line

---

[39] Cohen, "Materials for the Study of Factors Influencing the Social Security Amendments of 1958"; Phillip Hughes to President Eisenhower, 23 August 1958, DEL, White House Office, Reports to the President on Pending Legislation Prepared by the White House Records Office, Box 138, Folder: 8/28/58; U.S. Congress, House of Representatives, *Congressional Record*, 85th Cong., 2nd sess., 31 July 1958, 15745; L.A. Minnich, Jr. to Maurice Stans [Director of the Bureau of Budget], 12 August 1958 and L.A. Minnich, Jr. to Maurice Stans, 29 July 1958, DEL, Ann Whitman File, Legislative Meetings Series, Box 3, Folder: Legislative Minutes 1958 (4) [July–December].

[40] Cohen, "Materials for the Study of Factors Influencing the Social Security Amendments of 1958."

by line."[41] Mills usually obtained a closed rule from the Rules Committee, which meant that the House could only accept or reject, not modify, committee legislation. He argued that the "technical complexity" of fiscal legislation and the danger of chaotic horse-trading in the House called for a closed rule.[42] To help demonstrate his own understanding of the bill and ensure support for the closed rule, Mills usually was accompanied to the Rules Committee by one of his experts, such as Myers or Laurence Woodworth, who attended as his personal advisor.[43] The closed rule was an extremely effective tool for passing legislation in the House, constituting one of the main procedural tactics that helped Ways and Means function as a "control committee" by curtailing the influence of congressional representatives outside the closed panel.

After his first few years as chairman, Congress knew that Mills would craft legislation to accommodate as many interests as possible. Other representatives were willing to delegate responsibility only to a leader they knew was competent and politically safe. As Mills once said: "A conscientious congressman knows he can't make an adequate personal study of all the complicated bills he's required to vote on. So when something comes up that's outside his field, he tries to find somebody he can rely upon to give him straight facts and intelligent judgments." He concluded: "After you've been here for a while, you're tabbed as either knowing your subject or not knowing it. I've sought to know my subject."[44] As a result, when Mills took a measure to the Rules Committee "it was a fait accompli."[45]

By the early 1960s, Mills thoroughly understood the parliamentary process. "There was no one," the congressional liaison Lawrence O'Brien once said, "more effective in handling legislation than Wilbur Mills."[46] Members from both parties praised Mills's "legislative

[41] Catherine E. Rudder, "The House Committee on Ways and Means," in *Encyclopedia of the American Legislative System: Studies of the Principal Structures, Processes, and Policies of Congress and the State Legislatures Since the Colonial Era*, ed. Joel Silbey (New York: Scribner's, 1994), 1039.　　[42] JMIC.

[43] John Manley's Personal Notes, 21 July 1964, LBJL, The John Manley Papers.

[44] Cassels, "This Man Shapes Your Tax Bill," 35; Joseph Alsop, "The Legislator," *The Washington Post*, 8 January 1962.

[45] Lawrence O'Brien, interview with Michael Gillette, 17 December 1986, LBJL, Oral History Interview Collection, Interview XVII, 19. On Mills's use of the closed rule see also Lammers, "The Role of Congressional Tax Committees"; Randall Strahan, *New Ways and Means: Reform and Change in a Congressional Committee* (Chapel Hill: University of North Carolina Press, 1990); Linda Katherine Kowalcky, "The House Committee on Ways and Means: Maintenance and Evolution in the Post-Reform House of Representatives" (Ph.D. diss., Johns Hopkins University, 1991).

[46] Lawrence O'Brien, interview with Michael Gillette, 24 July 1986, LBJL, Oral History Interview Collection, Interview XI, 36.

expertise" in addition to his knowledge of policy.[47] For instance, he helped pass the Technical Amendments Act of 1958 that created a new tax entity, the Subchapter S corporation, for the exclusive purpose of providing some businesses greater tax protection.[48] Mills also pushed through the Life Insurance Taxation Reform (1959), which cost the industry over $500 million in its first year of operation.[49] In 1961, moreover, he guided through Congress a 20 percent increase in the minimum OASDI benefit and an increase in widows' benefits. One executive official offered a revealing observation of the expectations that had developed among representatives:

> When congressmen see Wilbur Mills bringing out a bill, they know certain things. They know Wilbur Mills has done his homework. They know the Ways and Means Committee has worked on the bill. And with the closed rule and all, they can be sure the Committee has the situation well in hand. . . . When an Education and Labor bill is on the floor, things are so confused that the Members don't even know who is in charge of the bill. There are amendments coming out of your ears. . . . From the beginning every bill is accompanied by bickering. Powell, Mrs. [Edith] Green, [Carl] Perkins, and [John] Brademas are all talking at once, vying to see who will get what. And it shakes the confidence of the Members of the House.[50]

THE SOUTHERN EXPERT

To succeed in postwar congressional politics, legislators had to keep pace with an expanding number of policy arenas. Given the vast size of the federal government, changes were taking place constantly as specialized policy communities moved in different and often contra-

[47] JMIC. One survey of House members and the Washington Press Corps in 1964 voted him the single most effective U.S. representative, "Who Is Best? Who Is Worst?" *Pageant*, November 1964.

[48] Sheldon D. Pollack, *The Failure of U.S. Tax Policy: Revenue and Politics* (University Park: Pennsylvania State University Press, 1996), 205.

[49] Claris Adams to Wilbur Mills, 3 February 1959; Adams to Mills, 31 January 1959; Mills to Eugene Thore, 2 December 1958; Thore to Mills, 30 January 1959; Gerard Brannon to Mills, 3 February 1959; Brannon to Mills, 20 March 1959; Brannon to Mills, 27 January 1959; Dean Davis, "Report to Life Insurance Association Membership Meeting of December 19, 1958," all in WMPC, unprocessed. See also U.S. Congress, House Committee on Ways and Means, Subcommittee on Internal Revenue Taxation, *Report on the Taxation of Life Insurance Companies*, 31 December 1958, H1416 (Committee – Print), 3; "Taxation of Life Insurance," 1958, DEL, Bryce Harlow Papers, Box 23, Folder: Taxation – Life Insurance Companies.

[50] Fenno, *Congressmen in Committees*, 239–240.

dictory directions. Congressional representatives frequently had great difficulty in adjusting to these changes without alienating their districts. Like their colleagues, members of the tax-writing committees had to monitor these developments carefully or they would get into political trouble.

Negotiating civil rights with the district

Mills came close to getting into serious trouble at home. He encountered a problem between 1958 and 1962 when the national government, including many members of the tax community, began to shift to a more liberal position on civil rights.[51] The civil rights movement temporarily threatened Mills's political standing in the district, causing him to hesitate before taking action on any fiscal policies that might be considered too liberal in Arkansas. These included investment incentives, loophole-closing reforms, and deficit-financing. One Washington associate astutely noted, "Wilbur may look very conservative up here, but in his district people call him up and say, 'Wilbur, don't you go too far along with that crowd, now.'"[52]

Indeed, the chairman had a difficult time adapting to this particular transition because his constituency had little sympathy for federal intervention in racial matters, particularly after the Little Rock incident.[53] Although Mills identified ideologically with the burgeoning group of southern (and Arkansan) moderate leaders who were more concerned with regional economic development than the preservation of racial hierarchies, and who were in favor of incremental and local pressure toward integration, he consistently opposed federal involvement in racial issues.[54] In 1956, for instance, he signed the "Southern Manifesto," which denounced *Brown v. Board of Education*; this document was signed by the entire congressional delegation of Arkansas. The Little Rock incident put Mills and his Arkansas

---

[51] Hugh Davis Graham, *The Civil Rights Era: The Origins and Development of National Policy* (Oxford: Oxford University Press, 1990), 27–152; James L. Sundquist, *Politics and Policy: The Eisenhower, Kennedy, and Johnson Years* (Washington: Brookings Institution, 1968), 221–286.

[52] Edmond Le Breton, "Mills Holds Ground on Principle," cited in U.S. Congress, House of Representatives, *Congressional Record*, 87th Cong., Appendix, 26 March 1962, A2316–2317.

[53] For examples, see WMPC, Boxes 323 and 684.

[54] On southern moderates, see Numan V. Bartley, *The New South 1945–1980* (Baton Rouge: Louisiana State University Press, 1995), 147–297; 460–461; Jack Bass and Walter Devries, *The Transformation of Southern Politics: Social Change and Political Consequence Since 1945* (New York: Basic Books, 1976), 87–106; Earl Black and Merle Black, *The Vital South: How Presidents Are Elected* (Cambridge, MA: Harvard University Press, 1992), 145.

colleagues on the national hot seat. As pressures intensified, Mills remained adamant; the level of the resistance from his constituents to every civil rights measure was immense.[55] In 1960, Mills opposed the Civil Rights Act as unnecessary and unconstitutional.

The redistricting of Arkansas in 1960 compounded Mills's problems.[56] As a result of the 1960 census, Arkansas lost two congressional seats, and the ensuing redistricting threatened to derail Mills's career. Once preparations for the census had begun in 1958, he found himself obliged to defend strongly the outspoken segregationist Arkansas Representative Dale Alford (D-AR), a close friend of Governor Faubus. Otherwise, Faubus would have been able to use his power in the state legislature to redistrict Mills out of office.[57] Alford had recently defeated Representative Brooks Hays through a write-in campaign that focused exclusively on defending segregation. Alford, with the support of Faubus, upset the incumbent Hays, who was defeated as a moderate on civil rights who had attempted to mediate the Little Rock school conflict.[58] Mills was successful in meeting the Alford challenge, but he paid a price for this effort. Supporting Alford cost Mills status in Washington circles: Mills felt "besieged" by the accusation that he was a "captive of Southern discrimination tradition."[59]

After the redistricting, the pressures continued. With Little Rock added to his district, the civil rights question became even more prominent as the number of African-Americans increased to approximately 17 percent of his constituency by 1964; the Little Rock public school population was quickly reaching an even racial balance.[60]

---

[55] Wilbur Mills, "Extension of Remarks of Honorable Wilbur D. Mills of Arkansas in The House of Representatives," 4 April 1960, WMPC, Box 784, File 9; U.S. Congress, House of Representatives, *Congressional Record*, 86th Cong., 2nd sess., 23 March 1960, 6398–6400; Mills to J.K. Hale, 14 January 1960, WMPC, unprocessed. See also Mills to Marion Thomas, 22 February 1960, WMPC, Box 684, File 2; Mills to Martha Humphreys, 9 October 1962, WMPC, Box 323, File 14; Mills to J.K. Hale, 22 March 1960, WMPC, unprocessed.

[56] On the importance of the district to entrenched representatives, see Richard F. Fenno, Jr., *Home Style: House Members in their Districts* (Boston: Little, Brown, 1978).

[57] Wilbur Mills to John McCormack, 24 November 1958 and Mills to Henry Bailey, 22 December 1958, WMPC, Box 637, File 7; "Gerrymander Season," *Newsweek*, 1 May 1961, 37; "Integration Foes Wins in Arkansas," *The New York Times*, 6 November 1958; Brooks Hays, interview with John Luter, 27 July 1970, DEL, Oral History Interview Collection, Interview 3, 99–141.

[58] Bartley, *The New South, 1945–1980*, 241–242.

[59] Norman Ture, interview with Julian Zelizer, Washington, D.C., 13 December 1993; Editorial, "Mr. Sam's Chair," *The New Republic*, 30 December 1957, 5.

[60] *CQ Census Analysis: Congressional Districts of the U.S.* (Washington, D.C.: Congressional Quarterly Service, 1964), 1835; Stephen A. Merrill, *Wilbur D. Mills: Democratic Representative from Arkansas* (Washington, D.C.: Grossman Publishers, 1972), 7.

Meanwhile, Alford, who was now in Mills's district, threatened to challenge him in an election.[61] Once again, the chairman was forced to swing to the right on all issues that might be considered too liberal back in the district. Many of his colleagues and the press believed that civil rights and redistricting cost Mills the Speakership of the House after Rayburn's death in 1961.[62] It was virtually impossible to determine Mills's chances of becoming Speaker, especially as there was a tradition of having the Majority Leader ascend to the post. There was intense public speculation from the national media and among Mills's colleagues. Combined with the unpopularity of Majority Leader John McCormack (D-MA) within the House, the discussion fueled debate within Washington and, more important, it gave prominence in the national media to the question of Mills's opposition to civil rights legislation.

Redistricting doubled the size of Mills's constituency and added Little Rock's labor unions.[63] This brought a new interest group into his formerly rural constituency and forced him to change course again. Although union members remained a minority in his district, they were highly vocal and effective at political mobilization; the number of blue collar constituents, moreover, increased significantly.[64] Mills, who had become used to his safe and stable seat, was caught off guard with this development. In one incident, Mills seemed to have delayed hearings on an insurance-taxation bill because of union opposition. Preoccupied with redistricting and the unions, Mills made a couple of uncharacteristic "slip-ups." The unions continued to pressure Mills, particularly in the area of health care.[65] An AFL-CIO representative later warned President Kennedy that the redistricting issue might in fact paralyze Mills politically.[66] Mills himself conveyed a strong sense of being cross-pressured. He told George Ellison of the United Steelworkers of America that he would allow discussion of health care proposal for the elderly only if the

---

[61] Richard Lyons, "Redistricting Can Give 4 Arkansans Trouble," *The Washington Post*, 9 February 1961; Cassels, "This Man Shapes Your Tax Bill," 66.

[62] John McMillan to Wilbur Mills, 11 December 1961 and Mills to McMillan, 14 December 1961, WMPC, unprocessed; Mills to Emerson Schmidt, 4 September 1959, WMPC, Box 691, File 6; "Decline & Fall," *Time*, 7 September 1959, 11; Lawrence O'Brien, "Mills, Wilbur D.," 1961, JFKL, White House Staff Files, Lawrence O'Brien, House File: Mills, Wilbur (Folder 3).

[63] Merrill, *Wilbur D. Mills*, 7.

[64] *CQ Census Analysis: Congressional Districts of the U.S.* (Washington, D.C.: Congressional Quarterly Service, 1964), 1821.

[65] JMIC.

[66] Henry Hall Wilson to Lawrence O'Brien, 13 April 1961, JFKL, White House Staff Files, Henry Hall Wilson, Box 3, File: Memorandum 3/1/62–3/5/62.

union people promised to "cease stirring up grass roots complaints in his district."[67]

The chairman was resilient, however, and withstood the pressures of civil rights and redistricting. Several developments led him to success. First, in 1962, Alford unsuccessfully ran against Faubus for governor. This loss ended Alford's congressional career. Without Alford's electoral threat, Mills could concentrate more of his attention on federal policymaking and less on the district. Second, the chairman and his staff worked with well-situated government administrators at the local and national levels to satisfy the demands of crucial constituents and their interest groups, particularly local bankers and agricultural businessmen. Mills's office also sent new brides the Department of Agriculture's meal planning guide, new mothers the Department of HEW's child care manual, high school graduates a congratulatory letter, and letters of condolence to families whose relatives had died. During congressional recess, Mills always returned to the district to deliver speeches, attend dinners, and talk with constituents. The chairman often spent Sundays in Searcy, on his front porch or strolling down the streets, conversing informally with local residents.[68] Few individuals even attempted to challenge Mills; the chairman had never been opposed in a general election and, even more important for a one-party state, he had primary opposition only once after entering Congress. Mills also secured federal projects for his district, including a missile launching complex in Little Rock.[69]

The Ways and Means studies on tax reform

One of the most important factors behind Mills's success at overcoming the civil rights dilemma was his achievements with the tax

[67] James O'Brien to Lawrence O'Brien, 2 April 1962, JFKL, White House Staff Files, Lawrence O'Brien, Box 10, File: House File: Wilbur Mills, Arkansas, Folder 1.

[68] Merrill, *Wilbur D. Mills*, 2–3. Mills, for example, worked with Mortimer Caplin's staff in the IRS and Robert Goodwin in the Department of Labor to help Arkansas fish farmers with their tax problems. See Mortimer Caplin to Wilbur Mills, 6 June 1962 and 6 March 1963, WMPC, Box 155, File: Govt Dept. of Treasury: Inter. Rev. Service #1 Fish Farming 1962–67/2; Charles Donahue to Mills, 25 February 1963, WMPC, Box 155, File: Dept. of Treasury, Internal Revenue Service #1, Fish Farming, 1962–1967/3; Robert Goodwin to Mills, 19 March 1962, WMPC, Box 319, File: 12.

[69] Claude Desautels to Lawrence O'Brien, 5 December 1961; O'Brien to Henry Hall Wilson, 8 May 1962; Desautels to O'Brien, 20 December 1962, in JFKL, White House Staff Files, Lawrence O'Brien, Box 10, File: Mills, Wilbur D. (Folder 2); See also Claude Desautels to Lawrence O'Brien, JFKL, White House Staff Files, Lawrence O'Brien, Box 10, File: Mills, Wilbur D. (Folder 3); Staff, Office of the Congressional Liaison for Lyndon Johnson, 1963, LBJL, Congressional Favors File, Box 24, File: Mills, Wilbur D.

community and his growing reputation as a "fiscal expert." The chairman's highly praised work with the tax reform faction, including Stanley Surrey, Mortimer Caplin, and Joseph Pechman, diverted attention in the press and among his colleagues from his regional ties even though he continued to oppose most civil rights measures. He was able to walk the fine line between alienating the South and losing support in Congress. It was not always easy to stay on this line. Some southern colleagues expressed deep concern over his new identification. As one journalist commented, "Southern conservatives accuse him of trying to be an economic statesman – of being too greatly impressed by economists and other Northern eggheads."[70]

But Mills stayed on the line and strengthened his reputation through the widely publicized hearings on tax reform. Without ever changing his vote on civil rights, thereby securing his incumbency in Arkansas, Mills focused attention in Washington on his skills as a tax man; his staff continued to write constituents letters that opposed federal intervention on civil rights.[71] In January 1958 and November 1959, Mills brought together the various people who were working on tax reform, most of whom were drawn from the same pool of experts that he had used in previous years.[72] Mills had the staffs of the Joint Committee on Internal Revenue Taxation and the Treasury conduct a section-by-section analysis of the income-tax code in order to find small changes that could raise more revenue.[73]

Behind the scenes, Norman Ture, on loan from the Joint Economic Committee, and Stanley Surrey gathered participants and collected information in an "objective" fashion to avoid any "political" opposition.[74] While conducting these hearings, the committee intro-

[70] "The Man Who Steers Tax Policy," *Business Week*, 22 March 1958, 62.

[71] WMPC, Boxes 323 and 684. For a good discussion of the similar pressure the civil rights issue placed on another prominent Arkansan politician, and his similar response, see Randall Bennett Woods, *Fulbright: A Biography* (Cambridge: Cambridge University Press, 1995).

[72] Wilbur Mills to Stanley Surrey, 3 March 1958, SSP, Box 28, File 1; Surrey to Mills, 7 November 1958 and Mills to Surrey, 14 November 1958, WMPC, unprocessed; Surrey to Mills, 22 January 1958; Surrey to Mills, 30 July 1959; Surrey to Mills, 8 July 1959; Surrey to Mills, 26 August 1959 all in SSP, Box 28, File 1; Mortimer Caplin, "Address to the National Conference on Tax Reform of the Chamber of Commerce," 14 February 1968, SSP, Box 183, File 3.

[73] Fred Scribner to Wilbur Mills, 13 November 1959; Henry Wallich to Mills, 19 March 1959; and Mr. Eldridge to Fred Scribner, 1 September 1960, all in NAT, RG 56, Office of Tax Policy, Box 68, File: Tax Legislative Program For 1959.

[74] Stanley Surrey to Wilbur Mills, 24 December 1958, SSP, Box 40, File 5. See also Surrey to Mills, 17 November 1959; Surrey to Norman Ture, 25 September 1959; Surrey to Gerard Brannon, 31 August 1959, in SSP, Box 28, File 1. See also Mills to Norman Ture, 2 November 1959, WMPC, Box 784, File 7; Ture to Mills, 29 October 1959, WMPC, Box 784, File 7; Brannon to Mills, 10 November 1959; Staff, Com-

duced several new actors into the policy community, including Mortimer Caplin, a leading scholar on tax reform from the University of Virginia.[75] Mills, Surrey, and Gerard Brannon produced a highly praised, 2,382-page compendium on loophole-closing tax reform and rate reduction, with lead articles by Surrey, Walter Heller, and Joseph Pechman. There were also specialized articles and hearings on reforming the taxation of the aged, the taxation of interest on state and local bonds, the taxation of foreign income, and the taxation of capital gains.[76] To complete the research, Woodworth wrote several analyses of the feasibility of specific base-broadening reforms.[77] The compendium became a "tax law bible" for that generation of policymakers.[78]

The studies revealed that there were many different types of tax

mittee on Ways and Means, "Confidential Staff Document Digest and Commentary on Compendium of Papers on Broadening of the Tax Base," 9 November 1959; Norman Ture to Harry Kahn and Danny Holland, 11 May 1959, all in NA, RG 233, Box 6342, File: Income Tax Rates.

[75] Mortimer Caplin, interview with Shelley Davis and Kecia McDonald, 18–25 November 1991, Internal Revenue Service, Oral History Interview, 5–6; U.S. Congress, House Committee on Ways and Means, *Tax Revision Compendium: Compendium of Papers on Broadening the Tax Base*, 86th Cong., 1959; U.S. Congress, House Committee on Ways and Means, *General Revenue Revision: Hearings before the Committee on Ways and Means*, 85th Cong., 2nd sess., 1958. Regarding Mills's use of a common pool of experts, see Norman Ture to Wilbur Mills, 11 May 1959, NA, RG 233, 87th Cong., Box 6342, File: Income Tax: Rates; Norman Ture to Mills, 29 October 1959; Mills to Ture, 2 November 1959 and Ture to Mills, 5 November 1959, WMPC, Box 784, File 7; "Tax Reform Panel To Discuss Wide Range of Topics," *The Wall Street Journal*, 5 June 1959; Editorial, "Studying the Obvious," *The Wall Street Journal*, 20 May 1959.

[76] Wilbur J. Cohen, "Income and Tax Status of the Aged"; Joseph A. Pechman, "What Would a Comprehensive Individual Income Tax Yield"; Richard Musgrave, "How Progressive is the Income Tax?"; Dan Throop Smith, "Tax Treatment of Capital Gains"; John M. Sullivan, "Accounting Provisions"; J. Fred Weston, "Accelerated Depreciation and Opportunities for Tax Avoidance," all in the U.S. Congress, House Committee on Ways and Means, *Tax Revision Compendium: Compendium of Papers on Broadening The Tax Base*, 1959, H0603 (Committee – Print). See also Stanley Surrey, "The Income Tax Base for Individuals," 1959, NA, RG 233, Box 6342, File: Income Tax Rates.

[77] JCIRT Staff, *Alternative Plans For Tax Relief For Individuals*, 25 February 1958, NA, RG 233, Box 6342, File: Income Tax Rates; Joint Staff, JCIRT and Treasury Department, *The Technical Amendments Bill of 1960 H.R. 9625 and H.R. 9626*, 14 January 1960, H4790 (Committee–Print); Joint Staff, JCIRT and Treasury Department, *Staff Data: Notes on Background of Existing Provisions of the Federal Income and Employment Tax Laws*, 25 August 1960, H11261 (Committee – Print); JCIRT Staff, NA, RG 128, Box 336, File: Sec. 521; JCIRT Staff, *Internal Revenue Code of 1954 as Amended and in Force on January 3, 1961*, 3 January 1961, J0535 (Committee – Print).

[78] Mortimer Caplin, interview with Shelley Davis and Kecia McDonald, 18–25 November 1991, 5. See also Fred Scribner to Wilbur Mills, 18 December 1959, NAT, RG 56, Office of Tax Policy, Box 68, File: Tax Legislative Program For 1959.

breaks, all of which had to be considered during reform. First, there were technical errors in the code that provided lawyers with room to evade the laws. Second, vague statutory language enabled lawyers to work around the original intention of the laws. Third, there were provisions that Congress enacted with the intent of providing relief to one particular company or individual. Fourth, there were credits, exemptions, and exceptions designed to encourage entire categories of citizens and industries to invest their money in particular ways. During most discussions about reform, policymakers, reporters, and citizens paid little attention to the differences between these tax breaks, and randomly used a variety of terms to describe them, including "loopholes," "preferences," "credits," "incentives," "advantages," and "special allowances."[79] Nonetheless, in substantive efforts for reform, each type of tax break had to be considered through different criteria.

The Ways and Means studies made political headlines by effectively articulating the idea of tax reform. "Tax reform," according to the committee, should reduce tax rates "without sacrificing revenues required for responsible financing of government." This would create a more favorable climate for economic growth, stable prices, greater compliance, and "horizontal equity," the notion that equal incomes should pay equal taxes and that there should be fewer distinctions between different types of income. To achieve these controversial reforms, Congress needed to balance the "tangible" economic benefit of each provision against the "intangible" cost of impairing the income-tax structure.[80]

Until such reforms were completed, citizens would continue to convert their income into nontaxable money and to lobby for more loopholes for certain groups; as Walter Heller explained, the back door to government subsidies marked "tax relief" was "easier to push open than the front door marked 'expenditures' or the side door marked 'loans, guarantees, and insurance.' "[81] Lower rates, combined

---

[79] The term loophole was first identified in 1591 when it was used to describe a "narrow vertical opening, usually widening inwards . . . to allow of the passage of missiles." The first known usage to mean "an outlet or means of escape" was in 1663. J.A. Simpson and E.S.C. Weiner, *The Oxford English Dictionary*, volume IX (Oxford: Clarendon Press, 1989), 14.

[80] Walter Heller, "Some Observations On The Role and Reform of the Federal Income Tax," in U.S. Congress, House Committee on Ways and Means, *Tax Revision Compendium: Compendium of Papers on Broadening The Tax Base*, 1959, H0603 (Committee – Print), 189.

[81] Heller, "Some Observations on the Role and Reform of the Federal Income Tax," 190; U.S. Congress, House Committee on Ways and Means, *General Revenue Revision: Hearings*, 85th Cong., 2nd sess., 1958, 3074–3085.

with loophole-closing reforms, could thus raise more revenue than under the existing system. Ultimately, reform would create a tax system that operated with minimum interference in the "operation of the free market mechanism in directing resources into their most productive uses."[82] The studies filled out these broad principles with concrete suggestions for reform, such as Surrey's proposal for withholding on interest and dividends.

Outside of Congress, Mills promoted these ideas through the specialized media of fiscal policymakers. In September, for example, he published an essay in the *Prentice Hall Newsletter* warning that "our taxpayers – including businessmen – are becoming aware in searching the Internal Revenue Code, that the tax differentials and preferences now existing, which cut our tax base by billions of dollars, do not contain any privilege or benefit from them. They know that these differentials and preferences mean generally higher tax rates than would be necessary if . . . every dollar of income for tax purposes were treated alike."[83] If Congress broadened the definition of taxable income, he said, they could reduce rates by up to 40 percent.[84] At Caplin's invitation, Mills also published a preface for the *Virginia Law Review* in which he called for a "new beginning" to income-tax policy.[85] To simplify these ideas for reporters, Mills relied on the following concept: "We can think of our income tax as a triangle, the area of which is the revenue collected. The base of the triangle is taxable income and the height of the triangle is the rate schedule. We can get the same area from a narrow base and high rate schedule or a broad base and low rate schedule."[86]

Professional think tanks joined the effort to promote the rhetoric of tax reform. The Tax Foundation, for example, released *The Federal Individual Income Tax: Revising the Rate and Bracket Structure*, which it

---

[82] U.S. Congress, House Committee on Ways and Means, *Tax Revision Compendium: Compendium of Papers on Broadening the Tax Base*, 86th Cong., ix. See also Leo Irwin to Stanley Surrey, 29 October 1957, SSP, Box 28, File 1; Wilbur Mills, "How Your Income Taxes Can Be Cut," *Nation's Business*, November 1959, 71–76; Mills, "The Possibilities of Major Tax Reform," 7 November 1959, WMPC, Box 784, File 7; Mills, "Remarks of Wilbur Mills before the Annual Meeting of the Arkansas Savings and Loan League," 15 October 1960, WMPC, Box 781, File 10; "Rep. Mills Proposes Broadening Tax Base to Increase Revenues, Suggests Some Levies Might Be Boosted," *The Wall Street Journal*, 3 December 1958; U.S. Congress, House Committee on Ways and Means, *General Revenue Revision: Hearings*, 85th Cong., 2nd sess., 1958, 2–3.

[83] Wilbur D. Mills, "Possible Tax Legislation in the 86th Congress," *The Prentice-Hall Federal Tax Guide: Current Report* XXVIII, No. 36 (8 September 1958): 1–4.

[84] "The Man Who Steers Tax Policy," *Business Week*, 22 March 1958, 60.

[85] Wilbur D. Mills, "Preface," *Virginia Law Review* 44, No. 6 (October 1958): 835–838.

[86] Wilbur D. Mills, "How Your Income Taxes Can Be Cut," *Nation's Business*, November 1959, 72.

distributed to members of the tax-writing committees. The publication emphasized the importance of rate reduction to an overall agenda of reform; only by lowering rates could Congress "reduce inequities, to minimize distorting effects on economic decisions, and to promote economic growth."[87] Independent experts and academic scholars were also active in this process. Dan Throop Smith, now a professor at Harvard, told the American Economic Association that "the most important single reform is to reduce the excessive rates of the individual income tax and tighten the definition of taxable income to cut down on present abuses, legal and illegal, and assure more equal treatment of taxpayers." He assured economists that reform no longer meant the radical redistribution of wealth because the New Deal's "extreme economic egalitarianism" was dead. Even those who favored high rates "as a matter of social philosophy," he said, "have recognized that on balance they are bad because they distort personal and business decisions and lead to action and attitudes which may jeopardize the income tax itself."[88]

Although these ideas about tax reform were not new to the tax field, this was the first time that they had been synthesized so effectively and given so much attention in Washington. More important, they were completed under the aegis of a tax-writing committee that was known more for its work with oil lobbies than for its ties to Harvard economists. Certainly, there were problems with the studies. In 1959, for example, the House Republican leader Charles Halleck (R-IN) attacked the "radical" Senator Paul Douglas (D-IL) for infiltrating the studies by placing his expert, Norman Ture, on the staff of Ways and Means.[89] These sorts of struggles were understandable because on many occasions, committee members delegated authority to the experts to evaluate the demands of other policymakers.

Mills's expertise

But Mills handled these problems effectively, and they were overshadowed by his success during the hearings at creating new levels of

[87] Tax Foundation, *The Federal Individual Income Tax: Revising the Rate and Bracket Structure* (Washington D.C.: Tax Foundation, 1959); John Martin, Jr. to Herbert Miller, 10 February 1960; Miller to Members of Congress, 15 December 1959, in NA, RG 233, Box 6342, File: Income Taxes, Individual and Corporation. See also Committee for Economic Development, *Tax Reduction And Tax Reform – When and How*, May 1957, HTL, Papers of Paul G. Hoffman, Box 142, Folder: Committee for Economic Development.

[88] Dan Throop Smith, "A Program For Federal Tax Reform" (Speech delivered to the Annual Meeting of American Economic Association), 30 December 1959, WMPC, unprocessed.

[89] Unidentified McGraw-Hill representative to Wilbur Mills, 7 November 1959, WMPC, unprocessed.

"expertise" in the tax-writing process. In doing so, he defined his chairmanship in large part on his fiscal "expertise" rather than primarily on his partisanship or his ability to broker congressional deals. Mills, said colleagues, knew "the tax system just inside and out, backwards and forwards," and could "run circles around anybody in the country on the tax law and its problems."[90] Members of Ways and Means were convinced of the accuracy of such statements; as one representative said: "We have a chairman who is so thoroughly knowledgeable in his field. There isn't anything in taxes he fails to understand or fails to relate to what has gone before and tie it into today."[91] His knowledge was so thorough that government officials began to say he did not even depend on the experts. "He understands tax legislation better than any person I know," commented one lawyer, "He reads every bill and report as thoroughly as the staff. He can hold his own in a technical discussion with any tax attorney, or with any of the Treasury's experts."[92]

In practice, however, Mills carefully used experts to enhance this image. He relied on them to persuade other legislators to grant him authority over complex policies. One staff member recalled that during committee markups, "Woodworth would go over the staff pamphlet with Mills the night before. As a result, Mills and Woodworth had the material down cold. At the markup, Mills would say things like, 'Larry, didn't we try something like this back in 1954?' Woodworth had told him about that the night before." After that, "the rest of the members would just sit there dumbfounded, dazzled by the knowledge of Mills and Woodworth."[93] A prominent committee member remembered a similar encounter with Stam. "He and Stam would go back and forth on the bill section by section: what happened in '36, '37, '38. It was quite a performance."[94]

To improve his knowledge, the chairman also depended on experts to pass information between himself and the tax community and to analyze a flow of data that was admittedly "cryptic and technical."[95] In particular, he would work with a talented, albeit small, group of legal and economic experts at his committee's disposal. Leo

---

[90] Gardner Ackely, interview with Joe Franz, 13 April 1973, LBJL, Oral History Interview Collection, 4.

[91] JMIC. Almost all of the people whom Manley interviewed mentioned two factors beyond Mills's offical position that accounted for his influence: congressional skills and fiscal expertise.

[92] John Cauley, "Mills of Arkansas, Powerful Voice in Congress," *Kansas City Times*, 22 August 1961.

[93] Thomas J. Reese, *The Politics of Taxation* (New York: Quorum Books, 1980), 69.

[94] JMIC.

[95] Joseph Pechman to Wilbur Mills, 17 September 1959, WMPC, unprocessed.

Irwin was the chief counsel; John Martin, Jr., served as assistant chief counsel; and Gerard Brannon, James Riddell, and Raymond Conkling led the professional staff. Among others were Harold Lamar, James Kelley, William Fullerton, Charles Hawkins, Robert Hill, and William Kane, all of whom worked for the committee staff at some point during Mills's chairmanship. Ways and Means had several additional sources of expertise, including the House Legislative Counsel, the Library of Congress, and the staff of the JCIRT.

As chairman, Mills had discovered that the bipartisan staff of the JCIRT, which included skilled economists, lawyers, and tax accountants, was very influential in the tax-writing process; it included former private attorneys and economists as well as employees of the IRS, the Treasury, Justice Department, and Bureau of the Budget. The JCIRT staff helped Mills forge compromises between the House, the Senate, and the executive branch. Because of its influence, the staff attracted some of the most respected tax experts in the nation: Colin Stam led the group from 1938 until 1964; Laurence Woodworth took over in 1964, having served on the staff since 1944.[96] Both men were among the highest paid staffers in Congress. Starting in his first year as chair, Mills drew heavily on their analytical skills. Stam and Woodworth published several important studies on revenue-raising reforms, they interpreted proposals from the executive branch, and they provided important analyses of the budget.[97]

[96] JMIC; Joseph Barr to Claude Desautels, 25 February 1963, SSP, Box 177, File 2; Reese, *The Politics of Taxation*, 61–88; Manley, *The Politics of Finance*, 307–319.

[97] Colin Stam to Wilbur Mills, 28 January 1957, WMPC, Box 701, File 1; Staff, JCIRT, "Staff Study I: Simplification of the Individual Income Tax Return," 28 January 1957 and Stam to Mills, 13 May 1957 and Eugene Thore to Mills, 31 October 1957, WMPC, unprocessed; Leo Irwin to Members of the Committee on Ways and Means, 11 January 1958, NA, RG 233 [Papers of the House Committee on Ways and Means], 85th Cong., Box 6337, File: Budget – 1961; Stam to Mills, 19 February 1958, WMPC, unprocessed; Staff, JCIRT, 25 February 1958 and Irwin to Members of the Committee on Ways and Means, 26 February 1958, NA, RG 233, 85th Cong., Box 6342, File: Income Rates; Stam to Mills, 23 January 1959, NA, RG 128 [Papers of the Joint Committee on Internal Revenue Taxation], Box 460, File: Budget 1959; Gerard Brannon to Leo Irwin, 10 May 1958, NA, RG 233, 85th Cong., Box 6345, File: Taxation of Co-ops; Norman Ture to Irwin, 6 May 1959 and Ture to Harry Kahn and Danny Holland, 11 May 1959, NA, RG 233, 86th Cong., Box 6342, File: Income Rates; Brannon to Mills, 8 December 1960, NA, RG 233, 86th Cong., Box 6338, File: Economy; Irwin to Members of the Committee on Ways and Means, 23 January 1961, NA, RG 233, 87th Cong., Box 6337, File: Budget – 1961; Irwin to Members of the Ways and Means Committee, 8 March 1961, NA, RG 233, 87th Cong., Box 6338, File: Economy; Gerard Brannon to Irwin, 28 June 1961 and Irwin to Democratic Members of the Committee on Ways and Means, 30 August 1961, NA, RG 233, 87th Cong., Box 6337, File: Budget – 1961; Staff, JCIRT, "Treatment of Costs in Excess of Mineral Income," 1962, NA, RG 128, Box 337, File: Sec. 611 1956–1964.

Furthermore, they wrote the "guff" of committee reports, which included a general explanation, a history, and a summary of each particular bill.[98]

Through these projects, Stam and Woodworth mediated between the policymakers, who proposed legislation, and the "technicians" from the Tax Legislative Counsel, who drafted committee bills. Ed Craft and Ward Hussey, Mills's tax technicians, also maintained extensive files of "Limbo Drafts," bills that were kept on file until an opportunity emerged to propose them; Representative Eugene Keogh's (D-NY) plan to provide self-employed persons with tax deductible retirement plans, for example, remained in limbo for almost three decades.[99] The staff worked in seclusion while preparing confidential reports on tax legislation. Stam and Woodworth suppressed these "committee prints" until they were released in the Ways and Means executive sessions. Woodworth did not share the material with others in Congress or with committee members who were not in the sessions.[100]

Through his work with the tax policy community, Mills overcame the problem of civil rights and maintained smooth relationships with tax experts in Washington and voters in Arkansas. He presented one image in Washington and another in Arkansas. Mills went so far as to install a private phone in his office exclusively for local supporters. While speaking on the line, Mills literally changed his voice, turning "that Southern accent off and on just like hot and cold running water." AFL-CIO expert Nelson Cruikshank recalled an important meeting between Mills and a group of Social Security experts. As Mills spoke to the experts, he sounded like a "Harvard law graduate." When he picked up the phone, however, "the Southern accent and all these little colloquialisms will swing in and you'd hardly know it was the same person – even a different pitch of the voice, that you get from a Deep South cracker. He'll do that all the way through. Then without ever batting an eye he'll hang up the phone, turn to

---

[98] David J. Stern, "Congress, Politics, and Taxes: A Case Study Of The Revenue Act of 1962" (Ph.D diss., Claremont Graduate School, 1965), 218–219.

[99] Ward Hussey, interview with Julian Zelizer, 19 May 1994; David Lindsay to Wilbur Mills, 27 January 1960, DEL, Files of Gerald Morgan, Box 17, Folder: Legislation Pending. For further discussions of the congressional staff, see Michael J. Malbin, *Unelected Representatives: Congressional Staff and the Future of Representative Government* (New York: Basic Books, 1979); Susan Webb Hammond, "Congressional Staffs," in *Encyclopedia of the American Legislative System*, 785–800; Harrison W. Fox, Jr., and Hammond, *Congressional Staffs: The Invisible Force in American Lawmaking* (New York: Free Press, 1977).

[100] Richard Spohn and Charles McCollum, eds., *The Revenue Committees: A Study of the House Ways and Means and Senate Finance Committees and the House and Senate Appropriations Committees* (New York: Viking Press, 1975), 50.

you and talk to you again in the same tone of voice and accent of a Harvard law graduate . . . not the least bit abashed by this."[101]

SECURELY ON THE HILL

By 1962, Mills had overcome difficult professional challenges by relying on two important assets. First, his congressional acumen ensured the passage of most of the bills that he supported. He learned to take full advantage of the procedural advantages and political clout that were granted to the chairman of Ways and Means. He used these advantages to secure sufficient votes for committee legislation and to please interest groups who monitored his panel. Second, his reputation as an expert and his analytical skills enabled him to engage the complex, technocratic world of the tax community while designing everything from Social Security to income-tax reform. As one colleague astutely noted: "I had some misgivings when Mills took over as chairman from Cooper because I thought it might be better to have two men in the two roles. The two roles are the procedural chairman, and the technical. I thought it was better to have these separate, Cooper as chairman, Mills for technical matters. But it's worked out perfectly, beyond all my hopes. Mills is both, procedural and technical, and he does both beautifully."[102]

Certainly, Mills would have been influential as chairman of Ways and Means, regardless of whether he was a neophyte or an expert. Nonetheless, the reputation he developed diverted attention from his southern roots, enhanced the productivity of his deliberations with the tax community, and increased his political clout within Congress. Mills earned a reputation for having a set of professional characteristics that were highly valued in Washington, D.C. Within Congress, David Mayhew argued, "the hero of the Hill is not the hero of the airwaves. The member who earns prestige among his peers is the lonely gnome who passes up news conferences, cocktail parties, sometimes even marriage in order to devote his time to legislative 'homework.' "[103]

For the same reason that representatives depended on "control committees," they created an "internal currency" of prestige to reward workaholics such as Mills, who maintained the integrity of

---

[101] Nelson Cruikshank, interview with Peter Corning, 15 February 1966, COHP, Social Security Administration Project, Interview 2, 83–84; Wilbur D. Mills, interview with Lewis E. Weeks, 13 August 1980, Hospital Administration Oral History Collection, Library of the American Hospital Association (Chicago, Illinois, 1983), 34–35.

[102] JMIC.

[103] Mayhew, *Congress*, 147.

Congress and consulted respected policy experts in addition to
interest groups. While the tax community had little choice but to
work with Mills, given his position in the House, its negotiations
with the chairman were more intense, more frequent, and more
interactive than they might otherwise have been. This had become
evident during the process through which the Community devised
the Social Security Amendments of 1958 and conducted the tax
reform studies, which produced data and momentum that fueled
future tax reform efforts. In fact, Joseph Pechman later credited
Mills's studies for boosting the cause of tax reform from the start of
his chairmanship.[104]

Mills's position was such that by 1962 he would become even more
influential in the agenda-setting and legislative processes of the
national state. Rayburn's death, his replacement by a politically timid
John McCormack, and the reform of Howard Smith's powerful Rules
Committee created a congressional power vacuum. Mills stepped in.
When Kennedy became president, James Reston quipped: "The first
question for President Kennedy on the new year is not whether he
can get along with Chairman Nikita Khrushchev but whether he can
co-exist with Chairman Wilbur Mills."[105] In 1962, several major pieces
of legislation were on the floor under the jurisdiction of the Ways and
Means Committee including Social Security amendments, the trade
expansion act, public welfare reform, and the revenue act. One journalist noted: "This year, he [Mills] is somewhat reluctantly destined
for an unprecedented apotheosis. For the first time in living memory,
all four of the session's biggest, toughest bills must be handled by a
single congressional committee, the Ways and Means Committee,
headed by Mills."[106]

[104] Joseph A. Pechman, "Tax Reform: Theory and Practice," *Journal of Economic Perspectives* 1, No. 1 (Summer 1987): 12–13.
[105] Cited in Joe Purcell, "The Wilbur D. Mills Story," *The Arkansas Lawyer* 6, No. 2
(March 1972): 52.
[106] Alsop, "The Legislator."

5

The Postwar Fiscal Discourse

Throughout his tenure as chairman of Ways and Means, Mills operated through the tax community. By balancing the competing needs of its factions, and by translating their ideas into legislative victories, he expanded his influence. But the process through which these policies were formulated and implemented clearly was full of conflict, contest, and uncertainty. There were moments when Mills and his colleagues outside Congress could not have been farther apart on important issues, ranging from the War on Poverty to tax breaks. Despite highly contentious debates, the policymakers acted as a community: They recognized themselves as the legitimate figures in policymaking who shared certain approaches to politics.

Between the 1940s and 1970s, the ties among all of the policymakers were strengthened by a shared political discourse, which included its own vocabulary and certain conceptions of the political economy. As Mills's colleagues came to express their ideas in this discourse, they communicated with each other more effectively, and at the same time they limited access to their debates. They were, as one former Treasury official noted, a "community of like-minded people."[1] What they were like-minded about was the postwar fiscal discourse – what role fiscal policy should play in the economy and how fiscal policies should be decided. Because this discourse combined several important, and often contradictory, intellectual traditions, each policymaker selected the parts of the language that he wanted to use; each faction of the community, moreover, emphasized a different aspect of the discourse. But these choices tended to remain within the intellectual boundaries of the discourse that defined their policy community; the discourse transcended the divisions among policymakers.

This chapter turns to the content of the postwar discourse. In other chapters, I discuss the unexamined assumptions that shaped the "technical" components of the discourse. For example, Chapters 2,

---

[1] Stanford Ross coined this useful phrase during a 1993–1994 workshop at the Woodrow Wilson International Center for Scholars.

4, 7, and 10 show how the tax community maintained a rhetorical link between payroll taxes and social insurance benefits; Chapters 3, 6, and 8 look at how the community defined income taxation in economic terms, while Chapters 4 and 9 describe how the community articulated a particular concept of tax reform. This chapter turns to the second aspect of the postwar discourse – the larger context within which taxes were formulated. In particular, the discourse centered on a conversation about the relationship between the state, fiscal policy, and civil society. Unlike the rest of *Taxing America*, this chapter does not provide a chronological narrative. Instead, it provides an overview of the main, shared components of the discourse that shaped the tax community throughout its existence. The analysis focuses primarily on the words of Mills, while incorporating the language of other members, to highlight the areas in which he found agreement with the community. While there were many areas of disagreement, the discourse helped establish certain parameters of debate among members of the community. To define those boundaries, the final section of the chapter examines alternative world views that the community excluded.

Discourse looms larger here than in other chapters. Historians touching the subject of discourse step into a heated area of controversy. First, scholars must answer the question of the relationship between discourse and institutions. My thoughts are best expressed through the words of the historian Michael Kazin: "Political discourse does not speak itself; it is the creation of people engaged in institutions with varied resources and agendas."[2] Second, scholars must explain what exactly they are studying when looking at "discourse." On this matter, I rely heavily on the work of the historian Dorothy Ross, who argues that discourse is a conversation that develops around certain problems and issues. The language of discourse provides historical actors with a "distinctive logic" and "rhetorical armory" through which actors express their ideas. Most important, language is used to express different ideas; language also has effects other than the ones its users intended.[3] By "mobilizing the raw materials of emotions into enthusiasms, commitments, and prejudices," political discourse and the culture within which it exists encourage political actors to react in certain ways to particular events.[4]

---

[2] Michael Kazin, *The Populist Persuasion: An American History* (New York: Basic Books, 1995), 285–286.
[3] Dorothy Ross, *The Origins of American Social Science* (Cambridge: Cambridge University Press, 1991), xviii–xxii.
[4] Joyce Appleby, *Liberalism and Republicanism in the Historical Imagination* (Cambridge, MA: Harvard University Press, 1992), 19.

For scholars of politics, discourse offers a way to overcome debate about whether one should focus on the real "interests" of politicians or the ideas they promoted. In fact, both are important and closely related. The study of political discourse takes seriously what politicians said, how they used a particular language to express multiple ideas and, in turn, how that language shaped their interests and behavior. This type of scholarship also demonstrates how political interests were most effective at shaping policy when they presented their claims through language that carried the "intellectual bona fides of good public policy."[5]

TALKING ABOUT TAXES

The postwar fiscal discourse included a domesticated Keynesianism that was framed in terms of moderate government intervention to ensure the health and stability of the corporate capitalist economy.[6] The goal of "economic growth," rather than the threat of "stagna-

---

[5] M. Stephen Weatherford with Thomas B. Mayhew, "Tax Policy and Presidential Leadership: Ideas, Interests, and the Quality of Advice," *Studies in American Political Development* 9, No. 2 (Fall 1995): 287–330. See also Paul J. Quirk, "In Defense of the Politics of Ideas," *The Journal of Politics* 50, No. 1 (February 1988): 31–41; Judith Goldstein and Robert O. Keohane, *Ideas and Foreign Policy: Beliefs, Institutions, and Political Change* (Ithaca: Cornell University Press, 1993).

[6] Some scholars who stress the role of the corporate world in weakening Keynesianism use the phrase "commercial Keynesianism." Others, who place greater emphasis in their narratives on the role of academic scholars, think-tank participants, and politicians in transforming Keynesianism criticize the term "commercial" for placing excessive weight on business. I use the term "domesticated" (borrowed from Herbert Stein) to describe the ways in which Keynesianism took hold on the home front in the United States by focusing on tax cuts instead of spending increases and preserving an emphasis on long-term balanced budgets. For a fuller discussion of this issue, see Herbert Stein, "The fiscal revolution in America, part II: 1964–1994," in W. Elliot Brownlee, ed., *Funding the Modern American State: The Rise and Fall of the Era of Easy Finance, 1941–1995* (Cambridge: Cambridge University Press and Washington, D.C.: Woodrow Wilson Center Press, 1996), 194–195, and Herbert Stein, *The Fiscal Revolution in America*, revised edition (Washington, D.C.: AEI Press, 1990); John J. Coleman, *Party Decline in America: Policy, Politics, and the Fiscal State* (Princeton: Princeton University Press, 1996); Alan Brinkley, *The End of Reform: New Deal Liberalism In Recession and War* (New York: Alfred A. Knopf, 1995); Margaret Weir, *Politics and Jobs: The Boundaries of Employment Policy in the United States* (Princeton: Princeton University Press, 1992); Cathie J. Martin, *Shifting the Burden: The Struggle over Growth and Corporate Taxation* (Chicago: University of Chicago Press, 1991); Margaret Weir and Theda Skocpol, "State Structures the Possibilities for 'Keynesian' Responses to the Great Depression in Sweden, Britain, and the United States," in *Bringing the State Back In*, eds. Peter Evans, Dietrich Rueschemeyer, and Theda Skocpol (Cambridge: Cambridge University Press, 1985), 107–163; Robert M. Collins, *The Business Response To Keynes* (New York: Columbia University Press, 1981).

tion," was a central feature of the language: Growth, the policymakers argued, promised a larger piece of the economic pie for every
citizen.[7] To reach the full potential of the market, they said, the government should increase both private investment and consumer
demand, thus combining the ideas of Andrew Mellon and John
Maynard Keynes.

In the 1960s version of Keynesianism, the federal government
was called on to intervene occasionally, avoiding direct management of economic institutions and leaving corporate managerial
prerogatives unchanged. Government policymakers could help the
economy overcome "performance gaps" and reach its full potential
through expansive fiscal policies in three ways: by spurring capital
investment through government incentives such as tax breaks, by
stimulating demand through monetary adjustments and income-tax
reductions, and by increasing defense or automatic expenditures.[8]
Taxation, not spending, was thought of as the central instrument for
promoting investment and increasing demand. The fiscal discourse
looked on moderate budget deficits as useful, even in non-
recessionary times, because they could spur economic growth,
stimulate consumer demand, generate more tax revenue, and create
higher employment.

Although policymakers thus openly accepted deficits by the early
1960s, the ghosts of the traditional balanced-budget rhetoric and
the importance of "fiscal responsibility" lurked in the language of
the day. The continued influence of fiscal conservatism ensured the
persistence of this concern and limited the rhetoric of those who
embraced deficit finance. President Kennedy expressed this ambiva-
lence, proclaiming in 1963: "Our choice today is not between a
tax cut and a balanced budget. Our choice is between chronic deficits
resulting from chronic slack, on the one hand, and transitional
deficits temporarily enlarged by tax revision designed to promote

[7] Robert M. Collins, "The emergence of economic growthmanship in the United
States: Federal policy and economic knowledge in the Truman years," in *The State
and Economic Knowledge: The American and British Experiences*, eds. Mary Furner and
Barry Supple (Cambridge: Cambridge University Press and Washington, D.C.:
Woodrow Wilson International Center For Scholars, 1990), 138–170; Ronald F. King,
Money, Time, and Politics: Investment Tax Subsidies and American Democracy (New Haven:
Yale University Press, 1993); Collins, "Growth Liberalism in the Sixties," in *The Sixties:
From Memory to History*, ed. David Farber (Chapel Hill: University of North Carolina
Press, 1994), 11–44.

[8] Economic Advisory Group of the Department of Treasury, "Fiscal Policy: Broad
Issues," 2 May 1963, SSP, Box 176, File 1; Norman Ture, "Priorities in Tax Policy for
the Next Decade: Presented to 19th National Tax Conference," 5 December 1967,
SSP, Box 188, File 3.

full employment and thus make possible an ultimately balanced budget."[9]

In seeking faster economic growth, Mills and the community accepted a particular type of state. "When one looks at the specific issues of public affairs," Mills insisted, "slogans about conservatism or liberalism have very limited value."[10] Mills claimed that because of the "chronic and growing" economic problems of the post-World War II era, income taxation and contributory social insurance were integral to "competitive, private enterprise."[11] Mills often reminded audiences, "We live in a complex and dangerous age and there is no use pretending that on some happy day very soon we can cut government expenditures to the point where we will no longer need large tax revenues."[12]

In his language and voting record, Mills proved to be an ardent defender of expansive military programs, highway development, and contributory social insurance. "The good economic society," Mills said, "is fair and humane."[13] Regarding Social Security, Mills argued: "How can it be said that we are doing something for that individual [benefit recipient] for nothing? Certainly he is at least entitled to say he is buying and paying for that security against need in his old age."[14]

---

[9] John F. Kennedy, Press Release, "The White House: Special Message On Tax Reduction and Tax Reform," 24 January 1963, JFKL, Presidential Office Files, Box 52, File: 1/24/63 Special Message on Tax Reduction and Reform. See also Theodore Sorenson, interview with Carl Kaysen, 26 March 1964, JFKL, Oral History Interview Collection, 50–57; Henry Fowler, interview with David McComb, 10 January 1969, LBJL, Oral History Interview Collection, 19–24; Walter Heller, interview with David McComb, 20 February 1970, LBJL, Oral History Interview Collection, Interview I, 24; Wilbur Mills to Heller, 10 May 1968, WMPC, Box 508, File 4; Mills, "Some International and Domestic Aspects of Tax and Expenditure Policy," *Tax Review* XXX, No. 1 (January 1969): 1–4; Charles Murphy to Leon Keyserling, 19 December 1949, HTL, Leon Keyserling Papers, Box 8, Folder: White House Contacts – Charles Murphy.

[10] Wilbur D. Mills, "Remarks before the Chamber of Commerce," 16 January 1962, WMPC, Box 784, File 17.

[11] Wilbur D. Mills, "Let's Strengthen the Income Tax," 1956, WMPC, Box 408, File 16. See also Mills, "Remarks of the Honorable Wilbur D. Mills before the Little Rock Rotary Club," 29 November 1962, WMPC, Box 591, File: Mills Speeches; Mills, "Fiscal Policy and the Economy: Speech," 4 November 1965, WMPC, Box 658, File 6; Mills, "The Role of Employment Security in a Changing Economy: Address to the Institute of the IAPES, Little Rock, Arkansas," 27 October 1960, WMPC, Box 781, File 5.

[12] Wilbur D. Mills, "Are You a Pet Or a Patsy?" *Life*, 23 November 1959, 62.

[13] Wilbur D. Mills, "Fiscal Policy and the Good Economic Society," 20 April 1967, WMPC, Box 644, File 8.

[14] Cited in Martha Derthick, *Policymaking for Social Security* (Washington: Brookings Institution, 1979), 248–249. See also Wilbur D. Mills, "Improvements in Social Security Programs Made by the 86th Congress: Address to Meeting of State Welfare Department Employees of the State of Arkansas," 1960, WMPC, Box 784, File 11.

Mills spoke of financing social insurance programs that maintained the "traditional family structure" and that avoided interfering, as much as possible, with the market. Government assistance, he argued, should enable people to become "self-sufficient," and should avoid causing "dependency" on the government.[15]

More than any other issue in the postwar discourse, welfare created conflict within the community. For while Mills harbored a deep antagonism toward noncontributory welfare, colleagues such as Walter Heller were less hostile toward means-tested benefits. Nonetheless, there were areas of broad agreement even on welfare. Mills and Heller both talked about the destructive moral consequences that resulted from an excessive reliance on these types of benefits. During the 1960s, policy discussions shifted from "relieving" poverty to "rehabilitating" the poor from welfare.[16] The discussion of welfare played down the importance of economic and political power, while focusing on the issues of bad values and immoral behavior.[17] Mills's rhetoric about welfare can be gleaned through a speech about welfare reform. Two postwar developments, according to Mills, had necessitated reform. First, the massive migration of people from agricultural, rural areas to industrial, urban residences led to overburdened relief rolls. Second, most of these migrants, who were formerly "self-sufficient" farmers, had become "rootless" in the new urban environment, "completely unprepared for city life." To find support, generations took "refuge" in welfare as a "new way of life." While Mills avoided any overt racial language, his reference to the postwar migration of African-Americans was clear. Because of these changes, Mills warned, "the public welfare program of providing a monthly cash

---

[15] Wilbur D. Mills, "The Congress and the Demands For Service: Remarks before the Arkansas Conference of Social Welfare," 6 November 1964, WMPC, Box 590, File 7; Mills, "A New Charter for Public Welfare: Address to the Public Welfare Employees of the State of Arkansas," 13 December 1962, WMPC, Box 591, File: Mills Speech.

[16] Wilbur Cohen to the Secretary, 6 June 1967, WCP, Box 92, Folder 8; Abraham Ribicoff to W.L. Mitchell, 6 December 1961, WCP, Box 136, Folder 4; Wilbur Cohen, "Some Observations on the History of Welfare During the 1960's: Presented to a Joint Session of the American Historical Association and the Social Welfare History Group," 30 December 1969, WCP, Box 263, Folder 4; "Ribicoff Pushing Big Relief Change," *The New York Times*, Sunday, 18 February 1962, section I; "Kennedy Welfare Bill Meets Little Hostility As Ribicoff Explains It to House Committee," *The Wall Street Journal*, 8 February 1962; U.S. Congress, House Committee on Ways and Means, *Public Welfare Amendments of 1962: Hearings*, 87th Cong., 2nd sess., 1962, 66–93.

[17] Michael B. Katz, *The Undeserving Poor: From the War on Poverty to the War on Welfare* (New York: Pantheon Books, 1989), 3–35; Herbert J. Gans, *The War Against The Poor: The Underclass and Antipoverty Policy* (New York: Basic Books, 1995).

check is in danger of becoming merely a conduit to carry Federal and State money right down the drain."[18]

Public welfare was one of the few programs that Mills occasionally discussed in nonbudgetary terms. The chairman wanted to transform families that had become "dependent" on welfare into "self-supporting taxpayers and not tax eaters. . . ."[19] To illustrate the problems facing policymakers, Mills targeted the explosive growth of Aid to Dependent Children (ADC). During the 1930s and 1940s, he explained, ADC was composed primarily of widows and their young children who "needed" help after the tragic death of the father: Cash payments to meet their immediate needs had usually been sufficient. As Congress expanded social insurance, however, the survivors provision of OASI turned widows and their children into a diminishing portion of those on the welfare rolls; in 1942, for example, approximately one ADC family in three was receiving payments because of the death of the father; by 1958, this percentage had declined to one in eight. On the other hand, ADC payments to families whose father was "absent" from the home rose dramatically from "divorce, separations, desertions and illegitimacy. . . ."[20] According to President Lyndon Johnson's top aide, Mills once justified his 1967 proposed reduction in the number of out-of-wedlock children eligible for welfare as follows: "Across town from my mother in Arkansas a negro woman has a baby every year. Every time I go home, my mother complains. The negro woman's now got eleven children. My proposal will stop this. Let the states pay for more than a small number of children if they want to."[21]

Mills frequently linked welfare to the problems of "dependency" and "family breakdown."[22] Recent reforms, said the chairman, recognized that mother's pensions (programs that provided cash pay-

---

[18] Mills, "A New Charter for Public Welfare"; Mills, "The Congress and the Demands for Service."

[19] U.S. Congress, House of Representatives, *Congressional Record*, 90th Cong., 1st sess., 17 August 1967, 23052–23053. See also Abraham Ribicoff to Wilbur Mills, 5 December 1961, NA, RG 233, 87th Cong., Box 27654, File: H.R. 10032 (1 of 2); U.S. Congress, House Committee on Ways and Means, *Public Welfare Amendments of 1962: Hearings*, 87th Cong., 2nd sess., 1962, 158–165; U.S. Congress, House of Representatives, *Congressional Record*, 15 March 1962, 87th Cong., 2nd sess., 4270; U.S. Congress, House Committee on Ways and Means, *Public Welfare Amendments of 1962: Report*, 87th Cong., 2nd sess., 3.

[20] Mills, "A New Charter for Public Welfare." See also Mills, "Improvements in Social Security Programs Made By the 86th Congress."

[21] Joseph A. Califano, *The Triumph and Tragedy of Lyndon Johnson: The White House Years* (New York: Simon & Schuster, 1991), 245–246.

[22] "Tax Changes to Look For: Exclusive Interview with Wilbur Mills," 16 December 1968, 68–71; Wilbur D. Mills, "Speech before the Arkansas Conference of Social

ments to "needy" individuals) no longer applied to the needs of the modern ADC family. The problems of these "hard-core" welfare families were "only perpetuated by a relief-oriented way of life." As a result, relief rolls were loaded with "repeaters" and "chronically-indigent" people. "Checks only begot more checks," Mills warned, and "money appropriations – Federal and State – only begot more and larger money appropriations."[23] Instead, Mills supported a federal government that limited welfare expenditures financed through general revenue and that relied on earmarked payroll taxes to finance social insurance. On the relationship between welfare and economic growth, Wilbur Cohen explained the disappearance of the Great Depression as an element in welfare debates: "Rather than justify changes or improvement in social programs on the basis of a crusade against the threat of unemployment or depression, changes in the program can and must be justified on a high level of economic literacy which assumes a continued increase in productivity and wages, and the ability of the country to finance improvements in social welfare out of a growing national income."[24]

Mills argued that the American state helped create social stability in a pluralistic society. In his language, the federal government helped maintain a social equilibrium by forging compromises among competing interest groups that, according to Mills, embodied the desires of the entire populace. The basic principle of society, Mills said, "is the interdependence of its various parts – of the individuals and the groups which comprise organized society . . . throw any important part of the social mechanism out of adjustment with the other parts, and the repercussions are swiftly transmitted throughout the whole system."[25] Congress played a role in harmonizing different factions and maintaining order in the "social mechanism." Throughout his career, Mills spoke of the nation in functional, pluralistic terms. "American citizens," said Mills, consisted of "business, agricul-

Welfare," 6 November 1964, WMPC, Box 590, File 7. See also "After 30 Years – Relief A Failure," *U.S. News & World Report*, 17 July 1967, 44–47; John Gardner, "Reducing Dependency on Public Assistance," 1966, WCP, Box 194, Folder 1; Liaison Committee of the National Association of Social Workers, "A Proposal for Considering How Welfare Services Can Contribute to the Prevention of Family Disorganization and Dependency and to the Strengthening of Family Life," 2 May 1961, WCP, Box 136, Folder 4.

[23] Mills, "A New Charter For Public Welfare"; Mills, "The Congress and the Demands for Service." See also Wilbur Cohen to President Johnson, 2 May 1968, WCP, Box 96, Folder Unmarked.

[24] Wilbur Cohen to Herbert Seibert, 26 June 1957, WCP, Box 66, File 5.

[25] Wilbur D. Mills, "Ways and Means Toward Peace," 1940s (n.d.), WMPC, Box 215, File: Speeches.

ture, labor, and so on."[26] Mills even claimed that the largely white, male, wealthy members of the Ways and Means represented a "cross-section of the people of the United States."[27]

Pluralism was integral to the fiscal discourse. During debates, policymakers regarded pluralism as an ideal model of civil society, and their words assumed that the United States was in fact pluralistic. Almost every faction in policy debates claimed constantly that its programs were essential to pluralism. Defenders of tax breaks, for example, frequently defended their benefits as pluralist alternatives to the interventionist policies of communist societies. When the president of the Carnegie Corporation defended his tax-exempt foundation against stronger government regulations in 1969, he articulated this logic: "Governmental control such as this would have far-reaching and extremely dangerous consequences for the American pluralistic system, of which foundations constitute such an important part . . . We must, therefore, recognize that if we want a pluralistic society, if we want multiple, private centers of initiative for the public good, if we think the principle of friendly competition by private organization with an otherwise all-powerful, all-embracing Government is a good thing, we must be prepared to accept the consequences of that system." By attacking tax-exempt foundations, he added, Congress would undermine the "principle of pluralism" by curtailing the freedom of the "very class of tax-exempt institutions whose chief purpose is to enable pluralism to continued to survive."[28] In discussing the state, the chairman and his community thus drew on a comforting pluralistic discourse that described a republic consisting of interdependent groups harmonized through the market and the proper intervention of government.[29]

For Mills, one of the most important elements in a proper intervention was growth-oriented fiscal policy. Several scholars have characterized Mills as steadfastly opposed to the use of fiscal policy to affect the economy.[30] In doing so, they often quote Mills's statement, "I believe that the function of taxation is to raise revenue . . . I don't

[26] Wilbur Mills, interview with Joseph O'Connor, 14 April 1967, JFKL, Oral History Interview Collection, 10.

[27] Cited in Howard A. Winant, *Stalemate: Political Economic Origins of Supply-Side Policy* (New York: Praeger Publishers, 1988), 109–110; Wilbur Mills, interview with Stephen Horn for Westinghouse Broadcasting Company, 11 October 1967, JMIC.

[28] U.S. Congress, House Committee on Ways and Means, *Tax Reform, 1969: Hearings*, 91st Cong., 1st sess., 1969, 124–125.

[29] These ideas played an important role in the language of President Eisenhower. See Robert Griffith, "Dwight D. Eisenhower and the Corporate Commonwealth," *American Historical Review* 87, No.1 (February 1982): 87–122.

[30] See Introduction.

go along with economists who think of taxation primarily as an instrument for stimulating, braking or otherwise manipulating the economy." Mills, however, was more flexible than these studies or this particular quotation suggests. Although he was indeed cautious in advocating active fiscal policies, he talked about the need to spur economic growth and to reach high levels of employment. Revealingly, those who cite the previous quotation usually cut off the rest of his statement: "But I do believe that, when tax rates are as high as they are now, we must take into account the fact that any changes we make inevitably will have far-reaching economic effects."[31]

The chairman acknowledged that after the postwar expansion of the tax system, there was "not a single economic activity" that was "not affected and conditioned by our Federal tax laws." He added, "Without losing sight of the basic purpose of Federal taxation – raising revenue to defray the expense of Government – there is an ever-widening awareness of the significance of the Federal tax structure in shaping the complexion of our economic growth."[32] American economic performance since World War II, said Mills, confirmed "the importance of sound public policy in providing the setting in which this spirit" could "impel our private economy to new achievements."[33] Mills explained: "A great deal of the extreme conservative argument in the current debate has been against all Federal deficits . . . When one gets into the details of these things, it has become apparent generally to both political parties that a government deficit during a recession is quite a different thing from a government deficit during good times. It is the persistent deficit in good times which is the mark of fiscal irresponsibility and

[31] Louis Cassels, "This Man Shapes Your Tax Bill," *Nation's Business*, March 1956, 66. See also Wilbur D. Mills, "Remarks of Honorable Wilbur Mills before Chamber of Commerce Banquet," 4 December 1964, WMPC, Box 660, File 15; "The Man Who Steers Tax Policy," *Business Week*, 22 March 1958, 62; "How Taxes Will Be Cut," *Nation's Business*, October 1957, 60–64.

[32] Wilbur D. Mills, "The Challenge of Federal Tax Policy in 1957: Address to the Seventeenth Annual Federal Tax Dinner of the Federal Tax Forum," 6 December 1956, WMPC, Box 781, File 1.

[33] Wilbur D. Mills, "Federal Tax Policy for Economic Growth: Speech," 1 May 1956, WMPC, Box 783, File 20. See also Mills, "Federal Tax Policy for Economic Growth: Address to the 44th Annual Meeting of the Chamber of Commerce," NAT, RG 56, Office of Tax Policy, Box 33, File: Federal Tax Policy for Economic Growth and Stability; Research and Policy Committee, The Tax Council, "Needed: A Long-Range Approach To Federal Tax Policy," 1 March 1967, WMPC, Box 508, File 4; Mills, "Remarks before the Chamber of Commerce," 27 August 1968, WMPC, Box 420, File: 20; Mills, "Fiscal and Monetary Policy as Factors In Economic Growth," 2 December 1958, WMPC, Box 775, File 5; Mills, "Recent Amendments to the Internal Revenue Code and Possible Future Tax Legislation," 30 October 1964, WMPC, Box 591, File: Speeches.

the source of inflation."[34] Always calling for moderation, however, Mills continued to insist that "taxes should not be raised and
lowered from season to season like the hemlines of women's skirts
and dresses."[35]

Once he began to focus on taxation and its relation to growth, Mills
grew more insistent on limiting general-revenue expenditures, particularly on nondefense items.[36] As would become evident during the
budget debates of 1967 and 1968, "expenditure control" constituted
an essential component of the postwar discourse. General revenue
symbolized a component of the state that lacked strong internal
control, especially once the annual "balanced budget" had lost its currency. Without a commitment to expenditure control, Mills warned,
the government might expand to excessive size. More important,
expenditure control enabled Congress to enact stimulative tax reductions when the economy needed a boost. According to Mills, Congress should continually "re-evaluate" existing expenditure programs
in light of a "very objective" cost-benefit analysis of existing and future
appropriations.[37] While rejecting any "doctrinaire indictment of government spending," Mills argued that policies should be examined
with "constructive skepticism": "We should start with the assumption
that the production capability to be allocated to the program would
be better left available to meet demands arising in the private sector
of the economy and require the program's proponents to persuade
us otherwise."[38]

Increasingly, Mills acknowledged the necessity of temporary
deficits. By the late 1950s, chronic deficits had become a subject
of considerable discussion.[39] Mills once told a reporter: "I am not
one of those who believe that the budget must necessarily be balanced over each *12-month period*. Nevertheless, I do firmly believe
in a balanced budget *over a period of years*, or over a business

---

[34] Mills, "Remarks before the Chamber of Commerce."

[35] Mills, "Fiscal Policy and the Good Economic Society"; Norman Ture, "Issues in Fiscal
and Monetary Policy in 1968," WMPC, Box 508, File 4.

[36] Eileen Shanahan, "Mills Says Expanded War Could Force Rise in Taxes," *The Wall
Street Journal*, 1 March 1968.

[37] Wilbur D. Mills, "Expenditure Control and Tax Policy: Remarks to the 75th
Anniversary Celebration, Security Trust Company," 22 May 1967, LBJL, Henry
Fowler Personal Papers, Box 236, File: Briefing Books: Tax Surcharge, 1967;
Mills, "We *Must* Control Federal Spending," *Reader's Digest*, July 1968, 2–6;
Mills, "Expenditure Control and Priorities in Government Spending: Remarks
before the 34th Annual Oilmen's Convention," 15 November 1968, WMPC, Box
644, File 3.

[38] Mills, "Fiscal Policy and the Good Economic Society."

[39] Stein, *The Fiscal Revolution in America*, 281–371.

cycle."[40] Similarly, at a private meeting with President Kennedy in 1962, Mills commented: "I don't see anything wrong with having a deficit. . . . It's much better to have employment and the economy going, even if you have some deficits, providing it's not excessive and inflationary."[41] Like Kennedy, Mills argued by quoting Andrew Mellon that income-tax reduction would spur enough growth to generate budget-balancing revenues in the future. As he explained to his congressional colleagues, "Our long-range goal remains a balanced budget in the balanced full employment economy."[42] The term "balanced full employment economy" blended neoclassical and 1960s Keynesian discourse in a manner typical of Mills.

All of these debates were packaged within the context of the Cold War. Mills's generation discussed politics as part of a larger struggle between communism and capitalism. Mills told a graduating class at Harding College: "Our guidepost is our common interest in deterring the spread of Communistic aggression and subversion . . . Communistic aggression does not just challenge our freedom and security, but also our way of life – which is and always has been based upon religion. Communistic aggression challenges the roots of our strength and growth . . . The only stable and lasting basis for our stand is economic strength."[43] During the 1960s and early 1970s, Mills lashed out against those in the New Left who flirted with "collectivism" and attacked corporations. He promised the Commonwealth Club of California: "I have resisted – and will continue to resist the advocacies of those who would lead us down the road to economic regression – regression toward those oppressive times when men and women lived out their lives in subjugation to the state, denied the liberties, denied the individual dignity, denied the full fruits of their own labor."[44]

Members of the tax community defined their government in opposition to laissez-faire liberalism and communist statism. Of course, there was considerable room between these two extremes. The New

---

[40] Emphasis Source. "The Top Man on Taxes Tells What to Expect," *U.S. News & World Report*, 12 December 1958, 109–113; Allen Drury, "Capital Expects Economic Review To Be Optimistic," *The New York Times*, 20 January 1958.

[41] "Off-The-Record Meeting With Wilbur Mills," 6 August 1962, JFKL, Presidential Office Files, Presidential Recordings Transcripts: Tax Cut Proposals, Volume I, Audiotape 7, 7.

[42] U.S. Congress, House of Representatives, *Congressional Record*, 24 September 1963, 88th Cong., 2nd sess., 17907. See also U.S. Congress, House of Representatives, *Congressional Record*, 25 February 1964, 88th Cong., 1st sess., 3556.

[43] Wilbur D. Mills, "Address to the Graduating Class: Harding College," 3 June 1954, WMPC, Box 729, File 10.

[44] Wilbur D. Mills, "Remarks to the Commonwealth Club of California," 2 June 1972, WMPC, Box 404, File 1.

Deal had produced political rhetoric that moved toward the left of this political spectrum, such as President Roosevelt's attack on the "economic royalists" and Huey Long's call for the redistribution of wealth. During the Cold War, however, even the most liberal members of the tax community moved right politically by focusing on compensatory fiscal policy as the central part of a growth-oriented economic program.

Born out of the compromise of the New Deal and World War II, the tax community's rhetoric emphasized that fiscal policy offered the best means for the American state to distinguish itself from and to protect itself against communism. On the one hand, it claimed, an active fiscal policy allowed the federal government to raise sufficient funds for its scientific and military battles against communism. On the other hand, the voluntary, self-assessed, progressive income tax allowed politicians to maintain a strong government without resorting to more coercive means of extracting revenue. Tax reform, Mills and his colleagues claimed, aimed to restore faith among citizens in the voluntary tax system. For instance, Mills kicked off the reform studies in 1958 by warning: "With the harsh realities of Soviet technological and scientific advances, we are all . . . aware that perhaps the most important weapon in the arsenal of freedom is found in our Federal internal-revenue system. Our tax system provides the funds not only for the shield of defense but for the sword of retaliatory power which protects the free world."[45]

According to the fiscal discourse, sound tax policy thus played a pivotal role in the postwar state. In particular, the proper use of taxation, either through earmarking government benefits or stimulating economic growth, offered a way for politicians to create a middle ground between laissez-faire liberalism and communism. Through taxation, the community believed that it could harness the power of the state while maintaining the stability of a pluralistic society.

TECHNOCRATS AND TAX REFORM

For Mills and others in the tax community, public policy issues were to be debated and settled in a neutral, technocratic manner.[46] Previ-

---

[45] U.S. Congress, House Committee on Ways and Means, *General Revenue Revision: Hearings*, 85th Cong., 2nd sess., 1958, 2; 225–226; 558–559. See also Lyndon Johnson, "The Need for Tax Reform: Draft," 15 August 1967, LBJL, White House Office Aides File, Joseph Califano, Box 54, File: Tax Reform; Mills, "Let's Strengthen the Income Tax"; U.S. Congress, House of Representatives, *Congressional Record*, 83rd Cong., 2nd sess., 18 March 1954, 3528.

[46] This technocratic ethos had evolved during the progressive era. See Ross, *The Origins of American Social Science*; Guy Alchon, *The Invisible Hand of Planning: Capitalism, Social*

ous politicians and reformers had often discussed taxation as an issue of "social class" and "wealth distribution."[47] The postwar fiscal discourse, however, played down those issues. Instead, that discourse portrayed taxation as a technocratic problem: Professional experts were to determine fiscal policy using quantitative and legalistic analyses in an "objective," nonpartisan process. When the discussion became "emotional" or "partisan," for example, Thomas Curtis (R-MO) urged his colleagues to "get it off the demagoguery and back to economics."[48] As Mills's generation had come to believe through its professional training, technocratic knowledge could diminish partisanship, limit the influence of interest groups, and curtail the authority of political elites.[49] One Ways and Means Republican explained: "I like the spirit of the committee. No petty, parliamentary scheming. I don't mean to say we're intellectuals all looking with no politics . . . But I like the numbers."[50]

Technocratic expertise

Mills insisted that fiscal policy be handled by a small number of "experts" who knew the technocratic language and functioned in an insulated environment. To be sure, Mills often warned of the limits of economic knowledge: "I have watched economists miss every big turn of the economy. I am not criticizing them; I'm only saying we expect too much of them."[51] At the same time, however, Mills would tell audiences during other speeches:

Science, and the State in the 1920s (Princeton: Princeton University Press, 1985); JoAnne Brown, *The Definition of a Profession: The Authority of Metaphor In The History Of Intelligence Testing, 1890–1930* (Princeton: Princeton University Press, 1992).

[47] Four works that discuss the radical tone that political discourse on taxation often took during earlier periods include W. Elliot Brownlee, "Economists and the formation of the modern tax system in the United States: The World War I crisis," in *The State and Economic Knowledge*, 401–435; Brownlee, "Social investigation and political learning in the financing of World War I," in *The State and Social Investigation in Britain and the United States* (Cambridge: Cambridge University Press and Washington, D.C.: Woodrow Wilson Center Press, 1993), 323; Mark Leff, *The Limits of Symbolic Reform: The New Deal and Taxation, 1933–1939* (Cambridge: Cambridge University Press, 1984); Alan Brinkley, *Voices of Protest: Huey Long, Father Coughlin & The Great Depression* (New York: Vintage Books, 1982).

[48] U.S. Congress, House Committee on Ways and Means, *President's 1961 Tax Recommendations: Hearings*, 87th Cong., 1st sess., 1961, 369. See also Wilbur Mills to the Congress, 28 June 1957, WMPC, Box 703, File 1.

[49] Theodore M. Porter, *Trust in Numbers: The Pursuit of Objectivity in Science and Public Life* (Princeton: Princeton University Press, 1995), 8.

[50] JMIC.

[51] Gilbert Burck, "Capitol Hill's 'Show Me' Economist," *Fortune*, February 1968, 107.

Among all of the Government officials who have the responsibility for making economic decisions, I believe Members of Congress have their own unique challenges in the face of the lack of full understanding of economic principles and concepts among the general public. Over the more than 30 years that I have served in the Congress the great growth that has occurred in the number of Federal programs with which a Member of Congress must be familiar of the economic interests of his constituency is truly amazing . . . As Chairman of the Committee for the last 12 years I have come to have a deep appreciation for the contributions that the principles and concepts of the discipline we know as economics have made to the unprecedented growth this country has experienced in recent decades.[52]

Although Mills often wondered whose experts were correct, he rarely contested the importance of experts themselves. "Political bravery," said Mills, was the "skillful and objective analysis of the facts without prejudice, to recommend action on the basis of those conclusions." As an example of "political bravery," he lauded President Johnson for having shown a "deep understanding of hard economic analysis" in 1964.[53] Mills tried to do the same in his meetings with administration officials and lobbyists, relying heavily on expert data for evidence to bolster his position. The chairman reified the importance of expertise by using medical metaphors that linked his committee to a highly respected profession. Mills often asked hearing participants, "Is the medicine that you are suggesting we use here on the patient the proper medicine?"[54] This metaphor suggested that economic problems, like "diseases," were curable if expert "doctors," such as the Ways and Means, could apply the proper fiscal remedies.

Technocratic policymaking involved a ritual of deference to expertise. Members of the tax community normally prefaced their remarks with an assertion or denial of their expertise. The refrain of "I am not an expert" became commonplace during the Ways and Means hear-

---

[52] Wilbur D. Mills, "Address of Honorable Wilbur D. Mills to the American Bankers Association," 17 November 1969, WMPC, unprocessed.

[53] Wilbur Mills, Unmarked Speech, 1965, WMPC, Box 590, File 9.

[54] This observation was made in Julius Duscha, "The Most Important Man on Capitol Hill Today," *The New York Times*, Section 6, Sunday, 25 February 1968. See U.S. Congress, House Committee on Ways and Means, *President's 1967 Surtax Proposal: Hearings*, 90th Cong., 1st sess., November 1967, 105–130; "Mr. Mills Conducts Class for Would-Be Tax Boosters," *The Wall Street Journal*, 11 December 1967; "High Officials Argue Over Taxes, Spending, Inflation," *U.S. News & World Report*, 18 December 1967, 90–92.

ings. In one telling exchange, Bruce Alger (R-TX) asked Secretary of
Commerce Luther Hodges: "On page 11 you mention the business
cycle. How would you define the 'business cycle'?" Hodges
responded: "I will have to ask one of my experts on that. It will probably get you confused too, as it does me."[55] In the 1961 hearings for
a particular tax credit, John Byrnes commented to Douglas Dillon:
"Because . . . I just have not had a chance to absorb all the details, I
am going to limit myself today in my questioning. I feel in a way somewhat like Congressman Barden who expressed his frustration one
time when he said he wished he was smart enough to understand
what some people were driving at or dumb enough that it did not
bother him."[56]

Policymakers reinforced the concept of expertise by constantly distinguishing members of their community as either "technical" or
"political" people. Technical people, they said, worked "objectively"
on the data behind legislative proposals. Robert Myers and Laurence
Woodworth, for example, could evaluate policies on a neutral, bipartisan basis that was grounded in fact and not dogma. Political people,
on the other hand, tended to look for compromises that could be
supported by broad constituencies. They played with numbers and
technical data to satisfy political demands. Of course, an individual
such as Mills challenged the validity of this distinction. Nonetheless,
fiscal policymakers, in their rhetoric, paid great respect to the difference between technicians and politicians. This was evident during a
heated controversy when Robert Myers attempted to become Commissioner of Social Security under President Nixon. His campaign
stirred debate about the legitimacy of a "technical" person running
for a position that involved political and administrative decisions of
the highest order.[57]

In this linguistic context, policymakers attacked each other on the
basis of their expertise: To discredit someone's expertise was to discredit his position. Mills and other committee members challenged
the administration in these terms. One year, Mills had embarrassed
the Treasury experts by finding seventy errors in one of President
Eisenhower's tax proposals. He played that card again in the 1960s,
publicly revealing one hundred technical flaws in Kennedy's 1961 tax

[55] U.S. Congress, House Committee on Ways and Means, *President's 1963 Tax Message:
Hearings before the Committee on Ways and Means*, 88th Cong., 1st sess., 1963, 572. See
also U.S. Congress, House Committee on Ways and Means, *Tax Reform, 1969: Hearings*, 91st Cong., 1st sess., 3418.

[56] U.S. Congress, House Committee on Ways and Means, *President's 1961 Tax Recommendations: Hearings*, 87th Cong., 1st sess., 1961, 337.

[57] Arthur Altmeyer to Wilbur Cohen, 1 July 1969 and Cohen to Altmeyer, 25 June
1969, WCP, Box 6, Folder 5.

proposal. He used similar tactics against the early medical care proposals, questioning their numbers on future hospital costs and funding, as well as in the battle over the Revenue Act of 1968, where he criticized the incorrect forecasts of CEA. Other Ways and Means colleagues joined Mills in these challenges. Thomas Curtis (D-MO), for instance, accused the administration of "juggling statistics."[58]

Quantitative data, economic theory, mathematical analysis, and technical legal jargon were the principal mediums of communication for these experts. In particular, the postwar experts drew on macroeconomic analysis to explain the relationship between fiscal policy, national consumption, and national investment and actuarial economics to gauge the long-term relationship between taxes and expenditures in Social Security. Because this generation made far more extensive use of this type of macroeconomic rhetoric than did older generations of policymakers, one had to master the language in order to participate fully in the community. The language thus limited who could participate, and dictated how they should participate. Mills was a master of the new technical rhetoric. As one colleague commented, "Wilbur just doesn't like to get up there and talk unless he has all of his people right there behind him with charts and tables of figures."[59] In executive committee sessions, Mills went law-for-law and number-for-number with the interest groups and administration experts on the most detailed provisions of legislative packages.

Statistics, tables, economic rhetoric, and legislative laws were the texts that policymakers such as Mills read. Days before the passage of the Revenue Act of 1964, the staff of the JCIRT published crucial revenue estimates relating to each version of the legislation. The text included thirty-one pages of tables and statistics on the revenue effect of each reform; it contained virtually no nonquantitative narrative.[60] In this and other ways, Mills emphasized the importance of mastering the technical details, driving this

---

[58] U.S. Congress, House Committee on Ways and Means, *President's 1963 Tax Message: Hearings*, 88th Cong., 1st sess., 1963, 620; 634–635; 796. For another example, see U.S. Congress, House Committee on Ways and Means, *President's 1961 Tax Recommendations: Hearings, 1961*, 87th Cong., 1st sess., 1961, 3028; "Capitol Hill's 'Show Me' Economist," *Fortune*, February 1968, 106–107; 204–207.

[59] "Wilbur Mills: What's His Tax Strategy?" *Nation's Business*, February 1968, 51.

[60] Staff, JCIRT, *Revenue Estimates Relating to the House, Senate, and Conference Versions of H.R. 8363, The Revenue Bill of 1964*, 21 February 1964, J1046 (Committee – Print). See also Colin Stam to Wilbur Mills, 27 September 1962, NA, RG 233, 87th Cong., Box 15, File: H.R. 10650; Staff, JCIRT, *Staff Data*, 6 June 1963, NA, RG 233, 88th Cong., Box 31, File: Taxes – General; Staff, JCIRT, *Summary of the President's 1963 Tax Message*, 1963, NA, RG 233, 88th Cong., Box 31, File: Taxes – General; "The New Potentates Rule by the Numbers," *Business Week*, 6 January 1968, 56.

idea into the heads of new members to the committee.[61] The arcane nature of the discourse often made it difficult to comprehend the social assumptions that were embedded in the revenue code, such as the centrality of the male-headed, single wage earning family to statutes involving marriage.[62]

One can glean a sense of the complexity of this discourse through private correspondence. Surrey, for instance, explained a tax provision in the following terms: "Because of the 85 percent dividends received deduction, an intercorporate dividend is subject to tax to the recipient only to the extent of 15 percent of the amount of the distribution. Under existing law, the amount of the intercorporate dividend is limited to the basis of the property in the hands of the distributing corporation."[63] Staff experts communicated with other experts in even more technical language.[64] Because of its importance to the postwar fiscal discourse, technocratic information became a key medium of political exchange.[65] Not all of the legislators were

[61] JMIC.

[62] Edward J. McCaffery, *Taxing Women* (Chicago: The University of Chicago Press, 1997), 267.

[63] Stanley Surrey to Wilbur Mills, 26 June 1962, NA, RG 233, 87th Cong., Box 6348, File: Unmarked. See also Surrey to Mills, 12 September 1962, NA, RG 233, 87th Cong., File: H.R. 10650, Box No. 15; Surrey to Mills, 22 September 1961, NA, RG 233, 87th Cong., Box 13, File: Tax Revision 1961 Dividends and Interest; Surrey to Mills, 12 September 1962, NA, RG 233, 87th Cong., Box 13, File: H.R. 10650; Surrey to Leo Irwin, 8 March 1962, NA, RG 233, 87th Cong., Box 15, File: H.R 10650; Douglas Dillon to Mills, 8 January 1964, NA, RG 233, 88th Cong., Box 48, File: Public Debt 1963–64; Mortimer Caplin to Mills, 29 March 1963, NA, RG 233, 88th Cong., Box 38, File: Gross Income – Business Expenses; Laurence Woodworth to Mills, 14 November 1968, Mills to Henry Fowler, 16 October 1968 in WMPC, unprocessed.

[64] For examples of Mills's correspondence to other state actors and experts' correspondence with each other, see the following: Leo Irwin to Jim Wright, 15 November 1961, NA, RG 233, 87th Cong., Box 6338, File: Credit against Tax; Gerard Brannon to Harvey Brazer, 31 January 1962, NA, RG 233, 87th Cong., Box 13, File: H.R. 10650; Irwin to Martha Griffiths, 30 July 1962, NA, RG 233, 87th Cong., Box 6339, File: Exemptions: Income Tax; E.J. Enquist, Jr. to Irwin, 10 December 1962, NA, RG 233, 88th Cong., Box 31, File: Tax – Income; Wilbur Mills to Peter Rodino, Jr., 6 February 1963, NA, RG 233, 88th Cong., Box 38, File: Gross Income – Business Expenses; Mills to Frances Bolton, 28 April 1964, NA, RG 233, 88th Cong., Box 40, File: Gross Income – Interest; Alan Murray and Albert Bruckberg to Laurence Woodworth, 21 December 1966, WMPC, unprocessed.

[65] See for example, Keith Funston to Wilbur Mills, 16 February 1960, NA, RG 128, Box 322, File: Sec. 34; American Bar Association, "Report on the Problem of Underreporting of Income from Dividends and Interest," 1961, NA, RG 128, Box 207, File: Withholding (ABA); Keith Funston to Colin Stam, 10 November 1961, NA, RG 233, 87th Cong., Box 359, File: Sec. 1201–02; Charles Stewart to Mills, 16 January 1962, NA, RG 128, Box 322, File: Sec. 38; J.W. Fulbright to Mills, 6 September 1962 and Thomas Power to Mills, 11 September 1962, NA, RG 233, 87th Cong., Box 13, File: H.R. 10650; Robert Higgins to Mills, 17 September 1962, NA, RG 233, 87th

comfortable with this language. One committee member remarked: "When I first went on the Committee I used to leave the meetings with a headache, truly a headache! The stuff was just over my head . . . The things we deal with are so complex! Detail and technical, oh there's so much detail and it's so technical!"[66] Another recalled his first hearing: "I was sitting there one day not knowing what . . . was going on. Title 19, Title 18. You sit there trying to look smart and I really felt phony. I remarked to the Chairman that this was calculus and I hadn't had arithmetic yet."[67]

Mills was well aware of the complexity of this discourse. On occasion, he used his mastery of its vocabulary and its syntax to his political advantage. Politicians less comfortable with the rhetoric deferred to Mills because he could engage the experts on their own linguistic terrain. On Medicare, Lawrence O'Brien's assistant told him in 1964, "[Cohen] expects that before Mills starts his executive sessions he'll call in Cohen to brief him for half a day and then in the executive sessions he'll keep Cohen on the stand all week going over all the combinations till the committee is so groggy it'll throw up its hands and let Mills write the bill."[68] Mills occasionally warned that because of what Surrey once called a "technical curtain," taxation had become "increasingly remote to most Americans and . . . the exclusive province of a technically trained elite."[69] But he nevertheless used that elite and the remoteness of the discourse to his own political advantage.

Tax reform

The fiscal discourse was dense, difficult to understand, and conservative. Its definition of "tax reform" blended the concepts of Henry Simons, who argued that equal income should be treated equally, of Andrew Mellon, who claimed that lower tax rates would increase economic productivity, and of John Maynard Keynes, who promised that

Cong., Box 12, File: H.R. 10650; Douglas Dillon to Mills, 5 October 1962, NA, RG 233, 87th Cong., Box 15, File: H.R. 10650; William Keller to Mills, 18 February 1963, NA, RG 233, 88th Cong., Box 33, File: Tax Suggestions 1963–64; George Lee to Mills, 3 June 1963, NA, RG 233, 88th Cong., Box 28, File: Tax Correspondence – Capital Gains; William Goeckel to Mills, 16 August 1963, NA, RG 233, 88th Cong., Box 56, Unfiled.

66 JMIC.

67 Ibid.

68 Henry Hall Wilson to Lawrence O'Brien, 2 March 1964, LBJL, White House Office Aides Files, Box 19, Folder: M.

69 Wilbur D. Mills, "How Your Income Taxes Can Be Cut," *Nation's Business*, November 1959, 76; Surrey, "The Congress and the Tax Lobbyist," 1175.

rate reductions could stimulate consumer demand and bring full employment.[70] Successful tax reform should achieve all three of these objectives simultaneously. Gone from the public rhetoric were terms such as "redistribution of wealth," "social class," and "economic justice." The new language of tax reform played down the discussion of income redistribution and social justice while focusing on economic "efficiency" and "growth." Policymakers such as Mills disliked the fact that taxpayers in identical circumstances and with identical incomes sometimes paid different amounts of income tax. When they mentioned class, members of the tax community usually referred to different classes of taxpayers that existed within the same income bracket: One class earned nontaxable income, the other taxable.[71] Relationships between different income levels, however, attracted less attention. One journalist noted that the goal of the reforms of the early 1960s was to rid the internal revenue code of the "ghosts of the Depression," with its "the soak-the-rich tone."[72]

Tax reform pursued the twin goals of rationalization and tax reduction. As Joel Barlow of the U.S. Chamber of Commerce said, "Rate reduction – rate revision – is really the greatest reform."[73] In this rhetoric, tax reform would free up money for "investment" and "consumption," while compensating for part of the loss from tax reduction. Reform would also eliminate the inefficient investments prompted by tax shelters. Mills told one journal: "We should seek a tax climate favorable to economic growth, income taxes under which people with the same income should pay like amounts of tax, an income tax that interferes as little as possible with decisions of the market place. We seek a system . . . which will respond quickly to changes in economic conditions to restrain inflation and recession."[74]

The primary goal of reform, according to Mills, was not economic redistribution but to "bring greater fairness and equity to it [the tax

---

[70] Henry Simons, *Personal Income Taxation: The Definition of Income as a Problem of Fiscal Policy* (Chicago: University of Chicago Press, 1938); Andrew Mellon, *Taxation: The People's Business* (New York: Macmillan, 1924); John Maynard Keynes, *The General Theory of Employment, Interest, and Money* (London: Macmillan, 1936).

[71] Stanley S. Surrey, "The Federal Income Tax Base for Individuals," in U.S. Congress, House Committee on Ways and Means, *Tax Revision Compendium: Compendium of Papers on Broadening The Tax Base*, 1959, H0603 (Committee – Print), 2–14; Wilbur D. Mills, "Some Dimensions of Tax Reform," *Arkansas Law Review* 23, No. 2 (Summer 1969): 160–161; Mills, "How Your Income Taxes Can Be Cut," 69; Mills, "The Challenge of Federal Tax Policy in 1957."

[72] "An Idea on the March," *Time*, 11 January 1963, 20.

[73] U.S. Congress, House Committee on Ways and Means, *President's 1963 Tax Message: Hearings*, 88th Cong., 1st sess., 1963, 2369.

[74] "Wilbur Mills Talks on Taxes," *Nation's Business*, August 1964, 81.

code] in the interest of greater economic growth."[75] The existing high tax rates, said Mills, directed too much money away from investment and consumption and toward an excessive federal establishment. This "fiscal drag" clearly retarded economic growth. Reformers such as Mills and Surrey also argued that existing high tax rates (which were appropriate to the World War II economy) caused individuals and organizations in the higher brackets to avoid taxes by creating loopholes or by cheating. In 1959, Mills branded the tax code a "House of Horrors," filled with provisions that allowed individuals and corporations to escape their responsibilities.[76] He lamented: "These high rates are part of the vicious cycle in which the income tax has been ensnared. When we have rates so high, taxpayers make determined efforts to obtain preferential treatment for various types of income and expenses. To the extent that they succeed, the tax base shrinks, thereby reinforcing the need for high tax rates."[77]

Excessive progressivity had thus become a "problem" that reformers hoped to solve. As Mortimer Caplin told a group of business leaders: "As we review the fiscal history of the 1960s, it is clear that our tax policy has moved far beyond the tax philosophy of the 1930s. Our income tax is no longer the prime tool to redistribute the wealth of our citizenry. Even an ardent tax reformer has said: 'After more than 20 years of rates reaching beyond 80 and 90 percent, a rate schedule that stops at 70 percent is welcome respite.' "[78] To promote growth and prevent tax avoidance policymakers had to reduce the progressivity of the statutory income-tax rates. In an interview, Mills recalled, "The basic reform that we sought all the way through was not just the reform of a section of the law or a dozen sections of the law . . . but also reform of the tax rate structure."[79] The existing high tax rates were described by policymakers as "confiscatory,"

---

[75] Wilbur Mills to Harlow Sander, 25 July 1959, WMPC, Box 694, File 4. See also Mills, "How Your Income Taxes Can Be Cut," 70–76; "Outlook For A New Tax System," *Nation's Business*, March 1959, 70–77; "The Plan For New Taxes: Interview with Wilbur Mills," *U.S. News & World Report*, 26 May 1969, 40–45; Mills, "The Tax Reform Act of 1969," *Indiana Legal Forum* 4, No. 1 (Fall 1970), 26–43.

[76] Mills, "Are You a Pet or a Patsy," 51; Mills, "Preface," *Virginia Law Review* 44, No. 6 (October 1958): 835–838. See also Joseph Califano to President Johnson, 28 August 1967, and "What the Tax Reform Program Does," 29 June 1967, in LBJL, White House Office Aides File, Joseph Califano, Box 54, File: Tax Reform.

[77] Mills, "Federal Tax Policy for Economic Growth." See also Mills, "Remarks before the Annual Meeting of the Arkansas Savings and Loan League," 15 October 1960, WMPC, Box 781, File 10; Mills, "Are You A Pet or A Patsy," 62.

[78] Mortimer Caplin, "Address to the National Conference on Tax Reform of the Chamber of Commerce," U.S. Chamber of Commerce, Press Release, 14 February 1968, SSP, Box 183, File 3.

[79] Wilbur Mills, interview with Joseph O'Connor, 14 April 1967, 13.

"unrealistic," and "excessive." Of course, said reformers, few individuals would pay the top rate of 91 percent; taxpayers were practically "forced" to find avenues for tax avoidance. But if the statutory rates were lower, compliance and thus the "effective" rates – the amount of revenue actually collected by the government – would be higher. The reformers assumed that the wealthy would comply with lower tax rates. Because progressive rates were linked with tax breaks, the reformers also equated the term "progressivity" with "complexity," thereby playing down the more relevant relationship between the definition of taxable income and the arcane tax laws. Their rhetoric consistently presented "simplification" and "progressivity" as contradictory objectives.

Unlike certain tax reformers of the 1920s and 1930s, who had called for higher taxes on the wealthy and on corporations, Mills insisted that the proposed reforms did not entail "the imposition of a new tax but, rather, a vehicle for the purpose of collecting taxes . . . due under the Internal Revenue Code similar to the vehicle . . . in operation with respect to salaries and wages."[80] By raising more revenue, reform would allow for less progressive rates and economic growth. The conservative foundations of this version of reform resolved the paradox of "a conservative Congressman such as Chairman Mills strongly supporting the concept of tax reform."[81]

Actually, the words "progressive" and "reform" had become increasingly difficult to define. Even among policymakers, the meaning of those terms was unclear; for those outside the beltway, the terms were virtually impossible to understand. To be a "tax reformer," argued the policymakers, one needed the "technical" sophistication to comprehend the differences between "statutory" and "effective" rates, to grasp the rationale behind "base broadening," and to know the relationship between "horizontal" and "vertical" equity. Given the complexity of these issues, the "experts" said that they needed to "educate" and "lead" the public: "It is the duty of tax men," insisted Mills, "to inform the American people of the consequences of continuing to deal with the federal tax structure. . . ."[82] As Mills's statement indicates, even the once-explosive rhetoric of "tax reform" had been absorbed into the technocratic discourse of the postwar era.

[80] Wilbur Mills to B.L. Goad, 8 August 1961, WMPC, Box 735, File 4; U.S. Congress, House of Representatives, *Congressional Record*, 87th Cong., 2nd sess., 28 March 1962, 5305–5306.
[81] Joseph Barr to Claude Desautels, 4 March 1963, JFKL, White House Staff File: Lawrence O'Brien, Legislative Leaders Breakfast Material, Box 23, File: 5 March 1963, Folder 1.
[82] Wilbur D. Mills, "Remarks of the Honorable Wilbur D. Mills before the Society of Public Accountants," September 1958, WMPC, Box 775, File 9.

This version of reform gained widespread currency among policy-makers and activists. The "liberal" tax reformer Senator Albert Gore (D-TN), for instance, once wrote to the "conservative" Mills, "Frankly, I had no idea our views of existing inequities were so parallel."[83] While criticizing the Revenue Act of 1964, *The Nation* praised Mills for inject-ing sanity into the deliberations. He was scarcely a popular figure in liberal circles, but the editorial noted: "Nobody – except Mr. Mills – seems prepared to brave the anger of those whose tax privileges are to be taken away . . . It will be well to consider Mr. Mills' proposals when he is ready to put them before Congress. He is an extremely diligent legislator and he has another virtue which is rare in both the executive and legislative branch: he puts the horse before the cart."[84] Even the liberal Surrey wrote: "Very high rates of individual income taxation have come to be recognized as bad, even by those who in the past have favored virtually confiscatory tax rates on ethical grounds . . . Tax reform involving rate reduction and loophole closing will give a law that is in many respects simpler, and in all respects, fairer and more conducive to sound economic development."[85]

THE ALTERNATIVES REJECTED

Political discourse, one scholar explained, "suppresses the inconve-nient."[86] While the fiscal discourse provided the tax community with a framework through which to conceptualize and debate public policy, it also categorized some viewpoints as irrational, impossible, and unthinkable. The discourse, and those who spoke it, omitted certain worldviews that had been expressed by prominent figures in the twentieth century, including the 1960s. An analysis of these alternative worldviews helps to further define the parameters of the fiscal discourse.

Microeconomic management

The first alternative was the statist microeconomic management. This rhetoric gained considerable popularity within the American state at various points in the twentieth century, including World War I, the Great Depression, and World War II. This vision of politics claimed

---

[83] Albert Gore to Wilbur Mills, 21 December 1959, WMPC, unprocessed.

[84] Editorial, "Tax Reform First," *The Nation*, 19 January 1963, 48–49; Editorial, "Shelve It!" *The Nation*, 16 March 1963, 217–218.

[85] Stanley Surrey to Henry Fowler, 27 September 1961, SSP, Box 176, File 3.

[86] J.G.A. Pocock, *Politics Language & Time: Essays on Political Thought and History* (Chicago: University of Chicago Press,1989), 18.

that federal institutions were needed to manage the economy on a permanent basis. While accepting the reality of the modern corporation, this rhetoric contended that the economy would stagnate without proper microeconomic government intervention into the managerial affairs of business. Proponents warned of the chronic problem of "administered" prices that resulted from the new corporate economy, whereby managers maintained artificially high prices that "upset the traditional equilibrating role of the market mechanism."[87] As Bernard Baruch, businessman and head of the War Industries Board in World War I, once explained, it was the duty of government agencies "to encourage, under strict Government supervision, such cooperation and coordination in industry as should tend to increase production, eliminate waste, conserve natural resources, improve the quality of products, promote efficiency in operation, and thus reduce costs to the ultimate consumer."[88]

Under the National Recovery Administration of the first New Deal, the Roosevelt administration used this rhetoric when it attempted to unite business, economists, labor, and government leaders voluntarily through "industrial codes" that coordinated pricing, production, investment, and wages. As a result of weak compliance and failed implementation, however, these efforts failed.[89] Championed by such experts as Rexford Tugwell, Gardiner Means, Thomas Corcoran, and Leon Henderson, this type of managerial vision continued during World War II in the form of the War Production Board and the Office of Price Administration. But problems and controversy once again discredited statist microeconomic management.[90] Although this rhetoric lost popularity after the war, it reemerged temporarily under President Nixon with anti-inflationary wage and price controls. Nonetheless, the tax community seldom discussed such managerial experiments.

Social Keynesianism

The second alternative was "Social Keynesianism." This interventionist version of Keynesianism reached the height of popularity during

[87] Theodore Rosenof, *Economics In The Long Run: New Deal Theorists & Their Legacies, 1933–1993* (Chapel Hill: University of North Carolina Press, 1997), 34.

[88] Cited in Brinkley, *The End of Reform*, 35. See also David M. Kennedy, *Over Here: The First World War and American Society* (New York: Oxford University Press, 1980), 130–132.

[89] William J. Barber, *Designs within Disorder: Franklin D. Roosevelt, the Economists, and the Shaping of American Economic Policy, 1933–1945* (Cambridge: Cambridge University Press,1996), 53–102; Ellis W. Hawley, *The New Deal and the Problem of Monopoly* (Princeton: Princeton University Press, 1966).

[90] Brinkley, *The End of Reform*, 198–200.

the late New Deal and World War II. Social Keynesianism called for the stringent enforcement of labor policies that sustained high wages and consumer demand, stimulative public investment (rather than tax cuts), and a federal guarantee to a full employment economy. Social Keynesians had supported the Full Employment Bill in 1945, which would have required the government to achieve full employment and create a National Production and Employment Budget that adjusted levels of government spending to ensure a very low rate of unemployment. During the 1960s, Social Keynesianism found supporters outside the tax community, including UAW President Walter Reuther, Senator Paul Douglas (D-IL), economists Leon Keyserling and John Galbraith, and Secretary of Labor Willard Wirtz, all of whom emphasized a budgetary commitment to expansive public employment policies. They argued that the focus of economic policy – on stimulative tax cuts and contributory social insurance – posited an insufficient role for the federal government in the United States.[91]

Anti-growthmanship

A third alternative found support among left-wing politicians during the 1960s; this can be characterized as anti-growthmanship. Given the hierarchies of capitalism, these critics argued, the benefits of economic growth reached a limited portion of the nation. Policies that focused on growth failed to address the main needs of society. Public policy should thus focus on structural inequalities that persisted over time. Some activists highlighted rural America. In *The Other America*, Michael Harrington described the 40 million rural Americans who lived in extreme poverty at the height of the "American Century." Echoing these arguments, the Students for a Democratic Society

---

[91] Margaret Weir and Theda Skocpol, "State Structures and the Possibilities for 'Keynesian' Responses to the Great Depression in Sweden, Britain, and the United States," 107–163; Weir, *Politics and Jobs*, 27–61; Rosenof, *Economics In The Long Run*, 44–127; Michael Brown, "State Capacity and Political Choice: Interpreting the Failure of the Third New Deal," and Ira Katznelson and Bruce Pietrykowski, "On Categories and Configurations: Further Remarks on Rebuilding the American State," *Studies in American Political Development* 9, No. 1 (Spring 1995): 187–221; Steven Fraser, *Labor Will Rule: Sidney Hillman and the Rise of American Labor* (New York: Free Press, 1991), 409–412; Nelson Lichtenstein, *The Most Dangerous Man in Detroit: Walter Reuther and the Fate of American Labor* (New York: Basic Books, 1995), 221–222; Meg Jacobs, "The Politics of Purchasing Power: State-Building, Political Economy, and Consumption Politics, 1909–1959" (Ph.D. diss., University of Virginia, work-in-progress) and Jacobs, "'How About Some Meat?': The Office of Price Administration, Consumption Politics, and State Building from the Bottom Up, 1941–1946," *The Journal of American History*, 84, No. 3 (December 1997): 910–941.

warned in 1962: "We live amidst a national celebration of economic prosperity while poverty and deprivation remain an unbreakable way of life for millions in the 'affluent society,' including many of our own generation."[92]

Other activists pointed to problems of the urban ghetto. One group of intellectuals compared urban ghettos to Third World countries: "Wealth is extracted by 'outsiders' as profits from the sale of consumer goods and returns to invested capital. The outward flow of cash is partially offset by the wages of 'exported' labor, but the result is that no net financial accumulation takes place within the ghetto. This creates a situation of dependency. Much as the colony is dependent on its 'mother country,' so too is the ghetto dependent on the larger society for most of its material needs."[93] Third World countries and urban ghettos, this group said, experienced economic deprivation and exploitation even when surrounded by thriving economies. These anti-poverty and civil rights activists argued that the ghettos could not prosper because residents lacked political power and access to capital: Economic growth did not reach into urban neighborhoods and could even exacerbate the gap between income classes.[94] This radical critique of American society questioned the basic principle of the tax community – the centrality of economic growth to public policy – and insisted that national economic policies must be redirected toward the elimination of structural economic, political, and social inequalities. The critique helped spawn the National Welfare Rights Organization and the Poor People's Campaign, which promoted the rhetoric of welfare rights – any poor citizen, "deserving" or "undeserving," was entitled to government income assistance.[95]

Populism

The fourth alternative worldview centered on populist politics. Its rhetoric combined a belief in the virtue of local participatory politics with an attack on concentrated power. Dating back to the American Revolution, this rhetoric found support throughout the twentieth century. Upper middle-class budget reformers in the progressive era, for example, had promoted expertise in the public realm as a means

---

[92] James Miller, *"Democracy Is in the Streets": From Port Huron to the Siege of Chicago* (New York: Simon & Schuster, 1987), 338.

[93] Katz, *The Undeserving Poor*, 58.

[94] Ibid., 52–66.

[95] Gareth Davies, *From Opportunity to Entitlement: The Transformation and Decline of Great Society Liberalism* (Lawrence: University Press of Kansas, 1996), 3–9.

of enhancing citizen participation. Experts, they claimed, could enable citizens to understand complex government issues, such as expenditure and finance, so that they could monitor government activities on a regular basis.[96] During the Great Depression, Senator Huey Long, Father Charles Coughlin, Francis Townsend, John Lewis, and President Roosevelt all tapped into populist themes. They pitted "the people" and "the masses" against the "elites" who had corrupted politics. John Lewis, one founder of the Congress of Industrial Organizations, declared in November 1939: "The millions of organized workers banded together in the CIO are the main driving force of the progressive movement of workers, farmers, professional and small business people and of all other liberal elements in the community . . . They are also the backbone of the resistance to all the forces that threaten our democratic institutions and the liberty and security that Americans hold dear."[97] While Coughlin lashed out on the radio against "the enemy of financial slavery"[98] and urged radio listeners to join his movement, Long created a "Share Our Wealth" campaign that called for limits on wealth. Even Roosevelt, who worked with business leaders throughout the Depression, tapped into this rhetoric during the election of 1936 by attacking "economic royalists" and the "forces of selfishness and of lust for power."[99] Coughlin, Long, and Roosevelt often debated taxation in terms of class conflict. In 1935, for example, Roosevelt told Congress: "Our revenue laws operated in many ways to the unfair advantage of the few, and they have little to prevent an unjust concentration of wealth and economic power." He recommended "the very sound public policy of encouraging a wider distribution of wealth" through taxation.[100]

This type of populist rhetoric seemed out of place in the technocratic culture of the postwar state. But in other arenas it flourished. During the 1960s, the New Left and the Civil Rights movement renewed this language of protest. They called for a national grass roots mobilization of citizens and railed against military leaders, corporate executives, politicians, and experts who stifled participatory democracy and racial justice.[101] Indeed, the Community Action Program drew explicitly on this rhetoric as it called for the empowerment of local communities in political decision-making, as opposed to the rule of technocrats. This populist rhetoric also

---

[96] Jonathan Kahn, *Budgeting Democracy: State Building and Citizenship in America, 1890–1928* (Ithaca: Cornell University Press, 1997).

[97] Cited in Michael Kazin, *The Populist Persuasion*, 135.

[98] Ibid., 114.

[99] Leff, *The Limits of Symbolic Reform*, 187.

[100] Ibid., 137.

[101] Miller, *"Democracy Is in the Streets,"* 336.

shaped the Christian Right movement during the 1970s as it painted
a portrait of a political system that was governed by liberal elites
without the consent of the citizenry and that destroyed the fabric of
communities.

Radical conservatism

Finally, another worldview involved a radical free-market conservatism that branded almost any government program as communistic or a violation of sacred American principles. After years of being
relegated to the shadows of New Deal liberalism, this rhetoric gained
national attention through Barry Goldwater in 1964. As the Republican candidate for the presidency, Goldwater lashed out against
almost every domestic policy, ranging from Social Security to cotton
subsidies to the National Labor Relations Board to the Tennessee
Valley Authority. Goldwater's rhetoric seemed extreme even to conservative members of the tax community, such as Mills, who supported Social Security and federal income taxation. Responding to
the growth of radical conservatism and radical liberalism, Mills once
explained that his views, and those of his colleagues, fell toward the
pragmatic center:

> The area of public affairs is not like a Western on television.
> There are not a bunch of good or bad fellows threatening
> the fabric of our society on the left which is being defended
> by a bunch of good or bad fellows on the right. There are, in
> fact, new problems being thrown up by the tide of events. It
> is *true* that many of the solutions produce only short-term
> results. Many are inconsistent with elements of our traditional
> position that we want to maintain. The solution, however,
> requires study and understanding of the problems and picking
> and choosing among the many solutions proposed. This I
> sincerely believe is the true conservative yet progressive
> tradition.[102]

These world views – statist microeconomic regulation, Social Keynesianism, anti-growthmanship, political populism, and radical free-
market conservatism – were absent from the discourse of Mills and
the tax community. To be sure, these types of rhetoric were available
to the community, but they were concepts that did not fit into its
understanding or vision of the political economy. While divisions
emerged within the community over questions such as the timing and

---

[102] Mills, "Remarks before the Chamber of Commerce."

frequency of tax reductions, or the role of general revenue in social insurance, there were clear boundaries to these debates. Few members, for example, challenged the centrality of economic growth, and no one called for a complete retrenchment of the federal government. As much as its substance, the silences of the discourse helped define the community and its agenda.

DISCOURSE AND THE TAX COMMUNITY

Fiscal discourse served the tax community well. It articulated its desire to finance a state that maintained the stability of a pluralistic society and avoided the extremes of laissez-faire liberalism and communist statism. The state could help maintain stability through contributory social insurance programs that avoided "dependency." This discourse emphasized the use of taxation rather than spending to spur growth and achieve high employment without abandoning the balanced budget rhetoric. Most important, the language took an appealing technocratic approach to taxation that emphasized macroeconomic and actuarial economics; its version of "reform" helped rid fiscal policy discourse of the "ghosts" of class conflict. Although there were clearly bitter debates among policymakers, they usually occurred within the boundaries of the postwar discourse.

This political discourse was an important part of the culture of the tax community. The discourse helped Mills and other policymakers to communicate and devise substantive policies. This style of discourse also shaped the ways in which Mills and his colleagues perceived their political world. Discourse, as Dorothy Ross has argued, develops "over time, centering around certain problems, setting the terms of discussion for those who enter into it, and at the same time responding to the different intentions of participants."[103] This fiscal discourse led Mills to conceive of himself as involved in a common intellectual and political project with other policymakers. In this case, their project was to manipulate taxation to achieve economic growth and contributory social insurance without sacrificing political or economic stability.

In the following chapters, I will examine the history of income taxation and Social Security between 1962 and 1972 as the community and Congress designed legislation within the context of the postwar discourse. The discourse provided a broad conceptual framework for Mills to negotiate compromises among the factions within the tax community and between the community and Congress. The discourse also provided a rhetorical arsenal with which to conduct policy

[103] Ross, *Origins of American Social Science*, xviii–xix.

debates. As a result, the discourse played a role in an unusually productive political decade, beginning with the Revenue Acts of 1962
and 1964, the Social Security Amendments of 1965, the Revenue and
Expenditure Control Act of 1968, the Tax Reform Act of 1969, cul-
minating in the Social Security Amendments of 1969–1972.

PART TWO

The Politics of Policy

6

The Road to Tax Reduction

As chairman of Ways and Means, Mills played a significant role in devising the Revenue Acts of 1962 and 1964. The bills were attempts to promote higher levels of employment and to enhance economic productivity. Arising from the Joint Economic Committee and Ways and Means hearings of the 1950s, the bills were rooted in a particular economic understanding and analysis of the income tax. As Mills explained, the legislation adopted "a new theory in taxation . . . that the tax system should be used, under proper circumstances, as an economic tool and as an instrument of fiscal policy."[1]

The transformation of income taxation into macroeconomic policy represented a significant victory for the growth manipulation faction of the tax community, which included economists Walter Heller, Gardner Ackley, and Herbert Stein. The Revenue Act of 1962 enacted the first major tax break designed explicitly to stimulate national private investment. The measure also launched a long-term project of incremental tax reform that had been promoted by the tax reform faction since the mid-1950s. Consistent with this approach was the Revenue Act of 1964, which enacted the largest postwar tax reduction until 1981 and, for the first time, openly endorsed deficits in nonrecessionary times.

Despite having serious objections to both pieces of legislation, Mills advocated the measures and considered them important successes. The policies grew out of the proposals and the policymakers that had gained prominence through Mills's committee studies of 1955–1961. By repackaging the legislation, moreover, Mills helped craft policies that could appeal to both Keynesian economists and fiscal conservatives, as well as to both tax reformers and interest groups; politicians and policymakers who were influenced by either strand of thought could claim at least a partial victory from the legislation. In 1965, Mills praised the measures as a watershed in public

---

[1] Wilbur D. Mills, "Recent Amendments to the Internal Revenue Code and Possible Future Tax Legislation: Remarks to the Pulaski County Bar Association," 30 October 1964, WMPC, Box 591, File: Mills Speeches.

policy. Together, he said, the new laws had increased the nation's economic growth, lowered unemployment, and raised the chances of achieving a balanced budget.[2]

KENNEDY, MILLS, AND THE TAX COMMUNITY

The studies produced by Mills and the tax community between 1955 and 1961 played an important role in defining the tax agenda of the early 1960s. Eisenhower and his cabinet paid little attention to the macroeconomic uses of income-tax policy or the need for substantive reform of tax breaks. Those two policies, along with specific proposals and their advocates, gained considerable attention within Washington through the Joint Economic Committee and Ways and Means. Many participants who obtained prominence as a result of the studies – such as Mortimer Caplin and Stanley Surrey – found themselves in positions of considerable power in the executive branch. With Mills as chairman of Ways and Means, moreover, these policies found some support even if it was only temperate from the committee leadership. Certainly, Mills expressed strong opposition to those who advocated the aggressive manipulation of tax policy, such as frequent temporary tax cuts based on short-term economic prognostications or a full embrace of deficits. Regardless, Mills provided an opportunity for these positions to be heard within Congress and voiced his support for the moderate use of income-tax manipulation and temporary deficits to stimulate growth.

The tax community in power

When Kennedy arrived at the White House in 1961, he brought several members of the tax community into the executive branch. Following Kennedy's election, Theodore Sorenson, special counsel to the president-elect, put together the pre-presidential Taxation Task Force and Economic Policy Task Force by recruiting people directly from the community who had helped with the congressional studies. The task forces promoted the ideas and personnel of the community within the executive branch.

The Taxation Task Force, for example, included Stanley Surrey, Mortimer Caplin, Norman Ture, Adrian de Wind, and Richard Musgrave, with the economist Cary Brown assisting on an informal basis. Building on the studies of Ways and Means, the task forces developed three proposals that became crucial to the administration: a targeted,

---

[2] Wilbur D. Mills, "Remarks to the Kiwanis Club, Little Rock Arkansas," 14 December 1965, WMPC, Box 658, File 17.

15 percent investment credit to increase private capital formation, an across-the-board rate reduction to stimulate investment and demand, and such tax reforms as restricting business expense deductions and tightening the definition of capital gains to raise more revenue.[3] Stanley Surrey circulated these findings among colleagues in the executive branch and the leaders of the tax-writing committees; he also organized a series of seminars at the Brookings Institution dealing with issues raised by the Taxation Task Force.[4]

While in office, Kennedy placed several members of the community in important positions. Surrey became assistant secretary of the Treasury; Harvey Brazer became Surrey's deputy assistant secretary and director of the Treasury's Office of Tax Analysis; Henry Fowler was named under-secretary of the Treasury; Joseph Barr served as a legislative liaison; Walter Heller, Kermit Gordon, and James Tobin formed the Council of Economic Advisors; Robert Ball became commissioner of the Social Security Administration; Wilbur Cohen was made assistant secretary of Health, Education, and Welfare; and Mortimer Caplin became commissioner of the Internal Revenue Service (IRS). Meanwhile, Joseph Pechman moved into the position of director of Economic Studies at the Brookings Institution and Herbert Stein continued to head the Research Division of the CED.

Within the administration, the academic triumvirate that ultimately pushed hardest for tax reduction and reform – Surrey, Heller, and Caplin – had all been involved in the early Joint Economic Committee and/or Ways and Means hearings between 1955 and 1960. Stanley Surrey, together with the Office of Tax Analysis and the IRS, for instance, completed a study of 1959 federal tax returns. This report provided shocking statistical documentation about unreported income, such as the $500 million lost as capital gains and the $834 million as dividends. The study concluded, "Although our statutory marginal tax rates go up to 91 percent, the average tax rates actually

---

[3] Taxation Task Force, "Tax Policy For 1961: Contents, Listing of Matters Covered, Brief Summary of Recommendations, Detailed Discussion of Recommendations," 31 December 1960, JFKL, Pre-Presidential Papers, Task Force Reports, Box 1072, File: Taxation Task Force; Edward S. Flash, Jr., *Economic Advice And Presidential Leadership: The Council of Economic Advisers* (New York: Columbia University Press, 1965), 173–218; "Tax Policy Report for Kennedy Outlines Ways to Spur Economy, Cut Income Taxes," *The Wall Street Journal*, 10 January 1961; David J. Stern, "Congress, Politics, and Taxes: A Case Study of the Revenue Act of 1962" (Ph.D diss., Claremont Graduate School, 1965), 8–12; Mortimer Caplin, interview with Shelley Davis and Kecia McDonald, 18–25 November 1991, Internal Revenue Service, Oral History Interview, 5–9; Theodore Sorensen, interview with Carl Kaysen, 20 May 1964, JFKL, Oral History Interview Collection, 145–147.

[4] Stanley Surrey to the Files, 7 February 1961, SSP, Box 180, File 1. See also Surrey to Wilbur Cohen, 8 November 1961, WCP, Box 112, Folder 15.

paid at high income levels are relatively low."[5] Surrey also conducted monthly meetings on tax reform with Treasury consultants who were handpicked from the tax community.[6]

Kennedy on the offensive

After 1961, Mills thus encountered an aggressive executive branch armed with its own expertise from the tax community. Under Presidents Kennedy and Johnson, the executive branch repeatedly attempted to encroach on the fiscal powers of Congress. In many respects, this confrontation was merely another battle in a long-standing war between the executive branch and the legislature over control of the modern American state.[7] But it was an important battle, both to the presidents and to Mills. Kennedy, for instance, expanded the role of the CEA.[8] Although there were constitutional limits to the power the president could achieve, Kennedy attempted to expand executive power in taxation as much as possible.

The administration charged that Ways and Means was failing to respond to pressing national needs. Powerful interest groups, the White House said, controlled its members. Moreover, Ways and Means members were charged with holding outdated economic ideas, such as the centrality of annual balanced budgets.[9] Only the executive branch had the expertise and the "freedom" from interest-

---

[5] Stanley Surrey to Wilbur Mills, 22 September 1961, SSP, Box 163, File 1; Surrey to Douglas Dillon, 30 July 1962, SSP, Box 177, File 6; Harvey Brazer to Surrey, 26 October 1961, SSP, Box 176, File 5; "Pending Tax Matters: 1961," NAT, RG 56, Office of Tax Policy, Box 68, File: Tax Reform 1961–1962.

[6] Stanley Surrey to Seymour Harris, 23 October 1962, SSP, Box 178, File 1; Surrey, Handwritten Notes, 23 October 1962, SSP, Box 175, File 4; Michael McGreevy to Surrey, 24 September 1963, SSP, Box 126, File 1; Harvey Brazer to Cary Brown, 17 October 1961, SSP, Box 170, File 1; Brazer to Surrey, 24 October 1962, SSP, Box 781, File 1; Surrey, "Individuals with whom we have discussed, or may discuss, tax policy issues," 2 November 1962, NAT, RG 56, Office of Tax Policy, Box 69, File: Tax Policy 1961–1963.

[7] Stephen Skowronek, *Building a New American State: The Expansion of National Administrative Capacities 1877–1920* (Cambridge: Cambridge University Press, 1982); Sidney M. Milkis, *The President and the Parties: The Transformation of the American Party System Since the New Deal* (New York: Oxford University Press, 1993).

[8] Flash, *Economic Advice and Presidential Leadership*; Erwin L. Hargrove and Samuel A. Morley, eds. *The President and the Council of Economic Advisers: Interviews with CEA Chairmen* (Boulder: Westview Press, 1984), 163–215; Walter Heller to Lyndon Johnson, 1 December 1963, JFKL, Walter Heller Papers, Kennedy-Johnson Files, Box 4, File: The Heller Council 7/63–12/63.

[9] Merriman Smith, "Progress Robs President of Traditional Weapon," *Nation's Business*, July 1963, 23–24; Seymour Harris, "The Gap Between Economist and Politician," *The New York Times*, Sunday, 14 April 1963, Section 6.

group pressure needed to carry out effective fiscal policies, the administration said. The White House also engaged in aggressive political lobbying. According to Wilbur Cohen, officials like Ivan Nestingen (under-secretary of the HEW), felt that "all you had to do was chop Mills up, grind him up, put the pressure on him, and the thing would fall into Kennedy's hands."[10] The administration even organized a powerful interest group – the Business Committee for Tax Reduction – to lobby for its proposals; the group included Henry Ford II (Ford Motor Company), Stuart Sanders (Norfolk and Western Railway), and Frederick Kappel (AT&T).[11]

Key players in the Kennedy administration understood that on taxes, an "information program" was needed to sway Congress; Stanley Surrey insisted that "facts and answers" rather than "Madison Avenue techniques" and "public relations gimmicks" were the key to success. As Surrey explained: "Taxes are a gut issue, and one where the Congress rightly feels that its members alone have the right to decide what shall be done, and that this decision should be made solely on the facts of the case. That makes it very dangerous to attempt to bring pressure to bear on Congress through public opinion. The only way such pressure can be brought to bear, and one which the Congress itself would never object to, is by publishing the facts of the case in a fair and objective manner."[12]

Kennedy facilitated communication between the executive and legislative branch by strengthening the Office of the Congressional Liaison, headed by Lawrence O'Brien. Following Kennedy's election, O'Brien had brought in a talented and aggressive staff, which included Claude Desautels, Henry Hall Wilson, and Mike Manatos. In addition, O'Brien improved the daily operations of the office: He arranged weekly breakfasts with legislative leaders; he took influential Democrats on three-hour trips in the presidential yacht (the *Sequoia*); he specialized the staff along regional lines; and he held Sunday brunches in his home for media officials and congressional representatives. These changes helped to close the gap between the two branches of government during the policymaking process.[13]

In response to Kennedy's aggressive approach, Mills protected his position by working closely with the tax community, many of whom

---

[10] Wilbur Cohen, interview with William Moss, 20 July 1972, JFKL, Oral History Interview Collection, 86–88. See also Cohen, interview with Moss, 24 May 1971, 73.

[11] Cathie J. Martin, *Shifting the Burden: The Struggle over Growth and Corporate Taxation* (Chicago: University of Chicago Press, 1991), 52–80.

[12] Stanley Surrey to March Sheehan, 1962, SSP, Box 179, File 4.

[13] Claude Desautels, interview with Michael Gillette, 18 April 1980, LBJL, Oral History Interview Collection, Interview I, 3–9; Lawrence O'Brien, interview with Michael Gillette, 18 September 1985, LBJL, Oral History Interview Collection, 50–54.

were now in the executive branch, to influence every stage of the tax-writing process. He was in a position to do so, because as chairman of Ways and Means, he stood at the crossroads of the various factions in the community. All factions depended on him to sell their proposals to Congress. Mills had also developed close personal ties with experts such as Surrey and Pechman during the 1950s. Rather than passively accepting or rejecting what the community offered, Mills expanded his influence by participating actively in all phases of the policymaking process. This required exhaustive efforts; one colleague acknowledged of Mills at this point in his career: "[He is] so single minded, never goes out, no social life or cocktail parties. He's thoroughly absorbed, goes home and thinks about the legislation."[14]

Lawrence O'Brien recalled that "Wilbur Mills was a key player . . . you were always aware of the absolute need for us to keep in total and constant communication with him, and probably more than that – keep him apprised of what you were doing."[15] While devising the Revenue Acts of 1962 and 1964, Mills and the tax community interacted through staff studies, letters, memoranda, informal brunches, formal breakfasts and dinners, confidential meetings, and "stag dinners."[16] Congressional hearings and studies served as an important meeting ground. The Department of Treasury consulted Mills at all times; as one official said privately, "Mills is kept informed the most and, obviously, influences our pre-message deliberation."[17]

Throughout the deliberations, many of Mills's most important con-

[14] JMIC.

[15] Lawrence O'Brien, interview with Michael Gillette, 4 December 1985, LBJL, Oral History Interview, Interview IV, 9.

[16] Invitations, WMPC, Box 676, File 3; Lawrence O'Brien, interview with Michael Gillette, 5 December 1985, Interview V, 36; Walter Heller, interview with David McComb, 21 December 1971, LBJL, Oral History Interview Collection, Interview II, 22; Robert Solow to Walter Heller, Kermit Gordon, and James Tobin, 24 April 1961, JFKL, Walter Heller Papers, Kennedy-Johnson Files, Box 6, File: Tax Cut 4/61–11/61. For correspondence between Wilbur Mills and the Treasury, see Mills to Douglas Dillon, 26 August 1961, NA, RG 233, 87th Cong., Box 6343, File: Insurance Company Act; Mills to Dillon, 24 October 1961 and Mills to Dillon, 10 January 1962, WMPC, Box 734, File 2; Stanley Surrey to Mills, 26 June 1962, NA, RG 233, 87th Cong., Box 6348, File: Unmarked; Dillon to Mills, 11 July 1962, NA, RG 233, 87th Cong., Box 6341, File: Depreciation; Mills to Dillon, 26 November 1962, WMPC, Box 19, File 14; Mortimer Caplin to Mills, 29 March 1963, NA, RG 233, 88th Cong., Box 38, File: Gross Income – Business Expenses; Dillon to Mills, 8 January 1964, NA, RG 233, 88th Cong., Box 48, File: Public Debt 1963–64; Mills, interview with Joe Franz, 2 November 1971, LBJL, Oral History Interview Collection, 15.

[17] JMIC.

tacts were with key executive staffers, administrators, and experts. For instance, Henry Fowler, under-secretary to the Treasury, earned the title of "Ambassador to Arkansas" because of his frequent visits with the chairman. O'Brien also mediated between the chairman and the president on most policy matters. Mills even had the unprecedented privilege, for a congressional representative, of participating in Kennedy's policymaking Troika and Quadriad. These top-secret meetings included the secretary of the Treasury, the director of the Bureau of the Budget, the chairman of the CEA, and occasionally the chairman of the Federal Reserve. Moreover, all of the leading interest groups and think tanks bombarded Mills with technical information and position papers. Representatives from the oil industry, the insurance industry, commercial banks, and the stock market were particularly aggressive in this respect.[18]

Laurence Woodworth played an important role during all of these encounters. Like Robert Myers on Social Security, Woodworth emerged as Mills's chief confidant, serving as the key link between Mills, the tax community, and related interest groups. Every Saturday, for example, Woodworth met at home with Treasury's Tax Legislative Counsel to formulate compromises among the committee, the administration, and interested organizations.

SUBSIDIZING ECONOMIC GROWTH

The Kennedy administration began its push for a more aggressive macroeconomic fiscal policy on April 20, 1961, with its proposal to stimulate economic productivity and growth. The main components of the bill – the investment credit and tax-break reforms – had originated from Surrey's Taxation Task Force and from the Ways and Means hearings in 1958 and 1959; the studies had helped define the central problems, highlighted specific proposals, and directed the policy agenda toward strategic tax incentives and reform.[19] Those who

[18] See for example, Jerry Voorhis to Wilbur Mills, 4 August 1961, NA, RG 233, 87th Cong., Box 6345, File: Taxation of Co-ops; Dan Jones to Wilbur Mills, 16 May 1962, NA, RG 233, 87th Cong., Box 6340, File: Foreign Trade and Tariffs; William Hogan, *Depreciation Reform and Capital Replacement* (Washington, 1964) and The Research Institute of America, *Making the Most of Depreciation and Investment Credit* (Washington, 1964) in NA, RG 233, 88th Cong., Box 39, File: Gross Income 1963–64.

[19] In its public statements, the Kennedy administration repeatedly acknowledged the influence of the studies of Mills's committees. See U.S. Congress, House Committee on Ways and Means, *Our Federal Tax System: Message from the President of the United States Relative to Our Federal Tax System*, 87th Cong., 1st sess., 1961; U.S. Congress, House Committee on Ways and Means, *President's 1963 Tax Message Along With Principal Statement, Technical Explanation, and Supporting Exhibits and Documents*, 88th Cong., 1st sess., 1963, 28–30; Curtis, "The House Committee on Ways and Means,"

proposed the investment credit hoped to encourage businesses to invest in new assets by allowing them to deduct part of the cost of these purchases from their income liability. Many income-tax experts actively supported this proposal. But at the Ways and Means Committee hearings in April 1961, the majority of corporate interest groups rejected it because they feared that the credit would cost them liberalized depreciation rates, a benefit that business had grown accustomed to since 1954. Moreover, they were angered that the proposed credit would cover only some sectors of business.[20]

Selling the investment credit

Having helped promote macroeconomic tax manipulation and tax reform on the policy agenda, Mills now worked to repackage the administration's proposals and to lead negotiations with members of the committee and their interest groups. Like many business groups, Mills too feared that a targeted credit would distort market-oriented economic decisions and lose excessive amounts of revenue. At this point, he stepped in to reconstruct the Kennedy task force proposal. Mills wanted a smaller, broader credit. In the end, he forged a compromise assisted by George Terborgh (research director of the Machinery and Allied Products Institute) and Maurice Peloubet (a prominent tax accountant).

The Mills compromise transformed the 15 percent targeted credit into a 7 percent flat-rate credit, which capital-intensive industries found very attractive. Corporate interests were even more enticed by the liberalized depreciation allowances announced by the Treasury in July 1961. Treasury officials also helped to ensure legislative success by adjusting their "semantics" to convince business that the investment credit was "not a subsidy but a broadly applicable yet somewhat selective reduction in the effective rate of the corporate income tax." This, according to one economist, helped gain the support of the Chamber of Commerce.[21] Together, the credit and the

121–147; Douglas Dillon to Wilbur Mills, 2 August 1961, JFKL, Presidential Office Files, Departments and Agencies, Box 89, File: Treasury 7/61–8/61; Robert Solow to Walter Heller, Kermit Gordon, and James Tobin, 24 April 1961, JFKL, Walter Heller Papers, Kennedy-Johnson Files, Box 6, File: Tax Cut 4/61–11/61.

[20] For a nuanced discussion of the corporate reaction to these proposals, see Martin, *Shifting the Burden* and Robert M. Collins, *The Business Response to Keynes, 1929–1964* (New York: Columbia University Press, 1987). See also Republican Members of the Committee on Ways and Means, "Ways and Means Republicans Denounce Administration Tax Credit Scheme as Irresponsible Tax Reduction and Urge Abandonment of Plan," JFKL, Presidential Office Files, Box 107, File: Taxes.

[21] Harvey Brazer to Stanley Surrey, 28 November 1961, SSP, Box 92, File 1. See also Surrey, Handwritten Notes, 31 March 1961, SSP, Box 91, File 3; Surrey to Myer

liberalized depreciation provided the biggest reduction in corporate taxes since 1954. In return for his support, Mills had demanded from the administration that a Titan II missile base be built in Arkansas and that President Kennedy personally dedicate a public works project located in his district; he warned the administration staff that "no one else will be acceptable."[22]

Closing tax breaks

The sections of the proposal that spurred the most intense conflict were the tax reform measures. Led by Stanley Surrey and Joseph Pechman, the tax reform faction of the community pushed for limitations on foreign tax havens, higher capital gains taxes, and the withholding of income on dividends and interest, which were three major tax-escape routes for the upper-income brackets.[23] The staffs of the Treasury and JCIRT worked together to formulate the administration proposal for Ways and Means.[24] The reform proposals angered powerful interest groups whose privileges seemed to be threatened. For the first time in decades, substantive reform seemed possible, and in the hearings and in private correspondences, organizations such as the U.S. Chamber of Commerce and the National Association of Manufacturers vigorously attacked the plans. As the struggle indicated, this issue was driven largely from "inside the beltway." The chairman recalled: "You have so much pressure to preserve preferences within the law and so little pressure on the part of those who contend generally that they want tax reform and equality of taxation. They have no lobby."[25] Mills realized that reformers needed to stir demand for reform inside and outside of the tax community. When Ways and Means was ready to bring the bill to the House floor, for instance, he told administration officials to "gear friendly pressure groups into motion."[26]

Feldman, 5 January 1962, JFKL, White House Staff Files, Myer Feldman Files, File: Tax Proposals: 1/62–1/63.

[22] Cited by Cathie J. Martin, "American business and the taxing state: Alliances for growth in the postwar state," in *Funding the Modern American State, 1941–1995: The Rise and Fall of the Era of Easy Finance*, ed. W. Elliot Brownlee (Cambridge: Cambridge University Press and Washington, D.C.: Woodrow Wilson Center Press, 1996), 369.

[23] "Pending Tax Matters: 1961," NAT, RG 56, Office of Tax Policy, Box 68, File: Tax Reform 1961–1962.

[24] Stanley Surrey to Colin Stam, 27 September 1961, SSP, Box 175, File 5.

[25] Wilbur Mills, interview with Joe Frantz, 2 November 1971, 19. See also Mills, "Remarks of the Honorable Wilbur D. Mills, Chairman, Committee on Ways and Means, before the Society of Public Accountants," September 1958, WMPC, Box 775, File 9.

[26] Henry Hall Wilson to Lawrence O'Brien, 1 March 1962, JFKL, White House Staff Files, Lawrence O'Brien, Box 10, File: Wilbur Mills, Arkansas, Folder 1.

But a strong tax reform lobby did not materialize outside the tax community. In the end, the chairman was forced to give ground to the interest groups on many of the reforms in exchange for the investment credit and for retention of some of the reforms. But before he did, he demonstrated his willingness to confront entrenched interests and to promote the cause of tax reform. Mills staunchly defended the reform provisions, such as the withholding of income on dividend and interests and reforms on mutual savings banks. When Mills saw that he did not have the support he needed for his other reforms, he crafted the best compromise he could get in a measure he knew would pass. Determined not to repeat the mistakes of his first year as chairman, he negotiated yet another round of compromises among the interest groups and members of the tax community.

The Revenue Act of 1962

After Mills maneuvered to cut the investment credit from 15 percent to 7 percent, and to change it from a targeted provision to a flat-rate credit for all capital-intensive industries, the Rules Committee granted Ways and Means a closed rule. Several important reforms were passed: a crackdown on foreign tax havens, new limits on benefits for cooperatives, a more rigorous system for reporting income on interest and dividends, and tighter restrictions on travel and entertainment deductions.

By mid-March, Ways and Means passed the Revenue Act of 1962. On March 22, Kennedy sent the chairman a congratulatory letter thanking him for its passage, and soon after, the Senate approved the legislation.[27] Mills was forced to drop the withholding provision after the Senate Finance Committee soundly defeated it. At the urging of the administration, Mills decided not to pursue that reform in conference.[28]

In the Conference Committee, staff experts collected and filtered the mountains of data gathered from the tax community. In the final meetings of the committee, five representatives from Ways and Means and five representatives from the Senate Finance Committee met with legislative staff members and Treasury experts to formulate the specific language of the tax law. Each day focused on a specific set of technical provisions.[29] The staff forged compromises between the

[27] John F. Kennedy to Wilbur Mills, 22 March 1962, JFKL, Presidential Office Files, Departments and Agencies, Box 50, File: 3/21–31/62.
[28] Stern, "Congress, Politics, and Taxes," 397.
[29] Notes of John Martin on Conference Committees on H.R. 10650 in May and September of 1962 in NA, RG 233, 87th Cong., Box 15, File: H.R. 10650; Stern, "Congress, Politics, and Taxes," 217–221.

competing interests, leaving the bulk of the work of writing the actual text to Woodworth and the Tax Legislative Counsel. When the tax-revision battle heated up, Mills turned primarily to Woodworth for advice because Stam opposed the major tax-break reforms. In 1964, Woodworth officially replaced Stam as the chief of staff of the JCIRT.[30]

Even though Mills closely monitored the staff, it was very influential at this stage. This was particularly true under Kennedy, since his administration's proposals were written vaguely, leaving the staff with considerable room to shape the substance of legislation.[31] While the committee met, individual experts actively pursued provisions of their choice. Gerard Brannon, for example, pushed hard for the liberalization of depreciation rates because he thought they were "horribly out-of-date"; he also urged the reform of foreign taxation laws and generally supported the investment credit.[32] In the Senate, said one lawyer: "If Stam thinks there is no merit in the idea, the Congressman will usually drop it. If Stam thinks there is merit, the Congressman is likely to sponsor it."[33] Since the staff played such an important role, lobbyists occasionally bypassed representatives to work directly with the experts.[34]

---

[30] Until his retirement, Colin Stam remained very influential in the Senate. Stern, "Congress, Politics, and Taxes," 70; Stanley Surrey, "Tribute to Dr. Laurence N. Woodworth: Two Decades of Federal Tax History Viewed from this Perspective," *National Tax Journal* XXXII, No. 3 (September 1979): 226–228.   [31] JMIC.

[32] Brannon's activities and positions can be traced through the following documents: Gerard Brannon to Wilbur Mills, 5 November 1958 and Brannon to Mills, 27 January 1959, WMPC, unprocessed; Brannon to Mills, 1 March 1960, NA, RG 233, 86th Cong., Box 6341, File: Depreciation; Brannon to Leo Irwin, 1 March 1960, NA, RG 233, 86th Cong., Box 41, File: Gross Income – Exclusions; Brannon to Mills, 1 September 1960, NA, RG 233, 86th Cong., Box 13, File: Legislative File; Brannon to John Byrnes, 4 January 1961, NA, RG 233, 87th Cong., Box 39, File: Gross Income – Business Expense; Brannon to Mills, 20 June 1961, NA, RG 233, 87th Cong., Box 13, File: Leg. File Co-ops; Brannon to Mills, 23 June 1961, NA, RG 233, 87th Cong., Box 6339, File: Foreign Income Tax Treatment; Brannon to Stanley Surrey, 7 November 1961, NA, RG 233, 87th Cong., Box 13, File: H.R. 10650; Brannon, "Commentary on Committee Decisions on Revenue Act of 1961," NA, RG 233, 87th Cong., Box 13, File: H.R. 87A-D14, H.R. 10650; Brannon to Mills, 17 January 1962, NA, RG 233, 87th Cong., Box 14, File: H.R. 10650; Brannon to Mills, 17 February 1962, NA, RG 233, 87th Cong., Box 13, File: Leg. File Co-ops; Brannon to Mills, 21 March 1962, NA, RG 233, 87th Cong., Box 14, File: Income Tax Credit; Brannon to Mills, 26 March 1963, NA, RG 233, 88th Cong., Box 39, File: Gross Income – Deductions and Depletion.

[33] E.W. Kenworthy, "Special-Interest Tax Legislation: A Washington Mystery Unfolds," *The New York Times*, 11 November 1963. See also Kenworthy, "Colin Stam: A Study in Anonymous Power," in *Adventures in Public Service: The careers of eight honored men in the United States Government*, eds. Delia and Ferdinand Kuhn (New York: Vanguard Press, 1963), 107–136.

[34] C.F. Hotchkiss to Leo Irwin, 15 February 1960, NA, RG 233, 87th Cong., Box 6345, File: Small Business; Gerard Brannon to Wilbur Mills, 15 February 1960, NA, RG

The staff also helped determine how effective the reforms would be once enacted. One member of Ways and Means relied on experts to find out if a bill was a "giveaway for someone"; the experts helped Ways and Means "decide the *merits* of bills."[35] Capitalizing on this knowledge, the staff sometimes limited the choices of legislators. Mills understood their role, and relied on experts to lobby for particular provisions within Congress. Several senators at the Conference Committee, for example, were angered with Mills's decision to tighten restrictions on travel and entertainment deductions.[36] But Mills's provision was saved by the two men who drafted the legislation, Woodworth and Donald Lubick. When Woodworth and Lubick met with the senator who threatened to kill the reform, by prearrangement they brought three different versions of the bill to the meeting. The first two drafts they presented to the senator were clearly too strict for him to accept. After the senator emphatically rejected the first draft, Woodworth "convinced" Lubick that he should show a more lenient provision, but the senator again said "no!" Finally, Woodworth urged Lubick to show the senator an even more "generous" bill, which they had drafted just that morning. Lubick shook his head and responded, "Look, look Larry this is absolutely out, the administration won't take it!" This draft, of course, was the one they and Mills had wanted all along. After some prodding, Lubick changed his mind. The senator took the bait and insisted on that version of the bill.[37]

In the end, the base-broadening reforms and the investment credit were important achievements. The new investment incentives of the Revenue Act lowered corporate taxes from 4.2 percent of GNP in 1960 to 3.6 percent in 1962. They saved corporations almost $90 billion in taxes between 1962 and 1981.[38] Meanwhile, the Treasury had also liberalized depreciation allowance schedules in 1962. The successful reforms of a few major tax breaks, such as restrictions on foreign tax havens and travel and entertainment deductions, marked a significant break from the tax-break-oriented path of the previous decade; as Treasury economists told one reporter: "For the first time in many years . . . the tax battle has been waged in terms of closing

233, 87th Cong., Box 6345, File: Taxation of Co-ops; James Carr to Mills, 3 March 1962, NA, RG 233, 87th Cong., Box 6337, File: Accounting Method; Irwin to Mills, 19 April 1960, NA, RG 233, 86th Cong., Box 39, File: Gross Income, Business Expenses; Peter Heller to Irwin, 12 March 1963, NA, RG 233, 88th Cong., Box 48, File: Stock Options 1963–64.

[35] JMIC.

[36] Stanley Surrey to the Files, 9 March 1962, SSP, Box 92, File 2; Surrey to Files, 23 March 1962, SSP, Box 167, File 1.

[37] Donald Lubick, interview with Julian Zelizer, Washington, D.C., 16 May 1994.

[38] Martin, *Shifting the Burden*, 12.

up loopholes rather than poking fresh ones in the code."[39] Although the reforms of 1962 did not overhaul the system, they were well appreciated by policymakers, who understood the difficulties of eliminating any tax break from the code.

WE ARE ALL KEYNESIANS NOW

The next important step in Mills's career was the Revenue Act of 1964, which involved a push by the growth manipulation faction for a massive, across-the-board tax reduction, paired again with a continued drive by the tax reform faction for revenue-raising reform. The reduction was a measure that the growth manipulation faction had sought since the Joint Economic Committee studies of 1955. According to Surrey, the "avant garde thinking" in Washington was "a big reduction in rates."[40] This time, the proposed reduction was tied to reforms that included repealing the interest and dividend income credit and exclusion, taxing capital gains accrued at death, and limiting the mineral-depletion allowance.

Tax reform, once again

Mills faced two difficult challenges. First, corporate interests once again opposed the tax-break reforms. Now, the chairman openly acknowledged his limits; on the proposed reform of the oil depletion allowance, he privately told Kennedy, "You know that reform's going to have tough sledding, it's scratch double-ended depletion or one of those things and it's never going to, uh, never happen."[41] Corporate lobbyists, moreover, applied intense pressure on committee members to oppose any changes in the liberal treatment of lump-sum profit sharing and pension payments; in response to complaints from committee members, Mills asked the Treasury during a closed executive session to drop this reform.[42] Overall, Mills dealt with the administration primarily on the rate reduction, since this was so central to his agenda. The reduction might allow for future tax-break reforms,

---

[39] Douglass Cater, "The Ways and Means of Wilbur Mills," *The Reporter*, 26.

[40] Stanley Surrey, Handwritten Notes, October 1962, SSP, Box 178, File 1.

[41] "Off-The-Record Meeting With Wilbur Mills," 6 August 1962, JFKL, Presidential Office Files, Presidential Recordings Transcripts: Tax Cut Proposals Volume I, Audiotape 7, 7. See also "Off-The-Record Meeting With Wilbur Mills, Lawrence O'Brien, C. Douglas Dillon," 29 July 1963, JFKL, Presidential Office Files, Presidential Recording Transcripts: Tax Cut Proposals Volume II, Audiotape 101, 6; Lawrence O'Brien, interview with Michael Gillette, 5 December 1985, LBJL, Oral History Interview Collection, Interview V, 34–37.

[42] Stanely Surrey to the Files, 14 May 1963, SSP, Box 176, File 1.

and Mills thought it would stimulate economic productivity and higher levels of employment.

While concentrating on the reduction, Mills left the Treasury the difficult task of devising base-broadening reforms.[43] Treasury officials responded to the challenge with a program designed to stimulate economic growth and full employment, to reduce nontaxable income, and to simplify the tax system; the reform proposals built on work in the tax compendium that came out of the Ways and Means studies of 1958 and 1959. For political and ideological reasons, Surrey insisted that the program avoid any redistributive effect. He wrote: "The reform program should . . . leave the issue of vertical equity more or less undisturbed – that is, tax liabilities after the reform program has been enacted should be so distributed among income brackets that each income pays roughly the same proportion of the total tax bill as it does now."[44]

Some members of the tax community had trouble with the Kennedy administration's willingness to frame tax reform as a means of achieving rate reduction. Economist Richard Musgrave, for example, told colleagues in Treasury: "I am bothered by the Administration's failure to emphasize the importance of the equity objectives in the whole reform issue. To argue for base broadening as needed merely to permit rate cuts (required on incentive grounds) without exceeding the 'permissible' deficit, and not urge it on equity grounds, is a pretty weak position from which to defend the reform case. One cannot but note a change in flavor, in this respect, between the tax messages of '62 and '63."[45]

For his part, Mills still insisted on reforms to offset some of the cost of the rate reduction; he considered the reduction as a sweetener to interest groups who otherwise would oppose reforms.[46] Throughout the hearings, Mills tried to "drive home to the Committee the fact that the repeal of the dividend credit" could result in "substantially lower rates in upper brackets."[47] Several prominent business leaders, including the president of the New York Stock Exchange, G. Keith Funston, were enticed by this trade-off. Funston called the existing credit a "dead-end street." He urged the Treasury economists to

---

[43] JMIC.

[44] Stanley Surrey to Douglas Dillon, 19 July 1962, SSP, Box 177, File 5; Harvey Brazer to Surrey, 17 October 1962, SSP, Box 178, File 1.

[45] Richard Musgrave, "Comments on Tax Policy," 4 May 1963, SSP, Box 176, File 1.

[46] JMIC; Stanley Surrey to the Files, 10 December 1962, SSP, Box 179, File 4.

[47] Joseph Barr to Claude Desautels, 1 July 1963, JFKL, White House Staff Files, Lawrence O'Brien, Legislative Leaders Breakfast Material, Box 26, File: 2 July 1963, Folder 1. See also Lawrence O'Brien to John F. Kennedy, 2 July 1963, JFKL, Presidential Office Files, Box 53, File: Legislative Files 7/63.

analyze foreign systems to discover which was the most rational system for encouraging economic growth.[48] Mills also urged the Treasury to propose an elimination of the exclusion of sick pay from federal taxation. Finally, Mills indicated his support for a reform of the definition of capital gains income, in areas such as timber and live-stock.[49] As with the dividend credit, Mills told his committee that frequent abuses of the definition of capital gains were preventing Congress from enacting lower tax rates.[50]

Debating how and when to cut taxes

Mills's second challenge stemmed from disagreements with the Kennedy administration over the structure and timing of the tax reduction. There was a broad agreement that a tax cut was needed to stimulate the economy, but these issues divided members of the community. The administration's first move against Mills was a failed proposal in January 1962 for presidential authority to reduce tax rates.[51] In April, Mills warned Stanley Surrey that he "should not [again] be put in the position of 'ceding' jurisdiction of his commit-tee."[52] Beginning in the summer of 1962, Mills and Kennedy squared off in a heated battle over tax reduction. Since its early days in office, the administration had called for a massive tax reduction to end the problem of fiscal drag and to avoid future recessions. In the summer of 1962, the call for a quick and temporary tax reduction emanated from the CEA and other Kennedy experts who predicted a recession after the stock market crashed in May. During a speech at Yale University in June, Kennedy became the first president to challenge officially the sanctity of annual balanced budgets: "The myth persists that federal deficits create inflation and budget surpluses prevent it . . . what we need is not labels and cliches but more basic discussion of the sophisticated and technical questions involved in keeping a great economic machine moving ahead . . . What is at stake in our economic decisions today is not some grand warfare of rival ideolo-gies which will sweep the country with passion but the practical man-

---

[48] Harvey Brazer to Stanley Surrey, 17 October 1962, SSP, Box 178, File 1; Surrey to the Files, 13 May 1963, SSP, Box 58, File 4 and Box 176, File 1; Surrey to the Files, 10 December 1962, SSP, Box 179, File 4.

[49] Harvey Brazer to Stanley Surrey, 17 October 1962, SSP, Box 178, File 1.

[50] Stanley Surrey to the Files, 10 May 1963, SSP, Box 176, File 1.

[51] Stanley Surrey to Walter Heller, 24 January 1962, JFKL, Walter Heller Papers, Kennedy-Johnson Files, Box 21, File: Stand-By Tax Authority 1/62–6/64. For an excellent discussion of the administration's aggressive promotion of its fiscal poli-cies, see Martin, *Shifting the Burden*, 52–80.

[52] Stanley Surrey to the Files, 24 April 1962, SSP, Box 182, File 1.

agement of a modern economy."[53] Such management now required an immediate tax reduction.

In July and August 1962, the administration and key policymakers held a series of meetings about the possibility of a temporary tax reduction to spur investment and demand. Treasury officials concluded that raising the possibility of tax cuts as soon as possible was as important as the legislation itself: "The economic outlook is such as to make an immediate tax cut desirable, but it seems certain that calling for a tax cut in late summer this year, even though it is expected that it will not be enacted until eight to twelve months later, will do some good in that one can expect stimulative effects from actions taken by business and consumers in anticipation of the cut."[54] After Walter Heller formally suggested that a reduction would avert an upcoming recession, the Mills committee, beginning on July 26, held private hearings with members of the tax community and various interest groups; Mills decided to conduct the hearings in secrecy since he feared that the information presented might "psychologically" shake American confidence in the economy and thus cause a downturn. One reporter noted: "On the tax issue, Mills is the man to watch. Pres. Kennedy is relying on Mills' advice on whether to ask for a quick tax cut or to hold off until early next year."[55]

During Mills's hearings, the chairman drew on the pool of experts in the tax community to collect viable economic data to support the ultimate position of Ways and Means. As the hearings proceeded, several respected interest groups and macroeconomic experts in the community challenged Heller's analysis that a recession was imminent. Mills then developed a "coolness" toward the proposed cut, and used select quantitative data from the hearings to combat the administration. The best statistical indicators, Mills argued, did not show that a recession was just around the corner. The proposed deficits, according to "privy information" from government officials, would also aggravate the nation's balance-of-payments situation by causing foreign investors to lose faith in the American dollar.[56] Congress, said

---

[53] Cited in Iwan Morgan, *Deficit Government: Taxing and Spending in Modern America* (Chicago: Ivan R. Dee, 1995), 92.

[54] Harvey Brazer to Stanley Surrey, 23 May 1962, SSP, Box 179, File 2.

[55] "Hopes for tax cut take setback," *Business Week*, 4 August 1962, 27–28.

[56] Wilbur Mills, interview with Joseph O'Connor, 14 April 1967, JFKL, Oral History Interview Collection, 9–11; Lee Preston to Walter Heller, 7 August 1962, JFKL, Walter Heller Papers, Kennedy-Johnson Files, Box 6, File: Tax Cut 8/62. For the best look inside these hearings, see memorandums from Walter Heller to Kennedy in JFKL, Presidential Office Files, Departments and Agencies, Boxes 74 and 75, Files: Council of Economic Advisors Summaries of Ways & Means Testimony 7/62 and CEA 8/1/62–8/7/62; "Ways and Means," *The New York Times*, Sunday, 29 July 1962, Section 4.

the chairman, would certainly reject a quick, deficit-inducing temporary cut without clear indications of a recession, and the proposal would only damage the possibilities for a more comprehensive bill.[57] To make matters worse, Mills warned: "You've got business on the one hand, if they want a tax cut, wanting one type of tax cut. You've got the labor groups on the other hand wanting a tax cut, but a different type of tax cut. . . . Even if we made up our minds that we wanted a tax cut, we can't win."[58] Finally, Mills warned Joseph Pechman that even though he accepted the economic value of temporary deficits, the public strongly favored balanced budgets.

Instead, Mills insisted on the program that the growth manipulation and tax reform factions had developed since the mid-1950s: a permanent tax reduction tied to some tax-break reform to combat the problem of "fiscal drag." He also demanded expenditure reductions. At Joint Economic Committee hearings that summer, participating economists had testified in favor of a permanent, across-the-board reduction even "if we do not experience an actual downturn in the economy."[59] Relying heavily on Woodworth's data, Mills suggested that a revenue loss of roughly $11–12 billion might be acceptable if there were "firm" presidential assurances of expenditure control.[60] Mills feared that since the government could not control its propensity to spend, economically valuable temporary deficits would turn into inflationary permanent deficits during the second half of the decade. Some experts were unhappy with this language. Richard Musgrave noted: "I see little chance for the public to gain a better understanding of fiscal policy if the case for tax reduction is advanced under the banner of budget balancing, or if it is argued that the prospective upturn in G.N.P. makes the climate for tax reduction more ideal than it would be otherwise."[61]

Nonetheless, Mills insisted on emphasizing long-term balanced budgets and expenditure control. Committee Republicans pushed Mills and the administration on this issue. Thomas Curtis (R-MO) wrote Secretary of the Treasury Douglas Dillon that "if the benefits of the proposed tax cut are not to be wiped out by inflationary pressures on the consumer price index . . . the upward trend in federal expenditures must come to a stop here and now."[62] Expenditure

[57] "Off-The-Record Meeting With Wilbur Mills," 6 August 1962, 11.

[58] Ibid., 5–6.

[59] Harvey Brazer to Stanley Surrey, 15 November 1962, SSP, Box 178, File 2.

[60] Stanley Surrey to the Files, 27 August 1963, SSP, Box 48, File 4; "Off-The-Record Meeting With Wilbur Mills," August 6, 1962, 10–15; Surrey to the Files, 16 August 1963, SSP, Box 185, File 2; Curtis, "The House Committee on Ways and Means," 128–132.

[61] Richard Musgrave, "Comments on Tax Policy," 4 May 1963, SSP, Box 176, File 1.

[62] Thomas Curtis to Douglas Dillon, 1 August 1963, SSP, Box 185, File 1.

control was essential, according to Curtis and Mills, to legitimize the tax cut. Kennedy responded to Mills's requests for expenditure control by writing the chairman a widely publicized letter that promised "an even tighter rein" on federal spending and that assured him, "Our long-range goal remains a balanced budget in a balanced, full-employment economy."[63] Despite this promise, Mills referred to the economic indicators, and steadfastly resisted the temporary reduction. By August, he had forced Kennedy to back down.

Discussion of a temporary reduction had receded by November. According to one administration official, "Wilbur Mills really put the kibosh on the idea."[64] The policy agenda shifted back to the issue of a permanent tax reduction. Determined to push through an economic stimulus, the president now sought a permanent, across-the-board tax reduction to start in January 1963. Conflict quickly arose over the issue of timing. Mills did not want the cut to begin until January 1964, and insisted on tying tax reform and expenditure control to the package.[65] During a three-and-a-half-hour meeting in November, Mills told Fowler that he was keeping in "very close touch" with the economic situation. "Current indicators," said the chairman, showed economic improvement, making an immediate cut unnecessary. Mills added that he fully supported a permanent reduction tied to revenue-raising reforms and nondefense expenditure limitations, even if it meant large budget deficits. Existing rates, he told Fowler, were a major drag on economic growth, and prevented higher levels of employment. Following this meeting, the executive budget director told Kennedy, "We can probably make a very strong case of the kind that Mills is after . . . at the expense of deferring a number of things that really are needed."[66] On November 26, Stam and Surrey

[63] John Kennedy to Wilbur Mills, 21 August 1963, JFKL, Theodore Sorenson Papers, JFK Speech Files 1961–3, Box 76, File: Tax Message to the Nation (TV) 9/18/63; "Tighter Spending Rein Promised by President," *The Washington Post*, 22 August 1963.

[64] Gardner Ackley, interview with Joe Franz, 13 April 1973, LBJL, Oral History Interview Collection, 3.

[65] Joseph Barr to Claude Desautels, 13 May 1963, JFKL, White House Staff Files: Lawrence O'Brien, Legislative Leaders Breakfast Material, Box 25, File: 13 May 1963, Folder 1; Wilbur Mills, interview by Joe Franz, 2 November 1971, 10–12; Henry Fowler interview with David McComb, 10 January 1969, LBJL, Oral History Interview Collection, Tape I, 21–30.

[66] "Off-The-Record Meeting With Douglas Dillon, Henry Fowler, David Bell, Willard Wirtz, Walter Heller, Kermit Gordon, Edward Gudeman, Charles Schultze, Paul Samuelson, Robert Solow, James Tobin, Gardner Ackley," 16 November 1962, JFKL, Presidential Office Files, Presidential Recordings Transcripts: Tax Cut Proposals, Volume II, Audiotape 58, 12. See also Henry Fowler to Douglas Dillon, November 1962, JFKL, Presidential Office Files, Departments and Agencies, Box 90, File: Trea-

established joint staff subcommittees to draft each section of the proposal.[67] Meanwhile, Mills made explicit statements to constituents about his emerging, albeit hesitant, acceptance of deficit finance. "Government expenditure is not something like leprosy," Mills claimed. "One of the first results of a dispassionate look at this matter of government expenditure is the very clear implication of the current outlook situation that an unbalanced federal budget arising from expenditure in excess of tax revenues does not necessarily bring on inflation . . . While the existing budgetary deficit is large, there is no solid evidence that a somewhat larger budgetary deficit would in fact bring on an inflation."[68]

By December 1962, all sides agreed on the need for a permanent rate reduction with some expenditure control and tax reform, as long as the deficit did not exceed $12 billion.[69] The only issue that was not settled was the question of timing; this issue once again divided the tax community between those who supported an immediate cut, such as Walter Heller and Gardner Ackley, and those who wanted to wait until the following year and until the administration and Congress reached an agreement on expenditure reductions.

The president and Mills struggled over that dimension of the problem while Kennedy was drafting his December speech to the Economic Club. Kennedy planned to call for an immediate, permanent rate cut. But Mills still rejected immediate action. On December 5, he told O'Brien that tax cuts should not be effective until January 1964. He urged Kennedy not to focus on the reduction during his upcoming speech. Mills warned that since the economy was improving, Congress would have an "extremely adverse" reaction to an immediate, deficit-inducing reduction. To make matters worse, the CEA's faulty prediction of an economic downturn had raised serious questions within Congress about the quality of the administration's expertise.[70] Privately, even administration officials felt uneasy about their economic analysis; only a few days earlier, the Troika staff had given two contradictory predictions of the effect the reduction would have on GNP, predictions that were almost $10 billion apart.[71]

sury 11/11–12/62; Douglas Dillon to Wilbur Mills, 15 November 1962, WMPC, Box 19, File 14.

[67] Stanley Surrey to Douglas Dillon, 30 November 1962, SSP, Box 178, File 1.

[68] Wilbur D. Mills, "Remarks before the Little Rock Rotary Club," 29 November 1962, WMPC, Box 591, File: Mills Speeches.

[69] Stanley Surrey to the Files, 28 December 1962, SSP, Box 179, File 4; Warren Smith to Council of Economic Advisors, 3 December 1962 and CEA Staff Memorandum, 3 December 1962, JFKL, Kermit Gordon Papers, Box 11, File: Major Tax.

[70] Lawrence O'Brien to John F. Kennedy, 5 December 1962, JFKL, Presidential Office Files, Box 64, File: O'Brien, Lawrence 9/62–11/63.

[71] Robert Wallace to Douglas Dillon, 4 December 1963, SSP, Box 179, File 4.

Mills also sent a message to the White House in the form of an interview with *U.S. News and World Report*, in which he declared his opposition to an immediate cut. Mills cited the experts of the tax community: Both "business and Government sources," he said, indicated that there had not "been a deterioration" in the economy.[72] As the *Washington Post* headline commented, "Blow Dealt 1963 Tax Cut Plan."[73] On December 12, Mills and Kennedy met privately in the White House in an effort to resolve their differences. Following that meeting, Kennedy remarked: "Well, I think that Mr. Mills' interview should be read in its entirety. If you read the entire article, it does not suggest that the Administration, under some circumstances, and Mr. Mills, may be far apart." He added, "Quite obviously, Mr. Mills will have a very decisive voice in the final decision, but we hope to adjust our viewpoints so that we can get some action on this program next year."[74] Some administration officials were less conciliatory; they were angry with Mills, whose remarks were "not within the spirit of his commitment last summer and within the spirit of his relations with the President."[75]

On December 13, the Committee on Economic Development, drawing on the research of Herbert Stein, announced its support for the president's plan. But when Kennedy delivered his famous speech to the Economic Club on December 14, he backed off on the issue of an immediate tax reduction. Instead, he focused on permanent cuts, expenditure control, and long-term balanced budgets, announcing, "Our tax system siphons out of the private economy too large a share of personal and business purchasing power . . . Surely the lesson of the last decade is that budget deficits are not caused by wild-eyed spenders but by slow economic growth and periodic recessions . . . In short, it is a paradoxical truth that tax rates are too high today and tax revenues are too low. . . ."[76] For the time being, at least, Mills had won the battle. At this point, the administration was not inclined to continue the struggle with the powerful chairman of Ways

---

[72] "Why A Tax Cut Is Unlikely In '63," *U.S. News & World Report*, 17 December 1962, 42–45.

[73] "Blow Dealt 1963 Tax Cut Plan," *Washington Post*, 11 December 1962; Editorial, "Mills Says No," *The Washington Post*, 12 December 1962.

[74] "Tax Cut in '63? Here's The Argument," *U.S. News & World Report*, 24 December 1962, 23–24. See also Frank Porter, "President Still Resolved To Seek Tax Cut in '63," *The Washington Post*, 13 December 1962; Richard Mooney, "President Says Tax Plan Offers Cuts Next Year," *The New York Times*, 13 December 1962.

[75] Frank Porter, "Tax Cut Plan Heading For Major 'Hill' Fight," *Washington Post*, 12 December 1962; Frank Porter, "$11 Billion Cut in Taxes Urged by CED: Experts See Slash Aiding U.S. Growth," *The Washington Post*, 14 December 1962.

[76] Cited in Richard Reeves, *President Kennedy: Profile of Power* (New York: Simon & Schuster, 1993), 453.

and Means. As Kennedy told Sorenson, Mills "knows that he was chairman of Ways and Means before I got here and that he'll still be chairman after I've gone – and he knows I know it. I don't have any hold on him."[77]

During these heated debates, Mills continued to rely on his experts to help him stay on top of the deliberations. Experts, Mills understood, were the glue that held the large and growing tax community together. They provided him with access to vital information about the reduction and proposed reforms and ensured the dissemination of his ideas. He relied on their analyses during his meetings with the administration. Experts also kept him informed of the positions of other policymakers and interest groups, both inside and outside of committee hearings.[78] Mills made certain that his experts were well-situated in key meetings, hearings, and studies. He insisted, for example, that two Ways and Means staffers be included in the inter-staff meetings between the Treasury and the JCIRT, despite Stam's attempt to exclude them.[79]

By January 1963, Mills had secured a permanent rate reduction with limited tax reforms, to be implemented the following year. Within the committee, Mills accepted the appointment of Pat Jennings (D-VA) and Ross Bass (D-TN), two advocates of tax reduction. According to Lyndon Johnson's notes at a cabinet meeting, moreover, "Nothing here [in the Revenue Act] won't receive approval of Mills."[80] In the week of January 11, Mills's power was discussed in cover stories in both *Time* and *Newsweek* magazines. *Time* reported that Mills's special authority derived "from the sheer weight" of his expertise. The magazine added that he is beyond "dispute Congress' leading author-

[77] Theodore Sorenson, *Kennedy* (New York: Harper & Row, 1965), 426.

[78] Staff, House Committee on Ways and Means, *"The Revenue Act of 1962" Comparative Analysis of Prior Law and Provisions of Public Law 87–884 (H.R. 10650)*, 19 April 1962, H2128 (Committee – Print); Colin Stam to Wilbur Mills, 15 January 1963, NA, RG 233, 88th Cong., Box 39, File: Gross Income 1963–64; Staff, JCIRT, *Tax Tables and Charts Print No. 8*, 9 September 1963, H4789 (Committee – Print); Staff, JCIRT, *Summary of the President's 1963 Tax Message as Presented to the Committee on Ways and Means*, April 1963, J0510 (Committee – Print); Staff, JCIRT, *Staff Data: Listing of Certain Primary Items of Allowable Deductions Available to Individuals Under the Revenue Acts From 1913 through 1962*, 6 June 1963, H8832 (Committee – Print); Staff, JCIRT, *Digest of Testimony Presented and Statements Submitted to the Committee on Ways and Means With Respect to the President's 1963 Tax Message*, 12 June 1963, J0280 (Committee – Print).

[79] Wilbur Mills to Henry Fowler, Stanley Surrey, and Colin Stam, 4 December 1962, WMPC, Box 18, File 2; Surrey to Fowler, 13 November 1962, SSP, Box 178, File 2; Surrey to Douglas Dillon, 30 November 1962, SSP, Box 178, File 1.

[80] Lyndon Johnson, Handwritten Notes, 10 January 1963 at 10:00 A.M, LBJL, Handwriting Files, Box 2.

ity on taxation."[81] That power was there for all to see later in the year
when Kennedy spoke at the Little Rock fairgrounds and participated
in the dedication of the Greer's Ferry Dam on the Little Red River
at Mills's request. One White House aid half-joked, "If Wilbur wanted
us to go down to Heber Springs and sing 'Down by the Old Mills
Stream,' we'd be glad to do it."[82] By this time, most administration
officials had accepted Mills's argument that the reduction should be
permanent, that it should begin in 1964, and that it should be tied
to tax reform and expenditure limits.[83] On January 9, Mills urged that
the tax program include $4–5 billion in reform to offset part of the
deficit, or else it would be "wrong to reduce rates." Surrey convinced
Mills that these figures were too high.[84]

The compromise

The president presented his final plan to the Congress on January
24, 1963. Individual tax rates were to be cut by $11 billion and cor-
porate taxes by $2.6 billion. Reforms, including changes in the divi-
dend credit and exclusion and in the mineral depletion allowance,
were to produce $3.4 billion in revenue.[85] Surrey and O'Brien reit-
erated that the administration had to sell this tax cut to Congress and
to the public as beneficial to the entire country: "Remember [we] are
selling a tax cut – question is how [to] convince people that something personally helpful is good for [the] country."[86] The administration also realized that it needed to keep close ties to the Ways and
Means staff as the committee hearings proceeded in the next few
months. In a letter to one of Kennedy's legislative liaisons, Joseph
Barr explained: "The Committee under the Chairmanship of Congressman Mills has developed a protective and rather fraternal
instinct. If a witness has a friend on the Committee, he is usually
treated rather gently and there is little or no attempt to break down
a friendly line of questioning. However, after two years' work on the

---

[81] "An Idea on the March," *Time*, 11 January 1963 and "Wilbur Mills. . . . 'Mr. Taxes'
in the Congress," *Newsweek*, 14–18.

[82] Tom Wicker, "President Visits Arkansas Today," *The New York Times*, 3 October 1963.

[83] Stanley Surrey to George Porter, 4 April 1963, JFKL, White House Central Subject
Files, Box 225, File: FI 11-4-1-63-5-10-63.

[84] Stanley Surrey to the Files, 12 January 1963, SSP, Box 58, File 4.

[85] John F. Kennedy, "Special Message on Tax Reduction and Tax Reform: To the Congress of the United States," JFKL, Presidential Office Files, Box 52, File: 1/24/63
(Special Message on Tax Reduction and Tax Reform), 2; Martin, *Shifting the Burden*,
72.

[86] Stanley Surrey, Handwritten Notes on Meeting with Lawrence O'Brien, January
1963, SSP, Box 176, File 6.

last tax bill, the Committee has acquired a broad knowledge of many of the issues." Barr added: "The Committee is very well staffed and an uncovered witness in a controversial area such as stock options can find the going very difficult indeed. We are making every attempt to cooperate with the Committee staff to see to it that members are supplied with all the information they need to question witnesses . . . They obviously are determined to plow through the witnesses and get down to work in executive sessions."[87]

During the Ways and Means Committee hearings, which began on February 6 and lasted until September 10, a number of interest groups opposed the revenue-raising reforms. The oil companies, for example, campaigned aggressively against a change in the depletion allowance, and even purchased advertisements on Arkansas radio stations to protest the measures.[88] Despite these threats, Mills felt confident that his seat was secure. The chairman privately told Kennedy about a constituent who had said to him: "It doesn't make a bit of difference to me or to anybody in Arkansas what you do about taxes. We think you know what oughta be done. Now, if you were against the tax bill, we're not gonna argue with you about it." After such encounters, Mills told Kennedy, "I feel pretty good that they've got that degree of confidence and they are *not* twisting my arm."[89] This allowed Mills to continue defending controversial reforms, such as limiting capital gains, and to push hard to bring individual tax rates down to a range of 15 percent to 65 percent.[90]

In July 1963, Mills promised the administration that he could pass the bill within a few months, but only if the president stressed his commitment to expenditure control.[91] In mid-September, before the

---

[87] Joseph Barr to Claude Desautels, 25 February 1963, SSP, Box 177, File 2.

[88] "Off-The-Record Meeting With Wilbur Mills, Lawrence O'Brien, C. Douglas Dillon," 29 July 1963, 6.

[89] Ibid., 32. For the views of colleagues who recognized this independence, see Wilbur Cohen, interview with William Moss, 20 July 1972, JFKL, Oral History Interview Collection, 113; Lawrence O'Brien, interview with Michael Gillette, 24 July 1986, JFKL, Oral History Interview Collection, Interview XI, 50.

[90] Stanley Surrey to the Files, 10 May 1963; Surrey to the Files, 13 May 1963; Surrey to the Files, 14 May 1963 all in SSP, Box 176, File I. See also Surrey to the Files, 13 May 1963, SSP, Box 58, File 4; Surrey to the Files, 24 May 1963, SSP, Box 187, File 1; Surrey to Douglas Dillon, 13 May 1963, and Surrey to the Files, 14 May 1963 and Surrey to Dillon, 13 May 1963, all in SSP, Box 176, File l; Lawrence O'Brien to President Kennedy, 3 June 1963, JFKL, White House Staff Files: Lawrence O'Brien, Legislative Leaders Breakfast Material, Box 26, File: 4 June 1963 (Folder 1); Surrey to the Files, 13 May 1963, SSP, Box 58, File 4; Surrey, "Outline of Current Status of Income Tax Reform Program," 23 February 1962, SSP, Box 176, File 2.

[91] "Off-The-Record Meeting With Wilbur Mills, Lawrence O'Brien, C. Douglas Dillon," 29 July 1963.

House vote, Mills worked extensively with the Democratic whip, the administration, and John Byrnes to ensure that both parties would support the legislation.[92] Later that month, the House passed the measure by a vote of 271 to 155. The president was pleased with Mills's work; as the secretary of the Treasury noted, the chairman's statement on the legislation generally followed the "administration line" and was an "excellent description of the economics of tax reduction."[93]

Johnson accepts expenditure control

On November 22, 1963, President Kennedy was assassinated. On taking over the presidency, Lyndon Johnson promised to move aggressively on the unfinished business of the previous administration, including the income-tax reduction. Two days after the assassination, Secretary Dillon warned the new president that the tax bill was the main factor "holding back the private economic decision-making that is needed to assure confidence in the long-range prospects for the economy." Dillon argued that failure to enact the legislation would also have disastrous effects on international exchange markets, the stability of the dollar, and the stock market. He urged the president to make needed changes in the budget to obtain passage of the reduction.[94] At the same time, Walter Heller warned that holding the budget to \$99–99.5 billion, rather than \$101.5–102 billion, could be tolerated even though it would sacrifice up to 15 percent of the expansionary effect that was expected from the legislation.[95]

Led by top administration officials such as Lawrence O'Brien, Johnson and Congress designed a compromise on expenditure control.

Johnson committed his administration to expenditure control. On January 8, 1964, in the same speech that unveiled his poverty programs, Johnson presented a budget that reduced spending to \$97.9 billion, a figure slightly less than conservative Democrats and House Republicans had requested. The budget reduced or limited the rate of growth in defense programs, the space program, interest payments

[92] Ibid., 7; Randall B. Ripley, *Majority Party Leadership In Congress* (Boston: Little, Brown, 1969), 46–48; JMIC.

[93] Douglas Dillon to John F. Kennedy, 16 September 1963, JFKL, Presidential Office Files, Departments and Agencies, Box 90, File: Treasury 9/63.

[94] Douglas Dillon to President Johnson, 25 November 1963, JFKL, Kermit Gordon Papers, Box 13, File: The Tax Bill and Budget Expenditures.

[95] Walter Heller to Lyndon Johnson, 25 November 1963, JFKL, Kermit Gordon Papers, Box 13, File: The Tax Bill and Budget Expenditures.

on the debt, agricultural programs, and veterans programs – areas that had been the source of spending increases in 1963 and 1964 – and only allocated a modest amount of money to the poverty programs.[96] In conversations following the speech, Johnson boasted as much about the conservative nature of this budget as his poverty initiatives. He told Chairman Harry Byrd (D-VA) of Senate Finance, "I am going to try to stop the, and arrest the, spending and try to be as frugal as I can make them be . . . You are my inspiration for doing it."[97]

Many prominent fiscal conservatives responded positively to this budget. For example, Mills told Johnson that he was "very thrilled" with the proposal.[98] Henry Fowler, moreover, thanked Johnson for "making an honest man out of me and out of Wilbur Mills in one day." Fowler explained: "I have always said that our party is the party of responsibility and you made it true today . . . I have been a voice crying in the wilderness, as you know, on this thing for, for months now and the fact that it came through today really made me feel good . . . you have made a shambles out of those people up there and the business community is just ecstatic."[99] In meetings with Wall Street investors, Robert Anderson (former secretary of the Treasury and a confidant of Johnson's) reported that he had not heard a "single adverse comment" from "some of the most hard-headed people in the country." Anderson had not seen "any more remarkable display of confidence in the president in my lifetime than the financial community is showing at this moment."[100] He later added that John Byrnes called this the first opportunity for bipartisan support for tax reduction and achieving "real fiscal responsibility." Eisenhower wanted Anderson to tell Johnson "how very happy" he was about this reversal of the trend toward "bigger budgets, toward bigger

---

[96] Telephone Conversation, Lyndon Johnson and Kermit Gordon, 9 January 1964, Tape WH6401.10, #1297, LBJL, Recordings of Telephone Conversations – White House Series.

[97] Telephone Conversation, Lyndon Johnson and Harry Byrd, Tape WH6401.08, #1247, 8 January 1964, LBJL, Recordings of Telephone Conversations – White House Series.

[98] Telephone Conversation, Lyndon Johnson and Kermit Gordon, 8 January 1964, Tape 6401.08, #1235, LBJL, Recordings of Telephone Conversations – White House Series.

[99] Telephone Conversation, Lyndon Johnson and Henry Fowler, 8 January 1964, Tape WH6401.08, #1254, LBJL, Recordings of Telephone Conversations – White House Series.

[100] Telephone Conversation, Lyndon Johnson and Robert Anderson, 7 January 1964, Tape WH6401.07, #1220, LBJL, Recordings of Telephone Conversations – White House Series.

deficits."[101] To validate the budget in light of liberal charges that the administration was risking a recession, Johnson wanted business to show its support by lobbying Congress to support the tax reduction and by increasing capital investment.

Once Johnson assured Congress that spending would be controlled, the new measure moved through the Senate. The Finance Committee approved the legislation following Johnson's assurance of budget cuts; the Conference Committee and its staff drafted the final legislation. Johnson pressured the congressional Democratic leadership to speed up the bill. The president feared that the tax legislation would get caught up in a Senate filibuster against civil rights legislation. "If it gets behind civil rights," he told Mills, "God knows when it will be there!" Since Senate Finance had not added too many unacceptable amendments, Mills felt confident that the bill could be quickly passed.[102] Johnson reminded Lawrence O'Brien that every day Congress delayed the bill it cost the economy $30 million.[103] Allaying Johnson's fears, the Revenue Act of 1964, with permanent rate reduction, expenditure controls, and limited reforms, passed Congress in February 1964.

The Revenue Act of 1964

The Revenue Act of 1964 emphasized demand, not investment (as had been the case in 1962). This new legislation resulted in across-the-board tax reductions of approximately $10 billion out of a budget that was slightly under $100 billion, including corporate rate cuts from 52 percent to 48 percent; it also reduced personal income-tax rates from a range of 20 percent to 91 percent to a range of 14 percent to 70 percent. The legislation contained a handful of important revenue-raising reforms. John Watts (D-KY) and Hale Boggs (D-LA), for example, had negotiated a deal that reformed taxation on corporate dividend income by repealing the 4 percent dividend credit. The legislation also rescinded the privilege of grouping oil and gas properties to get extra benefits from the depletion allowance.[104]

---

[101] Telephone Conversation, Lyndon Johnson and Robert Anderson, 8 January 1964, Tape WH6401.10, #1288, LBJL, Recordings of Telephone Conversations – White House Series.

[102] Telephone Conversation, Lyndon Johnson and Wilbur Mills, 7 February 1964, Tape WH6402.08, #1921, LBJL, Recordings of Telephone Conversations – White House Series.

[103] Telephone Conversation, Lyndon Johnson and Lawrence O'Brien, 7 February 1964, Tape WH6402.09, #1955, LBJL, Recordings of Telephone Conversations – White House Series.

[104] Joseph Barr to Claude Desautels, 24 June 1963, JFKL, White House Staff Files, Lawrence O'Brien Papers, Legislative Leaders Breakfast Material, Box 26, File: 25 June 1963, Folder 1; Stanley Surrey to Files, 16 August 1963, SSP, Box 194, File 4;

In the Ways and Means and Conference Committee sessions, Mills had traded away most of the reforms to placate representatives and their interest groups in return for the rate reduction.[105] For example, Mills urged the committee to change one technical provision as a result of the concerns expressed by shoe companies, and John D. Rockefeller II had convinced Mills to water-down the reforms on the tax-treatment of foundations.[106] Whereas the 4 percent dividend credit was repealed, the $50 exclusion was doubled. John Martin's technical analyses helped derail several major reform proposals of capital gains taxation.[107] The committee also rejected a provision to increase the deduction for child care; Ways and Means, Surrey wrote, was "simply not interested in encouraging women to work."[108]

In the end, Mills had used the proposed higher tax on capital gains, the oil-depletion allowance, and the effort to curtail foreign tax havens as bargaining chips to ensure passage of the rate reduction, a central item on his larger agenda for reform. According to the studies of the 1950s, lower rates raised the incentives for people to pay their taxes. Interest groups were clearly more secure with the permanent tax reductions provided by their tax breaks than with the promised relief of future rate reductions. But in the end, most interest groups received both.[109] CEA economists did not mind this trade-off since, as James Tobin once wrote to Kennedy: "The stake of the nation and

Stanley Surrey to the Files, 8 May 1963, SSP, Box 58, File 4; Martin, *Shifting the Burden*, 56.

[105] Stanley Surrey to the Files, 4 March 1964, SSP, Box 193, File 5; Walter Heller to Theodore Sorenson, 8 July 1963, JFKL, Theodore Sorenson Papers, Box 59, Legislative Leaders Files 1961–64, File: Legislative Leaders 1963 (Meetings) 12/18/62–3/26/63; Heller to John F. Kennedy, 7 June 1963, Theodore Sorenson Papers, JFK Speech Files 1961–63, Box 76, File: Tax Reduction and Reform Message to Congress 1/24/63; Joseph Barr to Claude Desautels, 3 June 1963, JFKL, White House Staff Files: Lawrence O'Brien, Legislative Leaders Breakfast Material, Box 29, File: 4 June 1963, Folder 1; Arlen Large, "House Unit Votes to Drop 4% Dividend Credit Over Two Years; Sum Excludable Is Doubled," *The Wall Street Journal*, 16 August 1963; "Observer," *The New York Times*, 15 January 1963; John Morris, "Tax Reform: Outlook Dim," *The New York Times*, 16 June 1963; John Morris, "Tax Adjustments Kennedy Seeks Face Rocky Road in Congress," *The New York Times*, 8 January 1962.

[106] Stanley Surrey to the Files, 4 March 1964, SSP, Box 193, File 5; Surrey to Secretary Douglas Dillon, 17 September 1964, SSP, Box 124, File 4.

[107] Thomas J. Reese, *The Politics of Taxation* (New York: Quorum Books, 1980), 62; Joseph Bowman to Claude Desautels, 10 June 1963, JFKL, White House Staff File: Lawrence O'Brien, Legislative Leaders Breakfast Material, Box 26, File: 11 June 1963, Folder 1.

[108] Stanley Surrey to the Files, 10 June 1963, SSP, Box 175, File 1.

[109] Albert Gore to John F. Kennedy, 15 November 1962, JFKL, Presidential Office Files, Box 90, File: Treasury 11/11–12/62. See also Claude Desautels to Joseph Barr, 4 March 1963, JFKL, White House Staff Files, Lawrence O'Brien, Legislative Leaders Breakfast Material, Box 23, File: 5 March 1963, Folder 1.

the Administration in tax reform is small compared to their stake in economic expansion."[110]

Mills was pleased with this measure, particularly because it promised to stimulate economic growth and create full employment through moderate tax adjustments. On public spending, moreover, the Revenue Act of 1964 marked an important break for Mills and his community. The act turned to reduced taxation instead of increased public spending to spur growth. On the House floor, Mills called this legislation a "turning point" for just this reason:

> I am convinced that there are two roads the Government can follow toward the achievement of this larger and more pros-perous economy. I believe we are at the fork of those two roads today. One of these is the tax reduction road. The other is the road of Government expenditure increases . . . Although it is possible to achieve the prosperity we desire by either of the two routes I have outlined to you, nevertheless, there is a big difference – a vital difference – between them. The route of Government expenditure increase achieves this higher level of economic activity with larger and larger shares of that activity initiating in the Government . . . This road leads to big Gov-ernment, especially big Central Government.

Mills told Congress, "The route I prefer is the tax reduction road which gives us a higher level of economic activity and a bigger and more prosperous and more efficient economy with a larger and larger share of the enlarged activity initiating in the private sector of the economy."[111]

To be sure, the government continued to boost consumption by spending billions of dollars on military operations. The economies of California, Arkansas, and Colorado, for example, relied heavily on weapons manufacturing and military bases. But Mills and his col-leagues did not consider defense expenditures in terms of macro-economic policy. Instead, they categorized military spending as an "uncontrollable" necessity that was forced onto the nation by a hostile international environment. These expenditures, they argued, should be legitimized primarily on the grounds of national security, not eco-nomic growth. As a result, the tax community concentrated on other

---

[110] James Tobin to John F. Kennedy, 16 June 1962, JFKL, Presidential Office Files, Departments and Agencies, Box 74, File: Council of Economic Advisers 6/16/62–6/30/62.

[111] U.S. Congress, House of Representatives, *Congressional Record*, 88th Cong., 2nd sess., 24 September 1963, 17908–17909.

forms of domestic spending in its debates about stimulating consumer demand and private investment.[112]

Always straddling the line between southern representative and tax expert, Mills continued to speak in many voices. Back in his district, Mills demonstrated his command of Keynesian economics while simultaneously drawing on a less technical idiom to explain the legislation to his constituents. The following excerpt from one of his speeches reveals how Mills spoke about this legislation with constituents:

> Fiscal policy can help in achieving this expansion of job opportunities in an economy such as ours by stimulating investment and encouraging additional consumption. I like to think of it, however, in terms of lessening the restraints which prevent the American free enterprise system from itself generating necessary growth and increasing job opportunities. Economists have developed some fancy phrases to describe how this increased investment and consumption is brought about. Thus, it is said that a tax reduction which is likely to lead to additional consumption by the consumers of the country involves a "consumption multiplier." What they mean by this is that tax reduction which is likely to lead to consumption expenditures not only will increase incomes of businesses and employees, because of this initial increase in consumption, but that this increased income will in turn lead to additional consumption which will also increase incomes . . . In addition to the effect on consumption – and to many a more important factor – is the stimulating effect of tax reductions on investment. The economists refer to this as the "acceleration principle" . . . Frankly, I do not know how much faith we can put in these theories of economists but I do know that removing tax burdens on business and consumers does free them to expand investment and consumption. And I believe this is really the essence of the ideas that they are trying to express.[113]

---

[112] Michael S. Sherry, *In The Shadow of War: The United States Since the 1930s* (New Haven: Yale University Press, 1995), 47; 76; 136; 244; Gabriel Kolko, *Main \Currents in Modern American History* (New York: Harper & Row, 1976). Kolko coined the term "Military Keynesianism" to capture the importance of this type of spending to eliminating the problem of underconsumption. While the term is a useful analytical tool, it overstates the degree to which federal officials perceived military expenditures as part of macroeconomic policy.

[113] Wilbur D. Mills, "Remarks before the Chamber of Commerce Banquet," 4 December 1964, WMPC, Box 600, File 15.

Committed to bipartisanship, Mills made certain that key Republicans received credit for helping to pass the legislation. On February 26, President Johnson called Mills to thank him for supporting the bill. Mills agreed that Johnson's budget reductions helped to build support from John Byrnes and Senate Finance. The president invited Mills to attend a press conference thanking everyone who had helped to pass the bill. After exchanging compliments with the president, Mills reminded Johnson that Charles Halleck (R-IN) and Byrnes should be acknowledged for accepting the conference report. Although Byrnes had a tendency to "be political," Mills said, "he did exactly what he told you he would do." Once an agreement had been made on the budget and particular reform provisions, Byrnes had given his support.[114]

THE POLITICAL MILEAGE OF TAXES

By 1964, Mills's influence was openly discussed by many policymakers. He was no longer dependent even on the president to obtain services for his district: O'Brien commented: "Anything the White House could do to accommodate Wilbur Mills was done. Wilbur Mills didn't need the White House."[115] Kennedy privately acknowledged this, using the term "to Wilbur Mills" a tax bill, meaning to pass a bill that no one wants in an election year.[116] During the legislative deliberations, Mills had received increased funding for military installations and public works programs in Arkansas; he was in that regard immune from the limitations he proposed for others.[117] At this point in his career, Mills's power could be exercised in a variety of realms: One administration official recalled about health care reform, "I think that at no time, right up to the end of the road on Medicare, did we feel we could take on Wilbur Mills and try to override

[114] Telephone Conversation, Lyndon Johnson and Wilbur Mills, 26 February 1964, Tape WH6402.21, #2200, LBJL, Recordings of Telephone Conversations – White House Series.

[115] Lawrence O'Brien, interview with Michael Gillette, 24 July 1986, Interview XI, 38.

[116] Joseph Barr to John F. Kennedy, 2 April 1962, JFKL, White House Central Subject Files, Box 476, File: LE FI 11 9-26-61–4-10-62.

[117] Staff notes, 1963, LBJL, Congressional Favors File, Box 24, File: Mills, Wilbur D; WMPC, Boxes 141–42, 651; Claude Desautels to Lawrence O'Brien, 5 December 1961, JFKL, White House Staff Files: Lawrence O'Brien, House File: Wilbur Mills, Arkansas, Box 10, Folder 1; Desautels to O'Brien, 20 December 1962, White House Staff Files: Lawrence O'Brien, House File: Wilbur Mills, Arkansas, Box 10, Folder 2; Claude Desautels to Lawrence O'Brien, 12 July 1963, and Lawrence O'Brien to Henry Hall Wilson, 8 May 1962, in JFKL, White House Staff Files: Lawrence O'Brien, Box 10, File: Mills, Wilbur D. (Folder 3). This folder is full of material regarding Mills's demands for projects in the district.

him . . . there was nobody in that conference [committee] who was going to buck Wilbur Mills on the House side and probably there was little appetite to buck him on the Senate side either."[118]

Mills's status as the chairman of the Ways and Means Committee also gave him power that extended beyond fiscal affairs. In international relations, for instance, Mills overrode the demands of Ambassador George Kennan, who strongly requested favorable trade status for Poland and Yugoslavia. Mills single-handedly defeated this request with a provision in the Trade Expansion Act of 1962. When Kennan called the president to tell him how disastrous this action would be, Kennedy simply transferred Kennan on the telephone directly to Mills, who said there was nothing he could do.[119] Policy experts, interest groups, and congressional representatives agreed that if Mills opposed a bill it "would be dead."[120] In 1963, one reporter commented, "Not since the halcyon days of the late Speaker Sam Rayburn, has any one man so dominated a Congress as Wilbur Mills, by the sheer power of his office and his knowledge of tax matters, dominate[s] the 88th Congress."[121] By the time the Revenue Act of 1964 had passed, some were calling Mills the "Third House of Congress." One journal argued that he was "actually one of the three or four most powerful men in Washington." It added, "Indeed, one poll has ranked him only second to the President."[122]

Besides enhancing Mills's status, the Revenue Acts constituted an important stage in the development of economic policy. The stimulative tax policies promised to enlarge the "economic pie" without regulating managerial institutions, without redistributing income, and without increasing government spending. Contrary to the axiom that there is no such thing as a free lunch, stimulative tax reductions, through lower rates and targeted credits, promised economic rewards for every citizen without any apparent cost. In 1964, Walter Lippman

---

[118] Lawrence O'Brien, interview with Michael Gillette, 24 July 1986, Interview XI, 45. For media discussions on Mills's power in the health care debate, see Editorial, "Movement on Medicare?" *The New York Times*, 13 November 1964; Editorial, "One-Man Veto on Medicare," *The New York Times*, 26 June 1964; Marjorie Hunter, "Major Fight Is Due Over Medical Care," *The New York Times*, Sunday, 16 February 1964, Section IV; John A. Grimes, "Care for the Aged," *The Wall Street Journal*, 31 August 1961.

[119] George Kennan, interview with Louis Fischer, 23 March 1965, JFKL, Oral History Interview Collection, 70–90.

[120] John Manley's Personal Notes, 4 February 1964, LBJL, The John Manley Papers; Henry Hall Wilson to Lawrence O'Brien, 7 November 1961, JFKL, White House Staff Files: Henry Hall Wilson, Box 3, File: Memoranda 11/1/61–11/9/61; "Shifts in the Odds," *Business Week*, 5 January 1963, 15–18.

[121] "Man In The News," *Insurance News Week*, 12 January 1963, 57.

[122] "Key Man in the Medicare Battle," *Medical World News*, 26 February 1965, 33.

proclaimed: "A generation ago it would have been taken for granted that a war on poverty meant taxing money away from the haves and turning it over to the havenots . . . But in this generation . . . a revolutionary idea has taken hold. The size of the pie can be increased by invention, organization, capital investment, and fiscal policy, and then a whole society, not just one part of it, will grow richer."[123] By pushing workers into higher tax brackets through economic growth, the tax reductions would even generate higher government revenue and encourage long-term balanced budgets. Furthermore, the legislation played well within the nation's consumer culture since it presented increased consumer power as a solution to economic malaise.

Most important, the income-tax reductions appeared to be effective. Mills admitted publicly that he was amazed by the results: "I must confess that I was surprised at how successful tax reduction was. While ready to concede that a massive tax cut would stimulate the economy to move closer to full employment, I did not expect the economy's reaction to be quite so prompt and quite so vigorous."[124] The Gross National Product for 1965 exceeded the predictions of the CEA by almost $9 billion, while unemployment sank to a record low of 4.1 percent. The deficit fell to 0.2 percent of GNP in 1965. In 1961, moreover, an average of 71.6 million people were employed each month and 4.8 million were unemployed; by August 1965, the number of employed had grown to about 74.6 million and the number of unemployed had fallen by 1.4 million. During this same period, despite heavy outlays for new plant and equipment, the index of capacity utilization moved up from 86 percent to 90 percent, a figure close to the industry's optimal operating rate of 92 percent.[125] During the summer of 1964, Johnson told Mills that the tax reduction was having a positive effect on his presidential campaign. Although Mills quoted Roosevelt, who had warned, "you don't get any mileage politically out of taxes," Johnson said he was benefiting from the prosperity that the tax cut had produced. The president noted that low rates of unemployment for married men were electorally beneficial. During a recent appearance in Massachusetts, Johnson saw 200,000 of those employed married men and every one was

---

[123] Cited in Robert M. Collins, "Growth Liberalism in the Sixties," in *The Sixties: From Memory To History*, ed. David Farber (Chapel Hill: University of North Carolina Press, 1994), 23–24.

[124] Wilbur D. Mills, "Fiscal Policy and the Economy," WMPC, Box 658, File 6.

[125] Ibid; Allen J. Matusow, *The Unraveling of America: A History of Liberalism in the 1960s* (New York: Harper Torchbooks, 1986), 57.

smiling. Without the tax cut, Johnson believed, the Democrats would not have encountered that sentiment.[126]

Of course, there were doubts whether the income-tax reductions had actually caused the economy to improve. Some economists, such as Milton Friedman, located the source of growth in the expansive monetary policies of the Federal Reserve, while others insisted that spending for Vietnam was responsible for the booming economy. Regardless, the convergence of dramatic growth with the tax credit and tax reduction led Mills and his colleagues to believe that stimulative income-tax policies could produce significant improvement. Until such policies failed to achieve favorable results, income taxation remained the central mechanism of economic policy within the state.

During an interview with the Chamber of Commerce's *Nation's Business*, in August 1964, Mills boasted that the Revenue Acts complemented his views of public policy. "My philosophy has not changed. We should seek a tax climate favorable to economic growth, income taxes under which people with the same income should pay like amounts of tax, an income tax that interferes as little as possible with decisions of the market place. We seek a system of fairness, relative ease of compliance and which will respond quickly to changes in economic conditions to restrain inflation and recession." He added: "tax policy can be used to combat inflation" and that "if inflation should reach a point, sometime in the future, that increased rates are necessary in order to prevent increase, or even bring a reduction in inflation, the Congress would certainly want to consider using tax policy as one possibility." Foreshadowing his future battle with President Johnson, Mills also warned the Chamber's reporter that "you can't form tax policy in a vacuum. You have to connect it with your spending policy. They have to go hand in hand."[127] When the issue of tax manipulation temporarily receded, however, Mills turned his attention to another pertinent question in the tax community: Could Social Security afford to incorporate health care into its system?

[126] Telephone Conversation, Lyndon Johnson and Wilbur Mills, 11 June 1964, Tape WH6406.06, #3686, LBJL, Recordings of Telephone Conversations – White House Series.

[127] "Wilbur Mills Talks on Taxes," *Nation's Business*, August 1964, 80–81.

7

Bringing Medicare into the State

A year after one faction in the tax community obtained a massive tax reduction, the Social Security faction pushed through one of the largest tax increases in the postwar period when it brought Medicare into the American state. This represented another stage of the long-term incremental expansion of social insurance. After passing the Social Security Amendments of 1950, the tax-writing committees had tenaciously protected the symbolic link between payroll taxes and Old-Age and Survivors' Insurance. Based on this linkage, Congress expanded OASI and transformed Social Security into the centerpiece of welfare policy; additionally, Congress added Disability Insurance to the program in 1956 with its own trust fund.[1] Through Social Security, the state provided a unique social benefit for the elderly and the physically disabled, which policymakers distinguished from welfare through earmarked taxation and the absence of a means test.

Some social insurance advocates, however, envisioned a broader program that the media would label "Medicare." Starting in 1952, a cadre of policy entrepreneurs from the Social Security faction demanded that Congress incorporate hospitalization and nursing home benefits into Old-Age Survivor's Insurance. Led by Wilbur Cohen, Robert Ball, Nelson Cruikshank, and Cecil King (D-CA), this group warned that large numbers of elderly persons lacked medical coverage. Within the private sector, insurance companies excluded the aged or charged high-risk premiums that few could afford. Within the public sector, vendor payments (federal grants-in-aid to states for the medical care of welfare recipients) and tax breaks for the cost of private coverage only helped selected segments of the population.[2] By financing health insurance through the Social Security tax,

---

[1] At this point, Old-Age Survivors' Insurance became known as Old-Age Survivors and Disability Insurance (OASDI).

[2] The Secretary of HEW, "Hospitalization Insurance for OASDI Beneficiaries: Report Submitted to the Committee on Ways and Means by the Secretary of Health, Education, and Welfare," 3 April 1959, NA, RG 233, 86th Cong., Box 469, File: HR 12580 (7 of 8); Charles Schottland to Senator Kerr, 8 February 1960, WCP, Box 274, File 11.

Medicare supporters argued, the state could ease the problem of elderly health care while avoiding socialized medicine.[3]

But Medicare proponents discovered that the earmarked tax system also constrained Social Security. Powerful members of the tax community, including Mills, feared that the Social Security tax could not withstand the high cost of health care. Medicare, according to Mills, posed two dangers to the system. First, by forcing Congress to raise payroll taxes beyond acceptable limits, it would lead to a constituent and corporate revolt against Social Security. Second, Medicare would weaken the relationship between taxes and benefits by using wage-related revenue to pay for non-wage related, *service* benefits. Because of its threat to Social Security, Mills believed that Congress would – and should – reject a program that already faced opposition on the grounds that it would pave the way for socialized medicine.

Within the tax community, the debate over Medicare was in large part about the soundness and legitimacy of the Social Security tax system. Certainly, one major component of the debate involved the constant accommodations the community made with the American Medical Association (AMA), which mounted a fierce campaign against federal involvement in private medicine. This aspect of the debate, which has been examined in great detail by scholars, presented a monumental challenge to Mills as he attempted to design a compromise.[4] Another crucial aspect of the debate within the community – one that has been under-analyzed and is the focus of this chapter – involved the threat Medicare posed to Social Security finance. Given the centrality of taxation to Social Security, debates about finance were more than narrow, arcane issues. Rather, they raised serious questions about the stability of Social Security, a program that most representatives and their constituents had come to embrace.[5]

[3] Wilbur Cohen to Harry Thompson, 18 September 1961, WCP, Box 75, Folder 3.

[4] James Sundquist, *Politics and Policy: The Eisenhower, Kennedy, and Johnson Years* (Washington: The Brookings Institution, 1968), 287–321; Robert B. Stevens and Rosemary Stevens, *Welfare Medicine in America: A Case Study of Medicaid* (New York: Free Press, 1974), 1–57; Paul Starr, *The Social Transformation of American Medicine: The Rise of a Sovereign Profession and the Making of a Vast Industry* (New York: Basic Books, 1982), 363–378; and Allen J. Matusow, *The Unraveling of America: A History of Liberalism in the 1960s* (New York: Harper & Row, 1984), 217–242.

[5] This chapter builds on the scholarship of Edward D. Berkowitz, *Mr. Social Security: The Life of Wilbur Cohen* (Lawrence: University Press of Kansas, 1995), 212–238; Lawrence R. Jacobs, *The Health of Nations: Public Opinion and the Making of American and British Health Policy* (Ithaca: Cornell University Press, 1993); Rashi Fein, *Medical Care, Medical Costs: The Search for a Health Insurance Policy* (Cambridge: Harvard University Press, 1986), 52–124; Martha Derthick, *Policymaking for Social Security*

As chairman of Ways and Means, Mills grasped the influence of the Social Security tax system on the politics and development of social insurance policy. Over the years, the program had created the notion that workers were entitled to receive wage-related benefits on retirement. Mills and the community learned that congressional representatives gave political credit to leaders who helped to protect the actuarial soundness of Social Security.[6] After all, the electorate "contributed" taxes with the expectation that they too would receive wage-related and non-means tested benefits upon their retirement. Because of the way Congress defined Social Security in relation to welfare, defending the payroll tax system held considerable political appeal to legislators, even if that meant opposing health insurance for constituents.

The struggle over Medicare deepened an intractable division within the Social Security faction. Chief Actuary of the Social Security Administration Robert Myers had warned of this problem in the 1940s, when he complained about the expansionary pressures that bureaucrats placed on actuaries. Program administrators, whose success depended on the proliferation of benefits, were often in conflict with the program's financial guardians, who were committed to the soundness of the earmarked tax system that controlled long-term costs and prevented any undue burden on income taxes. Medicare exacerbated this tension by threatening the tax system.

The battle over Medicare reached a climax in 1965, when the pressure for reform from the Social Security faction and its congressional allies became so intense that Mills decided to compromise. The final legislation demonstrated that Mills understood how to use the positive power of the chairmanship to shape particular administrative proposals and to redesign Medicare. In the end, the chairman designed legislation that in the opinion of *The New Republic*, could "only be discussed in superlatives."[7] Through his strategic alliances with technical experts, Mills overcame the most significant divisions that existed within the community and Congress. Not only did the Social Security Amendments of 1965 protect the link between Old-Age, Survivors, and Disability Insurance [OASDI] and payroll taxes, but the legislation extended the use of earmarked taxes into the field

(Washington, D.C.: The Brookings Institution, 1979), 316–338; and Theodore R. Marmor, *The Politics of Medicare* (Chicago: Aldine Publishing, 1973).

[6] John Ferejohn, "Congress and Redistribution," in *Making Economic Policy in Congress*, ed., Allen Schick (Washington, D.C.: American Enterprise Institute for Public Policy Research, 1983), 140–141.

[7] Cited in Marmor, *The Politics of Medicare*, 70.

of health insurance. At the same time, the struggle preceding the victory showed that the earmarked taxes, which provided Social Security with much of its political strength, simultaneously constrained the program.

THE ONE MAN VETO, 1961–1963

Like most members of Congress, Mills agreed that the government should provide some type of medical assistance to those who lacked adequate care. Once the lobby for Medicare began in 1952, Mills had put forth various alternatives during his deliberations with Cohen, Myers, and Ball that kept health care out of Social Security. In 1960, for example, the chairman helped push through the Kerr-Mills Act, which provided states with federal grants-in-aid for the "medically indigent." Based on public assistance, Kerr-Mills benefits were funded through general revenue.[8] But the program never fulfilled its promise. Most states were unwilling to adopt the legislation or used the funds to subsidize pre-allocated expenditures.[9] Despite these failures, Mills insisted that the program just needed time to take effect.[10]

The campaign for King-Anderson

Dissatisfied with Kerr-Mills, the Kennedy administration allied itself with Representative King and Senator Clinton Anderson (D-NM) to reintroduce contributory medical insurance for the nearly 14.8 million people receiving OASDI. The proposal was called King-Anderson. Based on the work of the transition Task Force on Health

[8] U.S. Congress, House Committee on Ways and Means, *Medical Care for the Aged*, 1960 in NA, RG 233, 86th Cong., Box 468, File 12580 (4 of 8).

[9] "Senator McNamara Releases Report Evaluating Kerr-Mills Program," 20 June 1962, WCP, Box 133, Folder 4; U.S. Congress, Senate Special Committee on Aging, *The Kerr-Mills Program, 1960–1963: Report of Subcommittee on Health of the Elderly*, 88th Cong., 1st sess., 1963; U.S. Department of HEW, Press Release, 28 March 1962, WCP, Box 133, Folder 4; Stevens and Stevens, *Welfare Medicine in America*, 33; 45–48; Marmor, *The Politics Of Medicare*, 36–37; Edward Berkowitz, *America's Welfare State* (Baltimore: Johns Hopkins University Press, 1991), 169–171.

[10] Office of the Minority Counsel, "Reasons for a Vote Against: The Medicare Program (The King-Anderson Bill)," 1 October 1962, in the JMIC. See also Wilbur Mills, " 'A New Charter For Public Welfare': Remarks at the Annual Banquet of the Public Welfare Employees of the State of Arkansas," 13 December 1962, WMPC, Box 591, File: Mills Speech; Mills to Caleb Adcock, 7 March 1962, WMPC, Box 730, File 1; Mills to Anna Batten, 23 March 1962, WMPC, Box 730, File 16; Mills to Bertha Robinson, 9 February 1962, WMPC, Box 742, File 4; "The Great Medicare Debate," *Newsweek*, 4 June 1962, 28–34.

and Social Security (directed by Wilbur Cohen), the federally administered benefits were to include hospital care, skilled nursing home care, and home health care visits. By excluding the cost of physicians, Medicare would not infringe on the jurisdiction of the medical industry that was dominated by private practice doctors, and hence might make it past the powerful AMA.[11] To finance the benefits, this version of King-Anderson included a higher payroll tax and wage base schedule. For those who retired before paying these additional taxes for hospital insurance, benefits would still be financed by the Social Security tax revenue.[12] At a rally in Madison Square Garden, President Kennedy repeated that this was not a "campaign against doctors" and the bill would not create socialized medicine.[13]

Mills's opposition

From the time Kennedy took office until the election of 1964, Mills branded Medicare, as proposed in King-Anderson, as a crusade that was doomed to failure.[14] The chairman focused much of his opposition on the danger that health benefits posed to the payroll tax. Skyrocketing prices combined with constituent pressure for liberalized benefits – once recipients discovered that Medicare did not include the cost of physicians – would force Congress to raise Social Security taxes beyond reasonable levels (considered to be 10 percent of the payroll). Faced with this crisis, Congress would turn to general revenue and weaken the distinction between social insurance and welfare.[15]

There were also technical problems with King-Anderson that caused great concern to Mills. In several areas, Medicare tampered with the complex actuarial logic behind Social Security. For example, SSA actuaries could not use the level-wage assumption, which had traditionally ensured sufficient revenue to liberalize cash benefits: Actu-

---

[11] Task Force on Health and Social Security, *Health and Social Security For The American People*, 10 January 1961, WCP, Box 72, Folder 10.
[12] Robert J. Myers, "Total Health Benefits That Will Be Received By Persons Who Do Not Contribute to Health Insurance Trust Fund," 9 July 1962, WCP, Box 142, Folder 16.
[13] *John F. Kennedy: Address on Social Security*, 20 May 1962, The Museum of Television and Broadcasting (New York, NY) T77:0181, 004026.
[14] Lawrence O'Brien, interview with Michael Gillette, 24 July 1986, LBJL, Oral History Interview Collection, Interview XI, 49.
[15] JMIC; Robert Myers, interview with Peter Corning, 8 March 1967, COHP, Social Security Project, 8 March 1967, Interview 1, 20–21; 30–53; "Mills Denies Move To Aid Medical Care," *The New York Times*, 1 June 1963. See also L.A. Minnich, Jr., "Legislative Meeting," 12 January 1960, DEL, Ann Whitman File, DDE Diary Series, Box 47, Folder: Staff Notes – January 1960.

aries assumed that wages would remain static, so that when wages rose, the program generated an "unanticipated" surplus of tax revenue that could be distributed as benefits.[16] But the level-wage assumption did not work with Medicare because the cost of hospital insurance was independent of the earnings of participants.[17] Since labor costs constituted the bulk of hospital expenses, moreover, a rising wage level would only mean increases in the cost of King-Anderson by increasing the salaries of hospital personnel.[18]

To compensate for this problem, Myers assumed that the revenue gained from future wage base increases (the amount of income on which payroll taxes were levied) could be used to finance rising hospital costs.[19] In the past, Congress had used this additional revenue to boost cash benefits without raising tax rates. The assumption that Congress might rely on this revenue to pay for health insurance, however, troubled Mills. Before considering any version of Medicare, Mills wanted statutory assurances that the revenue gained from wage base increases would be used primarily to pay for OASDI.[20]

Making matters more unpalatable, King-Anderson provided service benefits in exchange for wage-related taxes, thereby weakening the relationship between the tax and the benefit.[21] As John Byrnes recalled, what "you were talking about was a benefit that had no relationship to the wage level. Everybody was entitled to the maximum. They could go to the limit. Your benefits weren't scaled to what your

[16] Robert J. Myers, *Social Security* (Bryn Mawr, Pennsylvania: McCahan Foundation, 1975), 168.

[17] Robert J. Myers, "History of Cost Estimates for Hospital Insurance," December 1966, RMP, unprocessed; Myers, "Underlying Factors in Long-Range Actuarial Cost Estimates for OASDI System," 8 June 1962, RMP, Box M83–106, unprocessed; Myers and Francisco Bayo, "Hospital Insurance, Supplementary Medical Insurance, and Old-Age, Survivors and Disability Insurance: Financing Basis under the 1965 Amendments," *Social Security Bulletin* 28, No. 10 (October 1965): 24–26; Derthick, *Policymaking For Social Security*, 328–334.

[18] Wilbur Cohen to Wilbur Mills, 13 June 1968, WMPC, Box 97, File: Unmarked.

[19] Robert J. Myers, "Actuarial Cost Estimates for Hospital Insurance Bill," July 1963, RMP, unprocessed; Myers, "Actuarial Cost Estimates for Hospital Insurance Bill Under Rising Earnings and Rising Hospitalization-Cost Assumptions," 2 December 1963, WCP, Box 146, Folder 11; Myers, "Interrelationship of Predicted Future Hospital Costs and Our Cost Estimates," 2 April 1963, WCP, Box 146, Folder 11; Myers, "History of Cost Estimates For Hospital Insurance"; Myers, "The Case for Revision of the Estimates of Health-Benefit Costs," 7 March 1962, RMP, Box M83-106, unprocessed; Henry Hall Wilson to the Files, 24 January 1964, LBJL, White House Office Aides Files, Box 3, File: Medicare (Henry Hall Wilson).

[20] See, for example, Robert J. Myers, "Estimated Level-Costs of Various Health Benefit Proposals," 11 July 1962, WCP, Box 142, Folder 16.

[21] Henry Hall Wilson to the Files, 24 January 1964, LBJL, White House Office Aides Files, Box 3, File: Medicare (Henry Hall Wilson).

wage had been ... And so there was no justification."[22] The cost of service benefits was unpredictable, given the wide range of factors outside the control of government that affected medical prices.[23] This problem was compounded by the fact that health benefits, financed by payroll taxes on current workers, were to be distributed to people who retired before paying additional Social Security taxes.

Given these problems, Mills warned in 1961 and 1962, Congress would reject the measure, especially since representatives were terrified of antagonizing the AMA; this indicated that Mills would not support the bill.[24] Most estimates of congressional votes indicated that Mills was correct. In 1961, for example, the Department of HEW calculated that Medicare was twenty-three votes short of a simple majority.[25] Within Ways and Means, the legislation was at least three votes short of passage each year before 1965. Most officials trusted Mills's legislative judgment since, as Joseph Barr noted, "Wilbur has demonstrated that he possesses one of the keenest political ears in Congress, and I am inclined to be guided by his judgement as to the effort we should be prepared to make."[26] Mills refused to cast the deciding vote so that he could tell the losing side: "You see they have this without my vote, I just modified it."[27] Recalling the legislative fiasco of 1958, the chairman refused to sponsor a bill that only commanded weak support within the House. In addition, Mills did not want to alienate the state medical society of Arkansas.[28]

[22] John Byrnes, interview with Peter Corning, 23 February 1967, COHP, Social Security Project, 8–11.

[23] Myers, *Social Security*, 307–311; U.S. Congress, House Committee on Ways and Means, *Medical Care for the Aged: Executive Hearings*, 89th Cong., 1st sess., 1965, 84. If anything, Myers had underestimated future costs by assuming that in the long-run, skyrocketing hospital costs would slow down as a result of better care, improved health, and more efficient services. See Robert Myers to Wilbur Mills, 6 March 1960, WCP, Box 274, Folder: 12; Myers, "Actuarial Cost Estimates for Hospital Insurance Bill under Rising Earnings and Rising Hospitalization-Cost Assumptions," 2 December 1963.

[24] Lawrence O'Brien, interview with Michael Gillette, 30 October 1985, LBJL, Oral History Interview Collection, Interview III, 49–53; Wilbur Mills, interview with Joseph O'Connor, 14 April 1967, JFKL, Oral History Interview Collection, 16; JMIC.

[25] Marmor, *The Politics of Medicare*, 41.

[26] Joseph Barr to Claude Desautels, 22 April 1963, JFKL, White House Staff Files: Lawrence O'Brien, Legislative Leadership Breakfast Material, Box 24, File: 23 April 1963, Folder 1. See also, JMIC; Henry Hall Wilson to John F. Kennedy, 12 June 1963, JFKL, Presidential Office Files, Box 67, File: Wilson, Henry Hall; Nelson Cruikshank, interview with Peter Corning, 15 February 1966, COHP, Social Security Project, Interview 2, 96–97.

[27] JMIC.

[28] Richard Harris, *A Sacred Trust* (New York: The New American Library, 1966), 108.

Negotiation

While some Medicare supporters tried to force Mills into endorsing King-Anderson through electoral and interest-group pressure, more experienced officials in the Social Security faction of the tax community relied on negotiation.[29] Avoiding confrontation, Cohen and Ball redesigned their proposal in an effort to satisfy Mills's demands without sacrificing the integrity of the bill. For example, they studied alternative plans such as the option to choose additional cash benefits instead of health insurance or the creation of a separate trust fund to finance hospital insurance.[30] Cohen also worked to gain the votes of representatives who were wavering, including Representatives Clark Thompson (D-TX), Burr Harrison (D-VA), Albert Sidney Herlong (D-FL), and John Watts (D-KY).[31]

By the summer of 1963, these efforts began to pay off. During a White House meeting, Mills outlined a compromise to finance hospital insurance under OASDI through a one-half of 1 percent increase in the payroll tax and increasing the wage base. To save money, lessen federal influence, and provide for the least disruption in hospital cost accounting, the program would be administered by a private, nonprofit insurance agency such as Blue Cross.[32] Mills told Cohen that a successful proposal would cover its entire cost through

[29] Wilbur Cohen, interview with William Moss, 20 July 1972, JFKL, Oral History Interview Collection, 86; Cohen, interview with William Moss, 24 May 1971, JFKL, Oral History Interview Collection, 73; Cohen, interview with David McComb, 8 December 1968, LBJL, Oral History Interview Collection, Tape 2, 2–3; Lawrence O'Brien, interview with Michael Gillette, 24 July 1986, LBJL, Oral History Interview Collection, Interview XI, 45–46.

[30] Ida Merriam to Wilbur Cohen, 14 February 1961, WCP, Box 140, Folder 5; "Optional Cash Benefits in Place of Health Insurance Benefits," 1962, WCP, Box 142, Folder 18; Cohen to John Baker, 4 January 1962, WCP, Box 142, Folder 19; Cohen to Jerry Verkler [Senate Chief Clerk, Committee on Interior and Insular Affairs], 4 May 1962, WCP, Box 76, Folder 7; Cohen, "Current Status of the Health Insurance Legislation before the Ways and Means Committee," 1962, WCP, Box 76, Folder 7; Robert Myers to Robert Ball, 19 June 1962, RMP, Box M83-106, unprocessed; Mike Manatos to Lawrence O'Brien, 27 April 1961, JFKL, White House Staff Files: Mike Manatos, Box 1, File: Memoranda 4/6/61–5/31/61.

[31] Wilbur Cohen to John F. Kennedy, 2 June 1962, WCP, Box 142, Folder 18; Robert Myers to Burr Harrison, 22 January 1962, WCP, Box 142, Folder 19; Alvin David to Cohen, 30 June 1962, WCP, Box 143, Folder 1; Henry Hall Wilson to John F. Kennedy, 12 June 1963, JFKL, Presidential Office File, Box 67, File: Wilson, Henry Hall.

[32] Robert Novak, "Compromise Medical Care Plan Outlined By Mills; Passage Likely If He Pushes It," *The Wall Street Journal,* 14 June 1963. See also Wilbur Cohen to Theodore Sorenson, 11 June 1962 and Secretary of HEW to Sorenson, 20 June 1962, WCP, Box 142, Folder 13; Henry Hall Wilson to the Files, 24 January 1964, LBJL, White House Office Aides Files, Box 3, File: Medicare, Henry Hall Wilson.

payroll taxes.[33] Meanwhile, the chairman considered new tax incentives that promoted the purchase of private insurance. In June 1963, for example, he studied Byrnes's proposal for allowing all people to fully deduct any premiums paid on private insurance policies (people over sixty-five were already allowed to take such deductions).[34] Each time he proposed the income-tax deduction, however, the committee defeated the plan.[35] Although hesitant to liberalize another tax break, Mills encouraged Byrnes to explore more inexpensive versions of the proposal.

The chairman sent other signals to the community that he was willing to compromise. For example, he allowed Ross Bass (D-TN) and Pat Jennings (D-VA), two outspoken advocates of Medicare, instead of the conservative Phil Landrum (D-GA), to be placed on Ways and Means in 1963.[36] Back in his district, Mills issued statements that indicated a shift in position. On one occasion, he told the Arkansas Chamber of Commerce that "in the area of public affairs, the solution will only be found through serious work on the problem and it will not develop out of a slogan that 'I am a conservative,' or 'I am a liberal.' I believe now that the general approach of our medical program in 1960 following the public assistance approach was correct but as time develops we will have to see how these things work and see what modifications are called for."[37]

In the end, Mills postponed further discussion until 1964. On September 18, 1963, he informed the Rules Committee that he did not intend to ask his panel to clear the bill that session. At this time, Cohen reported, Mills's "lack of enthusiasm for hospital insurance" eliminated any chance of Congress passing King-Anderson.[38] Following Kennedy's assassination in November, Johnson urged Wilbur Cohen, Robert Myers, and Robert Ball to design a politically feasible version of King-Anderson. Given the stunned mood of the electorate and Congress, the time seemed ripe to complete the domestic agenda that had been defined between 1961 and 1963.[39]

---

[33] Wilbur Cohen to the Secretary of HEW, 23 April 1963, WCP, Box 112, Folder 7.

[34] Henry Hall Wilson to John F. Kennedy, 12 June 1963, JFKL, Presidential Office File, Box 67, File: Wilson, Henry Hall.

[35] See, for example, Stanley Surrey to the Files, 10 June 1963, SSP, Box 175, File 1; Surrey to the Files, 10 June 1963, SSP, Box 194, File 4; Surrey to the Files, 24 May 1963, SSP, Box 187, File 1; Wilbur Cohen to the Secretary, 3 July 1963, WCP, Box 146, Folder 11.

[36] JMIC; Lawrence O'Brien, interview with Michael Gillette, 24 July 1986, LBJL, Oral History Interview Collection, Interview XI, 21.

[37] Wilbur D. Mills, "Remarks before the Chamber of Commerce of Stuttgart, Arkansas," 16 January 1962, WMPC, Box 784, File 17.

[38] Wilbur Cohen to Theodore Sorenson, 25 October 1963, WCP, Box 146, Folder 14.

[39] Berkowitz, *Mr. Social Security*, 188–189.

1964: MOVING TOWARD A COMPROMISE

The next year, Mills accelerated negotiations with Cohen and Ball. From the start, Johnson granted full authority to these men to represent the administration before Ways and Means. As a former senator, Johnson understood fully the political advantages to negotiation over confrontation. By this point, many administration officials felt that "we might as well let Mills tell us what he'd go with and then send it up as ours."[40] Lawrence O'Brien warned the president: "this actuarial soundness thing is likely crucial to solving Mills."[41]

Placating the chairman

But Mills refused to "tell" the administration or other policymakers exactly what he wanted. By withholding clear statements about his own position until the final stages of negotiation, Mills avoided backing himself into a corner through hasty promises to interest groups or to policy experts. By keeping colleagues off-guard, Mills created room to maneuver around emerging proposals and to design effective compromises. During heated debates such as the one over Medicare, moreover, the ambiguities of Mills's position weakened opposition attacks since they lacked clear evidence of his agenda and remained uncertain whether the chairman was even against them. Wilbur Cohen, according to his biographer, "read the transcript" of Mills's speeches "the way that Sinologists studied statements from Mao."[42]

At this point in the debate, Mills demonstrated the positive power of the chairmanship by pushing policymakers to revise particular aspects of their proposals. Additionally, he demonstrated his command of the actuarial logic behind Social Security. These skills enabled him to help redesign very specific aspects of the administration proposal. Between March and August, Cohen and Ball had Myers meet Mills's actuarial concerns by adjusting his estimates.[43] First, Myers assumed that Congress would refuse to raise the wage base in the coming years, so that proposed benefits would have to be funded almost entirely through the payroll tax. Myers agreed that should

[40] Henry Hall Wilson to Lawrence O'Brien, LBJL, White House Office Aides Files, Box 3, File: Legislative Programs 64–65 (Henry Hall Wilson). See also Henry Hall Wilson to Lawrence O'Brien, 8 June 1964, LBJL, White House Office Aides Files, Box 3, File: Medicare, Henry Hall Wilson; Wilson to O'Brien, 2 March 1964, LBJL, White House Office Aides Files, Box 19, Folder: M.

[41] Cited in Berkowitz, Mr. Social Security, 213.

[42] Ibid., 225.

[43] Myers, "History of Cost Estimates for Hospital Insurance."

Congress increase the wage base, only a small portion of the revenue could be used for Medicare.[44] Second, he estimated that utilization rates for Medicare would be 20 percent higher than in the original proposal.[45] Third, Myers agreed that the cost of hospital services would rise faster than wage earnings for the next ten years.[46] Fourth, he based his long-range cost estimates on a twenty-five-year period, as opposed to a seventy-five-year period. Fifth, Myers devised a tax schedule that earmarked hospital insurance as a separate item from OASDI, to be deposited in a separate trust fund. This meant that a portion of the monthly payroll tax revenue from Social Security taxes would pay for monthly hospital insurance, while some additional tax revenue would remain in the trust fund as a contingency reserve.[47]

While Myers worked on actuarial compromises, Johnson encouraged cordial relations with Mills. Knowing Mills's dislike of confidential information being leaked to the press prematurely, the president was infuriated by articles on behind-the-scenes delibera-

[44] Robert Myers, interview with Peter Corning, 8 March 1967, COHP, Social Security Project, Interview 1, 7–8; 72–73. See also Henry Hall Wilson to the Files, 24 January 1964, LBJL, White House Office Aides Files, Box 3, File: Medicare, Henry Hall Wilson; Myers, "Earnings Base Required under OASDI System in Order to Finance Adequately Hospital Insurance Benefits," 22 April 1964; Myers, "Cost Estimates for King-Anderson Bill," 23 April 1964; Myers, "Cost Estimate for Proposal Discussed by Chairman Mills Yesterday at the Executive Session of the Ways and Means," 23 April 1964 all in WCP, Box 150, Folder 10; Myers, "History of Cost Estimates For Hospital Insurance"; Myers and Bayo, "Hospital Insurance, Supplementary Medical Insurance, and Old-Age, Survivors, and Disability Insurance: Financing Basis Under the 1965 Amendments," *Social Security Bulletin* 28, No. 10 (October 1965): 17–28; U.S. Congress, House Committee on Ways and Means, *Medical Care For The Aged: Executive Hearings*, 89th Cong., 1st sess., 1965, 80–88; Myers to Robert Ball, 6 March 1964, WCP, Box 150, Folder 8; Staff Paper, "Actuarial-Cost Situation for Hospital Insurance Benefits System Under Rising Earnings and Hospital-Cost Assumptions"; SSA Staff, "What Is To Prevent Social Security Hospital Insurance From Being Expanded to Cover All Health Services For The Aged," 23 April 1964; SSA Staff, "Actuarial-Cost Situation for Hospital Insurance Benefits System under Rising Earnings and Hospital-Cost Assumptions"; "Suggestions Made by Mr. Mills in Meeting," 24 January 1964 all in WCP, Box 150, Folder 10.

[45] Myers, "History of Cost Estimates For Hospital Insurance"; Myers, interview with Peter Corning, 8 March 1967, COHP, Social Security Project, Interview 1, 74–75.

[46] U.S. Congress, House Committee on Ways and Means, *Medical Care For The Aged: Executive Hearings*, 89th Cong., 1st sess., 1965, 8; Myers, "History of Cost Estimates for Hospital Insurance"; Myers, "Cost Estimates for Hospitalization Benefits Under Modified Dynamic Assumptions," 30 January 1964, WCP, Box 151, Folder 12.

[47] U.S. Congress, House Committee on Ways and Means, *Medical Care For The Aged: Executive Hearings*, 89th Cong., 1st sess., 1965, 80–88; Wilbur Cohen to Lawrence O'Brien, 28 September 1964, LBJL, White House Office Aides Files, Box 3, File: Medicare.

tions with the chairman. Johnson complained to Secretary Celebrezze that the Associated Press had reported on a private conversation he had had with Mills encouraging him to compromise with Wilbur Cohen. The article claimed that HEW was the source. Johnson ordered Celebrezze to stop the leaks until final decisions were made because he feared that the stories would "run Mills off" and "make Mills mad." This was especially important because he sensed positive momentum regarding Medicare. After spending two days with Mills in Little Rock, Celebrezze found him to be "a fine gentleman." Mills, said Johnson, was "real complimentary" of Celebrezze, and said that he would do "anything" he could to work with HEW. Celebrezze responded that he could work with Mills "if some other people will keep their noses out of it."[48]

In late March, the president indicated that Mills was controlling the deliberations. In a telephone conversation, Johnson told Wilbur Cohen that he intended to work as long as necessary to obtain medical care for the elderly. He instructed Cohen: "You get him [Mills] something, though . . . if labor will buy it, that he can call a Mills bill, that's what it amounts to, and you're smart enough to do that." Cohen responded: "I think we can . . . Mr. President. I'm, I'm positive of that."[49]

By April 1964, members of the Social Security faction and the tax-writing committees appeared to be reaching a compromise. It even seemed likely that Mills could obtain Representative Watts's support as the thirteenth vote within the committee.[50] To maintain this momentum, Mills worked to resolve all remaining issues with the HEW, including the amount of the deductible, the age of eligibility for health insurance, and a proposed liberalization of cash benefits.[51] The chairman also accepted the possibility of "blanketing-in" the aged uninsured through general revenue, although this method of

[48] Telephone Conversation, Lyndon Johnson and Anthony Celebrezze, 9 March 1964, Tape WH6403.05, #2409, LBJL, Recordings of Telephone Conversations – White House Series.

[49] Telephone Conversation, Lyndon Johnson and Wilbur Cohen, 21 March 1964, Tape WH6403.15, #2612, LBJL, Recordings of Telephone Conversations – White House Series.

[50] Henry Hall Wilson to Lawrence O'Brien, 27 April 1964, LBJL, White House Office Aides Files, Box 3, File: Medicare; Wilson to O'Brien, 20 April 1964, LBJL, White House Office Aides Files, Box 3, File: Medicare. Mills and Watts worked out an agreement on two important issues: first, they would have King-Anderson benefits begin at age sixty-five, drop a few minor amendments, and raise the wage base to perhaps $6,000; second, they would increase OASI benefits by 5–6 percent, financing it by increasing contributions on both sides to 5 percent.

[51] Henry Hall Wilson to Lawrence O'Brien, 8 June 1964, LBJL, White House Office Aides Files, Box 3, File: Medicare.

finance was "distasteful" to him.[52] In secrecy, he and Byrnes discussed the possibility of combining Medicare with a voluntary plan that covered physicians.[53]

On May 18, 1964, Johnson had a lengthy conversation with Lawrence O'Brien about the status of the proposal. O'Brien told the president that Wilbur Cohen had been "living" with Mills for several months. Mills, according to O'Brien, had promised to have a package to discuss by the end of the week. When O'Brien questioned Mills about disturbing articles that nothing was happening on Medicare, the chairman said that O'Brien knew better than to pay attention to such stories. Mills warned, however, that the administration could not have everything it wanted, and that ultimately the bill would need "the Mills stamp on it." O'Brien replied that the president's door was "wide open" whenever the chairman wanted to talk. Mills said he would take up the offer once he had a proposal of interest that he could "spell out" and that "makes some sense."

During this important conversation with Johnson, O'Brien stated Mills's concern with specific portions of the legislation (such as an option for recipients to take a cash benefit instead of hospital insurance), and indicated that Mills was "certainly in the Medicare ball park." Nonetheless, O'Brien reported that Mills was still "feeling his way along very slowly" and "manipulating and maneuvering . . . but he isn't pinning anything down that can't be unwound." O'Brien told Johnson that they should have confidence that Mills would contact them soon; Cohen did not think that there was any "hanky-panky" in Mills's position. Many Medicare supporters on Ways and Means who were optimistic that something "would work out" remained nervous because Mills would not tell them anything about the deliberations. O'Brien reminded the president that that was how Mills always operated. Although rumors were circulating in the press that Mills would come out with an extension of Kerr-Mills that bypassed Medicare, the chairman insisted to O'Brien that his goal was to include Medicare in the bill. Johnson asked O'Brien to remind Mills again not to make any commitments without consulting with him. Johnson mentioned an article about Mills's proposal to increase Social Security benefits.

---

[52] Lawrence O'Brien to Lyndon Johnson, 11 May 1964, LBJL, White House Office Aides Files, Box 3, File: Medicare (Henry Hall Wilson).

[53] JMIC. Moreover, Mills wanted to expand Kerr-Mills to include dependent children. "Revision of Kerr-Mills Legislation," 28 May 1964, WCP, Box 150, Folder 9; Wilbur Cohen, "Meeting with Congressman Mills," 17 April 1964 and Staff SSA, "Possible Improvements in Provision of Medical Assistance to Needy Aged Persons Under OAA and MAA," 21 April 1964 in WCP, Box 150, Folder 10; John Morris, "New Health Plan For Aged Drafted," *The New York Times*, 16 May 1964; Editorial, "Still Blocking Medicare," *The New York Times*, 26 May 1964.

Cohen had told O'Brien that this just meant Mills wanted to have his "imprimatur" on the legislation. Frustrated with Mills's autonomy, Johnson ordered O'Brien: "Now tell him, god dammit, if they're [Ways and Means] getting to where that is getting out [in the press] I would like to know what he has in mind . . . tell him they're asking me questions and I don't know what the hell he's doing. A Democratic President ought to know what a Democratic chairman is doing. . . ."[54]

It seemed that a compromise was in the works in early June. Under this proposition, each individual would have the option of receiving additional cash benefits in lieu of hospital insurance.[55] Blue Cross/Blue Shield would administer the benefits, while excess tax revenue would be deposited into a separate trust fund where the money would be invested in government securities.[56] Cohen believed that this modified version of King-Anderson had better than a 50/50 chance of getting Mills's approval. At this point in the debate, according to Cohen, the negotiations had been trying because of "liberal friends continually giving me the advice – don't sell out on any bad compromise." On the other hand, if Cohen failed, liberals would "tell everybody how it was our fault for not being able to get it through the Committee when we only needed one additional vote."[57]

After asking how the "Mills Bill" was doing on June 9, Johnson made a bold appeal for the chairman's support:

> The single most important popular thing is the bill you are working on. No question in my mind about it. If you get something you can possibly live with and defend, that these people will not kick over the bucket with, it will mean more than all the bills we passed put together. And I think it will mean more to posterity, and to you, and to me. So I am not trying to go into details and I am not trying to write a new section every morning or title. I just let it go since I talked to you last time . . . but I have looked at some of the stuff that has been considered, from the press and other people, and it looks like to me that you are

---

[54] Telephone Conversation, Lyndon Johnson and Lawrence O'Brien, 18 May 1964, Tape WH6405.08, #3472, LBJL, Recordings of Telephone Conversations – White House Series.

[55] Lawrence O'Brien to Lyndon Johnson, 11 May 1964, LBJL, White House Office Aides Files, Box 3, File: Medicare (Henry Hall Wilson).

[56] "The Mills Social Security Bill of 1964," June 1964 and Wilbur Cohen to the Secretary, 9 June 1964 and Cohen to the Secretary, 5 May 1964 and Cohen to Lawrence O'Brien, 4 May 1964, WCP, Box 150, Folder 9; Cohen to Theodore Sorenson, 5 May 1964 and Cohen to the Secretary, 15 May 1964, WCP, Box 81, Folder 3.

[57] Wilbur Cohen to Arthur Altmeyer, 26 May 1964, WCP, Box 81, Folder 3.

approaching it right and that you are getting it in shape and I
will just say this, that there is not anything that has happened
in my six months or that will happen in my whole term, in my
judgment, that will mean more to us as a party or to me and you
as individuals in this piece of legislation. Now . . . the details, if
you don't know more about it than I do . . . Now you work it out
and anything you want me to do let me know . . . If you want
Walter or Dillon or anybody to give us any estimates let's do it,
let's make it sound and solid. But let's move in this direction
and it'll be a bill that you and your folks will never forget and I
will come in and applaud you.

Mills, who was afraid of the reaction of "working people" to scheduled Social Security tax increases, said that "we are making every
effort to do something." Johnson responded: "grind something out
of there."[58]

Mills was searching for a program that he "could say" was different
from King-Anderson to enable "those of us who have repeatedly said
we would not vote for the King bill" to endorse the legislation. The
president, who agreed on this strategy, urged Mills to move forward
with King-Anderson once he had thirteen or fourteen Democratic
votes. But Mills wanted some Republican votes as well. When Johnson
said that Mills should never expect Republican support for any administration proposal since they opposed every poverty program, Mills
responded: "They are not always against Social Security. I got them in
a bind if they vote against this bill." Committee Republicans, Mills said,
all supported a cash benefit increase. The president felt that Republicans would not be against hospitalization insurance once they had a
"taste" of it just as they had come to accept Social Security despite their
opposition in 1935. Mills added that Secretary Celebrezze had talked
to Ways and Means about a "three-pronged approach" that combined
hospitalization insurance, increased cash benefits, and improvements
of Kerr-Mills. Johnson expressed concern that if the House passed
cash benefits and improvements in Kerr-Mills without a hospitalization insurance program they would "murder" Medicare, which had
the most "sex appeal", and make it difficult to pass in the future. The
president did not think that the Senate would add hospitalization
benefits to a House bill.[59]

---

[58] Telephone Conversation, Lyndon Johnson and Wilbur Mills, 9 June 1964, Tape
WH6406.03, #3642, LBJL, Recordings of Telephone Conversations – White House
Series.

[59] Telephone Conversation, Lyndon Johnson and Wilbur Mills, 11 June 1964, Tape
WH6406.06, #3686, LBJL, Recordings of Telephone Conversations – White House
Series.

A deal falls apart

But the compromise fell through when Mills lost the votes needed to pass the bill. Trouble began when Representatives Watts and Herlong told Mills that they might oppose Medicare in light of the November election.[60] Likewise, several pro-Medicare representatives urged Mills to wait until after the elections before proposing any legislation so that they could avoid having to take a definitive stand. Representatives from New Mexico, Idaho, southern Illinois, Pennsylvania, Ohio, Indiana, and Texas – non-southern rural Democrats who supported the bill – suggested to the chairman that they opposed a vote at this time.[61] Watts, Harrison, and Herlong each informed Mills that they could not cast the thirteenth vote since the electoral cost was too high. Many constituents believed AMA warnings that Medicare would lead to socialized medicine.[62] After speaking with Mills, legislative liaison Henry Wilson warned O'Brien that "All of Mills' reactions and activities that we have seen point toward his shrinking from a floor showdown, and my guess would be that he'll be quite slow to come charging back to the floor."[63] When Representative Eugene Keogh (D-NY) asked Mills how he intended to vote on the bill, the chairman responded: "I am only the Chairman of the Committee. It is up to somebody else to make the motion."[64]

On June 22, Lawrence O'Brien informed Johnson that "the Wilbur Mills situation is deteriorated, I would say at this moment totally." Mills told Wilbur Cohen "that he can't put this thing together" because he had lost the votes of Watts and Herlong. Instead of King-Anderson, Mills was going to support a Social Security cash benefit increase. Mills suggested either taking King-Anderson off the table until the following year or attaching it to the Social Security bill once it reached the Senate. At that point, Mills indicated that he could conceivably convince the AMA that something strong was going to come out of conference, and he could act as a mediator by cutting back

[60] Wilbur Cohen to the Secretary, 9 June 1964, WCP, Box 150, Folder 9; Nelson Cruikshank, interview with Peter Corning, 15 February 1966, COHP, Social Security Project, Interview 2, 96–97; Henry Hall Wilson to Lawrence O'Brien, 8 June 1964, LBJL, White House Central Files, Box 3, File: Medicare, Henry Hall Wilson. See also Cohen, "Meeting with Congressman Mills," 17 April 1964, WCP, Box 150, Folder 10.

[61] Henry Hall Wilson to Lawrence O'Brien, 20 April 1964, LBJL, White House Office Aides Files, Box 3, File: Medicare.

[62] JMIC. For earlier signs of defection by Watts and Herlong, see Wilbur Cohen, "Meeting with Congressman Mills," 17 April 1964, WCP, Box 150, Folder 10.

[63] Henry Hall Wilson to Lawrence O'Brien, 20 September 1964, LBJL, White House Office Aides Files, Box 3, File: Medicare (Henry Hall Wilson).

[64] Wilbur Cohen to the Secretary of HEW, 9 June 1964, WCP, Box 150, Folder 9.

and helping them to avoid a debacle. In addition to this conversation, one Democrat told O'Brien that short of a meeting between Johnson and Mills, "there wasn't anything that could happen tomorrow morning except to lose this thing totally, that the best that could happen is that they do not take a formal vote." O'Brien was at a loss over what to do in this "dismal situation." The AFL-CIO's Andrew Biemiller had left a message for O'Brien that "all hell had broken loose and things had fallen apart" in the Ways and Means Committee. As usual, O'Brien complained with considerable frustration, Biemiller told him "how bad things are without any answers."[65]

In response to these developments, O'Brien and Johnson considered two strategies: The first was to try to postpone the next Ways and Means meeting and search for more supporting votes. Johnson did not think that this would make a difference. So they opted for the second strategy, which was to prevent the vote in committee and attach King-Anderson in the Senate as an amendment to the Social Security increase. Although they chose this strategy, O'Brien expressed several concerns. First, he warned that ardent Medicare supporters in Ways and Means would force a vote and it would be defeated. Second, O'Brien feared that critics would complain that Johnson had "succumbed to Mills" by asking Medicare supporters to shelve the bill. Third, Mills had not promised to protect an amendment in Conference Committee. O'Brien, who believed the administration could get an amendment in the Senate, explained his feelings about Mills's support as follows: "I don't see daylight where Mills is suggesting that he will be helpful in the conference . . . if Mills would say well 'hell in conference I will play ball totally to get a good piece of this thing accepted and run it through the House,' that's one thing . . . I'm afraid what he's getting at is that this role would be, that at the point of conference that we could convince, or become convincing, that this thing was in the process of full settlement and our way, that then Mills moves in on behalf of the AMA and he is the guy cutting back and he is a hero with the AMA and at the same time he is indicating, of course, that he is a big help to us. That's a pretty tricky operation." Nonetheless, Johnson and O'Brien decided this was their only viable choice.[66]

Johnson later told O'Brien that he wanted Senator Anderson to "slug it out, all the way, let all the chips in . . . move in on King-Anderson, go to conference, and then be willing to be reasonable."

[65] Telephone Conversation, Lyndon Johnson and Lawrence O'Brien, 22 June 1964, Tape WH6406.12, #3804, LBJL, Recordings of Telephone Conversations – White House Series.
[66] Ibid.

At conference, Johnson would let Mills "scare the living hell out of the doctors and everybody else and then he could come up with a compromise . . . and I think you would establish the first health insurance that way if you could get it over." Nonetheless, in addition to having a version of King-Anderson attached to the bill, Johnson warned, the Democrats needed to have a prepared compromise because "Wilbur Mills will take your pants unless you got something that he got to trade for."[67] Senator Abraham Ribicoff (D-CT), former Secretary of HEW, had put forth such a compromise with a bill providing recipients an option to take a cash benefit of lesser value instead of hospital insurance.

On June 24, Mills announced that he could not support King-Anderson at that time, since it was not known how much the wage base and tax rate might have to be increased in the future. More important, he simply did not have the votes in the House to pass the measure.[68] Two weeks later, Ways and Means reported out a bill that provided a 5 percent increase in OASDI benefits, along with an increase in the wage base to compensate for a small actuarial imbalance. The cost of the liberalization in benefits threatened to prevent Congress from enacting health insurance at that time.[69] Medicare advocates were outraged. The editors of *The New York Times* branded Mills as the "One-Man Veto on Medicare."[70]

Action in the Senate

A bipartisan coalition of senators, led by Albert Gore (D-TN), Clinton Anderson (D-NM), and Jacob Javits (R-NY), attached a modified version of Medicare as a rider to the Social Security bill.[71] The Senate stunned federal officials by passing the measure by 49–44, marking the first time that either chamber had passed any version of Medicare. Mills warned the administration that "if any legitimate question be raised as to the soundness of the financing of the Senate bill, the

[67] Telephone Conversation, Lyndon Johnson and Lawrence O'Brien, 14 August 1964, Tape WH6408.19, #4921, LBJL, Recordings of Telephone Conversations – White House Series.

[68] JMIC.

[69] Wilbur Cohen to Social Security Experts, 2 July 1964, WCP, Box 81, Folder 6.

[70] Editorial, "One-Man Veto on Medicare," *The New York Times*, 26 June 1964. For media discussions on Mills's power in the health care debate, see Editorial, "Movement on Medicare?" *The New York Times*, 13 November 1964. See also "Medicare," NA, RG 233, 88th Cong., Boxes 1–26.

[71] Wilbur Cohen to the Secretary, 10 July 1964, WCP, Box 278, Folder 7; Cohen to the Secretary, 8 July 1964 and Cohen to the Secretary, 13 July 1964, WCP, Box 81, Folder 7.

opponents would be in excellent shape to have the conference drop the whole thing."[72] Before the measure reached conference, however, Mills did not support the measure and had secured enough votes to block its passage.[73]

But Mills was more than just a one-man veto. For the remainder of 1964, the chairman encouraged Medicare supporters to continue negotiations. For instance, in a widely publicized speech in Little Rock, Mills once again suggested how officials could satisfy his concerns: "I want to make it clear that I have always thought there was great appeal in the argument that wage earners, during their working lifetime, should make payments into a fund to guard against the risk of financial disaster due to heavy medical costs . . . One of the difficulties that has actually impeded the reaching of a sound solution is the insistence by the proponents of medical care on proceeding toward a solution through the existing OASDI system . . . I would be hopeful that the basic prepayment concept might lead us in the direction of sound approaches to this matter."[74] At this time, Mills confessed to another group, "I am acutely aware of the fact that there is a problem here which must be met."[75]

The election of 1964

On November 3, these messages gained new urgency when the Democratic party scored a stunning victory. Democrats gained 38 seats in the House, reducing the Republicans to their lowest level since the Democratic landslide of 1936. The new congressional balance was 295 Democrats to 140 Republicans in the House and 68 Democrats to 32 Republicans in the Senate. Additionally, three anti-Medicare Republicans on Ways and Means were defeated. The morning after the election, Mills promised reporters that he "would

---

[72] Henry Hall Wilson to Lawrence O'Brien, 21 June 1964 and Wilbur Cohen to O'Brien, 13 August 1964 and O'Brien to Lyndon Johnson, 13 September 1964, LBJL, White House Office Aides Files, Henry Hall Wilson, Box 3, File: Medicare; Henry Hall Wilson to Lawrence O'Brien, 20 September 1964, LBJL, White House Office Aides Files, Box 3, File: Medicare (Henry Hall Wilson).

[73] Marmor, *The Politics of Medicare*, 56.

[74] Speech is excerpted in *Congressional Quarterly Almanac*, 88th Cong., 2nd sess., 1964, 231–232. The text of the speech was reported in Marjorie Hunter, "Aged Care Action Is Expected Today," *The New York Times*, 30 September 1964; "Medicare Funds From a Separate Tax Again Urged," *The Wall Street Journal*, 30 September 1964.

[75] Marjorie Hunter, "Mills Gives Way on Aged Care Bill," *The New York Times*, 12 November 1964; Wilbur Mills, interview with Joseph O'Connor, 14 April 1967, JFKL, Oral History Interview Collection, 16. See also Mills, "Recent Amendments to the Internal Revenue Code and Possible Future Tax Legislation: Remarks to Pulaski County Bar Association," 30 October 1964, WMPC, Box 591, File: Mills Speeches.

be receptive to a Medicare proposal" in the upcoming session.[76] When the Democratic Caucus altered the party ratio within Ways and Means from 15(D)-10(R) to 18(D)-7(R), the chairman did nothing to oppose this change, despite the bitter protest of the AMA.[77] These electoral developments, noted one representative, loosened Mills's "constraints" on his "freedom of maneuver."[78] On December 2, Mills announced that he could support a payroll tax for financing health benefits "just as I have supported a payroll tax for cash benefits."[79]

The congressional election, combined with Mills's speeches back in the district, inspired the Social Security faction to design another version of King-Anderson.[80] One colleague predicted that "Wilbur has a big, fat compromise in his pocket for medicare."[81] At Mills's direction, the Social Security Administration prepared a new hospital insurance plan with a separate trust fund and a higher tax schedule.[82]

[76] *Congressional Quarterly Almanac*, 89th Cong., 1st sess., 1965, 237; Marjorie Hunter, "Mills Gives Way on Aged Care Bill," *The New York Times*, 12 November 1964.

[77] JMIC; John Manley's Personal Notes, 16 March 1965, LBJL, the John Manley Papers. See also "House Democrats Seeking 3 GOP Seats On Ways-Means to Lift Total to 18 of 25," *The Wall Street Journal*, 21 December 1964.

[78] JMIC; Editorial, "Movement on Medicare?" *The New York Times*, 13 November 1964; Tom Wicker, "What Changed Mills's Mind?" *The New York Times*, Sunday, 11 April 1965, section IV.

[79] "Remarks of Congressman Wilbur D. Mills before the Downtown Little Rock Lions Club," 2 December 1964, WMPC, unprocessed; Marjorie Hunter, "New Payroll Tax Urged for Hospital Care of Aged," *The New York Times*, 3 January 1965; "Mills Says He Could Support Tax For Health Care, Doubts Adequacy," *Arkansas Gazette*, 3 December 1964.

[80] John Byrnes, interview with Peter Corning, 23 February 1967, COHP, Social Security Project, 13–16.

[81] "Chairman Wilbur Mills & the Shape of the Next Tax Bill," *Forbes*, 15 December 1964, 15.

[82] Wilbur Cohen to the Secretary of HEW, 25 November 1964; Robert Myers to Robert Ball, 8 December 1964; Myers, "Principles and Operation of Potential Dynamic Cost-Sharing Provision in Hospital Insurance Plan," 25 November 1964; Ball to the Secretary of HEW, 23 December 1964; Cohen to Wilbur Mills, 17 December 1964. All the aforementioned documents are in WCP, Box 154, Folder 1; The Secretary of HEW to President Johnson, 25 November 1964, WCP, Box 82, Folder 5; Cohen to Clinton Anderson, 3 November 1964, WCP, Box 82, Folder 4; Myers to Cohen, 17 November 1964 and Alvin David to Myers, 8 December 1964, WCP, Box 153, Folder 9; Sidney Saperstein to Cohen, 12 November 1964, WCP, Box 150, Folder 8; Cohen to the Secretary of HEW, 5 November 1964, WCP, Box 82, Folder 4. See also Myers, "Special Maximum Provisions to Safeguard HI System Against Rising Hospital Costs," 8 June 1964, WCP, Box 150, Folder 8 and Myers, "Short-Range Estimate for Hospital Insurance Under Social Security by Adding it Along Lines of the Administration Proposal," 17 July 1964, RMP, Box M83–106, unprocessed.

MEDICARE, BETTERCARE, AND ELDERCARE

Deliberations resumed on January 3, 1965, when the Advisory Council on Social Security recommended a separate payroll tax to finance a $2.2 billion program of hospital care for the aged under OASDI. The combined tax rate for cash retirement and hospital benefits, according to its plan, would reach 10.4 percent in 1971.[83] The wage base, it added, should be increased to $7,200. Council members received encouragement when Mills announced over the AP wire, "I assume the committee would be able to work something out. . . ."[84]

The day after the council issued its report, the administration introduced a revised version of King-Anderson that provided 60 days of hospital care (with the patient paying the national average cost of one day's care), 60 days of extended facility hospital care, home health-care visits, and outpatient hospital diagnostic services (with the patient paying one-half the deductible for inpatient hospital benefits).[85] These federally administered benefits were to be financed through a higher payroll tax, with general revenue supporting the elderly not receiving OASDI. Although the bill did not enact a tax exclusively for health insurance, it established a separate trust fund for the health program and provided W-2 forms that distinguished the amount of money going toward health insurance.[86] Mills's imprint on this bill was visible to all those who were involved.

---

[83] Myers, "History of Cost Estimates For Hospital Insurance"; "Report of the Advisory Council on Social Security: The Status of the Social Security Program and Recommendations for Its Improvement," *Social Security Bulletin* 28, No. 3 (March 1965): 3–41.

[84] Berkowitz, *Mr. Social Security*, 227. See also Henry Hall Wilson to Lawrence O'Brien, 5 January 1965, LBJL, White House Office Aides Files, Henry Hall Wilson Papers, Box 9, File: Medicare; "Medicare by Easter?" *Newsweek*, 25 January 1965, 52.

[85] U.S. Congress, House Committee on Ways and Means, *Medical Care For the Aged: Executive Hearings*, 89th Cong., 1st sess., 2–15; Myers, "History of Cost Estimates For Hospital Insurance."

[86] U.S. Congress, House Committee on Ways and Means, *Medical Care For the Aged: Executive Hearings*, 89th Cong., 1st sess., 1965, 8; Henry Hall Wilson to Lawrence O'Brien, 5 January 1965, LBJL, White House Office Aides Files, Henry Hall Wilson Papers, Box 9, File: Medicare; Wilson to Lawrence O'Brien, 5 January 1965, LBJL, White House Office Aides Files, Lawrence O'Brien Papers, Box 17, File: Mills, Wilbur; Marjorie Hunter, "Medicare Plan To Be Expanded," *The New York Times*, 4 January 1965; Charles Mohr, "Johnson Health Program Gives Medicare Priority; Regional Centers Sought," *The New York Times*, 8 January 1965. Contrary to the advice of Advisory Council, Cohen and the AFL-CIO's Nelson Cruikshank agreed that if Mills wanted to create a separate tax for hospital insurance, distinct from the existing Social Security tax, he would have to fight for it on his own. See Wilbur Cohen to John McCormack, 19 November 1964, WCP, Box 154, Folder 1; Cohen to Clinton Anderson, 18 November 1964, WCP, Box 82, Folder 5.

The actuarial estimates for the proposal were based on the assumptions that Myers, monitored closely by Mills and Cohen, had devised
the year before.[87]

The AMA and Eldercare

Secretary of HEW Celebrezze packaged the legislation as another
victory for contributory social insurance in the battle against public
assistance.[88] Through this rhetoric, Celebrezze attempted to overcome Mills's fear that health insurance contradicted the principles
behind Social Security, and suggested that it represented a logical out-
growth of the program. In contrast, the AMA now embraced the
public assistance approach. Sensing the inevitability of reform,
the organization proposed a bill called "Eldercare" that expanded
Kerr-Mills: The bill offered voluntary medical insurance for the
elderly, distributed on the basis of need in participating states. People
over sixty-five could purchase Blue Cross/Blue Shield or commercial
insurance, paying all or none of the cost depending on their income;
the states, drawing on federal and state general revenue, would
pay the entire cost for people with incomes below a level set by law.
While coverage depended on the private insurance policy specified
by each state, it could include the cost of hospitals, doctors, and prescription drugs.[89] Representatives Thomas Curtis (R-MO) and Albert
Herlong introduced the plan, estimating it would cost $2.1 billion
per year.[90]

Dissecting the administration's proposal

On January 27, Ways and Means started its hearings. During the hearings, Mills continued to apply pressure on policy experts to devise
stronger safeguards to protect Social Security finance. For the next
three months, policymakers vigorously debated what types of taxes
should support what types of benefits, fluctuating between the social
insurance and public assistance approach. Experts tested the actuarial assumptions designed to prevent the social insurance approach

---

[87] Robert Myers to Wilbur Cohen and Robert Ball, 10 February 1965, RMP, Box
M83–106, unprocessed; Myers, "History of Cost Estimates for Hospital Insurance."
[88] U.S. Congress, House Committee on Ways and Means, *Medical Care For the Aged:
Executive Hearings*, 89th Cong., 1st sess., 1965, 3–4; 487.
[89] Austin Wehrwin, "New Health Plan Offered By A.M.A," *The New York Times*, Sunday,
10 January 1965, section 1; Wilbur Cohen to Nelson Cruikshank, 25 February 1965,
WCP, Box 83, Folder 1.
[90] Sydney Herlong and Thomas Curtis, Press Release, 27 January 1965, LBJL, John
Manley Papers, Box 5, File: Medicare.

from undermining the payroll tax. These experts found that they still needed to convince the committee that a higher tax rate and wage base would not reach a point where, as one member feared, "the worker no longer sees Social Security as a bargain and will become disillusioned with the system itself. If he pays in more than he can expect to get out in retirement benefits he will reject the system."[91]

The chairman dreaded this outcome. Mills worried that since doctors were not covered under King-Anderson, enraged constituents would demand liberalized benefits. As a result, he warned, Ways and Means could be forced to raise the payroll tax above the maximum acceptable limit.[92] Even Cohen admitted that "we do recognize this problem and I think it has been complicated by the use of the term 'medicare' which is an erroneous term when applied to this program . . . We didn't invent the term 'medicare.' I consider it to have been invented by headline writers because it fits into a headline, and we have tried very conscientiously not to fall into that error."[93]

Another safeguard against unexpected costs involved a Social Security tax schedule that was large enough to finance monthly hospitalization benefits and to maintain a contingency reserve within the hospital insurance trust fund. Mills insisted to Myers and Cohen that "I have never had any hesitancy at all in fixing the tax so as to take care of the cost. I just want to be certain that we do it. That is all I have ever wanted to do. Whatever the tax is, I am perfectly willing to vote for it, and I do not think any of us should have any hesitancy about it, but let us not do what I thought was a weakness in the thing last year and get ourselves right back, Mr. Cohen, where we were then, of not doing enough. . . ."[94] The proper tax rate would establish a small cushion in case of a fiscal crisis. Nonetheless, Mills did not want an emergency fund so large that it seduced Congress to liberalize benefits without considering the actuarial soundness of Social Security.[95]

Throughout the hearings, Medicare opponents played to Mills's fears by warning of massive tax hikes. The AMA devoted much of its testimony not only to the threat of socialized medicine, but to the argument that hospital insurance was "unpredictably expensive" and that "enactment of this program would impose an unfair

[91] JMIC.
[92] JMIC. See also Wilbur Cohen to the Secretary of HEW, 28 January 1965, WCP, Box 82, Folder 9.
[93] U.S. Congress, House Committee on Ways and Means, *Medical Care For The Aged: Executive Hearings*, 89th Cong., 1st sess., 1965, 104.
[94] Ibid., 85.
[95] Ibid., 86.

burden on the Nation's wage earners and their employers to finance health care benefits for millions of older Americans who are self-supporting. . . ."[96] "We are dealing with a tax increase," warned the AMA president, Donovan Ward, "of major proportions. By 1971, Social Security taxes will reach 10.4 percent of payroll on the first $5,600, to be shared by worker and employer. And no one knows what the ultimate cost of this program would be as the costs of living rise and the aged population grows."[97] Most important, when constituents found out that doctors were not included in Medicare, they would demand an expensive liberalization of health benefits.

The Social Security experts responded that their bill provided a safety net.[98] Acting as an interpreter, Mills helped Myers to explain his actuarial estimates to the committee.[99] Myers replied to the AMA by explaining that the proposed tax schedule could finance health insurance through the 1980s and that it would create an adequate contingency reserve in the trust fund.[100] Since 1952, the financing in the various Medicare proposals had increased significantly.[101] In sum, Myers claimed to have strengthened Medicare by assuming "dynamic" economic change in its cost estimates, unlike earlier proposals, which had assumed that "nothing changed in the future; the hospital costs didn't go up. . . ."[102]

Medicare supporters also relied heavily on the symbolic value of the Social Security tax to support this liberalization in social insurance. When one representative challenged HEW to distinguish health insurance benefits from other types of welfare, Robert Ball admitted that, rationally, it was impossible to answer this question. Nevertheless, he said, there were distinctive qualities to the payroll tax. "There are many governmental interventions," Ball explained, "in the wage structure and in the benefit arrangements of society where people get from those interventions of government something back that is more than they would have earned in the open marketplace, the minimum wage law, the veteran's program, the social insurance

[96] Ibid., 742–744.

[97] Ibid., 744; Austin Wehrwin, "A.M.A. Questions Medicare Funds," *The New York Times*, 16 February 1965.

[98] U.S. Congress, House Committee on Ways and Means, *Medical Care For The Aged: Executive Hearings*, 89th Cong., 1st sess., 1965, 80–87.

[99] Ibid., 80–89.

[100] JMIC; U.S. Congress, House Committee on Ways and Means, *Medical Care For The Aged: Executive Hearings*, 89th Cong., 1st sess., 1965, 8–9; 80–87; Robert Myers to Robert Ball, 11 February 1965, WCP, Box 154, Folder 8.

[101] Myers, *Social Security*, 262–63; U.S. Congress, House Committee on Ways and Means, *Medical Care For The Aged: Executive Hearings*, 89th Cong., 1st sess., 1965, 13; 95–97.

[102] Robert Myers, interview with Peter Corning, 8 March 1967, COHP, Social Security Project, Interview 1, 17.

program, and it does not seem to me that these interventions add up to charity." When a citizen "contributed" payroll taxes to Social Security, moreover, he earned the "right" not only to the benefits offered at the time of the payment, but to any liberalization that occurred in his lifetime.[103]

Likewise, Robert Myers explained that congressional representatives should view social insurance as a "prepayment in advance on a collective group basis, so that the younger contributors are making their contributions with the expectation that they will receive benefits in the future – and not necessarily with the thought that their money is being put aside and earmarked for them, but rather that later there will be current income to the system for their benefits."[104] When some members suggested that the service benefits should be financed through general taxation, Cohen responded that while it might be completely logical to use general revenue, Congress had maintained a policy "of not wanting to pay out of general revenues for the people who had contributed to the system. . . ."[105]

Voicing his support, Mills warned that using general revenue without imposing a means test remained "untenable" and contradicted the basic principles behind social insurance.[106] For Mills, the contributory method of finance had produced the most effective programs since the New Deal. As he explained to his committee:

> Haven't we done a better job, actually, of financing the cost of the social security program out of a separate fund, paid for by a payroll tax, than we have some other expenditures of Government . . . whenever you have a program financed by a specific tax, the willingness of people to pay that tax, that specific tax, limits the benefits of that specific program . . . if you put a program, then, into the general fund of the Treasury, there is less likelihood that you control the package of benefits initially enacted than there is if you put it in a trust fund . . . I can't help but reach the conclusion that a specific fund, supported by a payroll tax, is a more conservative method of financing something than to do it out of the general fund of the Treasury.[107]

While Mills sympathized with the argument that "too great a burden is being placed on payroll taxes as the welfare programs financed by these taxes increase," he expressed greater concern about containing

[103] U.S. Congress, House Committee on Ways and Means, *Medical Care For The Aged: Executive Hearings*, 89th Cong., 1st sess., 1965, 98.
[104] Ibid., 20.
[105] Ibid., 117.
[106] Ibid., 116–117.
[107] Ibid., 803.

"the inroads on general revenues" should the money be used in social insurance.[108] Director of the Bureau of the Budget Kermit Gordon agreed, adding that in contributory programs taxpayers knew that they had the benefits as "a matter of right" and that "they know and can see that their own contributions are financing it. It is maintained as a separate account, and it has the special integrity that a separate account makes possible."[109]

Ideally, according to Mills, health insurance for the elderly should be financed under the same system. The chairman even indicated some flexibility regarding the 10 percent figure that he had previously perceived as the maximum limit for the payroll tax: "I can remember when I was on this committee that we sought as diligently as we could not to break the 5 percent. We froze the tax rate for many, many years. Maybe after many of you came to Congress we continued to freeze the rate, all indicating the desire on our part that the tax rate itself not go up too high too soon, but for the life of me I have never thought there was any determinable dollar limit to any tax rate." Mills continued, "It is all based upon the willingness of the taxpayer to pay, and we may find that 10 percent is that rate; we may find $10\frac{1}{2}$ percent is that rate; or we may find that the existing maximum is that rate before we get through."[110] To conclude, Mills argued that "if the payroll tax itself could be absorbed by the economy without increasing prices, and without making it more difficult for us to sell goods abroad, it seemed that was a preferable way of having this benefit, if it is to be had, than putting it in the general fund of the Treasury."[111]

But arguments about actuarial assumptions and symbolic values failed to persuade many antagonistic interest groups. Rather than criticizing the concepts behind King-Anderson, some opponents focused on Myers's expertise. Aetna Life Insurance, for example, charged that his estimates were incorrect and misleading. To prove its case, it brought its own actuary into the hearings to review each estimate contained in the bill. Mills then moderated a technical, yet emotionally charged, debate over each of the estimates. The Aetna actuary, for example, noted that Myers had predicted that in 1967, the cost of Medicare would reach $1.8 billion; in fact, he showed, the predicted cost was $2.9 billion. By 1990, he claimed that costs would reach $5.8 billion, not $2.5 billion.[112]

---

[108] Stanley Surrey to the Files, 25 October 1965, SSP, Box 182, File 2.

[109] U.S. Congress, House Committee on Ways and Means, *Medical Care For The Aged: Executive Hearings*, 89th Cong., 1st sess., 1965, 803.

[110] Ibid., 29.

[111] Ibid., 806.

[112] Ibid., 397–398; 402–425; Joint Letter from the Division of the Actuary, Social Security Administration, American Life Convention, Health Insurance Association of

In fact, both men had underestimated the cost of hospital insurance by billions of dollars.[113]

Some committee Republicans focused their attack on the "insurance" rhetoric that disguised this massive tax increase. The payroll tax, argued Representative Curtis, did not differ from other types of taxes because Congress did not retain the money in a trust fund. Curtis also rejected claims about the distinctive nature of the payroll tax, urging his colleagues to formulate policies in a more realistic language. If this was done, Curtis explained, the public might realize that policymakers were proposing the largest tax increase in the postwar period without considering its economic effects, only one year after they had enacted an income-tax reduction to accelerate economic growth.[114] Byrnes agreed with this critique. When administration budget director Kermit Gordon accused the Republicans of ignoring the "contributory" aspect of social insurance, Byrnes curtly responded: "What is contributory in the system? It is proposed in H.R. 1 [King-Anderson] to provide a benefit for all people who are today over 65 with no participation on their part, and give them the same package of benefits given to someone 20 years from now who has paid the new tax that would be imposed under this system . . . where is the prefunding?"[115] Responding to earlier discussions about a "prepayment," Byrnes said:

> I wonder whether the concept of prepayment is based on the idea that under the OASDI program and the social security program everybody has at least paid something, where under the income tax some people may never pay an income tax. Beyond that I have great difficulty in finding where the prepayment exists because the benefit is not, even under the OASDI program, completely tied down to what the individual has paid or that he has prefunded his benefit. I think this creates a problem of understanding, possibly semantic. But there is a misconception that the social security tax gives benefits a different complex and gives you something that you paid for.[116]

America, Life Insurance Association of America, and the Life Insurance Conference to the House Committee on Ways and Means, February 1965, WCP, Box 154, Folder 8.

[113] *Budget of the United States Government: Historical Tables*, (Washington, D.C.: U.S. Government Printing Office, 1994), 228. There is significant controversy among policy experts about the actual size of the miscalculation. See Robert J. Myers, "How bad were the original actuarial estimates for Medicare's hospital insurance program?" *The Actuary*, February 1994, 6–7.

[114] U.S. Congress, House Committee on Ways and Means, *Medical Care For The Aged: Hearings*, 89th Cong., 1st sess., 1965, 29–39; 43–79.

[115] Ibid., 822.   [116] Ibid., 822–823.

In fact, this particular proposal undermined the only truly distinctive feature of Social Security – namely, that monthly expenditures on benefits were related to specific payroll tax revenue that was collected from wage-earners.[117] Now, Congress was threatening to guarantee service benefits with unpredictable costs.

Byrnes's alternative – Bettercare

On February 4, 1965, Byrnes introduced a more expansive alternative to the AMA's Eldercare that was a hybrid of social insurance and public assistance. Under this federally administered plan, retirees could choose to participate in a program that covered hospital and doctors bills, as well as selected patient services. Refusing to use the payroll tax to finance service benefits, Byrnes planned that the government would pay two-thirds of the cost through general revenues, while participants would match that contribution with a graduated premium. The premium would distinguish the benefits from welfare and would limit the program's growth by imposing a significant cost on the beneficiary. To avoid a means test, the contribution was based on the Social Security payments the individual received.[118]

While designing the blueprint for his plan – often called "Bettercare" – Byrnes was denied access to actuarial expertise. Since his bill was an alternative to Medicare, the HEW refused to provide technical assistance.[119] Neither could he seek help from Blue Cross/Blue Shield, since they "were already in bed with HEW."[120] Even the AMA ignored Byrnes since he had rejected two principles that they had spent thousands of dollars to get into the 1964 Republican platform: health care benefits based on need and local administration.[121] In the end, Byrnes turned to the Aetna Life Insurance Company and the Civil Service Commission to assist him with his actuarial data; these groups had devised a similar program for federal employees on which this proposal was based.

A legislative challenge

By late February, it became clear that Ways and Means intended to pass some type of comprehensive reform.[122] When the closed execu-

---

[117] Ibid., 820–823.

[118] Wilbur Cohen to the President, 29 January 1965, WCP, Box 82, Folder 9.

[119] John Byrnes, interview with Peter Corning, 23 February 1967, COHP, Social Security Project, 26–27.

[120] JMIC.

[121] John Manley's Personal Notes, 16 March 1965, LBJL, The John Manley Papers.

[122] Charles Mohr, "President Urges Public To Press Medicare Action," *The New York Times*, 17 February 1965.

tive sessions came to a end, there were three options before the committee: Medicare, based on the social insurance approach, offered
hospital coverage financed through a higher Social Security tax;
Eldercare, built on the public assistance approach, expanded means-
tested assistance to the "medically indigent" by relying on general
revenue; Bettercare offered voluntary hospital and doctor coverage
that was financed through general-revenue appropriations and
premium contributions by participants.

During an executive session on the morning of March 2, Democrats and HEW experts had a "very hard time poking holes" in the
Byrnes plan.[123] To be sure, Republicans were surprised by the "coop-
erative atmosphere" that emerged. Cohen stunned the committee
when he acknowledged that the Byrnes plan offered higher benefits
than Medicare and at a lower cost to participants; of course, general
revenue would subsidize two-thirds of the program.[124] Mills, who had
long opposed financing social insurance through general revenue,
"enthusiastically went along" with the plan on the grounds that
medical benefits were somehow "different" than cash benefits and
could thus be paid for as insurance even while using general revenue.
The premium would also help contain the cost of the program by
imposing a fee on the beneficiary.[125] He did so despite Myers's continued admonition that the cost to the Treasury would rise more
rapidly than through a contributory plan.[126]

Faced with the task of reconciling three very different bills, Mills
searched for a compromise to avoid political disaster. At the heart of
this compromise would be a program that relied on earmarked taxes
to distinguish Medicare from welfare, but one that did not threaten
the earmarked tax system that was already in place for OASDI.

CONGRESS PASSES A "THREE-LAYER-CAKE"

Although Mills could simply have said yes or no to the various bills at
this point in the deliberations, instead he put forth his own proposal.
While he had already influenced the construction of the finance in
the administration bill, he now redefined the Social Security Amendments of 1965 to include physicians coverage, hospital insurance, and

[123] JMIC; John Manley's Personal Notes, 15 March 1965, LBJL, The John Manley
Papers.
[124] JMIC; John Manley's Personal Notes, 2 March 1965, LBJL, The John Manley Papers.
[125] Wilbur Cohen, interview by David McComb, 8 December 1968, LBJL, Oral History
Interview Collection, Tape 2, 15–16.
[126] Robert Myers to John Byrnes, 1 March 1965, RMP, Box M83–106, unprocessed;
Myers, "Actuarial Balance of OASDI System Under H.R. 7057," 6 April 1965, RMP,
Box M83–106, unprocessed.

increased coverage for the medically indigent. Toward the late-morning hours, Mills stunned his colleagues by moving forward with an idea that he had mentioned to John Byrnes back in 1964. At 3:00 p.m. he proposed that Congress combine Medicare, Eldercare, and Bettercare into a "three-layer-cake."[127] Just moments into the session, the Arkansas Democrat leaned back in his chair, turning to Wilbur Cohen, and said: "Well, now let's see. Maybe it would be a good idea if we put all three of these bills together. You go back and work this out overnight and see what there is to this."[128] Byrnes just sat there with his mouth wide open.[129]

The Mills bill

The announcement took participants by surprise. While they were aware of Mills's talent for compromise, few expected him to suggest a proposal that was more expansive than King-Anderson. When Mills offered the plan, one committee member recalled: "It was fantastic. It was Wilbur Mills at his best. His maneuvering was beautiful, and I don't mean maneuvering in a bad sense – he just said why don't we take it all."[130] Right then, according to another participant, everyone in the room knew "that it was all over. The rest would be details. In thirty seconds, a $2 billion bill was launched, and the greatest departure in the social security laws in thirty years was brought about."[131] As Mills told Cohen, the action was partially due to the AMA's argument that limited benefits contained in Medicare would lead to calls for expensive liberalizations.[132]

For Mills, the combination solved many of his fiscal and legislative

---

[127] JMIC; John Manley's Personal Notes, 2 March 1965, LBJL, The John Manley Papers; Wilbur Cohen to Lawrence O'Brien, 5 March 1965, WCP, Box 83, Folder 3; Wilbur D. Mills, interview with Lewis E. Weeks, 13 August 1980, Hospital Administration Oral History Collection, Library of the American Hospital Association (Chicago, Illinois, 1983), 29–30.

[128] JMIC; Robert Myers, interview with Peter Corning, 8 March 1967, COHP, Social Security Project, Interview 1, 92; John Manley's Personal Notes, 2 March 1965, LBJL, The John Manley Papers.

[129] Harris, A Sacred Trust, 187–188.

[130] JMIC; Lawrence O'Brien, interview with Michael Gillette, 24 July 1986, LBJL, Oral History Interview Collection, Interview XI, 36; Arlen Large, "Doctor-Bill Insurance for Elderly Is Proposed by House Republicans," The Wall Street Journal, 3 March 1965; "Three-Part Package of Medical Care Takes Firmer Shape in House," The Wall Street Journal, 4 March 1965; Edmond Le Breton, "Congress Eying New Health Plan," The Washington Post, 6 March 1965; Arlen Large, "'Medicare' Plan With Doctor-Bill Coverage Expected to Clear House Panel This Week," The Wall Street Journal, 8 March 1965.

[131] JMIC.

[132] Wilbur Cohen to Douglass Cater, 10 March 1965, WCP, Box 83, Folder 3.

concerns by restricting the burden that could be imposed on the Social Security tax. Since medical benefits – here meaning the reimbursement of doctors' fees – were only to be offered under the voluntary and public assistance portions of the legislation, those unpredictable costs would remain outside preexisting social insurance taxes. Assuming that Myers's estimates were now correct, the legislation promised expansive federal assistance on a sound fiscal basis.[133] In Mills's mind, Myers recalled, "people have been led to believe they're getting a lot more than just hospital benefits. And instead of having continual pressure put on us [Ways and Means], let's broaden the scope of the program and develop it the way we want under our own initiative, rather than under pressure from bureaucrats or the public."[134] Politically, the bill seemed invincible. By absorbing the proposal of each constituency in this debate, the chairman neutralized their opposition.[135] "Like everyone else in the room, I was stunned," Cohen explained, "It was the most brilliant legislative move I'd seen in thirty years. The doctors couldn't complain, because they had been carping about Medicare's shortcomings and about it being compulsory. And the Republicans couldn't complain, because it was their own idea. In effect, Mills had taken the AMA's ammunition, put it in the Republican's gun, and blown both of them off the map."[136] To cover his bets, Mills secured support for Bettercare should the Democrats reject his proposal.[137]

The Golden Ring Council of Senior Citizens, the first major interest group to represent senior citizens on matters of Social Security, arranged an elaborate luncheon in the committee room to celebrate Mills's accomplishment. During the festivities, Mills issued his first public statement of support for government health insurance.[138] As media pundits reported these events, it became evident that Mills had stolen the political spotlight from the experts who had promoted Medicare since 1952. Tom Wicker wrote in *The New York Times*: "Mills, by waiting, managed to become the architect of victory for medical care, rather than just another devoted but defeated supporter."[139] One

[133] Robert Myers to Robert Ball, 5 March 1965, WCP, Box 154, Folder 8.
[134] Robert Myers, interview with Peter Corning, 8 March 1967, COHP, Social Security Project, Interview 1, 90–91.
[135] Wilbur Cohen to the President, 2 March 1965, WCP, Box 83, Folder 3.
[136] Harris, *A Sacred Trust*, 187.
[137] JMIC.
[138] John Morris, "Mills To Support Revised Medicare," *The New York Times*, 11 March 1965; Editorial, "Improving Medicare," *The New York Times*, 12 March 1965; Arlen Large, "Old Folks Whoop Up Victory on Medicare At Scene of Battle," *The Wall Street Journal*, 11 March 1965.
[139] Tom Wicker, "Medicare's Progress," *The New York Times*, 25 March 1965.

committee member privately boasted, "The stimulus for all of these changes has come from the Committee and not from HEW – Wilbur Mills and the Committee are telling HEW what to do and initiating the changes."[140]

Medicare versus Keynes

Nonetheless, there were still crucial issues that needed to be resolved before bringing the bill to the House floor. One was the debate between the growth manipulation faction and the Social Security faction over the potential effect of the payroll tax increase on economic growth. This was rooted in ongoing tension between the growth manipulation and Social Security factions over whether social insurance finance should be evaluated in terms of economic growth or its actuarial soundness. After the debates about the income-tax reduction in 1964, policymakers were unable to ignore this issue. Traditionally, the Social Security faction had avoided considering the payroll tax in this respect since its main concern was raising sufficient revenue to finance OASDI. But the size of this tax increase led some officials to reconsider their position.[141] On several occasions, Mills stated that "all taxes, including Social Security, must be examined in light of their impact on the economy. Almost everyone in government thinks that way now."[142] Privately, Mills confided to Stanley Surrey and Gardner Ackley (the new chairman of the CEA) that the tax hike would drain purchasing power only one year after the stimulative income-tax reduction. In addition to proposing an excise tax reduction, Mills proposed a $3 billion rate reductions for people with incomes under $5,600, and an increased standard deduction to offset any detrimental economic effects. Mills felt that the income-tax reductions would be more effective than excise taxes, "psychologically if not economically," in offsetting the $5 billion payroll tax hike.[143]

---

[140] JMIC.

[141] "New Bills on Social Security Aim at Over-All Fiscal Policy," *The New York Times*, 26 March 1965.

[142] "Social Security: A Growing Giant," *Business Week*, 6 February 1965, 76. See also, U.S. Congress, House Committee on Ways and Means, *Medical Care For the Aged: Executive Hearings*, 89th Cong., 1st sess., 1965, 798.

[143] Gardner Ackley to Lyndon Johnson, 12 May 1965; Stanley Surrey to Henry Fowler, 13 May 1965; Ackley to Fowler, 21 April 1965, in SSP, Box 115, File 1. See also Surrey to Henry Fowler, 14 May 1965, SSP, Box 182, File 2; Ackley to Lyndon Johnson, 12 May 1965, LBJL, Legislative Background: Tax Increase, Box 1, File: Tax Increase – January–August 1966; Wilbur Cohen to Lawrence O'Brien, 17 March 1965, WCP, Box 154, Folder 8.

The growth manipulation faction, led by Ackley, warned Johnson
that the Mills bill threatened to create economic difficulties by building a $1 billion surplus in the Medicare fund during the first half of
1966. To achieve this surplus, Congress was to raise Social Security
taxes before distributing any benefits. "It is clear," Ackley warned Mills
and Johnson, that "the *economy could not take so large a drain of purchasing power.*"[144] The CEA wanted Ways and Means to reduce the size
of the tax increase and to delay its implementation until Congress
began to distribute benefits (this would offset the tax increase with
higher expenditures). If necessary, Congress should guarantee a
contingency fund through a standby budget appropriation from the
general revenue.[145]

Yet the Social Security faction still felt that issues of actuarial soundness outweighed economic growth. Despite concerns about the economic effect of Medicare taxation expressed to Surrey and Ackley, for
example, Mills insisted on financing health insurance through higher
payroll tax rates, even though wage base increases were better for
the economy.[146] Secretary Celebrezze explained to Ackley that the
Keynesian critique ignored the distinctive character of the payroll tax.
While designing social insurance, Celebrezze said, Social Security policymakers could not engage in deficit-spending or use general revenues to pay for benefits. "It is impossible to run a social insurance
system on a sound basis if it must create a fiscal stimulant to the
economy ever year by running a deficit of $1 billion annually . . . Mills
feels *very* strongly about this point," Celebrezze wrote Ackley, "I am
convinced that many of the congressional proponents of the legislation would be most disturbed if the program were to start off
on a basis that would require borrowing money from the General
Treasury, let alone even having the possibility of doing so. Mr. Mills
is vigorously opposed to this."[147] The chairman insisted on "the need
to accumulate a $1 billion 'nest egg' in the hospital insurance
fund before benefits start, and rejected other proposals to ease
the impact."[148] The advantages of sound financing and its bearing on

[144] Gardner Ackley to Lyndon Johnson, 17 March 1965, LBJL, White House Central
Files, Box 15, File: WE 6, Social Security 11/23/63–3/31/66. See also Gardner
Ackley to Henry Fowler, 21 April 1965 and Robert Myers, Memorandum, 16 August
1965, SSP, Box 115, File 1.

[145] Ibid. See also Arlen Large, "Social Security Tax Could Be Over Double '65 Levy if
Proposed Medicare Bill Passes, *The Wall Street Journal,* 19 March 1965; Harley Lutz,
"Mistake in Medicare," *The Wall Street Journal,* 17 March 1965.

[146] U.S. Congress, House Committee on Ways and Means, *Medical Care For the Aged:
Executive Hearings,* 89th Cong., 1st sess., 1965, 800–806.

[147] Anthony Celebrezze to Gardner Ackley, 13 March 1965, LBJL, White House Central
File, Box 15, File: WE 6, Social Security 11/23/63–3/31/66.

[148] Gardner Ackley to Lyndon Johnson, 17 March 1965, LBJL, White House Central
Files, Box 15, File: WE 6, Social Security 11/23/63–3/31/66. See also Ackley to

public opinion "far more than outweigh any economic impact aspects, which should be handled in other ways."[149] Therefore, Celebrezze argued that Congress had to determine payroll tax rates on the basis of balancing the Social Security budget rather than on the basis of managing economic growth.

Closing the deal

The final days of closed hearings were filled not with dramatic debates about the rights of the elderly to health insurance or about the threats of socialized medicine, but focused on how each technical provision would affect Social Security taxation. Between March 12 and March 19, Mills's committee met in the Longworth Building to reexamine the actuarial assumptions, reassess cost estimates, and review the cost-control devices contained in the 253-page bill. Ways and Means evaluated the bill line by line, covering about 40 pages each day. The only officials present at these closed hearings came from the committee, HEW, and the Treasury. During these final sessions, the discussion was filled with actuarial jargon that few of the representatives could understand without expert help. The chairman dazzled his colleagues with his mastery of the data, as one Democrat recalled, "You should have seen him when we had the executive people in on Medicare. He just knew so much more than they did it wasn't funny."[150]

During the final sessions, Stanley Surrey and Lawrence Woodworth appeared before the committee to oppose Representative Byrnes's proposed liberalization of tax deductions for private health insurance. Mills privately supported Surrey and Woodworth, agreeing that the provision imposed a cost to the Treasury of over $70 million. Nonetheless, he frustrated Surrey and Woodworth by publicly supporting the liberalization in order to secure Byrnes's support for the overall health insurance package.[151]

Henry Fowler, 21 April 1965, SSP, Box 115, File 1; Robert Myers, "Cost Estimates for Possible Changes in H.R. 6675 and in Procedures Thereon to Reduce Fiscal Drag," 16 August 1965, SSP, Box 115, File 1.

[149] Anthony Celebrezze to Gardner Ackley, 13 March 1965, LBJL, White House Central Files, File: WE 6 Social Security 11/23/63–3/31/66. See also Ackley to Lyndon Johnson, 12 May 1965 and Robert Myers, "Cost Estimates for Possible Changes in H.R. 6675 and in Procedures Thereon to Reduce Fiscal Drag," 16 April 1965, SSP, Box 115, File 1.

[150] JMIC.

[151] Wilbur Cohen to Lawrence O'Brien, 12 March 1965 and Cohen to O'Brien, 19 March 1965 in WCP, Box 83, Folder 3; Executive Sessions on H.R. 1, 18–19 March 1965, LBJL, John Manley Papers, 3137–3145; 3170; Stanley Surrey to the Files, 19 March 1965; Surrey to the Files, 12 March 1965; J.A. Stockfisch to Surrey, 5 March 1965; Surrey to Joe Bowman, 10 April 1965. Aforementioned documents all in SSP, Box 115, File 1.

Ways and Means also tested Myers for one last time on his actuarial assumptions. Some members, for example, wanted to know how the exact cost of the Byrnes plan changed under different levels of participation.[152] When Mills sought assurances that the payroll tax revenue for Medicare would be distinguished from the portion for OASDI, Myers outlined the two distinct tax schedules that were to be listed on the revised W-2 forms, and he discussed the two separate trust funds established by the bill.[153] Overall, Mills said, "we can say on the basis of this enactment that if nothing else is ever done for this 25-year period, our best estimates are that we will have ample fund to take care of these benefits."[154]

On March 17 and 18, the chairman turned to the problem of cost-control. According to Mills, "I don't happen to feel the need to know why we should let any doctor who wants to prescribe a drug he wants to because of the cost elements that are involved, and that is the determining factor. If it were not for the cost we could do everything that everybody asks us to do. . . ."[155] Ways and Means agreed that hospitals would nominate "fiscal intermediaries" to distribute reimbursements from the federal government and to conduct audit services in conjunction with local committees. The committee also concluded that Blue Cross should pay hospitals for their costs rather than according to a schedule of negotiated rates. Both of these methods for cost-containment were highly favorable to hospitals and to the private insurance industry, although many involved parties were uncertain which method would benefit them the most.[156] Finally, the committee debated the potential problems that might result from different cost accounting procedures, and explored the strengths of different methods of tax administration.[157] On March 19, the committee

---

[152] Myers explained that with 100 percent participation, the estimated cost was $3.65 billion in the first year of operation. At 80 percent participation, the cost would fall to about $2.9 billion in the first year. Either way, Social Security could finance the program through a combination of general revenues and premium contributions, without touching the money from the payroll tax. See John Manley's Personal Notes, 15 March 1965, LBJL, The John Manley Papers; Executive Sessions on H.R. 1, 16 March 1965, LBJL, The John Manley Papers, 2810–2853.

[153] Executive Sessions on H.R. 1, 16 March 1965, LBJL, The John Manley Papers, 2814–2816.

[154] Ibid., 2816. See also Wilbur Cohen to Lawrence O'Brien, 18 March 1965, LBJL, White House Office Aides Files, Henry Hall Wilson Papers, Box 9, File: Medicare.

[155] Executive Sessions on H.R. 1, 17 March 1965, LBJL, The John Manley Papers, 2913.

[156] Starr, *The Social Transformation of American Medicine*, 375–376. See also Wilbur Cohen to Lawrence O'Brien, 11 March 1965, WCP, Box 83, Folder 3.

[157] The discussion of these issues can be found in Executive Sessions on H.R. 1, 16–18 March 1965, LBJL, The John Manley Papers.

tentatively approved Byrnes's tax deductions, while Mills accepted Myers's figures for the tax schedule.[158]

At this stage in the policymaking process, Mills inserted several provisions into the amendments that won the interest-group support of physicians and other medical providers. For instance, over the objection of the administration, the bill defined radiologists, pathologists, and rehabilitation therapists as "doctors" instead of "hospital services" to avoid the charge that the mandatory part of the program, which covered the cost of hospitalization, interfered with private medicine.[159] Furthermore, Mills consulted with blood bank organizations to see whether Medicare's coverage of blood costs would hamper voluntary blood-giving drives: When they informed him that it would, his experts inserted an amendment that forced Medicare beneficiaries to pay for, or to replace, the first three pints of blood used during hospitalization.[160]

By the evening of March 22, the technicians finished drafting the legislation. In Mills's opinion, "we have done such a complete job here . . . that it will be utterly impossible for the Senate to conceive of any possible amendments to this bill," while staying within the proposed tax rate.[161] The following afternoon, Ways and Means approved the legislation by a straight-party vote of 17 to 8.[162]

The Social Security Amendments of 1965

The final bill contained three sections: Part A (Hospital Insurance) provided insurance for sixty days of hospitalization and related nursing care to all people after age sixty-five. Part B (Supplementary Medical Insurance) provided optional coverage for doctors fees. Part C (the expansion of Kerr-Mills later called Medicaid) broadened Kerr-Mills to extend coverage for the poor to dependent children and to the blind and permanently disabled; it required all participating states to provide hospital and physicians services; and liberal-

---

[158] Wilbur Cohen to Lawrence O'Brien, 19 March 1965 and Cohen to O'Brien, 18 March 1965, LBJL, White House Office Aides Files, Henry Hall Wilson Papers, Box 9, File: Medicare; Executive Sessions on H.R. 1, 19 March 1965, LBJL, The John Manley Papers.

[159] Wilbur Cohen to Lawrence O'Brien, 16 March 1965, WCP, Box 83, Folder 3.

[160] Marmor, *The Politics of Medicare*, 67.

[161] Executive Sessions on H.R. 1, 19 March 1965, LBJL, The John Manley Papers, 3247.

[162] John Morris, "Expanded Medicare Bill Is Voted by House Panel," *The New York Times*, 24 March 1965; Arlen Large, "House Panel Passes 'Medicare' Plan Financed By Social Security; Pensions Would Rise 7%," *The Wall Street Journal*, 24 March 1965; "Medicoup," *Newsweek*, 5 April 1965, 28–29.

ized the means test for inclusion of more elderly citizens into the program.[163]

To finance the $6 billion package, the committee turned to general revenue and payroll tax financing, and introduced a new type of earmarked tax. Part A (Hospital Insurance) was funded through increased Social Security payroll taxes; Part B (Supplementary Medical Insurance) was funded through a combination of general revenue and monthly premium contributions by participants; and Part C (Kerr-Mills) was funded through the general revenue.

The legislation distinguished Social Security from Medicare, even though the two were actually part of one larger social insurance program. While the original plan had been presented in terms of incorporating Medicare into Social Security, the final legislation appeared to separate Medicare from Social Security. Although the legislation did not establish a new tax for hospitalization insurance, it distinguished the cost of hospital insurance from the cost of OASDI. The schedules of tax rates for OASDI and for hospital insurance were inserted into separate subsections of the Internal Revenue Code. Hospital insurance had a separate trust fund. As with OASDI, monthly revenue was used to pay for monthly benefits (along with a small excess of revenue to be placed into the fund); this contingency reserve was invested in government securities. The act stated that the tax schedule on W-2 forms would show what proportion of the total contribution went to hospital insurance.[164] The financing basis for the hospital insurance program was determined by a different approach than that used for the OASDI system, reflecting the differences in the two programs. Rising earnings and rising hospitalization costs in future years were assumed, instead of level earnings, and the estimates were for twenty-five years rather than for seventy-five years.[165]

To pay for Supplementary Medical Insurance, the legislation created a new type of earmarked tax that combined equivalent general revenue and participant contributions. For the initial period of operation, the premium rate was established at $3 a month; the total income of the system per participant per month was thus to be $6 per person. The premium was paid through a payroll deduction from a recipient's Social Security benefit. All financial operations for the

[163] U.S. Congress, House Committee on Ways and Means, *Summary of Major Provisions of H.R. 6675: The "Social Security Amendments of 1965," As Introduced and Ordered Reported To the House of Representatives By the Committee on Ways and Means*, 24 March 1965, H7496 (Committee – Print).

[164] Ibid.

[165] Myers and Bayo, "Hospital Insurance, Supplementary Medical Insurance, and Old-Age, Survivors and Disability Insurance," 24–26.

program were handled through the Supplementary Medical Insurance Trust Fund. Importantly, the program relied on a different concept of actuarial soundness than OASDI. In essence, the program was financed on a current-cost basis rather than on a long-range cost basis, since costs and the premium rate were subject to change.[166]

On the floor, Byrnes still criticized Part A as a threat to Social Security.[167] He warned that the proposed "separation" of the cash and health tax systems involved a duplicitous political mechanism; as he explained, "you can put in gimmicks that look like you are separating it, you can do all of the rationalization you want, but you will still have them both (hospital and Social Security retirement funds) tied together. . . ."[168]

The chairman responded that these distinctions were more than just fiction. Clearly, his committee had gone to great lengths to ensure that the portion of money that went into each program was clearly earmarked. By doing so, Congress could provide hospital insurance for the elderly and limit the growth of the benefit. While the OASDI Trust Fund had been actuarially sound for the past twenty-five years, Mills reminded his colleagues, "how many times have we had a balanced budget of the general fund of the Treasury into which the gentlemen proposes to put this system?"[169] In the end, the House rejected the Byrnes substitute by a vote of 191–236.[170]

On March 31, Mills asked Myers to show the principal aspects of the actuarial assumptions that showed the amendments were financed "more conservatively than any of its predecessors."[171] Upon calling for a vote on the committee bill, Mills argued that the challenge of health care could best be met by "the combined efforts of voluntary organizations and the Government."[172] Once again, he assured those who feared the bill might jeopardize OASDI, "without any hesitation, without any equivocation, that there is not one single, solitary thing in this bill which would permit or allow for $1 of the money which is set aside to go into the old-age and survivors disability insurance trust funds to ever get into the hospital insurance trust fund. . . ."[173]

---

[166] Ibid., 24–26.

[167] U.S. Congress, House of Representatives, *Congressional Record*, 89th Cong., 1st sess., 7 April 1965, 7223.

[168] Ibid., 7222.

[169] Ibid., 7223. See also, pages 7210–7211.

[170] U.S. Congress, House of Representatives, *Congressional Record*, 89th Cong., 1st sess., 8 April 1965, 7443–7444.

[171] Wilbur Mills to Robert J. Myers, 31 March 1965, RMP, Box M83–106, unprocessed.

[172] U.S. Congress, House of Representatives, *Congressional Record*, 89th Cong., 1st sess., 7 April 1965, 7211–7214. [173] Ibid., 7213.

On the House floor, Mills's speech to the members sealed the compromise that he had designed. One reporter recounted: "Mills received a standing ovation from both sides of the aisle when he went to the rostrum in the well of the House to describe what had by now become known as the Mills bill. He quickly justified the reputation he had acquired for always being in command of his material. Speaking without a trace of an accent – it is reported that he has an unusually strong one whenever he talks to a group of his constituents – and only rarely referring to notes, he outlined the provisions of the bill, which was two hundred and ninety-six pages long."[174] The House passed the measure by a vote of 313–115 on April 8. The amendments received further support when Congress enacted a $4.8 billion excise tax reduction in mid-June. Since the reduction affected the same income-brackets that were going to pay the higher payroll tax, the legislation mitigated the problem of "fiscal drag." Only a week after enacting the excise reduction, the Senate passed the Social Security amendments (raising the wage base to $6,600 in 1966).[175]

During April, Mills continued to promote the use of earmarked taxation in this bill. In the dentist association's journal, for example, he wrote, "Properly designed, this tax has some points to recommend it. The breadth of its base produces considerable sums of money. The cost burden is not placed on the General Fund, already overburdened. It is visible and capable of easy classification, which focuses public concern on the proper expenditure of the funds. It is a way through which the worker can take cognizance and pride in his contributions." Through separate trust funds and accounting mechanisms, moreover, the cash benefit could not be compromised and health care would not come at the expense of "the root factors of food, shelter, and clothing."[176]

The Conference Committee met only six times before reaching an agreement. During the sessions, Mills continued to make key concessions to the AMA to ensure its lukewarm support of the bill. Mills secured passage for a provision that allowed doctors and hospitals to

[174] Harris, A Sacred Trust, 191–192.

[175] U.S. Congress, Senate Committee on Finance, Brief Description of Senate Amendments to H.R. 6675, 1965, S1506 (Committee – Print); Edwin Dale, Jr., "Smaller Tax Drag," The New York Times, 18 June 1965; "'Medicare' Plan Of House Backed By Senate Panel," The Wall Street Journal, 24 June 1965; Arlen Large, "'Medicare' Plan Approved 12 to 5 By Senate Unit," The Wall Street Journal, 25 June 1965; Eve Edstrom, "Senate Unit Approves Medicare," The Washington Post, 25 June 1965; "'Medicare' and Increased Pensions Under Social Security Near Final Passage; Amount of Tax Rise Is Still at Issue," The Wall Street Journal, 12 July 1965.

[176] "Mills on Medicare: How to Raise the Money? How to Spend it Best?" Dental Management, April 1965.

maintain control over their fees rather than having the government set up a rate structure.[177] Meanwhile, Mills successfully kept chiropractors, podiatrists, and even radiologists outside of the hospital insurance program.[178] Although the first concession handcuffed Congress if it desired to control the cost of Medicare, it was crucial if Mills wanted to avoid an intensified attack by the AMA. Mills's actions revealed the political limits to his fiscal conservatism by rejecting substantive cost regulation in exchange for interest-group support. As a legislative leader and an opponent of direct government controls on markets, Mills understood that such compromises were essential to success. Nonetheless, based on the current prices of medical care, Mills believed that the proposed taxes and the restrictions in coverage would contain the cost of the program within reasonable limits.

During the closed conference sessions, representatives from each tax-writing committee and from the administration went over the House and Senate bill. Following the lead of the Senate, the Conference Committee raised the wage base to $6,600 in 1966. According to the final tax schedule, combined tax rates for cash and health benefits would reach 8.4 percent in 1966, 8.8 percent in 1967–1968, 9.8 percent in 1969–1972, and 10.8 percent in 1973–1975.[179] The tax increase was effective on January 1, 1966, six months before hospital benefits became available; to satisfy some of Ackley's concerns, Mills made the 7 percent increase in cash benefits retroactive to January 1 1965, thereby releasing an extra $3 billion into the economy.[180]

---

[177] Lawrence O'Brien, interview with Michael Gillette, 24 July 1986, LBJL, Oral History Interview Collection, Interview XI, 45.

[178] Wilbur Cohen to Lawrence O'Brien, 21 July 1965, WCP, Box 84, Folder 4; Cohen to O'Brien, 20 July 1965, WCP, Box 84, Folder 4.

[179] U.S. Congress, House Committee on Ways and Means, *Summary Of Major Provisions Of H.R. 6675, The Social Security Amendments of 1965 As Agreed To By The House, Senate, and Conference Committee*, 21 July 1965, H4485 (Committee – Print); "Conferees in Agreement On All Main Provisions Of 'Medicare' Package," *The Wall Street Journal*, 21 July 1965; John J. Morris, "Conferees Clear Bill on Medicare," *The New York Times*, 22 July 1965; Robert J. Myers, *Actuarial Cost Estimates And Summary Of Provisions Of The Old-Age, Survivors, And Disability Insurance System As Modified By The Social Security Amendments Of 1965 And Actuarial Cost Estimates And Summary Of Provisions Of The Hospital Insurance And Supplementary Medical Insurance Systems As Established By Such Act*, 30 July 1965, H0701 (Committee – Print).

[180] Robert J. Myers, "Cost Estimates for Possible Changes in H.R. 6675 and in Procedures Thereon to Reduce Fiscal Drag," 16 April 1965, RMP, Box M83-106, unprocessed; Robert Ball to the Secretary, 24 April 1965, RMP, Box M83-106, unprocessed. See also "Wrapping Up the Medicare Bill," *Business Week*, 27 March 1965, 32; "New Bills on Social Security Aim at Over-All Fiscal Policy," *The New York Times*, 26 March 1965; Myers, *Social Security*, 117–118.

On July 10, Myers published a report about this tax schedule to Ways and Means. In the document, he affirmed the actuarial soundness of the legislation, concluding that "there is close to an exact balance, especially considering that a range of variation is necessarily present in the long-range actuarial cost estimates and, further, that rounded tax rates are used in actual practice." To assure that the program remained sound, Myers announced that HEW would conduct a small, continuous actuarial sample to check whether the program was working according to schedule.[181] On July 20, the Conference Committee agreed to the bill, which then moved through the House and Senate with relative ease.[182] Mills called the amendments "one of the most significant and far-reaching measures which had been before this or any recent Congress."[183]

MEDICARE'S MIXED PRECEDENTS

Despite its success, Medicare opened up serious questions about social insurance and its relation to the payroll tax. In response to the pressure from the Social Security faction to provide hospitalization benefits, Mills had endorsed significant modifications to social insurance that weakened its distinctions from other public expenditures. At the time of Medicare's passage, the compromises seemed acceptable to Mills, given the layered protections and the internal fiscal controls that were built into the program. Furthermore, Medicare was by no means akin to welfare or food stamps given the absence of a means test, the presence of earmarked monies, and the number of middle-class beneficiaries.

In the long-run, however, the problems associated with Medicare became ammunition for future attacks by fiscal conservatives, economists, and left-wing activists on Social Security. Foremost, the Social Security Amendments of 1965 contradicted the propaganda of the payroll tax as a wage-related premium for a wage-related benefit since the revenue was now going to finance service benefits that had absolutely no relation to past wages. When policymakers analyzed this large $5 billion annual payroll tax increase within the context of the income-tax reductions of 1962 and 1964, they could no longer ignore

---

[181] Robert J. Myers, *Actuarial Cost Estimates For The Old-Age, Survivors, And Disability Insurance System As Modified By H.R. 6675 And For The Health Insurance System For The Aged Established By H.R. 6675, As Passed By The House of Representatives And As According to the Action of the Senate*, 10 July 1965, H1409 (Committee – Print).

[182] Wilbur Cohen to Lawrence O'Brien, 21 July 1965, WCP, Box 84, Folder 4. Soon after, the House passed the Social Security Amendments of 1965 by a vote of 307–116 and the Senate by a vote of 70–24.

[183] *Congressional Quarterly Almanac*, 89th Cong., 1st sess., 1965, 269.

the economic consequences of the payroll tax. "Just as the oppressive size of the income tax forced a rethinking of its place in the economy in the first half of the 1960s," one economist predicted, "the growth of the Social Security tax will force some rethinking about its proper role in the second half of the 1960s."[184] In future years, the tax community would have to focus on how payroll taxes affected economic growth, just as they did with the income tax.

Most important, Congress had compromised on a basic Social Security principle by authorizing the use of general revenue to finance a portion of the social insurance program – namely, Supplementary Medical Insurance. Although Mills contended that the voluntary nature of the program and the monthly participant contribution distinguished the benefits from welfare and limited its growth, the amendments nonetheless established a precedent for the use of general revenue to pay for social insurance. Policymakers immediately picked up on this precedent, and began to consider the use of general revenue in other types of insurance programs. For example, a joint staff study in the executive branch raised questions about the limited and regressive supply of revenue offered by the payroll tax.[185] While economists thought it futile to discuss the use of general revenue in OASDI since traditional Social Security insiders believed in the role of payroll taxes to maintaining the "right" to benefits, they were more optimistic about experimenting with unemployment insurance.[186]

Even in a moment of great triumph, it was clear to some that the Social Security Amendments of 1965 had unraveled some of the logic behind the tax policies of the American state. Despite Mills's achievement in expanding earmarked taxes into the realm of private medicine without destroying OASDI, the legislation raised delicate questions about finance: Medicare challenged the limited capacities of the payroll tax to finance public welfare, it undermined the myth that payroll tax policies could not be considered for their economic affects, and it contradicted the beliefs that general-revenue money

---

[184] "Social Security: A Growing Giant," *Business Week*, 6 February 1965, 77; Stanley S. Surrey, "Federal Tax Policy in the 1960s: Remarks to the State University of New York at Buffalo," 21 April 1966, reprinted in *Tax Policy And Tax Reform: 1961–1969, Selected Speeches and Testimony of Stanley Surrey*, ed. William F. Hellmuth and Oliver Oldman (Chicago: Commerce Clearing House, 1973), 115–134.

[185] Joint Staff, Bureau of the Budget, Council of Economic Advisors, Department of Commerce, and the Treasury Department, "Letter to Report: The Long-Range Implications for Payroll Financing of Social Insurance," 29 July 1965, SSP, Box 114, File 3.

[186] Stanley Surrey to Henry Fowler, July 1965, SSP, Box 114, File 3. See also Gerard Brannon to Stanley Surrey, 26 July 1965, SSP, Box 115, File 1.

could not be used in social insurance and that payroll taxes must be tied to specific benefits.[187]

For the moment, these problems were overshadowed by the promise of the new legislation. Federal officials from all ideological persuasions agreed that the legislation constituted a historic achievement. The amendments extended assistance to the elderly and to the medically indigent in areas that had heretofore remained outside the scope of the state. By linking these programs to the payroll tax, the benefits were not stigmatized as welfare. Mills and his colleagues claimed that these special contributory benefits, like OASDI, assisted the elderly without encouraging dependence on government handouts. The elderly received health benefits in return for the contributions they had made during their working years. After retirement, those who chose to participate could also contribute a portion of their Social Security benefits toward a voluntary insurance program that covered the cost of physicians. Finally, through symbolic distinctions such as the separate trust fund, Congress had promised to protect Social Security from excessive health care costs.

Since the beginning of this debate, Mills had expressed strong concerns about the effect of Medicare on Social Security. By the end of the debate, as a result of the layered tax system and separate trust fund, it appeared that Medicare and Social Security were two distinct programs, each safe from the other. With this accomplishment in his legislative pocket, Mills entered into a historic battle with President Johnson about the survival of the Great Society.

[187] For an excellent analysis of Medicare's post-1965 history, see Jonathan Bruce Oberlander, "Medicare and the American State: The Politics of Federal Health Insurance, 1965–1995" (Ph.D. diss., Yale University, 1995).

8

The War on Inflation

Between 1966 and 1968, inflation replaced economic growth at the top of the national political agenda. After half a decade of promoting investment and demand, the tax community turned to the problem of restraining economic growth without imposing price controls. "In my view," Mills told the House as early as 1966, "inflation is a major threat to the domestic economy at this time."[1]

Although the entire tax community agreed on the need to curb inflation, it was divided over how the state should design its fiscal policy in this effort. Most members of the growth manipulation faction, led by the Council of Economic Advisors, argued that the nation was experiencing "demand-pull" inflation. According to their analysis, industrial supply was unable to keep pace with booming consumer demand. Based on Keynesian logic, a temporary tax increase with spending cuts would dampen demand by taking income away from consumers. The CEA, together with the Department of Treasury, combined Keynesian arguments with a neoclassical concern for balanced budgets. Without the tax increase, they warned, the deficit would reach over $29 billion as the government attempted to provide guns (Vietnam) and butter (the Great Society).

Other members of the community also disliked inflation and deficits, but located the source of the nation's economic problems in collective bargaining and government spending. Led by Mills, this group claimed that the economy was experiencing "cost-push" inflation. They targeted collective bargaining agreements as a major source of higher prices. According to this analysis, business was passing along the expensive cost of wage settlements to consumers through higher prices. Thereafter, consumers reacted by insisting on higher wages and perpetuating a cycle of inflation. The most effective way to end "cost-push" inflation was a substantial reduction in public expenditures. Unlike a tax increase, this would remove money from the economy without squeezing personal and corporate income.

[1] U.S. Congress, House of Representatives, *Congressional Record*, 89th Cong., 2nd sess., 30 September 1966, 24549.

Mills also believed that expenditure reduction was essential even if
the "demand-pull" analysis turned out to be correct; otherwise,
increased public spending would offset the decline in personal
income from the tax increase. Finally, some economists argued that
a tax hike would only lead consumers to reduce their personal savings
in order to maintain stable levels of consumption.[2]

The debate took place within an unstable international financial
environment, which involved the U.S. balance-of-payments deficit
and the related depletion of U.S gold reserves. The rising balance-of-
payments deficits meant that more American dollars were being
invested abroad than at home as a result of tourism, low national
interest rates, overseas military operations, foreign aid, and improved
investment opportunities overseas. Since too many dollars were being
held abroad and inflation weakened the dollar at home, foreign
investors grew concerned that the dollar would be devalued and that
individuals holding dollars would lose money.[3] The balance-of-
payments deficit produced dramatic losses in the U.S. stock of gold
when foreign investors exchanged their dollars for gold in response
to the potential devaluation of the dollar. Speculators hoped that the
U.S. would increase the price of gold as the government exported too
much gold (during the Bretton Woods conference in 1944, the U.S.
agreed to exchange gold for dollars at $35 per ounce to foreign gov-
ernments). The balance-of-payments deficits, combined with the loss
of gold, pressured federal officials to improve the stability of the
dollar by curbing inflation, raising interest rates, and improving
investment opportunities within the United States.[4]

The heated battle over taxation and spending ended when Mills
forced the administration to accept over $6 billion in expenditure
reduction to fight "cost-push" inflation in exchange for a temporary
10 percent tax increase to fight "demand-pull" inflation. The
Revenue and Expenditure Control Act of 1968 reestablished the principle of expenditure control temporarily by gutting the Great Society

[2] Wilbur D. Mills, "Remarks before the Chamber of Commerce," 27 August 1968,
WMPC, Box 420, File 12; Council of Economic Advisors to Lyndon Johnson, 12
March 1966, LBJL, Confidential File, Box 44, File: FI 11, Taxation; Mills, "Remarks
before the American Institute of Certified Public Accountants," 16 October 1968,
WMPC, Box 644, File 3. For a explanation of "cost-push" inflation, see Allen J.
Matusow, *The Unraveling of America: A History of Liberalism in the 1960s* (New York:
Harper Torchbooks, 1984), 156–165; 178.
[3] Cathie J. Martin, *Shifting the Burden: The Struggle over Growth and Corporate Taxation*
(Chicago: University of Chicago Press, 1991), 21.
[4] In this chapter, I draw much of my understanding of the international context from
Robert M. Collins, "The Economic Crisis of 1968 and the Waning of the 'American
Century'," *American Historical Review* 101, No. 2 (April 1996): 396–422.

and by slashing spending increases that had been built into existing appropriations laws. In contrast to Medicare, Mills here relied primarily on the negative power of the chairmanship, working around the tax community to block legislation. At the same time, however, he helped place the issue of expenditure control on the political agenda. In doing so, he demonstrated how the negative and positive power of the chairmanship were often so related as to be indistinguishable.[5]

Not only did the struggle reveal to the public the power of tax-writing committee chairmen, but it showed how the language of macroeconomics had saturated national debates about tax policy. While members disagreed over what type of fiscal policy could stop inflation most effectively, they all relied heavily on macroeconomics as a rhetorical weapon (rather than calls for microeconomic intervention, or a rights-based opposition to tax increases, or a liberal needs-based defense of public spending). In short, the tax community agreed on the need for the state to dampen inflation through macroeconomic fiscal policy, but members differed on how much expenditure reduction was necessary within that equation.

GUNS *OR* BUTTER?

To shift from a policy of "stimulus" to a policy of "restraint," federal officials experimented with a variety of fiscal measures.[6] At first, President Johnson rejected the advice of the CEA for an across-the-board income-tax hike, and instead obtained support for smaller measures.[7] In 1966, for example, Congress accelerated corporate tax payments and temporarily repealed the investment tax credit to discourage capital expenditures.[8] But these measures were too mild. In the State

---

[5] Steven S. Smith and Christopher J. Deering, *Committees in Congress*, 2nd edition (Washington, D.C.: Congressional Quarterly Press, 1990), 12.

[6] Stanley Surrey, Handwritten Notes, 1966, SSP, Box 189, File 1.

[7] James D. Savage, *Balanced Budgets & American Politics* (Ithaca: Cornell University Press, 1988), 180.

[8] U.S. Congress, House Committee on Ways and Means, *President's Proposal on Suspension of the Investment Credit and Application of Accelerated Depreciation: Hearings*, 89th Cong., 2nd sess., 1966; U.S. Congress, House Committee on Ways and Means, "Press Release: Chairman Wilbur D. Mills (D., Ark.), Committee on Ways and Means, Releases Committee Decisions Relating to Suspension of the Investment Credit and the Allowance of Accelerated Depreciation," 23 September 1966 and "Press Release: Wilbur D. Mills (D., Ark.), Committee on Ways and Means, Announces Committee Has Ordered Reported to the House H.R. 12752, The 'Tax Adjustment Act of 1966,'" both in NA, RG 128, Box 497, File: Ways and Means 1960; Albert Buckberg to Laurence Woodworth, 6 May 1966, in NA, RG 128, Box 465, File: Economic Clippings, Forecasts 1967.

of the Union message in January 1967, Johnson proposed a 6 percent tax surcharge to reduce consumer demand and to lower the budget deficit. But the Ways and Means Committee rejected the surcharge because of its traditional opposition to tax increases, hostile constituent mail, weak support in the House, and mixed economic forecasts.[9] As late as June, one congressional staffer wrote that the economy was in a state of "apathy."[10] Even a close administration ally, the AFL-CIO, opposed the surcharge on the grounds that its experts did not predict continued inflation. Should a tax increase be imposed, moreover, the AFL-CIO argued that the burden should be placed on the upper-income brackets through tax-break reform.[11] Given these problems, the administration postponed any formal request for a surcharge until it gathered more compelling economic evidence that inflation was going to continue at dangerous levels.[12]

Johnson pushes the tax surcharge

When inflation returned during the summer of 1967 at an annual rate of about 4 percent, the president requested a 10 percent income tax surcharge and almost $2 billion in expenditure reduction.[13] Without the surcharge, Johnson warned, "ruinous inflation" would rob the poor and elderly of their fixed incomes while the deficit would soar to unprecedented heights. During Ways and Means hearings, administration economists teamed up with Keynesian scholars to promote the surcharge as a solution to "demand-pull" inflation.[14] As with the 1964 tax reduction, Secretary of the Treasury Henry Fowler mobilized business groups to lobby in favor of this effort. On August 24, these business executives, including leaders of the American Bankers Association, the Mortgage Bankers Association, and the National Association of Home Builders, sent a telegram

[9] JMIC; M. Stephen Weatherford with Thomas B. Mayhew, "Tax Policy and Presidential Leadership: Ideas, Interests, and the Quality of Advice," *Studies in American Political Development* 9, No. 2 (Fall 1995): 287–330.

[10] Laurence Woodworth to William Forti, 15 June 1967, NA, RG 128, Box 465, File: Economic.

[11] Stanley Surrey to the Files, 30 June 1967, SSP, Box 184, File 2.

[12] Donald F. Kettl, "The Economic Education of Lyndon B. Johnson: Guns, Butter, and Taxes," in *The Johnson Years: Volume Two*, ed. Robert A. Divine (Lawrence: University Press of Kansas, 1987), 54–78.

[13] William Forti to Laurence Woodworth, 4 August 1967, NA, RG 128, Box 465, File: Economic; Joseph Barr to Lyndon Johnson, 11 August 1967, NAT, RG 56, Office of Tax Policy, Box 68, File: Tax Increase.

[14] Walter Heller to Wilbur Mills, 4 August 1967, WMPC, Box 508, File 4; Mr. White to Stanley Surrey, 3 October 1966 and Henry Fowler to Lyndon Johnson, 25 August 1966, NAT, RG 56, Office of Tax Policy, Box 68, File: Tax Increase.

urging Mills to support the tax increase and expenditure control package. Their letter warned that continued inflation would destabilize the international and domestic economy.[15]

Mills objects to the proposal

From the start of the hearings, Mills warned that the surcharge lacked strong support within Congress, especially after the Democrats had lost forty-seven seats in the House in the election of 1966.[16] Besides the perennial political danger of increasing taxes, and Mills's ongoing desire to reduce public spending, Mills disliked the surcharge on economic grounds. He still viewed frequent manipulations to the tax code, based on questionable economic forecasts, with extreme caution. He warned colleagues: "We must not let ourselves be placed in the position of raising and lowering the hemline of taxation, from season to season, merely to make the merchandise more salable . . . it is essential that these laws have a certain degree of stability, if our system of substantially voluntary tax collection is to continue functioning effectively on that basis."[17]

Mills's opposition stemmed from challenges by his own economic experts to the analysis of the CEA. Detailed studies by the JCIRT staff showed that most of the economic forecasts, including predictions of continued inflation, were highly uncertain: Slight adjustments to CEA assumptions produced dramatically different pictures of the economy. Should the assumptions behind the surcharge be incorrect, the staff warned, Congress might dampen an economy that was already heading into recession.[18] Mills used this data to question the

[15] For the best discussion of the alliance between the administration and business groups, see Martin, *Shifting the Burden*, 81–106. See also Eileen Shanahan, "113 Business Leaders Back a Temporary Rise in Taxes," *The New York Times*, 25 August 1967.

[16] JMIC; "Mills Is Doubtful On Tax Surcharge," *The New York Times*, 14 August 1967; "Johnson Tax-Rise Plan Faces Uphill Battle In Congress, Ways and Means Chief Says," *The Wall Street Journal*, 14 August 1963.

[17] U.S. Congress, House of Representatives, *Congressional Record*, 90th Cong., 1st sess., 16 March 1967, 6891. See also Wilbur D. Mills, "Fiscal Policy and the Good Economic Society: Remarks Delivered to the American Enterprise Institute," 20 April 1967, WMPC, Box 644, File 3.

[18] See the following documents: William Forti to Laurence Woodworth, 27 February 1967 and Forti to Woodworth, 10 May 1967, in NA, RG 128, Box 465, File: Economic Forecasts, 1967; Woodworth to Wilbur Mills, 28 December 1966; Alan Murray and Albert Buckberg to Woodworth, 3 January 1967; Woodworth to Mills, 6 January 1967; Woodworth to John Byrnes, 6 January 1967; Murray and Buckberg to Woodworth, 27 January 1967; Buckberg and Murray to Woodworth, 21 July 1967; Buckberg to Woodworth, 6 December 1967; Murray to Woodworth, 4 August 1967; Murray to Woodworth, 8 April 1966, all in NA, RG 128, Box 465, File: Economic Clippings, Forecasts 1967; Forti to Woodworth, 10 October 1967; Forti to

soundness of the CEA proposals. "From Truman's day on," he remarked, "I have watched economists miss every big turn of the economy. I'm not criticizing them; I'm only saying we expect too much of them."[19]

Mills often repeated the story of how CEA chairman Gardner Ackley allowed Johnson to make a presentation that used a figure of $83 billion for 1967 corporate profits. Although the actual estimate was less than $80 billion, Ackley feared that such a low figure would imply that there was an economic recession. During a meeting with the president in early 1967, Mills challenged the prediction on continued high profits, and enticed Johnson to call Ackley about his analysis. The president put Ackley on an intercom, without telling him that Mills was in the room, and asked if the report had been too optimistic. In response, Ackley admitted, "Well, Mr. President, you know it's very difficult to forecast profits. My own guess is that they'll probably be down a little bit, but we thought it was appropriate to say that they're going to be at about the same level." Clearing his throat, Johnson informed Ackley that Mills was in the room and that the "squawk box" was on. Ackley recalled being terribly embarrassed.[20] Even the Bureau of the Budget admitted that its economic outlooks were "necessarily tentative" because of the "uncertainties" of Vietnam and the "uncontrollable" costs of public assistance, farm price supports, health insurance, and veterans pensions.[21] Mills also distrusted CEA economists after their flip-flop on the investment tax credit. In 1966, Mills had reluctantly supported an administration request to suspend the investment tax credit despite strong opposition from business interests. Within a few months, Johnson and the CEA asked Ways and Means to restore the credit since the administration forecasts had been incorrect.[22]

Woodworth, 11 September 1967; Forti to Woodworth, 10 March 1967; Forti to Woodworth, 7 April 1967, all in NA, RG 128, Box 465, File: Economic, Woodworth to Mills, 28 December 1966, WMPC, unprocessed, Gardner Ackley, interview with Joe Franz, 13 April 1973, LBJL, Oral History Interview Collection, Interview I, 33–34; Ackley, interview with Franz, 7 March 1974, LBJL, Oral History Interview Collection, Interview II, 16–20.

[19] Gilbert Burek, "Capitol Hill's 'Show Me' Economist," *Fortune*, February 1968, 107.
[20] This story is recounted by Ackley in Erwin L. Hargrove and Samuel A. Morley, eds., *The President and the Council of Economic Advisers: Interviews with CEA Chairmen* (Boulder: Westview Press, 1984), 256.
[21] Charles Schultze to William Proxmire, 17 August 1967, LBJL, Henry Fowler Personal Papers, Box 236, File: Briefing Books, Tax Surcharge, 1967. See also Richard Janssen, "Foggy Forecasts," *The Wall Street Journal*, 12 September 1967; Schultze, interview with David McComb, 10 April 1969, LBJL, Oral History Interview Collection, Interview II, 10; 19–21; Gardner Ackley, interview with Joe Frantz, 13 April 1973, LBJL, Oral History Interview Collection, Interview I, 34–35.
[22] Kettl, "The Economic Education of Lyndon B. Johnson," 69.

Yet Mills relied on like-minded economists to challenge the administration. Indeed, Mills had no trouble invoking the predictions of Norman Ture, Arthur Burns, and Paul McCracken, all of whom argued that the surcharge would have little effect on the two main sources of inflation: increased government spending and collective bargaining settlements.[23] Throughout the debates, the chairman synthesized such analyses to challenge the CEA. On one occasion, Mills invited Ture to visit his office without any further explanation. When Ture arrived, he found that the chairman was talking with Lawrence O'Brien (legislative liaison for the administration) about the economic value of tax increases. Acting surprised by Ture's visit, Mills casually asked Ture about the economy. "So," Ture recalled, "I gave the answers that he expected which is the reason why he called me in the first place." He explained that the threat of inflation could not be handled by a tax increase since consumers would not reduce their spending, only their personal savings. This would lead consumers to demand higher wages, and business would have to pass along the cost of those wages through increased prices. At that point, Ture realized that it was "time for me to leave the room. So I did."[24] Mills, who had carefully planned this exchange, reminded O'Brien, an influential presidential advisor, that he had respectable economic data contradicting the CEA.

Mills's main problem with the surcharge was related to his desire to reestablish control over general revenue.[25] Congress had lost control of general-revenue spending after Johnson had taken office. Within the Johnson administration, a group of bureaucrats and economists who had few ties to the tax community, including Robert Lampman and Burton Weisbrod (CEA) and David Hackett and Richard Boon (President's Committee on Juvenile Delinquency and Youth Commission), had helped create new antipoverty initiatives

---

[23] See, for example, Norman Ture, "Issues in Fiscal and Monetary Policy in 1968," 21 February 1968, WMPC, Box 508, File 4; Ture to Wilbur Mills, 22 November 1966, WMPC, Box 236, File: Ways and Means Committee/1; Arthur Burns, "The Economic and Financial Outlook: Remarks at the Manufacturers Hanover Trust," 2 December 1966, WMPC, unprocessed; Ture, interview with Julian Zelizer, Washington, D.C., 13 December 1993; "Cautious Eye on the Tax Package," *Business Week*, 4 February 1967, 124; "Taxes: To Boost or Not to Boost," *Newsweek*, 19 December 1966, 87–88; "Three Experts on the Outlook," *Newsweek*, 10 January 1966, 52–53.

[24] Norman Ture, interview with Julian Zelizer. See also Lawrence O'Brien and Henry Hall Wilson, 19 August 1966, LBJL, Legislative Background: Tax Increase, Box 1, File: Tax Increase, January–August 1966.

[25] Wilbur D. Mills, "Fiscal Policy and the Good Economic Society" and "Expenditure Control and Tax Policy: Remarks at 75th Anniversary Celebration, Security Trust Company," 22 May 1967, LBJL, Henry Fowler Personal Papers, Box 236, File: Briefing Books: Tax Surcharge, 1967.

such as the Economic Opportunity Act.[26] Meanwhile, Congress had expanded funding for existing welfare programs, including AFDC and Medicaid, in response to higher case loads. Mills referred to Medicaid as the most expensive mistake of his career because physicians' fees had soared since 1966 and the states had implemented liberal definitions of the "medically indigent."[27] The administration and congressional spenders were joined by military strategists who directed the nation's intervention in Vietnam, a military adventure that constituted the largest expenditure in the federal budget.[28] Finally, this debate came at a time when many liberals shifted from the concept of opportunity toward one of entitlement. In doing so they championed an idea that was anathema to Mills – namely, that the poor had an unconditional right to a guaranteed income from government.[29]

Together, welfare and military expenditures had reversed a two-year trend toward lower budget deficits. According to the new unified budget (which combined trust fund and general-revenue expenditures), spending had been relatively stable between 1961 and 1965, increasing from only $98 billion in 1961 to $118 billion in 1965. But from 1966 to 1968, Mills said, expenditures had "taken off like a rocket to the moon," rising from $135 billion to $179 billion. Mills warned, "The fact of the matter is that the budget has not set tough priorities. The United States is simultaneously battling communist aggression in Vietnam and trying to give help not only to the poverty-stricken but to many other groups as well." The chairman added: "There are demands for help with education, air pollution, wildlife conservation, dams, supersonic transport planes, travel to the moon. Each of us can argue that we have a right to these things. But what good will the expenditures do us if we endanger the position of the dollar in the process?"[30]

Record deficits under Johnson led Mills to reinvigorate his attack

[26] Carl M. Brauer, "Kennedy, Johnson, and the War on Poverty," *The Journal of American History* 69, No. 1 (June 1982): 98–119.

[27] JMIC; American Enterprise Institute, "For Release," 18 September 1967, WMPC, unprocessed.

[28] David Halberstam, *The Best and the Brightest*, 4th ed. (New York: Ballentine Books, 1992), 607–609.

[29] Gareth Davies, *From Opportunity to Entitlement: The Transformation and Decline of Great Society Liberalism* (Lawrence: University Press of Kansas, 1996).

[30] Wilbur D. Mills, "We *Must* Control Federal Spending," *The Reader's Digest*, July 1968, 2–6; Mills, "Remarks to Central Arkansas Chapter, National Association of Accountants," 10 December 1968, WMPC, Box 420, File 10; Mills, "Some International and Domestic Aspects of Tax and Expenditure Policy: Remarks to the Tax Foundation," 3 December 1968, WMPC, Box 420, File 17. See also "How the Budget Deficit Could Escalate," *U.S. News & World Report*, 5 June 1967, 44.

on unbalanced budgets. After starting his presidency by supporting expenditure control, Johnson would allow the deficit for fiscal year 1968 to reach approximately $25 billion. This deficit, 3 percent of GNP, was a record for the postwar period. High chronic deficits, according to Mills, were causing inflationary prices and undermining the stability of the dollar. As domestic prices increased, he warned, the United States was pricing itself out of world markets and making the domestic market more attractive for imports. Foreign investors were also losing confidence in the value of the dollar. Government borrowing to finance deficits, moreover, placed a heavy burden on financial markets at a time when the expanding economy increased demands for funds in the private sector. This dynamic created upward pressure on interest rates.[31]

The chairman feared that the "paved road of tax reduction ends in the Vietnam jungle."[32] Without deep cuts in spending, Mills explained, a surcharge would place fiscal policy in a "straightjacket" by limiting the prospects for periodic, stimulative income-tax reductions.[33] Mills was disturbed by his insight that the surcharge would not be temporary. Based on the experience of World War II and Korea, Congress would use the additional tax revenue as an excuse to finance new domestic programs once the conflict in Vietnam subsided.[34] By forcing Congress to keep taxes high, these developments would ultimately undermine the stimulative effects of the Revenue Acts of 1962 and 1964.

While understanding the dampening value of a tax increase, Mills insisted that expenditure control was essential to the war on inflation and to reduce deficits.[35] In September 1967, he privately told the president to announce on television that the nation had to choose between guns and butter, and that Johnson was choosing guns.[36] On Keynesian grounds, Mills argued that it made little sense to reduce

[31] Mills, "Some International and Domestic Aspects of Tax and Expenditure Policy."

[32] Stanley Surrey to the Files, 10 January 1966, SSP, Box 55, File 5.

[33] Mills, "Expenditure Control and Tax Policy." See also Mills, "Remarks before the Chamber of Commerce."

[34] Mills, "Fiscal Policy and the Good Economic Society"; U.S. Congress, House Committee on Ways and Means, President's 1967 Tax Proposals: Hearings, 90th Cong., 1st sess., August-September 1967, 14–16; 76–77; 581; Lawrence O'Brien, interview with Michael Gillette, 22 April 1987, LBJL, Oral History Interview Collection, Interview XIX, 27.

[35] For early evidence from the JCIRT on the value of a tax increase to dampen consumer demand, see Albert Buckberg and Alan Murray to Laurence Woodworth, 26 April 1966, NA, RG 128, Box 465, File: Economic Clippings, Forecasts 1967.

[36] Cited in Matusow, The Unraveling of America, 171; U.S. Congress, House Committee on Ways and Means, President's 1967 Tax Proposals: Hearings, 90th Cong., 1st sess., August–September 1967, 580.

consumer demand through a tax increase if Congress ultimately returned the money to the economy through its own expenditures. This contradicted economic logic. Furthermore, it was politically undesirable to ask that constituents tighten their belts when Congress refused to do the same.[37]

Seeking to control expenditures

Mills and his supporters on the committee were in a difficult position. Given that Ways and Means only had formal jurisdiction over taxation and Social Security, Mills could not force Congress to reduce general-revenue spending. Instead, the chairman needed to persuade the Appropriations Committee and the administration to make the cuts themselves. The chairman could only pass the surcharge and hope that Appropriations would follow through on the spending reduction. Or Mills could sit on the bill until other members accepted his demands. For the time being, it seemed that the latter option would have to suffice.

Outside the committee hearings, negotiations between Mills and the administration were disastrous. Although Johnson's advisors understood that Mills's support was essential, they could not find a satisfactory compromise on expenditure reduction.[38] As deliberations proceeded within Congress, the relationship between Johnson and Mills deteriorated into public hostility. Mills frequently told colleagues that the president wanted to exclude him from any meetings.[39] When asked about the breakdown of direct communication between himself and the president, Mills responded bluntly: "He knows my number."[40] Budget Director Charles Schultze, on the other hand, felt that Mills and Ways and Means were playing "chicken" in an "eyeball-to-eyeball confrontation." According to Schultze, "I can't be positive – and obviously I'm not the world's greatest expert on what moves the Congress – but I think that if we are willing to take a strong and unyielding stand, they will blink first. They won't blink right away

---

[37] "Will Congress Raise Taxes?" *U.S. News & World Report*, 9 October 1967, 52–55; Henry Fowler, interview with David McComb, 10 January 1969, LBJL, Oral History Interview Collection, Tape #1, 13–15.

[38] Barefoot Sanders to Lyndon Johnson, 31 August 1967, LBJL, White House Central Files, Box 53, File: LE/FI 11-4 7/1/67–8/31/67.

[39] Walter Heller to Lyndon Johnson, 12 October 1967, LBJL, Legislative Background: Tax Increase, Box 5, File: Legislative Struggle – Vol. III, October 5–November 18, 1967; JMIC.

[40] John Herbers, "Mills Feud With Johnson Creates Crisis in House," *The New York Times*, Sunday, 15 October 1967, Section I.

until they test our resolve. More economic signals will be necessary. But blink they will."[41]

But Mills refused to blink until the administration and the Appropriations Committee agreed to at least $5 billion in expenditure reduction.[42] Without the spending cuts, House Republicans and conservative Democrats would certainly reject the measure. On October 2, Daniel Rostenkowski (D-IL) warned the administration: "The way Mills has been acting, the tax bill is in very, very bad shape."[43] He was right. The following day, Ways and Means shelved the surcharge.[44] The motion to shelve the bill, introduced by John Watts (D-KY), received strong support from Mills, ten Republicans, and eight Democrats.[45] Following this decision, Mills explained to a group of reporters that "these actions are not irresponsible, bullheaded, or spiteful nor are they maneuvers for partisan advantage. They are, on the contrary, an expression of the anxiety which many Members of the Congress feel – fortified by the uneasiness they found in their constituencies over the recent Labor Day recess – about the recent sharp rise in federal outlays and the proliferation of federal government activity."[46]

The chairman tackles "built-in" spending

At this point in the negotiations, Mills raised the ante by attacking the spending "pipeline" that was built into the existing appropriations laws. Besides limiting discretionary spending for the next fiscal year,

---

[41] Charles Schultze to Lyndon Johnson, 16 September 1967, LBJL, White House Central Files, Box 53, File: LE/FI 11-4 9/1/67–10/15/67.

[42] Joseph Califano to Lyndon Johnson, 7 October 1967, LBJL, White House Office Aides Files, Files of Joseph Califano, Box 25, File: Califano, Taxes; O'Brien to Johnson, 17 October 1967, LBJL, White House Central Files, Box 53, File: LE/FI 11-4, 10/16/67–12/31/67; Charles Schultze to Johnson, 19 October 1967, LBJL, White House Central Files, Box 53, File: LE/FI 11-4, 10/16/67–12/31/67; "Text of Mills Statement on Federal Spending and Growth of Government," and "Mills Demands President Cut Long-Term Spending," *The New York Times*, 7 October 1967; Editorial, "Mr. Mills Makes a Point," *The Wall Street Journal*, 10 October 1967; "Will Congress Raise Taxes? Interview with Representative Wilbur Mills," *U.S. News & World Report*, 9 October 1967, 52–55.

[43] Charles Roche to Lyndon Johnson, 2 October 1967, LBJL, White House Central Files, Box 53, File: LE/FI 11-4, 9/1/67–10/15/67.

[44] Marjorie Hunter, "House Unit Votes To Delay Action on Surcharge," *The New York Times*, 4 October 1967; Norman Miller, "Mills Says Johnson Is Unlikely to Yield to House Panel Demand He Cut Spending," *The Wall Street Journal*, 5 October 1967.

[45] JMIC.

[46] "Text of Mills Statement on Federal Spending and Growth of Government," *The New York Times*, 7 October 1967.

Mills wanted to cut into spending increases that Congress had, explicitly or implicitly, authorized in previous appropriations legislation. In doing so, the chairman raised serious questions about the process through which existing programs received automatically increasing appropriations over time without congressional scrutiny. In 1970, for example, these "built-in" increases – trust fund expenditures, scientific research programs, non-Vietnam military expenditures, federal employee salaries – were to raise expenditures by some $10 billion.[47] Mills pointed to normal workload increases in agencies that would inevitably require more funding due to the "ever-expanding use of our parks, the need to provide more traffic controllers for the expanded use of our airways, the additional employees required by our ever-expanding postal volume and even the need for increased Internal Revenue Service personnel for processing the growing volume of tax returns."[48] Congress would devote a substantial part of future revenue increases to these types of expenses.

Much of this spending had resulted from programs that Mills had helped expand, including some that directly benefited his district. During his tenure, Mills helped obtain a variety of federal funds for Arkansas, including approximately $24 million for the 8th Street Freeway (called "The Wilbur D. Mills Expressway"); a $1.3 million combination loan and grant for a national folk cultural center in the Ozarks, a $4 million Forest Service project to develop Blanchard Springs Caverns in the Ozark National Forests; model cities grants for Little Rock, funds for the construction of the Arkansas River Navigation Project, $350,000 from HEW for an addition to the White County Memorial Hospital, and funds for the new Kensett Community Center. By 1971, the Second District claimed 37 percent of Arkansas' federal payments.[49]

Nonetheless, Mills demanded overall reductions in almost all domestic programs except Social Security. Substantive expenditure control, Mills said, required a deep reduction in "built-in" increases. He repeatedly called for $6 billion cuts in previously appropriated revenue and a $14 billion cut in future appropriations contained in the current budget proposal. The chairman also proposed the establishment of an independent bipartisan commission (based on the Hoover Commission) to review the efficiency of established programs and determine whether their appropriations should remain the

[47] Mills, "Some International and Domestic Aspects of Tax and Expenditure Policy," 1–4.
[48] Ibid., 4.
[49] Stephen A. Merrill, *Wilbur D. Mills: Democratic Representative from Arkansas* (Washington, D.C.: Grossman Publishers, 1972), 3–4.

same.[50] "Today tax policy is like the tail of a dog," Mills complained to a reporter, "It is being controlled almost completely by expenditure policy. This is one of the basic concerns to me, to try to find some effective way to bring about a change in the rate of increase in expenditures. I would think that if any good came from it, you would have a greater part to be played by tax policy than can be played by an over-all fiscal policy, where the tax policy is of secondary concern in relation to expenditure policy."[51]

Upon hearing such statements, Charles Schultze urged Johnson to demand new hearings so that the administration could blame any economic crisis on an obstinate Mills.[52] Other officials believed that the chairman might agree to a $4 billion expenditure reduction if the administration secured enough support on the House floor.[53] The New York financial community regarded these negotiations as "purely political," and expected a strong tax bill to be passed.[54] For the time being, however, Mills returned to Arkansas and told the Democrats that he had no need to be in Washington.[55]

His trip did not last long. On November 18, Britain devalued the pound. The devaluation stimulated a further loss of confidence in paper currency. Investors demanded more gold in exchange for their dollars. Policymakers understood that the only way to prevent the run on gold was to maintain faith in the American dollar.[56] To do so, they needed to lower inflation immediately to increase the value of the dollar. Without the surcharge, warned the administration, speculators would continue to exchange their dollars for gold, the price of American goods would continue to rise, exports would suffer, imports would thrive, and the balance-of-payments deficit would

[50] Joseph Califano to Lyndon Johnson, 7 October 1967, LBJL, White House Office Aides Files, Files of Joseph Califano, Box 25, File: Califano, Taxes.
[51] "Congressman Wilbur Mills On A Way Out of the Spending Crisis," *Nation's Business*, October 1967, 48–49.
[52] Charles Schultze and Gardner Ackley to Lyndon Johnson, 13 October 1967, LBJL, White House Central Files, Box 53, File: LE/FI 11-4, 9/1/67–10/15/67.
[53] Walter Heller to Lyndon Johnson, 6 November 1967, LBJL, Confidential File, Box 34, File: FG 411, House Committees; Gardner Ackley to Johnson, 13 October 1967, LBJL, Legislative Background: Tax Increase, Box 5, File: Legislative Struggle – Vol. III, October 5–November 18, 1967; Charles Schultze to Johnson, 19 October 1967, LBJL, White House Central Files, Box 53, File: LE/FI 11-4, 10/16/67–12/31/67.
[54] Gardner Ackley to Lyndon Johnson, 10 October 1967, LBJL, Legislative Background: Tax Increase, Box 5, File: Legislative Struggle – Vol. III, October 5–November 18, 1967.
[55] Joseph Califano to Lyndon Johnson, 17 November 1967, LBJL, White House Central Files, Box 53, File: LE/FI 11-4, 10/16/67–12/31/67.
[56] Collins, "The Economic Crisis of 1968 and the Waning of the 'American Century'," 396–422.

worsen. The administration proposed a 10 percent tax surcharge, a $4 billion reduction in expenditures for fiscal 1969 (up from the $2 billion in the previous proposal), and a task force to evaluate prior appropriations.[57]

Mills's economics

To justify his position before other members of the tax community, Mills drew on macroeconomic analysis to challenge the existing package. Using data from the staff of the JCIRT, Mills continued to focus on "demand-pull" inflation. During committee hearings in late November, he showed that standard economic indicators including rapidly rising wholesale prices, the utilization of plant capacity, retail sales, and business plans for future investment, still failed to confirm the arguments of the CEA.[58] Mills warned that the surcharge was not the "proper medicine" to "take care of the type of price increases that we are this year experiencing." Even Fowler confessed to the committee that retail prices might continue to rise at the same rate despite a tax increase. This complex debate was reprinted in various newspapers and magazines, all of which commented on the sophisticated level of the economic arguments that were presented by the administration and Mills.[59]

Instead of the surcharge, the chairman contended that the government needed to reduce its spending as a cure for "cost-push" inflation. According to Mills, business was passing along the higher costs of wage settlements to consumers through higher prices. Thereafter, consumers reacted by insisting on higher wages and perpetuating a cycle of inflation. The most effective way for the government to end "cost-push" inflation was a substantial reduction in public expenditures, which, unlike a tax increase, would remove money from the economy without squeezing personal and corporate income. Some administration officials had previously responded that the sur-

---

[57] Edwin Dale Jr., "Mills To Restudy Tax Rise Plan, Revised In Light Of Cut In Pound; Prime Bank Rate Begins To Go Up," *The New York Times*, 21 November 1967; "Texts of Announcement and Address by Representative Mills on Taxes and Expenditures," *The New York Times*, 21 November 1967; "Scheduled House Tax-Panel Meeting Indicates Possible Surcharge Break," *The Wall Street Journal*, 21 November 1967.

[58] U.S. Congress, House Committee on Ways and Means, *President's 1967 Surtax Proposal: Hearings*, 90th Cong., 1st sess., November 1967, 105–130. For the source of Mills's analysis, see the following documents: William Forti to Laurence Woodworth, 9 December 1967, NA, RG 128, Box 465, File: Economic; Henry Fowler to Mills, 19 December 1967, WMPC, Box 337, File 15.

[59] "Mr. Mills Conducts Class for Would-Be Tax Boosters," *The Wall Street Journal*, 11 December 1967; "High Officials Argue Over Taxes, Spending, Inflation," *U.S. News & World Report*, 18 December 1967, 90–92.

charge would even cure "cost-push" inflation by limiting the market for goods and thus stiffening business resistance to wage increases (since management would not be so confident of its ability to pass the higher costs to consumers through higher prices). A lower cost of living would also reduce the pressure on unions to obtain wage increases.[60]

Following the hearings, Mills informed reporters that Ways and Means would not consider the surcharge until January 1968.[61] Although the administration had shown an "increasing awareness" of the need for expenditure reduction, Mills felt that its proposal remained almost $3 billion short of a proper compromise.[62] According to his experts, moreover, the optimistic economic forecasts of the administration were of dubious value.[63]

Appropriations defends its turf

Some members of Congress were enraged by Mills's actions. In particular, the chairman of the Appropriations Committee, George Mahon (D-TX), "blew sky high" when he heard that Mills had encroached on his jurisdiction by demanding higher spending cuts. Mahon believed that he had already cut enough money from the budget, and that any slim chance of passing the existing cuts would be "completely eliminated" if Schultze and Fowler circumvented the Appropriations Committee.[64] Mills, Mahon felt, should stick to issues of taxation, while his committee would remain in charge of public spending. Backing the Appropriations Committee, Johnson said that Mills would live to "rue the day" he decided to oppose the income-tax hike.[65]

All sides in this debate actually agreed on the need for anti-

---

[60] Mr. White to Stanley Surrey, 3 October 1966, NAT, RG 56, Office of Tax Policy, Box 68, File: Tax Increase.

[61] Eileen Shanahan, "Mills Indicates Rise In Tax Is Out, At Least Till '68," *The New York Times*, 1 December 1967; "House Unit Dashes President's Plan For Tax This Year," *The Wall Street Journal*, 1 December 1967; "Tax Rise Blocked Again – How and Why It Happened," *U.S. News & World Report*, 11 December 1967, 8.

[62] Barefoot Sanders to Lyndon Johnson, 28 November 1967, LBJL, White House Central File, Box 53, File: LE/FI 11-4, 10/16/67–12/31/67; Norman Miller, "Income Tax Bill Appears Stalled In House for 1967," *The Wall Street Journal*, 29 November 1967.

[63] William Forti to Laurence Woodworth, 9 December 1967, NA, RG 128, Box 465, File: Economic.

[64] Joseph Califano to Lyndon Johnson, 27 November 1967, LBJL, White House Central Files, Box 53, File: LE/FI 11-4, 10/16/67–12/31/67.

[65] "Chairman Mills – He Wouldn't Budge When LBJ Pushed," *U.S. News & World Report*, 4 December 1967, 19.

inflationary fiscal policy even though they differed on how much of an expenditure reduction the economy needed. On December 14, Fowler, Mills, and Byrnes agreed on the need for an "austere" budget to make the tax bill successful. The chairman promised to reintroduce the surcharge within the context of the international crisis and the balance-of-payments deficit.[66]

EXPENDITURE CONTROL

By January 1968, it was clear that Congress intended to pass some combination of tax increase and expenditure reduction. At this point in the debate, there was a consensus within the tax community that tax increases and expenditure reduction both needed to be in the final package. The question was how much expenditures should be reduced. While Mills had agreed that a surcharge would have a positive effect on inflationary consumer demand, the administration now conceded that expenditure reduction was also necessary to lower prices. All that remained to be settled was the spending figures to be included in the package. During the next six months, the administration and Appropriations pushed for a $4 billion reduction in spending for 1969, while Mills held out for a $6 billion cut. For the administration and the Appropriations Committee (which had originally proposed an absolute maximum of $2 billion in spending cuts), Mills's $6 billion figure (out of a $184 billion budget) seemed intolerable. That figure would force them to eliminate significant elements in the War on Poverty. Nonetheless, they needed Mills's support to pass the bill.[67] This struggle offered the nation a clear view of the power of the tax-writing committees.

Mills accepts the "demand-pull" thesis

At the start of 1968, no one was quite sure what to expect from Mills. As one journalist commented: "'Reading Wilbur' as the pastime is called, is a hazardous business on a par with China-watching."[68] In committee hearings, the chairman surprised pundits by admitting that the administration had presented a strong case for "demand-

---

[66] Henry Fowler to Lyndon Johnson, 14 December 1967, LBJL, White House Central Files, Box 53, File: LE/FI 11-4, 10/16/67–12/31/67.

[67] Barefoot Sanders to Lyndon Johnson, 24 February 1968, LBJL, White House Central Files, Box 53, File: LE/FI 11-4, 2/1/68–4/30/68.

[68] Norman Miller, "Mills & the Tax Bill," *The Wall Street Journal*, 22 January 1968. See also Tom Wicker and Marjorie Hunter, "Wilbur Mills Takes on the New Economics," *New York Times*, 8 January 1968.

pull" inflation.[69] Backed by the data of the JCIRT staff, however, Mills released figures that indicated the power of "cost-push" inflation and the need for steeper expenditure reductions.[70] By hiding his specific agenda from the media and top-level officials, Mills allowed himself room to maneuver in the subsequent negotiations.

In the end, Ways and Means reported out a mild bill that did not include a surcharge. On the House floor, Mills restated that any tax increase needed to be coupled with expenditure control in "spirit and deed." Without a $6 billion reduction, he said, there were still not enough votes to pass the surcharge.[71] Nonetheless, he admitted that a "substantial acceleration of war expenditures" or "inflationary pressures generated from an excess of demand" might "force" Ways and Means to increase taxes.[72]

The international monetary crisis

Problems continued on the international front. In mid-March, speculators increased their exchange of gold for dollars in an attempt to force the United States to increase the price of gold in relation to the dollar. In response, members of the Federal Reserve and the Department of Treasury convinced London to close its gold market temporarily, and convened an international meeting to handle the emerging crisis. The U.S. government decided to abandon its single-price system for gold, in which the price of gold was pegged at $35

[69] U.S. Congress, House Committee on Ways and Means, *President's Surtax Proposal: Continuation of Hearing*, 90th Cong., 2nd sess., January 1968, 128–130. See also Leon Klud to Laurence Woodworth, 9 February 1968, NA, RG 128, Box 465, File: Economics 1968; "Now the Year of the Worried Bull," *Newsweek*, 8 January 1968, 51–55.

[70] U.S. Congress, House Committee on Ways and Means, *President's Surtax Proposal: Continuation of Hearing*, 90th Cong., 2nd sess., January 1968, 128–166; Norman Ture, "Issues in Fiscal and Monetary Policy," 21 February 1968, WMPC, Box 508, File 4; *Transcript: ABC's Issues and Answers*, 11 February 1968, LBJL, White House Central Files, Box 53, File: LE/FI 11-4, 2/1/68–4/30/68. For samples of JCIRT studies, see William Forti to Laurence Woodworth, 12 January 1968; Leon Klud to Woodworth, 9 February 1968; Klud to Woodworth, 12 February 1968; Forti to Woodworth, 13 February 1968, in NA, RG 128, Box 465, File: Economics 1968.

[71] Barefoot Sanders to Lyndon Johnson, 24 January 1968, LBJL, White House Central Files, Box 53, File: LE/FI 11-4, 1/1/68–1/31/68; Sanders to Johnson, 1 February 1968, LBJL, White House Central Files, Box 53, File: LE/FI 11-4, 2/1/68–4/30/68; Sanders to Johnson, 24 February 1968, LBJL, White House Central Files, Box 53, File: LE/FI 11-4, 2/1/68–4/30/68; Henry Fowler to Johnson, 27 January 1968, LBJL, White House Central Files, Box 53, File: LE/FI 11-4, 1/1/68–1/31/68.

[72] Eileen Shanahan, "Mills Says Expanded War Could Force Rise in Taxes," *The New York Times*, 29 February 1968; "Vietnam Spending Jump Could 'Force' Rise in Taxes, Mills Says; House Clears Excise," *The Wall Street Journal*, 1 March 1968.

an ounce, and adopt a new, two-price system.[73] Under the new system, the gold market was separated into an official market – where monetary gold for banking purposes was governed by a rate of $35 an ounce – and a private market – where the cost of gold would be dictated by the laws of supply and demand.[74]

A more permanent solution to the gold crisis was to ensure a stable dollar by controlling inflation. After all, should the dollar maintain its value in international markets, investors would hesitate to trade in their currency for gold. Within days, Mills admitted that since the economy needed a stable dollar, the situation might force him to reconsider his position on the surcharge.[75] After hearing this, Fowler said that Mills was "persuaded now of the key relationship of the tax bill, real or psychological, to the international monetary system."[76] Legislative liaison Barefoot Sanders concluded: "There is enough concern in the House right now that if a tax bill were on the floor we could pass it."[77]

Mills, Fowler, Mahon, and William McChesney Martin, Jr. (chairman of the Federal Reserve) discussed the relationship between the international monetary crisis and the tax increase on March 22. During this luncheon, Mills complained that he was "despondent" and "disgusted" with Congress for its attitude toward the appropriations process. The Appropriations Committee did not seem concerned with the dramatic increase in general-revenue spending that had taken place since 1964, nor did it care about the problem of built-in increases in appropriations. Mills again warned that the House would reject the surcharge unless Appropriations accepted $6 billion in spending cuts for 1969, along with a significant reduction in automatic expenditures. These actions would result in a $14 billion reduction in future appropriations and a $6 billion reduction in existing appropriations. Despite these obstinate demands, Fowler sensed that a compromise was possible. About Mahon and Mills, he wrote to Johnson: "I do not believe either one of them want to block the

[73] Henry Fowler to Lyndon Johnson, 8 March 1968, LBJL, Confidential File, Box 63, File: Legislation LE/FI 11-4; "Gold Rush Dusts Off the Tax Bill," *Business Week,* 23 March 1968, 33–34; Wilbur Mills to William Colmer, 20 March 1968, WMPC, Box 675, File 4.

[74] Collins, "The Economic Crisis of 1968 and the Waning of the 'American Century'," 396–422.

[75] "Rep. Mills Hints Continued Gold Outflow Could Prompt Congress To Vote Tax Boost," *The Wall Street Journal,* 12 March 1968.

[76] Henry Fowler to Lyndon Johnson, 8 March 1968, LBJL, Confidential File, Box 63, File: Legislation LE/FI 11-4.

[77] Barefoot Sanders to Lyndon Johnson, 15 March 1968, LBJL, White House Central Files, Box 53, File: LE/FI 11-4 2/1/68–4/30/68.

parade – that both want to achieve a result not far different from our objective – but that neither one is particularly anxious to assert the type of 'gung ho' boldness in leadership that it may take."[78]

The battle reaches a climax

On March 31, 1968, Johnson changed the political situation drastically by announcing that he would not seek the Democratic nomination for the presidency. The president believed that this decision would strengthen his hand by enabling the administration to concentrate on issues such as the tax increase and Vietnam without having to fear electoral defeat. Senator John Williams (R-DE) and Senator George Smathers (D-FL) took matters into their own hands by adding an amendment to the House bill that called for a 10 percent surcharge combined with an expenditure cutback of $6 billion. Some colleagues and pundits believed that Mills had made a deal with Senators Williams, Smathers, and Chairman Mahon to insert this amendment successfully into the bill. This amendment offered him a way to control spending without having to rely on the Appropriations Committee. The chairman was certain that he could control the conference and send the bill back to the House floor with a closed rule, under which representatives would have to vote "up or down" without amendment. The Johnson administration also endorsed the amendment since it expected to regain $4 billion of spending cuts in conference.[79]

During the conference deliberations, the struggle over spending continued. Some officials made inflammatory speeches that pressured Mills. On April 19, William Martin announced that the nation was in the "worst financial crisis since 1931."[80] Meanwhile, Mahon insisted that the maximum cuts his committee would allow were $4 billion in 1969 expenditures with a $10 billion cut in built-in appropriation increases; this was opposed to Mills's figure of $14 billion.[81] Should the administration accept the $6 billion reduction in 1969,

---

[78] Henry Fowler to Lyndon Johnson, 22 March 1968, LBJL, Confidential File, Box 63, File: Legislation LE/FI 11-4.

[79] Henry Fowler to Lyndon Johnson, 22 March 1968, LBJL, Confidential File, Box 63, File: Legislation LE/FI 11-4; Fowler to Johnson, 10 February 1968, LBJL, White House Central Files, Box 53, File: LE/FI 11-4, 2/1/68–4/30/68. See also Fowler to Johnson, 10 April 1968, LBJL, Confidential File, Box 63, File: Legislation LE/FI 11-4.

[80] "Mills Renews Demand for Spending Cuts, Terms Senate Tax-Rise Bill Unacceptable," *The Wall Street Journal*, 24 April 1968.

[81] Barefoot Sanders to Lyndon Johnson, 22 April 1968, LBJL, White House Central Files, Box 53, File: LE/FI 11-4, 2/1/68–4/30/68.

House Majority Leader Carl Albert (D-OK) warned, it would lose two-thirds of the Democratic vote because of the devastating cost to the War on Poverty.[82] During a secret White House meeting on April 30 with Democratic leaders, Johnson said that Mills had agreed to a compromise (offered by Mahon) that included a reduction of $4 billion in government expenditures in 1969 and an almost $18 billion reduction in prior and future appropriations.[83]

But Mills would not budge, especially on the $6 billion figure for expenditures, since he could no longer back down without losing significant clout.[84] The chairman "belittled" the White House resolution as inadequate, particularly since it did not cut sufficiently existing appropriations. Instead, he proposed a series of changes. One included new appropriations reductions.[85] Mills also said that he could obtain somewhere between 60 and 100 Republican votes for a conference bill with the $6 billion expenditure reduction for 1969.[86]

Although some advisors urged the president to continue his opposition, others feared a worldwide economic disaster should the surcharge fail to pass Congress. CEA member Arthur Okun warned that if the tax bill failed, the atmosphere of financial emergency would end up giving conservatives the "upper hand" in "choking" high-priority domestic programs. Johnson, he said, might as well accept the spending cuts demanded by Mills and get the best compromise possible.[87] Fowler argued: "The stakes for the economy and the

[82] Barefoot Sanders to Lyndon Johnson, 2 April 1968, LBJL, White House Central Files, Box 53, File: LE/FI 11-4, 2/1/68–4/30/68.

[83] Joseph Califano to Lyndon Johnson, 30 April 1968, LBJL, White House Central Files, Box 53, File: LE/FI 11-4, 2/1/68–4/30/68; "Congress faces the tax facts," *The Economist*, 11 May 1968, 17.

[84] Henry Fowler to Lyndon Johnson, 24 April 1968, LBJL, Confidential File, Box 34, Folder: FG 400, Legislative Branch; Fowler to Johnson, 26 April 1968, LBJL, Confidential File, Box 63, Folder: Legislation, LE/FI 8-LE/FI 11-3; Charles Zwick to Johnson, 24 April 1968, LBJL, WHCF, Box 53, File: LE/FI 11-4, 2/1/68–4/30/68; Barefoot Sanders to Johnson, 3 May 1968, LBJL, White House Central Files, Box 54, File: LE/FI 11-4, 5/1/68–5/15/68; "Tax Bills Is Still The Key," *Business Week*, 27 April 1968, 33; "Mills Renews Demand for Spending Cuts, Terms Senate Tax-Rise Bill Unacceptable," *The Wall Street Journal*, 24 April 1968; Editorial, "Mr. Mills Marks Time," *The New York Times*, 25 April 1968.

[85] Charles Zwick to Lyndon Johnson, 2 May 1968, LBJL, White House Central Files, Box 54, File: LE/FI 11-4, 5/1/68–5/15/68. See also Wilbur Mills to Walter Heller, 10 May 1968, WMPC, Box 508, File 4; Barefoot Sanders to Johnson, 27 April 1968, LBJL, White House Central Files, Box 53, File: LE/FI 11-4, 2/1/68–4/30/68; George Mahon to Mills, 3 May 1968, WMPC, Box 506, File 7.

[86] Barefoot Sanders to Lyndon Johnson, 9 May 1968, LBJL, White House Central Files, Box 54, File: LE/FI 11-4, 5/1/68–5/15/68.

[87] Arthur Okun to Lyndon Johnson, 27 April 1968, LBJL, The President's Appointment File [Diary Backup], Box 97, File: 29 April 1968. See also Barefoot Sanders

country are entirely too high to risk a loss on the legislation or a long, drawn-out delay. Either or both might be the consequence of a failure on the part of the Administration and the leadership to back up the Conferees package."[88]

Faced with this dilemma, President Johnson decided to compromise. Behind the scenes, he ordered his cabinet to "take the bull by the tail and get the tax bill now" by considering how $6 billion in spending cuts could be made.[89] Johnson continued to use a more confrontational rhetoric before the media. He was encouraged by trusted assistants such as Joseph Califano. "The current tax fight," Califano wrote, "may be a critical turning point in your Presidency, not only vis-à-vis the Congress, but on a much broader scale." Despite Johnson's having dropped out of the next presidential race, Califano added:

> This remarkable accretion of power in a lame duck status could deteriorate rapidly if Wilbur Mills rolls over us on the tax legislation . . . If my instinct is right, then the importance of winning the tax fight transcends our fiscal problems . . . Like it or not, the White House and the Presidency are identified with the Mahon Package. If that package loses and if you get stuck either with no tax bill or with provisions of the kind Mills is now peddling, I think the ball game may well be over on the Hill for the rest of the year.[90]

Heeding this advice, Johnson attacked Mills on national television, warning: "Don't hold up the tax bill, until you can blackmail someone into getting your own personal viewpoint over on reductions." He told members of Congress to "stand up like men" and do "what ought to be done for the country."[91]

Ultimately, however, the administration acceded to Mills's $6 billion figure and to most of his demands for reducing automatic expenditures.[92] Although Barefoot Sanders told Johnson that "it is

to Johnson, 1 May 1968, LBJL, White House Central File, Box 54, File: LE/FI 11-4, 5/1/68–5/15/68.

[88] Henry Fowler to Lyndon Johnson, 14 May 1968, LBJL, White House Central Files, Box 54, File: LE/FI 11-4, 5/1/68–5/15/68.

[89] The Presidential Cabinet, "The Cabinet Meeting of May 1, 1968," LBJL, Cabinet Papers, Box 13, File: Cabinet Meeting 5/1/68 (2 of 3).

[90] Joseph Califano to Lyndon Johnson, 2 May 1968, LBJL, White House Central Files, Box 54, File: LE/FI 11-4, 5/1/68–5/15/68. See also John McCormack to Lyndon Johnson, 4 May 1968, LBJL, Legislative Background: Tax Increase, Box 6, File: Legislative Struggle – Vol. VII, May 7–May 27, 1968.

[91] "President Lyndon B. Johnson's News Conference #124," LBJL, Legislative Background: Tax Increase, Box 6, File: Legislative Struggle, Volume VI; Frank Porter, "LBJ Castigates Hill On Taxes," *The Washington Post*, 4 May 1968.

[92] Joseph Califano to Lyndon Johnson, 15 May 1968, LBJL, White House Staff Files, Box 54, File: LE/FI 11-4, 5/1/68–5/15/68; Douglas Cornell, "New LBJ Tax Plea Accepts Budget Cut," *The Washington Post*, 6 May 1968.

very tempting to let Mills lie in the bed which he has made" by attempting to undermine the conference report, the president understood that any further confrontation would risk severe economic problems.[93] "We'll look like Hoover if we don't use all the horsepower we've got," the president explained to his cabinet, "This is a question of survival. It is not Democratic or Republican. It is not public relations, it is a matter of survival for the country."[94]

The House passed the conference report by a 268-159 vote. Speaking in favor of the legislation, Mills warned that the failure to exercise "fiscal responsibility" with the combination tax increase and expenditure reduction formula might well create an underheated economy with high levels of unemployment.[95] The chairman was convinced that the surcharge would reduce the deficit, slow down inflation, and restore international confidence in the dollar.[96] He privately suggested to the Bureau of the Budget where it should make its cuts in spending. Budget Director Zwick believed that the chairman was "increasingly anxious" to show that reduction could be made without affecting social programs since he wanted to place the burden on the president for any unpopular cuts.[97]

To justify to House colleagues why he had decided to accept the surcharge, Mills continued to draw on the macroeconomic discourse of the tax community rather than focusing his attack on a conservative rights-based rhetoric against tax increases and public spending. Mills told the House of Representatives that there had been a definite change from "cost-push" to "demand-pull" inflation. To demonstrate his point, Mills highlighted several indicators of excessive consumer demand, including the rise in prices on a steady basis by over 4 percent, and an increase in the GNP of $19.4 billion during the first quarter of the fiscal year. One of the most dangerous problems was the decline in the savings rate of Americans from a fourth quarter level of 7.5 percent to a first quarter 1968 level of 6.6 percent.[98] Equally important, the administration had agreed to the deep spend-

[93] Barefoot Sanders to Lyndon Johnson, 9 May 1968, LBJL, WHCF, Box 54, File: LE/FI 11-4, 5/1/68–5/15/68.

[94] The Presidential Cabinet, "The Cabinet Meeting of May 29, 1968," LBJL, Cabinet Papers, Box 13, File: Cabinet Meeting, 5/29/68 (2 of 3). For CEA data behind these predictions, see Charles Maguire to Lyndon Johnson, 29 May 1968, LBJL, Legislative Background: Tax Increase, Box 6, File: Legislative Struggle-Vol. III.

[95] U.S. Congress, House of Representatives, *Congressional Record*, 90th Cong., 2nd sess., 20 June 1968, 18000–18003.

[96] Ibid., 18001.

[97] Charles Zwick to Lyndon Johnson, 10 June 1968, LBJL, WHCF, Box 54, File: LE/FI 11-4, 6/9/68–6/30/68.

[98] U.S. Congress, House of Representatives, *Congressional Record*, 90th Cong., 2nd sess., 20 June 1968, 18000–18004.

ing cuts in addition to the surcharge, which Mills believed were essential for a sound economic future.

The Revenue and Expenditure Control Act of 1968

The Revenue and Expenditure Control Act of 1968 promised to increase federal revenues by $15.5 billion in 1969, with about $11.6 billion coming from the surcharge. Using the unified budget, the legislation contained a surplus of $3.2 billion. Tied to the surcharge was a ceiling on federal spending for fiscal 1969 of $180.1 billion that contained $6 billion in spending reductions from the previous budget. This figure had been the one Mills wanted all along. The legislation required that requests for future "built-in" spending increases be reduced by $10 billion, and that the president submit recommendations in his budget message to cut back $8 billion in spending authority the Appropriations Committee had previously approved.[99] To protect the bill's supporters from any direct connection with specific expenditure cuts, Congress had required the Appropriations Committee to make the reduction in its upcoming review of the budget rather than specifying the cuts in the legislation itself.[100] The total of $18 billion reduction in appropriations and a $6 billion cut in expenditures satisfied Mills and frustrated the administration, since the figures were far higher than they had expected when this debate began in 1967.

Some programs were protected from the harsh budget cuts. To be excluded were such programs as the war in Vietnam, interest on the debt, payments of veterans benefits, and Social Security and Medicare payments.[101] In fact, although Mills had demanded serious reductions in general-revenue spending, he had also helped pass legislation in 1967 that raised payroll taxes and increased Social Security

---

[99] U.S. Congress, House and Senate Conference Committee, *Revenue and Expenditure Control Act of 1968*, 10 June 1968, 90th Cong., 2nd sess., H1174 (Committee – Print); U.S. Congress, Joint Publication Committee on Finance, *Summary of the Decisions of the Conferees on H.R. 15414: Revenue and Expenditure Control Act of 1968*, 9 May 1968, 90th Cong., 2nd sess., S1643 (Committee – Print). See also Wilbur Cohen to the President, 5 June 1968, WCP, Box 97, Folder Untitled.

[100] R. Douglas Arnold, *The Logic of Congressional Action* (New Haven: Yale University Press, 1990), 165.

[101] U.S. Congress, House Committee on Ways and Means, *President's Proposals For Revision in the Social Security System*, 90th Cong., 1st sess., 1967; Wilbur Cohen to Lyndon Johnson, 14 July 1967, LBJL, White House Central Files, Box 164, File: LE/WE 6, 11/22/63–8/31/67; Cohen to Johnson, 3 November 1967, WCP, Box 94, Folder 4; Cohen to Joseph Califano, 8 December 1967, WCP, Box 161, Folder 9; "As Social Security Benefits – And Taxes – Go Up . . . ," *U.S. News & World Report*, 18 December 1967.

benefits.[102] The legislation constituted the largest total dollar increase in cash benefits in history.[103] On military expenditures, Mills said, "some of the increased costs are connected with our military operations in Vietnam, and I am certainly not talking about expenditures in that category. I have made this very clear. We simply have to do what is necessary there, whatever the cost, as far as spending is concerned."[104] Without any symbolic distinctions or controls to protect expenditures, and often with the weakest, least organized members of society receiving the benefits, the portion of general revenue earmarked for nonmilitary expenditures had proven to be the most vulnerable component of the state.

The final legislation constituted an important achievement for Mills. It was the last time Congress passed a balanced budget.[105] Mills helped to reestablish, temporarily, the principle of expenditure control in the national agenda, and scored an important victory in this dramatic battle with the president and the Appropriations Committee. Al Ullman, a liberal Democrat from Oregon, praised Mills for promoting a program of "intelligent budgeting" that considered tax policy in combination with budget policy and that tackled the difficult problem of built-in government expenditures. The title of the legislation – the Revenue and Expenditure Control Act of 1968 – itself reflected Mills's influence on the debates. By relying on his professional assets – the power of the committee chairmanship, his alliances with technical experts, and his own economic expertise – Mills helped undermine Johnson's vision of postwar liberalism: a federal government that provided both guns and butter through expansive general-revenue spending in addition to the social insurance programs already in place.[106] This vision would become increasingly obsolete as the nation entered into an era of stagflation and budgetary retrenchment.

---

[102] U.S. Congress, House Committee on Ways and Means, *President's Proposals For Revision in the Social Security System*, 90th Cong., 1st sess., 1967; Wilbur Cohen to Lyndon Johnson, 14 July 1967, LBJL, White House Central Files, Box 164, File: LE/WE 6, 11/22/63–8/31/67; Cohen to Johnson, 3 November 1967, WCP, Box 94, Folder 4; Cohen to Joseph Califano, 8 December 1967, WCP, Box 161, Folder 9; "As Social Security Benefits – And Taxes – Go Up . . . ," *U.S. News & World Report*, 18 December 1967.

[103] Wilbur Cohen to Joseph Califano, 7 December 1967, WCP, Box 161, Folder 9.

[104] Wilbur D. Mills, "Remarks at the Fifth Congressional District of Indiana," 26 January 1968, WMPC, Box 240, File 1.

[105] James D. Savage, *Balanced Budgets & American Politics* (Ithaca: Cornell University Press, 1988), 290–291.

[106] Bruce J. Schulman, *Lyndon B. Johnson and American Liberalism: A Brief Biography with Documents* (Boston: Bedford Books, 1995), 82–87; 155–166.

THE TEMORARY TRIUMPH OF EXPENDITURE CONTROL

In the summer of 1968, Mills continued to promote expenditure control on the political agenda through the national media. In an article for *Reader's Digest* entitled "We *Must* Control Federal Spending," Mills argued that the United States needed an independent commission to evaluate every federal program. Mills warned of recurring fiscal crises if this was not done. Huge budget deficits and massive borrowing needed to pay federal bills, he claimed, would propel prices into an inflationary spiral and turn foreigners against the American dollar. In addition, Mills continued to raise concerns about built-in spending increases. By writing future increases into the appropriations laws, portions of the government seemed outside the control of Congress. Without constant vigilance over these programs, and without occasional cutbacks, the federal government and its deficits would expand to unprecedented size. Mills continued to call for a twelve-man independent bipartisan Government Program Evaluation Commission drawn from American leadership outside the government, modeled on the Hoover commission. "Clearly," Mills wrote, "the fight for *sensible* spending can be won only if the American people themselves become conscious of the need for establishing priorities."[107]

During the coming years, Mills continued his campaign for expenditure control.[108] He used the Revenue and Expenditure Control Act as an example of sound public policy and a "blueprint" to put the government back on the "path of fiscal soundness." The legislation marked the logical outcome to the Revenue Acts of 1962 and 1964 and the Social Security Amendments of 1965, each of which had given priority to the growth of social insurance programs, the reduction of income taxation, and the control of general-revenue spending.

Besides the issue of expenditure control, the Revenue and Expenditure Control Act of 1968 stimulated the national media to write about the overwhelming power that Mills held as chairman of Ways and Means. *The Wall Street Journal,* for example, published a piece entitled "Wilbur Mills, Enigma," which captured the sentiment

---

[107] Mills, "We *Must* Control Federal Spending," 2–6.

[108] "Tax Changes to Look for: Exclusive Interview with Wilbur Mills," *U.S. News World & Report,* 16 December 1968, 68–71; "Congress Raises Its Voice," *The Economist,* 21 June 1969, 41–42; Mills, "Some International and Domestic Aspects of Tax and Expenditure Policy," *Tax Foundation's Tax Review* XXX, No. 1 (January 1969) 1–4; Mills, "Remarks to Central Arkansas Chapter, National Association of Accountants"; Mills, "Remarks before the American Institute of Certified Public Accountants"; Mills, "Remarks before the Chamber of Commerce"; Mills, "Remarks before the Little Rock Rotary Club," 29 August 1968, WMPC, Box 420, File 13.

of many policymakers who were not in his closest circles. Journalists focused on Mills's massive technical knowledge as a key source to his success. One reporter concluded:

> An understanding of the tax laws that few, if any, other law-makers can match; a craftsman's approach to legislation that stresses painstaking attention to details; untiring cultivation of other Congressmen of both parties, particularly members of his own committee; an almost unfailing correct judgement of what legislation can and cannot pass Congress; a pragmatic political attitude that allows him to switch positions without regard to ideology; a flair for compromise; a sense of caution that leads him to use his influence only sparingly, so it hasn't been dissi-pated when really needed on major issues . . . During 29 years in Congress, in short, this bespectacled Congressman has managed to create a mystique about his commanding role in tax legislation and that intangible factor is probably his greatest asset. In a sense, it makes little difference whether Mr. Mills has all the qualities his colleagues credit him with. The fact that other lawmakers think he has them makes it so.[109]

During other policy debates, Mills earned the wrath of New Left activists in his battle to reduce welfare. There were intense protests, for example, against the spending reductions and the controversial freeze on Aid to Families with Dependent Children welfare benefits – limiting the number of out-of-wedlock children eligible for pay-ments – that the chairman had helped to enact in 1967.[110] Over 500 people from the Poor People's Campaign marched to Mills's apart-ment on Connecticut Avenue to protest his role in attacking the War on Poverty.[111]

When the dust settled, Mills emerged as a winner, and Lyndon

---

[109] Norman Miller, "Wilbur Mills, Enigma," *The Wall Street Journal*, 14 August 1967. For more examples, see "Pied Piper of Taxes," *The New York Times*, 13 August 1967; Julia Duscha, "The Most Important Man on Capitol Hill Today," *The New York Times*, Sunday, 25 February 1968, Section 6; Murray Seeger, "The Most Powerful Man in Congress," August 1969, *The New Republic*, 81–82; William Novak and Robert Evans, "Mills Quiet Winner on Budget Cuts But President Achieves His Surtax," *The Washington Post*, 13 May 1968; Irwin Ross, "Most Powerful Man in Congress," *Reader's Digest*, January 1971, 101–105.

[110] For an insightful analysis of this episode, see Davies, *From Opportunity to Entitlement*, 157–210.

[111] Willard Clopton, Jr., "40,000 to March Today; Peaceful Protest Pledged," *The Washington Post*, 19 June 1968. See also, Leslie Carter to the Secretary, 7 August 1967, WCP, Box 279, File: 6; National Welfare Rights Organization, "NOW! Questions and Answers about the New Anti-Welfare Law," 2 February 1968 and Wilbur Cohen to Lyndon Johnson, 2 May 1968, WCP, Box 110, Folder 6.

Johnson had compromised his own role in history. Mills had helped move the policy agenda toward the problems of inflation, deficits, and expenditure control. Even though social welfare spending continued to rise in the next decade, and even though Congress failed to enact many of the spending cuts, the enthusiasm for expanding social programs had been quelled. "What was left," concludes the historian Robert Collins, "was not the powerful reform surge of mid-decade but only its inertia." [112]

Nonetheless, the legislation of 1968 was too mild and too late with regard to inflation. Indeed, the nation entered into a period of unprecedented inflation, coupled with high rates of unemployment and falling rates of economic growth. By 1980, the growth rate of real income was almost zero, unemployment was 7.5 percent, and inflation reached 10 percent.[113] The Great Inflation continued until the wrenching changes of the early 1980s. These rates of inflation transformed the national economy, its workforce, and its government. In 1968, however, the extent of the economic situation could not be foreseen. Many members of the tax community believed that they had put the brakes on inflation.

As he had done on previous occasions, Mills had attempted to frame the legislation in such a way that many different policy activists, ranging from Keynesian economists to budget-cutters to southern conservatives, could all perceive the bill as a partial vindication of their efforts. Despite his bitter conflict with the CEA, Mills continued to voice his appreciation for economists. He told a group of powerful bankers in 1969 that "I have come to have a deep appreciation for the contributions that the principles and concepts of the discipline we know as economics have made to the unprecedented growth this country has experienced in recent decades."[114] Above all, Mills believed passionately in the value of political and intellectual compromise on fiscal policy. Following the battle, he explained:

> The proper role of our tax system in the shaping of national
> fiscal policy is still open to debate and will no doubt continue
> to be the subject of controversy. On the one hand, there are
> those who would use the tax system as a positive "economic tool"
> to achieve preconceived economic goals. On the other hand,
> there are those who maintain that the tax system should never

[112] Collins, "The Economic Crisis of 1968 and the Waning of the 'American Century,'" 422.

[113] Martin, *Shifting the Burden*, 109–110.

[114] Wilbur D. Mills, "Address to the American Bankers Association," *Proceedings of a Symposium on Public Policy and Economic Understanding*, 17 November 1969, WMPC, unprocessed.

under any circumstances be used to influence overall policies or goals of the Nation. While I do not adhere to either extreme because I do not think that either position is realistic or practical, surely we can all agree that the primary or overriding role of the Federal tax system is to raise in a fair and equitable manner the necessary revenues without which government cannot operate. At the same time there also is a widening agreement that with moderation, our tax system can also be used to provide economic stability and growth for the private economy.[115]

In 1969, Mills would fight one of his last major income-tax battles before succumbing to alcoholism. During that year, the tax community took up the controversial issue of tax reform. Together with Laurence Woodworth and Stanley Surrey, Mills used the expertise of the community to raise important questions about the economic cost of tax breaks and about the problematic structure of the tax code. Continuing a dialogue that began in the mid-1950s and culminated in 1986, these three redefined tax breaks as hidden government expenditures that subsidized private investment.

[115] Mills, "Remarks before the Chamber of Commerce."

9

Spending through Taxes

Southern congressmen often compared tax reform to the childhood game of plucking feathers off a chicken. In both games, they told colleagues, the winner was the person who plucked the most feathers without causing the chicken to squawk.[1] Indeed, closing tax breaks was a monumental challenge. By narrowing the definition of "taxable income," tax breaks benefited broad categories of taxpayers, such as middle-class homeowners, and profited powerful economic interests, including the oil industry and the New York Stock Exchange. By eliminating any tax break, Congress removed the barrier that protected some citizen or organization from high tax rates.

Compared with Sweden and Britain, the American state had distinguished itself by the number of tax breaks it enacted.[2] Given the appeal of tax breaks to the legislator and the beneficiary, policymakers needed to articulate a compelling rationale to convince the tax-writing committees to embrace some reform. Reformers within Congress also needed to build strong alliances within the tax community and to marshal an effective combination of technical knowledge and appealing rhetoric. Between 1965 and 1969, the tax reform faction – led by Mills, Laurence Woodworth, chief of staff of the Joint Committee on Internal Revenue Taxation [JCIRT] and Mills's chief confidant, Joseph Pechman, director of Economic Studies at the Brookings Institution, and Stanley Surrey, assistant secretary to the Treasury – demonstrated that Congress could enact substantive reform, despite the opposition of powerful economic and political interests.

Woodworth and Surrey revitalized the rhetoric of reform by producing comprehensive studies on the tax code. The studies, written

---

[1] This saying has its origins in the following statement by Jean-Baptiste Colbert, the Finance Minister to Louis XIV: "The art of taxation consists of plucking the goose so as to obtain the largest amount of feathers with the least amount of hissing." Cited in Sven Steinmo, *Taxation and Democracy: Swedish, British, and American Approaches to Financing the Modern State* (New Haven: Yale University Press, 1993), 19.

[2] Steinmo, *Taxation and Democracy,* 35–40; 103; 135–144. See also R. Douglas Arnold, *The Logic of Congressional Action* (New Haven: Yale University Press, 1990), 198–200.

with the Treasury and JCIRT staff, built on the compendium developed under Ways and Means during Mills's first year as chairman. For decades, reformers, reporters, and citizens used the term "loophole" to describe provisions that enabled citizens to escape their tax obligations. Their terminology implied that Congress did not anticipate the consequences of legislation, but that astute tax lawyers had manipulated laws to their advantage. The Treasury and JCIRT studies, however, suggested that Congress played a more active role in this process. These avenues of tax escape were hidden expenditures made through the tax code; in this way, tax breaks constituted an important form of government financial assistance.[3]

These tax breaks became known inside the policy community as "tax expenditures." Unlike most normal budget expenditures, Congress did not have to reauthorize tax expenditures every few years. The studies supplemented this argument with massive statistical documentation on the budgetary cost of each expenditure. The data showed the effect of tax breaks by documenting their role in the investment decisions of various industries. No longer did reformers focus on the tax breaks of particular individuals or companies, examining instead how national industries had structured their investment practices around the benefits accorded by the federal tax code. Had Ways and Means and the Treasury considered the cost of tax expenditures, according to defenders of the Great Society, Congress would have been pressured to achieve many of its revenue-raising objectives without cutting spending for the poor.[4]

The intellectual efforts of Surrey, Pechman, Woodworth, and others in the tax community, together with Mills's legislative skills, culminated in the Tax Reform Act of 1969. The legislation eliminated some tax expenditures, reduced others, and lowered rates for almost every citizen. The reform did not attempt to destroy the tax-break system. Rather it aimed to preserve and to cleanse the existing tax system by distinguishing "legitimate" tax breaks – defined as those provisions that were currently endorsed by the tax-writing committee leaders and their experts – from those that could no longer be defended on economic or political grounds. For representatives, tax reform was exactly the type of action that they expected from the "control committee," armed with its special privileges such as the closed rule and executive sessions, to maintain the institutional

---

[3] Defined in Stanley S. Surrey and Paul R. McDaniel, *Tax Expenditures* (Cambridge, MA: Harvard University Press, 1985), 25; Surrey, *Pathways to Tax Reform: The Concept of Tax Expenditures* (Cambridge, MA: Harvard University Press, 1973).

[4] Surrey, *Pathways To Tax Reform*, 2.

integrity of Congress.[5] Although the bill excluded many important reforms, it constituted an important achievement for the tax reform faction. Most reformers understood, realistically, that Mills needed to negotiate their proposals with the demands of interest groups if any reforms were to survive. As the editors from *The New York Times* noted: "The Tax Reform Act of 1969 – which, for all its imperfections, deserves passage by the House today – is a classic example of how the citadel of special privilege can be stormed by the skillful marshaling of an opposing force."[6]

By guiding some of the community's intellectual concepts through the legislative process, Mills helped to eliminate several flaws that his colleagues perceived in the tax structure. Just as important, the deliberations advanced an intense conversation within Washington about the need for ongoing tax reform and for an understanding of taxation in the context of general economic and budgetary policy. The legislation, and the debates surrounding it, kept the potentially explosive issue of tax reform on the agenda. The legislation also revealed how difficult tax reform had become by 1969. Given the centrality of income taxation to the postwar state, organized interests and voters guarded each provision with the same intensity with which they would protect any other government benefit.

STUDYING REFORM

The United States income tax system [Stanley Surrey told a group of finance specialists in 1967] is a powerful factor in our society, in our business and in our households. Viewed in the aggregate, its importance for fiscal policy purposes has been demonstrated in recent years, notably in the 1964 revenue reduction – and we hope again this year through the tax surcharge. American business is intimately aware of its importance in the particular, and tax planning is an integral part of business planning. About 90 percent of our adult population is involved in filing an income tax return and 75 percent in paying an income tax – a coverage broader than in any other country.[7]

---

[5] David R. Mayhew, *Congress: The Electoral Connection* (New Haven: Yale University Press, 1974), 154–158.

[6] Editorial, "Tax-Cut Lubricant," *The New York Times*, 7 August 1969.

[7] Stanley S. Surrey, "The United States Income Tax System – The Need for a Full Accounting," in *Tax Policy and Tax Reform: 1961–1969: Selected Speeches and Testimony of Stanley Surrey*, eds. William F. Hellmuth and Oliver Oldman (Chicago: Commerce Clearing House, 1973), 575–576.

To achieve an efficient and equitable tax system, the tax reform faction argued that Congress needed to reform the code periodically to maintain its integrity.[8] Ongoing reform, it explained, could stimulate economic growth, stabilize prices, improve compliance, and achieve "horizontal equity" – the notion that equal incomes should pay equal taxes, and that there should be fewer distinctions between different types of income. When speaking of "tax reform," the tax community referred to two different actions: tax reduction to stimulate growth and lower the incentives to avoid taxes, and closing tax breaks that politicians could no longer justify on economic grounds, or that political interests were unable to defend. Of course, Congress privileged tax reduction because it offered an opportunity to distribute benefits without any apparent cost. Eliminating tax breaks, on the other hand, required Congress to rescind benefits from powerful interests. Most legislation during the 1960s attempted to combine reform on tax breaks with a tax reduction program. The tension between the types of changes in the tax structure that should receive greatest attention had generated conflict between the tax reform and the growth manipulation factions of the community since the early 1960s. This was similar to the division between administrators and fiscal conservatives within the Social Security faction.

The tax reform faction made its greatest contribution to this legislative debate by placing reform on the policy agenda by means of the comprehensive studies on the budgetary and economic effect of tax breaks. Between 1965 and 1968, Stanley Surrey and Laurence Woodworth, at the request of Mills, helped to strengthen the reform agenda by directing studies on the tax system. Conducted through the Treasury and the JCIRT staff, these studies drew on experts in the tax reform faction such as Joseph Pechman, Gerard Brannon (the Treasury), Daniel Throop Smith (Harvard University), Jerome Kurtz (the Pennsylvania Bar), Mortimer Caplin (private Washington attorney), Richard Musgrave (Harvard University), Harvey Brazer (the Treasury and University of Michigan), Sheldon Cohen (IRS), and Edwin Cohen (University of Virginia). In the process, these studies built on the work completed under the auspices of Ways and Means in 1958 and 1959, and drew on the same pool of tax experts.

The concept of "tax expenditures"

Foremost, the studies introduced a new concept into the vocabulary of reformers. The term "tax expenditure" highlighted the fact that

---

[8] Mortimer Caplin, "Address to the National Conference on Federal Tax Reform of the Chamber of Commerce," reprinted in U.S. Chamber of Commerce, Press Release, 14 February 1968, SSP, Box 183, File 3.

the government spent money through the tax code. These hidden expenditures played a crucial role in the investment decisions of many industries. Tax expenditures were very attractive because they remained active until Congress repealed the measures. Most budgeted expenditures, on the other hand, had to be reauthorized periodically. "Loopholes," the studies said, were a type of government assistance provided by Congress to particular interests. According to Surrey, the "tax expenditures represent tax revenues being 'spent' (through being lost to the tax system) to achieve the specific nontax goals represented by the special roles. In this regard, the tax expenditures stand as alternatives to the direct Government expenditures – in the form of loans, grants, guarantees, and the like – that could have been utilized to achieve these same goals."[9] By defining this type of expenditure in what Surrey called the "tax language," few citizens or legislators perceived tax breaks as government financial assistance.[10] As one member of the Ways and Means Committee staff noted of the oil depletion allowance: "It was easier to induce exploration through the tax structure than to go and get an appropriation for money to give oil developers to try to find new sources of oil . . . a direct subsidy would be much more efficient than working through the tax structure . . . but that you'd never get an appropriation for hundreds of millions to prompt new sources of oil."[11] The investment tax credit of 1962 had proven that tax breaks could have dramatic effects on private investment.

To supplement the idea of "tax expenditures," the study designed new accounting methods that incorporated the cost of these expenditures into the federal budget.[12] Economists attempted to quantify the existing tax expenditures in the same way they identified direct government expenditures. They found, for example, that the formal budget of the Commerce Department and the transportation program excluded the more than $1 billion spent through the tax system.[13] Furthermore, the studies applied cost-benefit analysis to compare the efficiency of "tax expenditures" with the efficiency of direct spending in various areas of public policy.[14] With the help of

[9] Stanley S. Surrey, "Past and Prologue in Tax Policy: Remarks before the Federal Tax Institute," in *Tax Policy and Tax Reform*, 171.

[10] Surrey, "The United States Income Tax System – The Need for a Full Accounting," 575–586.

[11] JMIC.

[12] Stanley Surrey to William Hellmouth, 26 August 1968, SSP, Box 182, File 3; Gerard Brannon to the Files, 29 December 1967, SSP, Box 184, File 2.

[13] Surrey, "The United States Income Tax System – The Need for a Full Accounting," 575–576; Surrey, "The Tax Expenditure Budget: A Conceptual Analysis," in *Tax Policy and Tax Reform*, 587–623.

[14] Surrey, "Past and Prologue in Tax Policy," 171; Gerard Brannon to the Files, 29 December 1967, SSP, Box 184, File 2.

Professor Henry Aaron, an economist at the University of Maryland, the Treasury staff prepared a "tax expenditure budget" that provided a systematic tally of tax expenditures arranged by traditional budget categories.

By the late 1960s, according to the Treasury-JCIRT studies, tax expenditures had become an extremely popular method for Congress to distribute benefits across income brackets and generations. One of the most costly tax expenditures was for the elderly. In 1967, there were 20 million people, over the age of sixty-five, with only 4 million filing returns and/or paying income taxes. As a result, the government provided almost $2.3 billion in special benefits to the elderly through a series of provisions in the tax code that included the $600 exemption for those over sixty-five, the tax credit for all retirement income, and the exclusion of Social Security benefits from taxation.[15]

Business also received tax expenditures as a reward for investment. The depletion allowance remained the most potent symbol of this assistance; Mills called it "a symbol of inequity – of all that is wrong in the tax law itself."[16] The allowance enabled oil producers to deduct $27\frac{1}{2}$ percent of their capital losses from taxable income and to deduct part of the cost even of successful ventures. During the 1950s, organized groups had begun to design special funds through which wealthy citizens could invest directly in oil exploration rather than in stocks or bonds.[17] Another industrial group that benefited from tax breaks was housing developers. One real estate operator, whose total income reached $7.5 billion over a seven-year period, had paid only $800,000 in taxes, which constituted 11 percent of his income. Meanwhile, a married wage earner with two children earning $10,000 paid the same percentage of taxes on his income.[18]

Wealthy citizens were equally dependent on the tax expenditure dole. For example, many individuals relied on the liberal definition

---

[15] Stanley S. Surrey, "Testimony on Tax Treatment of the Elderly," in *Tax Policy And Tax Reform*, 259–267; Surrey to Melvin White, 15 June 1966, SSP, Box 114, File 3; Anthony Celebrezze, "Tax Provisions for the Aged," 1963, WCP, Box 136, Folder 11. For earlier, detailed discussions of this issue, see the following documents from the WCP, Box 136, Folder 11: Ida Merriam to Wilbur Cohen, 7 January 1963; Cohen to Robert Ball, 16 July 1963; Cohen to the Secretary, 29 November 1962; Surrey to Cohen, 21 June 1966. See also Cohen, "Tax and Benefit Treatment of the Elderly," WCP, Box 263, Folder 1; "Tax Provisions Favoring Older Persons," 1962 and Gerard Brannon to Mr. Leahey, NAT, RG 56, Office of Tax Policy, Box 58, File: Tax Treatment of the Aged.

[16] Wilbur Mills to Joe Kardsmuir, 22 July 1969, WMPC, Box 483, File 4.

[17] "Drilling Against Taxes," *The Economist*, 10 May 1969, 38.

[18] Stanley S. Surrey, "Tax Assistance for Housing: Its Implications for the Federal Tax Structure and the Federal Budget," in *Tax Policy and Tax Reform*, 631.

of capital gains to protect their wealth.[19] The treatment of capital gains at death constituted a particularly problematic area for reformers. Under the laws, the wealthy were able to transfer income at death to their heirs without having to pay much in taxes. This legal arrangement cost the federal government almost $2.5 billion a year. Surrey considered these laws to be the "single most important tax reform issue."[20] In fact, high income taxpayers regularly defined a broad range of income as "capital gains" to avoid higher taxes.

Besides raising revenue, the Treasury-JCIRT studies argued that a reduction in tax expenditures could achieve another important goal: tax simplification. The proliferation of tax expenditures had resulted in an extraordinarily complex code. Mills argued that the complexity was an inevitable product of the nation's legislative process:

> Another factor which undoubtedly accounts for much complexity in the tax laws is the very nature of the legislative process. While the suggestion that the art of legislating is the art of compromise is a well-worn phrase, nevertheless, there is much truth in it. Much of the legislation passed, tax or otherwise, is obtained only by synthesizing varying points of view. Frequently, these differing points of view develop at different times during the various stages of the legislative process. As a result, legislation may start in one direction and then through a series of modifications be materially changed until the end product differs substantially from the initial proposal. Consequently, in some cases, it may be possible to find a solution for the end result which is simpler than the one achieved by adding the series of modifications to the initial provision.[21]

The nature of the legislative process provided a need for the tax-writing committees to periodically reform the code.

Mills promotes tax reform

To promote simplification, Mills published an article in the Chamber of Commerce's *The Nation's Business* that received widespread praise within the tax reform faction. Woodworth, who wrote the original draft of the article, circulated it among the Treasury economists, including Surrey, and incorporated their revisions before publica-

---

[19] Stanley Surrey to Gerard Brannon and Lawrence Stone, 16 August 1965, SSP, Box 184, File 3; Surrey to Henry Fowler, 23 August 1966, SSP, Box 182, File 2; Surrey to Brannon, 22 August 1966, SSP, Box 183, File 2.

[20] Stanley Surrey to Henry Fowler, 8 December 1966, SSP, Box 182, File 2.

[21] Wilbur D. Mills, "Good News for Taxpayers: Top Lawmaker Explains," *Nation's Business*, December 1965, 52.

tion.[22] The final article warned that the complexity of the tax code had alienated citizens and placed taxation under the control of a professional tax elite. Complexity allowed for the existence of "deadwood" – provisions that had outlived their original economic purpose and now served only as blatant tax breaks. Those provisions, he said, gave "legitimate" tax incentives a bad reputation among politicians and the public. Once again, Mills implied that "legitimate" incentives were those that the tax-writing committee leaders and their experts deemed essential for economic growth.

In the article, Mills insisted on the simplification of the language contained in the tax code. Much of the deadwood resulted from the interest group driven Members' Bills that Mills had turned into a regular feature in his committee. Acknowledging the effect of Members' Bills, the chairman argued that these exemptions occasionally needed to be reviewed in order to maintain the code's integrity. Mills also argued that the committee should simplify the abstruse language in the tax code. As an example of unnecessary jargon, he highlighted one line that described ordinary income as follows: "gain from the sale or exchange of property which is neither a capital asset nor property described in section 1231."[23] Mills received support from Senator Russell Long (D-LA), the chairman of the Senate Finance Committee, who proposed that Congress offer a maximum tax rate below 50 percent for taxpayers who opted to forego all tax breaks.[24]

The Treasury-JCIRT agenda

The Treasury-JCIRT studies produced several concrete areas of agreement within the tax community. First, most officials agreed that any reform legislation should be "revenue neutral," meaning that it would raise as much money through closing tax breaks as it would lose by reducing rates. Revenue neutrality could prevent opponents from accusing reformers of increasing the deficit or of using reform to increase the size of the government.[25] Second, the reforms should

[22] Stanley Surrey to Henry Fowler, 2 November 1965, SSP, Box 182, File 2.
[23] Mills, "Good News for Taxpayers," 50–57; Stanley Surrey to Henry Fowler, 25 August 1966, Box 182, File 2. See also Mills, "Tax Simplification from the Viewpoint of the Legislator," in *Essays on Taxation: Contributed in Memory of Colin Stam* (New York: Tax Foundation, Inc., 1974), 74–117.
[24] Laurence Woodworth to Milton Young, 18 October 1968, NA, RG 128, Box 493, File: Tax Simplification; Stanley S. Surrey, "Federal Tax Policy in the 1960's," in *Tax Policy and Tax Reform*, 123.
[25] Lyndon Johnson, "The Need for Tax Reform: Draft," 15 August 1967 and Stanley Surrey to Joseph Califano, 29 June 1967 in LBJL, White House Office Aides File, Joseph Califano, Box 54, File: Tax Reform.

include some version of a "minimum tax" and a "maximum tax." While the minimum tax would specify a percentage of income that all taxpayers would have to contribute, the maximum tax would establish a top limit for all taxpayers regardless of the type of income they earned. Third, Mills explained, comprehensive reform still included tax reduction: "We must remember that, to the extent the tax base is constricted, the *rates* have to be higher, and that the broader the base the lower rates can be."[26] Reformers agreed that unlike 1962 or 1964, now Congress should direct a significant portion of this reduction to lower income taxpayers by raising their principle tax break, the standard deduction.[27]

The studies also revealed a consensus about how the reforms should affect different income groups. For the high-income brackets, the legislation was to reduce the main escape routes that enabled some groups to avoid all or most of their taxes, while it would also make certain that different types of high income were treated as equally as possible by the law. For middle-income taxpayers, the reforms would restore the relationship between taxpayers who used itemized deductions and those who drew on the standard deduction. Finally, policymakers generally agreed that Congress should reduce the tax burden for lower-income groups.[28] Explaining these ideas to the media, Mills told *U.S. News & World Report*:

> What we're doing now is to try to eliminate some of the preferences that exist within the law that have become tax shelters for many, many of our citizens. That's a very appropriate thing. That's in the interest of greater equity in the law. I hope we will not do so, but as we do this, we may be adding page after page to the Internal Revenue Code. We may end up by further complicating the Internal Revenue Code. We might also be further complicating the tax return itself for many people. I hope not. True tax reform means more to me than the establishment of equity, as important as that is. Simplicity is a great part of reform. Neutralization in decisions of taxpayers is an important matter. By that I mean that tax laws should never be such as to predominate over the marketplace in decision making. We know that no business decision of any magnitude is now going

---

[26] Wilbur D. Mills, "Remarks before the American Institute of Certified Public Accountants," 6 October 1968, WMPC, Box 644, File 3.

[27] For broad discussions about all of these reforms, see the following documents in the SSP: Stanley Surrey to Henry Fowler, 25 August 1966 and Surrey to Fowler, 8 December 1966 in Box 182, File 2; Surrey to Fowler, 16 June 1967, Box 184, File 2; Surrey to Fowler, 2 July 1968, Box 183, File 1; Surrey, Handwritten Notes, 28 June 1967, Box 183, File 2.

[28] Stanley Surrey to Henry Fowler, 2 July 1968, SSP, Box 183, File 1.

to be made without consulting the tax lawyer. In time I would like to see us get our law as simple as it can be. That is very important with the type of tax system we have, where a person voluntarily complies. At least, if he's asked to comply voluntarily, let's give him something that he can understand, so that he doesn't have to go pay somebody $5 or $25 and upward to help him fix up a return.[29]

In the studies and subsequent proposals, the Treasury and the JCIRT decided to include as many proposals as possible because, as one official warned, "anything that we omit from the reform package will have little or no chance of being acted on in the future since the reply would always be 'Even Stanley Surrey didn't object to that.' "[30]

Although President Johnson encouraged the studies, he displayed little enthusiasm for the reform legislation. He believed that it was too dangerous politically for him to say anything about controversial provisions such as the depletion allowance.[31] Rejecting calls for immediate reform, Johnson agreed to a statement in the Revenue and Expenditure Control Act of 1968 that required the Treasury to submit proposals to the Congress by December 31.[32] Although the Treasury sent its recommendations to the White House in late 1968, Johnson withheld them from Congress.

Turning the tax reform agenda into public policy

Facing presidential reluctance to take on this issue, Mills, Woodworth, and Surrey attempted to translate the ideas of the tax community into legislative outcomes themselves. On a moderate scale, they fought against campaigns from the political left and the right to use tax credits to establish domestic programs, including manpower training, social welfare, urban and rural development, and low-income housing.[33] While supporters promised that these credits were an alter-

[29] "Interview with Wilbur Mills. . . . The Plan for New Taxes," *U.S. News & World Report,* 26 May 1969, 40–45.

[30] Mr. Gibb to Stanley Surrey, 13 November 1968, SSP, Box 184, File 1.

[31] Stanley Surrey to the Files, 4 November 1966, SSP, Box 182, File 2.

[32] Treasury Department, Press Release, 31 December 1968, SSP, Box 184, File 1; Henry Fowler, "Statement of the Honorable Henry H. Fowler, Secretary of the Treasury For the Congress of the United States on the Tax Reform Program. . . . 1968," 11 December 1968, LBJL, Personal Papers of Henry Fowler, Box 205, Folder: Briefing Books – Tax Reform; Editorial, "Evading Tax Reform," *The New York Times,* 10 January 1969.

[33] Surrey, "Past and Prologue in Tax Policy," 171. See also Wilbur Mills, "The Tax Reform Act of 1969," *Indiana Legal Forum* 4, No. 1 (Fall 1970): 26–43; Klaus Peter Kisker, "A Note on the Negative Income Tax," *National Tax Journal* XX, No. 1 (March

native to expansive governmental intervention, Mills and Surrey warned that they would ultimately cost more than direct expenditures.[34] "I consider it [the credits]," Chairman Mills warned, "a form of backdoor spending."[35] The chairman insisted that every proposal should be put to a simple test: "Do you get more actual return for the dollars involved than you do through a direct expenditure out of the Government?"[36]

Meanwhile, Stanley Surrey's Task Force on Tax Reform had offered several legislative proposals. First, the task force proposed tightening the liberal treatment provided to capital gains income transferred at death, and urged reforms of the estate and gift tax laws. The task force concluded that "a change in the treatment of capital gains at death" was the "single most important tax reform." They were aware that such reforms were "difficult because the public generally does not think of this area as a crucial issue compared to, say, percentage depletion." But the 1963 reform proposals on capital gains, although they failed, "did improve the climate and made many aware of the need for change."[37] Second, the task force proposed a minimum tax and reforms on the treatment of tax-exempt foundations. Additionally, Surrey's group wanted to provide low-income tax reduction through a liberalized standard deduction.

Behind closed doors, Mills and Woodworth conducted intense negotiations with the Treasury about what should be proposed in upcoming legislation.[38] From the start, Mills warned how difficult it

1967): 102–105; Task Force on Income Maintenance, "Toward Greater Security and Opportunity For Americans," 14 November 1964, WCP, Box 189, Folder 6; Income Maintenance Task Force, "Negative Tax," 1 September 1964, WCP, Box 189, Folder 1.

[34] Stanley S. Surrey, "Taxes and the Federal Budget: Speech before the Dallas Chapter of the Financial Executives Institute," in *Tax Policy and Tax Reform*, 613–623; Eileen Shanahan, "Tax Incentive Fight," *The New York Times*, 21 December 1967; Eileen Shanahan, "Mills Denounces Tax-Credit Moves," *The New York Times*, 15 December 1967; "Mills Assails Income-Tax Credit Proposals, Fears a 'Catastrophic' Loss of Revenue," *The Wall Street Journal*, 15 December 1967.

[35] "Will Congress Raise Taxes? Interview with Representative Wilbur Mills," *U.S. News & World Report*, 9 October 1967, 52–55.

[36] "Nixon, Mills, McCracken – A Look At Policies Of The Future," *U.S. News & World Report*, 23 December 1968, 34; "Tax Changes to Look For: Exclusive Interview with Wilbur Mills," *U.S. News & World Report*, 16 December 1968, 69.

[37] Stanley Surrey to Henry Fowler, 8 December 1966 and Task Force on Tax Reform, "Report," 25 October 1965 in SSP, Box 182, File 2; Task Force on Tax Reform, "Administratively Confidential Report," October 1965 and Surrey to Joseph Califano, 13 August 1965, SSP, Box 184, File 3.

[38] Stanley Surrey to the Files, 25 October 1965, SSP, Box 182, File 2; Surrey to Henry Fowler, 10 August 1965, SSP, Box 184, File 3; Surrey to the Files, 11 January 1965, SSP, Box 184, File 2; Surrey to the Files, 25 April 1966, NAT, RG 56, Office of Tax Policy, Box 68, File: Tax Reform Proposals; Surrey to the Files, 29 June 1966, SSP,

would be to reform the tax code: "We run into much opposition when we endeavor to make dollars subject to taxation that are not now subject to taxation. A great pressure is built up. People have vested rights and feel that they have, over the years, fully justified those rights. They don't want to give them up."[39] Throughout their discussions, Mills and Woodworth argued that Congress should attack tax breaks directly rather than relying on indirect methods such as the minimum tax. While indirect measures were politically attractive because Congress did not have to challenge any particular interest group, these measures left too much room for continued avoidance and failed to restructure the code. To weaken existing tax breaks, the chairman urged colleagues to "keep the 'tax preferences' on the defensive."[40] Woodworth, along with JCIRT staff members Albert Buckberg and William Forti, met regularly with Treasury officials such as Gerard Brannon, Michael Bird, and John Wilkins. Drawing on Mills's request for concrete data to use in his presentation before the committee, these six men produced extensive statistical tables documenting the provisions that allowed individuals with adjusted gross incomes of over $100,000 to escape their tax burdens.[41]

Throughout these negotiations, Surrey saw Mills as his ally. In 1965, he wrote in his files, "I would still regard Mr. Mills as still basically in favor of improving the tax system. He does, obviously, need Administration support for this and would want it. But the basic fact remains that he is the Ways and Means Committee Chairman who will work to improve the tax structure."[42] Surrey could point to numerous cases to support his claim. Mills had even opposed Senator William Fulbright's (D-AR) amendment to liberalize the depletion allowance for Arkansas aluminum interests on the grounds that the break would be too costly and inequitable.[43]

Box 182, File 2. See the following documents in the NA: Bob Shapiro to Laurence Woodworth, 10 December 1968 and Shapiro to Woodworth, 12 December 1968, RG 128, Box 493, File: Tax Simplification; Wilbur Mills to Woodworth, 21 November 1968, WMPC, Box 158, File: Govt. Dept. of Treasury General, 90th Cong., 1967–68/3; Surrey, Handwritten Notes, 28 June 1967, SSP, Box 183, File 2; Surrey to the Files, 23 January 1967, SSP, Box 118, File 2; Surrey to Henry Fowler, 10 October 1967, SSP, Box 184, File 2.

[39] "Wilbur Mills Talks on Taxes," *Nation's Business*, August 1964, 78.

[40] Stanley Surrey to the Files, 5 January 1967 and Surrey to the Files, 31 January 1967, SSP, Box 184, File 2. See also Surrey to Henry Fowler, 10 August 1965, SSP, Box 184, File 3.

[41] Stanley Surrey to William Hellmouth, 26 August 1968, SSP, Box 182, File 3; Gerard Brannon to the Files, 29 December 1967, SSP, Box 184, File 2.

[42] Stanley Surrey to the Files, 25 October 1965, SSP, Box 182, File 2.

[43] David E. Price, *Who Makes the Laws? Creativity and Power in Senate Committees* (Cambridge, MA: Schenkman, 1972),187–188.

During meetings with the Treasury, Mills pushed for specific reforms. For example, he stressed the need to remove numerous transactions that were not sales or exchanges of capital gains from being classified as capital gains. Mills told Surrey, Joseph Barr, and Jerome Kurtz at the Treasury that they should propose the elimination of the unlimited charitable deduction. Mills pointed out that the deduction permitted taxpayers to give away greatly appreciated assets, but then to buy new stock with their tax savings and thus change appreciated assets to assets with a basis closer to real value. Mills strongly believed that the unlimited charitable deduction could be reformed despite adamant opposition from interest groups. He also insisted on reforms to eliminate the abuses by foundations and their supporters.[44] At the same time, Mills convinced the Treasury to abandon its proposed reforms on tax-exempt state industrial development bonds. Although this reform even had the support of John Byrnes, Arkansas relied extensively on them to attract business.[45]

In October 1967, Surrey and Woodworth announced to Mills that the reform legislation proposal consisted of a balanced revenue package, and had four objectives: to relieve the lowest income groups from the burden of income tax; to respond to charges that a large number of the wealthy were not contributing their fair share of tax payments; to ease the burden on those in the higher income brackets who were paying excessive taxes because of the type of income they held; and to achieve a complete revision of the estate and gift taxes. Although Mills was "guarded" during this conversation, he seemed receptive to the estate and gift tax revisions, to the proposal for a 50 percent maximum tax, and to limits on charitable contributions.[46] Treasury officials wanted to hold off on some reforms, such as the withholding of dividend and interest income, because those measures seemed too controversial.[47]

While negotiations took place between the Treasury and Ways and Means, others in the tax community struggled to influence this debate. Umbrella business and financial organizations, for example,

[44] Stanley Surrey to the Files, 5 January 1967, SSP, Box 184, File 2.

[45] Stanley Surrey to the Files, 11 January 1967, SSP, Box 184, File 2; Surrey to the Files, 17 July 1968, SSP, Box 184, File 1; Surrey to the Files, 4 August 1966, SSP, Box 57, File 2; Bruce J. Schulman, *From Cotton Belt to Sunbelt: Federal Policy, Economic Development, and the Transformation of the South, 1938–1980* (New York: Oxford University Press, 1991), 65.

[46] Stanley Surrey to the Files, 30 October 1967, SSP, Box 184, File 2.

[47] U.S. Department of Treasury, "The Possibilities for Legislative Proposals in 1967 for Tax Reform," 1967, NAT, RG 56, Office of Tax Policy, Box 68, File: Tax Reform Proposals.

sent Mills detailed studies arguing that particular provisions were
essential for economic growth.[48] Meanwhile, professional think tanks
spent considerable amounts of time working on reform, including
economists at Brookings and the National Bureau of Economic
Research. For instance, the Urban Coalition worked out cost-benefit
analyses that compared tax expenditures with direct expenditures.[49]
The Treasury used many experts in the tax reform faction, including Richard Musgrave, Herbert Stein, Joseph Pechman, and
Norman Ture, as regular consultants to help them design politically
feasible reforms.[50]

Finally, professional journals published debates about tax reform.
The *Harvard Law Review*, for example, published an exchange over
the notion of "broadening the tax base." Yale's Professor Boris Bittker
argued that terms such as "preferences" and "exceptions" were so
vague as to be meaningless, and that most reformers targeted particular tax breaks while leaving others untouched. Given the power of
interest groups in the legislative process, and the commitment of
reformers to some tax breaks, Bittker felt that numerous tax breaks
would always exist: After all, "legitimate" tax breaks were simply the
provisions supported by the reformers. Bittker endorsed a continued
system of countervailing "preferences" that distributed tax breaks
across income brackets.[51] Rejecting Bittker's pessimism, Surrey wrote
to Pechman:

> I think it is a wrong view of the tax world and certainly is not
> one upon which the Treasury Department can operate. Nor
> should a Congress operate on those premises. The world may
> be pragmatic but I doubt if it is as pragmatic as Bittker made it
> out to be, and without theory or principle. In the reaction of
> Congressmen and Senators – including a great many of the tax
> committees – there is still a strong intuitive pull grounded in
> tax equity and fairness that they feel when they consider a new

---

[48] See, for example, Keith Funston to Wilbur Mills, 10 February 1967, WMPC, Box
336, File 4 – Ways and Means, Interest Equalization-HR 3813-90th Cong/3.

[49] Laurence Woodworth to Wilbur Mills, 1967, WMPC, Box 339, File 5.

[50] Treasury Memo, 14 March 1968 and William Hellmuth to Stanley Surrey, 17 December 1968 and Cary Modlin to William Hellmuth, 10 December 1968, SSP, Box 182,
File 3.

[51] Boris I. Bittker, "A 'Comprehensive Tax Base' as a Goal of Income Tax Reform,"
Harvard Law Review 80, No. 5 (March 1967): 925–985. See also Bittker, "Comprehensive Income Taxation: A Response," *Harvard Law Review* 81, No. 5 (March 1968):
1032–1043; Stanley Surrey to William Hellmuth, 26 August 1968, SSP, Box 182, File
3; Richard A. Musgrave, "In Defense of an Income Concept," *Harvard Law Review*
81, No. 1 (November 1967): 62; Joseph A. Pechman, "Comprehensive Income Taxation: A Comment," *Harvard Law Review* 81, No. 1 (November 1967): 63–67.

tax issue. That really is the premise that underlies the idea of a comprehensive income tax base. This public is not always present – but if it were not there a good deal of the time, all would be chaos in the Congress. And yet we know that there is considerably more order than chaos, even in the very difficult area of taxes.[52]

These discussions about reform within the tax community gained momentum during the debates over the Revenue and Expenditure Control Act of 1968. The legislation enacted such dramatic reductions in general-revenue spending, particularly in Great Society programs, that it caused some policymakers to question why tax breaks had escaped the debate. By categorizing the issue of tax breaks under "tax reform" rather than "expenditure control," Congress had protected these provisions from serious reduction. Within this context, Surrey introduced the term "tax expenditure" during a speech on November 15, 1967 to a New York financial group. He lamented: "When Congressional talk and public opinion turn to reduction and control of Federal expenditures, these tax expenditures are never mentioned."[53]

In the end, Surrey, Woodworth, Mills, and the other members of the community who had contributed to the studies, provided unprecedented statistical documentation on the cost of tax breaks to the federal budget. They also introduced a powerful concept into the vocabulary of tax reformers: The notion that the federal government spent monies through the tax code. As a result of the negotiations by Surrey, Woodworth, and Mills, moreover, tax-break reform had gained strong bipartisan support, including ranking Ways and Means Republican John Byrnes.[54] Mills wanted to wait on tax reform so that it would not become a mechanism for opponents to stifle the tax

---

[52] Stanley Surrey to Joseph Pechman, 29 November 1967, SSP, Box 47, File 4. Similar debates were published in the *National Tax Journal.* See also Lawrence M. Stone, "Comprehensive Income Tax Base For the U.S.? Implications of the Report of the Royal Commission on Taxation," *National Tax Journal* XXII, No. 1 (March 1969): 24–38; Boris I. Bittker, "Accounting for Federal 'Tax Subsidies' in the National Budget," *National Tax Journal* XXII, No. 2 (June 1969): 244–261; Surrey and William Hellmuth, "The Tax Expenditure Budget – Response to Professor Bittker" and "What Is a Comprehensive Tax Base Anyway?" in *National Tax Journal* XXII, No. 4 (December 1969): 528–537; 543–549; William Hellmuth to Boris Bittker, 11 March 1969, NAT, RG 56, Office of Tax Policy, Box 33, File: Budget.

[53] Stanley S. Surrey, *Pathways to Tax Reform* (Cambridge, MA: Harvard University Press, 1973), 3.

[54] Stanley Surrey to the Files, 17 July 1968, SSP, Box 184, File 1. See also Surrey to the Files, 23 January 1967, SSP, Box 184, File 2; Gibb to Surrey, 13 November 1968, SSP, Box 184, File 1.

surcharge and expenditure control bill. Furthermore, Mills said, the
Democratic Study Group (a group of congressional Democrats
devoted to liberal policy and congressional reform) would be more
willing to support the regressive surcharge and expenditure control
legislation if they knew that Ways and Means was working on a proposal to plug up tax breaks that benefited the wealthy.[55] By 1969, the
time seemed ripe for reforming tax expenditures.

A TASK WORTHY OF SOLOMON[56]

Armed with the studies from the community, Mills began the difficult
task of selling tax reform to Congress. When the year began, he
moved quickly to outflank the opposition. The chairman scheduled
committee hearings before the newly elected President Richard
Nixon had appointed an assistant secretary to the Treasury. When
Norman Ture, who was heading Nixon's Task Force on Tax Reform,
asked Mills if it didn't seem unfair to hold hearings before the president had an opportunity to organize his economic team, Mills
replied "yes" with a grin.[57]

Joseph Barr warns of a taxpayer revolt

On January 20, 1969, the outgoing Secretary of the Treasury Joseph
Barr captured media headlines when he warned that a "taxpayer's
revolt" was brewing among middle-class wage earners. Before the
Joint Economic Committee, Barr warned that "the revolt will come
not from the poor but from the tens of millions of middle-class families and individuals with incomes of $7,000 to $20,000, whose tax
payments now generally are based on the full ordinary rates and who
pay over half of our individual income taxes." To dramatize his argument, Barr revealed that in 1967, no income taxes were paid on 155
tax returns with gross incomes of $200,000 or more.[58] When Mills's
staff investigated the returns, they found that 21 of those taxpayers
were millionaires.[59]

---

[55] Stanley Surrey to the Files, 30 October 1967, SSP, Box 184, File 2.

[56] This is the phrase Joseph Pechman used to describe loophole-closing tax reform.
George F. Break and Joseph A. Pechman, *Federal Tax Reform: The Impossible Dream?*
(Washington, D.C.: The Brookings Institution, 1975), 15.

[57] Norman Ture, interview with Julian Zelizer in Washington, D.C., 13 December 1993.

[58] "Statement By the Honorable Joseph W. Barr, Secretary of the Treasury before the
Joint Economic Committee," 17 January 1969, NA, RG 128, Box 495, File: Secretary; "Treasury Secretary Warns of Taxpayers' Revolt," *The New York Times*, 18 January
1969. See also U.S. Congress, House of Representatives, Committee on Ways and
Means, *Congressional Record*, 91st Cong., 1st sess., 6 August 1969, 22563.

[59] Mills, "The Tax Reform Act of 1969," 26–43; Eileen Shanahan, "Mills Will Examine
Tax Returns of 155 Who Paid Nothing," *The New York Times*, 22 March 1969.

Barr supplemented these proclamations with the tax expenditure budget, a detailed economic analysis of government expenditures made through the income tax. Based on the Treasury-JCIRT studies, the document categorized tax expenditures under the same functional categories used in the federal budget. For example, the budget contained a category entitled "National Defense," which listed all the salary payments and reenlistment bonuses to military personnel serving in combat zones; these earnings were excluded from the income tax. Under the category of "Housing," the document listed the tax deductions for interest paid on home mortgages and for property taxes, items that cost the federal government annually $1.8 billion.[60] Together, tax expenditures totaled almost one quarter of the federal budget. If Barr had any evidence that an actual revolt was going to take place among the middle class, he did not produce it. Nonetheless, his statement provided rhetorical ammunition for policymakers to package tax reform as a moderate agenda that benefited a broad range of Americans.

In fact, according to Barr, Mills, Surrey, and their colleagues, even wealthy citizens and corporations stood to gain from a reduction in tax expenditures. Congress could use the additional revenue to lower statutory rates and thus reduce the need for complicated strategies of tax avoidance. By combining rate reduction with tax-break reform, Mills frequently explained, the federal government could raise more revenue than it did under the existing income-tax system. As a result of tax expenditures, Congress raised less tax revenue than the legal rates required. Policymakers pointed to the difference between "statutory rates" – the legal rates – and "effective rates" – the actual rates of income that the federal government captured. Although the statutory rates ran from about 14 percent to 70 percent, according to Pechman the "effective" rates ranged from less than 1 percent on the lowest income group, rose to only 29 percent on those with incomes of $150,000 to $200,000, and then fell to 27 percent for the wealthiest citizens. Surrey and Pechman frequently reminded audiences that taxes absorbed a smaller portion of the GNP in the United States than in any other industrialized country, with the exceptions of Japan and Switzerland.[61]

---

[60] "Statement by the Honorable Joseph W. Barr, Secretary of the Treasury before the Joint Economic Committee."

[61] Joseph A. Pechman, *Federal Tax Policy* (Washington, D.C.: The Brookings Institution, 1966), 52–104; Stanley S. Surrey, "The Federal Tax System – Current Activities and Future Possibilities," in *Tax Policy and Tax Reform*, 158; John G. Gurley, "Federal Tax Policy (A Review Article)," *National Tax Journal* XX, No. 3 (September 1967): 319–327.

Crafting a politically viable bill

With Mills and the community placing reform squarely on the policy agenda, Mills moved to sell a viable plan to his committee. Beginning on February 18, Ways and Means began the most extensive hearings on tax reform that had been undertaken since 1958. At the start of the sessions, Mills told *Newsweek* that they were being conducted in response to the different treatment of similar types of income: "The general attitude of the people is more favorable now on tax reform than it has been in the past. There is more discussion of it now. More people are interested in it. More people are interested in these higher and higher rates. What the President is interested in is what we all want – simplification in the tax-collection system, greater equity, with less preference as to source, like municipal bonds or capital gains, and as much neutrality as possible so we don't distort business decisions."[62]

The committee hearings forced policymakers to grapple with the complex relationship that had developed between the federal income tax and the economy. As the president of Gulf Oil told Ways and Means concerning the depletion allowance: "The tax structure is intimately involved in thousands of contractual obligations. And percentage depletion is a cornerstone, a major part of the foundation on which the industry has built its house. To dismantle it in whole or in part could very well jeopardize that whole structure and, to a serious degree, the economy dependent upon it."[63] One of the clearest examples of this relationship was the provision that rewarded conglomerate mergers. These provisions gained considerable attention in 1967 and 1968, when a flurry of conglomerate mergers attracted the attention of the press and government officials.[64] Opposing these mergers on the grounds that they restricted competition and encouraged speculative behavior, Mills targeted tax provisions that allowed companies to write-off much of the debt incurred during these transactions.[65]

---

[62] "'Major Tax Reform': A High Nixon Priority," *Newsweek*, 17 February 1969, 77.
[63] U.S. Congress, House Committee on Ways and Means, *Tax Reform, 1969: Hearings*, 91st Cong., 1st sess., 1969, 3181; Wilbur D. Mills, "Some Dimensions of Tax Reform," *Arkansas Law Review* 23, No. 2 (Summer 1969): 165–166.
[64] Wilbur D. Mills, "Press Release," 10 February 1969, NA, RG 128, Box 460, File: Budget 1961.
[65] "Mills Hints Opposition to 2 Tax Benefits That Lubricate Conglomerate Mergers," *The Wall Street Journal*, 11 February 1969; "Mills Squints at Conglomerates," *Business Week*, 8 March 1969, 30. This story was closely followed by Robert Metz at *The New York Times*; see the following articles by Metz: "Mergers, Mills, and Tax Laws," *The New York Times*, 12 February 1969; "Searching Look At Merger Bill," *The New York Times*, 5 March 1969; "Mills Bill Aims at Merger Debt," *The New York Times*, 1 March 1969; "Conglomerates: Tax-Bill Target," *The New York Times*, 28 February 1969. See

Each day during the hearings, Ways and Means focused on a different provision in the law, ranging from the tax-exempt status of foundations to the treatment of state and local bonds. On one occasion, participants discussed how foundations were abusing their tax-exempt status. They explained the problem of "self-dealing," through which donors made substantial contributions to foundations and then conducted private transactions with the foundation, such as renting property or borrowing money from it. Representative Wright Patman (D-TX) proposed a reform that imposed a 20 percent tax on the investment income of all private foundations and that restricted the activities of the institutions. Together, Mills and Byrnes backed these reforms, arguing that since the federal government had taken over activities in areas such as education and scientific research, the tax privileges for foundations had become outdated.[66] The hearings also raised the problem of "hobby farms." These involved wealthy individuals who operated farms as a hobby, and at a loss, to reduce their taxes. The Treasury estimated that plugging this tax break would raise almost $145 million a year.[67] As the hearings proceeded, Byrnes ordered Woodworth and his staff to continue their confidential sampling of returns to learn how high-income taxpayers ($200,000 or more) took advantage of particular tax breaks.[68]

Business organizations were surprised by the seriousness displayed by Mills regarding these reforms.[69] For the first time in history, the

---

also Harvey Segal, "Mills Takes Tax Aim at Big Mergers," *The New York Times*, Sunday, 16 February 1969, Section E.

[66] U.S. Congress, House Committee on Ways and Means, *Tax Reform, 1969: Hearings*, 91st Cong., 1st sess., 1969, 112–428; U.S. Congress, Staff, Joint Committee on Internal Revenue Taxation, *Summary of Testimony on Tax-Exempt Organizations*, H1489 (Committee – Print); "Tax-Exempt Status of Private Foundations Is Questioned by Byrnes at Panel Hearings," *The Wall Street Journal*, 20 February 1969; "House Unit Studying, Tax Reform Grills Ford Foundation Chief on Exempt Status," *The Wall Street Journal*, 21 February 1969; "Foundations feel heat of tax reform," *Business Week*, 8 March 1969, 72–76.

[67] U.S. Congress, House Committee on Ways and Means, *Written Statements By Interested Individuals and Organizations on Treasury Department Report on Private Foundations*, 2 February 1965, 89th Cong., 1st sess., H0745 (Committee – Print), 14; Stanley Surrey to the Files, 30 October 1967, SSP, Box 184, File 2; Surrey to the Files, 29 June 1966, SSP, Box 182, File 2; U.S. Congress, House Committee on Ways and Means, *Tax Reform, 1969*, 91st Cong., 1st sess., 1969, 2001; U.S. Congress, House Committee on Ways and Means, *Summary of Testimony On Other Deductions: Farm Losses, Moving Expenses, and Gasoline Taxes*, 14 May 1969, H1497 (Committee – Print); "Growth of Foundations," 14 November 1967, NAT, RG 56, Office of Tax Policy, Box 18, File: Private Foundations.

[68] John Wilkins to Mr. Rudney, 13 February 1968, NAT, RG 56, Office of Tax Policy, Box 58, File: Statistical Information on Individuals.

[69] David Vogel, *Fluctuating Fortunes: The Political Power of Business in America* (New York: Basic Books, 1989), 61–64.

committee seemed to be on the verge of seriously curtailing the oil depletion allowance.[70] When representatives from the oil industry argued that the provision protected domestic oil production and prevented dependence on foreign oil, Mills refused to back down. Drawing on proposals from the Joint Economic Committee, he suggested that there were ways to minimize the risk of oil drilling while simultaneously curtailing the privileges afforded to the industry. Mills wanted to reduce the allowance to 20 percent.[71] As the chairman warned: "I would not want you to leave here thinking . . . that just because something has been in the law for a long time it may stay that way."[72]

Another controversial issue involved the tax treatment of interest on state and local bonds. Reformers argued that the exemption on the interest offered a popular escape route for wealthy investors. According to one expert, 91 percent of these bonds were held by taxpayers whose incomes exceeded $50,000 a year.[73] When state and local officials responded that these tax privileges allowed local governments to raise revenue easily, Mills continued to pressure the committee for change.

The hearings also focused on the larger principles behind tax reform. Most participants agreed that Congress needed to reexamine the tax code continually to weed out provisions that could no longer be defended on economic grounds. To preserve "legitimate" tax breaks, participants said, the tax-writing committees needed to take the initiative and eliminate those provisions without any justification. Of course, the arbitrary distinction between "legitimate" and "illegitimate" tax expenditures often depended on which interests convinced the members of the tax-writing committees that their preferences benefited growth and reelection. Nonetheless, reformers still believed in this negotiated, incremental process. Sheldon Cohen,

---

[70] U.S. Congress, House Committee on Ways and Means, *Tax Reform, 1969: Hearings*, 91st Cong., 1st sess., 1969, 3175–3198. See also, John Nolan to Albert Gore, NAT, RG 56, Office of Tax Policy, Box 18, File: Petroleum Industry.

[71] U.S. Congress, House Committee on Ways and Means, *Tax Reform, 1969: Hearings*, 91st Cong., 1st sess., 1969, 3175–3197; William Proxmire to Wilbur Mills, 22 March 1967, WMPC, Box 490, File 4.

[72] U.S. Congress, House Committee on Ways and Means, *Tax Reform, 1969: Hearings*, 91st Cong., 1st sess., 1969, 3197. The chairman issued a similar warning to defenders of the existing capital gains taxes. "Interview with Wilbur Mills. . . . The Plan for New Taxes," 40–45. See also U.S. Congress, Staff of the JCIRT, *Summary of Testimony on Capital Gains*, 9 July 1969, Jo781 (Committee – Print).

[73] U.S. Congress, Staff of the JCIRT, *Summary Of Testimony On The Tax Treatment Of State And Local Bond Interest At Public Hearings*, 9 July 1969, H1482 (Committee – Print).

former IRS commissioner, explained that "taxes have an effect on business decisions and however you gear your tax structure it is going to have an effect on business decisions and therefore a lot of energy of business people is going to be spent on what are the tax and economic consequences of this decision."[74] As a result, Congress needed to minimize unnecessary provisions to strengthen those that were essential.

In response to the hearings, the Nixon administration sent proposals to Congress on April 21, 1969, that linked tax-break reform to a reduction in the tax surcharge and to a repeal of the investment credit. Nixon's reforms were significantly milder than those suggested by Ways and Means. Nixon's boldest measure was the "Limit on Tax Preferences" (LTP), a complicated version of the minimum tax that established a limit on how much income could be shielded from taxation. In total, the legislation would raise as much revenue as it would lose through reductions.[75] Mills disliked the LTP as an indirect measure that avoided substantive reform and left too much room for continued manipulation.[76] Mills also criticized the administration for leaving the existing tax schedules unchanged. Throughout these debates, he continued to promote the tradeoff between fewer tax breaks and lower rates. In particular, he wanted an average reduction of 5 percent in most income categories along with a cut in the top rate from 70 percent to 50 percent.[77]

By May 11, *The New York Times* explained that Washington had its eyes glued to Mills: "The Society of Wilbur Mills Watchers and Second-Guessers has convened again for what promises to be a long session. Membership in the nonexclusive society includes a horde of

---

[74] U.S. Congress, House Committee on Ways and Means, *Tax Reform, 1969: Hearings*, 91st Cong., 1st sess., 1969, 4214.

[75] U.S. Congress, House Committee on Ways and Means, *Tax Reform Proposals Contained in the Message from the President*, 22 April 1969, H1242 (Committee – Print). For a more detailed account of the position of the Nixon administration, particularly with regard to the repeal of the investment credit, see Ronald F. King, *Money, Time, & Politics: Investment Tax Subsidies & American Democracy* (New Haven: Yale University Press, 1993), 327–335.

[76] Wilbur D. Mills, "Remarks to Democratic County Committee, Bronx," 2 June 1969, WMPC, Box 645, File 21; U.S. Congress, House Committee on Ways and Means, *Tax Reform, 1969: Hearings*, 91st Cong., 1st sess., 1969, 5535–5690; Eileen Shanahan, "Mills Would Cut Tax Deductions And Reduce Rates," *The New York Times*, 8 May 1969.

[77] Editorial, "Toward True Tax Reform," *The Wall Street Journal*, 12 May 1969. For responses to this tradeoff from the district, see WMPC, Boxes 484, 491, and 494. See also David Kennedy to Wilbur Mills, 8 July 1969 and Gerald Ford to Mills, 1 July 1969 and Bill Becker to Mills, 27 June 1969, all in WMPC, Box 339, File: 9, Ws+Ws-Revenue-Surtax '69–70 91st Cong/3.

lawyers and lobbyists whose clients have a direct financial interest in proposed changes in the tax laws; a small army of journalists who are trying to tell their readers and listeners not only what Mr. Mills has said and done but what it portends; a large number of Government officials, up to and including the President himself; and a good many members of Congress, including most of the members of the House Ways and Means Committee." The *Times* article added: "In recent years, he has also seemed to enjoy more and more his growing reputation as an enigma – a man whose words do not always mean what they appear to mean and whose real objectives remain obscure until the moment he chooses to clarify them."[78]

Pushing tax reform through the House and Senate

During the closed committee sessions, Mills relied on the uncertainties about his position to guide his committee toward significant reforms without stimulating a backlash against the legislation. By making it difficult for interest groups to anticipate his response, Mills caught their representatives off guard before the committee. On July 21, Ways and Means stunned Washington pundits by voting 18–7 to reduce the oil depletion allowance, marking the first time since 1926 that the tax-writing committee had taken unfavorable action on this benefit. On August 2, Ways and Means reported out a bill that included income-tax cuts totaling $4.44 billion. The cuts included a reduction from 14 percent to 13 percent for the lowest income brackets and a 5 percent reduction for all individuals with income under $100,000. The bill also raised the standard deduction to 13 percent in 1970 and to 15 percent in 1972. The reductions were combined with tax-break reform, including the reduction in the oil depletion allowance, tighter definitions of capital gains income, restrictions on tax-exempt organizations, and less generous treatment for interest on state and local bonds.[79] The bill also fixed a maximum tax of 50 percent on earned income, thereby offering an incentive for the wealthy to reject the use of their tax breaks.

On August 5, the Rules Committee granted a closed rule to the bill. In an unusual move during the lunch recess, however, Ways and Means voted to amend the bill by adding an additional $2.4 billion

---

[78] Eileen Shanahan, "Wilbur Mills: He Has Great Power and Likes to Use It," *The New York Times*, Sunday, 11 May 1969, Section E. See also Anthony Lewis, "When Tax Justice Is Not Seen to Be Done," *The New York Times*, Sunday, 3 August 1969, Section E.

[79] U.S. Congress, House Committee on Ways and Means, *Summary List And Brief Description Of Provisions Contained In H.R. 13270 The "Tax Reform Act of 1969"*, H17109 (Committee – Print). See also "A First Look At House Plan For Tax Tightening: Who's Hit," *U.S. News & World Report*, 9 June 1969.

in tax reductions for middle-income wage earners. This was in response to an announcement by the liberal Democratic Study Group that people with incomes between $7,000 and $13,000 who itemized deductions were to receive very little in the way of tax breaks from the House legislation. Since this group constituted an important constituency for the Democratic party, these figures could prove to be politically damaging in the next election.

On the House floor, Mills took a strong stand for reform. He suggested to the House that these reforms promised strong electoral benefits. In a dramatic statement, Mills ordered members to say to their constituents: "'Have you been enjoying a tax preference or a shelter for all or a part of your income which allows you to avoid paying the full rate of tax on it?' If he says 'Yes,' you tell him 'This bill does affect you. It squares your situation with that of all other taxpayers.' Yes, that situation is changed. On the other hand, if you see a taxpayer back home and you ask him if he has been enjoying a tax preference, and he says 'no; I am subject to the withholding taxes and I have no income that is not fully subject to taxation,' then you tell him that the bill contains benefits for him because we have taken all of the revenue – more, in fact, that could be recouped through the limitation of the tax shelters and the preferences dealt with in the bill – and we have given this revenue back in many ways to all the taxpayers. As a result there will not be a taxpayer in your district who will not have his taxes reduced some way or other in 1971 and 1972."[80] Toward the end of his presentation, Mills added, "preferences and shelters are not sacrosanct by virtue of age. They are susceptible to reconsideration and reevaluation."[81] The House approved the bill on August 7 by a vote of 394–30. The bill provided $9.3 billion a year in tax reductions and $6.9 billion in tax-break reforms. "Although the bill did not make all of the sweeping changes desired by reform groups," political scientist John Witte later wrote, "its liberal nature and tone should not be underestimated."[82]

Some members of Congress criticized the legislation for falling short of its promise. Senator Long, for example, labeled the legislation as the "Attorneys' and Accountants' Relief Act of 1969" because of its "bewildering complexity."[83] Even more important, the legislation would lose more revenue than it produced, thereby threatening

[80] U.S. Congress, House of Representatives, Committee on Ways and Means, *Congressional Record*, 91st Cong., 1st sess., 6 August 1969, 22562–22563.

[81] Ibid., 22563.

[82] John F. Witte, *The Politics and Development of the Federal Income Tax* (Madison: University of Wisconsin Press, 1985),169.

[83] Frank Porter, "Your Income Tax," *The Washington Post*, Sunday, 25 September 1969, Section B. See also Stanley Surrey to Wilbur Mills, 1 October 1969, WMPC, unprocessed.

to increase deficits. Such action was fiscally irresponsible, and constituted yet another stage in Mills's ongoing campaign to starve the general-revenue fund. In response, Mills drew on the logic of the Revenue Act of 1964 to explain that in the long run, the economic improvements borne out of the bill would generate higher revenue. Many of the costlier provisions, moreover, were important for the goal of tax simplification. Raising the standard deduction, for example, would encourage more taxpayers to use one simple deduction instead of numerous itemized deductions.[84]

But Senate Finance only aggravated these problems when it heavily amended the bill to combine an annual $9 billion in tax reduction with only 5 billion dollars in tax-break reform.[85] When the bill came to the Senate floor, Senator Albert Gore (D-TN) argued that the 5 percent reduction in tax rates provided insufficient tax relief to the lower income brackets, so he proposed increasing the levels of personal exemptions from $600 to $800 by 1971. Long also surprised his colleagues by attaching a 15 percent increase in Social Security benefits that had been passed by Ways and Means.[86] The final Senate bill, which passed by a vote of 62–30, contained about $3 billion more in tax reductions than the House bill, with fewer reform measures.

The Tax Reform Act of 1969

Following the Senate vote, Mills kept the Conference Committee in marathon sessions that lasted up to eighteen hours a day. By the end of the closed sessions, free from the gaze of interest groups, Mills had eliminated many of the costly amendments that the Senate had adopted.[87] The legislation restored many of the reforms that were not included in the Senate bill. As passed by Congress, the Tax Reform Act of 1969 curtailed over seventy-five tax breaks. The legislation increased the personal exemption from $600 to $750 by 1973, and increased the maximum standard deduction from 10 percent of income, with a maximum deduction of $1,000, to 15 percent and $2,000 in stages by 1973. The bill also eliminated the unlimited char-

---

[84] Wilbur D. Mills, "Tax Simplification from the Viewpoint of the Legislator," in *Essays on Taxation: Contributed in Memory of Colin Stam* (New York: Tax Foundation, 1974), 78–79.

[85] David Kennedy, "Remarks before the American Petroleum Institute," 10 November 1969, NA, RG 128, Box 495, File: Kennedy, David.

[86] Editorial, "Tax Spree in the Senate," *The Washington Post*, 12 December 1969.

[87] Editorial, "Improved Tax-Reform Bill," *The Washington Post*, Sunday, 21 December 1969, Section B; "How Mills ran the tax makers' marathon," *Business Week*, 27 December 1969, 70–71.

itable contributions deduction and made sure that by prohibiting self-dealing, foundations used their huge wealth for the purposes for which they had secured a tax exemption. The bill also increased the maximum tax on capital gains, limited real-estate depreciation schedules, eliminated the tax credit for investments, reduced the oil depletion allowance to 23 percent, and restricted the tax benefits granted to corporate mergers.[88]

Congress imposed a maximum tax of 50 percent on taxable income. Despite Mills's previous lack of enthusiasm for the minimum tax, he incorporated it, at a rate of 10 percent, into the legislation to satisfy legislators who perceived its symbolic value.[89] There were smaller reforms as well. The legislation, for example, enabled more people to choose to have their tax computed by the Internal Revenue Service. According to the JCIRT staff, the Tax Reform Act of 1969 broke with the regressive precedents of previous legislation and offered the largest benefits to lower income brackets.[90] Finally, the legislation included a 15 percent boost in Social Security benefits. In 1969, Congress also increased the tax rates on married couples, thereby reducing the disparity with non-married wage-earners.

Nixon signed the legislation into law on December 30. Despite all the limitations, the reforms were significant. Given the structure of the tax code, any successful modification of the tax-break system represented a considerable achievement. The deliberations also served as an important foundation for tax reformers in the coming decades, particularly those who were to participate in the debates of the Tax Reform Act of 1986. To be sure, some defenders of the existing system criticized the concept of the tax expenditure for its comparison of tax breaks with direct expenditures. Critics said that public spending provided people with money that was not originally their own. But tax breaks were a way for citizens to avoid paying an obligation that had been imposed on their private property by the federal government. The ability of the government to tax income, they said, was a privilege in a democratic, capitalist society, while every citizen had a natural right to retain earned income.[91]

Nonetheless, the concept of a tax expenditure budget gained currency in the tax community and Congress and, to a limited extent, outside of Washington. Most policymakers agreed that despite its limitations, the legislation constituted an important victory. The tax expenditure concept revealed how wealthy citizens, elderly retirees,

[88] "Closing the Depletion Allowance," *The New York Times*, 24 July 1969.
[89] Mills, "The Tax Reform Act of 1969," 26–43.
[90] Witte, *The Politics and Development of the Federal Income Tax*, 172.
[91] Norman Ture, interview with Julian Zelizer in Washington, D.C., 13 December 1993.

middle-class consumers, philanthropic institutions, powerful economic organizations, and other segments of society profited from the "hidden" budget of the federal government. The concept also provided a new understanding of the role of the tax system in the national economy, for even the most arcane provisions in the revenue code produced a dramatic effect on private investment.[92]

THE REFORMERS MARCH FORWARD

In the coming years, Surrey continued to develop the concept of the tax expenditure as a Professor of Law at Harvard University. He maintained a particularly close association with Joseph Pechman and the Brookings Institution, with whom he conducted annual conferences on these matters in Washington, D.C. In several published articles, Surrey argued that the task of tax reform lay in a systematic exploration of the Tax Expenditure Budget. Reform, Surrey explained, had become inseparably linked with the problem of government expenditures. This new understanding raised a series of questions that reformers had previously ignored: "Is tax assistance really required by national priorities? If so, is tax assistance the preferred route, or should the assistance be given directly? Which method comes closest to the targeted goal of the assistance and does so with fairness and efficiency?"[93] The Treasury continued to publish the Tax Expenditure Budget annually for the tax-writing committees.

Just as Medicare stimulated proposals for the introduction of general revenue into social insurance, the tax expenditure studies intensified discontent among a younger generation of policymakers with the income-tax system. The debates planted the seeds for the attack on the tax code that took place in 1986. Indeed, the Tax Reform Act of 1986 saw the implementation of the ideas of Mills's generation through a sweeping revision of the tax-break system combined with a significant rate reduction.

The Tax Reform Act of 1969 also demonstrated how difficult it had become to weed provisions out of the tax code. Legislators were much more hesitant to retract hidden subsidies than they were to enact them. Some congressional representatives openly defended the existing tax structure. Representative George Bush (R-TX), for example, said that he favored tax incentives as a nonintrusive method for the government to encourage investment. In fact, Bush was "amazed to find many Members of Congress feeling that the tax free

[92] Mills, "The Tax Reform Act of 1969," 26–43. See also Editorial, "A Long Step in Tax Reform," *The Washington Post*, 23 December 1969.
[93] Surrey, *Pathways to Tax Reform*, viii.

features on municipal bonds was a loophole. At a time when the country is literally crying out for decentralized answers – for the 'new federalism' concept that President Nixon advocates – the House charged in and passed a bill which in effect considered tax-free municipal bonds as loopholes." Bush added: "I favor tax credits and tax incentives as the way to answer many of our problems as opposed to direct Government subsidy or starting some new bureau on the Potomac to try to solve all the Nation's problems."[94]

Certainly, Bush was not alone in his remarks. The Tax Reform Act of 1969 did not attempt to eliminate the tax-break system, only to reform and control it. Most tax shelters were reduced or tightened but not eliminated, as seen in the lowering of the oil depletion allowance. Other important reforms, such as the capital gains tax on income transferred at death, were lost in the legislative mills. Congress placed much emphasis on the minimum tax, which built on the existing provisions without fundamentally restructuring the code.[95] In 1972, Mills criticized the popular impression that tax breaks were only for the wealthy. In fact, he said, people from all income brackets enjoyed the benefits of these provisions. "I can't conceive of Congress denying the young couple just married, trying to buy a home, the right to deduct interest from their income – that is, the interest they pay on the mortgage, from their income before paying income taxes. That was done for an economic reason as well as a social reason." Mills explained this with an example: "The social reason was to get people to become homeowners rather than to live in rented spaces. In addition, the economic reason was to stimulate the housing industry. I think both purposes have been noticed by all as having been accomplished. I just can't conceive of Congress taking those types of preferences away from people."[96]

Ultimately, policymakers such as Mills and Surrey argued that tax reform was designed to maintain a modified progressive tax structure that contained some economically efficient and politically necessary deductions, exemptions, and exceptions. Reflecting on the 1969 legislation, Mills explained to a group of tax accountants: "Anyone who is at all familiar with the subject of taxes knows that tax reform is a continuous process. For one thing, it is necessary continually to revise the tax laws to conform to changing underlying economic and institutional conditions." Mills concluded: "As we gain experience with the effects of various provisions and can look at them in the per-

[94] U.S. Congress, House of Representatives, Committee on Ways and Means, *Congressional Record*, 91st Cong., 1st sess., 22 December 1969, 40883–40885.

[95] Witte, *The Politics of Taxation*, 173.

[96] *Transcript: Meet the Press*, 11 June 1972, WMPC, Box 397, File 3.

spective of time, we are better able to evaluate them. Provisions which may have been appropriate at the time they were adopted may not be appropriate now or in the future."[97]

This conversation highlighted the tension at the heart of tax reform. On the one hand, policymakers believed in the concept of tax neutrality, meaning that the tax code should have as little effect as possible on the private economy. On the other hand, these policymakers accepted that "tax expenditures" played an important role in private investment decisions since tax breaks were an alternative to more stringent government regulation. Successful tax reform, in the minds of Mills and Surrey, should achieve a balance between extreme tax neutrality and a sheer excess of tax breaks. While the tax laws should encourage certain types of investment decisions that would otherwise be stifled, such encouragement must be limited to particular areas of the economy. Mills later wrote:

> In drafting the tax laws, the legislator must take into account revenue, economic, equity, and other considerations as well as tax simplicity. It is a happy coincidence when all of these objectives coincide so that they can be achieved simultaneously. Often, however, the different objectives appear to conflict. A provision, which raises the necessary revenue, is equitable and has desirable economic effects, for example, may be complicated; while an alternative provision, which is relatively simple, may not be as fair or as desirable on economic grounds. In such cases, the legislator must make a tradeoff between the various goals in order to arrive at a provision which does justice but yet is not so complex that it is unworkable. The exact nature of the tradeoff in any particular instance, of course, becomes a matter of judgment and different people, including experts in the matter, often reach different conclusions as to what is the best combination of these factors in a given case.[98]

It would be the responsibility of tax-writing committees, assisted by their experts, to decide which provisions fit within this balance.

During the late 1960s, this type of balance seemed possible. Assisted by the special congressional rules that helped insulate Ways and Means from House members and their interest groups, Mills and his colleagues had been able to constrain the tax-break system. Because of the executive sessions, interest groups were unable to monitor the final deliberations of the committee. On the House floor,

---

[97] Wilbur D. Mills, "The Prospects for Tax Reform in the 93rd Congress," *The National Public Accountant*, February 1973, 10.

[98] Mills, "Tax Simplification from the Viewpoint of the Legislator," 76–77.

moreover, representatives could not propose amendments to legislation. As a result, the number of tax breaks in the tax code during the 1960s remained modest compared with what emerged during the following decade.

In the end, the legislation demonstrated to many Washington pundits that Congress, through the tax-writing committees, could enact substantive reform despite the opposition of powerful interests. Most important, tax reform was not part of the radical struggles taking place on the streets of urban cities, nor was it a call for redistribution of the nation's wealth from the rich to the poor. Rather, the tax reform faction presented its program as an essential component for economic growth and for providing equitable tax treatment to the middle class. In 1969, members of the tax community had provided a display of technical knowledge, appealing rhetoric, and bargaining techniques, ranging from Surrey's and Woodworth's studies on tax expenditures to Mills's negotiation techniques. Together, the community had transformed its studies into policy, and enacted one of the most significant tax reforms of the postwar period.

10

Expanding Social Security

While Congress completed the Tax Reform Act of 1969, the Social Security faction of the tax community initiated a massive expansion of OASDHI that transformed the program.[1] By most indications, Social Security was a major component of the welfare system in 1969: 24 million people were receiving cash payments from Social Security every year; 18.4 million of those receiving benefits were sixty-two or older; 2.2 million were disabled workers under sixty-two and their dependents; and 3.4 million were widowed mothers and children. In June 1968, the program cost the federal government almost $28 billion. To finance benefits, 92 million wage earners paid Social Security taxes.[2]

Despite these figures, the Social Security faction insisted that cash benefits were too meager in an inflationary economy. A rapid acceleration of prices had begun in 1965 following seven years during which consumer prices rose slowly and wholesale prices had experienced almost no increase. From 1958 to 1964, Congress had only adjusted benefits once. Since 1965, Congress increased benefits twice: once in 1965 by 7 percent, and again in 1968 by 13 percent. Toward the end of 1969, the rising price level caused the purchasing power of Social Security benefits to decline once again.[3]

Between 1969 and 1972, Congress responded to inflation by expanding Social Security. There were two intertwined components to this expansion. First, the expansion involved a partisan competition between congressional Democrats and the Republican President Richard Nixon to keep benefits up to date. This competition was

---

[1] OASDHI stood for Old-Age, Survivors', Disability, and Hospital Insurance.

[2] Wilbur Cohen to President Johnson, 12 September 1968, WCP, Box 97, Folder Unmarked; U.S. Congress, House Committee on Ways and Means, *The President's Proposals For Welfare Reform and Social Security Amendments 1969*, October 1969, H2200 (Committee – Print); Secretary of Health, Education, and Welfare, *Reports of the 1971 Advisory Council on Social Security*, 1971, 92nd Cong., 1st sess., House Document No. 92–80.

[3] Daniel N. Price and Robert O. Brunner, "Automatic Adjustment of OASDHI Cash Benefits," *Social Security Bulletin* 33, No.5 (May 1970): 3.

limited to the question of how, and by how much, to expand Social Security rather than whether the program should be expanded at all. Each time the Republicans called for benefit increases in proportion to the cost-of-living, the Democrats supported more generous increases. The increase began with the Tax Reform Act of 1969, which included a 15 percent boost in Social Security benefits. Based on a projected actuarial surplus, the legislation provided an $4.4 billion annual increase without higher taxes.[4] This competition ended in 1972 with a 20 percent increase in Social Security benefits.

The second component of the expansion also began in 1969, and resulted in the indexation of Social Security to the cost-of-living (termed a Cost-Of-Living Adjustment, or a COLA). As a result of indexation, every time that the cost-of-living rose by 3 percent or more, according to the Department of Labor's Consumer Price Index, Social Security benefits would increase by the same percentage. The wage base (the maximum amount of income on which Social Security taxes were levied) would also rise automatically to finance the higher benefits through earmarked taxes. Similar versions of indexation had been implemented through labor contracts negotiated in the General Motors-United Automobile Workers Agreement of 1948, in the Military Retirement Program, and in the Civil Service Retirement Program.[5]

Despite bipartisan support for indexation, including the endorsement of Nixon, the proposal encountered fierce opposition from Mills. Foremost, Mills feared that Congress would lose control of the annual decision to raise benefits and taxes, a feature that had helped to contain the cost of the program since its inception. Before indexation, retirees' pensions remained fixed unless Congress decided to raise benefits, along with taxes. With indexation, however, that decision would be made automatically in response to the Consumer Price Index. As a result, continued inflation would guarantee a dramatic expansion of Social Security regardless of its economic cost or the desires of Congress. Even worse, Mills warned, neither Congress nor his committee would receive credit for the liberalization of social insurance benefits, an institutional prerogative he had protected throughout his tenure. Finally, indexation would make it more difficult for Congress to combat inflationary spending increases.

---

[4] Robert Ball to Wilbur Cohen, 11 October 1968; Ball to Cohen, 14 October 1968; Robert Myers, "Actuarial Cost Aspects of Keeping OASDI Benefits Up-to-Date with the Cost of Living," 16 September 1968, all in WCP, Box 129, Folder 7.
[5] Price and Brunner, "Automatic Adjustment of OASDHI Cash Benefits," 3.

In the end, Mills failed to block the passage of indexation. The chairman's struggle with alcoholism, prescription drug abuse, and chronic back disease prevented him from waging a full-scale legislative attack. More important, Mills was overwhelmed by the popularity of a program that he helped to build. The chairman found little political support for his opposition to indexation since retirees assumed that their benefits would be adequate in relation to the cost-of-living. Social Security, a program that policymakers sold to the public through the metaphor of private insurance, had taken on a life of its own. Lower-income and middle-income constitutents expected benefits, adjusted to inflation, on retirement.

INFLATION AND SOCIAL INSURANCE, 1969–1970

The Social Security debate began in 1969, when members of the tax community, the tax-writing committees, and the Nixon administration agreed that Social Security pensions were inadequate because of inflation. As Social Security Commissioner Robert Ball explained: "It is really a settled policy by now that the benefits will at least be kept up to date with changes in the purchasing power of the dollar."[6] In 1969 and 1970, two proposals emerged: a rapid increase in benefits based on an actuarial surplus (this was the method Congress had used to adjust benefits for inflation since 1939), and automatic COLAs for Social Security. These proposals were at the center of a political competition between Nixon and Mills.

Nixon and the tax community

Elected to office in 1968, Richard Nixon was the thirty-seventh president of the United States. During his first term as president, Nixon supported several expansive domestic programs for the middle class. According to one scholar, the administration believed that it should

---

[6] Cited R. Kent Weaver, *Automatic Government: The Politics of Indexation* (Washington, D.C.: The Brookings Institution, 1988), 69. Throughout this chapter, I build on the foundation provided by Weaver's analysis of this debate. His brief account of the 1969–1972 debate focuses on why Congress accepted indexation even though it seemed to conflict with the electoral interests of most politicians – namely, the ability to claim credit for benefit increases. Weaver argues that scholars must broaden their understanding of what motivates policymakers to understand policies such as indexation. Congressional representatives, for example, were willing to forgo opportunities to claim credit for the liberalization of benefits if they were more concerned with avoiding blame for unpopular decisions and/or defending institutional prerogatives. Weaver also compares the fiscal dynamics of Social Security with indexation in other programs, ranging from food stamps to dairy price supports. See pages 67–92.

target "disaffected Democrats, blue-collar working class white ethnics. We should set out to capture the vote of the forty-seven-year old Dayton housewife."[7]

The Nixon administration had a lukewarm relationship with the tax community. Although several members of that community, including Wilbur Cohen, Robert Myers, and Stanley Surrey, returned to academia at the time Nixon took office, others such as Herbert Stein, Arthur Burns, and Robert Ball remained in official positions of power. Given their expert knowledge and the continued Democratic control of Congress, those who left to go to academia or into private practice, such as Wilbur Cohen, were consulted regularly by the tax-writing committees.[8] The administration even drew on some of the staff of think tanks, such as the Brookings Institution, which were central to the community.[9] Since the community maintained its presence within Washington, and since a new community had not yet emerged, its members provided continuity with previous administrations.

The failed attempt to reform welfare

One of the Nixon administration's most celebrated efforts involved welfare reform. The aim of the reform was to shift away from "welfare" toward "workfare."[10] Drawing on the work of a presidential task force, Nixon proposed in August 1969 that Congress replace Aid to Families with Dependent Children with the Family Assistance Plan (FAP). The FAP would provide a guaranteed annual payment of about $1,600 a year for needy families, including the working poor who were eligible. Whereas AFDC penalized work, according to the administration, FAP encouraged work by providing payments to those with

---

[7] Jill Quadagno, *The Color of Welfare: How Racism Undermined the War on Poverty* (New York: Oxford University Press, 1994), 159. See also Joan Hoff, *Nixon Reconsidered* (New York: Basic Books, 1994), 1–144.

[8] Myers told one reporter that Cohen's departure to the University of Michigan made little difference to the Social Security Administration since he continued to be consulted on all legislation. See Martha Derthick, *Policymaking for Social Security* (Washington, D.C.: The Brookings Institution, 1979), 347.

[9] When Brookings president Kermit Gordon heard that administration officials were calling Brookings a "government in exile" for the Democrats, Gordon reminded them that two key administration officials – Herbert Stein and Richard Nathan – had come from Brookings, and that "to complain about the lack of Republicans when the Administration has hired some away is a bit like the child who, after killing his mother and father, pleads for mercy in the courtroom on the grounds that he is an orphan." See Donald Rumsfeld to the President's File, 23 June 1972, NPM, President's Office Files, Memoranda for the President, Box 89, File: June 18 [1972].

[10] Julius Duscha, "Mighty Mills," *The Washington Post*, 12 September 1971.

low-income jobs. Although Mills opposed this particular solution as too costly, he ended up working with the administration to shepherd the bill through the House. Mills felt that FAP had strong bipartisan support, and he did not want to end up on the losing side of this battle, especially since he supported the principle of welfare reform and he was considering a run for the presidency.[11] Even though the House passed a version of this plan in 1970 and 1971, the proposal never made it out of the Senate, where liberals claimed that benefits were too meager and conservatives complained about its expense. By 1972, Congress gave up on FAP, which experienced a quiet death in Conference Committee. In July 1972, according to Secretary of HEW Elliot Richardson, welfare was a "non-issue."[12]

Throughout the debates over FAP, Mills had promoted the concept of welfare reform. Like Nixon, the chairman targeted AFDC as a major cost in the budget.[13] During one speech to the House, Mills spoke about the "runaway growth" of AFDC. In 1950, AFDC had cost $500 million; by 1969, the number of families who were on AFDC had risen to 1.7 million, and the total cost of the program was approximately $4.5 billion. Since states and localities controlled eligibility, Mills explained, "we are completely helpless to put any restraints, controls, or limitations" on the program.[14] Mills endorsed the federalization of welfare since the states could not seem to control costs.[15] He repeatedly told Cohen that he was "disappointed with the inability of the States to control caseloads and costs," and was considering a federal program that could implement "fiscal controls . . . as com-

[11] William Timmons to President Nixon, 19 February 1970, NPM, White House Central Files, Subject Files: Welfare, Box 40, File: Social Security (69/70); Telephone Call, Nixon to John Byrnes, 5 March 1970, NPM, White House Central Files, Subject Files: Federal Government, Box 14, File: FG 33–21 House Committees – Ways and Means; Dick Cook to John Campbell, 2 February 1971; Clark MacGregor to Nixon, 25 February 1971; George Shultz to John Ehrlichman and Clark MacGregor, 4 March 1971; Timmons to Nixon, 26 April 1971; Nixon to Gerald Ford, 21 June 1971, all in NPM, White House Central Files, Subject Files: Welfare, Box 40, File: Social Security 1/1/71–12/71. See also Elliot Richardson to Nixon, 9 September 1971, NPM, White House Central File, Subject Files: FG 23, Box 3, File: FG 23 8/1/71–9/30/71.

[12] Elliot Richardson to Kenneth Cole, 31 July 1972, NPM, White House Central Files, Subject Files: Welfare, Box 11, File: WE 7/1/72–7/31/72.

[13] Richard Madden, "Relief Loss Here Put At 66-Million," The New York Times, 26 September 1969.

[14] U.S. Congress, House of Representatives, Congressional Record, 15 April 1970, 91st Cong., 2nd sess., 11878. See also Mary Switzer to Wilbur Cohen, 2 April 1968, WCP, Box 130, File 3.

[15] Fred Zimmerman, "Idea of a Federal Take-Over of Welfare Suddenly Gathers Strength in Congress," The Wall Street Journal, 5 February 1971; Joseph Alsop, "Wilbur Mills' Bombshell," The Washington Post, 21 February 1971.

pared with the 'open-ended' moral commitment to match State funds in the existing law."[16] AFDC, Mills added, encouraged the breakup of the family by providing incentives for fathers to leave home so that their wives and children could receive benefits. Mills emphasized that job training was important to reform: "Do not characterize these people generally as being lazy or shiftless or without motivation or desire. Most of them are without training. That is why they are where they are."[17] Mills also feared that recent attempts to encourage states to simplify their administrative methods for determining eligibility would converge with the welfare rights movement to further strain the coffers of government.[18]

Indexation and Social Security

Although FAP captured the attention of the media, the expansion of social insurance resulted in a more concrete transformation of public policy. The expansion began in September 1969, when President Nixon recommended the indexation of OASDI. During his message to Congress, the president proclaimed: "This Nation must not break faith with those Americans who have a right to expect that Social Security payments will protect them and their families . . . I propose that Congress make certain once and for all that the retired, the disabled and the dependent never again bear the brunt of inflation . . . This will instill new security in Social Security . . . By acting to make future benefit raises automatic with rises in the cost of living, we remove questions about future years; we do much to remove this system from biennial politics; and we make fair treatment of beneficiaries a matter of certainty rather than a matter of hope."[19]

Nixon explained that indexation would make Social Security "inflation proof."[20] The administration proposed a 10 percent

[16] Wilbur Cohen to Lyndon Johnson, 2 May 1968, WCP, Box 96, Folder Unmarked.

[17] U.S. Congress, House of Representatives, *Congressional Record*, 15 April 1970, 91st Cong., 2nd sess., 11879. See also, U.S. Congress, House of Representatives, *Congressional Record*, 31 March 1970, 91st Cong., 2nd sess., 9889–9890; U.S. Congress, House of Representatives, *Congressional Record*, 21 June 1971, 92nd Cong., 1st sess., 21089–21093.

[18] Wilbur Mills to Wilbur Cohen, 27 September 1968, WCP, Box 137, Folder 4. See also "Mills Says Nixon Agrees to Changes in Welfare Bill," *The Washington Post*, Sunday, 28 March 1971, section A.

[19] U.S. Congress, House Committee on Ways and Means, *The President's Proposals for Welfare Reform and Social Security Amendments 1969*, October 1969, H2200 (Committee – Print), 1.

[20] Paul O'Neill to Ken Cole, 22 March 1972, NPM, White House Central Files, Subject Files: Welfare, Box 40, File: Social Security [1/72–6/72] and John Ehrlichman to President Nixon, 1969, NPM, White House Central Files, Subject Files: Welfare, Box 40, File: Social Security (69/70).

increase in Social Security along with the indexation of benefits and the wage base beginning in 1972.[21] By indexing the program, according to the president, Congress would protect Social Security from partisan politics. By delegating its authority, Congress could prevent decisions about benefits from turning into a "political football" during an era of inflation.[22] Indexation would contain future spending increases by preventing partisan bidding wars over liberalization. These statements echoed Lyndon Johnson, who declared in 1968 that Congress should increase benefits by 50 percent within the coming decade and index benefits for inflation.[23]

Much of the administration's proposals were rooted in the findings of the tax community. Robert Myers and Wilbur Cohen, for example, claimed that a 15 percent increase in benefits would be actuarially sound without any significant change in the tax rates.[24] Myers explained, despite his own opposition to liberalized cash benefits, that Congress continued to generate an excess of revenue through the "level-wage assumption." Should Congress abandon the level-wage assumption and predict continued wage increases, Myers added hesitantly, it could even afford to raise benefits by 50 percent.[25] But Myers warned that if the assumption of higher wages turned out to be incorrect, Congress would have to rely on a general-revenue contribution or enact a massive tax increase.[26] Finally, Myers claimed that the earmarked tax system could support indexation without a change in the tax rates if the wage base rose automatically with benefits.[27]

[21] Kenneth Cole to Peter Flanigan and Bryce Harlow, 17 March 1970, NPM, White House Central Files, Subject Files: Welfare, Box 40, File: Social Security (69/70).

[22] U.S. Congress, House Committee on Ways and Means, *The President's Proposals for Welfare Reform and Social Security Amendments 1969*, H2200 (Committee – Print), 1.

[23] Wilbur Cohen to Joseph Califano, Jr., 5 October 1968, WCP, Box 97, Folder Unmarked.

[24] Robert Ball to Wilbur Cohen, 25 September 1968 and Robert Myers to Manuel Levine, 13 September 1968 in WCP, Box 129, Folder 7; Wilbur Cohen to Herman Schneebeli, 4 October 1968, WCP, Box 98, File: Unmarked. See also, Cohen to President Lyndon B. Johnson, 24 October 1968, WCP, Box 97, File: Unmarked; Cohen, interview with David McComb, 8 December 1968, LBJL, Oral History Interview Collection, Tape 2, 16; Marjorie Hunter, "20 percent Benefits Rise For Aged Favored," *The New York Times*, 20 November 1969; John Nolan to Robert Mayo, 19 May 1969, NAT, RG 56, Office of Tax Policy, Box 36, File: Social Security Amendments of 1969.

[25] Robert Myers to Robert Ball, 26 September 1968; Ball to Wilbur Cohen, 25 September 1968; Ball to Cohen, 14 October 1968. Aforementioned documents are in WCP, Box 129, Folder 7.

[26] Robert Myers to Robert Ball, 26 April 1968 and Ball to Wilbur Cohen, 26 April 1968, WCP, Box 129, Folder 1.

[27] Myers, "Actuarial Cost Aspects of Keeping OASDI Benefits Up-to-Date with the Cost of Living"; Robert Myers to Robert Ball, 26 April 1968, WCP, Box 129, Folder 1.

Leading economists at Brookings, including Joseph Pechman, also published a study that endorsed indexation.[28]

Mills's alternative and his concerns

To combat the problem of inflation, Mills supported an across-the-board increase in Social Security benefits by 15 percent. The chairman wanted to raise the wage base to $12,000 by 1972.[29] In his statements, Mills agreed that benefits were inadequate, and that Congress should raise benefits based on the actuarial surplus, as it had done five times since 1950. As long as the earmarked tax system remained intact, Mills was prepared to support the expansion of social insurance for the elderly. John Byrnes urged that Ways and Means limit the increase to 10 percent.[30] Nonetheless, Republican House leader Gerald Ford (R-MI) favored Mills's 15 percent increase, and even Byrnes admitted that there was a strong possibility of a 20 percent increase if the 15 percent figure were rejected.[31]

At the same time, Mills expressed three reservations about the expansion of Social Security. First, he was concerned about recent proposals to use general revenue to subsidize benefit increases and to reduce the tax contribution of low-income workers.[32] The tension between the program's administrators, who depended on the expansion of benefits, and its fiscal guardians, who depended on controlling payroll taxes and avoiding strain on income taxation, had become more intense. A group of economists at the Treasury and Brookings, for example, had endorsed general-revenue finance to make the tax system more equitable. Robert Ball, moreover, said that after Congress enacted a graduated 50 percent increase in benefits, along with an automatic adjustment of the wage base, policymakers should consider a general-revenue subsidy to increase benefits further.[33] Based on his efforts since 1950 to exclude general revenue, Mills could not accept such proposals, "If we keep this system wage-related, then I think that Social Security can go down into the

---

[28] Joseph A. Pechman, Henry J. Aaron, and Michael K. Taussig, *Social Security: Perspectives For Reform* (Washington, DC.: The Brookings Institution, 1968), 220.

[29] Edwin Dale, Jr., "Mills Will Seek 1970 Benefit Rise in Social Security," *The New York Times*, 5 May 1969; "If Wilbur Mills Gets His Way on Spending and Taxes," *U.S. News & World Report*, 19 May 1969, 78–80.

[30] Bryce Harlow to President Nixon, 8 December 1969, NPM, White House Central Files, Subject Files: Welfare, Box 40, File: Social Security (69/70).

[31] Lamar Alexander to the Staff Secretary, 10 December 1969, NPM, White House Central Files, Subject Files: Welfare, Box 40, File: Social Security (69/70).

[32] "Who Foots What Bill For Social Security?" *Business Week*, 13 January 1968, 110–111.

[33] Robert Ball to Wilbur Cohen, 26 April 1968, WCP, Box 129, Folder 1.

future as a great program . . . If we are going to make out of it a welfare program, then I doubt very frankly that the American people will submit to this periodic increase in taxes, and this periodic increase in the wage base." [34]

Second, Mills opposed indexation on a variety of grounds. Foremost, indexation would bypass the power of Congress over Social Security taxation.[35] Throughout his chairmanship, Mills had repeatedly opposed any proposal that curtailed the constitutional right of the Congress to control taxation. Indexation, Mills added, was unnecessary since Congress had raised benefits frequently over the years to compensate for the cost-of-living: "I have thought that the Congress itself has done a pretty good job of enacting Social Security increases to take care of cost-of-living increases. . . . The American people can rely on the Congress to continue without us having to enact automatic adjusters."[36] Finally, Mills warned that indexation was fiscally irresponsible. Since the tax-writing committees would lose control over Social Security, they would find themselves paralyzed if inflation, in addition to continued discretionary increases above and beyond indexation, raised the cost of the program to unbearable levels.[37]

The chairman received support from many umbrella business organizations that argued that indexation would make it difficult for the government to control inflation.[38] The Chamber of Commerce's Henry Chase warned: "If the cost-of-living escalator is incorporated in the social security program, it will inevitably spread to other public programs, private pension plans, and, conceivably, to the entire wage structure . . . It is difficult to visualize a more likely means of institutionalizing inflation, barring, of course, a flat mandate that the total wage structure in this country be predicated on a cost-of-living escalator."[39] Arthur Burns, one of Nixon's top economic advisors, branded

[34] Cited in "Who Foots What Bill For Social Security?", 110–111. See also Wilbur Cohen, interview with David McComb, 8 December 1968, LBJL, Oral History Interview Collection, Tape 2, 15–16.

[35] Weaver, *Automatic Government*, 72–73.

[36] "Nixon, Mills, McCracken – A Look At Policies of the Future," *U.S. News & World Report*, 23 April 1968, 34. See also Marjorie Hunter, "Mills to Oppose Linking Pensions to Living Cost," *The New York Times*, 27 September 1969; Marjorie Hunter, "G.O.P. Urges Jan 1. For Pension Rise," *The New York Times*, 25 September 1969; "One-upping Nixon on Social Security," *Business Week*, 11 October 1969, 42–43.

[37] Robert J. Myers, *Social Security* (Bryn Mawr, Pennsylvania: McCahan Foundation,1975), 103–106.

[38] Derthick, *Policymaking for Social Security*, 349.

[39] Cited in Weaver, *Automatic Government*, 72. See also John Ehrlichman to President Nixon, 1969, NPM, White House Central Files, Subject Files: Welfare, Box 40, File: Social Security (69/70).

automatic COLAs as "bad economics."[40] From a different perspective, the AFL-CIO opposed indexation since the Consumer Price Index did not adequately reflect the cost-of-living. They found some support from Cohen, who argued that indexation was "settling for too little that was too inadequate and inconsistent with an expanding dynamic economy."[41]

Third, Mills was concerned with the rising cost of Medicare, a program that was partially financed through the same Social Security tax that paid for cash benefits. As a result of skyrocketing medical prices, the cost of hospitalization insurance had grown much faster than the portion of revenue allotted to the program. Medical prices were increasing faster than any expert had predicted in 1965.[42] The principle causes of this increase were higher utilization of hospitals (partially attributable to Medicare) and the rising wages of hospital workers and physicians.[43] Until Congress addressed this problem, Medicare threatened to strain the earmarked tax system.

Together, these problems – the threat of general-revenue finance, the problems of indexation and inflation, and the financial burden Medicare imposed on payroll taxes – caused Mills to be cautious in his support for expanding Social Security. "I just want to become convinced," Mills explained to reporter Sam Donaldson, "that it will not do to the cash Social Security program what has been happening to the Hospital-Medicare program, wherein we have been unable to keep it correctly financed."[44] Mills ultimately lost control of the expansion as a result of personal problems, political ambition, and the sheer popularity of Social Security.

The debate over how to expand Social Security

When Ways and Means conducted hearings between October and November, all sorts of policymakers supported the expansion of OASDHI. Secretary of HEW Robert Finch endorsed indexation as the

---

[40] Rogers Morton to Bob Haldeman, 15 May 1969, NPM, White House Central Files, Subject Files: Welfare, Box 40, File: Social Security (69/70).

[41] Wilbur Cohen, interview with David McComb, 8 December 1968, LBJL, Oral History Interview Collection, Tape 2, 16.

[42] "HEW Report Analyzes Medical Costs," *Medical World News*, 17 March 1967, 32–33; Howard West, "Five Years of Medicare – A Statistical Review," *Social Security Bulletin* 34, No. 12 (December 1971): 17–27.

[43] Wilbur Cohen to Wilbur Mills, 13 June 1968, WCP, Box 97, Folder Unmarked; William Gorham to Cohen, 29 February 1968 and Dorothy Rice to Cohen, 22 April 1968, WCP, Box 109, Folder 4; Cohen to Lyndon Johnson, 17 December 1968, WCP, Box 98, Folder Unmarked.

[44] *Transcript: ABC's Issues and Answers*, 7 November 1971, WMPC, Box 397, File 18.

ultimate solution to inflation.[45] Finch, accompanied by Ball and
Myers, explained that the 10 percent increase covered the 8.2 percent
increase in the cost-of-living since August 1969. Under existing conditions, Ball and Myers insisted that the OASI Trust Fund would accumulate a surplus of over $15 billion by 1973. This money, they
thought, should be spent for a benefit increase.[46] Commenting on the
administration's proposal to raise benefits without increasing taxes,
one observer aptly explained: "The Social Security trust fund is
actuarially so sound that it runneth over, by tens of billions of
dollars yet."[47]

During the hearings, the AFL-CIO favored a 50 percent increase
in benefits. Andrew Biemiller, the organization's lobbyist, explained
that "the unpleasant truth is that social security benefits, which should
be a main bulwark against poverty, have not been adequate at any
time in the history of the program." Turning to the traditional
rhetoric, Biemiller warned that the failure to expand social insurance
would force more people to rely on welfare. He insisted that current
problems could not be solved by "periodic tinkering with the system,"
and his experts called for a 20 percent increase in 1969, to be followed by a 30 percent increase in the next two years. "Social security
beneficiaries," Biemiller concluded, "have the right to maintain the
real value of their benefits in the face of rising living costs as well as
to participate in the Nation's increasing standard of living." Regarding finance, the AFL-CIO proposed that Congress use the actuarial
surplus to increase benefits without raising taxes. Congress, moreover,
should incorporate general revenue into social insurance until it
financed one-third of the total cost.[48]

Throughout the hearings, Mills articulated his concerns about the
expansion. Using his actuarial knowledge, Mills repeatedly turned
the committee's attention to the mounting cost of Medicare and the
burden that program placed on the Social Security tax. In a heated
exchange with Ball and Myers, the chairman grilled the two experts
about medical inflation. He reminded them that the Hospital Insurance Trust Fund would be depleted by 1973 unless Social Security
taxes were increased.[49] While questioning Myers, Mills asked:

[45] U.S. Congress, House Committee on Ways and Means, *Social Security and Welfare Pro-
    posals: Hearings*, October 15-November 13, 1969, 91st Cong., 1st sess., 130–131.
[46] Ibid., 175.
[47] "Social Security's Galloping Surplus," *Business Week*, 18 October 1969, 41–42.
[48] U.S. Congress, House Committee on Ways and Means, *Social Security and Welfare
    Proposals: Hearings*, October 15-November 13, 1969, 91st Cong., 1st sess.,
    1778–1785.
[49] For the best data concerning this issue, see Board of Trustees of the Federal Hos-
    pital Insurance Trust Fund, *1971 Annual Report of the Board of Trustees of the Federal*

Do you remember the interrogation that occurred when we were considering this matter in 1965 [Medicare], when former Secretary Celebrezze sat there and he was surrounded by some of the finest looking, most intelligent men I had seen up to that time – you, and Mr. Ball, and Mr. Cohen, and a few others – when I was interrogating you about the costs of this hospital program and whether or not there was a possibility that for 5 or 6 years of hospital costs might rise at a rate of about twice the increase of the earnings level? Do you remember all that . . . Without trying to make myself the one with the white hat and somebody else with a black hat, who turned out to be more nearly correct? Have hospital costs gone up over a 5-year period at about twice the rate of the rise in earnings levels?[50]

Myers responded: "That, unfortunately, is correct." Mills reminded Myers that in 1967, Congress had borrowed from the OASI Trust Fund and transferred extra revenue into the Hospital Insurance Trust Fund. When Myers challenged the statement on technical grounds, Mills replied: "That may not be the technical way to describe it, but down in my country I think they would have said they had taken water out of one pail and put it in the other with a gourd or something. It is immaterial how we discuss it or how it happened. I know we did find ourselves short in the hospital trust fund on that occasion. Now we find ourselves short just 2 years later." The chairman found this situation "alarming" since there was no prospect of the rising cost leveling.[51]

Mills also continued to attack indexation. He told Ball that "I have tried to find some precedent for this idea of an automatic increase in the taxable base, which is an automatic increase in taxes of certain individuals, that you could look to, to justify this, and I have been unable to find any precedent where the Congress ever in the past has, without certainty and definiteness, passed legislation that would provide for automatic increases in the taxes of individuals . . . And I have never known of any time in the past when the Congress has ever left to such indefiniteness and uncertainty the matter of future taxes."[52] Mills feared that the wage base might rise to unbearable

---

Hospital Insurance Trust Fund, 1971, 92nd Cong., 1st sess., House Document No. 92–87. See also Board of Trustees of Federal Supplementary Medical Insurance Trust Fund, *1971 Annual Report of the Board of Trustees of the Federal Supplementary Insurance Trust Fund*, 1971, 92nd Cong., 1st sess., House Document No. 92–89.

[50] U.S. Congress, House Committee on Ways and Means, *Social Security and Welfare Proposals: Hearings*, October 15–November 13, 1969, 91st Cong., 1st sess., 187.

[51] Ibid., 187–189.

[52] Ibid., 197.

levels within a few years as a result of inflation. Myers, under Mills's prodding, admitted that existing rates of inflation could push the wage base up to $18,000 by 1989.[53]

The expansion of Social Security begins

On December 5, 1969, Ways and Means reported out a bill that increased Social Security benefits by 15 percent without a tax increase.[54] The House passed the bill by a vote of 398 to 0. Soon after, the Senate attached an amendment to the Tax Reform Act of 1969. Mills urged the House to support the amendment in light of the 9.1 percent increase in the cost-of-living that had taken place since the last benefit increase in February 1968.[55] The increase was to be financed through the "unanticipated surplus." Byrnes supported the increase while he urged future support for indexation. The ranking Republican painted a partisan portrait of the economic situation when he explained to his colleagues: "Runaway inflation was a part of the fiscal mess the new administration inherited when it took office earlier this year."[56] Congress passed the Tax Reform Act, along with the Social Security amendment, on December 22, 1969. Eight days later, Nixon signed the tax bill into law.

By January 1970, Ways and Means worked to expand Social Security further. On May 14, 1970, the committee reported out the Social Security Amendments of 1970, which provided a 5 percent increase in cash benefits without indexation.[57] The bill raised the wage base from $7,800 to $9,000 and raised tax rates to 5.2 percent in 1971 from 4.2 percent. Finally, the legislation contained several measures to reduce the cost of Medicare, including an option for Medicare beneficiaries to use Health Maintenance Organizations, an increase in the portion of Social Security taxes going to the Hospital Insurance Trust Fund, and additional limitations on physicians' fee increases.[58]

---

[53] Ibid., 204–205.
[54] U.S. Congress, House Committee on Ways and Means, *Social Security Amendments of 1969: Report*, 91st Cong., 1st sess., 1969.
[55] U.S. Congress, House of Representatives, *Congressional Record*, 15 December 1969, 91st Cong., 1st sess., 39008.
[56] Ibid., 39010.
[57] William Timmons to Ken Cole, 1 April 1970, NPM, White House Central Files, Subject Files: Welfare, Box 40, File: Social Security (69/70).
[58] U.S. Congress, House Committee on Ways and Means, *Press Release Announcing Summary of Decisions With Respect to Amendments To The Social Security Act*, 4 May 1970 H8659 (Committee – Print); "House Panel's Republicans Decry Approval of Bill to Lift Social Security Benefits 5 percent," *The Wall Street Journal*, 15 May 1970.

On the House floor, Mills lost control of the bill when the Republicans secured enough votes to push through an amendment for indexation. On May 21, 1970, the House passed the Social Security bill by a vote of 344 to 32 after adding a measure to index benefits and taxes. Before the final vote, Mills desperately tried to convince his colleagues that indexation would harm the program: "What they are asking the Congress to do is to give up the last restraining, sole possession that it has of all the functions that were given to the Congress in the Constitution and that is, namely, determining what an individual's tax will be." Mills added: "I hope that my colleagues in the House will fully understand before they pass judgment that they are giving up control of the social security tax; they are giving up control of social security benefits, and Congress will be out of business unless they want to go along with the administration, whatever administration may be in office, and say we are not satisfied with just the increased cost of living for which we have already used all possible increase in the base within the tax, we are out of business because we just cannot raise the tax itself at the same time that they do it downtown."[59] The chairman had stressed that this was not a partisan issue since he refused to cede the power to tax to Kennedy or Johnson when they requested it for income taxation.[60] When Mills sensed an impending loss, he made one final appeal to self-interest: "This is what it boils down to: Is the Congress going to get any credit for the future adjustments of benefits, or are we going to do what the gentleman from Wisconsin (Mr. Byrnes) suggests: Let the Secretary of Health, Education and Welfare get all of that credit – and be accused in the forthcoming election of having voted in 1970 to fix the amount of income subject to tax at better than $22,000?"[61] But in the end, the House passed legislation that included automatic COLAs.

The Senate Finance Committee conducted hearings on the House bill between June and December. These deliberations were slow since the Senate was also considering the controversial Family Assistance Plan. On December 11, the committee reported out a bill that included a 10 percent increase in benefits (as opposed to the 5 percent increase of the House bill) and an indexation provision. Under the Senate bill, benefits adjustments were to be financed through an automatic increase in tax rates and through an automatic increase in the wage base; the House bill had relied entirely on the

[59] U.S. Congress, House of Representatives, *Congressional Record*, 21 May 1970, 91st Cong., 2nd Sess., 16582.

[60] Ibid., 16582.

[61] Ibid., 16582. See also Weaver, *Automatic Government*, 73; "Tying Social Security To Cost of Living: The Prospects," *U.S. News & World Report*, 8 June 1970, 57–59.

wage base. Finally, the Senate bill included reforms of Medicare, including a revised tax schedule for hospital insurance and a peer review system to monitor Medicare services. On December 29, the Senate passed the legislation, including indexation, by a vote of 91 to 0.

But Mills delayed the legislation's passage by claiming that it was "utterly impossible" for a Conference Committee to negotiate a compromise within a few days.[62] The chairman received praise from Nelson Cruikshank, now president of the National Council of Senior Citizens, who wrote that his organization was relieved that Congress had not taken "hasty action" by settling for an inadequate bill. Cruikshank reminded the chairman that the modest increase in benefits that passed the House had already been negated by inflation.[63] In response, Mills promised that Social Security would be the first item on the committee's agenda in the coming year.

Robert Myers resigns

Some fiscal conservatives, including Robert Myers, voiced their opposition to these developments. At the time, Myers was involved in a heated personal battle with Robert Ball. When Nixon had become president, Myers wanted to replace Ball as commissioner of Social Security. Although, according to Cohen, Myers had been "so important to Mills in giving Mills assurance that any social security bill Mills approved was actuarially and financially sound," Mills supported Ball for the position.[64] During this controversy, Myers attacked Ball and the expansionist mind set of the Social Security Administration. He warned that if the "expansionists" had their way, "the federal government's programs will be expanded to the point where the already overgrown social welfare octopus would be further increased with a commensurate crippling reduction in the opportunity of the private sector of the economy."[65]

When Myers failed to garner enough support for the nomination, he resigned from the Social Security Administration in 1970, dis-

[62] Warren Weaver Jr., "Senate Votes Pension Bill, But Hope of Rise Now Dims," *The New York Times*, 30 December 1970.

[63] Nelson Cruikshank to Wilbur Mills, 23 December 1970, NPM, White House Central Files, Subject Files: Welfare, Box 40, File: Social Security (69/70).

[64] Wilbur Cohen to Arthur Altmeyer, 25 June 1969, WCP, Box 6, Folder 5.

[65] Peter Flanigan to Robert Finch, 21 October 1969 and E.J. Faulkner to George Cook, 7 October 1969 both in NPM, White House Central Files, Subject Files: Welfare, Box 40, File: Social Security (69/70).

gusted with the "irresponsible" increase in benefits.[66] Cohen avoided any response since he feared that a public conflict would "endanger the integrity of the Social Security system."[67] Charles Trowbridge, an actuary from the private insurance industry, replaced Myers. Since Trowbridge was less attached to the traditions of Social Security finance, Myers's resignation had significant implications for public policy as Congress moved to liberalize the program.

RETHINKING FINANCE, 1971

During the early months of 1971, the Senate attached an amendment to a bill that extended the public debt ceiling, increasing Social Security benefits by 10 percent.[68] On the Senate floor, Russell Long (D-LA), chairman of Senate Finance, pleaded with his colleagues to take immediate action. Within a month, the House and Senate enacted the increase. Congress financed the increase by raising the wage base, scheduling a future tax increase, and drawing on the actuarial surplus from rising earnings.

The threat of general revenue returns

The increase whetted the appetite of those seeking to redesign Social Security. There were new proposals for general-revenue finance. In April, the Democratic majority on the Special Senate Committee on Aging urged Congress to consider financing another increase in benefits out of the general-revenue fund to avoid burdening the payroll tax. A network of economists from the Treasury, Brookings, MIT, and Yale University, moreover, perceived this expansion as an opportunity to restructure Social Security finance on a more equitable basis. They argued that the pressures of inflation, and the precedent established by Supplementary Medical Insurance, supported the use of general revenue.[69] Former Ways and Means economist Gerard Brannon complained that Social Security taxes hurt middle-class workers who paid high contributions, but would not receive weighted benefits.[70] Arguing that it was a "conceptual defect"

---

[66] Edward Berkowitz, *Mr. Social Security: The Life of Wilbur J. Cohen* (Lawrence: University Press of Kansas, 1995), 290.

[67] Wilbur Cohen to Arthur Altmeyer, 25 June 1969, WCP, Box 6, Folder 5.

[68] Richard Nathan to Bill Gifford, 20 January 1971, NPM, White House Central Files, Subject Files: Welfare, Box 40, File: Social Security 1/1/71–12/71.

[69] J. Douglas Brown, *An American Philosophy of Social Security: Evolution and Issues* (Princeton: Princeton University Press, 1972), 104–107.

[70] Gerard Brannon to Mr. Nolan, 8 April 1971 and "Meeting of Advisory Council on Social Security," 1 June 1970, NAT, RG 56, Office of Tax Policy, Box 40, File: Advisory Council on Social Security.

to equate Social Security with private insurance, Brannon claimed that general revenues could be used without undermining the program.[71] General-revenue subsidies gained momentum through legislation proposed by Senators Edmund Muskie (D-ME) and Walter Mondale (D-MN) that incorporated nonearmarked monies into Social Security.[72]

The Advisory Council on Social Security

The next important development occurred in March 1971, when the Advisory Council on Social Security issued its report.[73] The Council, which had been established by the Social Security Administration, included Gabriel Hauge (Manufacturers Hanover Trust Company), Charles Siegfried (Metropolitan Life Insurance Company), Douglas Brown (Princeton University), Walter Burke (the United Steelworkers of America), Kermit Gordon (Brookings Institution), and several other Social Security experts. During two years of meetings, Gordon headed the subcommittee on Social Security Finance. The subcommittee consulted with several economists and independent actuaries, including Otto Eckstein of Harvard University, Nancy Teeters of the Brookings Institution, and Murray Latimer, an actuary who helped design Social Security in 1934.[74]

The Advisory Council's final report offered several recommendations. Most important, it suggested that Congress abandon the level-wage assumption. They argued that it was time to abandon this actuarial practice, which limited scheduled benefits, given skyrocketing inflation. By doing so, Congress could schedule higher benefits by assuming that revenue would rise along with wages.[75] This proposal would have encountered fierce resistance within the Social Security Administration had Myers, a strong advocate of the level-wage

---

[71] "Summary of Issues Covered in Memoranda Submitted to the Advisory Council on Social Security," 14 August 1970, NAT, RG 56, Office of Tax Policy, Box 40, File: Advisory Council on Social Security.

[72] Wilbur Cohen, "Comments on S. 2656-Social Security Financing Bill," 2 February 1972, WCP, Box 223, Folder 11; Wilbur Cohen to Walter Mondale, 19 November 1971, WCP, Box 242, Folder 2; Mr. Gold to Mr. Bailey and Mr. Ott, 29 November 1972, NAT, RG 56, Office of Tax Policy, Box 36, File: Social Security.

[73] Secretary of Health, Education, and Welfare, *Reports of the 1971 Advisory Council on Social Security*, 1971, 92nd Cong., 1st sess., House Document No. 92–80.

[74] Derthick, *Policymaking for Social Security*, 353; Secretary of Health, Education, and Welfare, *Reports of the 1971 Advisory Council on Social Security*.

[75] Secretary of Health, Education, and Welfare, *Reports of the 1971 Advisory Council on Social Security*; C.L. Trowbridge to Robert Ball, December 1971 and "Background Material for the Advisory Council on Social Security," 1971 in NAT, RG 56, Office of Tax Policy, Box 40, File: Advisory Council on Social Security.

assumption, remained in office.[76] Trowbridge, however, seemed willing to abandon the practice.[77]

Second, the Council urged Congress to adopt a "current cost" basis of finance. This recommendation legitimized the "pay-as-you-go" system that had been used in 1950, the system that used monthly taxes to pay for monthly benefits and for a small contingency reserve.[78] Under the "current cost" plan, Congress would schedule taxes and benefits on the assumption that wages would rise. In short, this would maintain the pay-as-you-go system while no longer accumulating "unanticipated surpluses." The Board of Trustees would report when the Trust Fund grew outside the range of 75 percent to 125 percent of the following year's estimated expenditures so that Congress could adjust the system accordingly.[79]

Through this modification of the system, the Council wanted to be more honest about Social Security finance. "Current-cost financing should result in better public understanding and better long-range public relations than a similar policy somewhat disguised."[80] The Council wanted the Social Security Administration to conduct a public relations campaign to explain to citizens how the "pay-as-you-go" system actually worked: "Presentation of OASDI to the public should deemphasize the accumulation of funds, and interest on the trust funds; and more directly recognize the pay-as-you-go and transfer nature of the system."[81] Kermit Gordon also supported a stricter "pay-as-you-go" system since it partially offset the program's economic

---

[76] Paul O'Neill to Director of the Executive Office of the President, 27 December 1971, NPM, White House Central Files, Subject Files: Welfare, Box 40, File: Social Security 1/1/71–12/71.

[77] C.L Trowbridge to Robert Ball, December 1971, NAT, RG 56, Office of Tax Policy, Box 40, File: Advisory Council on Social Security; Derthick, *Policymaking for Social Security* 354–357.

[78] Secretary of Health, Education, and Welfare, *Reports of the 1971 Advisory Council on Social Security*. Paul O'Neill to Director of the Executive Office of the President, 27 December 1971, NPM, White House Central Files, Subject Files: Welfare, Box 40, File: Social Security 1/1/71–12/71.

[79] Secretary of Health, Education, and Welfare, *Reports of the 1971 Advisory Council on Social Security*, C.L. Trowbridge to Robert Ball, December 1971, NAT, RG 56, Office of Tax Policy, Box 40, File: Advisory Council on Social Security.

[80] C.L Trowbridge to Robert Ball, December 1971, NAT, RG 56, Office of Tax Policy, Box 40, File: Advisory Council on Social Security.

[81] Ibid. See also U.S. Department of Treasury, Office of Tax Analysis, "Report of Meeting on Advisory Council on Social Security," 14 April 1970; U.S. Department of Treasury, Office of Tax Analysis, "Report of Meeting on Advisory Council on Social Security," 3 February 1970; U.S. Department of Treasury, Office of Tax Analysis, "Briefing Paper: Relevant Issues in the Report of the 1971 Advisory Council on Social Security," 2 April 1971. All the aforementioned documents in NAT, RG 56, Office of Tax Policy, Box 40, File: Advisory Council on Social Security.

impact by spending most of the monies that came into the system.[82] Nonetheless, the Council agreed that economic considerations should have "secondary priority" to balancing the Social Security budget.[83]

Finally, the Council divided over automatic COLAs. Although the final report endorsed indexation, some members openly dissented. Gabriel Hauge, for instance, opposed automatic COLAs since they would make controlling inflation more difficult. Automatic adjustments, Hauge argued, would shield large groups within the population from the effect of inflation, and thus reduce the public's willingness to support anti-inflationary economic measures.[84] In addition, Hauge questioned the equity of insulating one group from inflation while leaving others unprotected.[85] Nonetheless, the majority endorsed the proposal on the same grounds as the Nixon administration did.

Although this report by Social Security experts did not constitute legislation, its findings provided a rhetorical arsenal for Mills and Nixon in their final showdown in 1972. Both the administration and Mills agreed to implement some version of these objective, expert recommendations.[86] Nixon used the report to criticize Congress for failing to support indexation.[87] Mills used it to support a dramatic liberalization in benefits without appearing to raise taxes.

The path to that showdown began in May of 1971, when Ways and Means passed a 5 percent benefit increase and an increase in the wage base to $10,200. Sensing that indexation was extremely popular

[82] Mr. Rudney to Assistant Secretary Weidenbaum, 8 February 1971, NAT, R.G. 56, Office of Tax Policy, Box 40, File: Advisory Council on Social Security.

[83] U.S. Department of Treasury, Office of Tax Analysis, "Report of Meeting of Advisory Council on Social Security," 14 April 1970 and Mr. Rudney to Assistant Secretary Weidenbaum, 3 February 1970, NAT, RG 56, Office of Tax Analysis, Box 40, File: Advisory Council on Social Security.

[84] Elliot Richardson to President Nixon, 1 April 1971, NPM, White House Central Files, Subject Files: Welfare, Box 40, File: Social Security 1/1/71–12/71.

[85] Secretary of Health, Education, and Welfare, *Reports of the 1971 Advisory Council on Social Security*; Mr. Rudney, "Briefing Paper: Relevant Issues in the Report of the 1971 Advisory Council on Social Security," 2 April 1971, NAT, RG 56, Office of Tax Policy, Box 40, File: Advisory Council on Social Security.

[86] Paul O'Neill to Director of the Executive Office of the President, 27 December 1971, NPM, White House Central Files, Subject Files: Welfare, Box 40, File: Social Security 1/1/71–12/71. See also Board of Trustees of the Federal Old-Age and Survivors and Disability Insurance Trust Funds, *1971 Annual Report of the Board of Trustees of the Federal Old-Age and Survivors Insurance and Disability Insurance Trust Funds*, 1971, 92nd Cong., 1st sess., House Document No. 92–88.

[87] Tod Hullin to the Staff Secretary, 22 March 1971 and John Ehrlichman to President Nixon, 16 March 1971, NPM, White House Central Files, Subject Files: Welfare, Box 40, File: Social Security 1/1/71–12/71.

within the House, and remembering the successful Republican amendment one year earlier, Mills finally accepted its inclusion in the bill. The bill also contained Medicare reforms, in addition to an extension of coverage to the disabled.[88] Once again, however, the legislation never made it through Congress. On June 22, the House passed the bill by a vote of 288 to 132, and the Senate Finance Committee held public hearings soon after. But the Senate delayed action on the Family Assistance Plan, which was part of the committee bill, and it took another year before the final stage in this struggle over Social Security.

The media covers candidate Mills

While the Senate deliberated, the national media began to report on Mills's presidential aspirations. The stories started when a group of legislators, led by Representative James Burke (D-MA), organized the "Draft Mills for President" movement. When Burke announced his activities at a press conference, reporters thought he was joking. Indeed, there is no evidence that Mills had considered seriously running as a candidate before the movement emerged, nor did he put much effort into the campaign once it began. Rather, Mills was, at best, an ambivalent traveler as "Draft-Mills" intensified its efforts.

Nonetheless, Mills encouraged speculation through the media. "I'm not a candidate," Mills frequently told the press, "but if my party should ask me to take it, I would. And if I did, I would be as active a nominee as the party's ever had."[89] On the television shows "Meet the Press," "Issues and Answers," and "Face the Nation," the chairman claimed that he could defeat the president by sweeping the South and the border states, drawing the vote of both the business community and organized labor, and winning the support of black Americans who would certainly choose a Democrat over Nixon.[90] Mills even believed that he could overcome the civil rights issue, which reporters raised in most of these interviews: "Segregation is a dead issue. I voted as I did over the years because it was necessary to vote that way if I was to stay in Congress. If I were a national candidate, I would be

---

[88] U.S. Congress, House Committee on Ways and Means, *Social Security Amendments of 1971: Report*, 92nd Cong., 1st sess., 1971. See also "Tax Cuts . . . Social Security . . . Welfare Reform," *U.S. News & World Report*, 15 March 1971, 42–48.

[89] "Mills for President? Darkest of Horses Is Off and Walking," *The Wall Street Journal*, 20 May 1971.

[90] "Mills Urges the Democrats to Nominate Middle-Roader," *The Washington Post*, 19 July 1971; Elsie Carper, "Nixon's Policies Putting Democrats in Position to Win in '72, Mills Says," *The Washington Post*, 6 June 1971.

receptive to the wishes of the people of the United States as I was to the people of my state."[91] The political commentator Kevin Phillips predicted that Mills could have a significant effect on the election. "Granted that Wilbur Mills lacks the charisma to become the new superstar of Southern politics," Phillips wrote, "he may be positioning himself for a strong impact on the Tennessee, North Carolina, and West Virginia primaries."[92] Mills hoped to return the Democratic party back to its vital center.

Reporters continued to comment on Mills's technical expertise as an important personal and professional asset. Building on the dominant media image of the chairman, *Life* published a lengthy article on his potential as president, entitled "The Wooing of Wilbur Mills," that explained:

> His committee has always been known as "the salt mines of Congress," dealing as it does with the wan and inert materials that are the essence of Ways and Means. Mills sits through these stultifying recitations and browsings with a seemingly omnivorous and unfaltering alertness, an epic patience, which leaves its other member stunned. "He just keeps going," declares one of them, "and going, and going – he outlasts you." Mills has accumulated whole reservoirs of expertise, vast bins and silos of knowledge, hoards, caches, archives of references. The reach of his familiarity with the bleak terrain of federal tax law is beyond the perception of anybody else in Washington; during committee sessions, in fact, he is wont to recite without falter whole sections of the tax code. "Hell, every time I bring up some point," says one of his committee members, "he knows more about it than I do. Doesn't make any difference what it is, he's going to know more about it than me."[93]

The media reports were most significant for their effect on Mills's reputation. Since they appeared in the press at the same time Mills was opposing Nixon on several measures, including the indexation of Social Security and Revenue Sharing, critics speculated that Mills was being obstinate for electoral purposes. In 1971, these accusations lurked just beneath the surface. Many reporters seemed willing to

---

[91] Richard Lyons, "Mills: A Non-Candidate on the Stump," *The Washington Post*, 2 June 1971. See also *Transcript: ABC's Issues and Answers.*

[92] Kevin Phillips, "Mills Gets Set To Influence '72," *The Washington Post*, 21 October 1971. See also Phillips, "Mills Sees High Office," *The Washington Post*, 20 March 1971; Rowland Evans and Robert Novak, "Mills Emerging as a Democrat," *The Washington Post*, 7 April 1971; Phillips, "Mills Means It," *The Washington Post*, 15 May 1971; Joseph Kraft, "The Mills Campaign," *The Washington Post*, 20 May 1971.

[93] Marshall Frady, "The Wooing of Wilbur Mills," *Life*, 16 July 1971, 57.

believe Mills when he promised to support changes in Social Security once "we become convinced that we are not jeopardizing the whole of the program."[94] In the coming year, however, such signs of trust were seriously challenged.

THE FAILED CAMPAIGN

After years in the grind of policymaking, Mills decided reluctantly to try his hand at presidential politics in the winter of 1972. On February 11, Mills announced that he would run for the Democratic presidential nomination. A write-in campaign had already begun in New Hampshire, where the first primary was to take place on March 7.[95] At the same time that Mills announced his candidacy, he changed several of his positions dramatically. For example, he announced his support for Revenue Sharing. For almost a decade, Mills opposed this proposal as fiscally irresponsible; as one administration official commented in 1971: "We might consider announcing that revenue sharing, as proposed, has been killed by Wilbur Mills. It's over, that's it. The wrath of the governors, mayors and county officials will be on Mills' head."[96] But facing criticism from the editors of the influential New Hampshire *Manchester Union Leader*, Mills suddenly switched his position.[97]

Mills shocked the policymaking world once again with his proposal for Social Security. On February 23, 1972, Mills proposed a 20 percent increase in Social Security benefits, a reduction in the scheduled tax rates, an increase in the wage base to $10,200 in 1972 and to $12,000 in 1973, and automatic COLAs. The proposal was packaged as a massive benefit increase combined with a significant tax reduction. The chairman claimed that Congress could finance this liberalization by assuming that tax revenue would rise in the next seventy-five years; he pointed to the Advisory Council report as the basis of his recommendation.[98] As usual, Mills packaged his proposal in the language of actuarial economics to give it legitimacy; he used the Council's report to build political support.

For years, Mills had built his reputation on a technocratic

---

[94] *Transcript: ABC's Issues and Answers.*

[95] "Mills Announces He's a Candidate," *The Washington Post*, 12 February 1972.

[96] Charles Colson to John Ehrlichman, 23 July 1971, NPM, White House Central Files, Subject Files: Federal Government, Box 14, File: FG 33–21 House Committees – Ways and Means.

[97] Wilbur Mills, "Address in Concord, New Hampshire," 15 February 1972, WMPC, Box 401, File 12; David Broder, "Mills Changes Signals," *The Washington Post*, 22 February 1972.

[98] Editorial, "Wilbur Mills' 20 Percent," *The Evening Star*, 25 February 1972.

bipartisan approach to politics. Now, that reputation seemed questionable. The proposal came a few weeks before the New Hampshire primary and only a few days after George McGovern, another Democrat running for president, had called for a 20 percent increase in Social Security benefits. The relationship between Mills's campaign and public policy distressed many of his colleagues, particularly those who had seen the chairman as a bipartisan technocrat who stood above the vagaries of electoral politics. It seemed as if Mills had finally become a politician, less concerned with fiscal responsibility and legislative compromise than with reckless political self-promotion. Of course, Mills had always been a politician and often pursued his own interests; Members' Bills were one example of such action. Yet he had always appeared to balance his own needs with a concern for sound public policy, legislative negotiation, and broad political consensus.

The convergence of the Social Security bill with the New Hampshire primary stimulated intense criticism in the national press. *The Wall Street Journal*, for example, published some of the strongest attacks on Mills. The newspaper appeared to feel betrayed by the chairman: "For years it's been a stock proposal of presidential candidates to raise the cash payments to the 27 million Americans on Social Security. Just as regularly, Mr. Mills, chairman of the House Ways and Means Committee, has thwarted such big increases because of a determination to keep the Social Security 'actuarially sound.' But this year the Arkansas Democrat is a presidential candidate himself."[99] The editors of *The Wall Street Journal* urged Mills to "Come Home" and they lamented:

> During his 30 years in Congress Chairman Mills has complied an awesome record of responsible public service. He has been steadfast in this commitment to fiscal conservatism. Yet he's been progressive without succumbing to demagoguery. When, from time to time, Capitol Hill has been awash with a mad, euphoric craving to raid the Treasury for giveaway programs, Rep. Mills has been among the few in Congress the nation could depend on to keep their heads. It is thus doubly discouraging, even alarming, to observe the Arkansas Democrat having been nipped by the presidential bug, cavorting like a mere politician . . . It's useless to speculate on Mr. Mills' motives, for he is an exceedingly complex man. But whatever his reasons, we hope this is a passing phenomenon, and before

---

[99] "Mills Proposes 20 Percent Benefit Rise In Social Security," *The Wall Street Journal*, 24 February 1972.

too long the Chairman will return to the Ways and Means Committee with the healthy skepticism that has marked his redoubtable career; his proposal for a 20 percent boost looks like the kind of pie in the sky on which he himself has long cast a beady eye.[100]

Washington Post columnists Rowland Evans and Robert Novak speculated that "Mills, the master legislative craftsman, has become bored with the world of Ways and Means. True or not, there is no doubt that his mind today is consumed not by tariffs and taxes but by the drama of presidential politics."[101]

Ignoring these complaints, Mills intensified his media campaign. Given his busy schedule in Washington, he relied heavily on television and radio promotions. He also made use of a computerized direct-mail campaign, which was the state of the art in campaign technology.[102] Several high-powered tax lobbyists assisted with the campaign in New Hampshire and a few other states. For example, James Riddell, the former tax counsel of the Ways and Means Committee, volunteered as a spokesman for Mills in New Hampshire; Riddell had spent the past ten years as a registered tax lobbyist for more than a dozen international firms.[103] Other lobbyists included Michael Daniels, the Washington agent for the Japanese government and a representative of Japanese and European textile and industrial exporters, and Carl Arnold, former lobbyist for the American Petroleum Institute.[104]

Mills's campaign ended in failure. In New Hampshire, he received 4.8 percent of the vote. In Massachusetts, he won 3.6 percent of the vote, and fell far behind George McGovern, Edmund Muskie, and George Wallace. Soon after, he dropped out of the race. Mills nominally remained in the campaign for the possibility of working for another Democratic president. Senator McGovern, for example, announced that should he win the election, he would appoint Mills to be secretary of the Treasury.[105] Mills also suggested that he would run with Edward Kennedy if a "Draft Ted Kennedy for President" succeeded at the Democratic convention.[106] Except for

[100] Editorial, "Come Home Wilbur Mills," *The Wall Street Journal*, 2 March 1972.
[101] Rowland Evans and Robert Novak, "Effect of Mills' Candidacy," *The Washington Post*, 9 March 1972.
[102] Dan Oberdorfer, "Absentee Mills' TV Blitz," *The Washington Post*, 1 March 1972.
[103] David Broder, "Lobbyists Aid Mills in N.H.," *The Washington Post*, 2 March 1972.
[104] Stephen A. Merrill, *Wilbur D. Mills: Democratic Representative from Arkansas* (Washington, D.C.: Grossman Publishers, 1972), 27.
[105] George Lardner, Jr., "Tax, Welfare Plan Unveiled By McGovern," *The Washington Post*, 30 August 1972.
[106] *Transcript: Meet the Press*, 11 June 1972, WMPC, Box 397, File 3.

these possible appointments or nominations, Mills dropped out of the competition.

There were several reasons for Mills's loss. First, he never took the candidacy seriously, nor had he completed the type of strategic planning that most candidates devote to campaigns. Second, as an alcoholic, Mills did not have the stamina needed to conduct an effective campaign. During the late-1960s, Mills began to drink heavily, and became addicted to prescription drugs, originally prescribed to ease the pain from a chronic back disease. Moreover, the chairman had discovered that his electoral appeal remained weak outside the second district of Arkansas. Mills was a creature of Washington. Having devoted his career to building an image as a technocratic bipartisan legislator, he did not have the type of image that went over well in the world of electoral politics. As *Life* magazine explained:

> In his three decades in Washington, he has left behind him a wake uncannily bereft of flair or anecdotes. Inevitably over the years, awed notice has been taken of Mills – occasional news-magazine covers, extensive newspaper profiles – but they were like match flares against a sheet of sandpaper: no reflection, no shimmer was given off. He seems to have a presence that defies celebration, that resounds about as vibrantly as a plank of cork. Despite his staggering clout, he has remained a resolutely unassertive figure, possessed by an implacable shyness. To expect from such an eminently unpresumptuous creature that most towering presumption of all – to run for President of the United States – could not have seemed more unlikely.[107]

Finally, Mills's campaign came at a time when Democrats were moving away from the labor-progressive business-southern coalition that party leaders had nurtured since the New Deal. Democrats began to court new constituency groups including women, Hispanics, and young, liberal, middle-class whites. The party also liberalized its agenda, and focused on the issue of "identity politics" rather than economics. Like other centrist Democrats, Mills had little appeal in this new Democratic age.[108] His voting record reflected his growing distance from the party. His party unity score, as calculated by the *Congressional Quarterly*, declined significantly during the second half of the 1960s after a career high of 89 percent in 1962.[109]

---

[107] Cited in U.S. Congress, House of Representatives, *Congressional Record*, 15 July 1971, 92nd Cong., 1st sess., 25522.

[108] Ronald Radosh, *Divided They Fell: The Demise of the Democratic Party 1964–1996* (New York: Free Press, 1996), 133–182.　　　[109] Merrill, *Wilbur D. Mills*, 10–11.

When Mills entered presidential politics, it was a game he knew little about. Because he devoted so much energy to the tax community, he rarely communicated with the electorate on issues other than taxation. In short, the campaign turned out to be a monumental failure. As the political scientists John Makin and Norman Ornstein explained:

> To presidential campaign operatives and veteran political reporters, his attempt seemed ludicrous. Mills had no experience in national party or presidential politics, no base of delegate support, no team of experienced and proven advisers. His support came from a group of about thirty colleagues in the House, who themselves were not major players in national Democratic party affairs. Mills's legendary reputation and his power in the corridors of Congress were virtually unknown outside the Beltway and his native state of Arkansas. His owlish, bespectacled appearance made him something less than an ideal candidate for the television age.[110]

Despite his loss, Mills still held considerable power as chairman of Ways and Means. Some pundits and colleagues joked that Mills had risked "stepping down" to take the position of president. Mills himself reportedly said about the presidency: "You don't need the title to run things in Washington."[111]

POLITICS AND PENSIONS, 1972

Even after Mills dropped out of the presidential race, the 20 percent Social Security increase and indexation package remained on the table. Mills continued to promote his proposal with vigor. During a speech to a senior citizens organization in New York, for example, he called Social Security his greatest "satisfaction" and he boasted to his audience:

> The social security program today protects workers and their families at all income levels. When I first came to Congress, the program covered less than half the civilian labor force and it provided only for retirement benefits for workers. Today more than 9 out of 10 jobs are covered and over 90 percent of the population aged 65 and over are eligible for benefits . . . In the

---

[110] John H. Makin and Norman Ornstein, *Debt and Taxes: How America Got into Its Budget Mess and What to Do About It* (New York: Random House, 1994), 153–154.

[111] Cited in Donald R. Kennon and Rebecca M. Rogers, *The Committee on Ways and Means: A Bicentennial History, 1789–1989* (Washington, D.C.: Government Printing Office, 1989), 324.

fourteen years that I have been Chairman of the Committee on Ways and Means, social security benefits have been broadened and improved in numerous ways and new beneficiaries have been added. During this time, the number of beneficiaries on the social security rolls has increased from eleven million to more than 27 million men, women and children – about one out of every eight Americans. Just as important, improvements have been made in the benefits paid under the program. The average benefit received by workers, for example, has doubled in amount since 1958 – increasing from $65 to $133 a month ... The need to modify the Social Security Act still exists, of course.[112]

When challenged about the size of the proposed increase, Mills responded: "If it were not for the fact that the cost of living has been going up in the last six months at the rate of about six percent ... If it were not for the fact that we are talking about people who are primarily retired and most of them unable to enjoy outside earnings ... I probably would not favor such an increase in spending. But ... these factors of need outweigh any argument to the contrary that we should not do it because of the increased spending that it would result in."[113]

The administration responds

The Nixon administration was divided over how to respond. Publicly, it presented a united front. It continued to support a 5 percent increase along with automatic COLAs.[114] The administration argued that Mills's proposal required a tax increase of almost 25 percent.[115] The bill could aggravate inflation by pouring too much money into the economy without raising taxes.[116] Finally, the increase would either shatter the budget ceiling or necessitate a $6 billion budget reduction in other domestic programs.[117]

[112] Wilbur D. Mills, "Remarks before the Senior Citizens' Town Hall Meeting," 17 April 1972, WMPC, Box 402, File 17.
[113] Transcript: Meet the Press.
[114] Arthur Fleming to John Ehrlichman, 12 June 1972, NPM, White House Central Files, Subject Files: Welfare, Box 40, File: Social Security [1/72–6/72].
[115] John Ehrlichman to President Nixon, 10 March 1972 and James Falk to Ken Cole, 7 April 1972 and Clark MacGregor to Patrick Buchanan, 29 June 1972 all in NPM, White House Central Files, Subject Files: Welfare, Box 40, File: Social Security [1/72–6/72].
[116] John Ehrlichman to the President's File, 24 April 1972, NPM, White House Central Files, Subject Files: Welfare, Box 40, File: Social Security [1/72–6/72].
[117] Paul O'Neill to Ken Cole, 22 March 1972 and Herbert Stein to President Nixon, 20 March 1972, NPM, White House Central Files, Subject Files: Welfare, Box 40, File: Social Security [1/72–6/72].

Behind closed doors, a split emerged between the Department of HEW and the Office of Management and Budget. On the one hand, the new secretary of HEW, Elliot Richardson, believed that Nixon could not afford to oppose Mills's proposal. He told the president that opposing the 20 percent increase "rejects a proposal which is very popular among the 20 million Americans over 65 – a key group in your reelection strategy . . . Through this approach, it is conceivable that you would end up signing into law a major benefit increase – for which you would not get credit – with a financing scheme that would have serious negative effect on the budget." Richardson reminded the president that even though an increase in the wage base constituted a tax increase, "It is worth noting that psychologically most people view social security payments not as part of a tax system, but as part of a contributory system which holds their future benefits in trust." Richardson, along with Ball and Cohen, proposed that Nixon support a modified version of the increase, with a 5 percent increase in 1972 and a 15 percent increase in 1973.[118] By using the finance mechanisms proposed by the Advisory Council, the administration could support the bill as fiscally sound.[119]

On the other hand, George Shultz, director of the Office of Management and Budget, adamantly opposed the increase. Shultz told Nixon that the "main substantive issue" was the increase in taxes. He argued that the administration had to help the public understand that "Social Security 'contributions' are taxes too . . . while it is occasionally useful to employ the antiseptic terms of polite conversation on Social Security, we must etch these plain public finance facts in our minds: Raising the 'maximum earnings base' *means increasing taxes*; increasing the 'contribution rate' *means increasing taxes*; and doing both at the same time *means increasing taxes substantially*." The director reminded the president that recent Social Security tax increases had offset nearly half of the personal income-tax reductions that Congress enacted since 1969.[120] "There is no magic actuary-alchemist," Shultz concluded, "who can provide benefits without

[118] Robert Ball to Elliot Richardson, 7 March 1972 and Richardson to President Nixon, 10 March 1972 and John Ehrlichman to President Nixon, 10 March 1972 all in NPM, White House Central Files, Subject Files: Welfare, Box 40, File: Social Security [1/72–6/72]; Wilbur Cohen to Wilbur Mills, 13 March 1972, WCP, Box 223, Folder 1.

[119] Elliot Richardson to President Nixon, 8 March 1972, NPM, White House Central Files, Subject Files: Welfare, Box 40, File: Social Security [1/72–6/72].

[120] George Shultz to President Nixon, 14 March 1972 and Shultz to Nixon, 7 March 1972 both in NPM, White House Central Files, Subject Files: Welfare, Box 40, File: Social Security [1/72–6/72]. See also "Nixon Aides, Others Puzzled By Mills Plan To Boost Social Security Benefits by 20 Percent," *The Wall Street Journal*, 29 February 1972.

incurring costs." Mills's claim of a 20 percent increase with lower tax rates was "partly sleight-of-hand and partly abuse. . . ."[121]

In his public speeches, Nixon took Shultz's advice, and went to great lengths to present his administration as the defenders of the elderly: total federal spending on the elderly, Nixon claimed, was nearly 50 percent greater than the $34 billion spent in 1969 when the administration came into office.[122] Besides his dramatic increases in spending for the elderly, Nixon reminded audiences that he had created the positions of special assistant to the president on the aged and a new cabinet-level Committee on Aging, and had organized a White House Conference on Aging. Nixon claimed that the elderly, under his administration, had become "A Generation No Longer Forgotten."[123] Privately, however, he acknowledged that there was little he could do to block the 20 percent increase. The president ordered budget officials to start looking for possible cuts in domestic programs involving agriculture, health, education, and social services.[124]

Indexation and expansion

On June 30, 1972, the Senate added a Social Security amendment to a bill extending the ceiling on the public debt.[125] The amendment, introduced on June 28 by Senator Frank Church (D-ID), chairman of the Senate Special Committee on Aging, was identical to the Mills bill. The amendment included a 20 percent increase in benefits and a provision for automatic adjustment of benefits and the wage base when the cost-of-living increased by 3 percent or more. Like the Mills bill, the Church amendment financed the cost of automatic benefit increases from a higher wage base; it also reduced future tax increases.[126] Once the Senate agreed to the amendment, Mills "placed

[121] George Shultz to President Nixon, 7 March 1972, NPM, White House Central Files, Subject Files: Welfare, Box 40, File: Social Security [1/72–6/72].

[122] Ibid.

[123] Richard Nixon, "To the Congress of the United States," 23 March 1972, NPM, White House Central Files, Subject Categories: Speeches, Box 66, File: Older Americans; Richard Nathan to John Ehrlichman, 24 May 1971, NPM, White House Central Files, Subject Files: Welfare, Box 40, File: Social Security 1/1/71–12/71.

[124] Caspar Weinberger to the President's File, 26 June 1972, NPM, President's Office Files, Memoranda for the President, Box 89, File: June 25 [1972].

[125] "Boost of 20 percent in Social Security Benefits Seems Imminent, Periling Welfare Reform," The Wall Street Journal, 26 June 1972; "Move to Tack a 20 Percent Social Security Boost To Debt Ceiling Bill Is Hit By White House," The Wall Street Journal, 28 June 1972.

[126] U.S. Congress, Senate, H.R. 15390: Amendments, 28 June 1972, 92nd Cong., 2nd sess., 1972.

his members on alert" to support the legislation without haste.[127] The Nixon administration attempted to convince members of the Conference Committee that the 20 percent increase in benefits would "seriously jeopardize the integrity of the Social Security Trust Fund."[128] But the Senate passed the legislation by 82 to 4, and the House by 302 to 35.

Nixon signed the legislation even as he attacked it as "fiscally irresponsible."[129] Since the amendments had been tied to the debt ceiling, Nixon had little choice. If he vetoed the bill, he would be rejecting an increase in the allowable debt ceiling as well as a popular benefit increase during an election year.[130] Representative Barber Conable (R-NY) attacked Mills and Congress for their fiscally irresponsible action: "In effect the chairman says, in recommending this increase on the basis of new dynamic actuarial assumptions, that 'all the experts agree.' I will not dwell on the question of whether the experts . . . are entitled to our confidence." Conable added: "I say only that we in Congress are not entitled to the confidence of the American people if we allow ourselves to be stampeded into this vote."[131] Even though the administration opposed the liberalized coverage contained in the bill, it realized that if Nixon didn't support the legislation "aging groups" would "scream traitor."[132]

The Social Security Amendments of 1972

The Social Security legislation of 1972 represented a watershed in public policy.[133] For contributory social insurance, the legislation meant expansion. First, the bill financed a 20 percent increase in benefits simply by changing actuarial assumptions. Although Congress raised the wage base, it lowered future tax rates. Second, the amendments implemented an automatic cost-of-living adjustment.

---

[127] Clark MacGregor to President Nixon, 30 June 1972 and Richard Cook to Mac-Gregor, 30 June 1972 in NPM, White House Central Files, Subject Files: Welfare, Box 40, File: Social Security [1/72–6/72].

[128] Ibid.

[129] "Nixon Signs Bill Raising Social Security Benefits 20 Percent But Blasts Congress For 'Fiscally Irresponsible' Act," *The Wall Street Journal*, 3 July 1972.

[130] Sheryl R. Tynes, *Turning Points in Social Security: From 'Cruel Hoax' to 'Sacred Entitlement'* (Stanford: Stanford University Press, 1996), 139–140.

[131] Derthick, *Policymaking for Social Security*, 364.

[132] James Falk to John Ehrlichman, 1 August 1972, NPM, White House Central Files, Subject Files: Welfare, Box 11, File: WE 7/1/72–7/31/72.

[133] U.S. Congress, Senate Committee on Finance, *Social Security Amendments of 1972: Report*, 92nd Cong., 2nd sess., 1972 and U.S. Congress, House and Senate Conference Committee, *Social Security Amendments of 1972: Conference Report*, 92nd Cong., 2nd sess., 1972.

According to the law, the Social Security Administration would use the Department of Labor's Consumer Price Index every year to determine whether the cost of living required an adjustment. Benefits would rise accordingly unless Congress passed an alternative increase.[134] Third, the amendments liberalized the retirement test (the annual amount of wages an individual could earn and still receive full benefits). Fourth, the amendments indexed the wage base so that it too would rise automatically as wages rose; this was designed to guarantee that general revenue would not be used to pay Social Security benefits.

For Medicare, the legislation meant both expansion and cost control. Foremost, it extended Medicare protection to the disabled. For cost-control, the amendments enabled Medicare participants to choose to be covered through a Health Maintenance Organization (HMO) – a prepaid group health plan that met prescribed standards. The amendments also created professional standard review organizations consisting of practicing physicians in a local area to review services covered under Medicare. Furthermore, the amendments enacted changes to the Supplementary Medical Insurance program; the premium would be increased only in the event of a general benefit increase. Additionally, Social Security beneficiaries would be automatically enrolled for SMI as they became entitled to hospital insurance (individuals would be given the opportunity to decline the coverage). Finally, the amendments increased the portion of Social Security tax revenue that went into the Hospital Insurance Trust Fund to compensate for the underfinancing of the program.

For welfare, the legislation meant greater federal control. While abandoning FAP, the amendments repealed the existing federal-state programs of aid to the aged, blind, and permanently and totally disabled. In its place, Congress created a Federal Supplemental Security Income Program designed to provide financial assistance to the needy aged, the disabled, and the blind. The means-tested program was to be federally administered by the Social Security Administration; this left AFDC as the only welfare program under the administrative control of the states. Individuals or couples were to be eligible for assistance if their monthly income was less than the full monthly payment.

Following these changes in public policy, Social Security loomed large over the American polity. The Social Security Amendments of 1969–1972 liberalized Social Security finance significantly and strengthened the notion of entitlement. By the mid-1970s, more than 80 percent of people over sixty-five were receiving income from Social

[134] Weaver, *Automatic Government*, 78.

Security.[135] Furthermore, politicians spoke about the Social Security "entitlement" as a right to benefits adjusted to inflation. Indexation, concluded the sociologist Paul Starr, provided "the political security that protects Social Security, which in turn protects the economic security of the elderly."[136]

The expansion of Social Security produced several important results. First, it confirmed the effectiveness of earmarked taxation by fostering the growth of contributory social insurance. Second, it cemented a new concept of Social Security entitlement. Because of the legislation, politicians now claimed that participants were entitled to pensions that were adjusted to inflation. Like the benefit, the adjustment was no longer perceived as a privilege to be granted by Congress. Politicians who challenged this right would encounter furious attacks at both the elite and grass-roots levels. Third, the expansion weakened the alliance between fiscal conservatives and Social Security by eliminating some of the fiscal controls that previously had been built into the system, such as the requirement that Congress control the growth of taxes and benefits and the conservative actuarial assumptions that had guaranteed an excess of revenue and limited guaranteed benefits. Finally, the expansion damaged Mills's technocratic bipartisan image. Critics accused him of placing his "political interests" – namely his presidential aspirations – ahead of the fiscal principles that defined Social Security.

A NEW TYPE OF SECURITY

The amendments placed the program on a long-term path of unprecedented growth. The results were staggering. According to one study, Social Security benefits rose an average of 2.7 percent per year in the fourteen years between 1952 and 1965. From 1967 and 1972, however, Congress enacted an annual average increase in benefits of 14.3 percent.[137] Between 1969 and 1977, Social Security benefits increased by almost 130 percent; benefit levels adjusted for inflation even rose by 23 percent.[138] With the Great Inflation of the

---

[135] Quadagno, *The Color of Welfare*; "Ahead in Social Security: Bigger Benefits, Higher Taxes," *U.S. News & World Report*, 26 June 1972, 68.

[136] Paul Starr, "Social Security and the American Public Household," in *Social Security: Beyond the Rhetoric of Crisis*, eds. Theodore R. Marmor and Jerry L. Mashaw (Princeton: Princeton University Press, 1988), 120. See also W. Andrew Achenbaum, *Social Security: Visions and Revisions* (Cambridge: Cambridge University Press, 1986), 59.

[137] Makin and Ornstein, *Debt and Taxes*, 154–155.

[138] Robert M. Ball, *Social Security Today and Tomorrow* (New York: Columbia University Press, 1978), 18–19; Keith Bradsher, "Partnership in the Deficit," *The New York*

1970s, and a technical error that overcompensated recipients for inflation, indexation resulted in a massive increase in the amount of cash the elderly received from the government and the amount of taxes workers contributed to the program. Between 1970 and 1990, for example, Social Security tax rates rose from 9.6 percent to 15.3 percent.[139]

The invigorated notion of entitlement, as promoted by this expansion, helped to define the lobby for the elderly. By the early 1970s, the elderly constituted roughly 15 percent of the electorate; few lawmakers could discount the influence of this "gray lobby."[140] The largest organization for older Americans, the American Association for Retired Persons (AARP), was founded in 1958; by 1992, it had over 28 million members and a paid staff of 1,300. This lobby joined others, such as the National Council of Senior Citizens and the National Committee to Preserve Social Security and Medicare.[141] These lobbies helped protect contributory social insurance from retrenchment. When politicians attempted to reform the program by reducing the percentage by which benefits automatically increased with inflation, they encountered fierce electoral resistance from the elderly lobby.[142]

But the expansion also destabilized Social Security finance. The indexing mechanism overcompensated for inflation, thereby imposing much higher costs than expected.[143] Furthermore, the debates about general revenue intensified. The group that Wilbur Cohen labeled as the "Harvard-Yale-MIT-Brookings" network had gained considerable attention within policymaking circles for its plan to replace the earmarked tax system with a more economically rational tax.[144] In a letter to Social Security expert Douglas Brown, Cohen compared these challenges to those of the 1940s:

Times, Sunday, 3 December 1995, Section I; Derthick, *Policymaking for Social Security*, 346; Quadagno, *The Color of Welfare*, 155–173; Kent Weaver, "Controlling Entitlements," in *The New Direction in American Politics*, eds. John E. Chubb and Paul E. Peterson (Washington, D.C.: The Brookings Institution, 1985), 312.

[139] C. Eugene Steuerle, *The Tax Decade: How Taxes Came to Dominate the Public Agenda* (Washington, D.C: The Urban Institute Press, 1992), 16; Steuerle, "Financing the American state at the turn of the century," in *Funding the Modern American State: The Rise and Fall of the Era of Easy Finance*, ed., W. Elliot Brownlee (Cambridge: Cambridge University Press and Washington, D.C.: Woodrow Wilson Center Press, 1996), 420–421.

[140] Achenbaum, *Social Security*, 58.

[141] Quadagno, *The Color of Welfare*, 163–165.

[142] Paul Light, *Artful Work: The Politics of Social Security Reform* (New York: Random House, 1985); Weaver, *Automatic Government*, 79–89.

[143] Weaver, *Automatic Government*, 79.

[144] Wilbur Cohen to Douglas Brown, 31 July 1972, WCP, Box 242, Folder 6. Edward Berkowitz, "Social Security and the financing of the American state," in *Funding the Modern American State*, 187–191, and *Mr. Social Security*, 292.

I am deeply troubled by the role that the macro-economists are playing with regard to the social security system. In some ways they have exactly the same approach that the earlier Townsend supporters had. They view the system from the standpoint of redistribution of income so that their entire basis for judging its social effectiveness is how much comes in, from whom, and how much goes out and to whom. Of course these are all important considerations, but in my opinion social security is much more than a tax system and this is a point that is very difficult to get the tax economists to really understand the real objectives of social insurance.[145]

But even Cohen recommended that Congress reenact the Vandenberg-Murray Amendment, which authorized a general-revenue subsidy should it be necessary, primarily to "allay the anxieties and doubts which have been stimulated by the current problems. No appropriation would have to be made unless it were necessary and no appropriation could be made without further action by Congress. But such a sentence would be a big helping removing concerns." Cohen pointed to the general revenue authorized to finance one-half of Part B in Medicare as a precedent.[146]

As the Revenue and Expenditure Control Act of 1968 weakened the growth manipulation faction, the Social Security Amendments of 1969–72 weakened the fragile alliance between fiscal conservatives and Social Security. Many fiscal conservatives attacked Social Security finance on the grounds that the expansion had been actuarially irresponsible. Mills himself later admitted that his motivation had been political and fiscally unsound:

I always believed that we should take in as much in Social Security trust funds each year as we spent. Since we had the power to tax we didn't have to have this big buildup of reserve that was initially considered necessary. I always felt like, so long as we took in a dollar more each year than we spent each year, that we were on sound grounds. I still believe that. I did always want that to happen and to that extent it was fiscally sound if that approach was fiscally sound. We did protect that. We did strive to attain that goal. There were times when I was maybe motivated a little too much by political consideration. I know, the time Nixon was in office . . . that was politically motivated. I didn't want Nixon to get the credit for the increase. I wanted

---

[145] Wilbur Cohen to Douglas Brown, 31 August 1972, WCP, Box 242, Folder 6. See also Cohen to the Editor of *Barons*, WCP, Box 98, Folder Unmarked.

[146] Wilbur Cohen, "Improving the Financing of the Social Security System," 19 June 1975, WCP, Box 244, Folder 5.

the Democratic Congress to get it. As I look back on it – see we did it without any increase in tax. As I look back on it, I'm a little concerned as to whether or not we were actually doing it on an actuarially sound basis. Everybody said we were, but the Social Security fund has been in trouble . . . since then we may have broken the barrier – that we always set up for the increases – that each increase be accompanied by some tax increase. This was the thing that I always harped on. But here I didn't do it on that occasion.[147]

The most notable public opponent was Myers, now a professor at Temple University, who continued to publicly attack the "expansionists" who were increasing the size of the program without regard to its fiscal instabilities. Myers was frustrated, for example, that Congress had abandoned the level-wage assumption. But his biggest fear involved the potential effect of the baby boomer retirement scheduled to begin in 2010 and end in 2040. Their retirement, along with the liberalized benefit structure, would strain the system beyond repair. In response to these demographic pressures, Myers predicted that general revenue would be introduced into the program and lead to uncontrollable expansion of benefits. It would also cause a sharp decline in private pension plans, personal savings, and other forms of personal security. The former actuary proposed alternatives, such as allowing individuals to place their money into private savings accounts rather than the trust fund.[148] These arguments were heard in the coming decades from supporters of Social Security reform.

But these types of questions had only started to emerge in 1972. For it was after Mills and his community had fallen from power that Social Security finance received full scrutiny at the highest levels of decision-making power. Even then, the power of the earmarked tax system, along with its increasingly broad base of middle-class beneficiaries, continued to protect the program from significant retrenchment. As a result of this expansion, Social Security remained the "sacred cow" of American politics in the coming age of political conservatism.

[147] Wilbur D. Mills, interview with Lewis E. Weeks, 13 August 1980, Hospital Administration Oral History Collection, Library of the American Hospital Association (Chicago, Illinois, 1983), 37–38.

[148] "Is It True What They Say About Social Security?" *Nation's Business*, June 1973, 53–55.

PART THREE

Coming Apart

11

Looking Backward and Forward

Wilbur Mills's failed presidential campaign in 1972, combined with the costly expansion of Social Security, harmed his reputation as a man who stood above politics.[1] It seemed to colleagues that Mills had abandoned the delicate balance between self-interest, interest-group politics, legislative negotiation, and sound public policy. While self-interest and interest-group politics had always been integral to Mills's career, he had gained much respect for balancing these factors with other aspects of tax politics. But media reports started to suggest that something had changed. In 1974, for example, the Watergate Special Prosecutor's staff reported that Mills's staff had accepted $55,000 in illegal campaign contributions from the dairy lobby and $15,000 from Gulf Oil.[2] There were also reports that two top executives from Texas millionaire Ross Perot's firm Electronic Data Systems, a major processor of health insurance claims, secretly funneled $100,000 into Mills's campaign to ensure their influence in any future national health care plan.[3] The campaign and subsequent revelations represented one stage in a long-term process of decline as Mills was soon engulfed in scandal and swept aside by a movement for political reform.

This chapter recounts the political reform of the 1970s. Fueled by Vietnam, stagflation, and Watergate, a group of "Young Turks" in Congress attacked the closed structure of federal politics. Unlike reformers of the progressive era who wanted to build a new government to replace the state of courts and parties, these reformers sought to expand participation within the existing system.[4] Unwilling

---

[1] Mary Russell, "Mills Image Undermined by Incident," *The Washington Post*, 13 October 1974; Rowland Evans and Robert Novak, "Challenging the Power of Wilbur Mills," *The Washington Post*, 21 December 1973.

[2] "Mills Backers Asked About Dairy Funds," *The Washington Post*, 19 March 1974; Brooks Jackson, "Milk Group Aided Mills Campaign," *The Washington Post*, 25 March 1974.

[3] "$100,000 Secretly Sent Mills '72 Unit," *The Washington Post*, 2 August 1974.

[4] On reform during the progressive era, see Steven Skowronek, *Building a New American State: The Expansion of National Administrative Capacities, 1877–1920* (Cambridge: Cambridge University Press, 1982).

to radically restructure the connection between the state and society, the reformers ultimately created a federal government that was even farther removed from the citizenry than before. At the same time, the reforms weakened the capacity of the state to enact new types of public policies.

LOSING THE WAYS AND MEANS, 1974–1976

Power acquired in the American state could be maintained over long periods of time, but it was tenuous. As Mills had learned in his first year as chairman, the fragmented political system created multiple points of access for reformers, under the right conditions, to challenge politicians in high office. In the early 1970s, Mills discovered the extent to which his influence depended on the support of his community and the committee system. Of course, the most visible factor behind his decline involved a highly publicized relationship with a stripper and their display of drunkenness in the Tidal Basin. The incident was particularly damaging to an individual who had built his professional reputation on technocratic expertise and a hard-work ethic.

Mills's sex scandal

At age sixty-five, Mills experienced a spectacular fall from power. While he was working on what might have become his most important achievement – a plan for national health insurance financed through earmarked payroll taxes – his career came to an abrupt halt.[5] His problems began in 1973 and early 1974, when back problems and surgery kept him away from the committee for long periods of time. Ranking Democrat Al Ullman (D-OR) acted as a temporary chairman while Mills was recovering from his illness, running the committee in a more decentralized and open manner. During Mills's absence, Ullman earned the respect of liberal Democrats by designing legislation without consulting Republicans; Ullman also created temporary subcommittees.[6] Even when he was healthy, Mills was suffering. In 1972, the Public Citizens' Tax Reform Research Group

---

[5] Nicholas George Laham, "The Elusive Reform: The Politics of National Health Insurance, 1915–1991" (Ph.D, diss., Claremont Graduate School, 1992), 348–366; Wilbur Cohen to Robert Ball, 29 May 1974, WCP, Box 223, Folder 1; Stuart Auerbach, "Health Insurance Package Is Unveiled by Wilbur Mills," *The Washington Post*, 15 August 1974; Editorial, "The Health Insurance Debate," *The Washington Post*, Sunday, 26 May 1974, section C.

[6] Randall Strahan, *New Ways and Means: Reform and Change in a Congressional Committee* (Chapel Hill: University of North Carolina Press, 1990), 37.

helped to block several million dollars in Members' Bills from passing for the first time under Mills's chairmanship.[7] In 1973, moreover, the House rejected a conference agreement on the debt ceiling that Mills brought to the floor. Despite these problems, no one predicted the scandal that was to come.

On October 7, 1974, the U.S. Park Police stopped Mills's 1973 Lincoln Continental, which was driving at "unreasonable speed with its lights off" near the Tidal Basin at 2 A.M. Mills, bleeding from the face and intoxicated, emerged from the vehicle. One of his fellow passengers, Annabel Battistella, a thirty-eight-year-old stripper who performed locally as "Fanne Fox, the Argentine Firecracker," jumped out of the car and into the Tidal Basin.[8] Battistella was taken to St. Elizabeths Hospital with two black eyes after a scuffle in which Mills tried to prevent her from leaving the car. A television cameraman arrived at the scene after hearing police reports, and captured the arrest on camera. Battistella later admitted that she was having an affair with Mills, who frequented the nightclub (the Silver Slipper) where she performed. After her romance with Mills began in the summer of 1973, Battistella stopped dancing and became his companion at the Silver Slipper. Battistella, who had immigrated to the United States from Argentina in 1965, lived next door to the Mills's in Arlington, Virginia.

On hearing the initial reports, members of Congress were shocked. Representative Sam Gibbons (D-FL) told reporters that "I've never seen him drink," while Speaker of the House Carl Albert (D-OK) called Mills an "outstanding member of the House" and said that "the loss of Wilbur Mills would be a great loss to the House of Representatives." Likewise, House Majority Leader Thomas P. O'Neill (D-MA)

---

[7] Richard Spohn and Charles McCollum, eds., *The Revenue Committees: A Study of the House Ways and Means and Senate Finance Committees and the House and Senate Appropriations Committees* (New York: Viking Press, 1975), xv.

[8] The story was widely reported by the media. For the coverage by *The New York Times*, see the following articles: "Mills Called Occupant of Car Police Stopped," 9 October 1974; John M. Crewdson, "Mills in Seclusion After Report He Was Intoxicated in Car Stopped by Police," 10 October 1974; Crewdson, "'Embarrassed' Mills Acknowledges That He Was in Limousine Stopped by Police," 11 October 1974; William Safire, "The Need to Know," 17 October 1974; Roy Reed, "Mills Apologized to His Constituents," 18 October 1974; "Mills Forced to Campaign Hard Following Tidal Basin Incident," 19 October 1974. For the coverage by *The Washington Post*, see the following articles: Alfred E. Lewis and Martin Wed, "Riders in Mills' Car Involved in a Scuffle," 9 October 1974; Stephen Green, "Mills Hurt, Intoxicated In Incident, Police Say," 10 October 1974; Green, "Mills Admits Being Present During Tidal Basin Scuffle," 11 October 1974; Margot Hornblower and Megan Rosenfeld, "Police Identify Driver In Rep. Mills Incident," 15 October 1974; "The Incident at the Tidal Basin," 20 October 1974.

told reporters that it "is hard for me to believe that Wilbur would be involved in anything of that nature; maybe he was just the victim of circumstances."[9] Although Mills's administrative assistant, Oscar Eugene Goss, first denied that the chairman had been present at the crash, the story quickly unfolded in the media, and it became clear that Mills and Battistella had a sexual relationship. Mills, moreover, had been an alcoholic since 1969 and addicted to prescription drugs since 1972. For the press, Mills's dramatic story helped stimulate a shift in the coverage of Congress away from policy and institutional issues toward personal scandals.[10]

Although Mills still won reelection in November 1974 against Republican opponent Judy Petty, he could not seem to control his drinking. In December, before shocked members of the media, Mills staggered onto the stage at Battistella's first public appearance in a Boston strip club.[11] Asked if his appearance at the burlesque theater would hurt him, Mills said: "This won't ruin me . . . nothing can ruin me."[12] The following day, House Democrats divested Ways and Means of its power to assign committee assignments. This reform had been in the works since 1970, and Mills's personal scandal provided the opportunity for reformers to push it through Congress.[13] Soon after the incident, Mills was forced by the Democratic leadership, including Speaker Albert, to step down from the chairmanship. Mills announced that he would not run for office in 1976, and left Congress with the distinction of having been chairman of Ways and Means for the longest consecutive period in the history of the committee (Doughton served about one year longer, but Harold Knutson took

[9] Stephen Green and Margot Hornblower, "Mills Admits Being Present During Tidal Basin Scuffle," *The Washington Post*, 11 October 1974.

[10] S. Robert Lichter and Daniel R. Amundson, "Less News Is Worse News: Television News Coverage of Congress, 1972–92," in *Congress, the Press and the Public*, eds., Thomas E. Mann and Norman J. Ornstein (Washington, D.C: American Enterprise Institute and The Brookings Institution, 1994), 131–140.

[11] "Mills Does a Walk-on With Stripper," *The New York Times*, 2 December 1974; "Mills Derided in Congress Over Link to Stripper," *The New York Times*, 3 December 1974; Anthony Ripley, "Mills Goes Into Hospital After Being Told of Plan To Oust Him as Chairman," *The New York Times*, 4 December 1974; Martha Hamilton, "Mills Appears on Stage With Stripper," *The Washington Post*, 2 December 1974. Battistella published her own account of her relationship with Mills. See Annabel Battistella and Yvonne Duleavy, *Fanne Fox* (New York: Pinnacle Books, 1975).

[12] *CBS News Special: 1974 A Television Album*, 29 December 1974, The Museum of Television and Radio (New York, New York), T81: 0089, 002908; Martha Hamilton, "Mills Appears on Stage with Stripper," *The Washington Post*, 2 December 1974.

[13] David E. Rosenbaum, "House Democrats End Mills's Rule Over Committees," *The New York Times*, 3 December 1974.

over the position in the middle of Doughton's tenure when the Republicans controlled the House).

When Mills decided to leave Congress, Wilbur Cohen wrote him a letter that captured the admiration many policymakers felt about this congressional leader. In the letter, Cohen wrote: "I am sure a great many people do not fully comprehend your personal role in the development of much of the social policy of the past 30 years. I know what contribution you have made over many years. While there were times when we disagreed and I was overruled, I knew I had never run for elective office and I recognized the practicality of accepting the legislative wisdom . . . I close this letter with many memories of exciting and important legislative developments in which we were engaged . . . all of these, and many more, are due, in part, to your help and understanding."[14]

Mills entered Bethesda Navy Hospital, and then transferred to the Palm Beach Institute, a Florida hospital that specialized in the treatment of alcoholism. Mills acknowledged that had become addicted to alcohol and prescription drugs.[15] He even admitted to having suffered a blackout following a meeting with President Gerald Ford. Once he recovered, Mills spent the rest of his life as a lawyer and a tax consultant in Washington, D.C. He also spoke across the country and testified before Congress on the dangers of alcoholism and the need for treatment programs.

Congressional reform

Nonetheless, as one scholar has argued, "The political climate in the House was such that Mills' centralized, consensus-oriented leadership regime and the committee's autonomy and extensive authority would likely have came under attack even if the Arkansas Democrat had spent all of his evenings in 1974 home studying the tax code."[16] During the era of Vietnam and Watergate, political reformers attacked Congress and the American state. Indeed, Ways and Means

---

[14] Wilbur Cohen to Wilbur Mills, 23 March 1976, WCP, Box 223, Folder 1.

[15] Richard Lyons, "Mills Quits as Chairman; Young Democrats Advance," *The New York Times*, 11 December 1974; Mary Russell, "Mills Will Lose Chairmanship, Albert Confirms," *The Washington Post*, 5 December 1974; Mary Russell, "Rep. Mills Gives Up Hill Post," *The Washington Post*, 11 December 1974; Jack Anderson, "Mills Doesn't Recall Boston Caper," *The Washington Post*, 26 December 1974; Marjorie Hunter, "Mills Reveals Alcoholism; Plans to Stay in Congress," *The New York Times*, 31 December 1974; Stuart Auerbach, "Mills Admits Drinking," *The Washington Post*, 31 December 1974; "Mills in Institution to Cure Alcoholism," *The New York Times*, 27 February 1975; "Mills Makes It Final: He Won't Run Again," *The New York Times*, 6 March 1976.

[16] Strahan, *New Ways and Means*, 38.

and the tax community had been partially responsible for several problems that reformers targeted, including the power of committees, the limits of public welfare, the loophole-ridden tax code, the failure of countercyclical tax policies, the influence of experts in policymaking, and the secretive culture of federal politics.

Foremost, the decentralized committee system came under attack, and along with it, the influential role of Ways and Means. In the early 1970s, a group of young House and Senate Democrats, which included Joseph Biden (D-DE), Thomas Foley (D-WA), Gary Hart (D-CO), Henry Waxman (D-CA), Edward Kennedy (D-MA), and Al Ullman (D-OR), participated in a movement for major political reform. Unlike Mills, who had entered politics at time when the nation believed in the promise of the government, the new generation was far more concerned with corruption and excessive power. Although they still retained the New Deal faith in government action, the reformers feared that an alliance between the military-industrial establishment, Republicans, and conservative southern Democrats had dominated the congressional process. Led by Richard Bolling (D-MO) and Phillip Burton (D-CA), these reformers used the House Select Committee on Committees, the Democratic Caucus, and the Democratic Study Group to break up the existing power structure.

The reforms built on the Legislative Reorganization Act of 1970. This legislation enacted a series of important changes: It increased the opportunity for noncommittee members to challenge bills reported out of committee, forced committees to record every vote, encouraged committees to hold open hearings, and spread staff among more committees. Through this legislation, reformers began to weaken committee chairmen, such as the leaders of Ways and Means and of Appropriations, and to decentralize power within Congress even further. As two congressional scholars noted in their study of this period: "The Legislative Reorganization Act of 1970, despite its somewhat limited effects, remains an important milestone in legislative reformers' efforts. It marks the end of an era when powerful committee chairs and other senior members could forestall structural and procedural changes that appeared to undermine their authority. And it marked the beginning of nearly a decade of continuous change in Congress, providing the opening wedge for further committee changes."[17]

During the next few years, the reformers continued to implement changes in the institutional structure of Congress. Bolling and his colleagues expanded participation within the existing policymaking

---

[17] Steven S. Smith and Christopher J. Deering, *Committees in Congress*, second edition, (Washington, D.C.: Congressional Quarterly Press, 1990), 47.

process, making politics more porous, chaotic, and decentralized. Foremost, they weakened the committee system by decentralizing power through subcommittees and dispersing staff among members of Congress (thereby weakening single groups such as the JCIRT). The reforms also made it easier for the caucus to remove committee chairmen, they weakened the closed rule, and they enhanced the role of the House Speaker and the Democratic Caucus.[18] While the reformers decentralized committee power, they simultaneously weakened the executive branch. For example, the Congressional Budget and Impoundment Control Act of 1974 restricted presidential authority to withhold congressional appropriations. The legislation also created the Congressional Budget Office to give independent expertise to the House and Senate on fiscal matters.[19] Congress also passed the War Powers Resolution, which required the president to report any commitment of American military forces to Congress within forty-eight hours, and obtain the legislature's approval within sixty days. The National Emergencies Act of 1976 ended presidential emergency authority and established congressional review for national-emergency declarations.[20]

Ways and Means was a target of many of the reforms. Along with Mills, Ways and Means had become a symbol of the distance that existed between the state and society. Two staffers on the Bolling committee later recalled: "The Ways and Means Committee's excessive power had been from the beginning a major target of reorganization. Speaker Albert and Minority Leader Ford certainly had Wilbur Mills's domain in mind when they proposed the reform effort, and the subject frequently found its way into the committee's

[18] Kenneth A. Shepsle, "The Changing Textbook Congress," in John E. Chubb and Paul E. Peterson, eds., *Can the Government Govern?* (Washington, D.C.: The Brookings Institution, 1989), 228–266; Richard Franklin Bensel, *Sectionalism and American Political Development, 1880–1980* (Madison: University of Wisconsin Press, 1984), 317–367; Steven S. Smith, "New Patterns of Decisionmaking in Congress," *The New Direction in American Politics*, eds. John E. Chubb and Paul E. Peterson (Washington, D.C.: The Brookings Institution, 1985), 203–234; Thomas E. Mann and Norman J. Ornstein, *The New Congress* (Washington, D.C.: American Enterprise Institute for Public Policy Research, 1981); Lawrence C. Dodd and Bruce I. Oppenheimer, eds., *Congress Reconsidered* (New York: Praeger Publishers, 1977).

[19] For an important study of expert knowledge within the legislative branch, focusing on the Office of Technology Assessment, see Bruce Bimber, *The Politics of Expertise in Congress: The Rise and Fall of the Office of Technology Assessment* (Albany: State University of New York Press, 1996).

[20] James L. Sundquist, "Congress and the President: Enemies or Partners," in *Congress Reconsidered*, 222–243; James Sundquist, *The Decline and Resurgence of Congress* (Washington, D.C.: The Brookings Institution, 1981), 199–414; Arthur Schlesinger, Jr., "After the Imperial Presidency," in *The Cycles of American History* (Boston: Houghton Mifflin Company, 1986), 277–336.

hearings."[21] Despite Mills's resistance, the reforms opened up the proceedings of Ways and Means. First, they weakened the chairmanship by enlarging the committee and by establishing subcommittees. Second, they pushed the committee to hold open hearings and markups in order to democratize the policymaking process. Third, they limited the use of the closed rule by Ways and Means, a provision that had allowed members to push bills through the House without any amendment. Fourth, the Democratic Caucus took over the function of the Committee on Committees; Ways and Means could no longer assign members to committee positions. Finally, bipartisan deliberations declined dramatically as these reforms took place. Bipartisanship had waned as early as 1973 when John Byrnes retired from the House and was replaced by Herman Schneebeli (R-PA), who was more partisan in his approach to politics and had a weaker relationship with Mills.[22] When Ullman took over the chairmanship in 1974, moreover, he continued to exclude Republicans from committee deliberations. With hearings and markups increasingly open to public scrutiny, party leaders and their interest groups were able to keep a closer eye and apply increased pressure on the decisions of committee members.

The congressional reforms of the early 1970s had two major effects on the legislative process. First, the decentralization of the legislative system had given access to a larger number of policy activists, interest groups, and congressional representatives. As a result of more democratic procedures, there were more points at which policymakers could push or block particular legislation.[23] The reforms thus produced a more porous political environment that invited an increased number of participants.[24] There were limits, however, to

---

[21] Strahan, *New Ways and Means*, 40–41.

[22] Ibid., 32–33.

[23] Catherine E. Rudder, "Committee Reform and the Revenue Process," in *Congress Reconsidered*, 117–139, and "The House Committee on Ways and Means," in *Encyclopedia of the American Legislative System: Studies of the Principal Structures, Processes, and Policies of Congress and the State Legislators since the Colonial Era*, ed. Joel Silbey (New York: Charles Scribner's Sons, 1994), 1033–1048; Strahan, *New Ways and Means*; Charles H. Stewart III, "The Politics of Tax Reform in the 1980s," in Alberto Alesina and Geoffrey Carliner, eds., *Politics and Economics in the 1980s* (Chicago: University of Chicago Press, 1991), 155–156.

[24] Marc K. Landy and Martin A. Levin, eds., *The New Politics of Public Policy* (Baltimore: The Johns Hopkins University Press, 1995); Chubb and Peterson, *The New Direction in American Politics*; James S. Fishkin, *The Voice of the People: Public Opinion and Democracy* (New Haven: Yale University Press, 1996); Robert Dahl, *The New American Political Disorder* (Berkeley: IGS, 1994); Hugh Heclo, "Issue Networks and the Executive Establishment," in *The New American Political System*, ed. Anthony King (Washington, D.C.: American Enterprise Institute, 1978), 90–121.

this partial democratization of politics. Ways and Means, for example, retained most of its jurisdiction despite the decentralizing reforms that had taken place. In a humorous note, columnist Russell Baker wrote in *The New York Times*: "This is the stripping of the powers of the powerful chairman of the powerful Ways and Means Committee. It is a powerful moment in the history of the Congress for now everything will be different until everything becomes the same again."[25] Congressional reformers, moreover, provided access largely to Washington-based organizations that maintained weak ties to the grass roots. As a result, many citizens remained alienated from the policymaking process at the grass-roots level. At the same time, voting continued its long-term path of decline.[26]

Second, the political reforms arguably made it more difficult for officials to enact coherent public policies. Ironically, the insulation of Ways and Means, and its monopoly of power and expertise, had enhanced its ability to push through legislation with limited opposition. This partial democratization short-circuited the ability of the American state to design coherent policies; however, the process did not integrate grass-roots political participation. These conditions were exacerbated by an increasingly partisan world in Washington that made debates over public policy more intense and delayed the passage of bills. This left citizens increasingly disenchanted with a federal government that seemed paralyzed.

Political reform

Important changes took place in other aspects of American politics during the mid-1970s. Reformers, for example, loosened the constraints on general-revenue spending that had been reimposed during the late 1960s, leading to increased spending on programs for the poor, such as Medicaid, and new programs for middle-class consumers and the environment.[27] Through judicial interpretation, the courts also expanded benefits in areas such as civil rights, education, and environmental regulation.[28] Continuing the agenda of reformers

---

[25] Russell Baker, "The Mills Picture Book," *The New York Times*, 7 December 1974. On the continued power of Ways and Means, see Linda Katherine Kowalcky, "The House Committee on Ways and Means: Maintenance and Evolution in the Post-Reform House of Representatives" (Ph.D. diss., The Johns Hopkins University Press, 1991); Strahan, *New Ways and Means*.

[26] Benjamin Ginsberg and Martin Shefter, *Politics By Other Means: The Declining Importance of Elections in America* (New York: Basic Books, 1990), 1–36.

[27] Joan Hoff, *Nixon Reconsidered* (New York: Basic Books, 1994), 1–144.

[28] R. Shep Melnick, *Between The Lines: Interpreting Welfare Rights* (Washington, D.C.: The Brookings Institution, 1994).

during the 1960s, the courts continued to increase federal control
over state and local government in conjunction with policies that
created legal mandates for the states to enact certain programs
and expenditures.[29] As a result, the deficit rose from 2.2 percent
of GNP to 4.3 percent in 1976, reaching $66.5 billion that year.[30]
Mills responded by promoting moderation. In 1979, he said: "The
great weakness, I think, of the people around the President is their
lack of knowledge of history. It has been proven and proven again
that the deficits can be controlled, can be changed into liquidity, from
the red into the black, and it can be done by government – where
there is a will to do it. You don't cut back on anybody. You just keep
the rate of growth from one fiscal year to the next at a lower percent
on the spending side than is your rate of growth on the revenue
side. It is the growth, the abnormal growth in government that kills
you . . . You can cut back on the appetite of the departments of government and not bring about a depression. Look what happened in
the Johnson Administration . . . We gave him the 10 percent surcharge, you remember, in return for just that one thing: his controlling the rate of growth and spending."[31]

Some reformers also fostered an intense cynicism toward several
aspects of the state that had previously been sacrosanct. One contested issue was the notion that limited groups of policymakers should
retain a monopoly on expertise. During the 1970s, reformers claimed
that technocratic expertise should be appropriated by as many
policymakers as possible. Rather than having a monopoly on expertise, they said, every activist should have his own expert. In debates
over atomic energy, for example, grass-roots organizations began to
hire their own scientists to challenge the experts of the establishment. Increasingly, public debates among experts diminished the
faith of citizens in the claims of experts to objectivity and neutrality.[32]
Within the economics profession, Keynesianism was discredited by
several competing theories, such as monetarism, supply-side economics, industrial policy, and fiscal conservatism. Combined, these
economic theories undercut the hegemony of Keynesianism within
the leading universities. None, however, replaced Keynesianism as a

---

[29] Martha Derthick, "Crossing Thresholds: Federalism in the 1960s," *The Journal of Policy History* 8, No. 1 (1996):64–80.

[30] Iwan W. Morgan, *Deficit Government: Taxing and Spending in Modern America* (Chicago: Ivan R. Dee, 1995), 132; Strahan, *New Ways and Means*, 26.

[31] Wilbur D. Mills, "Capital Formation," in *Dateline Washington* (Washington, D.C.: LTV Corporation, 1979), 102.

[32] Brian Balogh, *Chain Reaction: Expert Debate & Public Participation in American Commercial Nuclear Power, 1945–1975* (Cambridge: Cambridge University Press, 1991), 221–301.

single dominant model that provided coherence to the profession. Instead, economists fragmented into contradictory schools. In the minds of some scholars, this created a "crisis" in modern economic thought.[33]

Even with the general disillusionment with expertise, policy communities continued to serve as engines of the state. The political reformers had challenged the notion of a monopoly on expertise rather than the legitimacy of expertise itself. In the early 1970s, reformers had expanded participation within policy communities rather than challenging their role in formulating policy. Within the existing communities, the reform era witnessed an explosion in the number of participants. For example, the number of professional think tanks and interest groups involved in the policymaking process grew dramatically.[34] In addition, new policy communities formed around issues such as civil rights, deregulation, and environmentalism.[35] The interaction between policy communities and the media, moreover, changed significantly. Policy entrepreneurs became more adept at selling policies directly to the public through the media. At the same time, they learned to manipulate the media while conducting battles with other members of the community.[36] By debating through the media rather than in closed door sessions, policy communities provided the public with a clearer view of the political process in Washington.

The tax community found itself vulnerable as the nation entered into this new historical period. The community had achieved its power during the era of the closed committee system, economic growth, and Cold War; it maintained its autonomy, moreover, within

---

[33] Robert Heilbroner and William Milberg, *The Crisis of Vision in Modern Economic Thought* (Cambridge: Cambridge University Press, 1995); Theodore Rosenof, *Economics in the Long Run: New Deal Theorists & Their Legacies, 1933–1993* (Chapel Hill: University of North Carolina Press, 1997), 87–170.

[34] James A. Smith, *The Idea Brokers: Think Tanks and the Rise of the New Policy Elite* (New York: Free Press, 1991); Jeffrey H. Birnbaum, *The Lobbyists: How Influence Peddlers Get Their Way in Washington* (New York: Times Books, 1992); David M. Ricci, *The Transformation of American Politics: The New Washington and the Rise of Think Tanks* (New Haven: Yale University Press, 1993).

[35] Martha Derthick and Paul J. Quirk, *The Politics of Deregulation* (Washington, D.C.: The Brookings Institution, 1985); Samuel P. Hayes, *Beauty, Health, and Permanence: Environmental Politics in the United States, 1955–1985* (Cambridge: Cambridge University Press, 1987).

[36] Although the literature is limited, some useful discussions about the changing role of the press in national politics during this period can be found in the following work: Kathleen Hall Jamieson, *Dirty Politics: Deception, Distraction, and Democracy* (New York: Oxford University Press, 1992); Eric Alterman, *Sound and Fury: The Washington Punditocracy and the Collapse of American Politics* (New York: Harper Collins Publishers, 1992).

a national culture that valued specialized expertise.[37] But as the situation changed, the strength of the tax community diminished. In addition to the changes in the committee system and attitudes toward expertise, stagflation shattered the faith of all Americans in the power of the government to maintain economic growth. Despite active fiscal policies, wages stagnated, prices skyrocketed, productivity declined, and unemployment remained high. Without economic growth, the government lost the automatic revenue that rising wages had generated; this made stimulative income tax reductions more difficult and costly to achieve. Many conservative and liberal reformers challenged the belief that long-term economic growth was possible. At the same time, the Vietnam War had produced an intense cynicism about the Cold War and the legitimacy of the federal government. The nation's shock at Watergate only intensified the resentment of citizens toward their political leaders and institutions. According to one Gallup poll, 80 percent of the American people trusted Washington officials to "do what is right all or most of the time" in 1964. By 1994, the number of people who responded affirmatively to the question had dropped to less than 20 percent.[38]

Together, these economic, institutional, and cultural changes undermined the foundations on which Mills and his colleagues had established their influence. The reform movement pushed a number of leading tax officials, including Mills, out of office. Although a few of the tax community's officials stayed in politics until the end of the decade – including Laurence Woodworth, who directed tax policy for the Department of Treasury under President Carter – most gradually left the centers of decision-making power. Some, such as Stanley Surrey, Robert Myers, and Wilbur Cohen, moved into academia, where they could study policy and occasionally advise politicians without the constant pressure of decision-making. Others, including Henry Fowler and Stanley Ruttenberg, entered private practice in Washington to stay involved with the world of policy-making. By 1979, the era of Mills and the tax community had passed. With the election of President Reagan in 1980, a new generation of conservative policymakers took over the highest ranking positions of government.

---

[37] Elaine Tyler May, *Homeward Bound: American Families in the Cold War Era* (New York: Basic Books, 1988), 26–28.

[38] Cited in Dan T. Carter, *The Politics of Rage: George Wallace, The Origins of the New Conservatism, and the Transformation of American Politics* (New York: Simon & Shuster, 1995), 466. See also Seymour Martin Lipset and William Schneider, "The Decline of Confidence in American Institutions," *Political Science Quarterly* 98, No. 3 (Fall 1983): 379–402.

RECONSTRUCTING WILBUR MILLS

I began this book by asking how the American state accomplished what it did between 1945 and 1975, despite the nation's anti-statist culture and its fragmented political institutions. I have argued that four aspects of Mills's career provide some answers to this important question. This section reconsiders those aspects of his career to better understand the American state.

Congress and the state

First, Congress was essential to the institutionalization of the state constructed under Franklin Roosevelt. From 1945 to 1975, Congress retained a tight grip on many areas of policy, including taxation, where it never ceded jurisdiction to the executive branch. The decentralized committee system was at the heart of congressional influence. Mills's career demonstrates that the tax-writing committees and their chairmen were essential to the maintenance and expansion of income taxation and Social Security. Given his influence in the House and Senate, Mills was able to package and repackage legislation at all stages of the policymaking process. Despite the tensions between them, policymakers and even the president depended on him to secure congressional support. While Mills often used the negative power of the chairmanship to prevent programs from passing, he also used its positive power to direct the flow of policy.

Congress continued to influence many areas of the state besides taxation. For example, the agricultural committees were extremely influential in farm policy. The committees formed a key link in the "iron triangle" that existed between the farm lobby, the Department of Agriculture, and Congress. Eisenhower discovered the limits of executive power when he failed in his campaign to reduce farm subsidies in the 1950s.[39] On economic policy, the small business committees, whose members included Wright Patman (D-TX), William Hill (R-CO), James Murray (D-MT), and Robert Taft (R-OH), initiated small business programs at a time when most policymakers focused on the large corporation.[40] Likewise, the House Committee on Un-American Activities and the Senate committees loomed large during the anti-communist crusades of the 1940s and 1950s.[41]

[39] John Mark Hansen, *Gaining Access: Congress and the Farm Lobby, 1919–1981* (Chicago: University of Chicago Press, 1991); Louis Galambos, *America At Middle Age: A New History of the U.S. in the Twentieth Century* (New York: McGraw-Hill, 1976), 93–95.

[40] Jonathan J. Bean, *Beyond the Broker State: Federal Policies Toward Small Business, 1936–1961* (Chapel Hill: University of North Carolina Press, 1996), 89–98.

[41] Robert Griffith, *The Politics of Fear: Joseph R. McCarthy and the Senate* (Amherst: University of Massachusetts Press, 1970).

Policy communities

Second, policy communities facilitated policymaking despite the fragmented structure of American government. The community connected congressional committees to other parts of the state; the worldview of its members also provided some coherence to policymaking and an intellectual framework through which interests could debate legislation. To shape policies at every stage of the tax-writing process, Mills worked closely with the tax community, and mastered its culture. The community consisted of a generation of policymakers who had come of professional age around the time of the New Deal and World War II, and who were dedicated to the operation of the federal government. This generation included many different types of policymakers, from business representatives to economists to actuaries to lawyers to party officials, who were all interested in bringing together the best aspects of technical expertise and public policy. They were dedicated to developing macroeconomic fiscal policy and contributory social insurance as centerpieces of the state. As a result of their professional training and political beliefs, they also valued a role for neutral, objective expertise in the formulation of public policy.

During the 1950s, policymakers such as Mills, Stanley Surrey, Joseph Pechman, Laurence Woodworth, Walter Heller, Wilbur Cohen, Herbert Stein, Robert Ball, and Robert Myers formed a tax community through their work on landmark legislation, such as the Social Security Amendments of 1950; through comprehensive hearings and studies, such as those held by the JEC and Ways and Means between 1955 and 1959; and through the efforts of various institutions, including Ways and Means, presidential task forces, the Treasury, the CEA, and think tanks. By 1961, several members of the tax community were in key positions of power inside and outside governmental institutions.

Throughout his tenure during the 1960s, Mills negotiated with the various factions of the tax community. His reputation as a tax expert and his analytical skills, combined with his statutory power as chairman of Ways and Means, enabled him to fully engage the world of the tax community and to help shape the policy agenda on issues ranging from Social Security to income-tax reform. As a successful tactical politician, Mills also had the capacity and the willingness to negotiate with congressional representatives and their interest groups as he translated the ideas of the community into legislation. Mills's influence, with the tax community and with Congress, was evident in the repackaging of the tax reduction of 1964, in the restructured version of Medicare that emerged in 1965, in the prominence of expenditure control by 1968, and in the Tax Reform Act of 1969. At the same time, the tax community and its culture affected Mills's view of politics, pushing him to accept moderate deficit finance, anti-inflationary tax increases, substantive tax-break reform, and a sizable expansion of Social Security.

By the end of his career, Mills had found that policy communities could be used by him to expand his influence among policymakers within the state, even if one were the chairman of Ways and Means. While Mills could have wielded power without the tax community, he increased his influence in policymaking by developing a strong working relationship with its members: The relationship allowed him to shape policies, rather than simply react to them. The community depended on Mills since he was chairman of the tax-writing committee; policy communities in the American state never experienced the insulation from politics that existed in countries such as England.[42] But Mills also understood that congressional representatives who operated most successfully with these policy experts, those who drew most effectively on the discourse of their community, and those who embraced certain assumptions about policy and politics, could significantly enhance their positive influence in shaping the political agenda. By the mid-1970s, however, long-standing divisions within the community – such as the tension between the administrators and fiscal guardians of Social Security, and the conflict between aggressive Keynesian economists and moderate fiscal conservatives – intensified. As a result, the community started to disintegrate by the mid-1970s, and was replaced by a new community during the 1980s that focused on supply-side reductions, interventionist monetary policy, and the retrenchment of domestic programs, including social insurance.

Throughout the postwar period, the tax-writing committees always had an incentive to develop a close working relationship with the tax community. Congress had refused to delegate any authority over taxation to the executive branch. As a result, the committee chairmen needed as much advice as possible on the potential effect of legislation on social welfare and the economy; they also needed assistance to shape the national agenda on these issues without becoming subservient to the executive branch. There was a sharp contrast between the power of the congressionally based tax community and the executive-directed foreign policy community of this period that included Robert McNamara, Dean Acheson, Dean Rusk, and Walt Rostow.[43]

[42] Hugh Heclo and Aaron Wildavsky, *The Private Government of Public Money: Community and Policy Inside British Politics* (London: Macmillan, 1974).

[43] David Halberstam, *The Best and the Brightest*, 4th ed. (New York: Ballantine Books, 1992); Melvyn P. Leffler, *A Preponderance of Power: National Security, the Truman Admin-*

During the postwar period, there were other chairmen who formed close ties with the policy communities. At the Joint Committee on Atomic Energy, for example, Senator Brien McMahon (D-CT) worked closely with scientists and administrators to promote a federal commercial nuclear power program despite a lack of external demand.[44] On civil rights, Representative Emanuel Celler (D-NY) played an important role through the House Judiciary Committee, often moving past the Kennedy and Johnson administrations, as he worked with the evolving civil rights community and pushed for expansive legislation over the opposition of southern Democrats.[45] The chairman of the Senate Commerce Committee, moreover, played an important role in initiating legislation and policy debates on issues such as traffic safety regulations, marine resources, and engineering.[46] Finally, Senator Edward Kennedy (D-MA) worked closely in the 1970s with the deregulation policy community to dismantle entrenched programs.[47] While each member of Congress cultivated unique ties to his respective community, all these activities were evidence of the ties that formed between congressional leaders and policy communities.

By the 1960s, specialized policy communities had become central to the American state. Scholars have gathered considerable evidence on the emergence of similar communities around other issues such as health care, civil rights, environmentalism, agriculture, defense, energy, welfare, and deregulation.[48] Like the political party of the

---

istration, and the Cold War (Stanford: Stanford University Press, 1992); Charles E. Neu, "The Rise of the National Security Bureaucracy," The New American State: Bureaucracies and Policies since World War II, ed. Louis Galambos (Baltimore: Johns Hopkins University Press, 1987), 85–108.

[44] Balogh, Chain Reaction, 45–59.

[45] Hugh Davis Graham, The Civil Rights Era: Origins and Development of National Policy (New York: Oxford University Press, 1990).

[46] David E. Price, Who Makes the Laws? Creativity and Power in Senate Committees (Cambridge, MA: Schenkman, 1972), 25–104.

[47] Derthick and Quirk, The Politics of Deregulation, 40–41; 43; 65; 106–107.

[48] For the best evidence of other communities during this era, see the following: Jacob S. Hacker, The Road To Nowhere: The Genesis of President Clinton's Plan for Health Security (Princeton: Princeton University Press, 1997); William P. Browne, Cultivating Congress: Constituents, Issues, and Interests in Agricultural Policymaking (Lawrence: University Press of Kansas, 1995); Halberstam, The Best and the Brightest; Margaret Weir, Politics and Jobs: The Boundaries of Employment Policy in the United States (Princeton: Princeton University Press, 1992); Balogh, Chain Reaction; Graham, The Civil Rights Era; Michael B. Katz, The Undeserving Poor: From the War on Poverty to the War on Welfare (New York: Pantheon Books, 1989); Samuel P. Hayes, Beauty, Health, and Permanence: Environmental Politics in the United States, 1955–1985 (Cambridge: Cambridge University Press, 1987); Derthick and Quirk, The Politics of Deregulation; Allen J. Matusow, The Unraveling of America: A History of Liberalism in the 1960s (New York: Harper Torchbooks, 1984).

nineteenth century, the policy community perpetuated shared values among policymakers; it provided professional networks of communication; and it offered a means of uniting dispersed officials, their staffs, and their clients. Even though tensions regularly occurred among the members, the participants maintained a sense of themselves as a community through regular exchanges of information, through a shared political discourse, through their constant involvement with a common issue, and through similar legislative institutions. Political actors identified themselves increasingly around a particular issue, such as taxation or defense, rather than solely through partisanship or ideology. Mills and Surrey, for example, were as much "tax men" as they were Democrats, liberals, or conservatives.

Taxation as liberal policy

The third aspect of Wilbur Mills's career involved the use of taxation as a viable form of liberal domestic policy. Taxation proved to be an essential tool to state-builders. The Social Security tax system supported the expansion of cash and medical benefits to the elderly. During Mills's career, middle-class constituents came to expect these benefits on retirement as an earned right, paid for through their taxes and distributed without a means test. These characteristics gave the program a tremendous amount of political strength, and helped build a broad recipient base that opposed any cuts in the program. But the success of Social Security's earmarked tax system was not guaranteed, and had to be maintained, defended, and reconstructed over time.

Since its enactment during the New Deal, the tax system came under fire on several occasions, and Mills worked closely with the Social Security faction of the tax community to protect this distinct method of finance. Between 1949 and 1950, Mills, Cohen, and Myers helped to ensure the exclusion of direct general-revenue finance from the program, and protected the symbolic link between payroll taxation and Social Security benefits. Mills and the community, moreover, pushed the Social Security Amendments of 1958 through Congress, elevating the issue of actuarial deficits to the forefront of public policy. When the Medicare proposal raised a serious challenge to Social Security finance in 1965, Mills, Cohen, Ball, and Myers designed a layered tax system for Medicare that promised to protect OASDI while extending earmarked taxes into the realm of health insurance. Finally, between 1969 and 1972, the success of this contributory program stimulated a partisan battle to expand the system, including the indexation of cash benefits to rise automatically with the cost of living. Although the legislation left the earmarked system intact, this last development began to place unprecedented strain on the program, and marked a new era in Social Security politics.

But during the 1970s and 1980s, Social Security continued to thrive as federal officials protected the earmarked tax system and program participants became an increasingly large segment of the middle-class population. In 1983, Congress enacted legislation to raise $165 billion by increasing payroll taxes and delayed the annual cost-of-living adjustments to meet a predicted actuarial shortfall.[49] Between 1980 and 1990, the combined payroll tax rate increased from 12.26 percent to 15.3 percent of wages.[50] The 1983 legislation enacted significant changes to the system. For the first time, Congress agreed to tax the Social Security benefits of high-income recipients as they would any other type of income, and agreed to use monies from general tax revenue to pay for a portion of OASDI benefits. Nonetheless, the reforms maintained the integrity of the earmarked tax system that distinguished social insurance. As a result of these reforms and the political power of the elderly who demanded their "insurance" payments, OASDI remained immune to the budget cuts that affected many areas of domestic policy. Even policy experts who had been increasingly critical of the program's regressive fiscal structure during the 1970s now supported the fiscal structure of the program.[51]

Earmarked taxes and trust funds, similar to those in Social Security and Medicare, became an increasingly important part of domestic policy in the postwar period. In some policy domains, particularly social insurance, legislators used these fiscal devices to secure long-term political support for policy commitments. By the 1990s, nearly 40 percent of total federal revenues were committed to trust funds, mainly Social Security and Medicare, but also for programs such as interstate highway construction, airport development, health damage compensation, nature conservation, airport maintenance, and the Superfund cleanup of toxic waste sites. These complex fiscal devices played a significant role in maintaining long-term political support

---

[49] Paul Light, *Artful Work: The Politics of Social Security Reform* (New York: Random House, 1985).

[50] C. Eugene Steuerle, *The Tax Decade: How Taxes Came to Dominate the Public Agenda* (Washington, D.C.: Urban Institute Press, 1992), 63–65. See also C. Eugene Steuerle and John M. Bakija, *Retooling Social Security for the 21st Century: Right & Wrong Approaches to Reform* (Washington, D.C.: Urban Institute Press, 1994).

[51] Edward D. Berkowitz, "Social Security and the financing of the American state," in *Funding the Modern American State: The Rise and Fall of the Era of Easy Finance, 1941–1995*, ed. W. Elliot Brownlee (Cambridge: Cambridge University Press and Washington, D.C.: Woodrow Wilson Center Press, 1996), 190.

for their programs and in building constituencies that expected certain benefits as an earned right.[52]

Between 1945 and 1975, Mills and his colleagues also relied on income taxation as an instrument of economic policy. With all its limits as a regulatory policy, taxation played a key role in government efforts to stimulate growth and restrain inflation. This form of economic policy found considerable acceptance within Washington. JEC and Ways and Means hearings, combined with the efforts by the Council of Economic Advisors and academic economists, helped to popularize this version of economic policy within Congress following the Recodification of 1954. A moderate version of these theories turned into policy in 1962 with the investment tax credit, in 1964 with the demand-side tax cut and resulting deficit, and in 1968 with anti-inflationary tax increases and expenditure controls. Through these policies, the state took an active role in stimulating and restraining the economy.

Macroeconomic tax policy continued to be important into the 1980s, although in a much different form. Foremost, policymakers relied on stimulative tax reductions to boost growth rather than stronger regulation or employment programs.[53] To stimulate the economy, Congress passed the Economic Recovery Tax Act of 1981, which enacted the largest tax reduction in American history: it included a reduction of the top rate from 70 percent to 50 percent. The act also provided for a 23 percent across-the-board cut spread over three years for all other marginal tax brackets, and improved incentives for private investment, including a new kind of depreciation allowance and new investment credits.[54] While the reductions focused more on investment than demand (as opposed to the balance that had existed during the 1960s), they represented a continued reliance on tax manipulation as economic policy. Former JEC staffer Norman Ture and Reagan's under-secretary of the Treasury for Tax and Economic Affairs was a key architect of the 1981 legislation. Fiscal policymakers also continued to accept frequent budget deficits: Each budget of the Reagan administration, for example, was more than $100 billion in the red, and three ran deficits of over $200 billion.[55]

---

[52] Eric M. Patashnik, "Unfolding Promises: Trust Funds and the Politics of Precommitment," *Political Science Quarterly*, 112, No. 3 (Fall 1997): 431–452; "The Politics of Federal Government Trust Funds" (Ph.D diss., University of California, 1996).

[53] On the failure of employment programs, see Weir, *Politics and Jobs*.

[54] Cathie J. Martin, *Shifting The Burden: The Struggle over Growth and Corporate Taxation* (Chicago: University of Chicago Press, 1991), 107–193.

[55] Iwan W. Morgan, *Deficit Government: Taxing and Spending in Modern America* (Chicago: Ivan R. Dee, 1995), 114–181.

But stimulative tax reductions produced different results in an era of economic stagnation. During the "American Century" of economic growth, rising wages had pushed citizens into higher tax brackets and thus generated unanticipated revenue, which Congress could return as a tax reduction. But once wages stopped rising, and once taxes had been indexed to inflation (so that taxpayers would not be pushed into higher tax brackets as a result of inflation), continued tax reductions resulted in a gradual defunding of the state. This development has created a state with vastly diminished resources. This was the context in the early 1990s within which Congress had to enact large income-tax hikes, raid payroll tax revenue, or implement cuts in general-revenue spending or bigger deficits.[56] Even the budgetary surpluses of the late-1990s offer only temporary relief in light of the long-term entitlement commitments of the American state, the nation's changing demographic conditions, and the uncertainty of continued economic growth. Moreover, taxation took a back seat to monetarism as the adjustment of interest rates became central to economic policy.

During Mills's career, the tax community also helped to develop and maintain the tax-break system. By forgiving certain types of investment from taxation, tax breaks subsidized certain types of investment and discouraged others. To maintain this complex system, Mills and his colleagues supported an ongoing process of tax reform, in which some provisions were eliminated from the code while others were enacted on economic and political grounds. The Ways and Means Committee hearings of 1958 and 1959 brought new attention to the process and the necessity of tax reforms, some of which were implemented in 1962 and 1969. At the same time, Congress continued to implement tax breaks through Members' Bills and targeted credits that stimulated certain forms of economic activities.

Following Mills's fall from power, the tax-break system continued to shape economic activity. Before 1986, Congress had passed an unprecedented number of tax breaks for investment in social and business programs.[57] Since its enactment in 1975, for example, Congress has expanded the Earned Income Tax Credit, which provides a tax credit for low-income workers.[58] Ironically, the openness of the new Ways and

---

[56] C. Eugene Steuerle, "Financing the American state at the turn of the century," in *Funding the Modern American State, 1941–1995*, 409–444; Paul Pierson, *Dismantling the Welfare State? Reagan, Thatcher, and the Politics of Retrenchment* (Cambridge: Cambridge University Press, 1994), 149–155.

[57] Christopher Howard, "The Hidden Side of the American Welfare State," *Political Science Quarterly* 108, No. 3 (1993): 403–436, and Christopher Howard, *The Hidden Welfare State: Tax Expenditures and Social Policy in the United States* (Princeton: Princeton University Press, 1997).

[58] Christopher Howard, "Protean Lure for the Working Poor: Party Competition and the Earned Income Tax Credit," *Studies in American Political Development* 9, No. 2 (Fall

Means gave interest groups greater opportunity to pass tax breaks. Ways and Means lost some of its capacity as a "control committee." Between 1973 and 1986, for example, the revenue losses from tax expenditures rose from 4.4 percent of GNP to approximately 10 percent in 1986.[59] The Congressional Budget Office calculated that the revenue lost from tax expenditures increased from $37 billion in 1967 (21 percent of federal expenditures) to $327 billion (35 percent of federal expenditures) by 1984.[60] From his classroom at Harvard, Stanley Surrey lamented, "The consideration of tax legislation by the Congress has completely disintegrated. The picture has been one of almost utter chaos without responsible control residing anywhere."[61]

At the same time, tax reformers continued to promote a combination of rate reduction and tax-break reform. The Tax Reform Act of 1986 represented the logical outcome of tax policies that had been in motion since the mid-1950s. The legislation weeded out a massive number of tax breaks that had been the target of reform since Mills took over the chairmanship.[62] While providing some new credits to the growing high-technology and service industries, the legislation rescinded numerous benefits for real estate interests and capital-intensive sectors.[63] This time, Treasury economists teamed up with the chairman of Ways and Means, Daniel Rostenkowski (D-IL), to enact one of the biggest tax reform bills in history. Before the reform passed Congress, there were eleven tax rates, ranging from 11 percent to 50 percent. The tax reform of 1986 condensed these brackets into two, lowering the top rate to 28 percent. To compensate for the lost revenue, the bill eliminated many tax expenditures: the investment tax credit, the individual retirement account, differential taxation of capital gains, and accelerated depreciation allowances.[64] In the end,

1995): 404–436; C. Eugene Steuerle and Paul Wilson, "The Earned Income Tax Credit," *Focus* 10, No. 1 (Spring 1987): 1–8.

[59] Steinmo, *Taxation & Democracy*, 43; Witte, *The Politics and Development of the Federal Income Tax*, 292.

[60] Cited in W. Elliot Brownlee, "Tax regimes, national crisis, and state-building in America," *Funding the Modern American State, 1941–1995*, 100.

[61] Cited in Catherine E. Rudder, "Tax Policy: Structure and Choice," in *Making Economic Policy in Congress*, ed. Allen Schick (Washington, D.C.: American Enterprise Institute, 1983), 204.

[62] Joseph A. Pechman, *Who Paid the Taxes, 1966–85* (Washington, D.C: The Brookings Institution, 1985).

[63] Martin, *Shifting the Burden*, 159–193.

[64] Figures cited in Martin, *Shifting the Burden*, 159–188. For interesting accounts and interpretations of this legislation, see the following works: Jeffrey H. Birnbaum and Alan S. Murray, *Showdown at Gucci Gulch: Lawmakers, Lobbyists, and the Unlikely Triumph of Tax Reform* (New York: Vintage Books, 1988); Steuerle, *The Tax Decade*, 57–162; Joel Slemrod, ed., *Do Taxes Matter? The Impact of the Tax Reform Act of 1986*

the legislation created the type of modified, progressive income-tax system that had been envisioned by Mills and his colleagues as early as 1955. During the presidency of Bill Clinton, there has been a gradual increase in the number of tax breaks as many of the 1986 reforms have been undone. At the same time, a vigorous campaign for tax reform has emerged from the halls of Congress. This campaign includes a variety of ideas, ranging from proposals for reform within the existing system (along the lines of the Tax Reform Act of 1986) to proposals for eliminating the progressive income tax and replacing it with a consumption tax or a flat income tax.

Fiscal conservatism and the state

Fourth, the relationship between fiscal conservatives and the American state was the final aspect of a career that helped explain some of the success of state-building in the area of taxation. To be sure, there were many fiscal conservatives who rejected virtually every component of the modern state. For example, Lewis Douglas, Franklin Roosevelt's first director of the Bureau of the Budget, resigned in protest during the 1930s. He continued to attack publicly almost every aspect of the state, ranging from deficit financing to Social Security. From 1945 to the early 1970s, however, this type of extreme fiscal conservative remained on the margins of national political debate.

Since the New Deal, a group of moderate fiscal conservatives came to accept the federal government, and helped build broad support for particular policies. While doing so, they devoted their attention to devising ways to control long-term costs, contain deficits, and limit the budgetary growth of programs. For example, Mills helped defend the "pay-as-you-go" tax system for Social Security with the hope of providing expansive benefits while controlling the long-term cost of the program and limiting the amount of benefits that could be provided. Mills also supported moderate macroeconomic policy adjustments, but did so by continuing to emphasize the dangers of long-term deficits; he consistently fought against frequent, short-term tax adjustments, and insisted on expenditure control. Mills joined an influential group of fiscal conservatives, including Henry Morgenthau, Robert Myers, Harry Truman, Dwight Eisenhower, Henry Fowler, Herbert Stein, and Robert Dole, who fought for a particular

(Cambridge: MIT Press, 1990); Gary Mucciaroni, *Reversals of Fortune: Public Policy and Private Interests* (Washington, D.C.: The Brookings Institution, 1995), 28–66; Randall Strahan, "Members' Goals and Coalition-Building Strategies in the U.S. House: The Case of Tax Reform," *Journal of Politics* 51, No. 2 (May 1989): 373–384.

type of state that could maintain control over its own budgetary growth.

Political institutions such as the Treasury and the tax-writing committees tended to nurture fiscal conservatives because these institutions were responsible for tax rates, the debt, annual deficits, and the stability of the dollar. From the end of World War II to the early 1970s, moreover, the coexistence of fiscal conservatism and the American state seemed possible. Between 1945 and 1960, seven balanced budgets were enacted. Most of the deficits that occurred during the 1960s were approximately 1 percent or less of GNP (compared with 5–6 percent of GNP between fiscal years 1983 and 1986). Even with the record high deficit of fiscal year 1968 (3 percent of GNP), Congress produced a budget surplus for fiscal year 1969. Given this context, numerous fiscal conservatives believed during the postwar period that they could realistically constrain the American state. At the same time, by accepting the permanence of a modest state, they could protect themselves from political marginalization. By the mid-1970s, however, these types of fiscal conservatives started to break from the alliance. Certain legislative battles, such as the expansion of Social Security in 1972, led them to lose faith in their ability to control the expansionary tendencies of the federal government. They also found a new home in the conservative movement that took hold at the grass-roots, state, and national levels during the 1970s and 1980s.

THE PROMISE OF THE AMERICAN STATE

By the 1980s, Mills and his colleagues had left behind a significant legacy in American politics. Between 1945 and 1975, broad segments of society, including elderly retirees, middle-class consumers, private investors, and corporations came to depend on the economic and social assistance that the tax community had helped create. This included contributory social insurance, macroeconomic income-tax adjustments, and tax breaks. In short, Mills and the tax community had found ways to work within the limits of American politics. Even in a period of conservative power, Social Security and income taxation have been highly resistant from the destructive attacks and the retrenchment that beset poverty policy, public housing, atomic energy programs, and industrial regulation.[65]

Wilbur Mills died from a heart attack on May 2 1992. His death came at a time when citizens of all ideological persuasions seem more dissatisfied with the American state than ever before. For some

---

[65] Paul Pierson, *Dismantling the Welfare State?*

observers, the legacy of Mills and the tax community offers a symbol
for the failures of American politics. Mills and his colleagues demonstrated that federal policies remained limited during the postwar
period, as Mills and his colleagues failed to enact expansive economic
policies; they were beholden to a handful of interest groups; they
refused to move beyond the limits of social insurance; and they perpetuated the racial and gender bias in public policies. Critics also
argue that Mills's technocratic style of politics diminished democratic participation and established a foundation for the public disen-
gagement from federal politics between the 1970s and 1990s.[66] The
vast distance between state and society thus represents the technocratic legacy of Mills and his generation.

   While these criticisms point to the crucial problems of this period,
the story of Mills and the tax community is also a roadmap showing
how American government has worked. Rather than focusing on Mills
and his colleagues only as policymakers with extremely limited vision,
these policymakers must also be studied for their ability to achieve
significant accomplishments, such as macroeconomic fiscal policy, tax
reform, and contributory social insurance – notwithstanding the institutional and cultural obstacles they faced. Despite all their limits, this
generation must be examined for its ability to design viable compromises that seem impressive in the shadow of Ronald Reagan's conservative revolution. The history of Mills and the tax community
offers some important insights into the roots of the nation's current
political situation as the American state enters into the twenty-first
century.

---

[66] See, for example, Lawrence D. Brown, *New Policies, New Politics: Government's Response
   to Government's Growth* (Washington, D.C.: The Brookings Institution, 1983); John
   B. Judis, "The Contract with K Street," *The New Republic*, 4 December 1995, 18–25;
   Lawrence D. Brown, "Adventures in Governance: Policy Culture and Health Reform
   Politics," 30 November 1995 (Paper presented at the Woodrow Wilson International
   Center for Scholars); William Greider, *Who Will Tell The People: The Betrayal of Amer-
   ican Democracy* (New York: Simon & Schuster, 1992).

Index